HE LAND OF ASSUR & THE YOKE OF ASSUR

STUDIES ON ASSYRIA 1971–2005

NICHOLAS POSTGATE

Oxbow Books
Oxford & Philadelphia

Published in the United Kingdom by
OXBOW BOOKS
10 Hythe Bridge Street, Oxford OX1 2EW

and in the United States by
OXBOW BOOKS
908 Darby Road, Havertown, PA 19083

Paperback Edition: ISBN 978-1-78297-741-4
Digital Edition: ISBN 978-178297-538-0

First published 2007
Paperback reprint 2014

A CIP record for this book is available from the British Library

For a complete list of Oxbow titles, please contact:

UNITED KINGDOM
Oxbow Books
Telephone (01865) 241249, Fax (01865) 794449
Email: oxbow@oxbowbooks.com
www.oxbowbooks.com

UNITED STATES OF AMERICA
Oxbow Books
Telephone (800) 791-9354, Fax (610) 853-914
Email: queries@casemateacademic.com
www.casemateacademic.com/oxbow

Oxbow Books is part of the Casemate Group

Front cover: two strips from the bronze ornamentation of gates erected at the Temple of Mamu at Imgur-Enlil (modern Balawat) by king Assur-nasir-apli II in the early 9th century BC. The cuneiform captions tell us that the upper strip shows the King receiving the tribute of Kudurru the ruler of Suhu, and the lower strip has him standing before the gates of Imgur-Enlil receiving further tribute from the same ruler. Drawing by Marjorie Howard; see the forthcoming volume on The Balawat Gates of Ashurnasirpal II by R. D. Barnett et al. (British Museum Press). The strips were conserved at the Britsh Museum and placed on display in the Mosul Museum but were mostly looted in 2003.

CONTENTS

M. Brosius (ed.), *Ancient archives and archival traditions: Concepts of record-
keeping in the ancient world* (Oxford University Press 2003), 124–138.

FOREWORD

This collection of papers brings between two covers some thirty years of engagement with the nature of Assyrian society and government. Most of the articles included here are broadly synthetic, dealing with general issues, and in a sense this collection is not a substitute, but an apology, for having failed to bring my work on this subject together into a more general study of Assyria.

Not included are editions of, or articles centred round, individual texts, contributions on agricultural matters to the *Bulletin on Sumerian Agriculture,* or introductions to volumes of text editions, even though in some cases they might not have been out of place. Hence among other articles room has not been found for "The Inscription of Tiglath-Pileser III at Mila Mergi", *Sumer* 29 (1973) 47–59, "The bīt akīti in Neo-Assyrian Nabu Temples", *Sumer* 30 (1974) 51–74, "Assyrian Texts and Fragments", *Iraq* 35 (1975) 13–36, "Assyrian Documents in the Musée d'Art et d'Histoire, Geneva", *Assur* 2/4 (1979) 1–15, and "On some Assyrian ladies", *Iraq* 41 (1979) 89–103.

Most articles are photographically reproduced from the first publications, with the insertion of this volume's page numbers in addition to the original pagination. In the case of items 15 and 18 I have taken the opportunity to insert a brief addendum or corrigendum. Item 27 is published here for the first time, in advance of the proceedings of the Copenhagen conference (see p. 331).

For permission to reprint articles first published in their journals or collective volumes I am much indebted to the editors and publishers: The School of Oriental and African Studies, University of London (1), Prof. Norman Yoffee, as Editor of the *Journal of the Economic and Social History of the Orient,* and Brill Academic Publishers, Leiden (2), Librairie Orientaliste Paul Geuthner (3), Prof. Dominique Charpin and the *Revue d'Assyriologie* (4 and 8), Prof. Jorge Silva Castillo (5), Prof. MogensTrolle Larsen and the Akademisk Forlag (6 and 27), the Editors of *Anatolian Studies* (7), Aris and Phillips Ltd. (9), Dr. M. Weszeli, Editor of the *Archiv für Orientforschung*, Vienna (10 and 16), the Akademie Verlag, Berlin (11), the Editors of the *Journal of Semitic Studies* and Oxford University Press (12), Prof. J. Rodgers, and the American Oriental Society (13), Prof. Ph. Talon, M. Lebeau and L. de Meyer (14), Prof. Giovanni Lanfranchi (15), Taylor & Francis, and Prof. T. Gosden, Editor of *World Archaeology* (http://www.tandf.co.uk) (17); Otto Harrassowitz Verlag (18), Prof. Dr. Hartmut Waetzoldt and the Heidelberger Orientverlag (19), Prof. Dr. Manfried Dietrich and the Ugarit-Verlag (20); Prof. Mario Liverani and the University 'La Sapienza' Rome (21); Dr Dominique Collon and Prof. Andrew George, Editors of *Iraq,* and the British School of Archaeology in Iraq (22), Dr. Paolo Negri Scafa and Borgia Editore (23); Prof. Dr. J. J. Roodenberg and the Nederlands Instituut voor het Nabije Oosten (24); Dr Tim Whitmarsh and the Cambridge Philological Society (25); Dr Joan Oates and Dr Lamia al-Gailani-Werr (26); Dr Maria Brosius and Oxford University Press (28).

This seems a good opportunity to express my gratitude to the institutions whose support has enabled my study of Assyria – Trinity College, Cambridge, the School of Oriental and African Studies, University of London, the British School of Archaeology in Iraq, and the Faculty of Oriental Studies in the University of Cambridge, and not least the Iraqi Directorate-General of Antiquities and its successors – and to my teachers, in the first instance James Kinnier Wilson and Margaret Munn-Rankin, but also Wolfram Freiherr von Soden and Dietz Edzard on my visits to Münster and Munich respectively. I would also like to acknowledge the immense debt that I, like all those who work on Assyria, owe to the two great projects created by the vision and initiative of Kirk Grayson and Simo Parpola, the Toronto Royal Inscriptions of Mesopotamia and the Helsinki State Archives of Assyria.

Nicholas Postgate
June 2007

STUDIES ON ASSYRIA

1971 – 2005

LAND TENURE IN THE MIDDLE ASSYRIAN PERIOD: A RECONSTRUCTION[1]

By J. N. Postgate

This article is an attempt to assemble and reassess the evidence relating to the problems of land tenure in the Middle Assyrian period, and to show that all ' private ' land was normally held as a concession from the crown in return for the performance of *ilku* obligations. The subjects are treated in five main sections:

1: *ilku* and military service (pp. 496–502)
2: the Middle Assyrian laws, tablet A, § 45 (pp. 502–8)
3: allocation of tenures by the crown (pp. 508–12)
4: evidence from the land sale documents (pp. 512–17)
5: conclusions (pp. 517–19)

1: *ILKU* AND MILITARY SERVICE

Since this article is largely concerned with the association of land tenure with personal service for the state, it will be useful to start by considering *ilku*, the one word which seems at all periods to refer to personal service of one kind or another. As we have only a few scattered occurrences in Middle Assyrian texts, it is particularly necessary to treat these in detail, and this should help to clear the ground for a more general discussion. I have deliberately refrained from making comparisons with usages of the word in other groups of texts, since this would inevitably prejudice the conclusions.

The most problematic of the relevant passages is that in *KAJ* 7; the text has often been discussed, and in general I can refer to D'yakonov's treatment in *Ancient Mesopotamia*, Moscow, 1969, 231–32 [written in 1949], where ll. 20–6 are translated ' Asuat-Idiglat and her progeny are " community members " (*ālāiū*) of A.' (the slave's master) ' and of his children; they will perform the service of " community membership " for A. and his sons, . . . '.[2] This is a passage from a document in which a slave redeems (for marriage) a free-born girl from her ' owner '.[3] Unfortunately the text does not tell us of what their service might have consisted, but some conclusions do seem to be possible about their liability to that service. Since, however, there is no unanimity among scholars as to the exact meaning of the phrase *ilku ša ālāiūti*, it seems best to consider three possible interpretations of it first.

(1) According to D'yakonov's interpretation, the *ilku ša ālāiūti* was a

[1] This article is a considerably expanded and revised version of ideas put forward by me in a dissertation submitted to Trinity College, Cambridge, in August 1970, entitled ' Taxes and military conscription in Assyria '. I am indebted to the Master and Fellows of the College for permission to make use of this material in this article.

[2] *KAJ* 7, 20–6: ^{mí}*asuat-[idiglat] ū lidānu-[ša] a-la-iu-ú ša Amurru-[naṣir] ū mārē-šu šunu-[ma?] il-ka ša a-la-iu-ú-t[i] ana Amurru-naṣir ū mārē-šu illuku.*

[3] For her social position see D'yakonov, 224–5, and Oppenheim, *Iraq*, XVII, 1, 1955, 73–4.

state-imposed obligation, to which those who owned land in each village (' community ', *ālu*) were *ipso facto* liable; here, however, the owners of the land have transferred the obligation to inferior dependants of their house (D'yakonov, 232). This theory implies that, if they had not done this, they would themselves have been liable not just to *ilku*, but specifically to *ilku ša ālāiūti* ' service of community membership ', and moreover, that they would have been *ālāiū* ' community members '. However, in the preceding phrase the text states that the slave and his wife are ' villagers ' (*ālāiū*) of their master, Amurru-naṣir, and the natural assumption must be that *ālāiūtu* here means precisely this status of theirs as his dependent ' villagers '; such a meaning of *ālāiūtu* could obviously not be applied to Amurru-naṣir and his family, and so this exact interpretation cannot be accepted.

(2) In CAD, I (A), Pt. I, 391a, the passage is translated: ' fPN and her children will remain villagers of PN_2 and of his sons and will perform services as the village residents to PN_2 and his sons '. This seems to imply (although it is not stated unequivocally) that the *ilku* here mentioned is not the same as ordinary state *ilku*, but a kind of private service exacted by the house of Amurru-naṣir from these dependants, the slave and his wife.[4] Such an interpretation is not supported by any other occurrence of *ilku*, but the translation does have the advantage of giving due weight to the connexion between the use of *ālāiu* in the previous phrase and the *ilku ša ālāiūti*; the translation ' services as village residents ' must be substantially correct.

(3) In order to reconcile these two points of view, a more complicated solution is necessary, but one which I hope is nearer to the truth. As is obvious, *ālāiu* means a person who lives in a village, but the usage here suggests that it is not a term which would have been applied to any free man who owned land in the relevant village (and was thus a ' community member ').[5] As CAD has noted, *ālāiu*, both here and in the Middle Assyrian laws (see below, § 2), is a ' dependent villager '. It seems therefore that the ' villager of Amurru-naṣir ' (or ' of the palace ') must be a dependant whose prime characteristic is that he (or she) lives in a village (as opposed to one who lives in the family house or in a town, viz. Assur). We may fairly assume that his master does not live in the village himself, and that the function of the villager is to cultivate the land which Amurru-naṣir (in this case) owns. We need not suppose that he owned a whole village, but he may well have had property in a number of different places, in all of which he may have had ' villager dependants '; the existence of families in Assur which owned land in outlying villages is well attested in the

[4] This translation could mean either that, as the village-residents, they will perform services to PN_2 . . . , or (and this is perhaps what was intended), that, as the village-residents to PN_2 . . . , they will perform services. However, this second version would demand that *ana* PN_2 be taken as directly dependent on *ilka ša ālāiūti*, and not, as Akkadian requires, on the verb.

[5] D'yakonov (232) recognizes that the simple translation ' community member ' is too broad to fit the context, and says that the word here ' is defined by the lines that follow: they are those who perform " the service of community membership " '; he does not, however, make any attempt to justify this restriction in the word's meaning.

KAJ texts, and has recently been stressed in the study of H. J. Nissen on the seal impressions of these documents.[6] Our phrase may then be taken to mean not ' (they shall perform) services as *the* village residents *to* Amurru-naṣir ', but rather ' (they shall perform) for A. the services (which go with) their position as villagers . . . '. In other words, this is a kind of service that would similarly be performed by other ' villagers ', but happens in this case to be performed for, i.e. on behalf of, Amurru-naṣir.

Our conclusion then is, in effect, much the same as that of D'yakonov and Garelli,[7] which is that the slave and his wife are obliged to perform services for the state which would otherwise have fallen on the owners of the land. We should not conclude from this that the dependants have been granted any rights to the land: the family unquestionably remained owners, and indeed there is nothing in the text to show that they incurred any obligations to provide their dependants with subsistence in return for the service, although we may fairly assume this. The association of *ilku* with land tenure is therefore in no way proved by this text, but it would none the less be a perfectly acceptable position that a family which held land from the state in return for *ilku* service was able to have those services performed by its own dependants without losing its rights to ownership. Indeed, this would be the only plausible hypothesis if any one family owned a large area of land on such terms.[8]

Other occurrences of *ilku* are less complicated and may be dealt with more shortly. Evidence that *ilku* could consist of true military service is provided by TR 3005 (*Iraq*, XXX, 2, 1968, plate LVIII), which records the issue of various commodities (some kind of corn, wool, and pig's fat) for the ' army of Niḫria, who performed *ilku* with [their(?)] brothers '.[9] These are typical rations for men on campaign, and there seems no reason to doubt that the men in Niḫria were fulfilling their *ilku* obligations there. The verb *alāku* is also used with *ilku* in TR 3010 (*Iraq*, XXX, 2, 1968, plate LIX), which is unfortunately harder to understand;[10] the text does, however, show that *ilku* obligations could be recorded, and their fulfilment acknowledged in the same way as other, more tangible, debts were regulated. One of the parties to the transaction is

[6] In D. O. Edzard (ed.), *Heidelberger Studien zum Alten Orient: Adam Falkenstein zum 17. September 1966*, Wiesbaden, 1967, 111ff.

[7] See *Semitica*, XVII, 1967, 14, where however this *ilku* seems to be equated with payments (*redevances, contributions*) by the villagers, which is not demonstrable.

[8] i.e., in return for *ilku* service; for the question of performance of *ilku* service on lands which had been sold, see below, § 5.

[9] Ll. 4–8: *ša ḫu-ra*!*-di ša* ^{uru}*ni-iḫ-ri-a ša il-ka iš-tu* ŠEŠ.M[EŠ (*x x*)] *i-li-ku-ni*. The passage has been collated by D. A. Kennedy, who confirms the sign *ra* in l. 4; he also indicates that there is in fact no sign after *il-ka* in l. 6. *Ištu* is regular in MAss. for ' with ' as well as ' from ' (cf. the interchange with *itti* in the PN *Ištu/Itti-ili-a-šam-šu*, Tallqvist, *APN*, 108b; *Iraq*, XXX, 2, 1968, 191b).

[10] The text reads: ^{1}*iš-tu* ^{iti}*ḫi-bur* UD.11.KÁM ^{2}*li*!-[*me*?] $^{m.d}$IM.EN-*gab-be* ^{3m}*a-bu*-[D]ÙG.GA *iš-tu* ^{m}*si-ki* ^{4}(*x*) NÍG.KA$_9$.MEŠ-*šu-nu* ^{5}*ṣa-ab-tu* ^{6}*il-la-ak*?*-šu-nu* ^{7}*i-na* ŠU!^{m}*si*!*-ki* ^{8}*a-li-ik* ' From the 11th of Hibur, *limmu* of Adad-bēl-gabbe, Abu-ṭāb and Sikku have done their accounts; their *ilku* has been performed (lit. ' gone ') " in the hand " of Sikku '. The double *ll* in *illak-šunu* is hard to explain; the emendation in l. 7 follows a collation by D. A. Kennedy.

presumably an official, but there is some reason to suppose that both may have been,[11] and it is therefore conceivable that state officials did not have to fulfil their *ilku* obligations by going on military service in person, but were able to make some kind of substitute payment such as is attested for Neo-Assyrian times. But this is purely speculative at present, and must await further evidence.

Confirmation that *ilku* did not refer exclusively to personal service in the army may perhaps be sought in a couple of texts from Assur, *KAJ* 233 and 253. *KAJ* 233, 1–6, reads: ‘ Anum-šūma-ēreš has received 16 homers 4 *sūtu* of corn (as) horse-fodder, *ša ilki*, belonging to (i.e. from) Parparāiu ’ [12]; *KAJ* 253 is very similar,[13] but reads instead *ša il-ki ša* ŠU PN, ‘ in the charge of PN ’, which shows that the corn must have been an administrative issue made by that person, and therefore excludes the possibility of combining the first-named person in each text (the giver) with *ša ilki* and thus translating ‘ of the service of PN ’. The *ša ilki* can therefore only refer either to the horses or to the corn, and since the animals, for whom the corn is destined, must be the *raison d'être* of the issue, we must assume that in each case the recipient is drawing fodder for the horses; they will have been brought into the administration in connexion with, or in fulfilment of, *ilku* duties, and he will be only the ‘ government groom ’, applying for supplies from his superior department. It would be rash on this basis alone to suggest that the supply of horses could serve as a substitute for personal execution of *ilku* service, but these texts do at least confirm the association of *ilku* with the army.

ḫurādu

As we have just seen, TR 3005 connects *ilku* unequivocally with the term *ḫurādu*, and another Tell al-Rimaḥ text (TR 2021+) gives further interesting details about this word, which I am provisionally translating ‘ army ’. The text records the loan of a lance (*ulmu*) and accompanying item(s) to a certain Ṣilli-amurri; the final clause reads: ‘ at the return of the army he shall give (back the lance) and break his tablet ’ [14]. In other words, when the lance has been returned his obligation is acquitted. It seems certain that Ṣilli-amurri was an ordinary person being called up for military service in the *ḫurādu*, but unfortunately the terse phraseology of the text makes it impossible to decide whether we should envisage his service as lasting for a whole year or more, or

[11] Affiliations are not given, and there are no witnesses, both features restricted in general to transactions within the administration.

[12] 16 ANŠE 5-BÁN ŠE PAD-*at* ANŠE.KUR.RA *ša il-ki ša* ^{m}*pa-ar-pa-ra-a-e* ^{m}AN-*num*-MU.KAM DUMU ^{d}*sin-ni-ia ma-ḫi-ir* (envelope, *KAV* 207, is identical except for the omission of *maḫir*).

[13] 5 ANŠE ŠE *i-na* ^{giš}BÁN SUMUN PAD-*at* ANŠE.KUR.RA.MEŠ *ša il-ki ša* ŠU [^{m}*i-q*]*iš-ia* [^{m}*x x* -]*še*?-*ia* [*ma*]-*ḫi-ir*.

[14] *Iraq*, XXX, 2, 1968, plate XLV, ll. 10–14: *i-na tu-ar ḫu*!-*ra-di i-dan ù ṭup-pu-šu i-ḫap-pi*; the words *ina tuār ḫurādi* probably mean ‘ at the return of the army ’, but Akkadian idiom would also permit the rendering ‘ at (his) return from the army ’. Add to the references for *ulmu* ‘ lance ’ (ibid., 159) given by me to Professor Wiseman, another from an unpublished MAss. text kindly drawn to my attention by D. A. Kennedy.

merely for the duration of a seasonal campaign. In either case a comparison with TR 3005 makes it likely that he was hereby fulfilling his *ilku* obligations, and it is therefore particularly vexing that the exact length of his service cannot be established.

In view of these new instances of the word *ḫurādu*, it seems advisable to review the other usages of the word, references to which have been culled from the dictionaries. The derivation from the root *ḫrd* shows that *ḫurādu* must originally have meant ' watch ', ' guard ', or ' garrison '; this would fit well with some of the Middle Assyrian passages (see below), but the wider usage, roughly ' army ', which is found in the texts from El Amarna and Boğazköy, may also be derived from Middle Assyrian. From Assyria proper the word is not in fact very common, and the major source is *KAV* 119, which lists a total of ' 4 men missing, of the *ḫurādus*, in the charge of PN ' :[15] above this summation the men are described individually, with their names, villages, and commanding officers, and extra details are given: for the first three, ' the *ḫurādu* which brought provisions to Šinamu ',[16] and for the fourth man, ' the *ḫurādu* which laid(?) the bricks of Šinamu '.[17] Points to note here are that each *ḫurādu* was clearly a separate entity, whatever its functions; that each man is assigned to a different officer; and that they are all associated with a particular town, Šinamu.[18] This last point is echoed by a text, quoted in *AHw.*, 367, s.v., which gives three references to ' PN *ḫu-ra-di ša* LN (= name of land) ', and also of course by TR 3005 (above), where the unit is associated with Niḫria.[19]

A slightly different picture is offered by the text Billa No. 12, which is an administrative transaction and probably refers to the supply of provisions (of a rather exotic kind) to ' the king's camp of the *ḫurādu* which (is) in the land of Katmuḫi '.[20] We may deduce from this that the *ḫurādu* could operate in camps, as opposed to town garrisons, and that since it might be under the command of the king himself, it could constitute the chief fighting unit of Assyria. This is confirmed by the title of a dignitary called Ninurta-apla-iddina, who is called, not only on his own stele but also on that of his son, the *rab ḫurādi* and the *rab*

[15] Ll. 12–13 : ŠU.NIGIN$_2$ 4 ERÍN.MEŠ LÁ.MEŠ *ša ḫu-ra-da-te ša* ŠU ^{m}ÌR-^{d}*še-ru-a*.

[16] Ll. 6–7 : *ḫu-ra-du ša* ZÍD.KASKAL.MEŠ *a-na* ^{uru}*ši-na-mu ub-lu-ni*.

[17] Ll. 10–11 : *ḫu-ra-du ša* SIG$_4$.MEŠ ^{uru}*ši-na-mu il-be-ú-ni*; the translation given follows the emendation of von Soden (in *AHw.*, 552b) to *il-be-⟨nu⟩-ú-ni*. If SIG$_4$.MEŠ could be taken to refer to ' brick-work ', we might consider a derivation from *lawû*, which would then dispense with the need for emendation, and yield the general sense ' the *ḫurādu* which besieged Šinamu '.

[18] Šinamu is known to lie in northern Mesopotamia (see J.-R. Kupper, *Les nomades en Mésopotamie*, pp. 123, 230, n. 1).

[19] Niḫria is well known from Old Assyrian and Old Babylonian texts; it is variously located in the Urfa region (Garelli, *Les assyriens en Cappadoce*, 94), or in the neighbourhood of Mardin (see M. Falkner, *A f. O*, XVIII, 1, 1957, 20–2). It is therefore hardly likely to have lain in the same administrative district as Tell al-Rimaḥ, and in any case it was itself a local capital (later ?), *RLA*, II, p. 439, stele No. 66. This shows that the *ḫurādu* organization transcended provincial boundaries.

[20] See Finkelstein, *JCS*, VII, 4, 1953, 126, 153; ll. 16–20 must have read much as follows: [ ]*tu an-ni-tu* [(*x*) *ina m*]*adakti* LUGAL *ša ḫurā*[*di*] *ša*? *i-na*? KUR *katmuḫi ta*?*-ad-na-at*?? ŠU LUGAL *i-din*. . . .

kiṣri;[21] we do not know the meaning of *kiṣru* at this period, although it may already, as later, have referred to a standing unit closely associated with the king, but the title *rab ḫurādi* suggests that he held the post of ' commander of the armed forces ', a position of sufficient importance to deserve mention on the stele.[22]

To sum up then, we must recognize three possible meanings of the word: first, ' guard ' or ' garrison ', second, ' contingent ' (with plural *ḫurādāte*), and finally ' army ', the last of which was borrowed into the peripheral Akkadian dialects.

Returning to *ilku* we may now reconstruct the position briefly as follows. When an Assyrian was called on to perform his *ilku* service he became part of the *ḫurādu*—' army '—which was itself composed of separate units which might also be called *ḫurādu*. Probably most recruits performed routine defence and garrison duties in fixed localities (e.g. Niḫria), but they may also have taken part in an expedition. Although there is no evidence, we should certainly expect that military units of this kind were maintained all the year round, and that, at least initially, each man would serve a full year. The army for the major campaigns, which were recorded in the annals, will in general have been recruited on a different basis, by a much wider call-up after the harvest; this was called the *dikût māti* in Neo-Assyrian times,[23] when it seems that service for the army under such circumstances did not count as *ilku*. Whether the same applies in the Middle Assyrian period is doubtful, and in any case both types of force were probably called *ḫurādu*.

For the sake of completeness two further points should be made about military service. In the first place, we do not know of any regular corps composed of full-time soldiers; if such existed the men would have been unable to do any work on the land, and would thus probably have been landless (and therefore low-class) Assyrians, or foreign mercenaries. As already suggested above, the term *kiṣru* in the title *rab kiṣri* may, on analogy with later usage, have referred to a corps of this kind. The second point concerns state labour. Under the Sargonid kings *ilku* might take the form of simple labour on behalf of the state—earth-moving, brick-making, etc.—and this was strictly called ' the king's work ' (*dullu ša šarri*).[24] This invites comparison with the phrase *šipar šarri* encountered in the Middle Assyrian laws, where different periods of

[21] Ungnad, *RLA*, II, pp. 438–9, stele No. 67 and No. 57 (dated by Ungnad to Tiglathpileser II for reasons not specified).

[22] We should probably include in this category the passage from an annalistic text referring to Aššur-rēš-iši I, quoted in Weidner, *Die Inschriften Tukulti-Ninurtas I. und seiner Nachfolger* (*Af. O*, Beiheft 12), p. 58, No. 70: *⁹ḫu-ra-su*^{meš} ^{giš}GIGIR.MEŠ-*šu*, where *ḫurāsu* = **ḫurād-šu*. Here the word seems to be contrasted with ' chariotry ', and refers to infantry, although it may not necessarily *mean* foot-soldiers.

[23] See Postgate, *Neo-Assyrian royal grants and decrees* (Studia Pohl, Ser. Maior, 1), 10 ff., and references in index, 128. Whether the Shalmaneser I passage *KAH*, I, 13.i.30 *da-ku-ut* ERÍN.MEŠ-*ia aš-ku-un* belongs here is uncertain, see CAD, III (D), 141a.

[24] The best instance of this is Harper, *ABL*, 99, rev. 14′–16′, a passage which will be treated in the writer's study on Neo-Assyrian taxation.

the ‘ king’s labour ’ are imposed as a form of punishment. Although no reference to the king’s labour is known to me outside the laws, it is of course possible, though by no means certain, that some of those who were called up to perform their *ilku* service in Middle Assyrian times found themselves engaged in the non-military activities of the *šipar šarri*.

2: THE MIDDLE ASSYRIAN LAWS, TABLET A, § 45

Having considered the occurrences of the word *ilku*, we now turn to texts which deal with questions of land tenure, and in particular with the conditions under which land might be held from the state. We shall not return to *ilku* until the final section.

Our concern is first with the section of the Middle Assyrian laws mentioned above, which treats the problems encountered when the husband of a woman who has no other male relations to support her is taken captive.[25] As this is one of the most elusive and important of all the laws, I shall first give the Akkadian text in full, with my own translation.

46	[*šum-m*]*a* MÍ *ta-ad-na-at*	If a woman has been given (in marriage),
47	[*ù*] *mu-us-sa na-ak-ru il-te-qí*	and her husband has been taken by an enemy,
48	*e-mu-ša ù* DUMU-*ša la-áš-šu*	(and) she has no father-in-law or son,
49	2 MU.MEŠ *pa-ni mu-ti-ša ta-da-gal*	she shall belong to her husband for two years;
50	*i-na* 2 MU.MEŠ *an-na-te šum-ma ša a-ka-li*	during these two years, if there is not enough
51	[*l*]*a-*[*áš*]*-šu tal-la-ka-ma ta-qa-ab-bi*	to eat, she shall come and declare it.
52	[*šum-ma*]*a?-la-i-tu ša* É.GAL-*lim ši-it*	If she is a villager of a palace,
53	[(*x*) *x*]*x-ša ú-ša-kal-ši*	her [palace?] shall feed her,
54	[(*ù*) *ši-pa*]*-ar-šu te-ep-pa-áš*	and she shall do its? work.
55	[*šum-ma* (*x x*) *x*] *ša-a ḫu-up-še ši-i-it*	If she is the [wife?] of a *ḫupšu*,
56	[*ú*]*-ša-kal!-ši*	[. . . . .] shall feed her,
57	[ ]	[. . . . .];
58	*ù* [ ]	and, [if she is a free woman? and there is]
59	A.ŠÀ *ù* [É *x x x* (*x x x*)]	a field and [a house at her disposal (?)],
60	*tal-la-ka-*[*ma taqabbi*]	she shall come [and declare it]
61	*ma a-na a-ka-*[*li x x x x* (*x x x x*)]	saying: ‘ [I have nothing] to eat ’.
62	lúDI.KUD.MEŠ ⌜*ḫa-zi*⌝*-a-na* GAL.MEŠ *ša-a* URU	(Then) the judges shall ask the mayor (and)
63	*i-ša-’u-ú-lu*	elders of the village
64	*ki-i* A.ŠÀ *ù* É *i-na* URU *šu-a-tu il-lu-ku-ú-ni*	whether the field and house belong in that village,
65	A.ŠÀ *ù* É *a-na ú-ku-la-i-ša*	(and) they shall sell the field and house for
66	*ša* 2 MU.MEŠ *ú-up-pu-šu*	her maintenance during the two years, on
67	*i-id-du-nu-né-eš-še*	her behalf (*-še*).
68	*us-bat ù ṭup-pa-ša i-šaṭ-ṭu-ru*	She is ‘ in waiting ’ and they shall write a tablet for her (to that effect).
69	2 MU.MEŠ *tu-ma-al-la a-na mu-ut lìb-bi-ša*	She shall complete two years, (and) then
70	*tu-ú-uš-ša-ab*	she may be ‘ in waiting ’ for the husband of her choice,
71	*ṭup-pa-ša ki-i al-ma-te-ma i-šaṭ-ṭu-ru*	(and) they shall write a tablet for her as if she were an *almattu* (‘ widow ’).

[25] Cuneiform text: Schroeder, *KAV* 1, col. vi, 46–88 (p. 10); edited *inter alios* by Driver and Miles, *The Assyrian laws*, 412–15 (and discussion, 256–66); new translation and commentary by Cardascia, *Les lois assyriennes*, 217–30.

72	*šum-ma i-na ar-kàt* UD.MEŠ *mu-us-sa*	If, after a time, her lost husband returns
73	*ḫal-qu a-na ma-a-te it-tu-ú-ra*	to the land, he shall take (back) his wife
74	DAM-*su ša a-na ki-i-di*	who was married outside (his household),
75	*aḫ-zu-tu-ú-ni i-laq-qí-áš-ši*	
76	*a-na* DUMU.MEŠ *ša a-na mu-ti-ša ur-ki-e*	(but) he shall have no claim on any sons
77	*ul-du-tu-ú-ni la-a i-qar-rib*	she bore to her later husband—
78	*mu-us-sa-ma ur-ki-ú i-laq-qí*	it is her later husband who takes (them).
79	A.ŠÀ *u* É *ša ki-i ú*[!]*-kúl-la-i-ša*	The field and house which she had sold
80	*a-na* ŠÀM *ga-me-er*	outside (his household) for her maintenance,
81	*a-na ki-i-di ta-di-nu-ú-ni*	
82	*šum-ma a-na dan-na-at* LUGAL *la-a e-ru-ub*	if it? has not entered the . . . of the king,
83	*ki-i ta-ad-nu-ni-ma id-dan*	he shall pay as (much as) was paid (for it before),
84	*ù i-laq-qí*	and shall take (it back);
85	*ù šum-ma la-a it-tu-ú-ra*	and, if he has not returned,
86	*i-na ma-a-te ša-ni-te-em-ma me-et*	(but) died in another land,
87	A.ŠÀ-*šu ù* É-*su a-šar* LUGAL	the king shall give (away) his field and his
88	*id-du-nu-ú-ni i-id-dan*	house wherever he wishes to give (it).

Detailed notes to the translation

49: *pāni muti-ša tadaggal*: this is rendered by Cardascia as ' elle demeurera . . . fidèle à son mari ' (cf. CAD, III (D), 23: ' has to wait . . . for her husband '). Although the sense ' wait ' is possible, one should at least consider the alternative meaning of the phrase ' to belong to '; if this were correct the passage would stress the legal rights of the husband, although of course the general import of the passage would not be altered, and is not in dispute.

51: the text has *tallaka-ma*, which means ' she shall come ' and not (as Cardascia) ' elle ira '. The distinction is important, because with the translation ' come ' the clause suggests that she is to come forward to the very authorities who are responsible for drafting the law. Since it is not specified in the text where, or to whom, she is to come, this does not give us any direct evidence as to the identity of the promulgators of the law; but it is at least possible that they are the judges mentioned below in l. 62.

52: the case for *ālāyītu* is discussed by Cardascia (pp. 219–20); it is certainly the most plausible restoration so far proposed.

53: the sign before *ša* ends in (or is simply) a single horizontal; both [*a-b*]*u-ša* and [*ḫa-zi*]*-aš-ša* have been suggested, but these are rejected, on adequate grounds, by Cardascia. He concludes (p. 220) ' Selon toute vraisemblance, le texte contenait ici le nom d'un fonctionnaire du Palais '. A possible restoration is therefore [É.GA]L-*ša* ' her palace ', which would compel us to translate in l. 52 ' of *a* palace '. The only objection I see to this restoration is that *ēkallu* is usually feminine, while the verbal form, and especially the suffix *-šu* in l. 54 are both masculine.

64: the accepted interpretation of this line is unsatisfactory; in the first place the suggested subject for *illukūni* (the husband) is not mentioned in the preceding two lines, and possibly not at all, as such; in the second place, *alāku* is never elsewhere found with a field (or house) as direct object (see CAD, I (A), Pt. I, 313a, s.v. *eqlu* c); finally, the present tense, although it could be defended, is not expected, and a preterite would be much easier. According to my translation, I suggest that *alāku* is used here in a transferred sense rather similar to the known Middle Assyrian usage ' to be fitting ', for which see CAD, I (A), Pt. I, 312b (*alāku* 3 l.). Admittedly the exact nuance—' belong ', ' go with '—which I am suggesting is not found elsewhere either, and time alone can show whether it is correct.

66–67: *ú-up-pu-šu i-id-du-nu-né-eš-še*: these two verbs are perhaps the most crucial of the whole section. Both, for different reasons, are of uncertain translation; Cardascia elects to translate ' on attribuera . . . (et) on les lui délivrera ', thus following CAD, IV (E), 232a: ' shall assign a field . . . and give (it) to her . . . '. It is true that *uppušu* + *nadānu* is not otherwise attested in Middle Assyrian, but in Neo-Assyrian legal documents it is used in alternation with the more frequent *uppušu* + *laqā'u* as the technical term for ' to sell ' (thus e.g. ND 212, 5–7 (unpublished): PN_1 *ana* PN_2 *ú-tap-piš i-ti-din*). In this combination *uppušu* [26] must have a specific

[26] This is a regular form for the Assyrian D stem infinitive and permansive of verbs I ʿayin; cf. in NAss. texts *up-pu-šat* (von Soden, *GAG*, *Ergänzungsheft* (Analecta Orientalia, 47), p. 20**,

legal connotation which still eludes us, but which will have been similar (at least) to CAD's suggested translation (ibid., 231a) ' to conclude a sales agreement '. It is difficult to separate this Neo-Assyrian usage from the law's *uppušu* + *nadānu*, and hence I would maintain that our clause here must mean ' they shall sell '. However, it is evident from the remainder of the law that the house and field were not sold *to* the abandoned wife, and we must therefore render the dative suffix on the verb as ' for her ', ' on her behalf ',[27] and assume that the judges (or perhaps the mayor and elders) are acting in place of her husband in selling the property to someone else.

68: *us-bat ù ṭuppa-ša išaṭṭuru*: this phrase cannot simply be translated ' she shall dwell (there) and they shall write her tablet ', since this does not give the force of the use of the permansive; the permansive used before a normal tense has usually to be translated with a subordinate clause, sometimes temporal, and sometimes modal. The usage is best documented for Babylonian (M. B. Rowton, *JNES*, XXI, 4, 1962, 271ff., and R. Frankena, *Bibliotheca Orientalis*, XIX, 3–4, 1962, 164, references I owe to K. R. Veenhof), but certainly also existed in Assyrian (Rowton, art. cit., 277; *ṣaḫrāku-ma zittī ša bīt abī-ni ina ālim talqi* ' *while* I was small, you took . . . ', *CCT*, V, plate 14a, 6–8, quoted by Frankena, loc. cit.; and K. Hecker, *Grammatik der Kültepe-Texte* (Analecta Orientalia, 44), § 135). I can find no exact parallel to the usage with *ū* rather than *-ma*,[28] but the sense must be either ' while she is dwelling . . . ', or ' because . . . ', or even perhaps ' although . . . '. A final decision seems impossible at the moment.

Here and in l. 70 (*w*)*ašābu* must have a special meaning. This must be defined with reference to those passages where the verb is used with *ana muti* (laws, tablet A, § 36, and *KAJ* 9, 29f.; see CAD, I (A), Pt. II, 402); CAD, loc. cit., translates l. 70 ' she may live with a husband of her choice ', but this is difficult to reconcile with the use of *ana*. It seems better to translate ' she shall wait for the husband of her choice '. In *KAJ* 9, property is left by a man to his wife, on condition that *ana muti lā tuššab* ' she shall not wait for a husband '; if she does so, she shall take nothing away. Support for this translation, rather than ' she shall live with ', comes from Tell al-Rimaḥ, in the text TR 4251 (*Iraq*, XXX, 1, 1968, 93–5), where the writer remarks: [6]MÍ *ši-i an-ni-ki-e-em* [7]*a-na mu-tim wa-ša-ba-*[*am*] [8]*ú-ul ḫa-aš-ḫa-at* [9]*qa-du-um* DUMU.MEŠ-*ri-ša* [10]*a-na* É *ia-ba-mi-ša-ma* [11]*li-il-li-ik* ' that woman does not want to wait for a husband here; let her go with her sons to the house of her brother-in-law '.[29] All these passages go to suggest that a married woman who had lost her husband and wished to remarry was said to ' be waiting for a husband '; perhaps, if she did not wish to remarry, or (as here) was unable to, she was simply ' in waiting '. If this is correct —and it does at least give some significance to *usbat*—then the condition of ' being in waiting ' was legally recognized, since a tablet could be written acknowledging it, different from the kind of tablet which would be written if she were a woman with no surviving male support (*almattu*). For the duration of the two years, the deserted wife is treated as if she were a widow who had a father-in-law or sons to support her. We may note in passing that this use of *wašābum* reveals an Assyrian practice in the Old Babylonian text from Tell al-Rimaḥ.

79–84: the basic statement in these lines is *eqla ū bēta . . . ilaqqi* ' he shall take (back) the field and house ', where the *ilaqqi* is preceded by what is in effect a condition: ' (if) he (re)pays as was paid ' (*kī tadnūni-ma iddan ū*). In 79–81, Cardascia translates ' qui, au titre de son (= de la femme) entretien, ont été donnés au dehors pour un prix entier . . . '; this cannot be right, because *ta-di-nu-ú-ni* must be preterite (*taddinūni*) and not permansive (which would be *tadnūni*, as in l. 83), so that it is the wife who is here said to have sold the field and house.[30] This would

§ 97e); *urrubu* (*erābu*), *ABL*, 427, rev. 3; *uttuku* (*etāku*), *ABL*, 170 rev. 14; *uṭṭuru* (*eṭāru*), CAD, IV (E), 405–6 (in legal cases); *ul-lu-e* (*elā'u*), *Iraq*, XVII, 2, 1955, p. 127, l. 35; cf. also below, p. 510, n. 50.

[27] The use of a dative suffix to give this meaning does not require documentation, but cf. *išaṭṭuruniššu* ' they shall write for him ' in *KAJ* 177, 17.

[28] *KAJ* 177, 13–15 (*šumma ina pāni-šu mamma lā ēriš ū tadnaššu*) has a sort of apodotic *ū* which is also attested in Old Assyrian (Hecker, *Grammatik der Kültepe-Texte*, § 138a).

[29] This interpretation agrees well with the fact that she is to go *with her sons* to the house of her brother-in-law, thus joining his family group; she could hardly remove them from their father's authority if he were alive. We must assume, however, that the *be-la-sú-nu* of l. 20, whose husband is alive, is different from the *be-la-as-su-*[*nu*] of l. 4; this is supported by the *šanītam* of l. 20, which should introduce a new topic (or we could translate ' the other (= *šanītam*) Bēlassunu ' !).

[30] I know of no other instance where **parisūni* stands for *parsūni* in MAss., although it is

clearly be impossible according to earlier interpretations of the section, but if the land was sold on her behalf, as I have suggested, then she may easily be said here to have sold it herself. The weakness in Cardascia's translation is realized by the editor himself: he is forced to translate *kī tadnūni-ma iddan* as ' selon (les conditions auxquelles) ils avaient été (antérieurement) concédés, il paiera (un cens) et il (les) prendra '. This he has to take as referring to the payment of rent (or similar) by the first husband on the same terms as the second husband, and he rightly remarks that ' on s'étonne que le rédacteur ait éludé le vocable qui eût éclairé sa pensée: par exemple *biltu iddan* . . . '. The idea that we have to do with rent is in any case contradicted by the phrase *ana šīm gamer*, which is used regularly in Middle Assyrian documents with *nadānu* to describe a completed sale, and could not be applied to a pledge or payment of rent. The use of this phrase here is confirmation that in ll. 66–7 the property was indeed being legally sold, and not merely ' assigned '.

82: *šumma ana dan-na-at šarri lā ērub*: this phrase is still unclear. It has traditionally (and no doubt correctly) been compared with the similar phrase in the Code of Hammurapi (§§ 27–8), which is usually rendered ' in a fortress ' or ' in the armed forces ' (of the king). However, this rendering is itself uncertain, and *dannutu* (**dannatu*) or *dannātu* is not known elsewhere in Middle Assyrian texts with any such meaning; moreover, as realized by other commentators, it is awkward to have a man supposedly re-entering the armed forces even before he has reclaimed his wife and land. Rather, we require in this context a phrase which will in some way preclude the land's resale to its original owner, and such a condition is more likely to apply to the land than to the man. I therefore take it that the subject of *ērub* is the land, and this is supported by the preterite tense of the verb, which makes the action previous to the man's return (*eqlu* is used by itself, without *bētu*, in l. 64 also). Therefore I would propose that the phrase in some way describes the assumption of the lands into the royal domain, from which they cannot be redeemed by the original owner (exact semantic shift of **dannatu* uncertain).

Discussion

Since my version of the law differs considerably from that of earlier editors, it may be useful to summarize their position before drawing conclusions from my revised translation; this will define the points at issue. To do this I rely chiefly on the translation and commentary of Cardascia (219–26), who has selected the best of the previous versions and made improvements of his own.

In general there is agreement about the meaning of the opening section of the law (ll. 46–57). From l. 57 onwards, according to Cardascia (pp. 221 ff.), we are concerned with the case of a soldier who is provided with a ' fief ' in return for his military service;[31] he is of superior social standing to the two previously mentioned classes, since his wife is not required to work for her living during his absence. Further, during the two years which she must wait for him, her maintenance is provided for her, by the enjoyment of a house and field assigned to her by the authorities. Cardascia here takes analogies from Old Babylonian practice to support his contention that, in the absence of the holder (or any eligible substitute), the land must in theory revert immediately to the crown (here represented by the authorities, i.e. the judges and the mayor

quite acceptable in late NAss. Professor Garelli refers me for this passage to J. Lewy, *Das Verbum in den ' altassyrischen Gesetzen '* (Berliner Beiträge zur Keilschriftforschung, I, 4), p. 37, n. 3, and p. 72, n. 9, but this is in fact the only instance quoted.

[31] It should be noted that the only reason for supposing that the man was on military service is the phrase ' an enemy has taken her husband ' (l. 47); this could, however, also refer to a merchant (cf. Code of Hammurapi, § 103), and there are therefore no grounds for assuming *a priori* that the land in debate in the second part of the law is held by him in return for military service in which he is engaged.

and the elders of the village) before it can be reassigned to her for the period concerned. He concedes that the land she receives will almost certainly have been exactly the same as her husband's original 'fief'; the reason for the intervention of the local authorities is to ensure that the woman is indeed entitled to the land.

Ll. 69–78 deal with the remarriage of the woman who holds the 'fief', and various possible consequences. Cardascia rightly rejects Szlechter's hypothesis that the section concerns all remarriages. This passage is fairly straightforward, but the ensuing section has given much trouble. Broadly, Cardascia follows Szlechter, and supposes that the land (and house) which was given to the woman for her maintenance is somehow rented to a third person (although this is not stated in the text), so that her maintenance is in fact to be provided from the rent collected by her from the lease of the land (see above, p. 505, note to ll. 79–84). This theory is necessary because on the return of the first husband the land is clearly not in his wife's possession, but has to be recovered by him from a third party. Finally, Cardascia seems to agree with Driver and Miles that the clause in ll. 82–4 implies that the returned captive would be reinvested with the 'fief', even though no longer engaged in military service. It is surely correct, that he is reinvested with the land, although the difficulty they envisage is removed if we assume that the 'fiefs' of the kind here treated were held more permanently (as a hereditary right), and not, as they assume, only by men actively engaged in military service.

Detailed reasons for rejecting the basis of the views just described have been given in the commentary, and it now only remains to put forward my own reconstruction. The law is framed in the typical rambling, almost anecdotal, style of this legislator, and defies any quick analysis. For our purposes we may take it in two main parts, first, the provisions for the maintenance of the 'grass-widow' during her two years of waiting, and secondly, the procedure to be followed on the unexpected return of the first husband after her remarriage.

Ll. 46–71: the introduction to the law gives us the basic premises: a married woman has been left without means of support because she has no sons, or father-in-law, and her husband has been captured by an enemy.[32] In these circumstances she must wait for two years before she may reattach herself to another family, and this section determines how she is to be supported during that period. The method of support depends on her husband's social or legal status; in two cases (when the wife is a 'villager dependant of the palace', and when the husband is a *ḫupšu*), the position is simple, and the responsibility is fairly easily assigned, although the details are lost in the break. It is the third case which leads to complications, and from this point onwards the law concerns exclusively the third case, that of the woman whose husband held a field and house. The complications largely follow because the legislator has

[32] Not necessarily in battle; see p. 505, n. 31.

tried to describe simultaneously the fate of the woman and the fate of the property.

The provisions are as follows: like the other women, she has to come before the authorities (probably themselves the judges); the judges will then inquire of the local authorities of the village to establish that the property does belong there, and having done this they are to sell the property on her behalf in order to provide for her maintenance during the two years.[33] Presumably the proceeds of the sale are handed over to her, and would have been sufficient for two years' maintenance.

The question which confronts us here, is why the field (and house) had to be sold at all, and, initially, at least, two answers seem to be possible. The answer may be one of expediency, in that, without male relations, the woman may be unable to cultivate the land for herself, whether for physical or social reasons—such as an absence of rights to arrange for hired labour, etc.; if this is the case, then the intervention of the judges will have been necessary because she does not herself have the legal right to dispose of property owned by her husband. The alternative answer would postulate legal reasons why the woman should not be permitted to continue enjoying the land in her husband's absence.[34] This seems less likely, since men must often have been away for long periods without prejudicing their wives' right to derive their living from the property, and an extension of such a period for two years would not create great problems. More significantly, this whole section is drafted so that the measures described are only taken at the woman's own request, and it is explicitly stated that she is only expected to come forward if she has no means of support.[35] The former explanation must therefore be the correct one.

Ll. 72–85: if, after she has remarried, the wife's first husband returns, the law provides that he may recover both his wife and his property. The wife returns from her second husband's household (although her sons must stay), while his land has to be bought back from the man who acquired it from the judges acting on his wife's behalf; there is, incidentally, no reason to suppose that this man is the same as the wife's second husband.

Ll. 85–8 prescribe that if the man does not return, the king shall give the field and house to anyone he may choose. This introduces us to a central problem: it appears to contradict the previous statement that the property is to have been sold off 'for the full price' to the third party. As I have said, *ana šīm gamer nadānu* is the phrase used in an ordinary sale, and there is nothing in the text to indicate that this sale, made by the authorities, was any less permanent than an ordinary private sale.[36] We may therefore be justified

[33] The subject of *uppušu iddununešše* in ll. 66–7 is probably the judges, who are the subject of the preceding verb, and not the mayor and elders.

[34] Such as those adduced by Cardascia (222), by analogy with Babylonia.

[35] 'if there is not enough to eat . . .' (ll. 50–1).

[36] Except, of course, for the right of the previous owner to buy the land back, but this is specifically provided for by the law.

in deducing that even land sold normally was not held outright by the purchaser, but, under certain circumstances, was also liable to revert to the king.

A clue as to what such circumstances might be is given us by this very law. I hope to show below that lands held under a concession from the crown were liable to revert to the crown when no member of the family to which the concession was made survived. In this case, the first husband had not reappeared, and hence his family was effectively defunct and the lands would be expected to revert to the crown, as stated. Apparently the fact that they had already been sold to a third party (*ana kīdi*) does not affect this: once the original concessionaire's claim lapses, the grant is automatically cancelled, whoever may be holding the field at that moment. However, we need not suppose that the new owner in the law goes entirely without compensation for his loss—when the king 'gives' the field he may do no more than concede the rights to tenure, while the monetary value of the land could be subject to different arrangements.

3: ALLOCATION OF TENURES BY THE CROWN

The discussion of the final part of the law leads us to consider in greater detail the evidence for land tenure and its conditions under the Middle Assyrian monarchy. Recently Garelli has dealt with the question of 'feudal' land tenure at this period, and with the problems of private and public ownership.[37] He distinguishes three main categories of land: that owned by the (local or central) palace (i.e. the king, the state), private property, and land leased (or otherwise made over) by the palace to private persons.[38] While admitting that such categories must have existed, I try to show in the discussion below that those lands placed by Garelli in the last category should rather be considered normal 'private' property, and, in particular, that the texts relating to grants or concessions from the palace refer to ordinary private land tenure.

There is a small group of texts from Assur, mostly of a rather early date,[39] whose common feature is that they record the transfer of a right to land tenure by the state from one party to another;[40] three of the texts describe the property so transferred as *zitti ēkalli*.[41] While not all the tablets document all the possible stages in the transaction, as a group they attest four phases into which the procedure may be divided.

(1) The original 'ownership' of the land, under a man whose claim has lapsed for some reason. Here the chief problem is why the man's claim should

[37] *Semitica*, XVII, 1967, 5–27, especially 6–14.

[38] ibid., 6.

[39] Dating: Aššur-nirari II (1426–1420), *KAJ* 177, with mention of Aššur-rabi; Aššur-bēl-nišē-šu (1419–1411), tablets mentioned in *KAJ* 162 and 172; Erīb-adad (1392–1366), *KAJ* 183, *KAJ* 160 (also mentions [Aššur]-uballiṭ as crown prince); Aššur-uballiṭ I (1365–1330), *KAJ* 173, *KAV* 212 (dates after Brinkman in Oppenheim, *Ancient Mesopotamia*, 346).

[40] The texts referred to in this section are: *KAJ* 160; 162; 172; 173 (= *KAV* 210); 177; 183 (= *KAV* 93); *KAV* 212.

[41] ḪA.LA É.GAL-*lim* (*KAJ* 172); ḪA.LA É.GAL-*lim a-di* ŠE-*ša* (*KAJ* 173); ŠE-*um ša* ḪA.LA É.GAL-*lim* (*KAJ* 183; see below, p. 510, n. 51).

have lapsed. As Garelli has pointed out,[42] in three cases (*KAJ* 160; 162; *KAV* 212 [43]) the man is called a ^{lú}*na-ia-a-li(m)*, and this must be compared with the use of the same word in the Akkadian texts from Ugarit, where it seems to mean a ' feudal tenant from whom his land has been withdrawn ' (' Lehnsmann, dem das Land entzogen wird ', *AHw.*, s.v.; see Nougayrol, *PRU*, III, 29). It is obvious that in these three Middle Assyrian occurrences also the term must be connected with the withdrawal of the man's rights to the land. Two reasons have been suggested for his loss of these rights: death,[44] and forfeiture as a penalty.[45] While the evidence is not very conclusive, neither of these seems very satisfactory; the first is unlikely because at Ugarit the *naiālu* is known to be alive; the second suggestion is not impossible, but is questionable in view of the relatively frequent occurrence of the term. There is, however, a third possibility, not that the first holder was dead, but that he had no heir to inherit the concession on his eventual death. Without going into the etymology of the word, it seems possible that a *naiālu* may have been the male equivalent of an *almattu*—i.e. a man with no living father and no male heirs.[46] As such, on his death, there would under Middle Assyrian laws of inheritance be no available heir to his property.[47] This would furnish an explanation for the reversion of the land to the crown.

(2) The reversion of the land to the king. The only texts which help us here are those which refer to a *zitti ēkalli*. It is generally agreed that the phrase *zitti ēkalli* must describe land which has in some way reverted from private

[42] op. cit., 10.

[43] It should be noted at this stage that no text has both the term *zitti ēkalli* and the word *naiālu*. The connexion I make between the two is purely on the grounds of the similarity of the transactions.

[44] Opinion attributed to Koschaker by Garelli (10); but not expressed in *NKRA*, for which see below, n. 45. It seems rather to have been an idea discarded by Nougayrol (*PRU*, III, p. 29, n. 5).

[45] So Koschaker, *NKRA* (*Neue keilschriftliche Rechtsurkunden aus der El-Amarna Zeit* (Abhandlungen der Sächsischen Akademie der Wissenschaften, Phil.-hist. Kl., XXXIX, 5), Leipzig, 1928), 44 (with reference to *zitti ēkalli*), and Nougayrol, *PRU*, III, p. 29, with notes (4) and (5), p. 234 ' (exploitant) défaillant '.

[46] This proposal gains support from the difficult NAss. letter (from Assur) *KAV* 197, 58–60: *an-ni-u la* ^{lú}PAP-*u-ni šu-u na-a-a-lu*! *šu-u i-na* É ^{m}PAP-*u-a*-SU *e-tar-ba* . . . ' this man is not our brother, he is a *naiālu* (and) he has entered the house of Aḫua-erība . . . ' (emendation after von Soden, *AHw.*, 717a).

[47] Once (*a*) the father died and (*b*) the brothers had made the division, the separate brothers had no rights to property which had been divided, even if the line of one brother died out. This is indicated not only by tablet A, § 45, discussed above, but by § 25, where only the *undivided* brothers of an *almattu*'s husband have any right to property he gave her.

The role of the extended family in Middle Assyrian times has, in my opinion, been exaggerated. Most families probably stayed together during the life of the paterfamilias, but evidence that this state of affairs usually survived his death for any length of time is scanty. It is true that the laws often mention the case of ' undivided ' brothers (see Cardascia, 71), but this may equally well be taken to show that it was an uncommon situation which required legislation precisely because the solution was not accepted by tradition. I would compare the position in Assyria with that described in P. Stirling, *Turkish village*, New York, 1966, 131 ff., where he says ' The rule is clear. On the death of a household head, his sons are expected within a reasonable period to divide up the property between them and establish separate independent households '.

' ownership ' to the royal domain; the use of the word *zittu* ' share ' would seem to imply that only a part of the land concerned went to the state, and this is the view expressed by D'yakonov, for example, with reference to the case of Bur-šarru.[48] However, there is in fact no evidence that tenures called *zitti ēkalli* formed only a part of the property, and I suggest that the position is much simplified if we take *zittu* to mean, roughly, no more than ' inheritance ',[49] thus leaving it open whether one or more persons did in fact inherit. This allows us to take *zitti ēkalli* to mean ' an inheritance (of land) falling to the palace ', i.e. the normal term for land reverting to the state in default of any other heir(s).

In the other texts, which do not use the term *zitti ēkalli*, we only know that the land had previously been held by another owner because the land conceded is identified by reference to his name; particular interest attaches to *KAV* 212, which, although difficult, seems to document the transfer of *all* a man's property.[50]

(3) The redistribution of the land. Land which has reverted in this way to the king is formally reissued to a new holder in three texts, *KAJ* 173 (= *KAV* 210),[51] *KAJ* 177,[52] and *KAV* 212. Only in *KAJ* 173 is the land designated as

[48] op. cit., 216. He states: ' the existence of extended families almost excluded the possibility of death without an heir. Besides, in two of the cases when the documents mention the " share of the palace " (i.e. in the " house " of Pūr-šarri and in that of Šamaš-āmerī) there is not a shadow of doubt that this " share " was situated in the " house " of a man who had either nephews and other relatives, or several sons '. On the other hand

(1) Only sons would inherit (see p. 509, n. 47).

(2) Šamaš-āmerī is too common a name to prove that this Šamaš-āmerī (in *KAJ* 174) is identical with that in *KAJ* 1 (see Ebeling, MAOG, XIII, 1, 1939, 81); the same applies to the possible identity of Igāiu in *KAJ* 149, who was a grandfather, and the Igāiu called a *naiālu* in *KAJ* 160 (Ebeling, op. cit., 45).

(3) If it be argued (with Fine, *HUCA*, XXIV, 1952–3, p. 200, n. 11) that some of Bur-šarru's property was inherited by his nephews or their sons, this is incorrect. The only property known to have belonged to Bur-šarru is mentioned in *KAJ* 172, where it is a *zitti ēkalli*; the rest of the property referred to by Fine came from his brother, Kubi-ēreš, who presumably inherited it direct from their father, Bēlia.

(4) As to the name ' Būr(Pūr)-šar(ru) ' (thus Ebeling, D'yakonov, etc.) the copy in *KAJ* 172, 2, and 175, 10, makes it quite possible that we should prefer the (known) deity ᵈTIŠPAK to a ᵈ*bur*, particularly when we compare the sign read *bur* by Ebeling in *KAJ* 74, 3. The name should perhaps therefore be read Tišpak-šar.

[49] As we shall see below, *zittu* is commonly used to mean ' inherited property '; the shift of meaning from ' share ' to ' inherited share ' to ' inheritance ' is not difficult; cf. already the use in the late OAss. text quoted in p. 516, n. 78.

[50] 1–3: A.ŠÀ-*šu* . . . *ù x ú*?-*bi*?-*šu*? *a-šar ù*?-*zu-bu-ú-ni* ' his land and his? . . . wherever it is deposited '. For *uzzub* as D permansive of *ezābu* see above, p. 503, n. 26; the rare D stem will be due to the plural subject (' Poebel-Pi'el '); for *ù* used syllabically see *KAJ* 2, 12 (von Soden, Analecta Orientalia, 42, p. 51, No. 264).

[51] This text disposes of the *zitti ēkalli* together with its corn (see p. 508, n. 41). This must mean that the new recipient is also given the crops actually standing on the land. *KAJ* 183 mentions the corn of a *zitti ēkalli* by itself; in this case Iddin-aššur must presumably have been granted the crops (unharvested because of the death intestate of the owner) while the land itself was still undistributed.

[52] Here Koschaker translates *usaḫḫirūni* (l. 9) as ' überlassen hatte ' (*NKRA*, p. 47, n. 2) and takes it to describe the issue of the land to Kidinnia. Certain restoration of ll. 7–8 seems impossible, and the reason for the re-allotment of the land must therefore also remain uncertain; a simple rendering of *saḫḫuru* as ' to return ', ' to hand back ' might be considered.

zitti ēkalli, but in the other texts the previous owner is mentioned by name, and the king (*uklu*) was involved in each transaction. There can therefore be no reason to doubt that they too refer to *zitti ēkalli* land, although it is far from proved.

The chief problem about the reissue of land is whether it is given to its new owner on the same terms as those under which it would originally have been granted. On this point the evidence is rather scanty. The term used for the reissue is simply *nadānu*, which tells us nothing, and there are no provisions as to duties or restrictions which apply to the land. We should be in a better position to answer this question if we knew how the original holder could establish *his* claim to the land: it is natural to assume that he received a simple tablet with the royal seal, confirming his right to the land, but we have no example of such a text, and it is obviously also conceivable that some holdings of this kind were by custom long-established, and needed no such documentation. However, it is possible that a reference to such a tablet does exist: in *KAJ* 160 and 172 (for which see below, under (4)) tablets giving the rights to a tenure are mentioned, but it is not absolutely clear at what stage these documents were prepared and sealed by the crown; in *KAJ* 162, however, the tablets bearing the royal seal are definitely those ' of ' (*ša*) Šamaš-magir, who is described as a *naiālu*.[53] It therefore appears that the original owner could have a sealed tablet similar to (though obviously not identical with) those actually known to us in the case of a reissue.[54] Why in these instances the original tablet should also retain any validity after the land's redistribution is unknown; we can only say that although the land is ' given ' to the new ' owners ', some recognition is made of the fact that it had previously been another man's tenure.[55]

Note finally that in *KAV* 212, 10, and *KAJ* 177, 16, provision is made for the new recipient to dispose of other possible claims before taking undisputed possession.[56]

(4) Transfer of the deeds. Finally, in three of the texts we witness tablets such as those just discussed being themselves transferred. In two cases the tablet(s) concerned are simply sold, and with them the right to the possession of the land. In the third document (*KAJ* 162) the ' seller ' of the tablet does not in fact have the right to dispose of the property yet, but he is able to deposit the deeds confirming his eventual right to it in a house of his creditor to act as a security, and provision is made that if he gains the right to the land, he is to sell it to his creditor and to no other.[57] The reason why the ' seller '

[53] Ll. 2–4: [1 *ṭ*]*uppu ša* NA$_4$.KIŠIB$_3$ $^{\text{m.d}}$*aššur-bēl-nišē-šu ukli*(*m*) [*ša* $^{\text{m.d}}$]*šamaš-magir* . . . [^{lú}]*naiāli*.

[54] viz. *KAJ* 173, 177, and *KAV* 212.

[55] The explanation for this is probably that the original tablet contained an accurate description of the property, which was not necessarily repeated on the new one (e.g. *KAJ* 173).

[56] *KAV* 212, 10–11: *ú-za-ak-ka-ma i-laq-qí* ' he shall clear (it) and (then) take (it) '; *KAJ* 177, 16–17: *ú-za-ak-ka-ma ṭup-pa dan-na-ta i-ša-aṭ-ṭu-ru-ni-iš-šu* ' he shall clear (it) and (then) they will write a " valid tablet " for him '.

[57] See Koschaker, *NKRA*, 45–7.

(Ilu-tašmar) does not have the right to sell the tablets at once is because the property is not yet 'cleared' for him; various reasons for this could be suggested, but it may simply be that the *naiālu* (Šamaš-magir) was not yet dead, and that arrangements for the land's distribution could still be made in advance.

The noteworthy feature about these three texts is that private persons were able to make a transfer of the possession of a crown tenure without apparent royal intervention. It suggests that once the right to the land has been (re-)conceded the crown retains no further interest in it, unless the entitlement of the original holder (or his descendants) lapses.

To sum up, *zitti ēkalli* was a term applied to land which had gone to the crown in the absence of any other heir. There is no reason to suppose that the land was so designated before it became apparent that no heir was available, and hence there is no good reason to differentiate this kind of land, which may revert to the crown, from any other land held under normal conditions of private 'ownership'. This is opposed to the view of Garelli (*Semitica*, XVII, 1967, p. 9, n. 3), that in *KAJ* 172 and 173 the *zitti ēkallim ša bīt* PN may be a tenure conceded by the king, which reverted by law to the crown at the death of the holder, and is therefore not normal, privately 'owned', land. Rather, I would maintain that all privately 'owned' land was originally conceded by the crown to its 'owners', and that it therefore naturally reverts to the crown for concession when (and probably only when) the direct line of succession fails.

4: EVIDENCE FROM THE LAND SALE DOCUMENTS

Since we have broached the subject of land tenure, it is clearly desirable to consider the evidence of the land sale documents.[58] To deal with the procedure of land sale in detail is beyond the scope of this article, and I must therefore restrict the discussion to two main points: the distinction between inherited land (*zittu*) and purchases (*ši'amātu*),[59] and the evidence for the intervention of the state in the 'ordinary' land transaction.

zittu and *ši'amātu*. In *KAJ* 153 Šamaš-tukultī sells to Bil-kube (reading of name uncertain) 12 *iku* of land, which is to be taken either from his (Šamaš-tukultī's) inheritance, or from his purchases, or from the purchases of his father; a similar provision is found in *KAJ* 155, and in *KAJ* 149 the land being sold is described as 'from the purchases of Igāiu, his grandfather'. The fact that a distinction of this kind is remembered for two generations, and is mentioned in these legal documents, implies that it must have had some legal

[58] The texts which form the basis of the ensuing discussion are *KAJ* 146–55, 164, 174–5, and 179 (in addition to those already discussed in § 3). Note the paucity of the texts.

[59] *Zittu*: *KAJ* 148, 4–5, 30; 149, 4; 151, 8; 153, 5; 155, 5; 164, 7; 174, 8; 175, 16–17; 179, 9; also (?) 24, 14.

Ši'amātu: *KAJ* 149, 6; 153, 5–6; 155, 5–6; 164, 10; 175, 21 (?); 179, 10 (written *ši-ma-tu-šu*); this last variant spelling suggests that the usual writing stands for *ši'mātu* with the *aleph* creating an audible *a*-sound before the *m*.

It should be noted that these two terms are not found on their own; we always have *zitti*/*ši'amāt* PN or *zittu-šu*.

significance, and suggests that the two kinds of land are held under different terms. Given all that we know of the meticulous recording of the Assyrian scribes, we may thus fairly assume that there was documentary evidence to demonstrate the different nature of the two kinds of holding, and a clue to the kind of document may be found in *KAJ* 164. This text records the sale of two tablets together with the land to which they constitute the entitlement; the present owner of the tablets is Maṣi-šamaš, but he inherited them through his father from his grandfather, Itti-ili-balāṭu. He in turn had bought the land from two sons of Kubi-ērеš (probably his uncle of that name, so that the sons were his first cousins), who had inherited the property in the ordinary way.[60] The tablets concerned were presumably prepared at the time when Itti-ili-balāṭu bought the land, and they will therefore be tablets documenting the transfer of ' ownership ' to him from the brothers, Šamaš-naṣir and Urad-šerua (it is much less likely that the tablets were bought by Itti-ili-balāṭu from them as title-deeds, which would mean that they only recorded the entitlement of the two brothers to the land, and that a separate document would be needed to show the change of ownership).[61] In either case, we have the unusual situation that the tablets giving the entitlement can be passed on with the land from one ' owner ' to the next; we observed a similar procedure in the case of two *zitti ēkalli* texts (see above, p. 511, under (4)). I shall return below to the question of why tablets were handed on in these instances and not in others; for the time being our concern is with the distinction between *ši'amātu* and *zittu* lands.

This distinction has been discussed by D'yakonov (207–8), and he concludes that the ' difference between *zittu* and *ši'amātu* most probably consisted in that the former was a part of the common estate of the family, while the latter was in the private possession of the purchaser '. This distinction depends on D'yakonov's conception of the extended family, which I do not think can be demonstrated for the Middle Assyrian period, and it is therefore hard to accept.[62] He also maintains that ' a plot bought by one's father or grandfather became *zittu*, a hereditary share, in the following generations '.[63] This is also question-

[60] This is shown by the *zitti* (ḪA.LA) before the name of Urad-šerua; it may be accidental that the term does not also appear before his brother's name.

[61] *ši'amāt* (l. 10) stands closer to the mention of the land than to that of the tablets, and elsewhere it always refers to land.

[62] Despite the opinion of Koschaker (*NKRA*, 40) and D'yakonov (206 ff.), I see no reason to assume the existence of joint family holdings (after the death of the father) as a regular feature. Individuals disposed of land called *zittu* just as freely as *ši'amātu* land, which would be impossible if the former were shared with other members of the family (or *Eigentumsgemeinschaft*) or community, and the latter not. See p. 509, n. 47, and p. 516, n. 75.

[63] No evidence is given for this assertion, although support for it might be sought in *KAJ* 149, where property described as ' the purchases of his ' (the seller's) ' grandfather ' includes as the last item ' a well, his inheritance ' (ḪA.LA-*šu*). *Zittu* here might refer to the well only, but it could be taken to apply to the whole property, which would then, uniquely, be described both as *ši'amātu* and as *zittu*. If this is indeed so, it would mean that *zittu* was here understood to mean an ' inherited purchase ', and not a true ' inheritance '. The text referred to in p. 516, n. 78, may reflect a similar usage.

able: *KAJ* 164, just quoted, shows that the distinction was maintained over at least two generations, and *KAJ* 153 and 149 also refer to the 'purchases' of a man's father or grandfather. It is obviously conceivable that after some length of time purchased lands, which were of course also inherited by the next generation, may have been referred to as *zittu*, but what evidence we have points in the other direction. If all inherited land was identical, whether originally purchased or 'hereditary', there would be no purpose in retaining the distinction, nor in the long 'case-histories' we find in some of the texts.[64] It follows that *zittu* land means not just 'inherited', but more precisely 'non-purchased hereditary land', and my suggestion is that it corresponds to land which had been originally conceded directly to the family by the crown.

As D'yakonov has observed,[65] the legal effect of a sale of *zittu* land differed apparently in no way from that of the sale of purchased land. From the point of view of the new 'owner' this is perhaps not very surprising, since both would become 'purchases' for him without distinction, but it seems from texts where the buyer is given the choice of 'hereditary' or purchased land without any condition, that there was in fact very little difference between the two types for the seller also.[66] Why then was the distinction important? We have seen that in the law (tablet A, § 45) land sold outside the family (*ana kīdi*) was liable to revert to the crown if the original owner failed to return and reclaim it. As I suggested there, the law seems to show that once the original concessionaire's claim has lapsed (owing to death or disappearance), the land reverted to the state (becoming, according to my theory, a *zitti ēkalli*), and could then be re-conceded. Whether under such circumstances the party which lost the land received any compensation is unknown; in any case, if this reconstruction is correct, the purchaser would be aware of the risk he was running since it would be clear whether the family of the original concessionaire was liable to die out in the near future. If all 'ordinary' land was subject to these conditions, we should have a very clear distinction between *ši'amātu* and *zittu* since the former would theoretically be liable to revert to the crown due to causes unconnected with the new 'owner'; however, the evidence is very slender, and we cannot assert this with certainty.

State intervention. A regular feature of land sale texts is a set of provisions reading: 'he (/they) shall "clear" the land (from claims) and measure (it) with the royal measure, and he (/they) shall write the "valid tablet" (*ṭuppa dannata*) before (?: *ana pāni*) the king';[67] some texts add: 'until he (/they)

[64] In particular *KAJ* 164 and 175.

[65] op. cit., 207–8.

[66] *KAJ* 153; 155; *KAJ* 179, which offers a similar choice, is a gift to a man's son, and not therefore strictly relevant; cf. also *KAJ* 24, 14–17, which should probably be restored: *lu-ú i-na* ḪA.[LA-*šu*] *ù lu-ú i-na* [*ši'amāt*] ᵐDUMU.ᵈ·ⁱᵈ*idiglat a-bi-šu*.

[67] *eqla uzakka ina ašal šarri imaddad ū ṭuppa dannata ana pān*(*i*) *šarri išaṭṭar*—*KAJ* 14; 27; 35; 146–51; 153–5; plural (*uzakku'u, imaddudu, išaṭṭuru*)—*KAJ* 12; 66; 68; 152; other variants—for *eqla KAJ* 147, 19, has [*eqla*] *qaqqar āli ū kirâ*, *KAJ* 149, 18, has *eqla adra qaqqar āli būra*, *KAJ* 66, 30, has *šaprātu-šunu*; for *ana pāni*, *KAJ* 150, 16, and 151, 19, have *a*(*p*)*pāni*;

has (/have) written the " valid tablet " before (?) the king, this one is " valid " '.[68] The ' valid tablet ' is clearly the final document which will constitute the proof of the purchaser's claim to possession; the texts which contain this provision are therefore not themselves the final documents,[69] but they do record the payment of the purchase price, and the sale is considered effectively to have taken place.[70] What remains to be done is to ' clear ' the land of claims,[71] to measure out the land—apparently done by the seller, although the purchaser is usually entitled to select the property himself,[72] and to submit the final document to the authorities.[73]

We therefore know of the intervention of the authorities at two stages of the transaction: first, before the sale is made, they supervise the public announcement of it, and give official confirmation that the sale may proceed, as other claims are excluded; this we know from the laws, tablet B, § 6.[74] Secondly, after the *de facto* sale, they provide the ' royal measure ' (possibly witnessing the measurement), and validate the *ṭuppu dannutu.* In neither case is there any reason to suppose that the state takes an interest in the transaction on its own behalf: it is there to act as an impartial arbiter, and to lend its

for *ṭuppa KAJ* 12, 18, has *ṭup-pí*; *KAJ* 27 and 152 omit the second part of the clause (after *imaddad*).

[68] *adi ṭuppa dannata ana pāni šarri išaṭṭurūni annītu-ma dannat*—*KAJ* 12; 148; 151; 152 (prob. omitting *ana pāni šarri*); *išaṭṭurūni* may of course be either singular or plural.

The phrase *ana pāni* is generally rendered ' before, in the presence of ', although for this one might rather have expected *ina pāni*; *ana pāni* could also mean ' for ' or ' on behalf of '.

[69] As generally recognized; called by Garelli (7) ' promesses de vente ' (as opposed to ' actes de vente '), and by Koschaker (*NKRA*, 27) ' Kaufvertrag '.

[70] This is evident from the phrase ' he has sold for the full price ' (*ana šīm gamer iddin*), and the ensuing ' the field is acquired (?) and received ' (*eqlu uppu laqi*, cf. CAD, I (A), Pt. II, 202b); the occurrence of the second phrase in the consequences of failure to pay a debt on time (e.g., *KAJ* 12 or 14) is not relevant, since it is there effectively in a conditional apodosis.

[71] *zakkû* (or *zakku'u*) ' to clear (of claims) ' is used constantly in MAss. texts in a variety of contexts. It is unexpected here because the land should already have undergone a process designed to exclude other claims, because of the specific statement in the texts that ' there is no (further) withdrawal or litigation ' (*tuāru ū dabābu laššu*), and because the purchase price has already changed hands.

[72] That these processes were done by the seller is apparent from the texts where land is sold by more than one person, and the relevant verbs are consequently in the plural (see p. 514, n. 67).

[73] The simple phrase *ana pāni šarri* (see above, n. 68) does not tell us what was involved here. Exceptional is *KAJ* 177 (a royal concession), where the ' clearing ' is apparently done by the eventual recipient, and in the absence of a seller his ' valid tablet ' is to be written for him by the authorities (see p. 511, n. 56).

[74] Garelli's description of the process (7–8) is accurate at most points (as against, e.g. Cardascia, 269 ff.; for detailed comment see *BSOAS*, XXXIV, 2, 1971, 388–9), but it is incorrect to say that the officials named here prepare the ' acte de vente ': the only tablets mentioned are those which confirm that the proclamations of the herald have been made, and that any further claims are void. Either (against Koschaker, *NKRA*, 34, and Garelli), the land sale texts we have must have been written after this stage, because in them (one part of) the sale has already taken place (see above, n. 70), and *a fortiori* the *ṭuppu dannutu* (= ' acte de vente ') cannot be referred to in the law either, or we must assume that the ' promesse de vente ' *was* in fact prepared before the herald's proclamations etc., and that these procedures were treated merely as legal formalities which did not prevent the virtual completion of the sale (from one side) beforehand. In this case the *zakku'u* of n. 71 could refer simply to those procedures.

authority to render the sale valid in the eyes of the law. The crown does not visibly have any powers to halt the transaction or to influence it in any way, either in the relevant section of the law, or in the legal clauses of the sale texts.

It seems therefore that the 'valid tablet' differed only in two respects from the interim documents we possess: first, it gave evidence of the confirmation of the transaction by the authorities, perhaps in the form of seal impressions of the officials concerned; and second, it contained the exact details of the land or property sold, giving in particular its location, which obviously could not be determined until the purchaser had chosen it,[75] and its dimensions, which had to be established with a standard official measure.[76] No example is known to me of a Middle Assyrian tablet which answers to this description,[77] but one does survive from the late Old Assyrian period, which gives the precise dimensions and location of the plot, and is expressly described as a *ṭuppu dannutu*.[78] Confirmation of this conception of the 'valid tablet' comes from a consideration of some texts already discussed. In *KAJ* 164 the land was sold along with two tablets which gave entitlement to it; the land itself is specified more exactly than usual, and there are no provisions for the purchaser to make his own choice; further, the usual clauses about the preparation of a 'valid tablet', including the provision for measuring the land, are entirely absent. The reason for this is obvious: the two tablets are themselves 'valid tablets' (although this is not stated), and they give both the official confirmation and the location of the property; thus to have re-measured the land and submitted again for official confirmation would have been superfluous. Similar considerations apply to the two *zitti ēkalli* texts which were sold (see above, p. 511). In *KAJ* 149, the position is slightly complicated because the seller has lost the 'valid tablet' which records the land's sale; another valid tablet has therefore to be prepared, with the usual preliminaries, but the precise description of the plot, and the provision that if the old tablet turns up it must go to the purchaser,[79] show that it is a particular, well-defined plot being sold. That the right to land could be transferred entirely without reference to the state shows

[75] On the subject of the '*inassaq ilaqqi* clauses' see below, Appendix.

[76] A conceivable further difference would be a reference in the 'valid tablet' to the original holder of the tenure, which we might expect if my suggestion concerning *ši'amātu* is right.

[77] Unless BM 123367 (*Iraq*, XXXII, 2, 1970, plate XXXVI) is one; it is an unusually well-written tablet, and has as witnesses the mayor of Nineveh, the governor (rev. 2′: *bēl pāḫi*[*ti*]), and the herald (rev. 4′). *Limmu* probably ᵐ*bu-ut-nu*. The tablet is sealed, like NAss. land sale texts, and not enclosed in an envelope as was the late Old Assyrian text referred to in n. 78, below.

[78] See Gelb and Sollberger, *JNES*, XVI, 3, 1957, 163 ff.; lines (tablet) 35–7 read: *ki-ma ṭup-pì dan-na-tí lá-be-er-tí a-ni-tù ṭup-pu da-an-na-at* 'instead of the old "valid tablet" this tablet is valid'. As observed by Gelb (174), *ṭuppu dannutu* is characteristically Middle, not Old, Assyrian.

[79] *ṭuppu* KALAG.GA *eqli šuašu*(!) *ašar tilēni* (*elā'u*) *ana* PN-*ma zakku'at* (ll. 22–5). See also *KAJ* 132 (discussed by Koschaker *NKRA*, 33), where a [*ṭupp*]*u dannutu*(*m*) (l. 2) is being sold, but is (probably) lost; the seller is required to pass it on to the purchasers when found, but if he fails to do so, he shall bear the responsibility for 'clearing' the field; otherwise, the implication is obvious, the 'clearing' would not be necessary because the 'valid tablet' provides the evidence.

clearly that the intervention of the state in the final stage of a land sale was quite disinterested, and that it had no say in whether the property should or should not be sold.

5: CONCLUSIONS

So far we have been approaching the central problems from a number of different angles, without ever reaching a conclusion. Drawing together the results so far obtained, I think we may treat the following facts as sufficiently established:

(1) *ilku* could consist of military service;

(2) if a man who owned property vanished for good, his property went to the crown, even when it had been sold to a third party;

(3) other private lands might fall to the crown, and there is no evidence that these were not in other ways entirely 'normal' private lands;

(4) there was a distinction between hereditary and purchased lands which remained effective over at least two generations.

If we look for a pattern into which all these facts can be fitted, I would propose the following reconstruction, which must be treated as a theoretical and ideal solution, and, even if correct in theory, was not necessarily adhered to strictly in practice: all 'normal' private land was granted to free men by the crown, to be held in direct line from father to son only, in return for the performance of *ilku* services. The following conditions of tenure must be posited:

(*a*) if the direct line died out, the land reverted to the crown;

(*b*) the land could be sold, apparently without the intervention or permission of the crown; for the problem of the regulation of *ilku* in the case of land sales, see below;

(*c*) if the line of the original owner of land which has been sold dies out (or the last representative is lost), the land still reverts to the crown, even though it is actually in the possession of another;

(*d*) the owners of the land could have their *ilku* performed for them by their semi-free 'dependent villagers'.

Despite the fact that there is still no firm evidence of any connexion between *ilku* and land tenure,[80] the basic outline of this reconstruction is now seen to agree with what is known about *ilku* in Neo-Assyrian times,[81] and, perhaps even more relevant, with the conditions of land tenure at nearby Nuzu.[82] When the texts from Nuzu are set side by side with the evidence from Assur, one point in particular stands out: in Nuzu elaborate arrangements are made when the land is sold, in order to circumvent difficulties put in the way of the

[80] Despite assumptions to the contrary; cf. for example CAD, I (A), Pt. I, 391a, which, referring to § 45 of tablet A of the laws, says: 'the *ālajūtu* of the palace are distinguished from the *ālik ilki* who live in villages which do not belong to the palace', and also Garelli, 9. See also p. 505, n. 31.

[81] The connexion is best seen in the phrase *ilku ištu āli* (*lā*) *illuku* in texts from Tell Billa, and later in land sales, *ilku issu āli-šu lā illak* (e.g., TCL, IX, plate XXVII, l. 60); the subject will be treated in my study of Neo-Assyrian taxation.

[82] See for the Nuzu texts: F. R. Steele, *Nuzi real estate transactions* (American Oriental Series, XXV).

sale by *ilku* obligations, whereas in Assyria the sales do not mention the word once. It appears from the Nuzu texts that the state did not technically permit land held in return for *ilku* to be sold outside the family to which it was originally granted; in order to avoid this restriction the practice was to adopt into the family an intending purchaser, who could then inherit the land in direct line of succession. However, if the purchaser already held his own land, with its obligations, he was naturally unable (or at least unwilling) to assume more *ilku* service, and the sales therefore may specify that the *ilku* relating to the land will continue to be performed by the original owner and his sons. What happens at Nuzu if a family line dies out is unknown; since the land which is sold is still in the eyes of the state the holding of the original family, it may be that the land reverts to the state, as I suggested was the case in Assyria, but the possible legal complications of this are beyond elucidation at the moment. What is important to note is that, apart from this rather clumsy legal fiction of adopting the purchaser, the transaction appears to be very similar to that in Assyria.[83]

The comparison with Nuzu leads us to wonder how the *ilku* obligations were adjusted in the case of a sale in Assyria. For practical reasons I think we may safely assume that, as at Nuzu, the obligations stayed with the family which sells the land. Since *ilku* might consist of military service, there is no reason why a family should not continue to fulfil its obligations without any land. That the obligations remained with the first holders of the land can also be deduced from the silence of the documents on the subject: as the purchaser did not become a member of the seller's family as at Nuzu, there is no presumption that he might inherit the obligations, and thus no reason to mention *ilku* in the sale text, whereas, if the obligation were transferred, this would surely be specially mentioned. It seems then, that the separation of state service from land tenure was further advanced (at least in theory) in Assyria than at Nuzu, but this need not cast doubt on the original connexion between *ilku* and landholding.

The disintegration of the original pattern can be observed in another situation. As *KAJ* 7, where the 'dependent villagers' perform *ilku* on behalf of the legal owners of the land, indicates, it may be that in the course of time the richer or more powerful families were able to have their *ilku* performed for them by dependants. Exactly how this worked it is impossible to tell; it is conceivable that these dependants, as they owned no land of their own, were not in the first instance liable to *ilku* themselves. However, we can hardly suppose that all the lower members of the state, who owned no land, were exempt from state service, and it may be that the term *ilku* was extended to cover state obligations which were not associated with the holding of land. This will in practice have been the case where families had sold their lands; whether in *KAJ* 7 the 'dependent villagers' had their own obligations to the state as well as those they performed on behalf of Amurru-naṣir, cannot be determined.

[83] Note that Nuzu also knew the practice of public announcements before a sale (most recently, A. Shaffer, *Orientalia*, NS, xxxiv, 1, 1965, 32–4).

Finally, it must once more be stressed how unsatisfactory our sources on the subject are. Both the law and the legal documents relating to land date from early in the Middle Assyrian period,[84] while the sale texts in particular relate to a very restricted group of families and villages, and cannot be assumed to be typical.[85] Agricultural conditions round Assur itself are not typical of northern Mesopotamia as a whole, and procedures suited to this small vassal of the Mitannian kings cannot have been applied to the empire of Shalmaneser I without adaptation. It is true that the newly acquired regions, at least in the north and west, had like Assur itself been under Mitannian domination, and may therefore have known the same sort of land régime as we know from Nuzu, but this is only speculation. The documents from Tell Billa and Tell al-Rimaḥ, informative though they are, cannot be combined with the earlier texts from Assur (as I have had to do) without risk of oversimplification or distortion. How wide a range of conclusions the available souces permit may be gauged from a comparison of this article with those of Garelli and D'yakonov; it is because of the sparseness of the sources, and the divergent deductions from them, that it has been necessary to investigate them again in detail, although the ramifications of the subject have made it impossible to avoid using some unverified assumptions.

Appendix

One vexed problem of the Middle Assyrian land sales, which I have tried to circumvent in the main text, should perhaps be mentioned here. The problem is why the interim sale texts do not usually define exactly the area to be sold, but leave it to be chosen later by the buyer.

Much the most thorough attempt to solve this problem was made by Koschaker in *NKRA*, 36–52. It is a compact piece of legal argument, and cannot be fully discussed here, but, briefly, Koschaker's position is that the exact area to be sold cannot be determined in the interim document (*Kaufvertrag*) because the land from which it will come is jointly owned by a ‘ property association ’ (*Eigentumsgemeinschaft*), usually based on the extended family. When the ‘ property association ’ is eventually dispersed, but only then, will the seller have an absolute right of disposal over the land he is selling. Provision is therefore made in the interim document for the purchaser to receive the kind of land he requires when the division is made. This provision, Koschaker maintains, is contained in the *inassaq ilaqqi* clause (with several variants, see *NKRA*, 38–9) ‘ he shall choose and take ’, which uses the technical phraseology known from the laws to refer to the unilateral action of one member of a ‘ property association ’ who elects to take his share out. Since the actual purchaser is the subject

[84] While the exact date of the laws cannot be determined (Cardascia, 22), they clearly belong to a phase when Assur was not the capital of a large empire; the sale documents are mainly (if not all) from the fourteenth century B.C.

[85] Along with some associated loan and pledge texts, they mainly document the acquisition of land in a few villages by a few families (cf. D'yakonov, pp. 210–11 with nn. 28, 30, and the article by Nissen referred to in p. 498, n. 6).

of the verbs, however, Koschaker assumes that the right of the seller as a member of the group is effectively transmitted to the purchaser, so that he is himself able to initiate a division (p. 41, middle).

The starting-point for this rather tortuous hypothesis (worked out in great detail for the various situations reflected by the texts) is the idea that *inassaq ilaqqi* here should be used in an exactly similar way to its use in the laws, where it refers to the division of inheritance by brothers (38–9). Before this (37–8) he describes but rejects the possibility that we have here to do with ' Gattungskauf ', i.e. ' non-specific sale ', the sale of land specified as to quantity and quality, but not exactly defined, much like the sale of corn or silver. This possible solution is rejected (p. 38, middle) on purely theoretical grounds to do with the nature of land sale (and with pledge law), and no real attempt is made to see if it could have worked in practice. However, as Koschaker himself has implicitly admitted, by considering the hypothesis first, if the land sale documents could in effect be recording a ' Gattungskauf ' it would be the simplest explanation of the texts.

The fault in Koschaker's argument, that ' Gattungskauf ' or non-specific sale cannot be reconciled with the sale of land, is that he fails to distinguish sufficiently rigidly between the final land sale document, the *ṭuppu dannutu*, and the interim texts which are all we possess. The *inassaq ilaqqi* clause is not known to have occurred in the *ṭuppu dannutu*, which rather, as we have seen, would have specified exactly the dimensions and location of the land. The final transaction would therefore have been entirely ' specific '. Our texts, which record an obligation to pass over a specified quantity of land of a specified quality, are only final documents from the point of view of the seller, who has, as they record, received full payment for the land. Why then did the seller receive his payment before the purchaser received the land ? The answer to this central question must be sought in the economic background to the texts. As already mentioned (p. 519, n. 85), these texts come from a very restricted milieu, and they belong to an archive which also contains loans (frequently backed by a security of land) made by the same families as are known as purchasers of land in the sale texts. It cannot have been habitual to sell one's best land unless it was unavoidable, and this consideration together with the loan texts, suggests that in all these cases it was the sellers of the land who initiated the transactions because they stood in urgent need of the money. Our problem is thereby solved already : the seller required his purchase price in a hurry, and therefore in exchange for immediate payment he gave the purchaser the right to select the land which suited him best, so making it possible to leave the lengthy procedures of choosing and measuring the land, of ' clearing ' it and writing the ' valid tablet ' until later. Thus the interim sale was effectively a ' Gattungskauf ' or non-specific sale, because to have made it specific would have entailed waiting too long. In this way the ' *inassaq ilaqqi* clause ' may be taken rather as a privilege accorded to the purchaser, than a restriction on the rights of the seller to dispose of his land.

Journal of the Economic and Social History of the Orient, Vol. XVII, Part 3

SOME REMARKS ON CONDITIONS IN THE ASSYRIAN COUNTRYSIDE *)

BY

J. N. POSTGATE

(Baghdad)

In 1901 C.H.W. Johns published an interesting group of texts from the archives of the Neo-Assyrian kings at Nineveh, under the title of 'An Assyrian Doomsday Book or liber censualis of the district round Harran, in the seventh century B.C.'. In contrast to some of his later work, Johns' copy of the texts was remarkably good, and with the edition he gave a full discussion of the evidence provided by the group of texts in differing spheres. No doubt partly because this edition was so thorough, the Doomsday Book has received little attention from scholars since then, apart from passing references. Only quite recently, with the quickening interest in Neo-Assyrian studies, have serious attempts been made once more to investigate these texts (they constitute an important part of the evidence in Dr. J. Zablocka's discussion of the agrarian conditions of the Neo-Assyrian empire, and are discussed also in G. van Driel, Bi.Or. XXVII 3/4 (1970) 175; V.A. Jakobson, in I.M. Diakonoff (ed.) Ancient Mesopotamia 277-295; and in a forthcoming book by the reviewer 'Taxation and Conscription in the Assyrian Empire' Rome 1974). However, in none of these cases has a complete re-examination of the texts been attempted, and this is what the book under review has done; in addition, the author has included 'Schedules' from the Niniveh archives, which have never been properly edited before.

The book begins with a brief introduction on the nature of the texts (pp. 1-12), followed by the edition of the texts themselves (pp. 13-89). The second part of the book discusses the evidence provided by the texts in various fields; it covers the geographical and historical setting

* Review of: F. M. Fales, *Censimenti e catasti di epoca neo-assira* [Studi economici e tecnologici 2] Roma 1973 pp. x, 151 5 Figs.

(pp. 91-114: the major centres in the Liber censualis: Sîn and Harrān in Sargonid times; and the onomastic and cultural milieu), and the economic and social conditions (The men and the land, pp. 115-133: the family; the socio-economic conditions; movable and immovable property; and the village and landed property). The texts are in general competently edited, and collation has allowed some improvements to Johns' version, although nothing of great moment; the passing of 70 years has naturally allowed a better comprehension of some problems which baffled Johns. At the end of this review we have listed some detailed corrections or suggestions, based largely on an independent collation of the Doomsday Book texts some years ago; it is encouraging to note that in the majority of cases the results of the two collations were identical.

If we have a criticism of the text editions, it is that rather scant attention is given to the philological problems. This is reflected in the inconvenient absence of an index of Akkadian words, and may also be illustrated by two points of translation. The first concerns the word *tillutu*, correctly rendered 'vine' by the editor; in ADD Johns read this word as *be-lut* and translated 'lady-palm', which possibly does not require refutation. But R.C. Thompson retains this reading in DAB 249-50, and adopts the translation 'gall-oak', which has found its way into other works as well (e.g. D. Oates, Studies in the Ancient History of Northern Iraq, p. 46). Since neither of the two dictionaries has yet covered *t*, for the sake of non-cuneiformists some explanation of the translation 'vine' should have been given, especially since a single reference to Harra-Hubullu III would have sufficed (MSL 5 p. 94, ll.19, 22-5). The second word, *zamru* is admittedly allowed a brief note on p. 28, where it is suggested that the contrast between *zamru* and *urqu* (= vegetables) favours a meaning for *zamru* of 'fruit' (in general, rather than any specific kind). However, since this translation is tacitly accepted throughout the rest of the book, it should have been substantiated with more care. Evidence that could have been quoted in favour of the proposal is the mention of 'mixed *zamru*' in Iraq 14 (1952) p. 43 l.123; and the word is also known in Middle Assyrian texts (Sumer 24 (1968) 38 VAT

17892, 12; W. Andrae, Das Wiedererstandene Assur, Taf. 49a l.4), and in at least one Old Babylonian text from Tell Al-Rimaḥ (information from Dr. S. Dalley) in the form *azamru* (cf. also CAD A Pt.ii, 525b). In fact, the reviewer believes that the translation 'fruit', has a good chance of being right; this would explain, for instance, why the *zamru* figures in the Doomsday Book and similar contexts to the exclusion of any other kinds of fruit which we know were cultivated, such as the quince (*supargillu*). Nevertheless, some investigation of the known occurrences of the word would have been desirable, and one should also try to establish what fruits were covered by the term, and hence, what trees might be encountered in the orchards of Harran—did they include under *zamru* nuts, or figs, or olives, for example?

The second part of the book covers in considerable detail the background to the Doomsday Book (hereafter: DB), as far as it can be reconstructed from the evidence contained within it, and from other sources. On the historical and geographical side this is a relatively straightforward procedure, and the data are presented and discussed at length, furnishing fairly concrete results. Particularly useful is the author's familiarity with Aramaic, at least to one without that advantage, and we look forward to seeing his work on Aramaic personal names (cf. p. 107 note 93). Equally tangible information is extracted from the DB on the subject of the family, but in the closing pages of the work the author ventures on the more treacherous ground of the economic and social conditions, and it is inevitably about these subjects that opinions must diverge. We propose therefore to summarise and discuss the views set forward in this section (pp. 122-133).

Purpose and identity of the Doomsday Book

Before the data of the DB and the schedules can be used to promote a reconstruction of social and economic conditions, it must be established what purpose these lists really served. In no case is a heading or colophon preserved to give us direct evidence on this point, and we are forced to deduce what we can from the character of the texts. While all agree that the DB is indeed a census of some kind, agreement stops there. Van Driel is cautious, saying 'It is not difficult to imagine other reasons for drawing up lists of estates than taxation, e.g. proscription of owners after a revolt, or something like that' (loc. cit.); on the other hand Jakobson comments that 'The students of the Ḫarrān lists agree in defining them as a cadastral survey drawn up for purposes of taxation and corvée' (Ancient Mesopotamia p. 281).

One thing at least is clear, and that is that the lists were drawn up for, and probably by, the central administration at Nineveh; this follows from the place of discovery, and the well-written tablets which form a definite series (cf. p. 6). After discussing the problem, Fales concludes that it is most probable that the DB was an 'open-ended' register of lands, kept up to date and added to by occasional visits to the area by officials, rather than a complete listing which was periodically revised. So, on p. 8, he writes 'A nostro avviso, un'immagine complessiva per il 'Doomsday Book' è quella di uno *standing register*, di un registro sempre aperto, relativo ai possessi fondiari che per ubicazione potessero rientrare nella competenza della burocrazia di Ninive'. Finally, in G. *Gli scopi del 'Liber'* (pp. 8-9), he stresses that the uses to which the information contained in the texts was put, do not necessarily coincide with the purpose for which it was initially compiled. In the last paragraph he writes that among the twenty texts of the so-called 'Liber censualis' which have come down to us 'we can point to a possible residue of a Ninevite archive . . . . relating to the systematic registration of the landed property of the time, and arranged according to the landowners. As a primary source of information on the state of affairs in the matter of distribution and management of the land, the 'Doomsday Book' can be considered structurally preliminary to a series of other contemporary texts relating to land: contracts of real-estate purchase (v. ADB 13.ii.7), and also royal decrees assigning farms, possibly provided with fiscal exemption'.

While the difficulties are well described, it seems to the reviewer that the author has in fact stepped very gingerly round the central question, viz. the original purpose of the compilation. My own answer to this question has been given in brief in the book referred to above, pp. 36-8, and is that the DB is a list of lands which are exempt from taxation. After reconsidering this suggestion in the light of the new discussion, I see no reason to withdraw it, and since the purpose of the compilation is a crucial point for the correct exploitation of its data, I make no apology for making one or two general points here in support of my interpretation. Any explanation of the original purposes of the DB must account for the fact that (1) the texts come from the archives of the central administration, but refer to lands in a specific area of North-west Mesopotamia, and (2) that the texts list property according to its owners, and do not follow a geographical order. When we consider these two points, it seems clear that the list cannot have been prepared strictly for the purposes of tax-collection. All the evidence available indicates that the collection of agricultural taxes or the enrolling of men for state service was organised by the provincial administration and was not directly the concern of the central government at Niniveh or Kalhu; while a complete listing of lands and other property for the use of tax-collectors would undoubtedly be arranged geographically, village by village—this would be both the only way to compile such a list, and the only form in which it would be of service. On the other hand, it is difficult—despite Van Driel's doubts—to conceive of any purpose for which such a list would be drawn up which was not in some way connected with taxation. Consequently we are led to suggest that lands enumerated are those properties in the area in question, which were exempt from taxation. This provides a very satisfactory solution of both problems: for tax-exemption was usually granted by the king, and indeed references in the Neo-Assyrian letters show that the provincial authorities would consult the king in person if doubtful about the exempt status of lands which fell under their jurisdiction. It was on this matter, therefore, that the central administration was concerned with the organisation of tax-collection in the provinces—or that the 'possessi fondiari' would 'rientrare nella competenza della burocrazia di Ninive'. Equally, we can understand why the list of property is arranged by owners, since individual grants or lists of property were of course made out for each owner of the exempted lands. We might assume that to prepare a list like the DB the scribes need only have consulted the grant texts available to them in the royal archives, taking the details from there. However, it is more likely that the process was more complex: the grants which survive from late in the 7th century do list lands and persons, but they do not give details as specific as those in the DB; on the other hand, it has been observed before (e.g. NARGD p. 4) that the grants from Assurbanipal's reign do not list the property granted, and must therefore have been accompanied by a separate list, or possibly only by the original tablets of purchase. In this connection, one's thoughts turn to the 'schedules' (Fales Nos. 23-31), and in particular to the suggestion (p. 133 note 49) that Nabû-šarru-uṣur is to be restored in No. 23, 31, and identified with the beneficiary of the Assurbanipal grant NARGD No. 10. Admittedly even this text could not have been a source for a DB type list, since it covers more than one owner, and does not include the age-designations (Fales: 'segni'). All the same, we should point out that, contra Fales p. 9, the DB cannot have served as a source of information from which details of contracts were taken, since he himself has pointed out (p. 126) that the data of the DB are not as exact as those required for a legal document of sale.

The reconstruction of agrarian conditions

The foregoing discussion of the purpose of the DB is necessary, if we intend to consider the reconstruction of social and economic conditions, which is largely based on its evidence. That the proposed reconstruction is open to doubt can be best illustrated by comparing it with another opinion. In Bi.Or. XXVII (1970) 174, G. Van Driel writes: 'Incomplete though the material may be, some not unimportant conclusions seem possible: 1) the large estates did not form one block of territories, with the result that the local communities, probably with some degree of local selfgovernment, must have played an important role in the lives of the people in the countryside; 2) royal favour could contribute to the formation of large estates and could crown the process of acquisition by a grant of exemption; 3) small landowners did exist; 4) the legal position of those who tilled the land was not uniform.'

Against this let us set the opinion of Fales (p. 131) that 'We do not have to do in these texts with a dispersed agricultural horizon of at least partly economically self-sufficient settlements, in which court officials possess estates haphazardly; as we have said above (p. 124), we are confronted with a countryside in which the original village communities have given way to wide stretches of 'slave' communities, devoted to production on behalf of the officials, in an extensive series of adjacent lots'.

Inevitably, both these summaries must over-simplify both the actual situation and their writers' view of it, but we believe that the former is much nearer to the truth, and consequently we must examine the arguments which led Fales to this conclusion. The cardinal fallacy seems to have been that it is assumed that the DB gives a true picture of settlement for the entire countryside. As we have noted above, the arrangement of the entries by land-owner is enough to show that the listing was not a complete listing of all property. Naturally the author is aware that we do in fact have no more than a record of the property of certain 'latifondisti'; but for various reasons he has concluded that the picture of these estates derived from the DB is also valid for all property in the area. As far as the description of conditions on these estates goes (pp. 123 ff.), we are in complete agreement with Fales: the people listed were 'servi', serfs, or glebae adscripti—persons who belonged to the owner of the land, and could be sold or granted together with it. Similarly, the phrase *ana gimirti-šu* certainly indicates that an entire village could belong to one of the landowners, as can be surmised from the occasional sale of an entire village among the legal documents. The crucial point is reached on p. 124, where it is asked whether, when a plot listed does not coincide with an entire village, we should imagine 'la compresenza di proprietà fondiarie di membri del villaggio e del latifondista registrato nel 'Liber', oppure la divisione totale delle terre del villaggio tra vari latifondisti, quali quelli del 'Liber', cioè non identificantisi in alcun modo con i produttori residenti del sito?'.

In answer to this question it is first conceded (p. 124) that the DB does make mention of property belonging to the local villagers (*ša ramāni-šunu*); it is rightly maintained that the infrequent references to private property of this kind do more to confirm the picture of the domination of the landed proprietors over their 'slaves' than to contradict it: if none were listed, we might suppose it possible that the villagers listed had their own, unrecorded, land, but since it is occasionally mentioned the assumption is justified that in other cases they had no property relevant to the list. At this point we encounter the flaw in in the argument, however; for in the next breath the question posed above is answered, with the conclusion that we must imagine that an 'estate' bordered more frequently on other similar estates, than on land belonging to and tilled by untied members of the village community. This does not follow from what was said. Whatever the purpose of the DB, it is unquestioned that it lists estates belonging to individual landowners. If I am right, and they were specifically tax-exempted landowners, it is obvious that they are in no way typical of the rural scene. But even if I am wrong, it is clear that members of a village community who tilled their own lands independently of any 'latifondista' or landlord would not be listed along with their land in the DB. Moreover, to assume that the *ša ramāni-šunu* plots were as big as other local holdings is also to beg the question; presumbly they were as it were the *peculium* of the 'slaves', and unlikely to be as large as the holdings of untied farmers in the same village. Obviously, landed estates existed and could be of considerable size; but to suggest that they occupied the majority of the agricultural land in the large area concerned, is to go too far beyond the evidence of our sources.

Apart from this basic point, there are other respects in which the idea of a predominantly 'slave-cultivated' countryside could be called into question. We do not know, for example, how large an area a single family would cultivate: a theoretical possibility is that a land-owner might have possessed insufficient man-power on a given estate to exploit it to the full, and consequently employed hired labour. Therefore, even when a village was listed 'in its entirety' (*ana gimirti-šu*), it is conceivable that the estate could have supported untied cultivators who do not figure in the list since they do not belong to the land-owner.

Furthermore, if we accept the idea that the DB is a list of exempted property, we must also admit the possibility that the 'slaves' could have owned land of their own which does not feature in the text because it was not exempt also. This is of course very uncertain, but it is known that under the terms of some grants (e.g. NARGD Nos. 10-11) the 'slaves' also had their own property exempted, and it is equally possible that in other cases this was not so.

If the concept of a close lattice of estates owned by absentee landlords is rejected as unproven, we must also reject the conclusion on p. 131, quoted at the beginning of this section. Consequently, it is not necessary to stress the possibility that both *ālu* (URU) and *kapru* (URU.ŠE; for the equivalence see now AfO 24 (1973) 75) refer to points on the map or administrative divisions rather than towns and villages (so p. 129-130). Of course both types of settlement were used as administrative units, and the land listed under them was both physically and administratively attached to them, but this is no reason to doubt that they were also villages and towns in the normal sense; nor do I see any valid grounds for the assumption that villagers lived in primitive structures not worthy of the designation *bētu* 'house', as is maintained on p. 129. As far as the size of the settlements is concerned, we have next to no evidence, but at Elumu, in the Carchemish district, there were 16 heads of families; the two 'entire' villages mentioned in the DB no longer preserve their exact areas of land and size of population. Note, in passing, that the villagers of Elumu negotiate as a community with the officer (*rab kiṣri*) who sealed the contract, and certainly do not give the impression of being the property of one or more *latifondisti* (the text, from Carchemish, is re-edited in J. N. Postgate, op. cit., Appendix).

History of settlement in North Mesopotamia

In the course of his argument, the author more than once expresses the opinion that the conditions he reconstructs in the 7th century replaced a pattern of village communities based on the owner-cultivator, such as has been demonstrated by I. M. Diakonoff for Middle Assyrian times (see pp. 124, 130). This is certainly an oversimplification of the facts, and since the author has not discussed the rural conditions in the early part of the Neo-Assyrian empire, it may be of interest here to survey the historical evidence for settlement on the North Mesopotamian plains, albeit only briefly.

Let us first confess that we know remarkably little of conditions in North Mesopotamia during the Middle Assyrian period. Diakonoff's conclusions apply to the immediate surroundings of the city of Assur, where both political, historical, and agricultural conditions are quite distinct from those further north. We should not therefore assume without proof that settlement in North Mesopotamia conformed to patterns round Assur. However, the situation in Middle Assyrian times in fact has very little to do with Neo-Assyrian conditions, for we know that a radical change in the settlement of North Mesopotamia took place in the interval. The 'dark ages' around 1000 B.C. saw the greater part of Assyrian territory overrun by Aramaean tribes, and a simultaneous intrusion of non-Semitic groups from the mountains (e.g. at Tell Billa, as can be deduced from the personal names of its local population in the 9th century). Although the details of this process are understandably mostly lost to us, we can see the results of the incursions from the situation confronting the Assyrian kings when they sought to reassert their authority over the lands of North Mesopotamia.

The main political centres opposing this revival of the Assyrian empire were Naṣibīna and Guzāna (encountered by Adad-nirāri II), Amedi (Bīt-zamāni, Assur-naṣir-apli II), and Til-Barsip (Bīt-adīni Shalmaneser III). A characteristic of these Aramaean states is their designation as *bīt* PN: the type of geographical name is well known, and is found throughout the Near East wherever there were new states founded by the Aramaean dynasties. The word *bītu* (or rather its Aramaic equivalent) cannot be translated, but in the Assyrian annals, and no doubt in Aramaic usage as well, it has principally a political meaning, but also carries a geographical connotation. The *bītu* is more than a mere tribe, which might move at any time from one district to another, but its association with a personal name brings home the fact that the political and geographical entity is founded on a tribal system. A more than superficial comparison can be found in the situation in Northern Mesopotamia shortly after the Arab conquests, when the province of the Jazīra was divided into the 'abodes' (*diyār*) of three major tribes: the Diyār Bakr (Amida and district), Diyār Muḍar (the Middle Euphrates with Ḥarrān and Raqqa), and Diyār Rabī'a (the eastern Jazīra with Mosul and Mardin); cf. The Encyclopaedia of Islam Vol. II 343 ff.

Although the new Aramaean inhabitants were masters of most of the lands of North Mesopotamia, this does not imply that they were settled there. Certainly each state centred on a chief city—Naṣibīna, Guzāna, etc.—but there is little evidence that outside the fortified capitals there was any extensive new Aramaean settlement. Signs of a recent nomadic past are still apparent: Nūr-Adad of Naṣibīna had a 'golden tent, symbol of his royalty' which was captured by Adad-nirāri II, and when the same king took Guzāna, which seems to have been the capital of Bīt-Baḫiāni, he says that it was 'held' (*ukallûni*) by Abi-salāmu, *mār Baḫiāni*, implying, I believe, that it was not his permanent residence, and that for at least part of the year Abi-salāmu pursued a nomadic life.

The capital cities we have mentioned seem all to have been newly founded, or at least renamed. In this they contrast with other towns, which survived from Middle Assyrian times through the period of unrest and into the Neo-Assyrian period. The distribution of such towns is significant: they lie almost exclusively on the major rivers. Down the Euphrates we have towns like Carchemish, Ḫindāna, 'Āna, and Ḥīt, and nearer to Assyria on the Ḫabur a cluster of towns survives the dark age-Dūr-Iaggitlim (= Dūr-aduklimmu), Šadikanni, Ṭābta, Qatni, Kaḫat, Urakka, and possibly also Naḫur and Ašnakku (cf. R. Borger ZA 62 (1972) 136). For the Balih we have less evidence, but of course Harran remained important. The survival of these cities—mostly from the early 2nd millennium, indeed—shows that settlements along the rivers were more tenacious in face of the chaotic conditions than those in the intervening countryside. Apart from the additional natural protection afforded by a river-side site, the greater fertility of the river valleys and the constant presence of water allowed the growth of larger towns, which could support a population capable of self-defence and able to build its own walls even in the absence of a powerful central authority. Consequently, in the times of weakness of major empires, these smaller cities were able to defend themselves, and small states might grow up around them. An excellent example of this is provided by the dynasty of Šadikanni (Arban), which guarded its identity from Middle Assyrian times until late into the ninth century (cf. RLA IV 28-9; E. Unger, BASOR 130 (1953) 15ff.). Another probable reason for the survival of these isolated towns, is that the nomadic incursors had no immediate desire to take possession of them. Just as in the heart of Assyria proper, they were probably content to let the town-dwellers pursue their own lives without overdue interference, and when they did choose to settle themselves, it was in new places which accorded with their rather different requirements (cf. D. Oates, Studies pp. 19-20 for the considerations leading to the settlement of beduin tribes at the site of Assur in recent times). It should be added that this tendency is less marked on the Middle Euphrates, where choices for town sites were more limited; on the whole the nomadic intruders took over the control of towns like Ḫindāna and ʻĀna, although the existing population no doubt survived.

To sum up, the period of unrest left the lands of Northern Mesopotamia overrun by Aramaean tribes, only partially settled. In places, along the rivers, old town-communities held on, while non-Semitic populations probably maintained their independence in the mountains to the North. Despite the earlier penetration of the Tigris-Upper Zab triangle by the nomads, and pressure on it from the North, the 'Assyrian homeland' probably remained under Assyrian control most of the time, while to the South, below the Lower Zab, the tribes of desert and mountain as in the West divided the land between them.

Let us now turn to conditions in the countryside, which are the true concern of our discussion. Periods of unrest drastically affect the extent of settlement, and this is particularly true of Northern Mesopotamia. From the accounts of 19th century travellers we learn that the Jazira to the West of Mosul was then almost entirely in the hands of bedu tribes, and was empty of villages, although this land is fertile and well within the limits of profitable rainfall agriculture. A similar situation is betrayed by the annals of the early Neo-Assyrian kings. They rarely miss a chance to record their military achievements, and yet when Adad-nirari II marched across country from Naṣibīna to Guzāna and on to the head of the Habur, he makes no mention of plundering or receiving submission from any villages en route. When his successors Tukulti-Ninurta II and Assur-nāṣir-apli II marched along the river Habur, they have nothing to say of small towns or villages, and yet when in the mountains to the North, Assur-nāṣir-apli II does not fail to record his plunder of large numbers of villages (e.g. Luckenbill, ARAB §§462-4). The conclusion must be that at this date much of Northern Mesopotamia was entirely deserted, except for nomadic tribes and enclaves of settlement along the rivers.

In a positive way this desertion is confirmed by the 'resettlement programme' pursued energetically by the Neo-Assyrian kings. From Assur-dān II onwards, successive kings concluded their annals with an enumeration of the measures taken by them to restore military strength and agricultural prosperity to the country. The activity is four-fold: (1) the building of 'palaces', i.e. administrative and military centres, in strategic positions, (2) the provisions of ploughs, (3) the storage of grain reserves, and (4) the acquisition of draught-horses. This reflects a deliberate policy of first winning back and defending the deserted lands from their Aramaean invaders, and then cultivating them so as to permit the growth of population and improve agricultural prosperity. An example of this activity is provided by the site of Apku (Tell Abu Maria), which must have been one of the palaces 'on the edge? of the land' (*ša šiddi māti*) and was adopted as a strategic and administrative centre as early as Assur-rēš-iši (Grayson, ARI I §978), and later retaken and rebuilt by Assur-bēl-kala and Adad-nirari II; Assur-nāṣir-apli II also built a 'palace' there, and it is clear that in the 10th-9th centuries it served as a keypoint in the Assyrian North-west front (cf. D. Oates, *Studies*, p. 54).

So far we have been speaking of resettlement of territory very close to the major Assyrian cities of the Zab-Tigris triangle. As the boundaries of the empire shifted westwards, the same policy was adopted, and within the recovered lands efforts were directed to the re-occupation of the deserted but fertile lands west of the Tigris. One instance is provided by the early 8th century foundation of Dūr-bēl-harrān-bēlu-uṣur (Tell Abta), now in desert country, but the best example is supplied by the recent excavations at Tell al-Rimaḥ (probably Zamāḫu), south east of Jebel Sinjar. The stele of Adad-nirari III found at the site described the foundation of as many as 331 villages in the province of Raṣappa, which stretched from Apku to the Ḫabur, and southwards to the Euphrates valley. The areas affected by the resettlement programme cannot all be defined, but they included Laqê and Qatnu (on the Ḫabur), the lands 'behind Jebel Sinjar' (*ina ku-tal* KUR *s*[*a*]*ngāri*, l.18), and no doubt the area of Tell al-Rimaḥ itself. This picture agrees admirably with the evidence of surface survey, which attests the widespread re-occupation of these plains south of Jebel Sinjar in the 8th and 7th centuries B.C. (cf. D. Oates, *Iraq* 30 (1968) 130). Further testimony to the extent of cultivation and settlement in the Late Neo-Assyrian period is provided by the occasional mention of villages or crops 'in the desert' (*madbāru*/*mudāburu*). Two references must suffice here, *Iraq* 28 (1966) 183-5, a letter to the king which refers to raising corn from the 'towns in the desert' (*ina mad-bar* ll. 11-13), and a text listing areas of land which include '70 homers in the desert (*ina mu-da-bi-ri*) of Raṣappa province' (T. G. Pinches, *Hebraica* 2 (1885/6) 221 ff.). Of greater interest still is the letter NL 52 (*Iraq* 21 (1959) 162-3), in which the king is informed of the differing prices of corn at Nineveh (1 homer : 1 mina copper), Halahhu (Khorsabad area; $1^{1}/_{2}$ homers: 1 mina) and 'the desert' (*mu-da-bi-ri*; 2 homers : 1 mina). Although all these prices are considered good by the writer of the letter, it is worth noting that the corn was cheapest, and presumably most abundant, in the desert province, which probably included, for example, Dūr-bēl-harrān-bēlu-uṣur which was described by its founder as being 'in the desert'.

These references to the desert bring us back at long last to the Harran area, for in No. 9 (= ADB No. 8) a village is mentioned '*ina madbār ša*^{uru}*balīḫi*'. We should not of course assume that conditions here were identical to those we have described, and in the absence of any archaeological survey we are unable to surmise how complete the desertion of the area was, and how extensive the resettlement in late Neo-Assyrian times. Very little is known of the details of the annexation of this area by Assyria, but we presume it fell into Shalmaneser's hands at latest when he finally defeated Bīt-adīni, and we do know that in 814 B.C. the Harran district formed a part of the province of the *turtānu* (cf. pp. 94 ff.). From the campaign accounts of Shalmaneser there seems to be some reason to suppose that the Balih area and the region round Til-barsip (Tell Aḥmar) and Carchemish on the Euphrates had been partially resettled by the 9th century, no doubt in consequence of the relative strength of the state of Bīt-adīni, but apart from this, evidence for the settlement of the region is almost entirely restricted to the DB itself. It is only logical to assume that Adad-nirari III or his successors undertook resettlement schemes in the Harran area, just as they had further East, although probably for political and geographical reasons at a later stage. The Assyrian annals do not mention the settlement of any deported populations in the area, but in fact texts No. 5 (= ADB 6) and 21 (= ADB 5) make it clear that as late as the 7th century Gambulaeans were deported and settled here. Unfortunately, since the population present before the reconquest of the area by Assyria was Aramaean, and the newly resettled families, like the Gambulaeans, may also have had Aramaean names, it is difficult to make use of the onomasticon as a guide to the composition of the population, but it seems highly probable that the sort of land allocation attested by No. 21 (= ADB 5) was already in progress during the 8th century. If this is so, the problems facing those hoping to reconstruct rural conditions with the help of the DB become at once more specific and of wider application. For we must first try to determine the origin of any settlement or group of settlements, and then speculate on the differing social and legal status of the pre-Assyrian population, deported people, and any whose presence was due to other circumstances. Even with these categories allowed for, much will still have depended on the age of the settlement in question, and on its geographical location, which was probably closely correlated with its age, since the more dependable lands would have been settled first, with later settlements pushing down southwards and out away from the rivers.

Next to nothing is known of the conditions of land tenure in the Assyrian empire, but it is very unlikely that they were as homogeneous as they may appear to us. The lesson of other empires is that conditions varied from province to province, and depended as much from the historical traditions of the area as from any uniform policy imposed by conquest. However much the DB may seem to present the comparatively straightforward picture of glebae adscripti belonging to absentee land-owners, we must bear in mind that the compilation was manifestly designed as a record of a particular type of land holding, so that it could not be expected to illustrate other possible situations. Both on historical grounds, and by the analysis of the DB itself, we must plead against the over-simplification of the rural conditions as propounded in the book's concluding section.

Detailed comment

I give below, by page or text, some detailed comments. These chiefly consist of passages in which my collation of the Doomsday Book tablets differs from the transliteration given. It is not claimed that in all cases my version is to be preferred, but when there was doubt I have thought it better to indicate an alternative for consideration. No. 1.i.46: read *5* (not *ṣa*), as already suspected by Fales; i.47: instead of *4* read *7*. After l.47 there was a line before l.48 of which only traces survive, possibly reading 1 É; i.49: my collation favours the spacing shown in Johns' copy, rather than that implied by the transliteration: ii.27: read ÙZ (not UZ) here and elsewhere; ii.32: read *ina*$^{!uru}$*ḫa-sa-me*; ad ii.40: note that the element *-manāni* may occur in the name of the *limmu* for 699 B.C., Bēl-manāni (instead of Bēl-šarrāni); iii.44: after this line there is space for 2 more lines, and then the traces of a ruling concluding this column; vii.3: the number of camels is a low figure, perhaps 2.

No. 2.i.16': in place of PAP-*šú* my collation gives DUMU GA; ii.15: this line is admittedly difficult, but reading *uṣru* cannot assist since it is unclear what form of *naṣāru* it could represent. The traces would permit *us-b*[*u*], which gives some meaning, although the import of the clause is still unclear; ii.16: *Pa-li-*[*ṭu*] is impossible, but the traces permit *pa-li-ṭ*[*i*]; viii.4': perhaps better PAP[.

No. 3.i.3: not indented!; i.9: GIŠ *ḫi*^!^*-lu-pu* is a possible reading, and gives a closer connection with *ḫa*/*uluppu*; i.13: the line is not indented, and reads 2 MÍ.MEŠ P[AP^?^ 3^?^]; ii.1: ^I^15.BÀD(^!^); ii.3: the figure 3 is damaged, not absent^!^; iii.10: ^I^*su*^?^*-ra*^?^*-a-a* A . . . (i.e. three 'a's); iv.12: not indented; vii.6: our collation also favours reading 33 ERÍN.MEŠ Z[I], but the reading calls for comment. ZI in this context cannot equal 'a soul, person', but must be read *nasḫu* (or comparable word), meaning 'deported (person)', although this usage is not admitted for Neo-Assyrian in AHw. The translation is supported by the relatively large number listed; cf. on Nos. 5.vii.7' and 21.

No. 4.iv.5: the place name is ZA-*i-di-tú*/*te*^?^; vii.6: read simply *ina*^!^[^*uru*^.. (without PAP); vii.12: read [PA]P ^*I*^*X-rém-a-ni*; viii.4: the sign before *ši* is correctly copied and therefore *na* (not *ba*).

No. 5: We may observe at this point that the author has assigned the texts a serial number for the purposes of the publication, which does not necessarily coincide with the old Doomsday Book number. We certainly approve the renumbering of the texts, but it is aggravating that in the second part of this book the author does not use these numbers, but rather the old Doomsday Book text numbers, making it tedious to consult the texts in his own edition!; i.2: after SAL.MEŠ read *ṣ*[*a* PAP 7(?)]; in the next line too there is room for more after the É; vii.1': read ^*I*^*šá-la*-EN-*man*^!^*-nu*; vii.7': ZÁḪ.MEŠ if a noun means 'fugitives', not 'prigioneri'; however it is perhaps more likely to be the stative *ḫalqu* 'fled'; Col. viii is not inscribed at the base, but the upper part of the column is not preserved.

No. 9.ii.4: although the meaning remains obscure, *10-ú-tú*^!^ *ša* É[appears to be the better reading.

No. 10.i.12: [^*I*^*n*]*a-šuḫ*-MU A-*šu ṣa* (only one '*a*'); i.10: perhaps better URU *pi-gi*-DINGIR[*-a-*]*a*; ii.9: perhaps rather 1 GIŠ.ŠA[R . . . . .].MEŠ;

No. 11.iv.4: ^*I*^*su-ri*^!^*-ram-mu*; iv.11-13: 20 A.ŠÀ and 2 *lim til-lit* have dropped out of the transliteration at the end of ll. 11 and 13 respectively.

16

No. 12.vi.3: -PAP-*ir* is damaged and *-na-kab* looks preferable; viii.6: instead of PA_4 .MEŠ read certainly P]Ú.MEŠ.

No. 13.B.5: URU *ḫa-lu-li-i*!

No. 14.ii.6: read [1] SAL (no DUMU!)

No. 19.6:][I]*man-nu-le-e-me-*LUGAL LÚ *ma-ṣar* [*qabli*]

No. 21: This is a very interesting text, perhaps not given quite enough attention by the author. Working from Col. ii.27 ('Gambulaeans') in combination with No. 5.vii.4, we agree with G. van Driel (Bi.Or.27 (1970) 175) that the text lists 'parcels of land distributed among deportees'. Unfortunately the unexplained double or treble ditto signs conceal from us the exact significance of the text, but it can easily be made to conform with the remainder of the collection if we imagine that it lists lands recently assigned, together with its newly deported occupants, to the high officials named, and at the same time exempted from taxation; i.9: A-*šú ṣa* is also possible; i.17: PAP.MEŠ-*šú ṣa*! is also possible; i.23: read GAR-*nu* SAG.MEŠ 'offerings supervisor' with Fales himself who suggests the reading as an alternative on p. 63; ii.11: [I.d]MAŠ.BA!-*eš* A-*šú ṣa*!; ii.13: possibly read SU in place of ZU, and while the rendering of *ku* as 'in luogo di' (= *kūm*) may be correct, it requires justification and the resulting statement (PN in place of PN) requires explanation; ii.23: the place name is written UD.ḪA, not, as the transliteration implies, UD-*nun*; ii.28: although this transliteration was already suggested in the reviewer's collated transcription of the texts, it should be noted that the reading *ú* is deduced from the context, and although possible, is not certain (not, therefore 'chiaramente visible'); iii.5: 3 ANŠE GAL URU.M[EŠ; iii.21: a ditto sign is omitted after 3-BÁN.

No. 22.iii.12: [I]*ia-ba*!*-ba-a*; Margine sinistro.i.3: the figure 3 has been omitted after Si'-manāni; Margine sinistro.iii: the proposal to restore *l*[*abari* 'vecchio' attributed to the reviewer is based on a misunderstanding; the transcription of the Doomsday Book texts mentioned above (which we were glad to let Dr. Fales consult) does indeed suggest restoring these letters, but in the form *l*[*a bari* 'not collated'. 'Vecchio' is obviously out of the question since the word is *labīru*. Note that this line was added after the clay had dried somewhat.

No. 23. Verso.3: the copy (Fig. 5) clearly has NUMUN not *mu*; 7: the copy has ^{uru}*za-pár-ra*; 9: since the first sign has only one vertical, it is unlikely to be *ta*, and it seems probable that the wedges preserved in this line should be combined to read GIŠ].ŠAR[.

No. 24.Recto.10: it seems likely that the 2 sign is indeed a ditto, referring perhaps to Arbail, and that *qa-ba-si-i* is the ordinary adjective meaning 'central'; ad Recto.33: Izalla is also encountered as a source of wine in inscriptions of Nebuchadnezzar (S. Langdon, VAB 4 pp. 90, 22-6 and 154, 49-53), and in KAV 174.21.

P. 119: In the 3rd paragraph note that the Neo-Assyrian for milk is not *šizbu* but *zizibu* (AfO 18 (1957-8) 329.117; CTN I pp. 85-6). CTN II No. 113 gives another list of people of a similar type, and in particular uses the terms *batussu* (l. 12') and DUMU *ša* GAB (= *tūli* cf. KAJ 238.2). The suggestion of CAD quoted in note 10 is confirmed by my collation of No. 1.i.46 (apparent *ṣa* to be read *ṣ*), and the same may prove to be the case in No. 3.vi.17 also.

P. 120: Fig. 1 needs correction on some points. First, ERÍN.GURUŠ we believe to be a misleading transcription, since here the KAL sign is almost certainly no more than *dannu*, the normal Neo-Assyrian for 'big' and in this case 'adult'; cf. MÍ KAL 'adult woman' ADD 906 Rev.2, (collated). The transliteration *ṣaḫartu* in ADD 906 is incorrect, since the word is written *ṣa*-ḪUR-*tú* and *ṣaḫurtu* is the normal form. In ND 2485 the copy clearly has LÚ*.ÍR (as suggested by Fales on p. 121), and the misleading DUMU$^{?}$.ÍR should be deleted accordingly. With regard to the addition of persons in ADB 5, the situation is still unclear, but I should stress that an unknown amount of the tablet is missing at the head of each column.

P. 123: The 'prigioneri' of Gambulu in ADB No. 6.vii$^{!}$.4 are not in fact prisoners but deported persons or 'booty' (*ḫubtu*).

P. 130, note 41: It is of course a mistake to say that the towns and accompanying villages mentioned in the stele from Tell al-Rimaḥ were 'conquered', since the stele records their foundation.

Figura 4: the excellent map could profitably have been extended slightly further northwards, and it might also have indicated the location of Ḫadattu (Arslan Tash) since this is one of the fixed points in the Doomsday Book (cf. pp. 95-6).

ROYAL EXERCISE OF JUSTICE UNDER THE ASSYRIAN EMPIRE [1]

J.N. POSTGATE

Unlike the kings of Babylonia, those of Assyria rarely included among the royal titles any claims to be the source or instruments of justice. The titularies of the early neo-Assyrian kings — Assur-nāṣir-apli II and Shalmaneser III, for example — are more or less restricted to self-laudatory phrases which stress the king's military virtues, but never mention the exercise of justice. [2] It seems to be only under Sargon and his successors that we do find creeping into the Assyrian royal inscriptions such phrases as 'preserver of law and lover of justice' (*nāṣir kitti rā'im mīšari*). [3] It seems very probable that this innovation is a direct result of increased contact (both historical and literary) with Babylonia, and indeed it may be that the titles were consciously adopted so as to harmonize with the claims of the Assyrian kings over the South. [4]

Since the kings' own inscriptions are uninformative about their judicial role, we must approach the question from another side, and try to determine the regular legal machinery in Assyria at this date. Here too we are rather in the dark, but we can deduce something of the constitution of the courts by examining the surviving records of court proceedings (referred to hereafter for convenience as *Prozessurkunden*).

[1] The text is essentially unchanged from that read at Paris. It is therefore deliberately not an attempt to deal with the subject exhaustively, but is intended to put forward the argument for future discussion. The footnotes, added later, give illustration or substantiation for various points which seem to need them, and occasionally make additional comments where these are thought desirable.

[2] See e.g. M.-J. Seux, *Épithètes royales akkadiennes et sumériennes.*

[3] E.g. M.-J. Seux, op. cit., pp. 201f. and 236f.

[4] For the attitudes of the Assyrian kings towards Babylonia, see below. W.G. Lambert pointed out orally that the extension of the range of the royal titulary in the Sargonid period would of itself have led to the inclusion of titles such as these. This may be true, but it does not necessarily annul the significance which I suggest attaches to their selection.

The evidence afforded by these texts has been assembled by Prof. K. Deller in an article entitled '*Die Rolle des Richters im neuassyrischen Prozessrecht*' [5], of which he has most kindly lent me the proofs, and which I have used as the basis of the following details of the *Prozess-urkunden*.

In none of the known neo-Assyrian *Prozessurkunden* is there any sign of direct royal participation or intervention. The presiding officer of a court is not known as a judge (*dayyānu*), as this word is apparently obsolete in current usage, but is referred to by name, or, more often, by his administrative office. Thus the majority of cases are presided over by either the *sartennu* (with or without the *sukkallu*), or by the mayor of the town (*ḫazannu*) [6]; but we also find, according to Deller's list, an *abarakku*, a town-commander (*ša muḫḫi āli*), a deputy (*šaniu*), and a priest, all acting as judges; there is also an official called *ša pīn dēnāni/dēnāte* ('man in charge of legal cases'), who is the only one with a title specifically associated with the judicial system [7]. So we see that most judges are just ordinary members of the administration. We may illustrate this more vividly with the evidence of a recently published text in which 5 criminals are brought for trial in the first instance before 3 members of the civil (or perhaps even military) administration, who consist of 2 *ša qurbūti* (roughly : 'officers') and a deputy (*šaniu*). These three do not however attempt to judge the case themselves, but propose to refer it to higher authority, that is, to the *sukkallu* and the *sartennu* in Nineveh [8].

This then is a clear illustration of the point that ordinary justice was exercised within the regular framework of the administration, but it also focusses attention on the functions of the *sukkallu* and the *sartennu*,

[5] Due to appear shortly in *Studi Volterra*; I am most grateful to Prof. Deller for permission to make use of his article here.

[6] Although, for the sake of simplicity, I have suggested that the exercise of justice was solely in the hands of the central administration, it seems possible that within a single community a locally appointed official, the 'mayor' (*ḫazannu*), was able to preside over cases. In a small village the *ḫazannu* was probably the only resident official, but in larger places too he is found acting as judge (at Assur, Kalhu, Nineveh). If the *ḫazannu* as representative of the citizens of these cities retained any independence of the civil administration, we might have here a branch of the judiciary not immediately under royal control. Note also the occurrence of a priest as judge (at Assur, *RA* 24 (1927), 112-3).

[7] Discussed by Deller in his article.

[8] See *Iraq* 32 (1970), 131ff. (No. 2).

whose connection with justice has long been noticed. Perhaps the best example of their activities is in *ABL* 716, where we hear that the king (Assur-bān-apli) appointed the two of them together to sort out the legal confusion which had resulted from disturbances in Babylonia, but they are found working as a team in other contexts too. Their duties were not however exclusively legal : the *sukkallu* at least is known to have had other administrative functions, and seems at times to have been the king's deputy in his absence. [9] The point I want to stress here, is that these two officials, who are the nearest we know to the state's highest legal authority, are directly subordinate to the king.

Both in the lower reaches of the judicial system, therefore, and at the top, it was members of the administration who were in charge, and it does not need to be demonstrated that the administration was just the arm of the king, and hence, as we should have expected, that the supreme judicial authority must have resided in the king's own person. This means that the king would certainly have been able to intervene in the normal legal processes, and the fact that he is never seen to do so in the sources available to us means simply that he customarily delegated this part of his rule to his governors or to the *sukkallu* and *sartennu.*

If the king does not appear in any *formal* legal context, his accepted position as righter of wrongs and the source of justice is reflected by the frequent letters of the Kouyunjik archive where private persons apply to the king for his assistance in one way or another. [10] These letters are never actually requests for intervention in a specific lawsuit, but are often rather complaints against a member of the administration who, it is claimed, has treated the writer of the letter unfairly. In a system where the administration is responsible also for the exercise of justice, some device through which the private citizen might reach the ears of the king and by-pass the officials directly superior to him was an obvious necessity, and, as we shall see, such 'safety-valves' did exist. Writing letters was one means of reaching the king directly, but even so those letters we have ask not so much for justice in law, as for help : they ask to have the case settled in their favour by the king not as the

[9] See e.g. *ABL* 844, where the *sukkallu* is addressed on Babylonian affairs which also concern the king, presumably because of the king's absence.

[10] e.g. in Assyrian : *ABL* 84; 177; 353; 390; 421; 620; 916; 1250; in Babylonian : *ABL* 530; 587; 716; 852; 880; 928; 1255(?); 1285. *ABL* 415 (Ass.), although not strictly in this category, is also of interest.

ultimate source of justice, but as the ultimate source of power or authority. Hence we find that many such letters are written in a very humble, not to say cringing, tone, while more than once the writer complains that he has received no answer to previous efforts of his to engage the king's attention. [11] Where the author of a letter is more straightforward with his requests, it is usually a high official who is writing simultaneously to the king on routine business, and has reason to expect that the king will listen to him in view of his position in the administration. [12]

One feature of these 'appeal' letters is the high proportion of Babylonians among their writers; perhaps the only letters from truly 'private' correspondents are from Babylonia, and it is only these which even make mention of lawsuits. [13] An explanation for this is not hard to find. We have already noted that titles referring to the king's activity as a guardian of law are probably of Babylonian origin. The Assyrian kings were generally anxious to secure their position in Babylonia as much by diplomacy as by force, and they attempted to behave as inheritors of the Babylonian traditions should, so as to placate the inhabitants of the major cities, and earn their gratitude by the establishment of regular law, as well as by granting them their *kidinnūtu*, or special protected status.

If we look at Babylonian traditions, we will see that the kings may well have been more willing to intervene directly in the judicial system of Babylonia than they would have been in Assyria. As is well known, the Babylonian kings were traditionally law-givers, and legal cases in the Old Babylonian period might be referred to the king. [14] Later, legal disputes mentioned in the *kudurru* texts are brought before the king, sometimes more than once in the history of a particular dispute, [15] and in the first millennium, Prof. Brinkman points out, the citizens of major cities had a right to have their cases tried by the king. Under the Chaldaean dynasty the same tradition was given a very self-conscious expression in the curious text called by its editor 'Nebuchadnezzar, king of justice', where the king's re-establishment of justice is described, and details given of some of the cases which were decided by the king in

11 *ABL* 852 (Bab.); *ABL* 716, 5-6 (Bab. : 'Why have I appealed to the king once and twice, but no one has investigated (my complaint) ?').

12 e.g. *ABL* 84; 353.

13 *ABL* 928; 1255; 1285.

14 for this cf. for example Th. Jacobsen, *Analecta Biblica* 12 (1959), p. 140.

15 e.g. L.W. King, *Babylonian Boundary-stones*, No. 3 (pp. 7ff.).

person.[16] Of particular interest in this connection is the famous text 'Advice to a Prince' (W.G. Lambert, *BWL* 112ff.), which has been confidently assigned by Diakonoff to the reign of Sennacherib (AS 16, 343-9). This Babylonian composition makes it clear that the Babylonians (presumably with the agreement of at least some Assyrians, since as Diakonoff has pointed out,[17] the tablet bears one of those colophons of Assur-bān-apli which state that the text was selected for his own perusal) — that they considered that the king had distinct obligations to fulfil towards the inhabitants of the ancient cities they ruled. It may well be a reflection of the same ideas that in *ABL* 1285 a Babylonian writer requests that the 'king should give attention to his servant's case' (*šarru bēlī ana dīni ša ardi-šu liqūla*) in words which echo the opening lines of the other text : *šarru ana dīnim la iqūl* — in both cases there lurks a tradition that the king is obliged to act as a just arbiter to his subjects if he is required.[18] No trace of such an attitude to the king can be detected in an Assyrian context.[19]

Having now, however briefly, considered the king's position in the legal structure of Assyria and Babylonia, we can turn to some passages in the royal correspondence which show, in my opinion, that there existed a formal procedure by which an Assyrian subject might appeal to royal authority. I quote below 6 instances of the phrase *amat šarri qabû*, or, in Assyrian, *abat šarri zakāru*. In each of these letters a subject has 'spoken the word of the king', and the result of this, it seems, should be that the matter is passed on to the king by the official to whom 'the word was spoken'.

1. The *šatammu* of Esagila to Esarhaddon :
   PN_1 ^{lú}GAL *širaku* PN_2 ^{lú}ENGAR *ša* ^{d}EN PN_3 *u* PN_4 ^{lú}*kizû*^{meš} *ša* ^{lú}*qīpi a-mat* LUGAL *kī iq-bu-ú ana pān šarri altapraš-šunūti šarru ša pī-šunu lišme*

[16] W.G. Lambert, *Iraq* 27 (1965), 1-11.

[17] AS 16, 349, with note 24.

[18] It should be noted that I know of no occasion where an Assyrian king directly intervenes in a lawsuit in Babylonia, any more than in Assyria. That no instance exists would not be surprising, but I should stress that I have not looked in the nBab literature for this.

[19] In the Kouyunjik archive the king concerns himself with possibly judicial affairs only very rarely : in *ABL* 186 he seems to show some concern about the punishment of malefactors, but no more than would be compatible with a natural desire to see public order upheld. In *ABL* 550 there are interesting but broken references to a lawsuit. *ABL* 168, though written in Assyrian dialect, refers to events in NE Babylonia.

"Because (these people) 'spoke the word of the king' I have sent them to the king's presence, so that the king may hear what they have to say".

[B. Landsberger, *Brief* ll. 26-32]

2. The *šandabakku* and the *mušarkisus* to Esarhaddon(?) :
PN *Larakūa ultu bīt kīli ša Larak*^{ki} *kī iḫliq ina* UKKIN *ša* UN.MEŠ *a-mat* LUGAL *iq-ta-bi adû ana pāni šarri bēlī-ni niltapraš-šu šarru liš'al-šu*

"After PN, a man of Larak, escaped from the prison of Larak, he 'spoke the word of the king' in the assembly of the people. (So) now we have sent him to the king's presence, so that the king may question him".

[*ABL* 344 rev. 1-10]

3. Nabû-balāssu-iqbi to Aššur-bān-apli :
anāku ḫīṭ ana šarri ūl aḫṭi adî lā nakrūti kī allika a-mat LUGAL *ana muḫḫi* ^{m}UB-*ra-bi aq-ta-bi umma dibbī-ia ana ēkalli ibašši ūl iplaḫ nikkassī-ia ittaši*......

"I have not committed a crime against the king my lord. When before the hostilities I went and 'spoke the word of the king' to UBrabi, saying : 'I have affairs for the palace', he was not afraid, but took away my property ......".

[*ABL* 716, 9-13]

4. Ubru(SUḪUŠ)-nabû to the king :
PN$_1$ DUMU PN$_2$ ^{lú}*mušarkis(u) a-bat* LUGAL *ina pāni-ia i-za-kar mā abū-a ina māt nakīri mēti* ...... *ūmā annurig ina pān šarri bēlī-ia ussēbilaš-šu šarru bēlī liš'al-šu kī ša abutūni ana šarri bēlī-ia liqbi*

"PN$_1$, the *mušarkisu*, has 'spoken the word of the king' before me, saying : 'My father died in enemy territory ......'. So now I have sent him to the presence of the king, so that the king may question him, and he may explain to the king how the matter stands".

[*ABL* 186,10-rev.7]

5. To the king; identity of writer lost :
^{lú}ÌR É.GAL *ina pānī-šunu aptiqidi* PN *uptatti-šu a-bat* LUGAL *i-za-kar mā* A.ŠÀ.GA.MEŠ *šarru iāši uzakki* ....] *ina pān šarri bēlī-ia a*[......] *šarru bēlī liš'al-šunu šummu* A.ŠÀ.MEŠ LUGAL EN *uzakki ana* PN *ittidin*

"I have appointed a 'palace-servant' over(?) them, but PN

has sent him away, and has 'spoken the word of the king', saying : 'The king exempted the land for me' ....] (so) I [have sent them(?)] into the presence of the king, so that the king may question them, whether the king did exempt the land and give it to PN".

[NL 68 (*Iraq* 25 (1963) 75-76), 5'-rev.6']

6. The deputy governor (*šaniu*) of Isāna to the king :
PN ...... *a-bat* LUGAL *i-zak-kar mā zakūka*......

"PN is 'speaking the word of the king', saying : 'I am exempt' (from corn-taxes mentioned above)".

[NL 74 (*Iraq* 27 (1965) 21-23), rev. 14'-16']

Looking at these examples in more detail, in Nos. 1 and 2 we have the highest Babylonian officials of Babylon and Nippur respectively, together with Assyrian officials in No. 2, writing to Esarhaddon on a number of unrelated topics. In the first letter some men are sent on for the king to hear their case *because* (*kī* — although of course other translations of *kī* are possible) they had 'spoken the word of the king', although we are not told why they had done this. In No. 2, however, it is clear that the man who 'spoke the word of the king' in the general assembly of Larak was thereby attempting to obtain a reversal of the decision which had confined him to the prison from which he had just escaped. By coming before the Assembly he presumably hoped to prevent the authorities from hushing up the affair and ignoring his appeal. This, however, is exactly what did happen in the third letter : instead of passing on the subject's complaints 'to the palace', the official did not respect (perhaps a more accurate translation of *ūl iplaḫ*) the appeal, but rather pursued his injustices further; and this is why the writer is forced to write directly to the king himself.

Moving from Babylonia to Assyria, in No. 4 Ubru-nabû (very likely a man known elsewhere as a high palace official [20]) passes on to the king the appeal of a man whose father had been killed fighting, and whose troops had disbanded together with their horses; the son here seeks royal intervention presumably in order to re-assert his father's authority. In the other two cases, in letters from Nimrud, we have appeals against taxation on the grounds that the land (or person) is exempt. As the author of one of these letters says, '(only) those who are mentioned

[20] See K. Tallqvist, *Assyrian Personal Names*, 104.

in the sealed decrees of the king are exempt' [21], and the matter must naturally be referred back to the king who either had, or had not, made the grant in the first place.

When these six passages, which are the only unmistakable ones I have noted [22], are placed side by side, it becomes clear that to 'speak the word of the king' implies an appeal to the king over the heads of those immediately concerned with one's case. How it achieves such a meaning is not clear; in Nos. 5 and 6 *abat šarri* could be taken to refer to a past decree of the king's, although this is unlikely, but this certainly cannot be correct in the other examples, and I do not believe we can offer an exact translation of the phrase at present. [23]

To define this institution of appeal more closely, then, we must consider the evidence of the passages quoted. While it is obvious that on each occasion the king is appealed to for just treatment, in a sense, the appeal is not in any way a part of the legal system. Appeals within a legal system to the head of state are of course possible; under the Roman empire a citizen might appeal to the emperor either before a trial or at the conclusion of a legal case. [24] However here, even in No. 2, where the appellant appears before the assembly to make his appeal, he is objecting not to any legal decision, but to the political act by which he was locked up, since prisons were not used for the constraint of criminals, but for the removal of political opponents of the régime. [25]

[21] Nimrud Letter 74 (*Iraq* 27 (1965) 21-23), Obv. 10-11.

[22] We should perhaps add : *ABL* 1032 (Bab.), Rev. 10 ('speak the word of the king to' (or : 'about' ?)'the brothers of PN'), and *ABL* 871 (Ass.), 8.

[23] Since the usual meaning of *ab/mat šarri* is not by itself sufficient to explain the usage, various different explanations seem possible. Two major groups of possibilities may be defined, depending on whether the words *ab/mat šarri* are seen as originally *oratio recta* ('he says : "The king's word"'), or not ('he speaks the king's word'). In the first case some words would have to be understood in order to complete the phrase, e.g. '(I appeal for) the king's word (on this matter)', or '(this matter is/should be) a case of the king' (although to my knowledge nAss does not use *abutu* for 'case'). If, on the other hand, the phrase is not direct speech, then *ab/mat šarri* must describe the man's appeal, and the man 'speaks the word of (= an appeal to) the king'. The uses of *zakāru* and *qabû* are sufficiently broad to allow of both. Cf. also *abat* (of the king) in mA, below, note 28.

Until we have some more evidence, it seems to me premature to try and decide between these and other possible explanations.

[24] For classical (i.e. Roman) parallels cf. J.M. Kelly, *Princeps Iudex* (Weimar 1957), 91f., and Pauly-Wissowa, *RE* XXIII.2.2444-2463, article '*Provocatio*'.

[25] This is my own assessment of the situation in *ABL* 344, but my statement about

It appears, therefore, that the procedure of 'speaking the word of the king' was intended to protect subjects from oppression by members of the administration. There must clearly have been an obligation on the local officials to whom the appeal was expressed, to pass it on to the king, and as we have seen, the appellants were in fact usually sent on to the king to put their own case in person. The failure of the official in No. 3 to perform his duties must have been relatively uncommon, since a letter to the king was presumably always an alternative for the subject. If this type of appeal was recognised by the kings in non-legal contexts, it may seem likely that a similar procedure existed for appeals in legal matters as well, but I can quote no instance of this.

There are of course many problems about this institution which are unsolved, but here I want only to ask one last question : is it of Babylonian or Assyrian origin ? I know of no parallels in either country, although they may of course exist. In view of what has been said of the king's traditional obligations in Babylonia, we might think the South a more likely breeding-ground for such a custom; but on the other hand the earlier texts are the Assyrian letters from Nimrud (Nos. 5 and 6), and a device of this kind displays the common sense which is typical of the efficient and often humane administration of the Assyrian empire.

To sum up, then, no instance survives of an Assyrian king's intervening directly in individual legal cases, whether in Assyria or Babylonia, but it seems likely that in both countries they were in theory able to do so. The basis for such an intervention is however different : in Assyria the exercise of justice formed a part of the administration, of the monolithic structure of government of which the king was sole head, whereas in Babylonia the king was traditionally obliged to act as arbiter of legal disputes when required. Justice in Babylonia was by no means a royal monopoly, however, since the assembly and other local courts were still active there. [26]

The other function of the king in this sphere was to correct the injustices of his own administration, and this too was doubtless

prisons' being used exclusively for political purposes does not hold good for at least the later periods in Babylonia : see M. San Nicolò, *Festschrift für Leopold Wenger II* (Münchener Beiträge zur Papyrusforschung und antiken Rechtsgeschichte 35), 1-17, on *bīt kīli*.

[26] See M. San Nicolò, *Babylonische Rechtsurkunden des ausgehenden* 8. *und des* 7. *Jahrhunderts v. Chr.*, pp. 146-7 (on No. 85).

considered an obligation. At least, letters were written to him by private citizens in Babylonia, and in both Babylonia and Assyria there was a recognised procedure, 'speaking the word of the king', for calling the king's attention to one's case.

I should like to conclude by quoting from two distinguished authors, in an attempt to place this rather brief summary in the perspective of the wider context to which it belongs. In his *Institutions des séleucides* (Paris, 1938), E. Bikermann wrote : 'On tenait la justice pour le premier attribut du roi, qui était lui-même "la loi vivante". Le roi devait juger partout et chaque fois qu'on l'en requérait. Pour cette raison non seulement les courtisans avaient l'occasion d'entretenir le monarque de leurs affaires personnelles, mais chaque solliciteur pouvait obtenir accès auprès du souverain. Evidemment, le roi ne rendait des sentences judiciaires que dans les cas exceptionnels; et en général il renvoyait les plaintes et les requêtes aux juges ordinaires' (p. 186). [27]

With this description of the Seleucid monarchy, which could apply word for word to the Assyrian kings, I should like to compare the peculiar position of Assyria in the history of the near East, recently admirably described by I.M. Diakonoff : 'There is a difference in quality between the Assyrian and the later empires, on the one hand, and the earlier kingdoms on the other. Previously, a stable centralized administration never reached outside the limits of the river basin. The conquests beyond these limits were either simple raids, or led at best to a loose hegemony over autonomous city-states.' (*Troisième conférence internationale d'histoire économique*, 1965, 28 [2]). As the first rulers of an empire of this kind and on this scale, the Assyrian kings met the problems it created for the first time, and their solutions were often those adopted by later generations of rulers too. [28]

[27] I owe this reference to Prof. A.D. Momigliano, to whom I am also most grateful to discussing the classical parallels with me.

[28] I have not considered any possible Assyrian traditions of the second millennium, which could have contributed to the King's legal position in the later period. For this subject I may perhaps refer to the contribution of M.T. Larsen to the Rencontre, for the old Assyrian period, and Prof. K. Deller kindly points out to me the article of C. Saporetti '*Un intervento del re in una questione giuridica medio-assira* (*KAJ 170 e KAV 211*)' in *Oriens Antiquus* 7 (1968), 51-55, which mentions a tablet recording a decision of Aššur-uballiṭ I and beginning *ina abat Aššur-uballiṭ* UGULA-*lim*.

J. N. POSTGATE : "*Princeps Iudex*" in *Assyria*.

In his recent volume of Neo-Assyrian letters, S. Parpola publishes two fragments of a letter to the Assyrian king, presumably Assurbanapli, although name of both writer and recipient are lost (*CT* 53, 78+426). The letter provides confirmation that subjects of the Assyrian king had a right of appeal to him in person, and since I discussed this topic in Paris in 1971 (see *Le palais et la royauté*, XIXe Rencontre assyriologique internationale, 417-426), I have asked for the hospitality of the *Revue d'Assyriologie* to present a brief treatment of the text. Since the join was made after the completion of the copies, collation was desirable, and did yield some results, which are incorporated in the following edition. My thanks are due to M. P. Garelli who made some valuable comments on a first draft of this note, and saved me from two actual errors.

1 ina UGU LÚ.ÉRIN.MEŠ ša a-bat-šar-ra-a-⌈te⌉ [iz-ka-ru-u-ni]
2 LUGAL be-lí lu la ú-ku$^{?}$-uš L[Ú$^{?}$.ÉRIN.MEŠ an-nu-u-te]
3 li-li-ku-u-ni li-iq-bi-ú ⌈ina de-e-n⌉ [i(-šú-nu) LUGAL be-lí]
4 li-ru-ub a-bu-tú š[a] ina IGI LUGAL maḫ-ra-tu-[u-ni]
5 ina ŠU.2-šú li-ṣi-bat ša [in]a IGI LUGAL EN-iá la maḫ-r[a-tu-u-ni]
6 LUGAL be-⌈lí⌉[lu-]⌊ra-a⌋m-mi šúm-ma ÌR ša LUGAL šu-u ina [UGU]
7 ^{lú}šak-ni-šu ina UGU L[Ú].NAM-šú iq-ṭí-bi bir-ti IGI.2.ME
8 ša ^{lú}šak-ni-šu ina muḫ-ḫ[i-š]ú lu-ma-di-du šúm-ma ur-du
9 [š]a aš-šur-a-a bir-te IGI.2.M[E] ⌊ša⌋ EN-šú lu-ma-di-du
10 [m]a-a ina lìb-bi LUGAL i-ti-i-la [ma-]a me-me-ni i-si-šú
11 la i-da-bu-ub ina lìb-[b]i e-ki-it la ta-ra-di
12 ⌊ú$^{?}$⌋ -la-a ú bi LUGAL be-lí É[RI]N.MEŠ-šú ú-ga-mar i-ḫal-li-qi
13 [i]-lak a-na me-eḫ-ri-šu i-qa-bi ma-a ina IGI LUGAL-ma
14 la-qa-bi ú-la LUGAL be-lí bir-te IGI.2.MEŠ ša LÚ.GAL.ME(Š)
15 ina muḫ-ḫi lu-ma-di-du bi-is i-šam-me-ú UN.MEŠ
16 ma-a['-d]u-te i-la-ku-u-ni ṣa-ḫi-it-tú ša LUGAL EN š[i$^{?}$-i]
17 ina da-ba-bi ma-a'-di ta-na-mar
ina UGU KÙ.GI ša [x x (x x)]
18 LUGAL EN-iá áš-pur-an-ni nu-uk šum-ma ṭè-e-mu ša[x x x]
19 an-ni-e ina IGI LUGAL EN-iá e-ta-rab nu-uk LUGAL [ ]
20 a-na ÌR-šú liš-pu-ra a-ta-a LUG[AL]
21 [šu]m-ma LUGAL be-lí ina$^{!}$ la da-ba-bi a[n$^{?}$-]
22 ⌈x⌉-te-e-ni a-na ^{lú}sar-tin-n[i]
23 [š]a$^{?}$ ^{uru}ḫar-ḫa-ra LUGAL be-lí[
24 ina IGI.2-[š]u-nu lu ina muḫ-ḫi-šú[

"As for the men who have [made] appeals to the king, the king my lord should not turn (them) away; let [these men] come and appeal, and let [the king my lord] go into [their] cases. Any matter which finds favour with the king, let him take into his hands, and any which does not find favour with the king my lord, let him dismiss.

[6]If he is a servant of the king (and) he appealed [against] his officer (or) against his governor, let them reprimand his officer about him; if he is the servant of an Assyrian, let them reprimand his master, saying: "... the king. No-one is to dispute with him. ..., do not harrass(?) (him)". Or else ... the king my lord will 'finish off' his men, and he will escape and go to his fellow(s) and say: "I shall appeal to the king himself". [14]Or else the king my lord should have them reprimand the nobles about it, so that they will hearken, (and) many people will come, (and thus) will this desire of the king my lord be achieved, through much disputing". [The remainder of the letter deals with another affair concerning gold].

There are several doubtful points about this translation, discussed in the following notes. However, it is clear that the writer is advising the king (presumably shortly after his accession) about his treatment of men who had "spoken the king's word" (abat šarri). The opening lines are fairly clear (1-5). The writer then considers two cases: he is either a royal servant, i.e. a state employee, and in this case he comes automatically under a government officer (*šaknu*) and any justifiable cause for complaint can be taken up with that officer. Otherwise, he will be the servant (or slave, if the term is preferred) of an Assyrian. If this is the case, the writer of the letter suggests the wording of the king's reprimand to the owner, but unfortunately it is obscure to me (ll. 10-11). In ll. 12-14 an alternative is proposed, probably applying only to the case of a private owner, and in ll. 14-16 another option described, involving the high state officials (LÚ.GAL.MEŠ), which could apply to both cases. We should not necessarily expect total clarity of thought and expression from the letter-writer.

As well as confirming the nature of the abat šarri institution, this short letter allows us a tantalizing glimpse of the social divisions in Assyrian society of which we are so amazingly ignorant. The persons appealing are called LÚ.ÉRIN.MEŠ (=ṣābu) and are either servants of the king, i.e. the state, or of an "Assyrian". We do not know the exact connotation of this word, but this letter makes it reasonable to propose a translation "free citizen of Assyria"; it is hardly likely to be restricted to the people of the city of Assur, but we remain quite ignorant of the qualifications for being an "Assyrian". Nevertheless, our passage does confirm that the term implied a precise social status. Apparently the letter-writer does not consider the case in which an Assyrian himself "spoke the 'king's word'": only royal servants or servants of Assyrians are mentioned. There is therefore an interesting contrast with the Roman empire, where it was only the civis Romanus who had the right to appeal to Caesar. Did "Assyrians" have other means of redress? Or were they simply not subject to the forms of bureaucratic or governmental injustice which the institution of the appeal to the king was designed to counteract?

1: the absence of introductory formulae shows that this is one tablet from a longer letter; for the phrase abat šarri and the different verbs used with it, see the article in Le palais et la royauté, quoted above. This is of course the first occurrence of the plural form.

2: although ukkušu is apparently not attested in Neo-Assyrian, there is little doubt about the ku; uš is followed by the first two horizontals of a sign, which could very well be L[Ú, but hardly an accusative suffix.

4: if li-ru-ub is 3. sg. then "the king" should almost certainly be restored at the end of l. 3; if however it is 3 pl. (which is quite possible in Neo-Assyrian orthography), then the translation should be emended: "... let them enter into judgement ...".

7-8: for the role of the šaknu in the Assyrian administration see J. N. Postgate in *Anatolian Studies* 30 (1980), forthcoming.

10: the signs in i-ti-i-la seem epigraphically beyond suspicion. An imperative from it'ulu? Or, as M. Garelli proposes to me, from têlu (*AHw* 1345*b*: "genau aussprechen")?

11: after renewed collation the sign after e ki must be IT — both da and ša were considered but rejected. We therefore probably require a verb ekād/t/ṭu, of which this would be imperative; no suitable verb seems to be known, unless we suppose a metathesized form from etāku "to be on guard" ...??

12: the simplest solution of the beginning of this line would be to emend to ú-la-a ina! lìb!-bi, but since the translation of the rest of the line is problematical, we would not really be justified in emending the perfectly clear ú. The translation we have offered for this line has the advantage of agreeing with the grammatical forms in the text, but it remains rather unconvincing otherwise.

15: for the nuance of bis, cf. *Iraq* 35 (1973), 25[9] on l. 18, where we suggest that ba-si has the nuance "so that", "in order that"; it seems probable to us that bi-is is no more than a graphic variant of ba-si.

16: at the end of the line ša LUGAL EN-š[ú(-nu)] would also be possible.

Nomads and Sedentaries in the Middle Assyrian Sources

J.N. Postgate

The following brief notes are offered in the consciousness that they contribute little to the theme of "economic symbiosis." Owing to the scarcity of written evidence, the role of the nomad in the Middle Assyrian state cannot yet be described in any detail. The few definite pieces of evidence, which are given below, are sufficient to reconstruct a plausible picture based on a comparison with other, better documented areas and periods, but are not in themselves the basis for a study of the relations between sedentary and nomad. Nevetheless, we appreciate that even our isolated scraps of evidence may prove of interest when placed alongside other contributions and, in order to present them in context, we have found it necessary to give a general summary of what is known of desert nomads during the period with which we are concerned, ca. 1400 to 1000 B.C.[1]

The sources

Although the written documents bearing on the Middle Assyrian period are relatively few in number and rather uniform in type, a brief description of them is needed to make clear any possible gaps in the records.

The *historical records* consist almost exclusively of the royal inscriptions of the Assyrian kings. The first major corpus comes from the three kings whose reigns spanned the thirteenth century: Adad-narari I, Shalmaneser I, and Tukulti-ninurta I. The only other king from whom a large body of inscriptions has survived is Tiglath-pileser I (1115-1077), although portions of the annals of his son, Aššur-bel-Kala, are also preserved. Apart from the royal inscriptions there are a few relevant passages in chronicles or historiographical texts.

Middle Assyrian *letters*, almost all of which come from the capital itself, Aššur, treat mainly daily business or administrative affairs and contain virtually nothing of importance for our topic. On the other

[1] We follow the dates given by J.A. Brinkman in A.L. Oppenheim, *Ancient Mesopotamia* (Chicago, 1964), pp. 346-7.

hand, there are references to the activities of nomads in the Syrian desert in the political correspondence from the chanceries of Ḫattušas and El Amarna.

Administrative and *legal* documents are often hard to tell apart, and can be considered here together. Again the main body of texts comes from Aššur itself, where in some cases distinct archives can be reconstructed with the help of the excavators' records or from internal evidence. Apart from some legal texts of the fourteenth century, the majority of these Aššur tablets come from the thirteenth century, in particular the reigns of Shalmaneser I and Tukulti-ninurta I. There is also one archive of over 100 tablets from the days of Ninurta-tukulti-Aššur (ca. 1135 **B.C.**), but little else as late as this.

From other sites too, the legal and administrative texts belong almost exclusively to the thirteenth century: some tablets from Kar-Tukulti-ninurta (opposite Aššur), small archives from Tell' Billa (Shibaniba, a provincial capital), from Tell al-Rimah (a local administrative center), and a very few tablets from Tell Fakhariyah on the upper Ḫabur.

It is not, of course, fortuitous that the best documented period historically is also that from which the majority of our administrative and similar tablets date. The effective maintenance of a strong government over a wide area has always bred vigorous scribal activity and the thirteenth century was the heyday of the Middle Assyrian empire. It is hardly necessary to point out also that it is precisely during such periods of strong central control that there will be the least military pressure exerted by the nomadic population on the settled lands, but the strongest incentives to promote peaceable intercourse, and that this should be reflected in the sources.

The nomadic populations

The superficiality of our sources is evident as soon as we search them for details about the nomad population. In fact, almost all the references to nomads employ one (or more) of three names: Sutians, Aḫlamu, and Aramaeans. All these are met during our timespan on Assyria's southwestern flank and since virtually all the evidence has been admirably summarised by J.R. Kupper, we need only sketch the position here.[2]

[2] J.-R. Kupper, *Les nomades en Mésopotamie au temps des Rois de Mari* (Paris 1957): pp. 83-145 For the geography of Assyria, see, in general, David Oates, *Studies in the Ancient History of Northern Iraq* (London, 1968).

The *Sutians*, who are known already during the Old Babylonian period, figure during the thirteenth and fourteenth centuries as the major nomadic group occupying the desert between Tadmor (Palmyra) and the borders of Babylonia. They are still in existence in ca. 1135 B.C., since they are among the vassals of Ninurta-tukulti-Aššur, but thereafter they fade out in the north, and reappear only later, probably only as an archaising name.

The *Aḫlamu* were of more recent origin, and the first certain mention shows them in Dilmun (Bahrain) as antagonists of the Kassites there, well down in the Arabian peninsula. In Assyria they are first mentioned by Adad-narari as opponents of his father, Arik-den-ili, along with the Sutians and Yauru. Towards the end of the reign of Adad-narari I, the Hittite Hattušilis III excuses himself for not having sent messengers to Babylon because the Aḫlamu were making the route down the Euphrates insecure, but later in the thirteenth century, Shalmaneser I encountered them in alliance with the Hittites and Hurrians in a desert area south of the major cities of Ḫanigalbat, perhaps near the lower Balih. Like the term *Sutian*, the name *Aḫlamu* survived into the first millennium as an archaic designation for nomad populations in both historical and "literary" (e.g., omen) texts, but already in Tiglath-pileser I's inscriptions, the term *Aḫlamu* is always qualified by *Aramaean*.

The *Aramaeans* (Assyrian: *Arumu*, *Arimi*, etc.) were evidently a subgroup of the Aḫlamu when they made their first appearance in our sources in the inscrptions of Tiglath-pileser. They penetrated as far as the district of Nineveh itself before the end of his reign and, as we shall see, Aššur-bel-kala (1074-1057) was obliged to meet them in several areas close to the Assyrian homeland. By this time the Aramaeans had established themselves so much as the main group that the prefix *Aḫlamu* is omitted.

To sum up, the evidence of the historical texts shows conflict between the Assyrians and the Sutians from the middle to the end of the fourteenth century, but no later. The Aḫlamu are first mentioned with the Sutians at the end of the fourteenth century and in the reign of Shalmaneser I (1274-1245), but not again until they are attacked as *Aramaean Aḫlamu* by Tiglath-pileser I, and the Aramaeans make their first appearance here and remain thereafter the major nomadic population.

To what extent the earlier groups retained a separate identity is impossible to say, especially because we have hardly any legal and administrative documents to illustrate internal conditions in Assyria after the reign of Tukulti-ninurta I. Characteristically, however, the Sutians may be found in the non-historical texts as late as the Ninurta-tukulti-Aššur archive (ca. 1135 B.C.), and it is possible that the relations with the Aḫlamu had already improved before they were swamped by the Aramaeans. In the absence of any reliable evidence on the subsequent fate of the Aḫlamu, however, we propose in the following section to concentrate on the Sutians and the Aramaeans, with particular emphasis on the geographical evidence.

Detailed attestations of nomadic presence

Although both northern Mesopotamia ("Assyria") and the south ("Babylonia") suffered from almost continuous nomadic pressure, their geographical circumstances were rather different. In the south, the undisputed territories of the desert nomad west of the Euphrates bordered directly on the central area with major cities like Sippar and Marad. The main urban cluster in the north was along and east of the Tigris, including, at our date, besides Aššur Nineveh, Arbil, Kalḫu, Kilizi, and Isana. These cities were separated from the western desert not only by the barrier of the Euphrates and the towns along it, but also by a wide belt of semi-desert, and, in periods of prosperity, by a fringe of small towns and villages pushing out towards the limits of viable rainfall agriculture. Put succintly, the heart of Assyria was one step more remote from the threat of bedouin *razzias*, and any relations with the nomads whether peaceful or hostile, would be predominantly on the borders of the country towards the desert.

Before plunging into detail, there is a further point which should be made. A constant dilemma of the Assyrian rulers was whether or not to annex the cities strung along the middle Euphrates and to police the river between them. In neo-Assyrian times, of course, this was done, but as far as our evidence goes there was no attempt by the Middle Assyrian kings. The land of Suḫi is sometimes mentioned as a vassal state, but direct government of the area was evidently not contemplated. The strategic considerations are complex. On the one hand it was pointless to try and prevent the nomads from pasturing their flocks in the vast expanses between the two rivers, and yet their presence east of the Euphrates greatly increased the exposure of the settled lands to nomadic infiltration. On the other hand, the river acted as an effective barrier in both directions, and even if shepherds, themselves might escape Assyrian vengeance by crossing the river, it is more difficult for the sheep to escape too. Our sources make no mention of conflict with nomads east of the river, and it is therefore possible that a mutually profitable modus vivendi was usually operating in the Jezirah.

The Sutians

Since the Sutians are mentioned in an Amarna letter as having detaneid messengers passing between the Egyptian and Babylonian courts, it is hardly doubtful that at this date (ca. mid-fourteenth century B.C..) they were occupying the strip of land running from Tadmor (Palmyra) past the Jebel Bishri to the current Babylonian border (at Rapiqu near modern Ramadi). This was perennially the home of independent nomadic groups, such as the Amorites, or, later, the Aramaeans, and they controlled the direct desert route from Babylonia to Syria which passed through Tadmor.

Except for a single reference to a campaign of Arik-den-ili against the Aḫlamu, Sutians, and Yauru, all remaining mentions of the Sutians in Middle Assyrian sources show them in a peaceful role. KAJ 39:7 refers to a trading-journey as a *KASKAL É LÚ su-ti-e* "journey (to) the 'house' of the Sutians," in which the term *house* may be an early instance of a usage which can be partly geographical but need only imply little more than *tribe.*[3] We know nothing of the exact geographical destination of this trading venture, which dates to about the middle of the fourteenth century, nor does the capital sum of silver advanced tell us anything of the nature of the undertaking.

Tribute (or simpley "payment"—*maddattu*) is brought by various foreigners including the *su-ti-e meš* (whose contribution is sixteen fat-tailed sheep) in KAJ 314, dating to Shalmaneser I.

In TR 2059 a government agent has received the customs duty payable on a donkey bought from a "Yaurian Sutian." The text dates to Shalmaneser I or Tukulti-ninurta I, and was issued at Qatara which is either Tell al-Rimah itself or perhaps more likely a town close by.[4]

The text TR 2083A + is an official document relating to a stolen

[3]For this usage cf. Journal ot the Economic Social History of the Orient[17]

[4]We acnowledge with gratitude Prof. Saggs' Kind permission to use the content this tablet, wich is mentioned in Iraq 30 (1968): 168

slave girl, who was sold to a Sutian and is to be recovered; this must also date to about the same period.[5]

In the Ninurta-tukulti-Assur *nāmurtu* archive (ca. 1135 B.C.), gifts of sheep are recorded from the Sutians on three separate occasions.[6] Once the donor is "the Sutians" (su-ti-u meš), but twice we have the phrase *DUMU na-gi su-ti-e*, usually understood to mean "son of the Sutian region," although we have doubts on this score.[7] In any case, these three texts show the Sutians in fairly regular contact with the Assyrian court, as friendly vassals or perhaps even subjects of the king.

The Aramaeans

Tiglath-pileser recounts that he crossed the Euphrates on at least fourteen campaigns in his efforts to intimidate the Aramaeans, whom he chased "from the Land of Suḫi to Carchemish" or "from the foot of Mt. Lebanon (to) Tadmor (and) Anat, and up to the border of Babylonia at Rapiqu." On one occasion he sacked six of their villages or towns which lay at the foot of the Jebel Bishri. Obviously the provocation for these campaigns came from Aramaean raids across the river into Assyrian territory, and these were only a foretaste of what was to come, since by the end of Tiglath-pileser's reign a chronicle fragment makes it clear that famine conditions in Assyria caused, of course, by bad harvests had led to desertion of settled parts of the Jezirah and enabled the Aramaean "houses" (whether "tents" or "tribes" is meant is not clear) to penetrate in search of grazing and spoil as far into Assyria as the district of Nineveh itself and the province of Kilizi between Arbil and the Tigris.[8] The extent of their

[5] The tablet is now composed of TR 2083A + B + C and TR 2084A + D; we hope to publish the resulting text before long.

[6] In E. Weidner, *Archiv für Orientforschung* 10 (1935-36): 31, VAT 9378; p. 38, no. 78; pp. 43-4, no. 105. For this archive in general, see recently J.N. Postgate, *Taxation and Conscription in the Assyrian Empire* (Rome, 1974), pp. 156-160.

[7] *Nagiu* is not found in other Middle Assyrian texts, but we would expect *na-gi-i/e* and, in any case, the designation "son of... district" seems unusual, and the exact meaning of this pharase must remain uncertain.

[8] For the latest edition see A.K. Grayson, *Assyrian and Babylonian Chronicles*

penetration is made clear by the annals of Assur-bel-kala, who within a couple of years was obliged to fight the Aramaeans at Pa'uza (at the foot of the Tur Abdin near Nisibis), at Shinamu (known to be near Mardin), and at a town whose name ends with *tigua* or *tibua* actually on the Tigris; also further west in the Ḫarran district, and at two places on the Ḫabur, Magarisi of the Yari land and Dur-Katlimmu (earlier Dur-Iaggit-lim). Extra details are supplied by the inscriptions of later kings: Shalmaneser III reports the loss of Pitru and Mutkinu on the Euphrates bend under Assur-rabi II (1013-973), and Adad-nirari II mentions that Gidara (Aramaic Radammate) had been lost under Tiglath-pileser II (967-935 B.C.).

Other minor groups

Among the opponents of Arik-den-ili were the "Aḫlamu, Sutians, (and) Yauru." TR 2059 now gives us a "Yaurian Sutian," showing that, to the Assyrians in the thirteenth century, the Yauru were considered a subgroup of the Sutians. In all probability, the same name is used by Assur-bel-Kala when he describes Magarisi on the Habur as being "of the Land of Yari," in which case this tribe was sufficiently sedentary by ca. 1050 B.C. to have specific district associated with it.[9]

Another subgroup of the Sutians seems to be represented in TR 2083A +, where the purchaser of the slave-woman is given as a *su-ti-e ta-ḫa-ba-ie-e*, presupposing a tribe Taḫabu or similar, but otherwise unknown. Possibly in the same category, but subgroups of the Ahlamu or Arameans, are the broken gentiliticus[*-mi-ra-ia*^{meš},]-*'a-da-ia* ^{meš}, and]*ḫa'-ma-a-ia* ^{meš}, all dating to approximately the reigns of Tiglath-pileser I and Assur-bel-kala.[10] The *nisbe* termination and/or plural sign tend to show that we have to do with

(New York, 1975). p. 189, with the reading *ki-li-zi* in the *Addenda et Corrigenda*, p. 289 We may mention here the possibility that at the beginning of the same line 12^{one} should restore ^{uru}*ta-i-di*.

[9] For the position of Magarisi on the Ḫabur, see F.M. Fales, *Censimenti e catasti di epoca neo-assira* (Rome, 1973). p. 97 *IA-ú-ru* may stand for /yūru/ but it is less certain that plain *IA-ri* in the Aššur-bel-kala text may do so.

10 Found respectively in VAT 9539 (AFO 6 (1930-31) 88 and 92: Iraq 32 (1970): 169:4': *Iraq* 32 (1970) Pl. XXXIV BM 122635 +. Rev. last line (coll.).

nomadic tribes in each case, and we may note that the habit of referring to an individual not by his own name but solely by his tribal affiliation indicates that the Sutians were still genuinely nomadic in the Tell al-Rimah region in the thirteenth century.

Lastly, we have two gentiliticus which are identical with tribes later qualified as Aramaean. In BM 122635, a Middle Assyrian tablet from Nineveh, there is mentioned a contribution from *KUR ru-qa-ḫa-ia*, a tribe known in the first millennium to have occupied the lands east of the Tigris below Aššur. [11] The tribe Ḫirana, found in Babylonia in the first millennium, acts as a military unit in a letter found at Dur-Kurigalzu, and elsewhere in Kassite texts is identified as a subgroup of the Aḫlamu. [12]

In general, though, we have so few specific designations of subgroups during these centuries compared to the first millennium, that we must conclude either that the nomadic populations were indeed less fragmented, which seems unlikely, or simply that the difference between subgroups was a matter of indifference to the Assyrian annalists.

The interaction of sedentary and nomad

With the very scant data at our disposal, we cannot hope to present anything solid on which to base conclusions about the "economic symbiosis," and it would be futile to enunciate general truths on so slender a basis of fact. All we can do, having set the scene at some length, is to quote the most relevant passages.

The practice of using nomadic soldiers in the armed forces of the urban states is well attested in the early second millennium and again in the neo-Assyrian empire. It is, therefore, hardly surprising to find Sutians serving as "auxiliaries" with the armies of the great powers during the latter half of the second millennium B.C. They are attested with the Hittite armed forces, and with some of the minor Syrian and Palestinian states involved in the Amarna correspondence. There is no evidence known to us that the Assyrians also employed the Sutians as mercenaries; the only remote hint of this is the *nāmurtu*

11 *Iraq* 32 (1970), Pl. XXXIII BM 122635 + :22': the precise date of this text is uncertain.

12. See O.R. Gurney, *Iraq* 11 (1949): 139-141.

contribution brought in to the Assyrian court by the Sutians three times in one year, showing that there were Sutians allied with or subject to the Assyrian king (ca. 1135 B.C.). The letter from Dur-Kurigalzu mentioned above refers to bodies of 500 Ḫ̌irana and Ḫ̌asmi soldiers, but it is difficult to ascertain from the text whether they are working with, or for, the Assyrians or the Babylonians.

Turning to commerce, we find no evidence of contact with any nomads except the Sutians. The two texts from Tell al-Rimah show that travelling Sutians did business with the townsfolk during the thirteenth century. The tax levied on the donkey in TR 2059 was a "customs duty," showing that the Sutian had brought it from outside the customs area within which taxes had to be paid. Parallels with other times would suggest that the Sutians here and elsewhere acted as shepherds for the sedentary population, but for this there is no evidence. At Aššur itself, the capital, there is even less sign of intercourse with the Sutians or other nomads. This may be blamed to some extent on the nature of the archives available to us, but we should bear in mind that a group of villages probably existed out west of the Wadi Tharthar, and that they may to some extent have acted as a buffer against nomadic penetration as far as Aššur itself, quite apart from any military measures taken with the same purpose. [13] The evidence from Aššur consists solely of the mention of a caravan to the "house" of the Sutians, and the contributions of sheep made by them at two dates. The caravan is interesting, but too isolated, and it is hard to reconstruct its economic incentive, while the sheep contributions tell us next to nothing, since sheep were the commonest of all gifts and are brought from every point of the compass.

Summary

The combination of evidence shows that after some initial hostility Sutian tribes during the thirteenth and twelfth centuries B.C. pursued a peaceful relationship with the Assyrian government on the

[13] Accepting H.J. Nissen's proposal to identify the river Šiššar in Middle Assyrian textx with the Wadi Tharthar (see *Heidelberger Studien zum Alten Orient* (Wiesbad 1967): 116.

western fringes of the country, but remained nomadic and distinct from the sedentary population. It may be thought likely that a process of assimilation had begun, e.g., in areas like Tell al-Rimah, on the fringes of settlement, but for this we have no evidence, and only very rarely are West Semitic names to be recognised in the texts. In any case, the Sutians, whether settled or nomadic, would have been swept away or absorbed in the flood of Aramaeans which all but overwhelmed the entire Assyrian state.

J. N. Postgate

THE ECONOMIC STRUCTURE OF THE ASSYRIAN EMPIRE

§ 0. *Introduction*

With one exception this paper is a fairly exact reproduction of that read at Copenhagen, combined with charts and some comments which were included in the preliminary abstract. The exception is the section on *kiṣru* (§§ 5.3–4), which has been expanded to supply background details which are not presented elsewhere. Throughout the paper footnotes have been included to give some basic references,[1] but it is very important that this should not lend it a spurious appearance of authority: it is conceived and presented as a speculative essay, not as a statement of accepted fact based on detailed research (which would have been impossible, as explained in § 2). It must therefore be read in a critical frame of mind, and the charts treated as reconstructions, not as exhaustive presentations of the evidence.

In view of the frequent misunderstandings which arise over terminology, we wish to clarify a few points at the outset, with special reference to words which might be given a more exact connotation than I have intended.

Although I believe it is justifiable to write about a 'government' in Neo-Assyrian times, it must not be forgotten that there is no Akkadian equivalent to our word. By 'government' we mean the body of royal employees or officials engaged in the king's business when it concerns the state as a whole and not the domestic affairs of his household. Although it may never have been formulated so clearly, it is our belief that in the later Assyrian Empire there did exist the concept of 'state business' as distinct from the king's private affairs.

Occasionally we have used the phrase 'central government' or 'central military administration'. The administration of the empire was based on the provincial system but there must have been some co-ordination from the centre, directly under the king, and this is especially true for the army, which no doubt came under the *turtānu* (cf. § 4.2.1). We have avoided discussing the exact links between the central government and the provinces because there is not enough evidence on this subject.

Following Diakonoff we have used the term 'helot' for the well-known tied cultivators.[2] The words 'free man' and 'citizen' are used interchangeably for subjects of the empire not so tied, and neither is intended to have any specific legal connotation beyond that.

§ 1. *Definitions*

For the purposes of this paper we are considering the Assyrian Empire only in its last and most extreme incarnation. At Rome Prof. Finley has distinguished between a 'conquest phase' and and 'imperial phase', and although the time scale is much shorter, this is a useful distinction in Assyria too. One might be tempted to consider the expansion of the Assyrian kingdom under Aššur-naṣir-apli II and Shalmaneser III as the 'conquest phase' of the Assyrian Empire; but in fact their achievements differed little from those of their Middle Assyrian ancestors, and we should not have been surprised, as distant observers of the scene, if after the reign of Adad-nirari III the Assyrian state had succumbed entirely to gradual attrition and a period of obscurity, and fallen prey to some new force in the north or east. Then we should probably have seen no cause to speak of an 'Assyrian Empire', or to place it alongside Macedon or Rome. Put another way, Assyria, unlike Rome, made several attempts, of which only the last was successful, at establishing and retaining an empire. For us, therefore, the true 'conquest phase' of the empire lasts from the accession of Tiglath-pileser III into the reign of Sargon, while broadly the 'imperial phase' spans the 7th century, under Sennacherib, Esarhaddon and Aššur-ban-apli. It is true that in administrative terms there is no clear break between 745 BC and the reign of Aššur-ban-apli – it seems accepted that Tiglath-pileser reorganized the provincial system and it is likely that the framework of the military and civil administrations was laid down in his reign as well – but in *economic* terms we must obviously draw a clear distinction between the decades during which the empire was regularly pushing its borders outwards and consolidating its conquests with an essentially military administration, and the later years when the main tracts of the empire had been under Assyrian rule long enough to have acquired a certain stability and to have adjusted their economic and civil life to the new conditions.

§ 2. *Sources*

There is a further reason for restricting ourselves to the latest phase of Assyria, and that concerns the source material. Our attitude towards the sources is illustrated in Chart 1, which is intended to show the non-Assyriologist (and remind the Assyriologist) what our statements have to depend on, and how much is lacking. The chart itself is self-explanatory, but there are two main points I wish to stress before plunging into the main part of the paper. One concerns the bias in our attitudes which results inevitably from the nature of the documents available to us: running the eye along the top of the chart, you will see that we are working from

Chart 1

	Royal inscriptions	*Royal decrees*	*Legal – sales etc.*	*Legal – loans etc.*	*Royal correspondence*	*Palace archives*	*'Doomsday book'*	*Archaeological data*	*Relative assessment*
Palace sector	x	o			x	x		x	good
Army	x				x	x		o	fair
State labour	o				x	x			fair
Administration	o			o	x	x			fair
Tribute	x				o	o		o	fair
Taxation	o	x	o		x	o			fair
Social structure			x				o		poor
City economy	o		o	x					poor
Village economy				o			x		poor
Land holding		x	x				x		fair
Non-state labour				o					bad
Crafts & industries				o	o	o			bad
Trade	o			o					bad
Prices & currency	o		x	o	o				poor

x = substantial evidence available
o = some slight evidence available

Chart 1: to show availability of source material

royal inscriptions, royal decrees, legal texts, royal correspondence, palace archives, a land census, and archaeological data. The monotonous recurrence of the word 'royal' merely reflects the archaeologists' concentration on royal palaces (and to a lesser degree, temples). Even the legal documents are predominantly – in the case of Nineveh virtually exclusively – from royal palaces, and the best private archive, from Nimrud, belonged to a man living on the citadel and obviously in close touch with the palace sector.[3] Private documents and letters have been found at Assur, but remain unpublished, and the only temple archive to speak of comes from the Nabu Temple at Nimrud. As will emerge below, we have split the economy into a palace, a government, and a private sector. Clearly the palace and government sectors are likely to be well represented in our sources, but the private sector *must* be under-represented, and we must accordingly do all we can to correct this imbalance.

My second point is perhaps more of an apology than anything else. When Dr. Larsen asked me to participate in the Symposium, the title 'The economic basis of the Assyrian Empire' was proposed. This I have deliberately replaced with the phase 'economic structure' as a token of the fact that I have made no serious attempt to assess the quantitative side of the evidence. This is for a variety of reasons. As Assyriologists will be aware, no detailed work exists on the economy of the Assyrian Empire as a whole: the best recent survey is that of Prof. Garelli,[4] and there are various specialist studies of topics such as land tenure, tribute, and taxation. Probably the best overall work, and even it is not all-embracing, is the book of I. M. Diakonoff,[5] but this is by now nearly 30 years old, and the Neo-Assyrian section is unfortunately not accessible to me, being in its original Russian. Since it was impossible for me to review all the primary sources for the benefit of this paper, it will therefore be obvious that any statements on the quantitative side are perforce fairly subjective, without the detailed study needed to back them up.

Moreover, the time for such a study is not yet ripe: the very important texts from Assur have still to be published, and the administrative documents from the palace at Nineveh, published by Johns, require total recollation before they can be safely used for quantitative purposes; some very interesting texts from the Arsenal at Nimrud are awaiting publication at the hands of the writer. Nevertheless, even when these deficiencies in modern publication are made good, I shall still be sceptical of our chances of reaching quantitative results: so many of our documents served ephemeral purposes which were not explained for us by their scribes, and even where a heading or a summary would have given us a clue, it is all too often lost because the most vulnerable parts of a cuneiform tablet are the beginning and end. Only for a very small percentage of the Nineveh documents in *ADD* II can their administrative context be described with any confidence, and the same is true of the Nimrud texts. The problem is epitomized in the 'Assyrian Doomsday Book': this is clearly some kind of census of rural estates, and it is unquestionably our main source for Assyrian rural conditions; but since those lines which would have told us the exact purpose for which the list was drawn up are missing, modern scholars are free to reconstruct the purpose for themselves, which they have indeed done, each with a different result.[6] It is of course true that the royal inscriptions may give us a generalized estimate of numbers of men and animals, or the quantities of precious metals etc. which came into Assyria as booty or tribute, and an excellent study based on such data has been made by Dr. Jankowska;[7] but my point here is rather that we do not have sufficiently explicit statements elsewhere in the documentation to enable us to determine how these quantities relate to the internal production or consumption of the empire. In other words, we can point to the existence of these imports, without being able to assess their significance.

It is true that we do have the occasional text which throws light on the internal sectors of the economy. There is a letter from the province of Zamua (the Shehrizor plain) listing its entire military establishment,[8] and one of the unpublished texts from the Nimrud Arsenal appears to record the disposition of cavalry-commanders throughout the separate provinces of Sargon's empire; but in each case we have the problem of weighing the undoubted authenticity of the statement against any number of temporary or local factors which may undermine its general validity. The same must apply to legal documents: for example, statistics on fluctuating slave prices in 7th century sales must have some meaning,[9] but there is very little with which to compare them and we cannot use them by themselves as an indicator of inflation. Evidence for the prices of everyday items is still exceedingly scarce in Neo-Assyrian times, and there are considerable problems about the relative value of silver and copper at different dates (see below, § 8.2).

§ 3. *Economic resources*

§ 3.1. The cultivated plains

It is too obvious to need stressing that the mainstay of the Assyrian Empire was its swath of corn-growing lands across northern Mesopotamia, which may be termed the 'cultivated plains'.[10] Only the existence of a healthy surplus of corn could supply the needs of the armies and secure the survival of the large cities. Of course the harvests varied in quality with the weather, and as we shall see below, the kings were keenly interested in the state of the crops (see § 7.4); but during the later empire their corn lands ranged from the real Jezirah in the south-west to the mountain fringes, so that a climatically disastrous year in one area could usually be compensated for to some degree elsewhere.

Although cereals were by far the most important component of the economy in the cultivated plains, the rural settlements (and nomadic population of the area) produced much that was of importance besides, both for the cities as such and for the administration with its problems of military and civilian supply. Chart 2 is designed to summarize the relationship of supply and demand between city, village and nomad; in particular we may underline the continual demand for straw, for both animal fodder and brick-making, which is reflected in numerous letters and other texts, while the production of leather and wool was also important.[11]

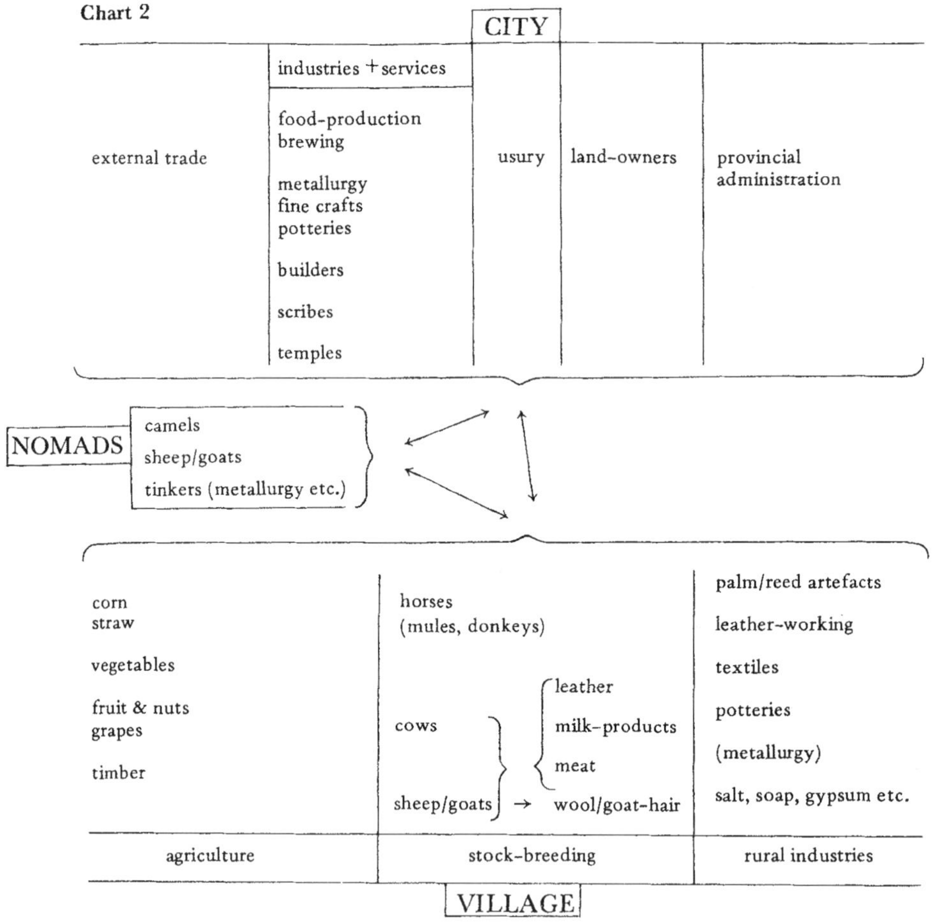

Chart 2: to illustrate economic resources & intercourse between city and village in the cultivated plains.

§ 3.2. The coastal strip

Even though local variations should not be forgotten, the basis of the economy was the same from the provinces of Arrapha and Lahiru (the Kerkuk plains) across the Euphrates and beyond to the Syrian saddle, down to Hamath and as far north-west as Sam'al: a strong village economy based on agriculture, and superimposed on this a fluctuating but probably always important long-distance trade. It was only with the incorporation of the Levantine seaboard and the Taurus states that the empire embraced any really different type of economy. The coastal towns, led by Tyre and Sidon, did have a different climate and therefore different agricultural produce to offer, but it was their rôle as trade centres that made the real difference: for the first time Assyria directly controlled the Mediterranean commerce, and although there is no reason to suppose that she tried to intervene in the traditional patterns, there must have been a healthy income from harbour dues. Whether or not this would have exceeded the annual tribute which had been forthcoming from Phoenicia in the past we have no means of knowing, but some changes must have resulted from having this income directed into normal government (provincial) channels rather than as an external contribution to the royal exchequer. Nor must we forget the North Syrian, Palestinian, Cilician and even on occasion the Cypriote ports which also participated in the same trade, and to which the same applies. It could of course be argued that the luxury goods available from these sources were irrelevant to the empire's economic needs, but that is to miss a crucial point. The dignity of the Assyrian king demanded that his capitals, his temples and his palaces should display his wealth, and the latest luxury items from the west, if not forthcoming as booty or tribute (which diminished inevitably with the growth of the empire), had to be provided in other ways, while the incorporation of these cities in the empire provided a new source of skilled craftsmen for the royal court to draw on.

§ 3.3. The Taurus

If we turn to the north-western mountains we meet a different situation. Mountain villages as such probably had little to contribute to the economic pattern of the empire, but in the Taurus were several mines which gave Assyria virtually her only direct access to metals. Once again it is not possible to suggest what quantitative effect this may have had, and the problem is not helped by the inadequacy of modern data on the mineral resources of the area.[12] As far as we are aware, Neo-Assyrian texts make no reference to the Ergani mines, which were close to the provincial capital of Amida (Diyarbakir) and could have been a major copper source; and although the existence of iron ores has recently been demonstrated close to the Iraqi-Turkish frontier north of Amadiyah, it is virtually certain that this region fell within Urartian territory.[13] There is however a very interesting, though tantalizingly fragmentary, section of Sargon's annals which describes how 'at that time the secret of the mountains of Hatti was revealed . . . '.[14] Unfortunately, except for Ba'il-sapuna (classical Mons Casius) the names of the mountains in the text are either too broken or too obscure for identification, but reference is clearly made to copper, iron, and lead; while at the close of the same passage Sargon says that he discovered how to smelt ores, and that he accumulated the metal in Dur-Šarrukin such that 'the purchase-price of copper was like (that of) silver in Assyria', implying perhaps that his discoveries had included silver deposits. This passage may reflect on the immense amount of iron discovered by Place in Sargon's palace, but for us the important point is that the discovery of these sources was of sufficient importance to merit mention in the annals, and that direct access to them may well have had a radical effect on the empire's economy and, in particular, on its currency system. Equally, the loss of direct control of these areas may have had the reverse effect, and have been seriously disruptive, in a way that the loss of a predominantly agricultural province would not.

§ 4.0. *Movement of commodities*

It is evident that the economy of the empire must have been closely restrained by its social and administrative structure. Owing to the character of our sources, most of our evidence on this score bears on the administrative channels through which the goverment controlled commodity supplies, and for the purposes of this paper it seems convenient to divide the empire into a palace sector, a government sector (including the army), and a private sector, with particular reference to the consumption, rather than the production, of commodities. This division seems specially valuable when considering the channels through which commodities moved, because of the different character of each sector; nevertheless there are great differences in their basic economy which makes the distinction useful in a wider context. It must be obvious that the borderline between palace sector and either government or private sectors will often be hard to define, and there is certainly an area of overlap, but I believe that in the following paragraphs it should be possible to justify the distinction.

§ 4.1. Palace sector

The components of the palace sector are set out in Chart 3, which is largely self-explanatory. The palace economy must include not only the king's various establishments and families in the different cities, but similar households belonging to his near relatives, such as the queen mother or the crown prince, and to those highly placed officials and courtiers whose remuneration was in the nature of domestic expenditure from the royal purse. To a certain degree, we may even count within the palace sector the household economies of highly placed officials whose position was not immediately dependent on the palace: they drew their income from similar sources, and were involved in similar expenses, although on a much smaller scale (at least in the 7th century). It would be misleading, however, to pretend that the palace sector was nothing more than a greatly enlarged household. On the income side we have the immense inflow of wealth

Chart 3

	PALACE SECTOR	
Income		*Expenditure*
	Royal palaces	
Booty	Nineveh	Subsistence of palace residents and staff
	Kalhu	
Tribute (*maddattu*)	(Dūr-Šarrukin)	
'Gifts' (*nāmurtu*)	Assur	Equipment of military staff
	Kilizi	
Land ownership	Tarbīṣu	
	Harrān (?)	*Luxuries*
Credit activities		foods
Slave sales	*Royal family*	wine and beer
	king	jewellery
Appropriations & confiscations	first queen	furnishings
	crown prince	clothing
	other relatives	*Gifts* to
	harem	high officers
	concubines' sons	visiting dignitaries
		temples
	Domestic staff	
	eunuchs	Regular temple offerings
	musicians	
	religious/medical	
	cooks etc.	Building operations
	porters	
	Admin. & military	
	ushers	
	guards	
	bodyguards	
	grooms etc.	
	messengers	
	scribes	
	interpreters	
	admin. officials	
	craftsmen	
	agents for crown lands in provinces	
	Court	
	courtiers (*ša qurbūti*)	
	high officers of state	
	foreign hostages	

Chart 3: components and economy of palace sector

from tribute, booty, and gifts: it could of course be argued that these are rather government income than private profit to the palace, but undoubtedly the gifts (*nāmurtu*), the booty, and some at least of the tribute (*mad-*

dattu) were the property of the king to dispose of as he chose. Even though he may generally have redistributed his profits outside the palace sector, this was the channel through which they entered the economy, and the preponderance of the profits of domination in the income of the palace sector gave it a structure quite different from the private sector. Precious metals and slaves in particular must have come into the palaces in considerable quantities, and although the slaves were frequently distributed elsewhere, the royal reserves in gold and silver surely constituted a significant component of the economy as a whole. Nor does it seem likely that much of this wealth found its way into the private sector even indirectly: royal building schemes were carried out largely with deported or conscripted labour, the many palace employees seem to have been on a rations and not a wages basis, and their subsistence was probably met from the palace estates and would not have needed to be purchased against currency.[15]

In this paper we have not considered the rôle of the temples within the economy, since *mutatis mutandis* it is very similar to that of the palaces, although quantitatively less important. There were inevitably great differences of behaviour between the temple and the palace, but viewed as part of the economic structure of the empire it seems permissible to include them in the same sector.

§ 4.2. Government sector

§ 4.2.0. The rôle of the government sector in the economy is primarily to draw on the private sector to provide resources for the state's civil and especially military organizations. As such, it may of course be administered by officials who themselves belong in the palace sector, but the activities of the government sector impinge on the entire population, whereas those of the palace sector affect only those individuals who are directly or indirectly dependent on the king's person. The separate identity of these two sectors, if accepted, points a significant contrast between the administrative procedures of the 13th century Middle Assyrian kingdom and the later empire: whereas under Shalmaneser I and Tukulti-ninurta I the government was in the hands of a number of 'houses' which, whether in origin merchant-houses or not, were run along commercial lines,[16] in the Neo-Assyrian period much of the fiscal and administrative work of the government was carried out by a 'civil service' with an existence quite distinct from family or firm.

The backbone of the government sector is the provincial system. The governor and his subordinates were responsible for the collection of payments of all kinds from their province, and for the conscription and supply of soldiers and civil labourers. Although some central control of these activities was obviously essential, it was through the provincial government that the state came into contact with the ordinary person. The administration certainly had civilian requirements – personnel to be fed, buildings to be constructed, accounts to be kept, etc. – but it was unquestionably the supply of the army which was the chief preoccupation of the provincial governments, in economic terms at least. In an often quoted passage, Sargon tells us how an eastern vassal had 'piled up stores of flour and wine to feed my troops, just like my eunuchs, the governors of the provinces of Assyria', and we know from the correspondence that the wall of Khorsabad (Dur-Šarrukin) was built in sections assigned to labourers from different provinces.[17] Moreover, some of the army's requirements must have placed a strain on the normal rural economy: provided the organization was efficient the supply of corn and other foods should not have presented a problem, and the correspondence which survives does not suggest that it did; rather it was the animals which led to trouble, since straw seems often to have been in short supply, and more than one provincial governor protests that he cannot feed the number of horses or mules assigned to him by the central government.[18]

§ 4.2.1. In view of the historical and economic importance of the way in which the Assyrian army was maintained, we have summarized the position as we reconstruct it in Chart 4. Although most of the 'channels' there fell directly under the provincial governor there was of course a central military administration (of which we know very little) under whose 'direct control' certain things remained. Principally these were the standing army, with its equipment and animals, and a reserve of horses (*nakkantu*) which seem to have been accorded a separate administration of their own, reflecting their importance.[19]

§ 4.2.2. The main heading under which the provincial governments were answerable to the central military administration was that of *ilku*. This was partly used, as in the past, to raise man-power in the shape of limited-period conscripted soldiers and civilian labour, and partly took a commuted form for privileged members of the administration, who contributed supplies and equipment for others actually performing state service. This system of commuted *ilku*-payments survived at least into the Achaemenid period, and is a characteristic bureaucratic device of the Assyrian Empire, which always seems to have made an effort to reduce the number of administrative procedures needed to route a given item from its origin to where it was to be used. Thus all available evidence indicates that the government would determine a man's *ilku* obligation and then leave it to the individual to make the relevant payment direct to its eventual recipient. Quite apart from the reduced administration, this system

Chart 4

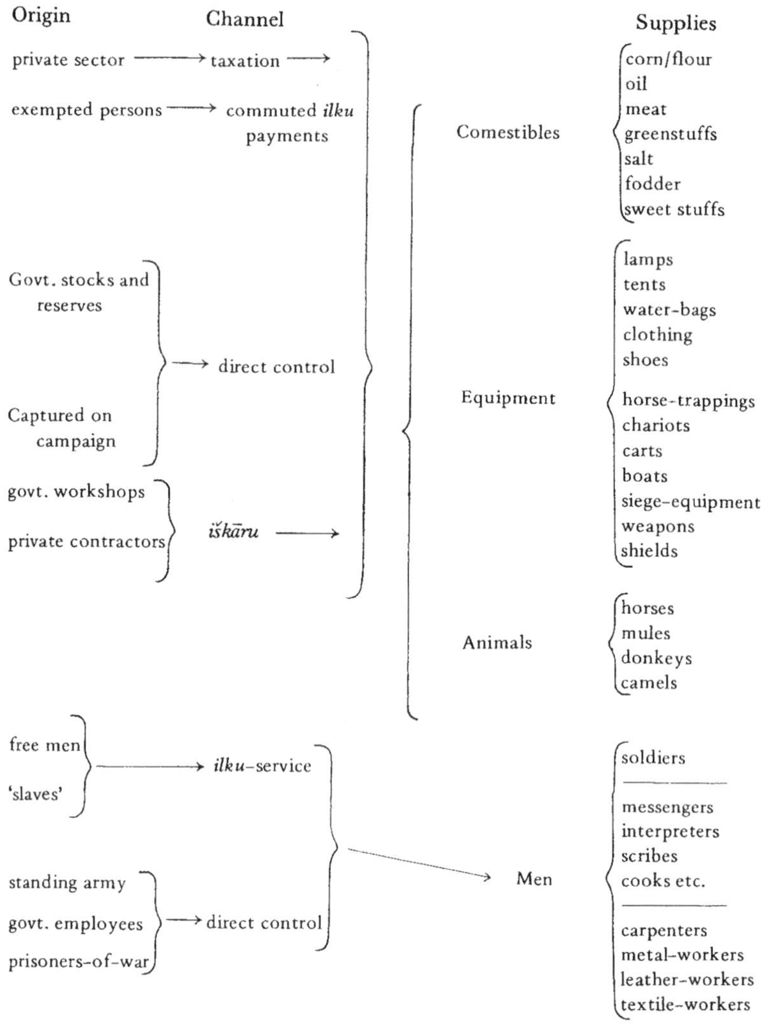

Chart 4: army requirements and means of supply

relieved the government of the physical burden of collecting and distributing the items, and enabled it, in theory at least, to calculate exactly how many soldiers and animals could be supported, without ever handling the relevant materials themselves. A similar policy is reflected in a practice attested at Assur, whereby cavalrymen from certain villages took their animals home with them for the winter, and fed them, although we do not know who actually bore the responsibility for the fodder.[20]

§ 4.2.3. Another procedure by which the administration tried to reduce the burden it shouldered was the *iškāru* system. Details of its working are still inadequate, but it was used to convert raw materials under the direct control of the government into the finished products needed by it. Instead of maintaining a large body of ration-drawing personnel, requiring considerable supervision, the policy seems to have been to allocate quantities of raw material to the craftsmen, and to define their obligation to supply the finished products with a commercial-style debt-note. This was certainly the procedure with independent craftsmen who were working as it were under 'government contract', but even for those who were more closely dependent on the government and were organized along military lines into 'cohorts' (see § 5), it is clear that supervision was minimal and that the system worked more on the principle of commercial, or rather fiscal, obligations.

§ 4.3. Private sector

§ 4.3.0. In the private sector of the economy the movement of commodities is much harder to document because of the scarcity of written evidence. There is of course some evidence for government taxation of the private sector, especially from administrative correspondence and the taxation exemption clauses which accompany royal grants of land. The evidence concerns the taxes on agriculture and trade, and is briefly discussed here.

§ 4.3.1. Direct taxation of the private sector was principally in kind, on agricultural produce, and these taxes probably furnished a large proportion of the reserves of grain required by the civil and especially the military administration. Evidence for the precise rates of tax is scanty, but it was usually if not invariably a fraction of the crop, and the attested rates are 10% for corn and 25% for straw, which no doubt reflects the relatively high demand for straw by the government. These rates do not seem oppressive, nor is there much evidence for arrears of tax, and in fact such correspondence as we do have on the topic rather suggests tax avoidance by the large landowner, not failure to pay by the small farmer. There is only very slight evidence for tax-farming,[21] a practice attested in Babylonia, and as a general rule it appears that the tax-collection structure was an arm of the provincial governments.

§ 4.3.2. Nothing is known of the taxation of town-dwellers without any agricultural lands, except that they were almost certainly liable to some form of *ilku* obligation (cf. § 4.2.2 and below, § 5). The royal land grants do however mention exemption from 'harbour, ferry and gate dues' (*miksē kāri nēbiri abulli* . . .) as well as other impositions lost by damaged texts,[22] and thus demonstrate in negative the existence of taxes on private trade.

It could of course be objected that 'ferry dues' may apply to the passage of persons only, although this is unlikely, but the only people liable to pay 'harbour dues' must have been those engaged in trade. The existence of substantial private trade during the Assyrian Empire is a point of controversy;[23] and we must admit at the outset that there is a most emphatic silence on this subject in the sources. No unequivocal reference to privately organized trade is known to me from the Neo-Assyrian letters, and although merchants are not infrequently mentioned, it is usually impossible to be certain whether they are in some way state-employed or independent agents. An unpublished slave-sale document from the house of an officer in the town at Nineveh (to be published soon by Dr. Bahijah Khalil Ismail) records his purchase of some slaves brought from Kummuh (Commagene) by a merchant, of whom there is no reason to suspect any involvement with the government, and other sources mention merchants from Carchemish, Tema, and elsewhere. Merchants (*tamkāru*) also figure not infrequently as witnesses at the end of sale documents, in a context which rather implies that they had some commercial rôle in the transaction – often, no doubt, the removal of the purchase price from the seller who was indebted to them – but of course the merchant need only have been a local businessman or money-lender, and was not necessarily involved in short or long-distance trade. Hence I can only make appeal to general considerations in an attempt to deny the existence of a government trade monopoly. Three or four passages seem to show that Assyrian kings actively encouraged private trade under their aegis: Tiglath-pileser's official in charge of the Phoenician coast writes to him to say that he was permitting the people of Sidon to 'bring down the timber' (from Mt. Lebanon) 'and do their work with it, but not to sell it to the Palestinians or Egyptians'[24] – implying that they might trade freely in the timber as long as they did not sell it to Assyria's potential enemies. A decade or two later Sargon describes how he tried to make the population of Samaria re-open trade with Egypt: 'I opened the sealed harbour(?) of Egypt, and I mixed the people of Assyria with the people of Egypt and made them engage in trade together'.[25] After describing how he restored Babylonia to normality and sent the citizens of Babylon back to their homes, Esarhaddon says that be 'opened the roads for them to the four winds'.[26] The phrasing of all these texts implies that the kings expected the merchants of the Levant and of Babylonia to carry on with their own mercantile activities without further interference from the government. They would of course have been liable to customs and other state dues (unless exempted), but there is no hint here of government monopoly. And if this applies to recently conquered lands, it must apply even more to the Assyrian homeland, where the tradition of private enterprise was surely too solidly established to have been superseded by state control of trade. It may be objected that the cities of the Levantine seaboard and of Babylonia were major centres of near eastern trade, but the Assyrian merchant was certainly active in the Middle Assyrian period, and it seems reasonable to surmise that during the later empire the inhabitants of the old Assyrian cities would have profited from their favoured position at the centre to expand, not reduce, their trading operations. They could not have viewed with equanimity the efforts of their kings to promote the commercial life of other parts of the empire unless they themselves were also prospering. Despite the suggestion of Dr. Jankowska,[27] that the Assyrian Empire had created a sort of trade vacuum, diverting routes round her frontiers and killing the regular exchange within them, I am very reluctant to admit that either of these was the case, or that the economic realities behind the age-old east-west routes up the Euphrates and across northern Mesopotamia had been annulled by the existence of the empire.

It would be superfluous in this context to try to reconstruct the actual items traded. The evidence from Assyrian sources is very scanty, although to some extent the major centres of production and crafts can be reconstructed by studying the tribute and similar payments recorded in the royal annals (as has been very thoroughly done by Dr. Jankowska). One or two administrative texts and letters do supply disjointed scraps of evidence, but since they belong to palace archives their value is hard to assess. Perhaps the most illuminating single source is the pair of Neo-Babylonian texts dating to the reign of Nabonidus, which record luxury and semi-luxury items imported to Babylonia from the west. As analysed by Prof. Oppenheim, the consignments consisted of: metals (copper, iron and tin), chemicals (dyes and alum), foodstuffs (wine, honey and other unidentified), fibres (dyed wool and linen), juniper resin and lapis lazuli.[28] Although these texts date from after the downfall of Assyria, the pattern of trade need not have changed much in the meanwhile, and we are justified in expecting that a similar type of consignment would have been finding its way to the Assyrian capitals and to Babylonia during the empire. Whether there was a parallel trade in coarser commodities is much less certain; all we can say for sure is that evidence exists in the Neo-Assyrian texts for trade in slaves and horses, two of the commodities most urgently needed to support the structure of empire.

§ 5. *Man-power*

§ 5.1. The army

Labour or the work-force can be treated in four major categories: the

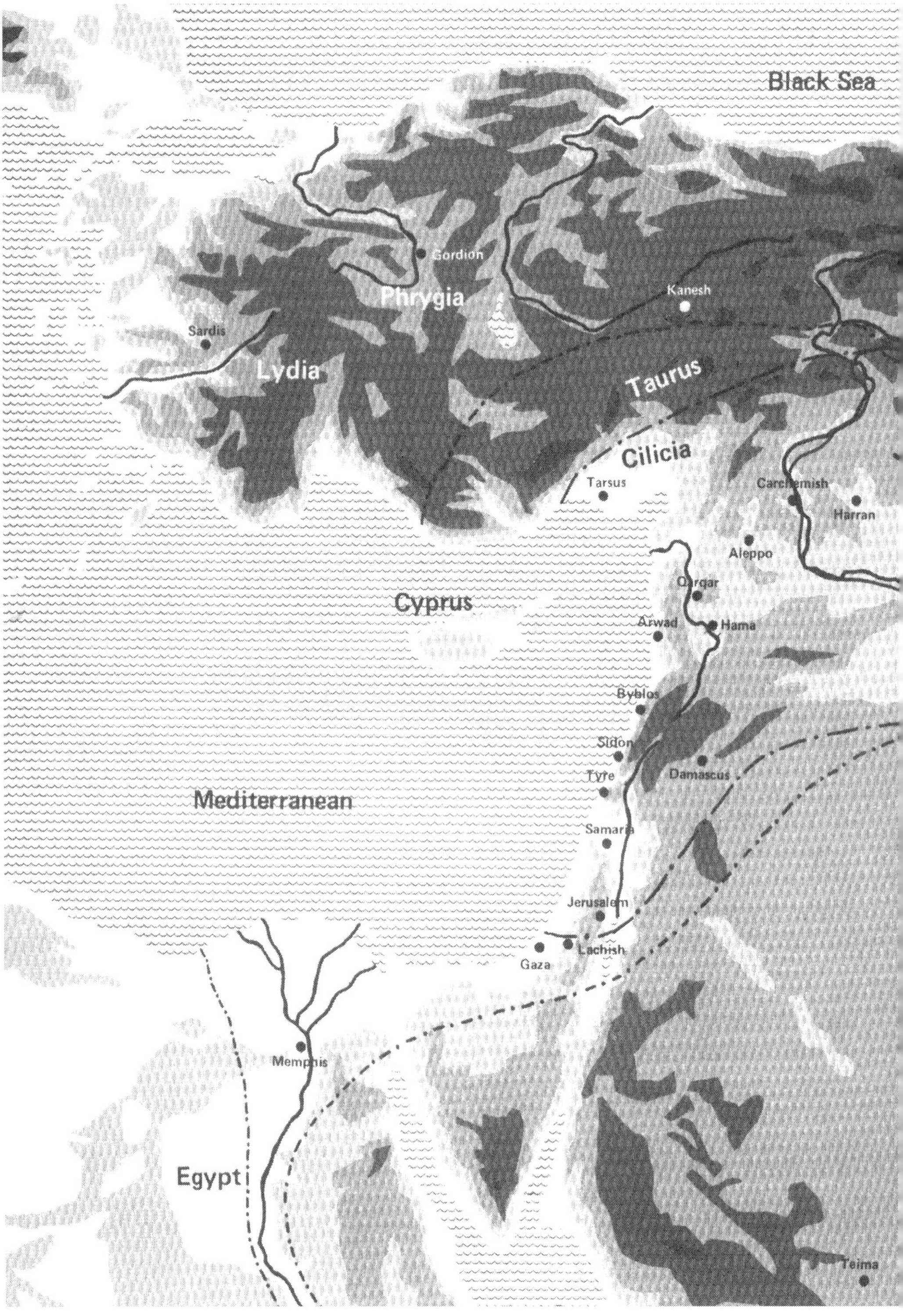

Black Sea
Gordion
Phrygia
Kanesh
Sardis
Lydia
Taurus
Cilicia
Tarsus
Carchemish
Harran
Aleppo
Qarqar
Cyprus
Arwad
Hama
Byblos
Sidon
Damascus
Tyre
Mediterranean
Samaria
Jerusalem
Gaza
Lachish
Memphis
Egypt
Teima

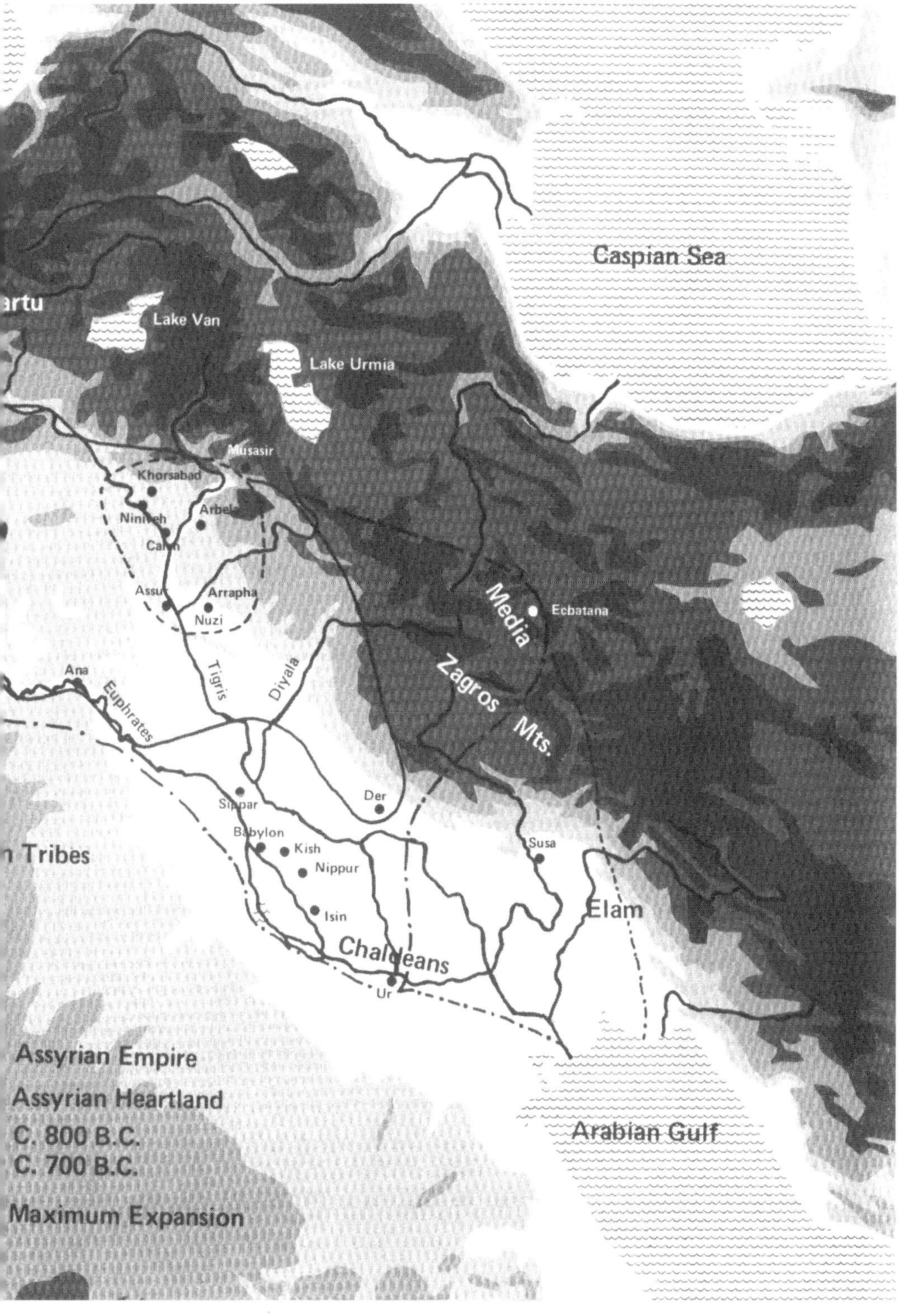
artu
Lake Van
Lake Urmia
Caspian Sea
Musasir
Khorsabad
Arbela
Assur
Arrapha
Nuzi
Media
Ecbatana
Zagros
Mts.
Tigris
Diyala
Ana
Euphrates
Der
Babylon
Kish
Nippur
Isin
Susa
Elam
Chaldeans
Ur
Tribes
Assyrian Empire
Assyrian Heartland
C. 800 B.C.
C. 700 B.C.
Maximum Expansion
Arabian Gulf

army, public works, crafts and skills, and agricultural labour. As for the army we must cut a long story short by noting merely that there is evidence that the chariotry and cavalry was drawn from full-blooded 'Assyrians' (the implications of this term are not known to us), who were probably in part full-time soldiers and in part men performing their periodic *ilku* service. The foot-soldiers were formed on a nucleus of permanent Aramaean mercenaries, in particular the Itu'āyu and the Gurrāyu. These were often used as a 'police-force' in the outer parts of the empire, and we simply do not know whether, and if so where, it was possible to use locally conscripted soldiers in the provinces. It is true that on several occasions the kings (Sargon, Sennacherib, Esarhaddon and Assurbanapli) state that they incorporated units from a conquered state into the Assyrian standing army, but this was certainly not the case for ordinary citizens of annexed territories.

§ 5.2. Public works

The ordinary citizen was either deported or – presumably more often – left to till his own fields, in which case he was certainly liable to 'corvée service like the people of Assyria'. If deported, prisoners-of-war were either employed directly on public works, such as the construction of Dur-Šarrukin or Sennacherib's irrigation schemes, or distributed among the population. The historical texts are quite explicit on this point: Assurbanapli states that 'the remainder I distributed like sheep between the cities, residences of the great gods, among my governors, my nobles, and all my camp',[29] while Esarhaddon writes 'the remainder of them I distributed like sheep to my palaces, my nobles, the entourage of my palace, and the populace of Nineveh, Kalhu, Kilizi and Arbail'.[30] The formulaic quality of this phrase shows that this was a regular and accepted procedure; it differs entirely from the policy of deportation, which was certainly used by Sargon, whereby dissident elements might be exchanged across from opposite ends of the empire, a political, not an economic, move. The continual channelling of conquered populations into the palace and the private sectors of the four great cities of Assyria was clearly a deliberate move to meet a labour shortage at the centre of the empire, a shortage which was probably most serious on agricultural estates.

§ 5.3. Craftsmen and the *kiṣru* system

§ 5.3.0. Occasionally royal inscriptions mention their treatment of the craftsmen among a conquered people. The most explicit statement is that of Esarhaddon, who says that, in addition to various military specialists,

'I added craftsmen, scribes, shield-bearers, scouts, farmers, shepherds and gardeners to the mighty forces of Assur and greatly increased the royal contingent of the kings my fathers before me' (R. Borger, *Asarhaddon* § 68)[31]

The phrase 'royal contingent' (*kiṣir šarrūti*) generally applies to the standing force directly under the king's command. It was thus the nucleus of the Assyrian army, and from the phrasing it is clear that people of a variety of skills were also incorporated within the permanent military establishment, which was divided into smaller contingents (also *kiṣru*) or, as I shall call them, cohorts. The purely military cohort is a well-established fact which does not require discussion here (although queries do persist), but the organization of craftsmen in the same system is of interest to us and requires a more detailed presentation.

§ 5.3.1. In his study of the Assyrian army, which has still not been superseded, Manitius discusses the 'specialist' cohorts, calling them Handwerkerabtailungen (*ZA* 24 (1910) 134). In addition to the royal inscriptions he was able to quote evidence for the existence of these cohorts from legal texts, but since then such evidence has increased and the following crafts and professions are represented: scribes, weavers, 'victuallers' (*karkadinnu*), shepherds, oil-pressers and leather-workers.[32]

Membership of the *kiṣru* does not seem to have been confined to any one social class. The scribes are not likely to have been slaves or 'helots', while the oil-pressers from Assur bear genuine Assyrian names suggesting that they too were, at least originally, free citizens. On the other hand we know from the royal inscriptions that conquered populations could be formed without delay into cohorts, and they can hardly have had better than 'helot' status; like the army, there was a single administrative system linking people working under different compulsions. It is possible that cohorts were formed of craftsmen fulfilling their *ilku* service (and so only available for a restricted period), but there may also have been free men committed to a lifetime of government service. The *kiṣru* system was not restricted to the towns; this is obvious in the case of the shepherds, and the penetration of villages is illustrated by the Carchemish text showing that the entire village of Elumu fell under the single captain (*rab kiṣri*) Šarri-taklak.

§ 5.3.2. Some at least of the cohorts were created from conquered peoples at the same time as purely military units were incorporated in the army, and all fall under the captain (*rab kiṣri*) which is a military rank. If there was a distinction between the military and civilian sides of the central and provincial governments (and this is uncertain) the cohorts of craftsmen will have come under the military side. However, their purpose was the production of materials or the provision of specialist services, and their organization must have differed from that of the army proper. The hall-mark of the system was the *iškāru,* which describes both the raw materials given to the craftsman and the finished product which he pays back: found at its simplest with wool or metal to be converted into textiles or weapons, the term was also applied to sheep, from which leather and wool could be rendered as the *iškāru,* or even horses.[33] The connection between the cohort and the payment of *iškāru* is best illustrated by the complex situation in *ABL* 1432: the author of this letter to the king, who was the governor of Naṣibina province, protests: 'About Ilu-uznēya-uṣur the shepherd, of whom the king wrote to me saying "You have demoted him from a captaincy. Why did you tell him to raise 1 talent of silver?", indeed I have not demoted him! He is still a captain! . . . . When Dugul-pān-ili [perhaps a royal agent] came to the shearing, that man withheld his *iškāru*; he did not come in to the shearing, but fled and took refuge in a temple. I sent and they brought him down, and I said "Let your *iškāru* be remitted you, but get your men and come, and do your work at Dur-Šarrukin" '. The position is clear: Ilu-uznēya-uṣur (who is known from *ABL* 639 to have been a 'captain of shepherds') is in charge of a cohort of shepherds and responsible for handing in their *iškāru* at the annual shearing. At the time of writing the governor has obviously been ordered to send contingents to help with the construction of Dur-Šarru-kin, and the captain is therefore required to collect his cohort and lead them off to join in this work, regardless of their specialist employment.

A contract found at Carchemish provides another instance in which the captain is responsible for collecting the *iškāru* from his cohort, and *KAV* 197 is probably a complaint by a cohort of oil-pressers abour the mal-practices of their captain(s), since their *iškāru* payments are mentioned twice (11. 19, 62) and 1.14 must be understood to mean '(why do you allow this behaviour) in a good cohort?' (*ina* ŠÀ *ki-ṣir* SIG_5). This last text also illustrates very clearly the fact that a large proportion of *iškāru* pay-ments were made in silver, at fixed times of year. Why this system had developed is not clear, but as observed above (§ 4.2.3) the tendency of the administration was to reduce bureaucracy by replacing personal super-vision with commercial-style written obligations, and the commuting of payments in kind into silver may well have been a further stage of the same process.

§ 5.4. *kiṣru* and *pirru*

§ 5.4.0. Although the word *kiṣru* 'a knot' or 'contingent (of men)' is known in Middle Assyrian texts,[34] we suspect that the very specific usage of the word in Neo-Assyrian times[35] dates only from the reign of Tiglath-pileser III.[36] The closest parallel in the Middle Assyrian texts seems to be the *pirru*, discussed below; but this does not hold good for Neo-Assyrian texts. In a recent survey of the known occurrences we concluded that they 'strongly favour the translation '(tax-)collection'.'[37] The word could refer to the assembly and review of horses for the army, but *KAV* 197 shows that the transaction in which a cohort of craftsmen delivered its produce (*iškāru*) was also called a *pirru*; passages from the Vassal Treaties of Esarhaddon and from liver omen queries refer to men 'coming in' (*erābu*) to the *pirru*, no doubt to deliver tribute or similar contributions. With one exception, the meaning 'tax-collection' is preferable to 'contingent' or 'cohort' in all Neo-Assyrian contexts, and must I believe be accepted, whatever the word meant in Middle Assyrian.[38]

§ 5.4.1. In *AHw* 855b s.v. W. von Soden offers the translation 'ein (Arbeits)-kommando' for the word *pirru*. As I have said, this does not agree well with the Neo-Assyrian usage, and I believe that it may also be unsatisfactory for the earlier occurrences. In the Middle Assyrian texts the word was not attested until the recent publication of administrative documents from Kar-Tukulti-ninurta.[39] These reveal two distinct usages: adjectival, in the phrase ERÍN.MEŠ *pir-ru-te*, and substantival in *bēl pirri* (only found in the plural, ERÍN.MEŠ EN.MEŠ *pir-ri*).[40] Unfortunately there is not sufficient variety in the contexts published to enable us to determine whether there is any significant difference between these two phrases. Although one might consider the possibility that *bēl pirri* 'master of a *pirru*' was equivalent to the later *rab kiṣri*, it does seem more likely that *pirrūte* and *bēlē pirri* are in fact interchangeable variants and both mean 'called-up' or 'conscripted'.

§ 5.4.2. The texts in which these phrases occur are lists of men (ERÍN.MEŠ) passing through the military administration at Kar-Tukulti-ninurta. Numbers are considerable, and most of them are doubtless destined to be ordinary soldiers. However, they do include builders, doctors, an incantation-priest, a seer, a scribe, an *aluzinnu* (cheer-leader), door-keepers, interpreters and runners.[41] Although we no longer believe that their presence in these texts as *bēlē pirri* means that they were formed into contingents (*pirru*, Arbeitskommando), which would have provided a close parallel with the Sargonid *kiṣru*, these 'specialists' were obviously conscripted under the same procedure as the ordinary soldier, and no doubt came under the same discipline. They do not include craftsmen, shepherds, or other purely civilian employees, such as we encountered in Neo-Assyrian times, and they were presumably enrolled specifically for work in or with the army.

§ 6. *Land tenure*

Since this has been discussed in print several times recently, we pass over the subject swiftly. We need only note that in various parts of the empire large private estates were built up by members of the palace sector, in addition to large tracts appropriated to members of the royal family and high officers of state. The income from such lands certainly depended on their cultivation by a large tied population.[42]

§ 7. *Government policies*

§ 7.0.
The economic structure of any empire will consist of the imposition of an administrative pattern upon underlying and largely unchanging economic realities. Much of the interest in each for the historian will lie in the interaction: in the constraints placed by the basic economy on the aspirations and achievements of government, and in the response of the government to these constraints, which may on occasions alter the economy itself. In more than one instance above we have suggested that the Assyrian kings were not much interested in manipulating the economy of either the central or the annexed regions of their empire, except in the crude sense of extracting wealth. There are however certain areas in which the state did intrude on the economy of the private sector, discussed below.

§ 7.1.
As was explained in § 4, there is no evidence of a conscious effort by the government to control or monopolize trade, but taxes were levied on the passage of goods, and there were normal agricultural taxes.

§ 7.2.
In the 7th century B.C., and by presumption earlier, we have the institution of *(an)durāru* which appears to consist of a royal edict cancelling the enslavement of free citizens for private debt.[43] It can hardly have effected the status of the great number of enslaved prisoners-of-war, nor is there any good evidence that it enabled the recovery of real estate sold under economic duress, although this latter is not inconceivable. The *(an)durāru* edicts go back into the middle of the 3rd millennium B.C. to our knowledge, and this was certainly no innovation of the Neo-Assyrian kings. It is therefore difficult to know whether its existence at this date was a deliberate economic policy, or a response to the traditional image of the Mesopotamian ruler as protector of the weak.[44]

§ 7.3.

There is evidence in the 7th and 8th centuries B.C. both in Assyria and in Babylonia for a legal provision in sales of persons which stipulated that the given sale took place in a year of economic hardship.[45] In Assyria this is usually expressed in terms of the current price of corn. The only purpose served by including such a clause in the document of sale must have been to facilitate its subsequent cancellation, or at the very least (and less likely) to enable an adjustment of the price in favour of the seller. It may be that these sales are specifically those affected by the *(an)durāru* edicts, but one has the impression that they are another, though similarly motivated, device, which must, of course, have depended on the backing of the government for its validity in the law-courts.

§ 7.4.

The health of the empire's economy naturally depended very much on the success of the harvest. Consequently it is not surprising to find that the kings were intensely interested in the state of the crops. Already in the earliest years of the Neo-Assyrian kingdom we see the rulers of the resurgent country boasting in their historical inscriptions of the ploughs they had set to abandoned lands, and although there may indeed have been religious obligations on the kings to concern themselves with such affairs, their daily correspondence makes it clear that they were kept accurately informed. Letters from distant parts may conclude with a fairly routine report on the state of the harvest; correspondents mention heavy rains, sometimes with precise details; and one letter from Kalhu gives the king information about the current prices of corn in at least three different provinces.[46] In his inscriptions Assurbanapli regularly refers to the great prosperity which resulted during his reign from what must have been abnormally heavy rainfall, since he adds the circumstantial detail that the luxuriance of the river thickets led to a dangerous proliferation of lions.[47]

However, despite this interest in market prices, there is no evidence for any serious attempt at price control. It is true that the same king more than once lists obviously idealised commodity prices,[48] but although genuine attempts at price-fixing are known from the Old Babylonian period, most such lists in royal inscriptions seem to be grossly exaggerated propaganda statements, aimed, one can only suppose, at posterity, since they can hardly have deluded their contemporaries. Here too the Assyrian kings were imitating a tradition at least 1000 years old, and although their concern for the price of corn, with its general implications for the economy, was unquestionably genuine, there is no evidence that it led them to interfere directly with the private sector. Here too they seem to have pursued a policy of laissez-faire, thus adhering to the traditions of ancient Assur.

§ 8. *Historical consequences*

§ 8.1. Town and country

In conclusion, we would like to single out one or two points of the empire's economic structure which may have had consequences outside the purely economic sphere. As we have seen, the collection of commodities required by the government sector was carried out through the provincial system. All our available evidence suggests that the administration of the province was concentrated at the capital city of each province: towns of some standing may have had separate administrative structures of their own, but most of the work seems to have been done by officials called 'village-inspectors' (*rab ālāni*) who were under the direct control of the governor. Through these officials each village will have been immediately answerable to the central government of the province, and there must have arisen a tendency for the economic life of each province to be focussed on its capital city, in consequence of its administrative set-up.

The intercourse between city and village was not of course a one-way affair. Although the city-dweller was dependent on the surrounding countryside for a great many commodities and the central government relied on materials collected through the provincial authorities for the equipment of the army, the villages were also tied to the cities by their needs. Many of the villagers will have been of slave status, cultivating land for its owners in the city, and others, still free, were forced into the towns in bad years to borrow, frequently losing their lands and even their freedom to their resultant creditors. The wealthy land-owners and usurers will certainly, for different reasons, have tended to cluster close to the centres of government, thus increasing the dominance of the provincial capital at the expense of possible alternative economic centres, and the same considerations will apply to the free intercourse between town and country represented by travelling merchants with perishable or imperishable commodities.

We would therefore suggest that the Assyrian provincial system, as reorganized by Tiglath-pileser III, tended to concentrate the wealth and economic activity of each province at the one provincial capital. In the absence of written sources, this must remain a mere hypothesis; there is only one small piece of evidence which might support it, by indicating that the old towns of the Assyrian homeland had lost much of their importance during the 8th century. When Šamši-adad V tells us of the revolt towards the end of his father's reign, about 830 B.C., he lists the cities which participated: Nineveh, Adia, Šibaniba, Imgur-enlil, Išpaluri, Bēt-šašširi, Šimu, Šibhiniš, Parnunna, Kibšuna, Kurbail, Tidu, Nabulu, Kahat, Assur, Urakka, Amat, Huzirina, Dūr-balāṭi, Dariga, Zabban, Lubdu, Arrapha, Arbail, Amedi, Til-abni and Hindanu, a total of 27 towns with their districts. We are entitled to assume that each of these was a town of some substance, and yet many of them are very rarely mentioned in the bulk of 7th century texts. A few (apart of course from Nineveh, Assur, Arbail and Arrapha) remained the capitals of provinces under Tiglath-pileser's re-organization, but if my assessment of the evidence is fair, his creation of smaller provincial units drained the life from those towns which had not become the capitals of provinces although they had in the past been local centres for a 'district' (*halzu*).

The sudden collapse of the Assyrian Empire has always excited comment. There does not appear to be any intrinsic economic reason why the vitality of the cultivated plains should have petered out, and yet the area never recovered its prosperity and importance. In the political sphere it is likely that the Assyrian domination ironed out local distinctions and killed local loyalties. We now wonder whether the empire's administrative framework did not contribute to the vacuum which followed its collapse by concentrating the economic life on its own administrative centres.

As we have already seen, a similar effect may have resulted from the conditions of land tenure. The cultivation of large areas of the corn-growing lands depended on the maintenance of tied cultivators, either of slave status from prisoner-of-war stock or subject to legal restraints resulting from economic depression. We have no way of calculating the importance of this sector of the agricultural population in quantitative terms, but it was certainly considerable, and any break-down of central control would have impaired the economy of the cities drastically, by cutting off not merely government revenue but also much of the private wealth.

§ 8.2. Problems of supply

Alongside the general dependence of the cities on the country, we should put some specific areas in which the central government relied on supply from a different part of the empire. Apart from corn, the staple requirements of the army were for men, animals, and straw. The provision of men and straw seems to have proceeded smoothly as long as the empire remained intact, but it is clear that the supply of animals, and especially of horses, was a constant anxiety to the kings of Assyria. Texts from the reign of Esarhaddon show that the horses were classed in two broad categories, riding (*ša pethalli*) and draft horses (*ša nīri*), and the latter type includes horses of the Kusaean and Mesaean breeds. There is no certainty of the identity of the places Kusu and Mesu from which these names derive, but the most plausible candidates are Cush (or the Sudan) and an area of north-western Iran.[49] Horses were certainly bred in Assyria as well, and elsewhere, but nevertheless the diminishing control over Egypt and the far north-eastern parts of the empire during the 7th century may well have led to a shortage of horses and thus have affected the whole country's military potential.

Finally there is the question of currency. Economic texts suggest that by the late 7th century silver was the generally accepted currency throughout the empire, having spread at the expense of copper (although the latter is still found).[50] Silver payments are encountered in various stages of the administrative procedure (e.g. *iškāru,* cf. § 5.3), and any severe disruption of the silver supply would certainly have affected the economy and caused administrative problems. Unfortunately we have no clear idea of how significant the metal supplies from the Taurus proved to be (cf. § 3.3.). We may discount Sargon's statement that silver became equivalent to copper, but it may well have been the increased supply of silver that led to the shift away from copper. In that case the loss of the area of supply, the Taurus, might well have resulted in serious problems for the empire's economy.

NOTES

1. To avoid continual references on points of detail, the reader is referred in general to the following works: J. Zabłocka, *Stosunki agrarna w panstwie Sargonidow* (Poznań, 1971; in Polish with German summary); id., "Palast und König", *Altorientalische Forschungen* 1 (1974) 91-113; G. van Driel, "Land and People in Assyria" in *Bibliotheca Orientalis* 27 (1970) 168-175; F.M. Fales, *Censimenti e catasti di epoca neo-assira* (Roma, 1973); review of same by J.N. Postgate in *JESHO* 17 (1974) 225-243; J.N. Postgate, *TCAE* (= *Taxation and Conscription in the Assyrian Empire,* Rome 1974; Studia Pohl, Series Maior 3); id., *FNAD* (= *Fifty Neo-Assyrian Legal Documents,* Warminster 1976).
2. See I.M. Diakonoff, "Slaves, helots and serfs in early antiquity" (*Acta Antiqua Academiae Scientiarum Hungaricae* 22 (1974) 45-78).
3. The archive of Šamaš-šarru-uṣur from TW 53 (see D.J. Wiseman, *Iraq* 15 (1953) 135ff.).

4. In P. Garelli & V. Nikiprowetzky, *Les empires mésopotamiens. Isräel* (Nouvelle Clio 2 bis; Paris 1974).
5. I.M. Diakonoff, Razvitiye zemel'nych otnošenii v Assirii.
6. See e.g. F.M. Fales, *Censimenti e catasti*; *TCAE* pp. 28-39; G. van Driel, *Bibliotheca Orientalis* 27 (1970) 175; V.A. Jacobson, in I.M. Diakonoff (ed.) *Ancient Mesopotamia*, 277-295; P. Garelli, op. cit. 266ff.; J. Zabłocka, *Altorientalische Forschungen* 1 (1974) 91-113.
7. N.B. Jankowska, in I.M. Diakonoff (ed.) *Ancient Mesopotamia*, 253-276.
8. Cf. *TCAE* 383-5.
9. Cf. P. Garelli, op. cit. 274-5.
10. See e.g. D. Oates, *Studies in the Ancient History of Northern Iraq*, Chapter 1 and 2.
11. The army needed clothing and equipment and hence wool and leather; note the leather-tax mentioned as *bitqu* KUŠ.MEŠ in the taxation exemption clauses (cf. *TCAE* 50 (1.19).)
12. Cf. J.D. Muhly, *Copper and tin*, 199-208 for a recent statement of known Anatolian copper sources.
13. K.R. Maxwell-Hyslop, *Iraq* 36 (1974) 139.
14. Lie, *Sargon* ll. 222-233 (needs improvement in several places); for the original text see P.E. Botta, *Monument de Ninive* IV Pl. 83, duplicated by Pl. 115 No. 13.
15. For the possibillity that royal land was allocated to royal employees for their subsistence, see S. Parpola's review of *TCAE* in *ZA* 65 (1976), 295, rejecting the derivation of *ma'uttu* (a type of field) from *mû* 'water' in favour of *mu'untu*.
16. For the family of Urad-Šerua see C. Saporetti, *Atti della Academia Nazionale dei Lincei, Rendiconti della Classe di Scienze morali, storiche e filologiche*, Serie VIII Vol. XXV (1970) 437-453.
17. See references under *pilku(m)* I 5 (*AHw* 863b).
18. *TCAE* 397.
19. See references under *nakkamtu(m)* 6 (*AHw* 722a) and *TCAE* 210; the most informative passage is *TCL* 3 l.191 where Sargon describes Urartian towns 'in which the reserve horses of his [the king's] royal contingent are stationed'.
20. See *TCAE* 209-210.
21. See *TCAE* Addenda opposite p. 1.
22. For the phrase *ha]r-ra-ni sa-x [-(x x) x x] la ú-ga[-mar* ?] see *Orientalia* NS 42 (1973) 441. If correctly restored, this could refer to payments for the use of, or compulsory labour on, the public roads.
23. See P. Garelli, op. cit. 269-273.
24. Quoted *TCAE* 391.
25. Cf. Lie, *Sargon* p. 6 l.18; Tadmor, *JCS* 12 (1958) 34.
26. R. Borger, *Asarhaddon* § 11 (p. 25 ll.38ff.).
27. In I.M. Diakonoff (ed.), *Ancient Mesopotamia*, 274-276.
28. *JCS* 21 (1967) 238.
29. M. Streck, *VAB* 7/ii, p. 60 ll.6-8.
30. R. Borger, *Asarhaddon* § 68 (pp. 105-6 ll.21f.).
31. Cf. also M. Streck, *VAB* 7/ii, p. 60, vii.2-5 (Assur-ban-apli).
32. Scribes: *ABL* 557 (cf. A.L. Oppenheim, *Centaurus* 14 (1969) 131[39]); Weavers: *ADD* 473 has Nergal-šallimanni as a weaver (LÚ.UŠ.BAR), whereas the duplicate *ADD* 474 makes him a 'captain' (GAL *k[i-ṣir]*); Nabû-le'i, GAL *ki-ṣir šá* UŠ.-BAR.MEŠ (*ADD* 59); cf. perhaps Arbailāyu, LÚ.GAL UŠ.BAR.MEŠ in *ADD* 453, and the LÚ.GAL 50 *ša māhiṣāni* in an unpublished sale text from Nineveh

(courtesy Dr. B.K. Ismail); 'Victuallers' (*karkadinnu*): *ADD* 618 (collated *FNAD* No. 50) mentions Assur-šūmu-iddina LÚ.GAL. *ki-ṣir ša* GAL SUM.NINDA 'captain of the chief victualler'; Shepherds; LÚ.GAL *ki-ṣir ša* LÚ.SIPA.MEŠ (*ABL* 639:16', with the same man in *ABL* 1432 and a similar situation in *ABL* 633 – cf. *TCAE* 287-9); Oil-pressers: *KAV* 197 (on which see below); Leather-workers: tablet from Carchemish connects Šarrī-taklak, a captain, with leather-workers (LÚ.ASGAB) as well as other employments (see new edition, *TCAE* 360-362, l.36).

33. See *TCAE* 100ff.
34. Cf. in particular the rank of the high official on Stele 57: GAL *hu-ra-di* GAL-*e* GAL *ki-iṣ-ri* and of his father on Stele 67: GAL [*ki-i*]*ṣ-ri* [G]AL *hu-ra-di* (*RlA* 2 'Eponymen' p. 439a). Here *kiṣru* is evidently a much larger unit, possibly even the 'conscripted army' as opposed to the 'standing army' (*hurādu*) – or vice versa. Note also the *kiṣir šarri* at Old Babylonian Mari (e.g. *ARM* 5, 70:25-8), and the use of *kaṣāru* for the assembling of troops in the recently published Middle Assyrian documents from Kar-Tukulti-ninurta (e.g. H. Freydank, *VS* 19, 73:15).
35. For reasons given in *TCAE* 221 we still consider that the *kiṣru* contained 50 men, but we could not exclude the possibility that it was of 100 (so J.V. Kinnier-Wilson in *CTN* 1).
36. We know of no certain occurrence of the cohort or the captain (*rab kiṣri*) before Tiglath-pileser III in the Neo-Assyrian sources; *CTN* 1 No. 6:48 is to be read *rab kisiti*, after *JSS* 21 (1976) 167. The *kiṣru* of Šamaš in the Nimrud wine lists is hardly military (cf. J.V. Kinnier-Wilson, *CTN* 1 p. 94). Instead, the earlier unit may have been a group of 10 (*eša/irtu*), as suggested in *TCAE* 225, with their commander the *rab eširti*.
37. *TCAE* 163-6, with the examples quoted there.
38. The exception being *ki-tul-lum pi-ir-ra* PN (Sargon, *TCL* 3, l.132). The passage is in any case obscure, but *pirru* here *could* mean a contingent, obviously (from the context) one larger than a mere *kiṣru*. However, we know from *ABL* 440 that under Sargon the army's horses were assembled at three separate *pirru* (at least) – Kalhu, Nineveh and Dur-Šarrukin – and since the same could easily have applied to the men themselves, a transfer from *pirru* = 'collection, assembly' to *pirru* = '(the army created at that) collection' does not seem too farfetched.
39. H. Freydank, *Altorientalische Forschungen* 4 (1976) 115ff.
40. *pirrūte*: *VAT* 18007:2,34, cf. 15; *bēlē pirri*: *VAT* 18007:59; 18099:11; 18105: 17,19. It is no doubt the adjectival usage which induces von Soden to normalize the word as *perru* (a pars form) but it seems probable that the substantive should remain *pirru* (a *pirs* form), and I have not wished to introduce confusion by writing *pirri* but *perrūte*.
41. See H. Freydank, op. cit. p. 116 (on *VAT* 18099 and 18007).
42. See the works of Fales, van Driel and Zabłocka quoted in footnote 1. At this point it may be worth mentioning a phrase in the Doomsday Book discussed by Fales (*Censimenti*, p. 123): it reads *issu libbi* LÚ.X(.MEŠ) and is used to describe farmers (LÚ.ENGAR) or gardeners (LÚ.NU.GIŠ.ŠAR). The X is either LÚ.NINDA.SUM (=*karkadinnu*, victualler) or LÚ.MU (=*nuhatimmu*, cook) or LÚ.UŠ.BAR *ṣiprāte* (a kind of weaver); there is little to add to Fales' discussion, but it may be that the men in question had been extracted from *kiṣru* composed of members of their respective professions.

43. Brief statement in *FNAD* pp. 21–2; cf. also *ABL* 387 (*du*$^{!}$*-ra-ru*) and *ABL* 1442 (in which it becomes clear that Sargon imposed a moratorium on all debts until the completion of the work at Dur-Šarrukin).
44. For the earlier edicts of this type see now D.O. Edzard, *Acta Antiqua Academia Scientiarum Hungaricae* 22 (1974) 145ff.
45. See *FNAD* p. 22.
46. Cf. e.g. *ABL* 93; 128; 157; NL 56 (*Iraq* 21 (1959) 166–8); the letter with corn (and wool) prices is NL 52 (*Iraq* 21), and cf. also *CTN* 2 No. 204. Under this same heading we should also consider those letters which show the kings taking an interest in the killing of locusts (e.g. NL 103 (*Iraq* 36 (1974) 214–16); *CTN* 2 No. 240; *ABL* 910,5).
47. M. Streck, *VAB* 7/ii p. 212 Rev. 6–8; more detail about the crops comes from A. Piepkorn, *AS* 5 p. 28, 27–38 (duplicating R.C. Thompson, *Iraq* 7 (1940) Fig. 6 No. 14, i. 23–9), where we read that the 'corn stood 5 cubits high in the furrows, and the length of the ears was five-sixths of a cubit', and are given (varying!) details of the cheapness of corn, wine, oil and wool. Another passage referring to the economy describes how the market was flooded with camels (and men) after the Arabian campaign (*VAB* 7/ii p. 376; Piepkorn, *AS* 5 p. 83, 12–22).
48. Cf. note 47, and E. Weidner, *AfO* 13 (1939–41) 210–3 (with 324–5), which is a prayer to Šamaš for the reduction of inflation, suggesting that not all of Assur-ban-apli's reign was as prosperous as he would have us think.
49. See *TCAE* 11–13.
50. See *CTN* 2 p. 25.

THE PLACE OF THE *ŠAKNU* IN ASSYRIAN GOVERNMENT

by J. N. POSTGATE

The legacy of the Assyrian empire consisted chiefly in the administrative structure inherited by its successors, and hence Assyriologists have always been conscious of the interest of the "army" of officials who appear in the correspondence and administrative documents found in the palaces of Assyria. In reconstructing this system the views of the Assyrian scribes themselves are obviously worthy of our careful attention, and a long-known "practical" list of officials, etc. from Kouyunjik (K 4395, hereafter "the Kouyunjik list") has been joined by two copies of a longer list from Sultan Tepe (STT 382 to 385, hereafter "the Sultan Tepe list"). Although parts of each are missing, and their arrangement is far from consistent, both lists give an invaluable idea of how the scribes viewed the different professions and appointments, and, within their own limits, they are obviously meant to give a fairly comprehensive account. Moreover, and this is of particular importance, they are lists of *Assyrian* terms, composed freshly from Assyrian sources and not dependent on the Babylonian lexical canon. Hence there is a reasonable expectation that they will give a picture of the situation at about the time in which we are interested, and we may even be allowed to hope that the lists may have been "up-dated" in the course of their existence to allow for changes. This hope does indeed seem to be fulfilled by the individual entries, which coincide very well with the repertoire of titles and their *Schreibweise* as these are known from 7th century documents. In this article devoted to a single title, *šaknu*, we shall have frequent occasion to refer to these practical lists, underlining their value to the "Neo-Assyriologist".

The word and its spelling. Of itself, the word *šaknu* should pose us no problems: it is of course no more nor less than the participial formation from *šakānu*(*m*) and means "an appointed person" (cf. AHw 1141a "Eingesetzter"). Our problems have two sources: first, the graphic ambiguity of the sign GAR, which also stands for NINDA "bread" and can be read syllabically *šá*, and, secondly, the very neutrality of the meaning "appointed person" which results in its use (or possible use) in a number of different contexts or meanings. Naturally, these problems solve themselves as more sources become available to us, for there cannot have been serious ambiguity for the scribes themselves, and it is our task to detect and define the criteria which helped the scribes to discard other interpretations of the signs for the right one, or distinguished one kind of *šaknu* from another. Only once we have done this will we be in a position to determine the function of the *šaknu* in the administration.

Without suffixes the writing of the word is entirely straightforward: LÚ.GAR, LÚ.GAR-*nu* and syllabic writings all give us the singular, Nom./Acc. form *šaknu*. In the Genitive this is as expected *šakni*. The plural is attested only as *šaknūte* (written for example LÚ.GAR.MEŠ, LÚ.GAR.MEŠ-*te*, LÚ.GAR-*nu-te*, LÚ.GAR-*nu*^{meš}, LÚ.GAR-*nu*^{meš}-*te*). There is no certain evidence for a form *šakni* or *šaknāni* of the plural, nor any reason to suppose such existed.

With personal possessive suffixes (i.e. usually *-šu, šunu*) the position is more complicated. In letters and some legal documents we are given the form *šaknu-šu*(*nu*) "his/their *šaknu*". However, in the penalty clauses of some legal texts we find an apparent *šakan-šu*: LÚ *šak-an-šu* (ADD 223:8), *šá-kan-šu* (ADD 478:3) and LÚ.GAR-*an-šú* (CTN II 27:15); cf. also in a letter LÚ *šá-kan-šú-nu* (ABL 610:5), and, doubtfully, *šá-ka-šú* (FNALD 22. A:10—but interpreted there as *šá* KA-*šú*). As far as the writer is aware, there are no cases of *šakin-šu*: the normal Assyrian form of the Nom. Sing. with suffix appears to have been *šaknu-šu*, while *šakan-šu* was an admissible alternative, perhaps felt to be "correcter". There does not seem to be any difference in meaning between the two forms.

Some red herrings. Before proceeding further, it is necessary to discuss in some detail various terms and writings which have been allowed to cloud the issue in the past.

1. LÚ.NINDA. It has been clear for many years that the signs LÚ.GAR *may* refer to a craftsman concerned with the preparation of bread, hence the convenient accepted transcription LÚ.NINDA. Thus in the Sultan Tepe list LÚ.NINDA and LÚ.GAL.NINDA occupy a section between the butchers and the brewers (MSL XII 234–5), while the LÚ.NINDA is seen receiving a large amount of corn in an administrative document (ND 5457:6 *Iraq* 19 [1957] 131). In many other instances it is clear from the context that this sign group has to be understood as the "baker", and not as the *šaknu* (=LÚ.GAR). Certainty can be achieved in the plural forms sometimes: LÚ.NINDA.MEŠ-*ni* is found only in those contexts where we expect a baker, while a plural with the syllabic complement -*te* may safely be taken to stand for *šaknūte*. Naturally one is led to wonder about the correct reading of the signs LÚ.NINDA, which, as an Assyrian innovation, do not figure in any of the canonical lexical lists. Various suggestions have been made recently: CAD A/i 296 gives several references for the logogram and writes that "Since the *alaḫḫinu* does not occur in any of the texts that list the LÚ.NINDA it seems likely that at least the functions of the officials were the same, even if it cannot be as yet asserted that LÚ.NINDA is to be read (*a*)*laḫḫinu* in NA". However, this suggestion founders on the known association of the *laḫḫinu* with temples, an association not shared by LÚ.NINDA. Another proposal was made by K. Deller, to read the logogram *ḫunduraja* (see *Orientalia* NS 33 [1964] 95), but this seems unlikely to be correct in general, especially as we have a LÚ.NINDA KUR *ár-ma-a-a* in ND 5457.

Having recently collated the Kouyunjik list, I would like now to put forward a third suggestion. Although at first sight it may well seem implausible, it has lexical evidence as its basis: K 4395. vi. 29 is given in MSL XII 240 as LÚ *šá* DUMU *mu-raq-qi-u*, but this rather peculiar entry does not correspond to any known title, and even before collation we were inclined to emend to LÚ.NINDA LÚ *mu-raq-qi-u*. Collation confirms that the third sign is in fact a "short" LÚ (and not DUMU), a form which this scribe appears to use entirely interchangeably with the full form. In this tablet two different spellings of the same word are often given, either on the same line or on two consecutive lines; only in one case are two different titles placed on the same line, and there they are marked as separate by the scribe, using two Winkelhaken (or Glossenkeil—see iv. 13). There is a priori therefore a strong reason to assume that the scribe intended LÚ *mu-raq-qi-u* as a syllabic writing of LÚ.NINDA (and accordingly, no doubt, *muraqqītu* as the equivalent of MÍ.NINDA). This however poses fresh problems, not the least being that Babylonian lexical sources give us the equation LÚ.Ì.RÁ.RÁ = *mu-raq-qu-u* (CAD M/ii 218), and that the LÚ.Ì.RÁ.RÁ is found in the Sultan Tepe list (v. 16) completely separated from LÚ.NINDA. Nevertheless, it is at least possible to reconcile the word *muraqqi'u*, conventionally "perfume-maker" with the occupation of "baker": ordinary bread would of course have been made in domestic ovens and probably by slaves in public institutions, and if we realize that the meaning of *riqqu* and its cognates embraces "(edible) spices" as much as "ointments, perfumes", it is reasonable that the *muraqqi'u* could have been a specialist bread-maker or pastry-cook.

There remains the problem of how to distinguish LÚ.NINDA from LÚ.GAR: provisionally the simplest rule of thumb will be to read it LÚ.NINDA unless the syllabic complement(s)—most often -*nu*—or the context indicate otherwise. We are not of course as well briefed as the Assyrian scribe, but frequently it is possible for us to decide on the basis of context which was intended, and failing that the great frequency of the writing LÚ.GAR-*nu* allows us, with only the rarest exceptions in the every-day administrative documents, to take the signs without a syllabic complement as standing for LÚ.NINDA.

2. *šakintu.* Evidence from the Nimrud documents shows that the *šakintu*, literally of course only "appointed woman", was an official responsible for the internal administration of palaces, and in particular for the female staff. Documents related to the work of the

šakintu come from Kouyunjik (unfortunately unprovenanced within the mound), from the North-West Palace (ZT) at Kalhu (B. Parker, *Iraq* 16 [1954]32 ff.; cf. *Iraq* 42 [1980] 99–100), and from Fort Shalmaneser (unpublished). Here we need only remark that although she may grammatically be the feminine equivalent of the *šaknu*, there is no equivalence of function. R. A. Henshawe rather hints, although he carefully does not state, that she could have been a "female *šaknu*", but as we shall see there does not appear to be a *šaknu* with this sort of administrative responsibility in the Neo-Assyrian palaces (cf. JAOS 88 [1968] 464). We cannot fully accept the recent conclusion of V. A. Jakobson that "the data presented points to the *šakintu* being a particular category of priestesses" (English summary p. 277 of his article in *Peredneaziatskiy Sbornik* III [1979] 243–5), although it is perfectly possible, as he also suggests, the *šakintu* was normally childless.

3. *šá* U.U. As a result of slightly careless copying this group of signs has often been misunderstood as (LÚ.)GAR MAN and taken as *šakin šarri*. This profession was identified in CTN II No. 31, note to l. 3, à propos the designation LÚ *ša šarri* (though we may take the opportunity to note that in this text we should perhaps prefer LÚ *ša-šar-ri* [cf. AHw. 1197 s.v. šašarû?]). As mentioned there, the title is found in the Sultan Tepe list in the same section as the coppersmith, stone-cutter and the engraver, and he must therefore be an expert craftsman. Unfortunately we are still unable to suggest a plausible interpretation of the logogram U.U. Unfortunately the letter recently published in CT 53, No. 149, tells us only that he could be entrusted with some ritual duties in a temple, and does not offer any hints as to the precise nature of his craft (see S. Parpola, LAS 310).

The two types of šaknu. With these irrelevancies cleared from our path, we may now turn to the administrative functions of the *šaknu* himself, and we see two distinct officials with this title: the provincial governor, and an official somewhat lower in the hierarchy. A similar conclusion was reached by R. A. Henshawe (JAOS 87 [1967] 517–525 and 88 [1968] 461–483), and indeed it has been clear for many years that not all the officials termed *šaknu* were provincial governors, but we hope to be able to bring some more precision to the function of the lower *šaknu*. Having discussed the governor and the ordinary *šaknu*, we shall turn to the occurrences of *šaknu* in the penalty clauses of legal documents, and finally draw some conclusions and point some comparisons with the later Babylonian sources.

Šaknu as provincial governor. By some historical accident Assyria seems to have acquired two words for the provincial governor, which are conventionally rendered as *bēl piḫāti* and *šaknu*. Neither of these renderings is strictly accurate for the late Neo-Assyrian period: in the first place, the Assyrian form is *pāḫutu* (i.e. *bēl pāḫiti*), and in any case writings such as LÚ.NAM-*su* (ARU 478) or LÚ.EN.NAM-*su* (ARU 617), as well as LÚ *pa-ḫa-ti* (cf. AHw 862b s.v. pīḫātu(m) I.5), prove that the *bēl* was dropped in speech, leaving *pāḫas-su* to mean by itself "his governor". This change is reflected in later Babylonian, and in the Hebrew derivative, as indicated in AHw., loc. cit. Secondly, with regard to *šaknu*, a more accurate rendering would be *šakin* + X = "governor of X": not invariably, but in the great majority of cases, *šaknu* without the name of a province after it will refer to the lower rank of *šaknu*, and the fact that it is not often found in letters or administrative documents meaning "governor", *pāḫutu* being much more usual, may indeed be because possible ambiguity was thereby avoided.

There is one ambiguity of which the scribes themselves must have been perfectly aware, and which in fact occasions no confusion except for the modern transcriber: are we to write, for instance, LÚ *šá-kìn* URU *ninua* or LÚ.GAR KUR URU *ninua*? The Assyrians knew perfectly well whether to say *šakin Ninua* or *šakin māt Ninua*; indeed, perhaps either was acceptable, and in any case the reality is unchanged. However, the ambiguity of the sign KUR has caused trouble in one context, that is the group LÚ.GAR.KUR by itself: this usually stands for *šakin māti* "governor of the land (of Assur)"—i.e. of the province of Assur itself.

Frequently it has been misunderstood as *šá-kìn*, but we have been unable to find any certain case where the two signs GAR.KUR form a "pseudo-ideogram" for forms of *šaknu* other than the construct *šakin* + X, which they can represent syllabically.[1]

It has often been asserted that there is some delicate distinction between the post of *šaknu* of a province and that of (*bēl*) *pāḫiti*. However, since the same person is at different times given each title apparently for the same post, this seems unlikely, and any difference in origin must have coalesced by the early 8th century (cf. CTN II p. 8[21]).

Šaknu as an official below the rank of governor. If the occurrences of the term *šaknu* on its own, not therefore referring to the provincial governor, are examined, certain clear categories emerge. The best attested is a *šaknu* acting as an officer connected with the cavalry of the Assyrian army, and after him comes a *šaknu* in charge of foot-soldiers. Other categories are less easy to define, so to begin with we will take these two.

A. *The cavalry šaknu*

1. GAR-*nu*^{meš} *ša pít-ḫal* (ADD 834:10; coll.) "cavalry *šaknus*" from a list of military and civilian officials; note on the other hand ibid. 12 GAR-*nu*^{meš} A.MAN "*šaknus* of the crown prince". [NB. ADD 815 (+900 + 986) mentions various LÚ *šá pít-ḫal*, who should probably be taken thus, as horsemen, rather than as LÚ.GAR *pít-ḫal* in view of the clear *ša* in ADD 834]
2. *lū* LÚ.GAR.MEŠ *zak-ki-e lū* LÚ.GAR.MEŠ *pít-ḫal lū* LÚ *qur-bu-ti lū* LÚ *ša* GÌR.2 (E. Klauber, PRT 44:6; coll.—copy has MI in place of *pít-ḫal*!) "whether the *šaknus* of the exempted (officials), or the *šaknus* of the cavalry, or the courtiers or the bodyguards".
3. PAP 4 LÚ *šak-nu-te ša pít-ḫal ma-'a-si* (ND 2386. iii. 6–7; coll. TCAE 372) "In all, four *šaknus* of the cavalry in the stables"—from a text detailing assignment of officials to posts, including *mušarkisu* and *šaknu.*
4. PAP 237 KUR.MEŠ LÚ *šak-nu-te* [*ša*] *ma-'a-si* (CTN I Pl. 53. ii. 11–13) "In all, 237 horses—the *šaknus* of the stables"—totalling a contribution of horses and mules from these *šaknus.*
5. [x LÚ.G]AR-*nu*^{meš} *ma-'a-si* (ADD 835:3)—in a list of miscellaneous officials.
6. L]Ú.GIŠ.GIGIR *qur-ub-te* LÚ *pít-ḫal qur-ub-te* LÚ.GAR-*nu-te ma-'a-si* (Borger, Ash. p.106:16) "the personal chariotry, the personal cavalry, the *šaknus* of the stables . . ."—from a list of military and civilian personnel from conquered lands added by Esarhaddon to his "royal corps" (*kiṣir šarrūti*).

These examples show quite clearly that there was a *šaknu* in charge of cavalry and a *šaknu* in charge of the stables; from example 3 we may be entitled to deduce that this is in fact one and the same office—the title in full being "*šaknu* of the cavalry-horses of the stables". When we write "cavalry" we do mean the horses and not their riders; for although in some instances ambiguity results from the fact that the word for "cavalry-man" was *ša pitḫalli*, these officials are in fact seen to be specifically concerned with the animals, not the men—e.g. examples 3 and 4—, and in example 2 there is no *ša* to create the ambiguity. Note also the seller in ADD 172 who was "officer of the horses of the new palace" (LÚ.GAR-*nu šá* ANŠE.KUR.MEŠ *šá* É GIBIL).

In addition to these explicit references, there are several occasions in our sources where the *šaknu* is concerned with horses, and we could reasonably assume that he was in fact the same official. Among the provincial governors and others sending in horses and mules to a collection-point in Nineveh before a campaign, we find Aššur-belu-taqqin

[1] We do not mean to state categorically that this is impossible, merely that we do not consider it proven. Even in K 4395.vi.30 LÚ *šá-kìn* may also be read LÚ.GAR.KUR = *šakin māti*, or rather *šakin māt*(-X), meaning "provincial governor".

LÚ.GAR-*nu* (No. 27) and the LÚ.GAR-*nu*^{meš} (No. 8; see TCAE 8 ff.; but note that here the animals are strictly yoke horses and not for riding, although the difference may not signify). In other contexts the *šaknu* is mentioned in the same breath as the *mušarkisu*, who was often connected with horses: so in ABL 153 (cf. TCAE 257) and in ABL 630, which is particularly unequivocal: "Now, should the team-commanders (*rab urāte*), whether a *šaknu* or a *mušarkisu*, who are going to their 'call-up' (*bitqu*), pass on, or should they [. . . . .]?" (ABL 630: 12′–18′; cf. TCAE 287). In CT 53, 136, which transmits an instruction from the king (to an official or officials whose name and rank are unfortunately lost), we read "gather together urgently your *šaknus* together with the commanders of your cavalry" (LÚ.GAR-*nu-ku-nu a-du*? *ša-pi-ri pít-ḫal-ku-nu ki-ir-ka-ni ár-ḫiš*, ll. 7–9). Unfortunately, the respective roles of the *šaknu* and the *šāpiru*—not a very common title—remain unclear in this letter.

In administrative documents from Fort Shalmaneser, as well as ND 10,001, mentioned above (CTN I, Pl. 53), we find L]Ú *šak-nu-te* in a list of personnel which is badly damaged, but includes a *rab urāte* (ND 10,003, as yet unpublished); while another list of personnel of uncertain purpose (ND 10,004) begins with ^{1}*aš-šur*-[*x*]-PAP GAR-*nu*, and includes also a certain Kiṣir-Aššur GAL *ki-ṣir* ŠU ^{1}*aš-šur-rím-ni* GAR-*nu* LÚ.GIŠ.GIGIR *taḫ-lip* (i. 17—19) "Kiṣir-Aššur, the captain, under the command of Aššur-rimanni, the *šaknu* of the armoured(?) chariotry". References like this one make it clear that there were *šaknus* responsible for the chariotry as well as for the riding horses, despite the apparent bias of the first six examples quoted towards the *pitḫallu*. A decision is sometimes difficult because it is clear from the following section that the *šaknu* could also be in charge of the men using the horses, rather than of the horses themselves.

B. *The šaknu in charge of troops*. This possibility is the more likely because in other contexts a *šaknu* is encountered who is clearly in charge of a body of soldiers (or of individuals who no doubt formed one of such a body). So in ABL 419 two *šaknus* of the Itu'ayu are disrupting life by camping outside the city wall of Assur. ABL 610, which is written to the king probably by a provincial governor, reports on the difficulty he is having in persuading some troops to come and fulfil their service obligations; the first steps were described thus: "now I sent their *šaknu* to them, saying "Come and I will review you, take you down into the . . . (*ummu*), and give you your equipment"—but they paid no attention, did not come, and maltreated their *šaknu*". In ABL 537 Shamash-belu-uṣur, quite possibly the governor of Arzuhina, writes to the king about reuniting some deported Babylonians (Labdudayu) with their families, and asks the king to issue instructions "to Balasu, their *šaknu*". Similar contexts are provided by ABL 1180 (cf. TCAE 295) and 1104, where stone threshold-blocks are being transported by the *rab-kallapāni*, the stone-engraver (*kapšarru*) and the officers (LÚ.GAR-*nu*^{meš}), the last presumably being responsible for the men providing the traction.

Since the *šaknu* commanded a body of men, it follows that each of these men came individually under the administrative jurisdiction of the *šaknu*. Hence we found Kiṣir-Aššur a captain (*rab kiṣri*), under the command of (*qāt*) a *šaknu* (see ND 10,004 above); similarly in ABL 567:10–12 a number (80+) of troops are *ša* ŠU.2 PN LÚ *šak-ni*, and in an important passage a weaver, seller of some land, is said to be *ša* ŠU.2 PN LÚ.GAR-*nu* (Mosul Museum tablet; No. 1 in forthcoming publication by Dr. Behijeh Khalil Ismail and the writer). An identical case is BM 123384 (*Iraq* 32 [1970] 142 No. 9): NA_4.KIŠIB PN LÚ *ṣi-du-na-a-a ša* ŠU.2 PN LÚ.GAR-*ni*, and very likely ADD 307 (see FNALD No. 13) is similar, although the title *šaknu* does not appear on the tablet. The association with a particular *šaknu* was not a transitory matter: the fact that it is worthy of mention in legal contexts shows this, and it also follows from phrases like LÚ.GAR-*nu-šú* PN "his *šaknu* PN" (ABL 639:6) or PN LÚ.GAR-*nu-šú šá* PN_2 (witness to sale of a woman, IM 76899) "PN, the *šaknu* of PN_2".

If we are to suggest that the *šaknu* was a military officer, the question immediately arises in what relation he stood to the other known officers, such as the *rab kiṣri* and the *rab ḫanšē*.[2] The evidence, though sparse, points unmistakably to the *šaknu* as the higher officer: in ND 10,004 we saw a *rab kiṣri* under the command of (*qāt*) a *šaknu*; in several contexts the *rab kiṣri* is mentioned after the *šaknu*, suggesting that he held the lower rank (ABL 557:20; IM 76882:26′–28′; and the examples from legal texts quoted below as 5, 6, and 7). Even more suggestive, though unfortunately too broken for certainty, is ABL 639:2′–8′, where the best sense may be given by translating "I appointed him (as) a second captain (*rab kiṣri*) with Naga"—and Naga is known from 1.6′ to be a *šaknu*.

This evidence therefore indicates that the *šaknu* could be an officer in the military hierarchy, whether in command of chariots, cavalry, or foot-soldiers, and beneath him were captains (*rab kiṣri*) as well as "commanders of 50". Like them, he had administrative responsibility for his men outside the sphere of military operations, and this can be reflected in his participation or at least his naming in legal documents relating to one of his men. The writer has recently drawn attention to the role of the "cohort" (*kiṣru*) in Assyrian central government, and it was established that this group of men, doubtless in origin a military unit, was used as the basis for the organization of a whole variety of civilian employments and trades which fell under the control of the central government (cf. M. T. Larsen (ed.), *Power and Propaganda* [Mesopotamia 7; Copenhagen 1979] 210–12). What applies to the *rab kiṣri* must equally apply to his superior officer the *šaknu*. Hence there is a *šaknu* in charge of government officials exempted from military service by the nature of their job (LÚ.GAR.MEŠ *zak-ki-e* PRT 44:6), and in the Mosul Museum text quoted above we find that Nabu-balassu-iqbi, named as the *šaknu* commanding the weaver Zabdi, is also described in the list of witnesses as LÚ.GAR-*nu ša* LÚ *ma-ḫi-ṣa-a-ni* (l. 41). It is probable that a great expansion of the *kiṣru* system took place in the reign of Esarhaddon, who claims himself to have "greatly increased the royal contingent (*kiṣir šarrūti*)" by adding "craftsmen, scribes, shield-bearers, scouts, farmers, shepherds and gardeners" to the personnel directly employed by the central government. It is certainly as a result of this procedure (whichever king was directly responsible) that we find Egyptians (IM Nineveh texts) and a Sidonian (*Iraq* 32 [1970] 142) under the command of a *šaknu*.

C. *The term šaknu outside Assyria.* In the Assyrian correspondence we do find mentions of a *šaknu* who was obviously part of the Babylonian or Urartian administration. In Babylonia he was clearly always a high official, but certainly not always a provincial governor. Space does not permit us to go into details, but anyone who considers ABL 287 (Nippur), 524 (Bit-Dakkuri), 763 (Larak), 846 (Zanaka), 863 (Sea-Land) and 1431 (Bit-Dakkuri) will, I hope, concur with this assessment. It is not often clear whether the official is locally appointed or sent in from Assyria: both were possible, since ABL 1215 r. 3 mentions "an Assyrian *šaknu*", and another *šaknu* at Nippur, with an Assyrian name, was appointed "to forward the sealed orders and messengers of the king in Nippur" (ABL 238 r. 8–10). No doubt the *šaknu* in ABL 414, who seems to have been in charge of a marching-post "in which there are no people"—except for a (*rab*) *kiṣri*—had much the same function in Syria.

As for Urartu, there is less evidence, but it seems equally clear there too that the *šaknu* was an important official, with military responsibilities. Presumably they were not, in fact, termed *šaknu*, but known by their native Urartian title, and the use of *šaknu* by the Assyrian scribes will reflect the meaning they assigned to the term in their own administra-

---

[2] In TCAE 221 it was stated that the *kiṣru* held 50 men; but this was with the mistaken assumption that the *rab kiṣri* = the *rab ḫanšē*. Evidently it is equally possible, and perhaps more likely, that the *kiṣru*, which we know was the basic unit of Assyrian chariotry, held not only 100 horses but also 100 men, two of each to each chariot: this would account for the passage quoted from ABL 273. Nevertheless, it seems improbable that the same system involved units of both 100 and 50 men, and hence an explanation of the *rab ḫanšē* needs to look outside the *kiṣru* system. Provisionally, we suggest that the military auxiliaries (e.g. Itu'aeans) and other, not necessarily military, groups of non-Assyrians in government service were divided into 50s. The correct explanation may of course be more complex; for the *rab ḫanšē* in Assyria (and Babylonia) see J. Zabłocka, *Stosunki agrarne w państwie sargonidów*, 104–5[312].

tive hierarchy. One of Assur-reṣua's letters from the Urartian frontier reports on the movement of "3,000 foot-soldiers, officers (LÚ.GAR-*nu-te*) and sappers (?—LÚ.GAL *kal-lab*meš)", making their military associations quite explicit. Note also CT 53, 95, in which Ša-Assur-duppu, governor of Tušhan and eponym for 707 B.C., talks about the "officers of the Urartians and the [Šubrians?]" (Rev. 23: LÚ.GAR-*nu*meš *ša* KUR URI-*a-a ša* KUR[—but possibly "of the Urartian (king)"). A similar use of the term *šaknu* to refer to officers of a foreign power is presumably to be seen in CT 53, 237.A.11′: L]Ú.GAR-*nu* LÚ.GAR-*nu*meš-*ia i-se-šú*["an officer (and) my officers with him", in a letter dealing with southern affairs in the area of Iqbi-bel.

D. *Šaknu in legal documents.* In the penalty clauses of Neo-Assyrian conveyances a provision is usually made that anyone who challenges the validity of the transaction shall undergo some penalty. Sometimes the "anyone clause" is as simple as *mannu ša ipparrikūni,* but more often this is expanded by adding "whether PN [=the seller], or his sons, or his sons' sons, etc.". The list can be prolonged by mentioning the brothers and nephews, and other persons, usually some kind of official, who might initiate legislation against the new purchaser or his sons. Among these officials we sometimes meet a *šaknu*, and we give below a list of such clauses which contain the term. No claim is made that the list is complete, for many broken and uninformative passages have been deliberately excluded, but it does fairly represent the available evidence. The passages are grouped according to the persons named, and the seller(s) with his (/their) relatives, who are generally mentioned at the head of the list, have been omitted.

1 *lū šaknu-šu*(*nu*) ARU 57; 102; 418; 624; BT 22
2a *lū šaknu-šu*(*nu*) *lū mammanu-šun*(*nu*) ARU 113; 37; 341; ND 3426
2b *lū šaknu-šunu lū mammanu-šunu qurbu* ARU 444
2c *lū šaknu-šu*(*nu*) *lū qurub-šu*(*nu*) ARU 41; 105(?)
2d *lū šaknu-šu lū qurub-šu lū mammanu-šu* ARU 159
3a *lū šaknu-šu*(*nu*) *lū ḫazannu* URU-*šu*(*nu*) ARU 89; ADD 1153 (!?)
3b *lū šaknu-šu*(*nu*) *lū ḫazannu-šu*(*nu*) *lū mammanu-šunu* ARU 68
3c *lū šaknu lū ḫazannu lū mammanu-šunu qurbu* CTN 2:15
3d *lū šaknu-šunu lū ḫazanna-šunu lū mammanu-šunu qurbu* ARU 211
4a *lū pāḫas-su lū šaknu-šu* [*lū ḫazan*]*nu* URU-*šu* ARU 133
4b *lū šaknu*-[*šunu lū*] *ḫazanna-šunu lū pāḫas*-[*sunu*] *lū mammanu-šunu qurbu* ARU 167
5 *lū šaknu-šu lū rab kiṣri-šu lū mammanu-šu* ARU 658
6 *lū šaknu-šu lū rab kiṣri-šu lū qurbu-šu lū ḫazannu* URU-*šu lū mammanu-šu* ARU 376
7 *lū šaknu-šu lū rab ḫanšē-šu lū* [ARU 44
8 *lū mammanu-šu lū šaknu-šu lū bēl ilki-šu* ARU 625; ADD 1181
9 *lū mamma qurub-šu* [*lū b*]*ēl ilki-šu lū šaknu* [*lū š*]*āpiru lū ḫazannu*[CTN 2:31
10 *lū šaknu lū šāpiru lū mamma bēl ilki-šu* ARU 96a
11 *lū mammanu-šu qurbu lū ša rēši bēl ilki-šu lū ḫazannu lū šaknu lū qēpu lū rab* URU.MEŠ *lū bēl pāḫiti lū mamma zaqpu* CTN 2:17
12 *lū bēl ilki-šunu* [(*lū x*) *lū ša*]*kan*-[*šunu* CTN 2:32
13 *lū šakan-šu lū* (*bēl-*)*pāḫiti* URU-*šu* CTN 2:27
14 *lū rubû urkû lū šaknu-šu lū qurub-šu lū mammanu-šu lū bēl-ilki lū bēl azanni-šu* ND 5550

Three broad possible translations suggest themselves for the term *šaknu* in these contexts: "(provincial) governor", "appointed person", and "officer". As to the first, the presence of the (*bēl-*)*pāḫiti* in the lists (cf. 4, 11, 13) makes it perfectly plausible that the governor should have been named among the persons possibly involved, but since *šaknu* is always given in these passages, and not always next door to the (*bēl-*)*pāḫiti*, it seems obvious that it does not mean "governor" here. Moreover, one would certainly expect *šakin māti-šu* in that case, rather than plain *šaknu*.

Šaknu, meaning "an appointed person", could indeed refer to a person entrusted by another to act on his behalf in a legal case. However, despite the weighty authority of von Soden ("Beauftragter von oder für", AHw 1141b), we do not believe that this can be the correct translation here. The decisive argument comes from ARU 658, a court document: Hani has been given in debt-slavery or pledge since he is unable to pay for the sheep he stole and the blood-money for the man he killed. The judge rules that whosoever wants him (*ú-ba-'u-šu-u-ni*), whether his *šaknu* or his captain (*rab kiṣri*) or anyone of his, shall pay these debts and release him. It is evident that Hani himself is in no position to release himself, since this possibility finds no mention in the text, and his family and land are also forfeit, and therefore he cannot have appointed another person to act in his interests either.[3] The evidence therefore points to the third choice of "officer": hence in these clauses the *šaknu* must, like the *rab kiṣri*, the *ḫazannu*, and the provincial governor, have been an official who by virtue of his administrative relationship with the person might have had some legal hold on him which could give him a claim on his person or his property.

Before proceeding to consider this relationship, let us first dispose of the possible objection that the variations in the formula demonstrate that we are not dealing with a rigidly determined list but rather a haphazard assemblage of titles, etc., drawn by the scribes from a hat. It must be admitted that there was no firm rule as to which titles were listed, and in what order; but this does not of itself condemn the legal accuracy of the scribes. It was not a careless repetition of jumbled phrases, as is shown by the occasional detail: where the seller was a eunuch, his sons were not listed (cf. CTN 2:17 or CTN 2:57, where the brothers, and not, as usual, the sons of the purchaser are mentioned, and he is a eunuch, as is known from No. 17). Similarly, the fact that the seller is a eunuch in CTN 2:17 (No. 11 above) is the reason why a eunuch is mentioned as his *bēl ilki*.

In any case, the origin of the legal link between the *šaknu* and the persons involved in the legal transaction is clear. Like the other officials, he was entitled to claim from them either personal service or payments which arose from his administrative powers. It is known that the powers vested in the *rab kiṣri* come from the *ilku* system (cf. for example CT 53:13 r. 12–17), and the same will apply to the *šaknu*; the connection with *ilku* is underlined by the use of the phrase *bēl ilki* in some of the texts (cf. Nos. 8; 9; 10; 11; 12; 14 above, and TCAE 67–8). In conclusion, the *šaknu* mentioned in these clauses may be confidently identified with the *šaknu* we have already described in the military hierarchy, and the fact that he precedes the *rab kiṣri* or the *rab ḫanšē* when they are mentioned together must reflect his higher position in the administration. That the mention of the *šaknu* in the penalty clauses was not an idle formality can be deduced from those legal documents mentioned above under B., in which one of the parties to the transaction is said to be in the charge of (*qāt*) his *šaknu*.

Conclusions. In the first instance the *šaknu* in the Assyrian empire was a military officer of fairly high rank, sometimes with specific responsibility for horses, but also in command of regular and auxiliary troops. His role also extended into civilian or peace-time administration[4] in two ways: as a military officer he was responsible for collecting the commuted *ilku* payments from those officials and others who had achieved exemption from military service in person, and, where the troops he commanded were Aramaean mercenaries (Itu'aeans, Gurraeans, etc.) or other, more recently conscripted members of the "royal contingent", he remained directly responsible for them in war and peace alike. In these respects he had the

---

[3] See also the dedication text, ARU 44, where much the same arguments apply.

[4] The mention of the *šaknu* in Exx. 9, 11, 12 and 13 above shows that the title's use reaches back at least into the early 8th century, although at this date his function may have been more purely military. For the high rank of the *šaknu* in later years, compare Assur-ban-apli's statement that "no governor was appointed and no officer commissioned without me" (LÚ.GAR-*nu*; M. Streck, VAB 7, 258, 28).

same function as the *rab kiṣri* or the *rab ḫanšē*, only at a higher level. The central role of the *šaknu* within the organization of the employees of the central government is vividly illustrated by the letter CT 53, 78 + 426, which must have been written by an elder statesman to the young Assur-ban-apli shortly after his accession. Referring to subjects who have appealed to the king for justice, the author writes: "If he is a servant (ÌR) of the king (and) has complained about his officer (LÚ *šak-ni-šu*) or his governor, let them give his officer (or) governor? a dressing-down; if a servant (*ur-du*) of an Assyrian, let them give his master a dressing-down".

We have already discussed, although rather inconclusively, the *šaknu* as he appears in Babylonia under Assyrian control. Under the Neo-Babylonian empire it is possible that he had a similar role, although we have not examined the evidence for this. However, the Achaemenid administration of the Nippur district, as reflected in the Murašû archive, does give a parallel which can hardly be fortuitous. There land-owners or tenants were liable to an annual payment of taxes to the state. These taxes were *ilku* obligations, either in the form of personal military service or as commuted payments: "Dans chaque canton . . . . . un *šaknu* (praepositus) assisté d'un 'second' (*šanû*) est responsable de la perception des impôts féodaux (*ilkû*)" (G. Cardascia, *Les archives des Murašû*, 7). Each *šaknu* was responsible for a group of tax-payers called a *ḫatru* (exact spelling uncertain); the groups were composed of officials (e.g. scribes), craftsmen (e.g. carpenters, shepherds) and ethnic groups (e.g. Cimmerians, Urartians; cf. CAD H 24). Much discussion has been devoted to the nature of the *ḫatru*, but it seems to us that San Nicolò is closest to reality when he doubts "the existence of associations formed on an autonomous basis" and prefers to see only "a bureaucratic organization of the artisans employed in state enterprises" (from the *Encyclopaedia of the Social Sciences*, 4, 204 ff., quoted after D. B. Weisberg, *Guild Structure and Political Allegiance*, 87). As far as the Murašû archives are concerned we would however go further than this: the taxes collected are exclusively *ilku* dues, of various kinds but all with their origin in the obligation to perform military service, and consequently, just as in Assyria some two centuries earlier, the officials responsible for collecting these taxes will have been *military* officers in the first instance. We therefore suggest that the *ḫatru* is the descendant of the Assyrian *kiṣru*.[5] Since there is one *šaknu* to each *ḫatru*, and there are some sixty of these round Nippur alone (see G. Cardascia, *Les Archives des Murašû*, 191[2]), the place of the Assyrian *rab kiṣri* must have been taken by the *šaknu*, who has thus suffered a drop in rank, although his essential role remains unchanged. In all other respects it seems to us that the Achaemenid system could have been taken directly from 7th century Assyria, where the *kiṣru* could also comprise officials and craftsmen, and the *šaknu* commanded contingents of recently conscripted foreigners. Since "the entire existing system of land tenure connected with service" was "evidently introduced by the Persian administration" (M. Dandamayev, *Ancient Mesopotamia* [Moscow 1969] 306), it is perfectly possible that the system did indeed come from Assyria, as a result of the years during which Media was incorporated within the Assyrian provincial system.[6]

---

[5] The equivalence *ḫatru* = *kiṣru* accords very opportunely with the recent suggestion of V. A. Livshitz that the first word derives from a Median word meaning "aggregate, union", a substantive from the Old Iranian root *hā(y)*-, "unite, connect" (Vestnik Drevnei Istorii 1979/4, 100). This would therefore be a simple loan translation of *kiṣru* into Persian or Median. On the *ḫatru* in general see recently G. Cardascia, *Armées et fiscalité dans la Babylonie achéménide* (in Colloques nationaux du C.N.R.S. No. 936: *Armées et fiscalité dans le monde antique*, Paris 1977).

[6] See also TCAE 224[2]; there are also literary and artistic influences which seem to have passed from Assyria to the Achaemenid empire without a Babylonian intermediary: see for example C. B. F. Walker, *Iran* 10 (1972) 159 or "despite the uncertainty about how Assyrian art influenced Achaemenid art, there can be no doubt that it was directly or indirectly of profound importance and formed the fundamental basis of the Persepolitan style" (M. D. Roaf, *Sculptures and Sculptors at Persepolis* [Oxford, D.Phil. thesis, 1978], I, 295; I am grateful to Dr. Roaf for enabling me to quote this concluding sentence of a ten-page discussion of the question.

Appendix

It will hardly have escaped the readers' attention that the question of the *šaknu* has often been discussed in the past, in particular by R. A. Henshawe, "The Office of *šaknu* in Neo-Assyrian Times", in JAOS 87 (1967) 517–525 and 88 (1968) 461–483. Naturally, many of the problems and passages we have dealt with were discussed by Henshawe and others, and their work has largely saved us the necessity of quoting all pertinent passages; there are also differences between us—otherwise this article would be superfluous—but considerations of space prevent us from mentioning all such points of disagreement. However, it does seem advisable to list here some of the major corrections where these result from fresh collations of the originals.

ABL 1239, 7: in place of **šá-ak-ni* read *šá ziq-ni* (coll.); similarly in ABL 566 r.8 one must restore *lu-u* LÚ *ša* [*ziq*]-*ni* [*lu-u*] LÚ.ÌR.É.GAL (coll.).

ADD 77 (=ARU 133), 6: read probably ^{I}DN-*la-*]*a-mur* (coll.), and cf. l. 1 -]*a*$^{?}$-*mur*$^{?}$ (not collated); the scribe must have forgotten the man's name and then inserted it after "his brothers". In l. 7 LÚ.GAR-*šú* is correct.

ADD 619 (=ARU 47), 8: read probably LÚ *šá* SAGŠU$^{!}$.MEŠ-*šú* "the hatter" after ABL 1224 r. 11–12 (not collated).

ADD 815 r. ii. 6: instead of 17 GAR-*nu* AN GIŠ.BAN read 19$^{?}$ *šá pít-ḫal* 1 GIŠ.BAN (coll.).

ADD 943 r. viii. 4–5: in place of LÚ.EN.NAM LÚ.GAR the tablet has LÚ.GAR KUR *ḫi-in-dan* (yes really ! !).

PRT 44, 6: instead of LÚ.GAR.MEŠ MI read LÚ.GAR.MEŠ *pít-ḫal* (coll.).

A plea for the abolition of *šeššimur*! — The mysterious substance *šeššimur* is to be found in E. Ebeling's edition of the chronicle of Arik-den-ili's reign (*IAK* No. XIX, 3, pp. 53-54). He writes (p. 53[16]) "*šeššimur (šêšimur)*, das nach Minen gewogen wird, dürfte ein Metall, ein Mineral oder ein Gewürz darstellen...". Whichever it is, it must be a durable substance for it survived half a century to feature in A. K. Grayson's new edition of the text (*ABC*, p. 186), and is admitted, with uncharacteristic docility, into the columns of *AHw* by W. von Soden (*AHw* 1220*b*: *šeššim/hur* (u.H.) ein Mineral?).

Now however I would like to propose its abolition, by reading the two lines in which it figures as follows:

18: [...]x 1 MA.NA.TA.ÀM ŠE *iš-ši-kin*...
27: [...]x *da*? MÍ.KAL.GA 2 MA.NA.TA.ÀM ŠE *i-ši-ki*[*n*...
18: .... corn was fixed at 1 mina (copper)...
27: ..... famine; corn was fixed at 2 minas (copper)...

That this is the correct interpretation, in spite of the fact that it seems to involve a new nuance of *šakānu*, seems to me to be demonstrated by the word *dannatu* (Assyrian: *dannutu*); inspection of the photograph in BRM 4 Plate IV suggests that MÍ is as probable as MU for the reading of the sign before KAL, but I cannot make any convincing proposals for what comes before.

Unfortunately, the existing "Getreidekursangaben" for the Neo-Assyrian period (see K. Deller, *Or NS* 33 [1964], 257-259; J. N. Postgate, *FNALD*, p. 22) are so varied that we cannot immediately suggest what quantity of corn cost a mina of copper, but 1 *sūtu* seems most probable. It is entirely understandable that it was not thought necessary to repeat this each time. The implications of this new reading are not negligible: for we must compare the first lines of two sections in Assyrian Chronicle Fragment 4 (*ABC*, p. 189, ll. 2 and 10) which deal with economic matters (famine, and the harvest), and this puts one in mind of the "Chronicle of Market Prices" (*ABC*, pp. 178-179) which also reflects a concern for economic history. This may tell us something about the composition of this document, and it is likely, in my view, that it shows that each section covers one year. How dearly one would love the rest of the text!

(J. N. POSTGATE, 4-12-1981.)

ILKU AND LAND TENURE IN THE MIDDLE ASSYRIAN KINGDOM – A SECOND ATTEMPT

J.N. Postgate (Cambridge)

Since access to and control of land was at all dates the paramount consideration in the Mesopotamian countryside, and *ilku* will usually have provided the main area of contact between the individual and the state, I hope I may be forgiven for making this second attempt at a subject which I discussed at some length less than ten years ago.[1] It seems worth doing partly because some new evidence is available, and partly in order to persuade I.M. Diakonoff that our views are perhaps not so irreconcilable as they seem at first sight. In the Middle Assyrian kingdom we would still define the *ilku* institution as a system whereby individuals owed personal service to the state for a specified length of time, as a condition of entitlement to land, and we shall now isolate some components of this definition and discuss them one by one.

The nature of ilku *service*

Was *ilku* military service? In accordance with the etymology of the word, the fundamental obligation it imposed was to "go", or serve the state, i.e. to place one's person at the disposal of the state for a period of time; even by itself the verb *alāku* retained this specific connotation, at least in Middle Assyrian times. What this personal service entailed varied: it was for the state to determine whether, having taken over a person, he should be employed on military or civilian duties, and the decision must have depended on economic and social conditions at the time, as well as on political events. Among scholars working on Old Babylonian texts there seems to be some reluctance to admit that *ilku* obligations could include military service,[2] but no such doubts seem to have afflicted Landsberger.[3] It is certainly the case at Nuzi, and under the Neo-Assyrian empire.[4] As for the Middle Assyrian system, the connection between *ilku* and military service was discussed in BSOAS 34 [1971] 496-502, but since it did not seem to a recent writer "that the evidence at present available supports his position",[5] it is necessary to review the evidence in some detail.

In certain receipts from Assur corn is issued as "rations for the *ilku* horses" (KAJ 233; 253; and now also VS 19, 44). Since even in Neo-Assyrian times horses were reserved for the army, it is a reasonable deduction that these animals were used by chariot-troops engaged on their *ilku* service. A badly preserved text from Tell al-Rimah confirms this in the closing portion of the contract:

TR 2087:10	[Š]E-*um* PAD-*at*	The corn, fodder
11	[AN]ŠE.KUR.RA.MEŠ	of the horses;
12	[(x) x]*na*? *ga ru*	the .....
13	*ša* LÚ.GIGIR *ù* A[NŠE]	of the charioteer and donkey?,
14	IN?.NU? *ša* 4 I[TI]	straw? for 4 months –
15	*i-na* UD-*me e-ri-šu-[ni]*	when he demands it
16	*i-dan*	he shall pay.

That this debt-note did refer to *ilku* obligations follows from TR 3023 (*Iraq* 30 [1968] Pl. LXIII), which also mentions corn, as horse fodder, straw (IN.NU) and oil (1 QA IÀ), received by Sikku "from the *ilku* of Abu-ṭāb" (KI *il-ki ša* A. : the same principals as in TR 3010, discussed below.

In VS 19, 72 javelins (*lištaḫu*) seem to be followed by the qualification *il-ku*; however, this is not epigraphically beyond doubt, and since one would expect *il-ki* or *ša il-ki* no argument can be based on this passage. On the other hand, we are probably entitled to take references to "goers" (*āliku*) as meaning persons performing their *ilku* service. The best examples of this usage are in VAT 18096, with the phrases ÉRIN.MEŠ BAN *a-li-ku-t[u] ša ḫu-ra-di* "archers, serving in the army" and 1 LÚ *a-li-ku ša ḫu-[ra-]di* "one man, serving in the army".[6] These passages underline the association of *ilku* with the term *ḫurādu*, first apparent from TR 3005, which mentions "the army of Nihria, who are doing *ilku* service with [their?] brothers" (cf. BSOAS 34 [1971] 49 n.9), and the meaning and importance of *ḫurādu* are supported by many new Middle Assyrian instances quoted by Freydank (AOF 4 [1976] 111-5; also KAJ 159:7 *i+na t[u-a]r ḫu-ra-di* [kindly collated for me by Dr. Freydank]). It appears beyond doubt that *ilku* service *could* lead to enrolment in the army, but the mere existence of a phrase like *āliku ša ḫurādi* tends to suggest that *ilku* duties could be performed in other, civilian, ways, and these would probably include the "king's work" (*šipar šarri*) which is threatened as a penalty in the Laws, and would correspond to the *dullu ša šarri*, known in Neo-Assyrian times to have been an alternative employment of those called up for *ilku* service.[7]

Exemption and substitution

At any period it is to be expected that those of sufficient social or administrative standing were able to avoid the performance of *ilku* service in person. The Neo-Assyrian sources offer clear instances of individuals exempted from *ilku* (among other obligations) as a personal favour from the monarch. This is probably how land came to have exempt status (*zakûtu*), which could be transferred with the land to a new purchaser, and the term rather implies that other land was normally liable to *ilku* obligations (as well as direct taxes on the crops). Quite different is the arrangement under which officials of a certain rank were entitled to commute their *ilku* service into payments in silver or in kind; we have suggested that these were the *zakkû*, a rather general term for the members of the administrative cadre (TCAE 241-3).

It is not likely that the same solution was adopted in Middle Assyrian times. Instead, there is evidence that one might engage another person to act as a substitute. As far as I know, there is no evidence for the length of time those performing *ilku* duties were needed by the state, but each individual's obligation must have been for a restricted period, and various texts prove that the time served was strictly accounted for, to the months and days. The most explicit text is TR 3010: "From day X, A and B have adjusted their accounts, and their *ilku* has been performed (*alik*) in the hand of (= by) B" (BSOAS 34 [1971] 498[10]). Although less clear, KAJ 246 obviously belongs in a similar context: "4 months 20 days in the hand of A, B has received..... of the army (*ḫurādu*) of .....". One suspects that a similar, though perhaps more complex, situation lies behind KAJ 137 too, which begins "from day X", and mentions "a month" as well as *il-ka* in l. 13; the tablet was kindly collated for me by Dr. Freydank, but it is lacking too many crucial signs to permit convincing restorations.

Although it does not contain the words *ilku* or *ḫurādu*, one of the most important documents in this context is KAJ 307 (also collated for me by Dr. Freydank).

1	KIŠIB ¹DI.KUD.ᵈ7.BI	Seal of Dayyan-Sibitti:
2	*iš-tu* ITI *al-la-na-te*	From 1st of Allanate,
3	UD.1.KÁM *li-me*	in the eponymate of
4	¹·ᵈ*šùl-ma-an*-UR.SAG	Shalmaneser (I):

5 ^{1}KAM.DINGIR *pa-aḫ-nu*	Eriš-ili, the *paḫnu*,
6 NÍG.KA$_9$.MEŠ *iš-tu ma-da-te-šu*	has settled his accounts
7 *iṣ-ṣa-bat*	with his payments.
8 ANŠE.KUR.RA *i-na pi-ti*	The horse will be fed in the
9 ^{1}KAM.DINGIR-*ma e-kal*	charge of Eriš-ili himself.
10 *ul-ma ù ḫa-ṣi-na*	A spear and an axe
11 *a-na pa-aḫ-ni-šu-nu*	they did not give
12 *la i-di-nu*	to their *paḫnu*,
13 *iš-tu* UD-*me an-ni-e-ma*	(but) from this day
14 *mul-te-ṣi-tu-šu-nu ša* GIŠ.GIGIR	their expenses on the chariot
15 *ki pa-ni-ti šu-nu-ma i-da-nu*	they themselves will pay, as before.

Seals and witnesses; no other date.

Notes on the text: 5: the reading *paḫnu* is secured by l. 11; it is probably to be recognized also in TR 3006, which records that "PN, LÚ *pa'-aḫ-nu* has received some tin and a horse(?)" [collated, but very worn]. 6: *maddattu* naturally does not mean "tribute" (any more than it does in VS 19, 49:4), but must bear the nuance "what *he* has to supply". 14: *multēṣītu-šunu* [-*ṣi*- and not -*ṣèr*- (contra CAD M/ii 289b) collated] more literally "their outlay".

This document records an agreement reached between Eriš-ili on the one hand and Dayyan-Sibitti representing an unspecified group on the other. It defines how certain expenses are to be shared between the two parties. The military connection is obvious, and it can hardly be doubted that Eriš-ili is going to the army on their behalf, with a horse and chariot, spear and axe. In these circumstances it seems probable that *paḫnu* was the technical term for a "substitute", and although it is not stated that the military service is an *ilku* obligation, this is a fair assumption, since there can hardly have been two parallel systems of this kind. Although it is conceivable that Dayyan-Sibitti represents the authorities responsible for *ilku* service, the text bears all the marks of a private transaction. Similarly in TR 3010 and KAJ 246 the phrase *ina qāt* points rather to the settling of accounts between the two parties in their private capacities, and hence to a substitution, than to a documentation of the individual's past or future *ilku* obligations to the administration.

The practice of employing a substitute to do one's *ilku* service, and the preparation of detailed accounts between the original bearer of the obligation (*qaqqad rēdîm*) and his replacement (*taḫḫum*) are attested in the Late Old Babylonian Ubarrum archive discussed by Landsberger, but neither the term *paḫnu* nor the practice of substitution in this form is found in the Neo-Assyrian sources.

Origin and transmission of ilku *liability*

Although we believe that all *ilku* obligations in the Middle Assyrian kingdom originated in theory from the tenure of land, it must be admitted that there is no proof of this connection, which is an assumption based on comparison with other regimes and on some circumstantial evidence. In Neo-Assyrian texts exemption from or liability to *ilku* is sometimes mentioned in documents concerned with land (see TCAE 81-2), showing that the *ilku* was an obligation specifically attached to particular pieces of land. Many of the Nuzi real estate adoption texts mention *ilku* duties which are obviously closely associated with the ownership or occupation of the land.[7] Both at Nuzi and in the Neo-Assyrian period it is known that *ilku* duties were inherited: a Nuzi text states "A's son is my son, with regard to my land, my house, and my *ilku*, and I have no other son"

(HSS 5, 48:28, quoted after CAD I/J 77-8), while a yet unpublished adoption text from the Nabû Temple at Kalhu includes the provision that the adopted son should share the profits and obligations of the father's house with any later sons:

10 *lū* DUMU.MEŠ-*šú* *ṣa* A, B ŠEŠ-*šunu* *dannu* *zittu* *issi-šunu* *ēkal* *il-ku* *issi-šunu* *illak* *ḫabullē-šu* *ušallam* *ḫabullē-šu* *ušaddana*

"Even if A (the father) has 10 sons, B is their eldest brother: he will enjoy a share (of the patrimony) with them, he will perform the *ilku* with them, he will repay his (A's) debts and recover his debts" (ND 5480, quoted by kind permission of Prof. D.J. Wiseman).

That *ilku* liabilities were inherited means that they were not imposed afresh by the authorities on individuals with regard to their own circumstances. Presumably each householder owed a measurable amount of *ilku* which was passed on from father to son, and which must have been determined by some pre-existent criterion. The mention of *ilku* in land sale documents means that the inherited *ilku* was attached to the father (and to his father, etc.) not as a person, but as a condition of the tenure of land. This appears to be the theoretical basis of the system at Nuzi and in the Neo-Assyrian period, and it may reasonably be assumed to have been current in the Middle Assyrian kingdom. However, this simple situation breaks down when the land is sold: since the original intention of the system was to secure personal service in return for land entitlement, it is obvious that the state would wish individuals to continue serving, even though landless. At Nuzi, therefore, the *ilku* obligations were not usually transferred to the new owner along with entitlement to the land, but had to be passed on to the next generation of the family selling the land, along with other debts and assets.

In the surviving Middle Assyrian land-sale texts there is no mention of *ilku*. There could be various explanations for this, but, for the same reasons as at Nuzi, it is clear that in practice the *ilku* obligation will have remained in most cases with the seller of the land. Although those land sale texts we have are only a very restricted group, as described below, we can be fairly certain that the cumbersome Nuzi real estate adoption procedure was not in use - rather they prepared explicit sale documents. Two solutions of the legal problem could be reconstructed: either the land entitlement was sold and the state officially recognized that the *ilku* obligation remained with the original titleholder - thus accepting the *de facto* separation of *ilku* from land tenure and attaching the *ilku* directly to the members of the family in question - , or, in the eyes of the state the new purchaser incurred the *ilku* along with the title to the land, but was somehow able to ensure that the actual service continued to be done by the previous owner. Whichever is right, one may guess that even after the transfer of titular ownership the same family would normally have continued to cultivate the land, although now as some kind of tenants under economic, if not legal, constraints to remain. This was probably the situation at Nuzi, where it can be proved to have happened in some cases.[8]

It was probably a relationship of this kind which lay behind the phrase *ilku* *ša* *ālāiūti* in KAJ 7. This passage was discussed at length in BSOAS 34 [1971] 496-8, where it was concluded that "a family which held land from the state in return for *ilku* service was able to have those services performed by its own dependants without losing its rights to ownership" (p. 498). The term *ālāiu*, which is found in this legal document and in the Middle Assyrian Laws, obviously had an accepted connotation precise enough to figure in legal contexts, and seems to refer to free-born persons subject to legal and economic dependence on another. This is presumably the relationship making large numbers of men dependent on wealthy families. The most explicit case of this is in VAT 15474 (see H. Hirsch, AfO 23 [1970] 79-80; H. Freydank, VS 19, 6), in which a total of 999 men (ÉRIN.MEŠ) is recorded as belonging to (*ša*) the three sons of Šamaš-aha-iddina and checked by state officials (*qīpūtu*).[9] Each son has a share (*zittu*) of men (respectively 426:230:150) and some extra men whose status is not made clear. The men are not slaves, and yet the family's hold over them is such that they can be inherited, and their dependent status is accepted by the state which employs officials to check them. Can these men all have been tenants, or at least erstwhile land-owners, whose lands have now passed into the possession of this family, leaving them to inherit only the *ilku* obligations attached to the land? It may seem improbable, but a parallel can be found in the land acquisitions of the Tehip-tilla family at Nuzi, and it is hard to know otherwise how the family could have built up so large a body of retainers.

Tenure of land – the sources

Any reconstruction of the system of land tenure in Middle Assyrian times must rely on two groups of sources: the land-sale documents and tablet B of the Laws. Since these are isolated from each other and from other sources, care must be taken to establish their exact nature and their *Sitz im Leben*, so as to avoid the danger of according them a validity wider than was in fact the case. The land-sale documents all come from a single provenance in the city of Assur, near the *Haus des Beschwörungspriesters*, and they may even belong to a single private archive: the lands in question are all in a group of villages "across the Šiššar", a river which H.J. Nissen has plausibly identified with the Wadi Tharthar.[10] The tablets are not the final deeds of sale (*ṭuppu dannutu*), but interim documents, probably made out hastily to enable the sellers to profit from the purchase price. This group of sales represents the establishment of rural estates by city families resident at Assur, a process equally attested during the 1st millennium BC for Kalhu and Nineveh. It was documents such as these which led to "a general division of society into two clearly defined strata: the more prosperous community members could now dispense with the necessity of fulfilling their obligations to the community ....., letting all these obligations rest solely on their impoverished neighbours who were dependent upon them as a result of debt or for other reasons" (I.M. Diakonoff, *Third International Conference of Economic History* [Munich 1965] 27).

The other major source for land tenure, tablet B of the Laws, as well as being much broken also has its inherent limitations. In the first place one has to bear in mind that no law can be expected to coincide precisely with currently prevailing conditions: they may either enshrine moribund traditions which have been outstripped by changes in society, or they may be freshly promulgated measures telling us more about the aspirations of their author than about the current social scene. A second point is that these are laws which apply to the city of Assur, and cannot be assumed to reflect conditions outside its immediate homeland: the land of Assur, or Assyria, was the creation of Aššur-uballiṭ I, and there is every reason to suppose that before him cities like Nineveh, Kalhu and Arbil had their own indigenous laws and traditions, probably even more strongly under Hurrian influence than Assur herself. It is therefore not surprising to find in an "interim land-sale" document from Tell Al-Rimah which includes formulae differing from those familiar from the Assur 14446 archive:

A.ŠÀ *ú-šal-ba*	"He shall delimit the field,
ki-i pi-i ri-ik-si	and according to the edict
ša LUGAL LÚ.NIMGIR *ú-sa-sa*	of the king he shall have the herald make an announcement."[11]

This use of *lawû(m)* Š is otherwise only attested at Nuzi (CAD L 76), and it here replaces the Assur phrases beginning *eqla uzakka* ..... (cf. BSOAS 34 [1971] 514[67]). Although too isolated to contribute any substantial information of its own, this outlying text serves to stress how rash it would be to consider the Assur 14446 archive as at all typical.

Land ownership – individual or communal?

All the evidence at present available suggests that the title to private land was in the name of an individual: single persons buy or sell the land in sale documents, and even if their relatives were present there is no indication that they played any legal role in the transfer of entitlement. Nor do the laws make any mention of "communal entitlement" to a piece of land, except in the case of "undivided brothers" (*aḫḫū lā zīzūte*). For obvious reasons state-controlled legal systems prefer to see the ownership of land (and any attached liabilities) registered in the name of an individual, and the property rights of the individual (even vis-à-vis his family) were of course recognized in the Old Assyrian city. *In law*, therefore, I still "see no reason to assume the existence of joint family holdings (after the death of the father) as a regular feature".[12]

This is not however to deny the importance of the extended family in the society of northern Mesopotamia. As we have stressed, laws and legal documents reflect actual social conditions only imperfectly, and *in practice* it is likely that much land was owned and tilled jointly by the consensus of extended families. This would be a normal situation for a rural society, and not implausible for families resident in the city. It was the extended family which formed the basis for Koschaker's theory of *Eigentumsgemeinschaft* (NKRA 36ff.), but we differ radically from him in that - although we admit that such joint ownership existed in practice - we cannot see how it would have achieved the legal status which would enable it *in law* to prevent a member with individual title to his land from selling it himself.

Nevertheless, there is one cogent point which shows that (whatever the legal position) land in some villages could not have been sold without the co-operation of others: "From the Law-Book (B) §5 we know that land could be delimited by a "great boundary of companions" (*taḫūmu rabi'u ša tappā'ī*) within which lay "lots" (*pūru*) divided by "small boundaries".[13] It is clear from KAV 125-129, for example, that these *pūru* were indeed pieces of land assigned to individuals by the drawing of lots, in a procedure similar to that used in the allocation of inheritance shares. This is a practice designed to achieve a fair distribution of the best land, and characteristic of villages with a regime of alternate fallow years, demanding that each cultivator's lands should be evenly disposed across the two halves of the village's land used in annual alternation. To illustrate the situation we may quote a parallel from the present century in the Hatay: "within the core and fringe villages there are anywhere from 25-30 permanent sections of the land which never change, and each head of a family has his inheritance scattered so that he has a plot in each of the permanent divisions. Within the fringe village land titles have been issued, and thus the plots are stabilized within the permanent divisions; in the core village these individual plots are changed every year according to a method whereby they draw from a hat for their position within the permanent large sections".[14]

There are two features here which need to be specially stressed: in the first place, we find a hierarchy of land-divisions - the permanent sections, evidently agreed by tradition among the heads of families, and separated by boundaries which may be taken as equivalent to the "great boundaries of companions" (implying that in this context *tappā'u* means another family-head in the same village community), and the sub-sections which may either be fixed by land-title or reassigned annually by lot. These latter correspond to the *pūru*, a term which does not apply to the larger sections, since the "small boundaries" are explicitly stated to be "of the lots" (*ša pūrāni*, MAL Tablet B §9).

The second feature of particular interest for us is the distinction between the "fringe" and "core" villages. The population on which Dr. Aswad is concentrating are "short-range herders", and she writes that "their village settlement and organization developed into a pattern of agnatic core and fringe villages. These are distinguished by the people as *merkez* (center) and *shoraba* (soup) villages respectively ..... The composition of a core or center village historically included the majority of a strong lineage plus sharecroppers, while that of a fringe village was more heterogeneous, reflecting the processes of expansion by the core into its lands and the acquisition of property by outside groups such as urban landlords to whom the core had aligned itself. Thus the agnatic core maintained its property corporately in the *merkez* village, but property in the fringe villages was owned by various groups" (pp. 24-5).

It would be naive to suggest that there is any deep-seated similarity between the 20th century Hatay and Middle Assyrian Assur, but it is still instructive to compare them. The agricultural activity of a core village is longer-established and more intensive, which would lead, even where the elder son received a double share of the patrimony, to a fragmentation of land holdings and intense competition for land, such as would call for a complex system of "lots" as described in the Middle Assyrian Laws, and militate against the assignment of stable land-titles. Such a system would make land sale a difficult procedure, to be undertaken only with the co-operation of the rest of the village, or at least of the family, but we cannot be sure whether the absence of land-sale documents referring to such villages is mere accident, or (less likely) because they were very rare or non-existent. In any case, we may guess that villages in the vicinity of Assur, to which the Laws probably were first applied, resembled the "core" villages. The Assur 14446 texts, on the other hand, slot almost too neatly into the category of a "fringe" village: probably geographically peripheral, recently established, with some evidence of provinciality in the inhabitants, and, as the documents themselves bear witness, open to the large scale encroachments of the urban landlord.[15]

In the Hatay the pattern of land tenure is inextricably entwined with factors such as historical events, ethnic origin, agricultural conditions, and the business and family connections with other villages and towns. It should serve as a warning not to try and impose a false homogeneity on Assyrian rural society, but being cuneiformists we are entitled to hope that evidence on just such factors may yet be recovered to bridge the immense hiatus between the two groups of texts on which we are forced to rely.

"Ultimate owner" – Village community or palace?

I.M. Diakonoff, and N.B. Jankowska, see the lands of villages round Assur and Nuzi as being the communal property of the "village commune".[16] While it may have been true in 3rd millennium Sumer that "The right of ultimate ownership of the land is exercised by the neighbourhood commune",[17] we seriously doubt that this can apply to Middle Assyrian Assur or to Nuzi. The disagreement is perhaps largely one of definition: it is quite true that the community, represented by a mayor and elders, was responsible for the village's territory both administratively and legally, but I can find nowhere any direct evidence that the community "owned" all this land.[18] We still believe that if there was such a thing as an "ultimate owner", it was the crown, or, in Assyrian phraseology "the palace".

Before enlarging on this point, we must first dispose of the *zitti ēkalli* "palace share", on which our previous position is in need of substantial correction. The *zitti ēkalli* texts have recently been treated by C. Saporetti, in *Egitto e Vicino Oriente* II [Pisa 1979] 151-172. Having considered the texts already known and the new VS 19, 41 (to which we shall return), he concludes that the land called *zitti ēkalli* had been conceded to individuals by the Mitannian overlords, and was forfeited to "the palace" when Assyria achieved her independence (*automaticamente considerate "eredità" del palazzo assiro*, p. 155). Without discussing his argument in detail, we must dissent from this view, but equally, we must admit that his criticisms of our own reconstruction are justified (p. 153f.). In particular, we were wrong to suggest that the *naiālu* was a childless man, and hence our idea that the entire property reverted to the palace on his death (as a *zitti ēkalli*) is invalid. Instead, I would now prefer to accept J. Nougayrol's assessment of the Ugaritic evidence and take *naiālu* as a defaulter (in his *ilku* liabilities), and the "palace share" as a part (or all) of the defaulter's property, confiscated at his death or during his lifetime, in compensation for the *ilku* he owed. That the forfeiture did not always include the entire property can be deduced from the new text VS 19, 41 (edited by Saporetti, loc. cit., 160): the crucial lines read "if he agrees to take (it) without a "divider" [LÚ *mu-zi-i-zi* - hardly = *muzzizu*, contra Saporetti], the ..... who denounced him shall take this palace-share" (ll. 8-13; in l. 12 one might collate for LÚ.A.LÁL+SAR.KI "an Assyrian"). It is entirely plausible that land which had been given to an individual in exchange for his performance of *ilku* duties, should be confiscated if he failed to perform those duties; this seems to have been the procedure at Ugarit, and the single occurrence of a *naiālu* in the Neo-Assyrian period may reflect the same situation then.[19] This sort of forfeiture does not prove that the palace was the "ultimate owner" of the land, but it makes it more likely.

But, it will be objected, if the palace "ultimately owned" *some* land, which it gave out to citizens in return for *ilku* service, this does not mean that it so controlled *all* land. My disagreement with the "village commune = ultimate owner" theory turns precisely on this point: they would see two classes of la one controlled by the palace and conditional on *ilku* performance for the state the other controlled by the "village commune" and conditional on performance c services for the commune.[20] I cannot see any reason to separate the two cate gories: admitting freely the control that in practice the commune could exercise over lands within its territory, I cannot see that in law this contradict the claim to "ultimate ownership" of the palace.

There is as yet no proof for either opinion, but we do feel that ours has a certain historical plausibility. The military successes of the Assyrian king could not have been accomplished without some administrative procedure for con scripting the rural population, and the *ilku* system as we describe it seems we adapted for this purpose: it is hardly likely to have excluded all those in villages with a strong traditional commune system. Hence we see the *ilku* sys tem as imposed from above on to an existing land regime: it would not have en tailed large-scale reassignment of land-ownership, merely the acknowledgement, in most cases, of the *status quo*. Nor need we envisage a Domesday Book opera tion, involving the issue of written land-titles by the state: clearly most existing entitlement to land would be unwritten, though fixed by custom, and the need for documentary proof probably crept in with the gradual encroachment of urban landlords.

At present the term *ilku* is unknown in Old Assyrian texts, although given their nature and provenance this is a dangerous argument *ex silentio*. Nevertheless, we cannot agree that "Die genaue Kenntniss der *ilku*-Verhältnisse in der altbab. Zeit bildet die Voraussetzung zum Verständnis der weiteren Entwicklung" (B. Kienast, RLA 5, 57-9). That is a rather Old-Babylonio-centric point of view, and if we look for parallels to the Middle Assyrian system we shall find them in Nuzi, Ugarit and Alalakh, rather than Babylonia. We believe that what we have at Assur is an adaptation of a system introduced throughout northern Mesopotamia by their Hurrian or Mitannian overlords, which may owe little more than the name to the institution of *ilku* in Hammurapi's Babylonia.[21]

AOF = *Altorientalische Forschungen* [Berlin]

MAL = *Middle Assyrian Laws* (see G.R. Driver & J.C. Miles, *The Assyrian Laws* [Oxford 1935])

TCAE = J.N. Postgate, *Taxation and Conscription in the Assyrian Empire*, Studia Pohl: Series Maior 3 [Rome 1974]

---

1 BSOAS 34 [1971] 496-520.

2 e.g. B. Kienast, RLA 5, 57-9 s.v. *ilku*; CAD I/J 80.

3 JCS 9 [1955] 128 ("*ilkum* .... purely military") with 10 [1956] 39b.

4 for Nuzi cf. JEN 327:12 *anāku ilka ina* ^{uru}X *našāk*, or 498:5 PN *ina āl ilki ašim-mi u aḫḫē-šu ana narkabāte ašbu-mi* (quoted after CAD I/J 75b); for NAss cf. TCAE 83; 218ff.; the new passages for *ilku* in CT 53, 10.r.12-13; 13.r.15-17; 87:8-14 do not necessitate any revisions.

5 M. deJ. Ellis, *Agriculture and the State in Ancient Mesopotamia*, 20[52].

6 See H. Freydank, AOF 4 [1975] 112; another new occurrence of *ḫurādu* is the *rab ḫurādāte* in VS 19, 5:1.

7 Space does not permit a discussion of the Nuzi situation, but an excellent summary of recent opinion is given in M.P. Maidman's dissertation, *A Socio-economic Analysis of a Nuzi Family Archive* [Pennsylvania 1976], 93ff. My thanks to Dr. Farouk al-Rawi for letting me consult his copy of this dissertation.

8 Cf. Maidman, op.cit., especially his comments on the views of Purves.

9 Unfortunately KAJ 306 [VAT 13623] is not directly relevant here, because the comparison with VS 19, 5:6 GAL *ša* É *ut-na-na-te* ("prayer-house", *utnennu* ?) shows that É UD-*na-na-*[here does not include a PN.

10 HSAO (Adam Falkenstein zum 17. September 1966), 115-6; the recent study of G. Simonet, *Irrigation de piémont et économie agricole à Assur*, is apparently unaware of Nissen's article and does not hold as much conviction (RA 71 [1977] 163-7).

11 TR 3004 (*Iraq* 30 [1968] Pl. LVIII):12′-14′; I am grateful to Dr. B.K. Ismail, head of the cuneiform section of the Iraq Museum, for permission to collate the Rimah texts quoted in this article.

12 BSOAS 34 [1971] 513[62].

13 Quoted from I.M. Diakonoff, *Ancient Mesopotamia* [Moscow 1969] 204ff., still the basic study of Middle Assyrian rural conditions. It will however be clear that we cannot accept his view that "the documents leave no doubt that these "lots" were large and comprised several smaller parcels. Hence we have the right to assume that the "great boundary" confined the entire territory of a community, *ālu*, which was divided into lots".

14 Barbara C. Aswad, *Property Control and Social Strategies in Settlers in a Middle Eastern Plain* [Ann Arbor 1971], 25. Note that R. McC. Adams also draws parallels with these conditions (see above in this Festschrift), independently but scarcely coincidentally.

15 See especially H.J. Nissen, HSAO 111-120.

16 e.g. the article in VDI 1963/1, translated in *Soviet Anthropology and Archeology* 2 No. 1 [New York 1963] 32-46; N.B. Jankowska, in *Ancient Mesopotamia* [Moscow 1969] and in JESHO 12 [1969] 233-82. But note that in everyday terms this view sees the "family community" as "collective proprietor of the means of production" (I.M. Diakonoff *Third International Conference of Economic History* [Munich 1965] 21).

17 *Soviet Anthropology and Archeology* 2 No. 1 [New York 1963] 38.

18 This does not of course exclude the possibility that some land in each village was the common property of the community - but note that land within the *ugār āli* of a village could be private property, to judge from MAL B §6.

19 For Ugarit see now M. Heltzer, *The Rural Community in Ancient Ugarit* [Wiesbaden 1976] 52-62; for the NAss reference cf. TCAE 366-7, 1.59. While on the subject of Ugarit, it should be observed that I can find no good reason for making a distinction between *ilku* and *pilku*, despite Heltzer, op. cit., 91.

20 I have yet to see any evidence at all that *ilku* could refer to services rendered to the community (as opposed to the state), despite (e.g.) I.M. Diakonoff, *Third International Conference of Economic History* [Munich 1965] 27: "obligations to the community (tax payments, partaking in community works, Ass. *ilku ša ālāiūte*)"; the most this latter phrase could be taken to prove is that *ilku* was owed in consequence of membership of the community (*ālu*) - not that it was owed to the community. For our own interpretation of the phráse see BSOAS 34 [1971] 496-8.

21 This article was completed before the writer saw the text AO 19.228 and the accompanying discussion in M.-J. Aynard and J.-M. Durand, *Assur* 3/1 [1980] 5-14. Although some of the same issues are discussed, neither text nor discussion necessitate any serious revision of my conclusions.

Sonderabdruck aus „Archiv für Orientforschung“ Band XXXII, 1985
In Zusammenarbeit mit Hermann Hunger herausgegeben von Hans Hirsch
Verlag Ferdinand Berger & Söhne Ges. m. b. H., A-3580 Horn

Khaled Nashef, Die Orts- und Gewässernamen der mittelbabylonischen und mittelassyrischen Zeit. XXVIII, 341pp., 1 Karte. Wiesbaden, Reichert, 1982. (=Répertoire Géographique des Textes Cunéiformes, Band 5, Beihefte zum Tübinger Atlas des Vorderen Orients, Reihe B (Geisteswissenschaften), Nr. 7/5).

With grammars, one completed dictionary, and an increasing number of volumes of the *Répertoire Géographique,* the historian who wishes to use Assyriological texts can now occasionally cease to worry about sheer survival in the jungle of new texts and can exploit them for historical purposes without serving a long apprentice as an indexing machine. This new volume from Tübingen covers ground which has never been properly indexed before, and does so extremely efficiently. A very few references may have slipped through Dr. Nashef's net, but this volume is quite up to the standard of its predecessors and will serve us well for years to come. Apart from the care and thoroughness with which the references have been selected, Dr. Nashef is to be congratulated, in the reviewer's opinion, on having struck the right mean in the discussion sections: earlier attempts at localization are briefly mentioned, and their validity discussed, but he has resisted the temptation to enter into long discussions. Dr. Nashef himself has asked me to mention, in this context, that he omitted to point out in his *Vorwort* that the texts covered are Middle Babylonian and Middle Assyrian in a narrow sense, and do not include the *Randgebiete:* Nuzi, Ugarit, Alalakh, Boğazköy, etc. Securely and less certainly identified places are marked on the map, which is now supplemented by the publication of the larger map in the Kartenwerk series of the Tübinger Atlas, prepared by Dr. Nashef himself (Blatt III B 7). As a general comment on the series, rather than this particular volume, it is perhaps to be regretted that a reverse index is not included: those who have attempted to restore broken place-names in the Neo-Assyrian sources know well how useful the reverse index provided by S. Parpola to *Neo-Assyrian Toponyms* can be; perhaps this can be made good for all volumes of the Répertoire at the end of the project.

The review was written in two sections: a discussion of the geography of the Middle Assyrian kingdom under Tiglath-Pileser I, which has profited from the new volume in association with the recently published text, VS 21 No. 21, and secondly, a list of additions to the volume from Middle Assyrian sources, most of which come from VS 21, which was published too late for Dr. Nashef to include them in it. On receipt of the review by the editors of *AfO*, it transpired that this list of new entries overlapped very substantially with a similar list prepared by Prof. K. Deller of Heidelberg, and it was therefore agreed that the discipline would be best served by amalgamating the two lists, which has accordingly been done.
(See above p. 68ff.)

VS 21: 21 and Tiglath-pileser's realm

VAT 18066 = Assur Fundnr. 18767 ac comes from the archive of Ezbu-lēšir, *rab ginā᾽ē* of the Assur Temple during the reign of Tiglath-pileser I (on which see provisionally *BiOr.* 37 (1980) 68–9). Most of the text is divided into five columns, of which the first four list amounts of different commodities, and the fifth names a town or province. The third and fourth columns are headed «sesame/linseed» (ŠE.GIŠ.IÀ) and «fruit» (*azamru*) respectively, and the first and second can be confidently restored «corn» (barley?: ŠE-*um*^{meš}) and «honey» (LÀL.MEŠ) by comparison with other texts from this archive, e. g. W. Andrae, *Das wiedererstandene Assur,* Taf. 49a, which have the same sequence. At the end of the text the columns are totalled, and the totals are described as *ma*]-*ah-ru ša pa-ha-te* «received, of the provinces» (1. 29). There follows only the date, which is rather broken, and the final line which has to be restored as [. . .*gi-n*]*a-ú mah-r*[*u ša l*]*i-me* ^{1}*pa-*᾽*u-zi* «[Total(?), offer]ings received [of the] eponymate of Pa᾽uzu». The obvious assumption is that this list covers *all* the offerings received from the provinces during this year, and, by implication, that the places mentioned in the fifth column constitute a *complete* list of the Assyrian provinces (*pa=hāte*) at the time. This may seem a rather bold assumption, and at present it can be no more than an assumption, but in its favour is Weidner's note (*AfO* 10 (1935–36) 21[148]) that this is not the only text with the same list of places: with the sources at his disposal he was only able to take the list down as far as the «lower province» (cf. the reviewer's note in *BiOr.* 37 (1980) 70[5]). Now however, with the publication of VS 21: 21, we have the reverse of a tablet giving us the complete list. The gazetteer of Tiglath-pileser's kingdom reads then as follows (the numbers are the lines in VS 21: 21):

2. ^{uru}*ar-ba-il*
3. ^{uru}*ki-li-zu*
4. ^{kur}*ha-láh-hu*
5. ^{uru}*tal-muš-šu*
6. ^{uru}*i-du*
7. ^{kur}*kat-mu-hu*
8. ^{uru}*šu-du*
9. ^{uru}*ta-i-du*
10. ^{uru}*a-ma-sa-ki*
11. ^{uru}*ku-liš-hi-na-áš*
12. URU ^{d}*a-šur*
13. *pa-hu-tu* AN.TA
14. KIMIN (= *pāhutu*) KI.TA

15. ᵘʳᵘtúr-šá-[an]
16. URU ŠÀ-bi URU
17. ᵘʳᵘni-nu-a
18. ᵘʳᵘkur-da
19. ᵘʳᵘap-ku
20. ᵘʳᵘad-da-ríq
21. ᵘʳᵘGEŠTIN.NA (= Karana)
22. ᵘʳᵘši-ba'-ni-be
23. ᵘʳᵘhi-iš-šu-tu
24. ᵘʳᵘši-mi
25. ᵘʳᵘhu-sa-na-nu
26. ᵘʳᵘkal-hu
27. ᵘʳᵘša-ṣi-li
28. ᵘʳᵘšu'-me-la

In the accompanying map I have indicated these cities, where they can be certainly located, by their numbers; where only an approximate location is known, I have put a number without a spot; and entirely hypothetical locations are shown by a number within a circle. Before discussing the significance of the resultant map, detailed comment is needed on some of the names (references to the literature may be found in RGTC 5 and are not repeated here).

4. *Halahhu.* The Neo-Assyrian evidence gives us the general location of this town, but Forrer's identification with Tell Abbasiyah, about 8 km. NE of Kouyunjik on the Khosr, seems over-

precise and rather too close to Nineveh. On the other hand, Reade's proposal to locate it north of the Ba'ashiqa-Maqlub range of hills is unlikely (RA 72 (1978) 52–3) because we know that the site of Sargon's later capital, Dūr-Šarrukīn, lay within the province (the village of Buruqu, part of which was bought by the palace-scribe for his Dūr-Šarrukīn residence, is known to have lain within the province of Halahhu in the early 8ᵗʰ century (cf. FNALD p. 81)).

5. *Talmuššu.* The location was discussed by Reade (RA 72 (1978) 157–61), favouring identification with Gir-e-pan, not far north of the Jebel Al-Qosh. This location does not conflict with any other evidence, and with the knowledge that Sennacherib's irrigation schemes reached this far it seems very plausible (cf. also Donbaz and Frame, *Annual Review of the Royal Inscriptions of Mesopotamia Project* 1 (1983) 4–5 for a new reference).

6. *Idu.* This is the Akkadian name of the modern Ḫīt on the Middle Euphrates. Nashef suggests that because it is listed between Talmuššu and Katmuhu «für die mA Belege ein *I. im Norden erwogen werden müßte» (p. 136). However, it is improbable that two Idus of such importance existed without being differentiated

Key to map

Lines   a.   maximum extent of lands known to have been with direct Assyrian provincial administration in the 13th/12th centuries.

           b.   extent of lands under Assyrian provincial administration at the time of VS 21 No 21.

           c.   hypothetical provincial boundaries: I have assumed that the obvious natural barriers were also used as provincial boundaries Obviously this assumption is less compelling, the less rugged the hills or more fordable the rivers, but even then the natural features supply obvious and mutually recognized lines. Other boundaries are usually postulated by bisecting the distance between two centres.

           d.   200 mm reliable annual rainfall limit.

Sites: *17 = (spot with number) = firm or probable identification with archaeological site
           17 (number without spot) = approximate location, probable
           ⑪ (number in circle) = approximate location, speculative
           ⑦ = possible provincial area, ancient name unknown

[Not entered on map, but known to have been provinces: Ḫiššutu (23), Šimu (24), Husananu (25), Šaṣili (27) and Šumela (28); also Buradhi (not under Tiglath-pileser)]

The map takes account of D. Oates, *Studies in the Ancient History of Northern Iraq*, H. Kühne, *AfO* 26 (1977–78); H. Kühne, *Beiträge zur Altertumskunde Kleinasiens: Festschrift für Kurt Bittel* (herausg. von R. M. Boehmer & H. Hauptmann, Mainz 1983), 296–308; P. Matthiae, *Studi micenei ed egeo-anatolici* 22 (1980) 35–51; and other general sources.

Nos.			
*3–28	Places in VS 21, 21 (see above)	*39	Šadikanni – T. Arban
*29	Arrahuna	40	Tābēte
30	Arrapha = Kerkuk	41	? – T. Fakhariyah
31	Lubdu	42	Harran
32	Ruqahu	43	Carchemish
33	Me-Turnat = T. Haddad	44	Emar = Meskene
34	Dur-Kurigalzu = Aqar Quf	45	? = T. Fray
35	Sippar = Abu Habbah	*46	Kar-Tukulti-Ninurta
36	Anat = 'Anah	47	Kahat = T. Barri
*37	Dur-katlimmu = Sheikh Hamad	48	Tušhan
*38	Qaṭnu/Qaṭṭunan	49	KIRruri = Hertz

[As well as known provincial capitals, marked with an asterisk (*), this list includes places beyond the Assyrian frontiers but known to have been active at the time.]

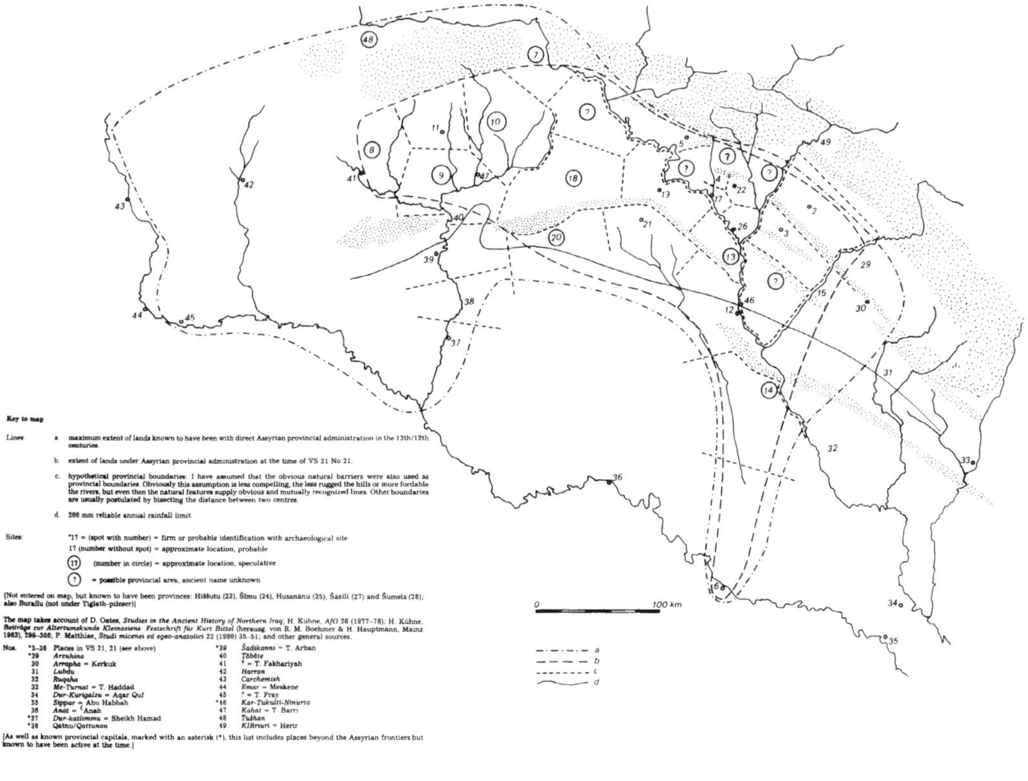

from one another, and since the list is in other cases demonstrably not founded on strictly geographical principles, and Idu on the Euphrates is explicitly described as an Assyrian fortress by the Synchronistic History for the reign of Tiglath-pileser's father, the traditional identification has to be retained.

7. *Katmuhu.* The precise limits of Katmuhu are uncertain and may have shifted across time. The capital in later times is apparently Šahuppa, a city not attested in mA texts. As Nashef suggests, the principal city in the 2nd millennium may well have been Tille, the location of which is unknown.

8. *Šūdu.* This name is found in this form only here in mA texts, but it does recur in two late nA lists, apparently as a place of some standing. In ADD 950: 8 it features as the seat of a *šakintu,* and therefore almost certainly of a palace, listed immediately before uru*te-ʾi-di* and uru*ka-hat.* While the use of such lists to deduce geographical locations is perilous, a connection with the Habur area is also hinted at by its listing between Ša-birē-šu and Tušhan in 2R 53.i.17–18. This brings some plausibility to the suggestion floated by Nashef that Šūdu in the 11th century and later may be the town called in the 13th century historical and administrative texts Šuduhu/i/a. In Adad-narari I's inscriptions, this town is listed among the cities of Hanigalbat between Hurra and Waššukannu; Taʾidu and Kahat also feature in these enumerations, and it is indeed tempting to equate the two forms Šūdu and Šuduhu (there cannot however be any connection with the «district of Sudu» which is mentioned in the same Adad-narari texts). If the equation is right, we have to take the final *-hu/i/a* as a Hurrian ending (cf. Durand, *Assur* 3/1 (1980) 47–8 on Šuri(ha) and Samanu(ha); this is however a procedure to be followed with caution – the same arguments could so easily lead us to equate Kummu with Kummuh!). Nevertheless, the Neo-Assyrian evidence allows us very plausibly to group Šūdu with the other towns which now follow in our text and are known to be in the Habur triangle.

9. *Taʾidu.* Royal city of Hanigalbat, identified by Kessler most recently with the Tīdu of the nA sources; however, this is now made improbable by a new text from Sheikh Hamad referred to by Nashef on p. 257, and to be published by W. Röllig, *Ein Itinerar aus Dûr-Katlimmu, Damaszener Mitteilungen* 1 (in press), giving clear evidence that Taʾidu was but two marches upstream, from Magrisi. The name survives into nA texts as uru*te-ʾi-di* (ADD 950) and uru*te-di* (a seat of Kumarbi, Frankena, *Tākultu* 8, VIII. 38), which rather invalidates Röllig's proposal to identify it with Tabite. A location on the central part of the Habur triangle seems plausible.

10. *Amasaki.* In Hanigalbat; identity with Masaka (nA) and hence close association with Kahat and Naṣibina suggest a location on the eastern side of the Habur triangle, but no specific identification is possible.

11. *Kulišhinaš.* Previously known only from these lists, this town has recently turned up in tablets from North-East Syria, perhaps specifically Tell ʿAmuda (see Nashef, s. v.; add Machinist, *Assur* 3/2 (1982) 100). While it can hardly be considered certain that these tablets do come from this very tell, about 19 km. west of Nisibis, the general area may perhaps be taken as correct.

12. URU d*a-šur.* The problem with this entry is simply how it is to be related to No. 16, URU ŠÀ-*bi* URU. I assume that *Libb(i)-āli* can only refer to the city of Assur itself, while the present entry reflects a usage such as *māt/pāhat āl-Aššur* «the province of the city of Assur», administratively separated from the inner city. If so, the governor of the province was probably the *šakin māti:* cf. Aššur-bel-ilani (C. Saporetti, OMA I, 107) who was *šakin māti* according to Stele 88, but *bēl pāhiti ša* URU d*a-šur* in the administrative documents KAJ 103, 106 and 133. While even in the Neo-Assyrian period *mātu* can refer to a province, it seems likely that in everyday parlance the normal term was *pāhutu,* and there may then have been a convenient distinction between *pāhat āl Aššur* «the province of Assur» and *māt Aššur* «Assyria».

13. and **14.** «*The Upper Province*» and «*The Lower Province*». The position of these entries, directly after Assur, and their simple designations, suggest that these two provinces may have been close to the capital, but as they are hardly attested elsewhere (for the lower province, see VS 19: 56. 43, 53), this is hard to prove. What, in any case, do «upper» and «lower» mean as topographical terms in Assyria? Probably, to judge from *mātu elītu* in the oB period and earlier, the contrast is between North(-West) versus South (-East), but one cannot *a priori* exclude the possibility that «upper» means closer to, and «lower» further from, the Zagros ranges.

Our list mentions no provincial capital directly north of Assur until one reaches Nineveh, and none further south. Hence I am inclined to identify the «upper province» with the Isāna district, and the «lower province» with the Tekrit area, where no obvious local centre is known, unless we count Kar-Ištar (see Reade, RA 72 (1978) 180). One argument in favour of this assumption is that Isāna is not otherwise represented, but was almost certainly a provincial capital (cf. the stelae Nos. 58 and 63, also implicitly described as a province in the reign of Ninurta-tukulti-Assur by the text TTKY 6/19: A. 113), and did send contributions to offerings (SISKUR.MEŠ) on other occasions (VS 21: 19. rev. 18').

15. *Turšan.* Location following Nashef; but note that the presence of Arrapha and Arzuhina confirms that it cannot have been much, if at all, south of the Zab.

18. *Kurda.* Well known in the Old Babylonian texts from Mari, and once or twice mentioned at Tell Al-Rimah (RGTC 3, 173). Listed here in a group with Nineveh, Apku and Karana, it is separated from the Habur cities given in 11. 8–11. This is not decisive, but in fact the reasons for placing Kurda in the Habur region (Kupper, RLA, s. v.) would be equally valid for a site further east, and I am therefore inclined to favour a location between Nineveh and the eastern affluents of the Habur.

19. *Apku.* A single, restored, writing is not sufficient grounds for reading this name Apqu, since all other writings suggest a *k*.

20. *Addariq.* This is the oB Andariq, frequent in the Mari and Tell al-Rimah texts. Dalley (OBTR 4^{25}) suggests that this town is close to Karana in the direction of either Tigris or Euphrates, in either case south of the line Jebel Sinjar – Jebel Sheikh Ibrahim – Jebel Najma (see Oates, *Studies,* p. 14).

22. *Šibaniba.* The location of Šibaniba at Tell Billa is not in doubt (Finkelstein, JCS 7 [1953] 114), but the extent of its administrative control is more of a problem. Towns mentioned in the Neo-Assyrian list of village headmen Billa No. 69 include two (^{uru}*gi-ir-mu-a* and URU *la-bi-ri*) which appear in a fragmentary inscription of Sennacherib to do with the Nineveh water-supply (^{uru}*a-lum-la-bir* and ^{uru}*gir-mu-a*, cf. Reade, RA 72 [1978] 167, where the 9th century references were not however noted, presumably because they have been accidentally omitted from Parpola, NAT along with some of the other nA toponyms from Billa Nos. 68–90). If the – admittedly attractive – suggestion that Girmua = Jerwan were right, this would imply that Šibaniba's administrative responsibilities stretched for some 25 km. across the Jebel Ba'shiqah to the north: this is not impossible, but it seems to contradict the natural terrain, and of course the nA provincial borders did not necessarily correspond with the mA ones. Note in passing that Ālu-eššu, mentioned in a late ND text (cf. NAT 126) and in Billa Nos. 72, 76 and 79, may also have belonged within the 9th century province, and that there is an Ālu-eššu in VS 21 No. 17 (see below); however, the name can hardly have been unique, and a firm identification of the two is as perilous as seeking to identify two Rēš-ēnis without confirmatory evidence.

24. *Šīmu.* Rarely attested, but it survives into the nA period, since it is one of the towns listed by Šamši-Adad V as participating in the revolt against Shalmaneser. There it stands between Bīt-šašširi and Šibhiniš, among other towns probably to be sought east of the Tigris, but no more precise location is possible.

27. *Šaṣili.* It is certainly tempting to identify this with Šasilu, despite the different sibilant. This town is mentioned by Tukulti-Ninurta I as being the far side of the Lesser Zab, and at the limits of his kingdom; it has also been identified by the reviewer with Šišil, but this seems to be contradicted by the writing ^{uru}*ši-ši-il* quoted from an Istanbul Assur text by Nashef.

Other cities

Before we consider the implications of this list, we must take account of some places which are *not* mentioned in it, because there are some which are known to be provincial centres in Middle Assyrian times. The first source is a document from Nineveh (BM 122635) published in *Iraq* 32 (1970) Pl. XXXIII-XXXIV. Many entries are lost, those which concern us may be tabulated thus:

A. 1	PN	KUR *kat-mu-ha-iu* (more than one)
2	PN	EN.NAM *ša* ^{uru}*i-[di]*
3	[PN]	EN.NAM *ša* ^{uru}*bu-ra-li*
4	[PN(?)]	KUR *ru-qa-ha-iu*
B. 1	PN	EN.NAM *šá* ^{uru}*ni-nu-a*
2	PN	[EN.NAM *šá*] ^{uru}*šá-di-kan-ni*
3	[PN]	EN.NAM *ša* ^{uru}*qat-ni*
4	PN	^{uru}DÙG.GA-*a-iu*
5	PN	EN.NAM *ša* ^{uru}*ha-láh-[hi]*
6	[	]*x-ma-a-iu*^{meš}

The text listed gifts (to the king?) from various governors and client rulers. The client rulers are regularly referred to as «the . . . ian» (A. 1; 4; B. 4; 6); the governors are named and their cities specified. Thus Katmuhu, Ṭābāte, the Ruqahaean tribe, and another tribe (B. 6) are client states, while Idu, Burallu, Ninua, Šadikanni, Qatnu and Halahhu are within the Assyrian provincial system. Despite the very fragmentary state of the text, there are notable differences from the picture given by our Tiglath-pileser list: Katmuhu is at least partly independent, while Burallu, Qatnu and Šadikanni are provincial towns.

This list cannot be certainly dated, although early in Tiglath-pileser's reign or before his accession seems probable. It is instructive to compare the geographical horizon of the well-dated Ninurta-tukulti-Assur archive Ass. 6096: here we have governors, or other strictly internal officials, of Amạsaki, Arzuhina [the «Arzuhinaeans» of KAJ 212: 6 are coming precisely because their governor has died, one suspects], Halahhu, Isana, Kulišhinaš, Ninua, Taʾidi and (?)Ahurra [this latter, if read right by Weidner, perhaps = Hurra (cf. (Ar)rapha, (A)masaki)]. Apparently with client status, or similar loosely subordinate standing, are: Arrapha, Suhu, various Sutians, and the ruler of Ṭābāte who is once signified with the title of «king». Here then we have Arzuhina (between the Lower Zab and Arrapha) and possibly (A)hurra, within the provincial system but not represented in the VS 21:21 list (for Isana, cf. above on entries 13–14). The four client areas are not within Tiglath-pileser's provincial system either, although obviously they may still have been subordinate to him.

Let us also mention some rather less coherent sources for the provincial capitals of the Middle Assyrian period. Stele 99 has a governor (*šakin*) of Tušhan. The new texts from Sheikh Hamad show that there was a governor (*bēl pāhiti*) of Dur-Katlimu, the ancient name of the site. Towns like Kahat and Nihria and Šinamu, also in the north-western region, are not actually attested as provincial capitals, and their absence from the list need not be considered significant. Kar-Tukulti-Ninurta, which did have a governor at one point, is presumably subsumed under one of the Assur provinces. Bīt-belti had a *hasihlu* and was probably in central Assyria (see above, p. 70, for references).

Geographical references in historical texts

The Synchronistic History reports for Tiglath-pileser's reign that
(1) he fought against the Babylonians first on the Lesser Zab in the region (*ina tarṣi*) of Arzuhina, and then at Gurmarriti (= Samarra?);
(2) he conquered (*ikšud*) Dur-Kurigalzu, Sippar, Babylon, Upi and their districts (*adi halzišunu*);
(3) he plundered the Ugarsallu as far as Lubdu;
(4) he ruled all the land of Suhu as far as Rapiqu. (Grayson, ABC 164–5).

The very fragmentary but important chronicle Assyrian Chronicle Fragment 4 (ABC 189) reports that in one year the Aramaeans captured Assyrian [cities(?)], and the [Assyrians] fled into the mountains of KIRriuri; and in the following year the Aramaeans [seized(?)] the district of Ninua, the land of Kilizi, and another city which could be Idu or [Ta]idi, while Tiglath-pileser was apparently still able to mount an expedition against Katmuhi.

Tiglath-pileser's own accounts do not present a very different picture, if one can read between the lines, especially since his texts mostly, if not exclusively, date from his earlier years. Quoted after Grayson, ARI II, his activities can be summarized as: hunting on the Habur and in the district of Harran (§§ 43–44); Aramaeans chased from Suhu to Carchemish and at Jebel Bishri (§ 70), or from Mt. Lebanon to Rapiqu and at Tadmar (§ 83); land of Suhu (§ 99); Karduniaš etc. (§ 100); and in the south-east, across the Lesser Zab, Ugarsallu as far as the city of Lubdu, and the mountains of Kamulla and Kaštilla (§ 98). This does not include the long extraneous marches to the Mediterranean, Malatya and Lake Van.

The borders of Assyria in Tiglath-pileser's reign

If we compare the area of direct Assyrian administration in the 13th–12th centuries with the situation revealed by VS 21 No. 21, the lesson is clear. Tiglath-pileser has lost control of the lower Habur, the lands between the Habur and Euphrates to the west, perhaps the western corner of the Habur triangle (Tell Fakhariyah), the Diyarbakir plain, Arrapha and Arzuhina. Of course, his victorious marches took him much beyond these limits, and the Harran area could well have been lost earlier in the 12th century, but by the time of our text, this seems to be all that he still ruled. The only contradictory evidence seems to come from the report of Shalmaneser III, that Mutkinu on the Euphrates (near Emar) had been built(?) by Tiglath-pileser and only lost to Aramaeans under Assur-rabi. If true, it must have been very isolated in the meantime, to judge from the evidence for

Aramaean penetration at the end of Tiglath-pileser's reign and under Assur-bel-kala.

On the Middle Euphrates only Idu ever appears to my knowledge as a provincial capital. The royal inscriptions make it clear that it was considered as a frontier garrison against Babylonia, but the Assyrian kings seem to have been content to accept the submissive attitude of the land of Suhu, with its principal town at Ana(t), and not to annex it. The only contradictory evidence might seem to come from the recent discovery of Middle Assyrian business documents by the French expedition to the Hadithah dam area, at the site of Diniyah not far upstream from ʿAnah; however, until they are published in full it would be rash to conclude that the town was within the provincial system, since they could equally well derive from a small merchant colony there.

Difficult areas are especially in the north and east. There could well be room for another provincial capital between Nos. 7, 10 and the Tigris, but we have no idea what towns may have been there. On the other bank, if a strip of Assyrian territory was held along the river to connect with Katmuhu, there may have been a province beyond Talmuššu to the north-west, somewhere south of the Zaho hills, near Bassetki where the Akkadian bronze statue was recently found; but it is also quite possible that Assyrian control did not reach this far when we consider the campaigns fought by Tiglath-pileser III and Sennacherib in this region.

Of the Eski Mosul – Al Kosh – Aqra strip we are equally ignorant. Whether we require a separate province between the Jebel Maqlub and Aqra, on the west bank of the Zab, will depend on whether the province of Šibaniba extended north of the jebel (a question discussed above, inconclusively). There is possibly room for provinces further west, in the Jerahiyah area, and in the bow of the Tigris at Jigan (a site which stands a good chance of being Neo-Assyrian Kurbail, but was also occupied in Middle Assyrian times to judge from the cup illustrated in M. Pillet, *Un pionnier de l'Assyriologie: Victor Place,* Pl. XXV Fig. 30, in which case it probably bore a different name since Kurbail is not attested in the 2nd millennium (cf. RLA s. v.)). Šimu is an obvious candidate for one of these putative provinces, and Hiššutu and Husananu are others. Another possible location for one of these is between the two Zabs, east of Arbail, but I have not included any of the mountainous area here within Assyrian borders because it seems probable that the Dasht-i Herir equals KIRriuri (whether the name is Habriuri of Kirriuri), and this land is never attested as a province, while the mountain range between Arbail and the Shaqlawa valley is a first-class natural barrier, which, again, there is no evidence that the kings penetrated.

Between Kilizi and Assur (or Kar-Tukulti-Ninurta) there is a stretch of some 100 km, which raises the possibility of an intervening provincial centre (e. g. near Makhmur). If Šaṣili could be identified with Šasili and/or Šišil, it could be a candidate for this area, but we have already seen that such an equation is very dubious, and the question is best left open. Bīt-belti might be another candidate.

Cambridge. J. N. Postgate

Altorientalische Forschungen	13	1986	1	10–39

JOHN NICHOLAS POSTGATE

Middle Assyrian tablets: the instruments of bureaucracy

Historians of ancient Mesopotamia are fortunate in the flood of light that is often shed on its social and economic affairs by commercial, legal and administrative records. In using this information it is always advisable to bear in mind the nature of the records themselves: cuneiformists are gradually realizing the importance of studying whole archives,[1] but this article will stress the necessity of examining the actual tablets, which are, as it were, the lens through which our illumination must pass, to enable us to make allowances for the distortions and variations of focus which are surely present. It is not sufficient to consider only the words written on each tablet: its physical appearance (shape, sealing, arrangement of the inscription, etc.) also conveyed a message of its own, but more than that each legal or administrative document was but one cog in the administrative machine, and the message of its written words was understood by both writer and reader in relation to its function within the system as a whole. For us to receive that message fully, we must at least try to reconstruct that system, so that we too can interpret the tablet's information with the same awareness of its wider context. This article was stimulated by preparing an edition of the 13th century family archive of Aššur-aha-iddina and his son and grandson (Ass. 14327), which includes both private and administrative documents.[2] It is not intended as an exhaustive survey, which could only successfully be done by examining all the Aššur tablets in person to see their physical characteristics, and in any case it is likely that much fresh evidence will accrue from the provincial archive of Dur-katlim-

[1] To the extent that the subject of the XXXe Rencontre Assyriologique Internationale at Leiden in 1983 was archives, not coincidentally foreshadowed by K. R. Veenhof's inaugural address "Spijkerschriftarchieven" (Leiden 1982).

[2] Although my interest in this particular archive dates to before 1970, the preparation of a complete edition, based on collation, is thanks to the encouragement of Dr. C. Saporetti and Dr. H. Freydank, who have also prepared new editions of particular Aššur archives for publication in the series "Cybernetica Mesopotamica: Data Sets: Cuneiform Texts" (Undena Publications, Malibu). The edition of Ass. 14327 will go to the press during 1986, it is hoped. I would like to pay tribute here to the kindness of Frau Dr. L. Jakob-Rost and other members of the staff of the Vorderasiatisches Museum, Berlin, for enabling me to make the necessary collations of the tablets comprising the archive, and for their hospitality during my stay; and to the Akademie der Wissenschaften der DDR and the British Academy for the academic exchange arrangements under which I was able to make the visit to Berlin in 1982. My thanks go also to Prof. Dr. H. Klengel and Dr. H. Freydank for their practical help and scholarly advice during that visit.

mu, now *ina qāt* W. W. Röllig, a kind fate for a cuneiform tablet.[3] We begin by considering the physical format of the documents (§ 1), then turn to look at the vernacular terminology for them (§ 2); the movement of information through the system is then considered (§ 3), and we end with a brief look at the terminology of account-keeping (§ 4).

§ 1 External features

In Neo-Assyrian times there is a clear distinction in practice between the tablet encased in an envelope, used for "contracts", and the "conveyance" tablets which record a transfer of ownership, and which have their sealing applied directly to a single tablet.[4] This distinction does not appear in the same form in Middle Assyrian times: "contract" tablets–loans, debt-notes, administrative obligations etc.–are not usually encased in an envelope, but are sealed on the tablets themselves. Nor are they of the same small (sometimes minute), cushion-shaped format usual for contract tablets of the late Neo-Assyrian period: even short and informal texts are generally inscribed on carefully formed rectangular tablets with a flat obverse and slightly convex reverse, and more or less square corners. The other big difference is in the sealing: in a Neo-Assyrian conveyance or contract it is usually only the seller or 'debtor' whose seal is impressed, but on Middle Assyrian tablets there may be witnesses' seals too. We shall consider now in more detail the use of seals and envelopes on our tablets, beginning with the seals.

§ 1.1 Sealing practice

Several writers have recently studied the sealing of cuneiform tablets at different periods, but the Middle Assyrian corpus has not been the subject of any special study.[5] However, the clear differences within Assyria from one period to the next show that it is a topic worth pursuing, since these are changes which are likely to reflect other more general trends in society and its organization as a whole. On a typical Middle Assyrian "contract" the scribe leaves a blank space at the top of the obverse for the "debtor's" seal, which is often identified by the simple ‚Siegelvermerk' "Seal of PN". The script of this Siegelvermerk is often smaller and less well impressed than the rest of the inscription, and in these cases at least it is clear that it was added only after the text had been written and the

[3] See W. W. Röllig, in: Orientalia 47 [1978], 419–430, and the same author's interim report on more recent finds at the site in the forthcoming proceedings of the XXXe Rencontre Assyriologique Internationale (Leiden, 1983).

[4] See J. N. Postgate, Fifty Neo-Assyrian Legal Documents (=FNALD), Warminster 1976, 3–9.

[5] Apart from contributions to McG. Gibson – R. D. Biggs(eds.), Seals and Sealing in the Ancient Near East, Malibu 1977 (Bibliotheca Mesopotamica 6), see also FNALD, 3–9 and J. Oelsner, Zur Siegelung mittelbabylonischer Rechtsurkunden, in: Rocznik Orientalistyczny 41/2 [1980], 89–95 and Zur neu- und spätbabylonischen Siegelpraxis, in: B. Hruška – G. Komoróczy(eds.), Festschrift Lubor Matouš, Budapest 1978, II, 167–186.

seal in question actually rolled.[6] Indeed, it was not formally part of the text, since this begins with the first line below the seal-impression space, which is indented (rather like a modern paragraph). It is curious that the same arrangement with sealing and accompanying Siegelvermerk at the head of the obverse, survives into Neo-Assyrian times, but only on conveyance tablets; the seal impression on a contract-envelope is usually further down, in the body of the text. Presumably Middle Assyrian conveyance tablets also had the seller's seal impressed at the head of the obverse, but until certain examples are known, this has to remain speculation (see below, § 2.2).[7]

Elsewhere on the tablet the witnesses' seals are rolled, with varying success. Sometimes every blank or inscribed surface is covered with impressions, often to the detriment of the text's legibility. Spaces are sometimes left between the name of one witness and the next for the appropriate seal to be rolled (e. g. KAJ 262), and not infrequently the scribe has divided the space along the left edge of the tablet into two or more fields with short single or double vertical strokes, each field then accommodating a different seal impression which may be identified by its owner's name as "seal of PN".[8] The names of the witnesses are usually introduced by IGI "in the presence of" (presumably *pān*), but it is not uncommon to find KIŠIB IGI PN;[9] quite how this would have been expressed in Akkadian is not clear. I suspect it may have no strict oral equivalent, and be simply scribal shorthand for "Seal of (and) in the presence of PN".

Self-evidently, tablets with the impression of more than one seal were witnessed transactions, but some sealed tablets are administrative documents without named witnesses. In those cases I have seen, these are sealed with only one seal, presumably by the person liable to the obligation the tablet records. An example is KAJ 108, a work contract in which Erib-Sin undertakes to supply nine chairs: this tablet is sealed all over by a single seal (published by A. Moortgat, in: ZA 47 [1942], 59f. with Abb. 14). Other examples from the 13th century Ass. 14327 archive are VAT 9005 (No. 33 in my forthcoming edition), KAJ 115 ("Seal of Ṣilliya"–on at least four surfaces), and KAJ 113, which has the same seal rolled on obverse, reverse, right edge, and probably originally the left and top and bottom edges too. There are plenty of exceptions though: the unwitnessed KAJ 102 is more of a legal than an administrative instrument, but has only impressions from a single seal; whereas KAJ 122, which is unsealed, very much resembles KAJ 117, also unwitnessed and also concluding with the phrase "he shall break his tablet", but with a seal impression (presumably that of Marduk-kitte-ide).[10]

6 One example of this is BM 123367, illustrated in photograph in: Iraq 35 [1973], Plate XVb.

7 Though cf. perhaps BM 123367 (note 16 below), or the inheritance tablet TR 2037 (most recently J. N. Postgate, in: Iraq 41 [1979], 89–91), both sealed at the top of the obverse.–TR is the siglum for tablets excavated at Tell al-Rimah; all the TR numbers quoted in this article were published by H. W. F. Saggs, in: Iraq 30 [1968], 154–174, and by D. J. Wiseman, in: Iraq 30 [1968], 175–205; in some cases the writer's version of the text is dependent on collations subsequent to the first edition of the tablets.

8 E. g. KAJ 54.

9 E. g. KAJ 110.

10 Given the care with which the seals of different witnesses and other parties were distinguished, it is not surprising that the use of hems or finger-nails instead was uncommon.

Before leaving the subject of seals, note that in KAJ 103 and 106 the name of the owner, Ehlipi, appears on the seal itself (collated), thus substantiating the Siegelvermerk of KAJ 103 : 1; while in contrast the traces of a seal inscription on KAJ 109 do not seem to include the name of either Kidin-Sin or his father, suggesting that the seal may have been borrowed or inherited.

§ 1.2 Envelopes

Although, as we have noted, Middle Assyrian "contracts" did not, like their Neo-Assyrian counterparts, have envelopes, we have a few examples of tablet + envelope among other kinds of Middle Assyrian texts. As in Old Assyrian times some letters were given an envelope which was sealed and had the "address" and other brief details written on it.[11] Presumably the reason for the envelope was not so much the physical protection it gave to the text on the inner tablet (although this may have played its part), but the concealment of the contents from unauthorized eyes; in this of course it differs from the purpose of an envelope on a legal text, where the wording is generally repeated on the outside. One letter with envelope (VS 19 No. 15) is concerned with an administrative matter; the envelope bears only the names of sender and recipient. A long letter about the fate of Kassite deportees in the north (VS 19 No. 71) is addressed on the envelope: "To PN_1, our master. Tablet of PN_2 and PN_3, servant of Shalmaneser". In both cases a seal was rolled in a space ruled off on the obverse between the two halves of the address, but also on the other surfaces of the envelope; according to Dr. Freydank's copies, the inner tablets were not sealed.

There is another class of letter which has no surviving envelope, but has been sealed on the tablet itself. The only examples I have noted are VS 19 No. 39, whose resemblance to an administrative document is enhanced by the ruling and date placed after the seal impression at the end of the text, and VS 21 No. 25, which was sealed in a space left at the head of the obverse. See perhaps on *našpertu*, § 2.8 below.

All the other envelopes I have noted come from receipts: that is to say, from documents in which the principal verb is *maḫir* "he has received", with more rarely *tadin* "has been given out" or forms of *akālu* = "consumed" (see the details of VS 21 No. 17, under 6. below). Before discussing these texts as a whole, it seems necessary to describe them briefly. First we list six administrative texts from Aššur:

1. KAJ 233 and KAV 207: The tablet (KAJ 233) is sealed, but not witnessed. It records the receipt of barley for horse-fodder. The envelope has a disjointed text, lacking the syntax of the tablet: „X barley, fodder of the *ilku* horses. (Space) Of PN_1. (Space) PN_2. (Space; no *maḫir*!) Date." The envelope too was „allseitig übersiegelt". This document belongs to the Ass. 14446 archive and is consequently probably 14th century in date.

However, (*pace* J. Renger, in: Gibson – Biggs, Seals and Sealing 78) I have noted textile impressions on some of the Ass. 14327 tablets, especially KAJ 77, 91 and 100, and two small texts from the Aššur Temple offerings archive (Tiglath-Pileser I) are introduced by the familiar Neo-Assyrian phrase: *kūmu kunukki-šu ṣupar-šu* (see B. K. Ismail, in: Sumer 24 [1968], 18–22, VAT 17889 and 17888) "instead of his seal, his nail". E. Ebeling notes nail impressions on KAJ 262, although I did not notice these myself.

[11] For the Old Assyrian evidence see M. T. Larsen, in: Gibson – Biggs Seals, and Sealing 96–98.

2. KAJ 241: The tablet is sealed, and witnessed. It records the receipt of oil and wool. The envelope is sealed, but the names of the witnesses not repeated. It repeats the essential data in a rather staccato fashion: *kiṣirtu*–of 1 *sūtu* oil and 10 minas wool–of PN_1–PN_2 has received (*maḫir*)–Seal impression–Date. From Ass. 14987, probably reign of Tukulti-Ninurta I.
3. VS 19 No. 25: The tablet is sealed at the top, and records receipt of "54 homers of barley, offerings of Idu, from the charge of PN_1 and PN_2, Ezbu-lešir has received (*maḫir*)". Date; no witnesses. The envelope is only fragmentary, but its wording was not identical because we meet the subjunctive *maḫrūni* in Rs. 5′ (cf. 4. below). There follows a wide space for the sealing, and the date. Like 4.–6. below, this document comes from the Aššur Temple offerings archive of Ezbu-lešir, dating to the reign of Tiglathpileser I (cf. J. N. Postgate, in: Bi.Or. 37 [1980], 68–70).
4. VS 19 No. 73: The tablet is sealed at the top, and lists the offerings received from three men of the city of Kulišhinaš by Ezbu-lešir. After *maḫir* (l. 13), we read "Aššur-kitti-šeṣi, provincial governor, has 'bound' (*iktaṣar*)" (see below, § 2.5). Date is stated in ll. 5–6. The envelope again is poorly preserved, beginning "Tablet (*ṭuppi*) of x [sesame and(?)] y . . .". After a seal impression it continues: "Offerings [of] Kulišhinaš (which), from the charge of PN, Ezbu-lešir has received" ([3]*gi-na-e* [*ša* u]ru*k*. . . . [10]*maḫ-r*[*u-ú*]*-ni*: a second *ša* = "which" seems to have been omitted but should probably be restored in the light of another minute fragment of envelope stored under VAT 16399, which reads [1]*ṭup-pí x*[ ] [2]*ša iš-tu* ITI.x[ ] [3]*li-me* [1]IGI + DUB.[ ] (ruling)). There follow another seal impression, and remnants of a date. Both tablet and envelope have the same seal (cf. Bi. Or. 37, 68[1]); this presumably belonged either to Ezbu-lešir or to Aššur-kitte-šeṣi, but only the study of the seal impressions on other tablets from the same archive is likely to determine which.
5. VS 21 No. 24: The obverse of the tablet is poorly preserved, and the structure of the text cannot be confidently reconstituted, though it includes such statements as [*ma*]*did* ("measured our", ll. 4, 7), *im-du-du* ("they measured out", l. 15), and *tadin* "was given out" (l. 20); l. 17 probably said "Ezbu-lešir received" ([*maḫi*]*r*). The tablet was not however sealed by him, but by Lu-dari-šarru, the servant of Haballani the diviner (l. 1). On the tablet, the seal impression is immediately after the Siegelvermerk, at the top of the obverse; on the envelope both the impression and the Siegelvermerk are at the centre of the obverse, and comparison with the letter-envelopes mentioned above suggests that this was a regular practice, no doubt the predecessor of that on Neo-Assyrian contracts. Unfortunately the text of the envelope is even more fragmentary than the inner tablet's and we can only say that as in 3. and 4. above, it is differently phrased.
6. VS 21 No. 17: This is a very big tablet (19.8 × 11.8 cm), with 114 lines of text. After an unidentified sealing at the head of the obverse, it lists issues of corn for a variety of purposes; some of the ruled sections end "given out" (*tadin*), but we also meet *ētaklu* "they consumed" and *ultakilu* "they arranged for the consumption of . . ." (at the king's command, l. 114). In one sense this is an administrative *Sammelurkunde*, and it is not just a list, but a functional cog in the machine, because it is sealed and also enclosed in an envelope;

like the other texts from this archive listed above, it is not witnessed. No doubt it was a tablet very similar to this one that is described in VS 19 No. 21 as "the big tablet of miscellaneous receipts" (*ša pī ṭuppi rabīte ša ma-ḫar/ḫir ma-ḫar/ḫir*, ll. 22f.; infin. status absolutus, or permansive), though of course this one is not a list of receipts.

In view of its size, it was surprising to find that this tablet had an envelope, although inevitably the thinness of its clay means that only fragments survive (Taf. XXX–XXXIV). The envelope, which was presumably sealed although this is not stated for any of the fragments copied, offered a complete (though not exact) duplicate of the text on the tablet (cf. Freydank, VS 21, p. 9).[12]
There were apparently no envelopes from Tell Billa, but a few of the tablets at Tell al-Rimah also had envelopes, and here too they are reserved for receipts or similar transactions. In TR 2057 the sum of 12 minas of *annuku* (tin or lead) out of an original loan of 30 minas is repaid by Nabudu, and the text prescribes that "they shall deduct (it) from his executed tablet for 30 minas of *annuku*" (*ina ṭuppi ṣabitte ša* 30 MA.NA AN.NA . . . *ukarrû*).[13] In such a case, there would one day be a final settling of accounts, and this receipt tablet (+envelope) would be set against the "executed tablet" (see § 2.3) recording the original debt. If it be asked why they did not simply cancel the original tablet and issue a new one for 18 minas, one reason is that the creditor in this case, Nabudu, came from another town (Uninu), and presumably did not carry the "executed tablet" around with him.

TR 2039 is an envelope fragment from a similar transaction between the same two principals. Another tablet+envelope acknowledges the receipt (*maḫir*) of 37 minas of *annuku* and 0.7 homers of corn (TR 2904 with 2083E+2084E+F). Finally TR 2062A+B with its tablet TR 2905, both sealed, is another receipt with the "they shall deduct" (*ukarrû*) clause, referring to an earlier debt. All the Rimah envelopes therefore come from receipts; the first three certainly belong to the archive of Abu-ṭab, since he is the man making the payment, and in whose possession we should expect the documentary proof of payment to have remained. In all these cases the payments are not from his own purse, but made in his official capacity "in the hand of Abu-ṭab" (*ša/ina qāt*); TR 2062A+B and 2905 are too broken to say whether or not Abu-ṭab was involved, or whether it was a private or an official transaction. By comparison with the other envelopes, both from Rimah and Aššur, the chances seem to be that it too was from government administration rather than private commerce, but there are not enough texts to assert this with any confidence. Similarly, the size of the sample is too small for us to detect any significance in whether or not the receipts were witnessed. TR 2904 (etc.) and KAJ 241 (above, 2.) had witnesses, but the majority did not. As at Aššur, both tablets and envelopes were sealed at Rimah; in the case of TR 2057 we have the impression at the centre of the reverse, in TR 2039 in the middle of the obverse (though probably also on the lost reverse as well). Despite the differences between the two towns, there is therefore an underlying consistency in their use of envelopes. They are used for receipts or similar transactions; they

12 I am very grateful to Dr. H. Freydank for showing the original tablet and envelope to me in Berlin.
13 For this phrase see below, § 2.3.

occur in administrative contexts; both tablet and envelope are sealed (sometimes with the same seal); unlike letters, the text of the tablet is repeated on the envelope, but on the Aššur documents it is usually rather differently formulated.

While the facts seem clear, I have to admit that the reasons for this practice escape me. Receipts are of course very different from "contracts" and were treated differently in Neo-Assyrian times (with a reversal of the earlier practice):[14] although in each case goods or currency may pass from one hand to another, with a receipt the payment is made in response to an existing obligation, either in full or in part. The recipient seals the document to acknowledge that payment was made, and the document remains in the possession of the payer, either for "ever", as proof that the obligation has been acquitted, or until actions are taken which make such a proof superfluous (such as the destruction of an earlier loan document on which the original obligation depends). We should not lose sight of the other ways in which an obligation might have arisen, though: most of the Aššur receipts refer to tax or offerings payments to a government official, and we have taxation receipts (for *miksu*) from Rimah and Aššur, although if they had envelopes these no longer survive.[15] Thus, although there are clear differences between the "contracts" (debt-notes, loans, work-contracts etc.) and our receipts, they do not obviously account for the use of envelopes in one case and not in the other: the advantages of an envelope are well known, briefly, the protection of the tablet from accidental damage or wilful falsification, but I fail to see why it was found more suitable for administrative receipts than for public and private loan transactions.

§ 2 The Assyrian terminology

Having described the external appearance of the documents, we turn now to the distinctions recognized by the Assyrian scribes themselves, and will hope to find some correlation between the two. The terms to be discussed are: *ṭuppu* (with its sub-classes *ṭuppu dannutu* and *ṭuppu ṣabittu*), *kanīku, kiṣirtu, lē'u* and *našpertu*. Perhaps we should not expect rigid distinctions to have been observed through different types of text and across three centuries, but despite some expected overlaps in their usage there are certainly some significant differences which we need to understand.

§ 2.1 *ṭuppu* (plur. *ṭuppāte*) The ordinary, all-embracing word for "a tablet", in common use in both formal and informal contexts. Unlike in Old Assyrian, it is uniformly feminine in Middle Assyrian texts, a change which had taken place already in the transitional Old/Middle Assyrian Geneva tablet published by I. J. Gelb and E. Sollberger, in: JNES 16 [1957], 163–175. Without further qualification *ṭuppu* may refer to a "letter" (often: e. g. KAJ 302; and frequently in the Babu-aha-iddina correspondence, e. g. KAV 98 : 40; 99 : 24, 38, 41), or to

[14] For the Neo-Assyrian receipt, with fresh legal terminology and a format similar to that of judicial documents, and no envelope, see FNALD 55–58.

[15] Most of the *miksu* texts were discussed in M.-J. Aynard – J.-M. Durand, in: Assur 3/1 [1980], 44–46; some additions and corrections in my review of P. Machinist, Assur 3/2 [1982], to appear in "Mesopotamia" (Torino) 18–19, [1983–1984], 229 ff.

legal/administrative "contract" tablets of various kinds (e. g. in the phrase *ṭuppu-šu iḫappi* "he may break his tablet", passim; other examples below). The type of tablet may be more closely specified, as in *ṭuppu našperti* "message tablet" (see § 2.8 below), or its particular characteristics described, as in *ṭuppu ša kunuk* PN (e. g. KAJ 7 : 30). Examples of tablets specified by their subject matter will also be quoted below in § 3.5. Here I want to single out for discussion two technical terms which are of basic importance, the "strong tablet" and the "executed tablet" (§§ 2.2–3).

§ 2.2 *ṭuppu dannutu* "strong tablet" In earlier discussions of this term I have followed others (e.g. CAD D and Gelb–Sollberger JNES 16, 165) in translating "valid tablet". However, this particular nuance, which is especially tempting in one of the phrases discussed below, cannot be considered proven, and the word "valid" is perhaps best avoided to prevent a *petitio principii*. As in Neo-Assyrian, where the term is shortened to simply *dannutu*, the "strong tablet" refers to the final document of land sale. Before such a tablet could be made out, certain formal procedures were necessary. These are described as "he shall clear the field (of claims), measure it by the royal measure, and shall write the "strong tablet" for(?) the king" (*eqla uzakka ina ašal šarri imaddad ū ṭuppa dannata ana pāni šarri išaṭṭar*; see J. N. Postgate, in: BSOAS 34 [1971], 514[67], and note that the *ū* here will have the implication "and then (and only then)" as with the phrase *ū ṭuppu-šu iḫappi*, making the first two procedures the precondition for the last). Some tablets also have the phrase "until they write the "strong tablet" for(?) the king, this one is "strong" " (*annītu-ma dannat*, see BSOAS 34, 515[68]); these are the cases where a translation "valid" is tempting, and it is a usage which goes back in time at least as far as the Geneva tablet which has "Like (or: Instead of) the old "strong tablet" this tablet is "strong" " (*kīma ṭuppi dannati labirti annītu ṭuppu dannat*, JNES 16, 164 165 ll. 35–37).

The formalities which preceded the writing of a "strong tablet" were partly actions (like the field-survey) and partly in writing. Among the contents of a storeroom belonging to Urad-Šerua at Aššur we read of "1 box of herald's proclamations for houses in the Inner City", and "1 box of the clearance(s) of persons and fields of the town of Šarika" (*1 quppu tazkīte ša* ÉRIN.MEŠ *ū* A.ŠÀ. MEŠ . . . , KAJ 310 : 19–20 and 11–12). The need for a "clearance" is mentioned by the land-sale documents mentioned above, and both clearances and herald's proclamations are referred to by the Middle Assyrian Laws, Tablet B § 6: this paragraph is too long to quote in full, but it prescribes that a proposed sale should be preceded by three successive proclamations by a herald, and it refers to tablets (*ṭuppāte*) which claimants should bring before the authorities to substantiate any claims they might have on the property being sold (ll. 16, 22), and to three tablets recording the herald's proclamations (l. 48).

We appear not to have any examples of actual clearance-tablets or herald's proclam tions, and indeed with only one possible exception, mentioned below, the only land-sale documents we possess are "interim" texts. We can only speculate, therefore, as to how a real *ṭuppu dannutu* might have looked. The Geneva tablet has an envelope, and both were sealed by the seller and the witnesses. On the other hand, the earliest attested Neo-Assyrian conveyances, called *dannutu*, had no envelope and were sealed by the seller only, at the top of the obverse. In the 1st millennium I have grouped transactions like slave sale, marriage, adoption etc., with real estate sales under the heading "conveyances" because they are similarly formulated and share a similar external format. However, in Middle Assyrian times such documents concerned with the transfer of title to persons do not seem to have required a "strong tablet", and their formulation and external format cannot be taken as typical of a *ṭuppu dannutu*. This is not surprising, since there is no reason to suppose that they required the same formalities. The only possible candidate for an actual "strong tablet" remains BM 123367, which resembles contemporary library tablets in appearance, is sealed, but does not look as though it can ever have had an envelope. It is particularly unfortunate that only the witnesses and date survive.[16]

Reverting now to the meaning of *dannu* in this phrase, we can reach only negative conclusions. If it indeed had the nuance "valid", this cannot have been its entire meaning, since most legal documents were presumably valid in their own way. Perhaps a more satisfactory translation would be "validated"; this would reflect a process of validation which would be called *dannunu* "to strengthen". No such usage is attested in Middle Assyrian, but *ṭuppam dannunum* is known (with and without *šībī* "witnesses") in Old Assyrian texts.[17] According to Larsen,[18] this can refer to the corroboration of the previous testimony of witnesses by means of an oath; but the evidence seems unclear, and we can only suggest diffidently that an Old Assyrian practice of validating documents officially survived into Middle Assyrian times in the context of real estate sale. In any case, one must assume that *dannu* did not of itself imply that the necessary preliminaries for the final document had been followed, since then the phrase *annītu-ma dannat* would involve too glaring a contradiction in terms.

§ 2.3 *ṭuppu ṣabittu* and *ṭuppa ṣabātu* Much new material for this usage has been made available by the publication of VS 19 and 21, and previous treatments need to be overhauled. AHw 1072a translated *ṣabtu* simply as 'genommen, gefangen', and for *ṣabātu* gives '(an sich) nehmen' (1067b III. 3a), which is understandable within the constrictions of a dictionary, but not satisfactory as a meaningful translation. CAD Ṣ offers "to take into safekeeping" for *ṣabātu* (18b) and "deposited" (45a–b). In the only longer discussion in recent years, K. Deller and C. Saporetti essentially accept the position of CAD and say of a *ṭuppu ṣabittu* "Si tratta di un documento consegnato a terzi per scopi che possono variare" (Oriens Antiquus 9 [1970], 306). All authorities therefore have retained the underlying notion of *ṣabātu* implying that the tablet enters someone's possession; I hope to show below that this is untenable, and I shall preempt my conclusions by translating *ṣabātu* as "to execute (a document officially)".

The "executed tablet" (*ṭuppu ṣabittu*) is found most often in phrases like that in VS 19 No. 8, where Urad-ilani acknowledges receipt of some of a total of

16 The text was published by A. R. Millard, in: Iraq 32 [1970], 173 and Pl. XXXVI, with a photograph and edition by the present writer in: Iraq 35 [1973], 16–18 and Plate XV a–b.

17 CAD Vol. 3 (D), 85b.

18 See Gibson – Biggs, Seals and Sealing 98 with note 52; but it should be said that the passages discussed by P. Garelli, in: RA 58 [1964], 128, relate to *šībī dannunum* but not *ṭuppam dannunum*.

"2 homers plus interest, in accordance with an executed tablet" (*ša pī ṭuppi ṣabitte*; for another example cf. KAJ 122 : 5; several instances from Tell al-Rimah are listed by Deller and Saporetti, loc. cit.). Now this same phrase recurs several times in the big accounts tablet VS 19 No. 1, in parallelism with its opposite: e. g. "85.45 homers, Ekur-reṣussu, in accordance with his executed tablet; 33.4 homers, Ekur-reṣussu–his tablet is not executed" (*ṭuppu-šu la ṣa-ab-ta-at*; l.7′–9′). The same opposition is repeated in the following sections of the tablet, with the curious hybrid solecism *ša pī ṭuppu-šu la ṣabtat*! Other relevant passages include KAJ 104 : 7 – 10 *ṭuppa ṣa-bi-ta iddan ṭuppa-šu iḫappi* "he shall hand over the executed tablet and may (then) break his (other, sc. un-executed) tablet"; TR 100 : 9 *ina ṭuppāte ṣa-ab-ta-*[*te*] *ša muḫḫi abi-šu ukarrû* "They shall deduct it from the executed tablets recording his father's debts"; and VS 19 No. 51 : rev. 12′–13′ *ina ṭuppi ši na*? (or: *ši-it*?) *ṣa-bi-ti ša muḫḫi-šina ú-kar*!*-r*[*u*?] "They shall deduct it from their(?) executed tablet (or: that tablet) recording their debts". These and other passages show that *ṭuppa ṣabātu* was not an occasional arbitrary act of seizure, but a well-recognized procedure which resulted in a particular kind of document, in most cases at least a "contract" tablet recording a debt.

It could of course be argued that the legal procedures of the time did indeed include the seizure of tablets as a regular event, but an examination of the passages for *ṭuppa ṣabātu* makes this unlikely. In VS 21 No. 20 : 19–20 we read "They shall bring the tablet of the corn which he took, they shall examine it, and execute his tablet" (*ṭuppa ša še'i ša iššianni ubbulūni ēmmuru, ṭuppu-šu i-ṣa-ab-bu-tu*). If we translate "execute" this passage makes good sense: having consulted the original document which specified his liability, they are able to establish the amount of his obligation remaining, and can then draw up a new "executed tablet" placing that amount on record; the details which follow in ll. 21 ff. are aimed at supplying the information needed for that purpose. In contrast, translating "they shall seize his tablet" makes no sense: the original contract tablet was in their possession already, so that they would have had no need to seize it; and in any case the tablet they are to "seize" is a different one, since the second *ṭuppu-šu* would otherwise be superfluous. While if they were meant to seize some other tablet of his, surely, some explanation of its identity would be required. A still clearer instance is afforded by KAJ 83 : 14–20: "He shall give the corn to Lulayu, and he shall execute a tablet of Lulayu. In the wording of the tablet he shall put as follows: to measure out the capital of the corn at the threshing-floors . . ." (*še'a ana L. iddan ū ṭuppa ša L. i-ṣa-ba-ta ina pī ṭuppi akia išakkan qaqqad še'i ina adrāte ana madādi*). The background to this is clear: the 'debtor' in this contract (Ištar-kidinni) has undertaken to deliver some corn to a third party called Lulayu. It is a loan, and on delivery of the corn another contract has to be made out transferring the debt to Lulayu, and Ištar-kidinni is charged with doing this, and is expected to include in the contract the correct repayment clause. There can be no question of his "seizing" any tablet already held by Lulayu, since he is to include the repayment clause in it and additions cannot be made to old, dry cuneiform tablets; and in any case, Lulayu would hardly have sealed a loan-contract before receiving the corn. Of course, it might be argued that the new tablet has to be taken back to the original creditor, Aššur-aha-iddina, and that Ištar-kidinni would "take" it in that sense, but this would usually be *ubālu*, and in that case this usage of *ṣabātu* could have no connection with the regular procedure from which the *ṭuppu ṣabittu* must derive.

The better solution is certainly to see *ṭuppa ṣabātu* as the formal procedure of preparing a contract tablet of this kind: it cannot be merely the 'writing' of the tablet, both because we regularly meet the verb *šaṭāru* in the same kinds of text, and because the *ṭuppu ṣabittu* constitutes a special category of document. Some of the same considerations must have influenced CAD's rendering of "deposit(ed)", but it is less satisfactory because there is no evidence from other sources of such a procedure, nor any obvious legal reason or cuneiform parallel for it. We conclude, therefore, that Middle Assyrian contracts could either be ordinary tablets, or specially "executed" ones. What then were the extra formalities entailed by executing a tablet? No certain answer can be offered to this as yet, but there is a striking, and probably not coincidental, similarity to the use of *ḫarāmum* in Old Assyrian, with its cognate *ṭuppum harmum*. Larsen wrote that the verb was not really used for the technical act of placing the tablet in its envelope, but "refers to the legal aspect of validation or certification" (Larsen in: Gibson–Biggs, Seals and sealing, 96). He adds that "... the most obvious difference between such texts" [e. g. sealed letters] "and those which could be referred to as tuppum harmum is that the latter were witnessed, and I suggest that this is the essential aspect of the certification of a tablet which made it a tuppum harmum". The same could be said for Middle Assyrian by simply substituting *ṣabittu* for *ḫarmum*: we have seen that neither sealing nor the application of an envelope can be relevant to this distinction, whereas the existence of plenty of legal and especially administrative tablets recording an obligation which are not witnessed, makes it probable that it was formalities involving the witnesses which constituted the "execution" of a tablet.

It remains unclear whether *ṣabātu* here means "to execute" or "to have executed". In KAJ 83, quoted above, it is the 'creditor', that is the person in whose favour the document is written, who "executes" it. The same is true of the Middle Assyrian Laws, B § 17, where a man has to "execute a tablet of the judges" (*ṭuppa ša* LÚ.DI.KUD.MEŠ *i-ṣa-bat*) "and then do his work" (ll. 14–15). However, in Neo-Assyrian texts the same usage of *ṣabātu* must survive in the epithet of the scribe "executor of the tablet "(*ṣābit danniti/egirti/kanīki/ṭuppi*); this cannot mean „Urkundenhalter, Notar" (AHw 1067b), but is the equivalent of the Neo-Babylonian *šāṭir ṭuppi/u'ilti* "writer of the tablet".[19]

[19] See already J. N. Postgate, in: Iraq 32 [1970], 147, for a justification of this position which assumes the continuity of usage from Middle to Neo-Assyrian times. The issue is complicated, however, by the question of the contemporary Middle Babylonian usage. Here the word for a sealed tablet is written NA_4.KIŠIB and construed as a plural (e. g. NA_4.KIŠIB-*šu iḫḫeppû* "his sealed document shall be broken", O. R. Gurney, The Middle Babylonian Legal and Economic Texts from Ur, British School of Archaeology in Iraq 1983, No. 75 rev. 9–10). Where NA_4.KIŠIB is used with *ṣabātu* Gurney writes "A private document was sealed by one party and given to the other, who was then said to have "seized" it ... For official documents, however, the recipient would have been the public registry. Thus in J. A. Brinkman, Materials and Studies for Kassite History (MSKHL), I, Chicago 1976, no. 8, no. 24, and probably no. 10 the phrase comes to mean "the document was taken into safekeeping" ..." (op. cit., p. 27 on

To sum up, *ṭuppa ṣabātu* describes a formal procedure by which a creditor (etc.) initiates, and a scribe carries out, the drawing up of a sealed and witnessed "contract" known as a *ṭuppu ṣabittu*. Like the contract tablet+envelope of Neo-Assyrian times, these documents provided the creditor with proof of loans or other obligations of a wide variety of kinds; but in contrast, there were also current in Middle Assyrian times informal tablets of similar content, most easily recognized by the absence of witnesses.

§ 2.4 *kanīku* (plur. *kanīkāte*) Not frequent in Middle Assyrian; indeed I know only the two examples:

1. *lubulta ammar ušēlûni ka-ni-ka-te šuṭrā ana libbi tupnināte ṣil'ā* "Write sealed (-tablets) (of) all the garments they get up, and put them in the chests" (KAV 98 : 23). The garments are being taken away, so it must be the *kanīkāte* that are to be put into the chests instead.
2. É *ka-ni-ka-a-te*^meš^ *ša* NÍG.ŠID.MEŠ *ša* LÚ.BAPPIR.MEŠ . . . "sealed(-tablet) container of the accounts of the brewers . . " (KAH II 64 : 1).

For etymological reasons there is an ***a priori*** assumption that a *kanīku* was a sealed document, which must be accepted without proof to the contrary. As it happens, these two examples refer to documents of internal administration from a private (1.) or public (2.) establishment. The sealing would not have been seen as a validation, or an acknowledgement of material liability for the goods in question, but rather as a means of identification and a sign of authentication. Two texts is not enough to establish a 'rule', but it may not be coincidental that the probably administrative text CTN 2, 100, dating to 835 B. C., should be referred to as a *kanīku*.

§ 2.5 *kiṣirtu* (plur. *kiṣrāte*) This is one of our most obscure terms, and it is scarce enough to justify quoting all the pertinent Middle Assyrian passages.

1. KAJ 241 (discussed above, § 1.2, no. 2.). The word *kiṣirtu* appears on the envelope only, prefixed to an abbreviated version of the main text. In BT 124 from the 7th century the envelope also has the word *kiṣirtu* prefixed to the text of the tablet proper.[20]
2. VS 19 No. 49 : 1–7: "[From] day X the accounts of Ezbu-lešir, the offerings-supervisor, – [ ] homers 2 *qa* corn from the gifts of the inhabitants of Aššur, according to the *kiṣirtu* with the seal(-impression) of Aššur-kitti-šeṣi, the provincial governor–have been settled (*ṣabtū*)".[21]
3. VS 19 No. 43 : 7: *ša pi-i ki-ṣir-te*, in a context too fragmentary to help much; an administrative text from the archive of Samnuha-ašared (Ass. 13058).[22]
4. KAJ 310 : 27: "1 box of *kiṣirtus* (*ki-iṣ-r*[*a*]-*te*) of Riš-Adad". An entry included in the total of "24 boxes of tablets (*ṭuppāte*)", ibid. 38.

No. 2 rev. 17). I can detect no reason in the attested Middle Babylonian examples why the Babylonian *kunukkī*(?) *ṣabātu* should differ in meaning from the Assyrian *ṭuppa ṣabātu*; as to the origin of the phrases, one might hypothesize an earlier usage with a second object now omitted, e. g. *ṭuppa kunukkī ṣabātu* "to grasp the tablet with seals" or perhaps *ṭuppa mamīta ṣabātu* "to swear the tablet"; but these are purest speculation.

20 See FNALD 117–122.

21 See further below, § 4.2.

22 For this, and other Middle Assyrian Assur archives, see the writer's contribution to the proceedings of the XXXe Rencontre Assyriologique Internationale (Leiden 1983) "Administrative archives from the city of Assur in the Middle Assyrian period" (forthcoming).

5. KAJ 311:15–16: "A total of 8 male and 3 female donkeys, according to 6 *kiṣirtus* (*ša* KA-*i 6 ki-iṣ-ra-te*) of Siqiya". An administrative document from the Ass. 14327 archive (13th century).

In their Assyrische Rechtsurkunden (ARU) 67 (=Zeitschrift für Rechtsvergleichende Wissenschaft 44 [1929], 371), E. Ebeling and M. David translated *kiṣirtu* without comment as „Hülle". This deduction from KAJ 241 is unexpectedly supported by the Balawat text of more than 500 years later, especially when one remembers that KAJ 241 is a receipt, whereas the later document is a delivery contract, so that their having an envelope is one of the few points of similarity. I have espoused the rendering "envelope" myself more than once, and still do so, but whether or not it be accepted, the examples quoted show that the *kiṣirtu* was a well-defined type of document which could be usefully distinguished by its contents as well as by its external appearance. This is not surprising, since the form and function of documents are often related, and if they were all envelopes (tablet + envelopes), § 1.2 above implies that they must have been administrative receipts. This is in fact entirely compatible with the available evidence, though proof is lacking.

kiṣirtu is obviously a derivative of *kaṣāru* "to knot", with the nuance of "bringing together" (e. g. *kiṣru* "a band (of men)"), rather than of "restraining", which belongs rather to *rakāsu* (yielding *riksu* "a bond"). While translating by etymology is a dangerous policy, there are two occurrences of *kaṣāru* in Middle Assyrian texts which are surely relevant (VS 19 No. 73 and A. 113 in V. Donbaz, Ninurta-tukulti-Aššur [=AfO 10, No. 95), see Bi.Or. 37 [1980], 68[1]). The two passages are parallel, in that the phrase "PN has knotted" (*iktaṣar*) comes at the end of the main section of each text, and the person in question is not one of the principals in the transaction (i. e. the recipient, Ezbu-lešir, in VS 19 No. 73, and the stock-fattener Mutta in A. 113, under whose authority the sheep "were consumed" (*i-na* ŠU [1]*m*[*u-ut-t*]*a* [*i*]*t-ta-ku-lu*, 23–24)), but holds a higher position in the hierarchy. We cannot here go into the detailed backgrounds of the two texts as shown by their respective archives, but whether or not *kaṣāru* is to be understood literally as "to apply the envelope", it seems probable that it implies some form of authentication or "endorsement" by a superior official. If so, it might fairly be compared with Ur III practice, where an official "at whose feet" (gìr) a transaction took place may also have had a similar function.[23]

§ 2.6 *lē'u* (plur. *lē'āni*), "a board". This is well-known in Neo-Assyrian and Neo-Babylonian contexts as a waxed tablet on which long cuneiform texts such as literary series or administrative lists might be written. Without doubt the use of waxed boards explains why there are no vast, many-columned cuneiform tablets from the royal palaces of Nimrud or Kouyunjik, compared with their existence in the Mari or Ebla archives. Actual examples of such boards have been found at Aššur and Nimrud, of 1st millennium date;[24] Frau U. Seidl points out to me that a hinged writing-board was already widely enough used in Babylonia

[23] A general meaning of this kind for gìr seems more probable to me than a specific connection with transport, despite the support for the latter theory from Larsen and Steinkeller (see P. Steinkeller, in: Gibson–Biggs, Seals and Sealing. 42 with note 12).

[24] See H. Hunger, Holztafel, in: Reallexikon der Assyriologie IV, 458f.; E. Klengel-Brandt, in: AoF III [1975], 169–171.

in the 12th century to feature on *kudurrus* as a symbol of Nabu.[25] There is therefore no reason to doubt that *lē'u* in our Middle Assyrian texts means a writing board, except that the word never has the GIŠ determinative in this meaning: we find GIŠ *le-a-ni ša erīni* (VS 21 No. 17 : 24) or GIŠ *le-a-ni ana igārāte* (ibid. 100) but these are clearly wooden boards for architectural purposes, and nothing to do with writing. The same slight doubt attaches to the examples of *lē'um* in Old Babylonian and even earlier texts (see CAD L 157a for references): without the GIŠ in front, we cannot be certain that *lē'um* does not refer to a particularly large type of clay tablet. No such doubts persist in the Boğazköy texts, where the problem is rather whether they were used for cuneiform or hieroglyphic script,[26] nor in the Middle Babylonian passages quoted by CAD, ibid,, where the GIŠ is regularly present. Despite the curious avoidance of GIŠ in the Middle Assyrian texts, therefore, it seems that *lē'u* was indeed a writing "board", and very likely hinged. Certainly, the mention of a sealed board in MDP 10, Pl. 11.I.17, suggests that it was possible to close them up for the protection of the contents, probably with a clay sealing on string.[27]

Wood or clay, the *lē'u* was an important cog in the administrative machine; there is no evidence in Assyria that it was used for legal documents (unlike Babylonia), although this cannot be excluded.[28] In the absence of any actual writing-boards, to define the character and purpose of the *lē'u* we have to consider the references to it in the clay tablets we do have.

KAJ 260 is a simple note, apparently unsealed, reporting that PN "has received (*imtaḫar*) 1.6 homers of corn: they have looked in the earlier and the later *lē'u* of corn received" (*ina*? *le-e ša* ŠE *maḫri pa*!*-ni*!*-e ū urki'e ēmuru*; emendation after CAD M/II, p. 33b). Evidently a simple matter of checking records of past issues to see how much the man had received; it is likely that the boards in question had long cumulative lists of issues to different persons (hence the need for a search), but this cannot be proved. Corn issues are also the subject of two texts from the Ass. 14327 archive concerned with rations for deported populations in the north, KAJ 109 and 113. The chain of administrative responsibility in these texts is too complex to discuss in this context, and has been studied before;[29] what concerns us here is that the original record of the issue of corn to the deportees was written on 13 writing-boards (KAJ 109) or 5 boards (in KAJ 113); large amounts are involved, and since these were rations, no debt was being incurred by the recipients. It would therefore have been senseless to prepare a separate sealed receipt tablet for each man, and the responsible official, Melisah

25 MDP 7.146ff. and BBSt. No. XVI Pl. LXXXII = U. Seidl, in: Baghdader Mitteilungen 4 [1968], Nos. 40 and 43 respectively.

26 For *lē'u* and *uṣurtu* in the Hittite sources, J. D. Hawkins refers me to I. Singer, The Hittite KI.LAM Festival, I (StBoT 27), 27, I, 40 with earlier literature. For the Old Assyrian period cf. also M. T. Larsen, in: Gibson – Biggs, Seals and sealing 96 on *iṣurtum*.

27 For actual clay sealings which might have been attached to wooden boards in the Neo-Assyrian period, cf. S. M. Dalley – J. N. Postgate, The tablets from Fort Shalmaneser, British School of Archaeology in Iraq 1984 (CTN III), 74f.

28 For Babylonian instances of *lē'u* in legal contexts see passages in *kudurrus* with the phrase *ina kanāk lē'u šuātu* and others, CAD L 157.

29 E. g. C. Saporetti, Una deportazione al tempo di Salmanassar I, in: Rendiconti della Classe di Scienze morali, storiche e filologiche, Ser. VIII, Vol. 25 (1970), 437–453.

or his son, would have been expected to account for the corn he had disbursed by supplying the list of disbursements. Such a document would resemble the envelope-receipts discussed above (§§ 1.2; 2.5); we have no way of knowing whether or not it was sealed, but the use of several writing-boards in each case presumably reflects the large number of separate disbursements which had to be recorded.

Let us see whether other instances of the use of boards are comparable. VS 21 No. 19 is an account of sheep-skins over a period of two years "in accordance with the writing-boards of offerings of the stock-fattener which he received on various occasions" (*ša pî le-a-ni ša* SISKUR.MEŠ *ša ša kurultie ša imtaḫḫurūni* rev. 11′–12′). Here the list is compiled from more than one writing-board kept by the official responsible for the sheep and added to as new details became available (note Gtn form). Sheep are also involved in KAJ 120 from the Ass. 14327 archive: "After his accounts had been settled and everything had been deducted or added to the accounts in accordance with his writing-board . . ." (*lū* [*ša p*]*î le-'i-šu ana nikkassē šaknūni*). Again, the board serves as a source of details for the compilation of administrative book-keeping, but the nature of the list is not known. Perhaps the entries in the board were those where a disposition was simply recorded unilaterally by the shepherd, without any reciprocal acknowledgement from a receiving quarter. This passage therefore fits into the same pattern: boards were used by officials to compile long lists of issues or receipts of goods of various kinds, and there is no evidence to say if they were sealed or endorsed in any other way. One reason for using the boards would obviously have been their size; but it is also possible that the wax remained soft for a much longer time than a clay tablet, so that entries could be made over a span of days or even weeks.

The other instances of writing-boards all concern lists of persons. One interesting entry comes in the *šulmānu*-text KAJ 91 (also from Ass. 14327). Here two brothers have made a gift to Erib-Aššur "so as to assign (lit.: pour) them to the writing-board of Lab'u" ([*aš*]*šum ana lē'i ša Lab'i tabāku-šunu* 16–18). While we are ignorant of the administrative positions of Erib-Aššur and Lab'u, there can be little doubt in the light of other passages that 'being on Lab'u's board' implies being under his ultimate command for military, or at least state, service. Thus in VS 21 No. 17 : 11 we read of more than 2,000 "men of the king's writing-board" (ÉRIN.MEŠ *ša le-e ša šarri*; cf. also VS 21 No. 10 : 5′). Elsewhere in the same large tablet we have 371 men called ÉRIN.MEŠ UD-*ru-te ša le-e ša šarri* (l. 2) and 560 ÉRIN.MEŠ UD-*ru-te ša le-e ša Adad-šam*[*ši*] (l. 34) and 1,604 ÉRIN.MEŠ *ša le-e ša Adad-šamši* (l. 46).[30] Some at least of these men are receiving corn rations for doing state work at Aššur (. . . *šipra ina* É.GAL-*lim eššite ša* [uru]*lìb-bi* URU . . . *ēpušūni*, ll. 47–48). In ll. 63–64 of the same text men of the writing-board of Šamaš-apla-uṣur are probably involved in work at Kar-Tukulti-Ninurta (l.66). Although the word *lē'u* is broken here, the restoration may be considered certain, because the same man occurs side by side with the king and Adad-šamši in at least two other places. In VS 19 No. 9 : 22–27 sesame issues are put

[30] For these passages see H. Freydank AoF 4 [1976], 115–118; I remain uncertain whether the adjective in use here was in fact *perru*, as proposed by Dr. Freydank, or *utru* "additional".

down to the "writing-boards" of Lulayu, Sin-ašared, Šamaš-apla-uṣur and Adad-šamši; the entire account is described as ". . . of the army which was imposed on Zamban-on-Diyala" (35–37).[31] A military connection is also implied by VS 19 No. 1.iv.27–35: this is one section of a big list of corn issued by the palace at Kar-Tukulti-Ninurta, and in place of the details of the destination of each amount given in other sections, we simply read: "162.4 homers of corn–board of the king; 70 homers–board of Lulayu; 105 homers–board of Sin-ašared; 105 homers–board of Šamaš-apla-uṣur; 105 homers–board of Adad-šamši". Clearly the single asyntactic statement "board of PN" conveys sufficient information to replace the details given in the other sections, but further explanation is offered after the total: "Total 447.4 homers of corn, to the herald for the writing-boards, received to give out to the inspected (?:or "starving", with H. Freydank?) men under their command who came for the army (going) to Karduniaš and were reviewed in the Inner City" (. . . ŠE *ana nāgiri ša le'āni ana* ÉRIN.MEŠ *ša qāti-šunu bari'ūte ša ana ḫurādi ša Karduniaš illikunini ina* [uru]*libbi-āli ašrūni ana tadāni maḫru*). While I have to confess that I am not sure of the exact sense of this passage, it is clear that the king and some high state officials (perhaps only these four) had separate corps of men under their command, whose names were presumably recorded on these writing-boards. The need for a board, not a tablet, is evident when one notes that the king's board included at least 2,000 men (see l. 11), and Adad-šamši's at least 1,604 (see l. 46: not all his men). Confirmation of the military context, and extra detail of the composition of the different corps, can be found in VS 19 No. 5: here a motley assemblage of officials (chief bird-catcher, chief Šuprian dragoman, chief diviner, etc.) is summed up as "officials of the men who have a mark" (GAL.MEŠ ÉRIN.MEŠ *ša simta šaknūni* [*simta* for *šimta*, AHw 1238b, 4a]). A smaller group are called "officials of the men who do not have a mark" (l. 29), and the tablet then concludes "Writing-board of Adad-šamši".

No doubt Dr. Freydank's work on the administrative documents from Kar-Tukulti-Ninurta will throw more light on this side of the organization of the Middle Assyrian army, and it would be premature to pursue the subject further here. For the present we need only observe that these lists of soldiers (or potential soldiers) served more than one purpose: as well as the essential record of persons under each command, they were used to supply the same information for the benefit of those responsible for the issue of rations to them. It would not be surprising if they existed in more than one copy. KAJ 245, not from Kar-Tukulti-Ninurta like VS 19 Nos. 1, 5 and 9, but from Ass. 14327, reflects the same system, but the names of the high officials are different, and among the persons "returned to their *tartennu*" are some women. It would be advisable therefore to consider the boards as listing persons assigned to each corps for "state service" rather than always service in the army, but either way it is clear that the bribe that is record-

[31] [ ]x-*tu ša ḫurādi* [*ša i-n*]*a* KUR *zamban aḫ Turan ēmidanni* (cf. H. Freydank, AoF I [1974], 80f.; I would propose restoring [*pi-š*]*èr-tu* in l. 35 (cf. VS 21 No. 23: 1, 5, 9 etc. *pišerti karu'ē*, although this is a slightly different usage connected with *karu'ē pašāru*, a difficult term on which see provisionally my review of VS 21 forthcoming in Orientalia).

ed in KAJ 91 was concerned to influence under whose command the two brothers would have to serve.

§ 2.7 *našpertu* This term is included principally because it was much used in Old Assyrian texts, both as a general word for a written letter or message, and as a type of legally binding document, when it was of course sealed (see the very full treatment in CAD N/II, 71–75, and discussion by Larsen, in: Gibson–Biggs, Seals and Sealing 97). Where commercial relations between merchants and their agents are concerned, the need for a secondary form of legal instrument with legally dispositive force is obvious, and such a type of document would presumably have been needed in Middle Assyrian times as well. The only occasions on which a *našpertu* is mentioned are in fact in an administrative context. Two "message-tablets" occur in the Tell Billa texts: in no. 13 a corn debt owed to Aššur-šadu-nišešu is paid to someone else "in accordance with the message-tablet of A. himself" (*ana pî ṭuppi našpi[rte] ša A.-ma*). Hubarzi in Billa no. 26 takes some corn and three yokes from the governor Sin-apla-ereš; he is acting on the instructions (*ši-p[i-ir-ti*, l. 4; see below § 3.3) of the herdsman, and the text concludes "[He shall give(?) a] message(-tablet), and then [may break] his tablet" (*na-áš-pi-ir-t[a iddan*(?)] *ù ṭup-pu-š[u iḫappi*(?)]). In other words, he needs to get a written authority from the herdsman, and once this has been delivered to the governor he, Hubarzi, will have fulfilled his role in the transaction. Two other Middle Assyrian contexts for *našpirtu* are known: in VS 19 No. 72 2,000 javelins are issued at the royal command, "in accordance with a message of Samnuha-ašared, the steward" (*ana pî na-áš-pír-te ša S.* AGRIG). The same phrase recurs in VS 19 No. 43 : 12, but in a context which is too fragmentary to contribute extra information.

As in Old Assyrian times, it is probable that some of these message-tablets were sealed. Indeed, as we have seen in § 1.2 above, letters were sometimes sealed, and some had envelopes as well. VS 19 No. 39, sealed on both faces but with no surviving envelope, is a particularly strong candidate to be considered as a *našpertu*, since it is also dated on the reverse in the manner of an administrative tablet.

§ 3 *The transmisson of authority*

§ 3.1 Public, private and the concept of responsibility

The examples of *našpertu* just mentioned exemplify the degree to which Middle Assyrian government was run along commercial lines, with administrative responsibilities being formulated according to patterns created for the regulation of private commerce. The business ethos, which had a long, healthy life already at Aššur, extended through all levels of government, and even the high offices of state and the provincial governorships were delegated to "houses".[32] It is not

[32] Cf. J. N. Postgate, in: M. T. Larsen(ed.), Power and Propaganda: A symposium on ancient empires, Copenhagen 1979 (Mesopotamia 7), 202; the comments on this passage by P. Machinist in: Assur 3/2 [1982], 32, appear to me to rest on a slight misunderstanding of my position, which I shall hope to rectify in the introduction to my edition of Ass. 14327.

difficult to offer an explanation for this: the royal house in Old Assyrian days had been but one among other family businesses, and these business houses had already established procedures for entrusting agents or subordinates with tasks involving commercial liability. In response to a sudden need for an administrative hierarchy capable of communicating decisions across a greatly enlarged Middle Assyrian kingdom, it was a natural step to adapt the commercial structure of the society of Aššur to the task of government. This, surely, is the origin of the elaborate system of written debt-notes and similar recorded obligations, which, although in legal guise, manifestly belong in our terms within the public sector.

It is at times difficult to know whether a particular document belongs to a public or a private transaction. The Ass. 14327 archive of Aššur-aha-iddina's family, for instance, contains both "private" and "public" documents, and we are entitled to wonder whether there was a clear demarcation between the two. Often we are forced to make a decision on this point by an intuitive assessment of the background as reflected by the document itself, and it is particularly hard to know whether a man's public obligations were technically distinguished in any way from his private debts.[33] Nevertheless, the distinction between the public and private sector did exist, and was formally recognized: at least two useful indicators that a transaction was "public"were described over 50 years ago by P. Koschaker.[34] First, the absence of witnesses is a clear indication that a contract is not a legally binding document (as we have seen, in other words, not a *ṭuppu ṣabittu*), and in general one would expect such a document to belong outside the world of commerce, in a context where other prior and subsequent relationships made the formality of a witness and document unnecessary. Secondly, we have the phrase *ša qāt*, often found in place of the simple *ša* "belonging to" which introduces the creditor in a regular private contract. Meaning literally "of the hand of" this refers in our texts, as elsewhere, to things which are under the administrative charge of someone; the phrase introduces not the owner, but the administrator of the items in question.

If asked to translate "public sector" into Assyrian, one's correct answer could presumably only be *ēkallu*, and some documents do indeed specify "the palace" as the creditor, as the owner of the goods owed. KAJ 121 records corn "belonging to the palace, in the charge of PN, the governor of Taidi" (*ša* É.GAL-*l*[*im*] *ša* ŠU PN).[35] Another phrase encountered in the Ass. 14327 texts is less easy to translate, but seems to mean "of the administrative-sphere of the granary" (*ša pitti ḫāšimi*: KAJ 101 : 5 *ša pi-it hašime*; VS 19 No. 47 : 2, 7, 11 *ša pi-*(*it-*)*te*/*i hašeme*, and 31 *ša pit hašeme*). This phrase was already discussed by Koschaker,[36]

[33] This uncertainty is exemplified by the mixture of private and public contract tablets and other, unsealed, administrative tablets within the Aššur-aha-iddina archives (Ass. 14327).

[34] P. Koschaker, Neue keilschriftliche Rechtsurkunden aus der El-Amarna-Zeit (NKRA), Leipzig 1928, 142, with footnote 3.

[35] For the correct interpretation of *ša ēkalli* in this context as indicating the owner of the commodity, not of the corn-measure, see C. Saporetti – K. Deller, in: Oriens Antiquus 9 [1970], 29 f.

[36] NKRA 114[1].

and the approximate meaning "sphere of administration" still seems correct, both in this particular phrase and in the other passages which refer to an individual's (even the king's) ‚Verantwortungsbereich' (AHw 870b; VS 19 No. 1.i.22′, 32′, etc; iv.6, 16, 23; No. 18 : 1; VS 21 No. 9 : 4′; No. 17 : 95).

§ 3.2 Oral authorization

The distinction between *ša* and *ša qāt*, and the word *pittu* itself are sufficient indication that the concept of a public sector was not entirely absent. This is at least *de facto* a recognition that the requirements of public administration differed from those of the commercial world, and hence it is not too surprising to find that there was still some place, however small, for an oral as well as a written chain of command. Even in the most rigid bureaucracy, from Ur III to Dickensian London and beyond, the desire of the lower officials to protect their future with written authorization from above for the least of their actions does occasionally have to yield to an unwritten instruction from on high. Their administrative records, anxious to assign the responsibility for decisions to their originators, often specify the source of such authorization. *ina abat šarri* "at the king's command" is not infrequent; it may occur in a legal context, with the king as *uklu*, supreme judge,[37] but more frequently it is an administrative order: "... corn which, on the orders of the king, PN_1 with PN_2, the representative of the king, gave to the deportees of Nahur" (KAJ 113 : 21–27). The representative, *qēpu*, is the high official who brought the order, and these representatives often figure in the administrative transactions, no doubt regularly bringing oral messages of this kind from the king. Except for Ninurta-tukulti-Aššur, who was effectively king at the time, few others are mentioned as having issued commands in this way, and where they are (as in KAJ 293 in particular), we may be fairly sure that they were senior officials, to whom one did not respond "may I have that in writing ...". The information about the orinator of the order is not included to enliven a dull text for the benefit of the modern cuneiformist, but to ensure that the authorization for the disbursement in placed beyond dispute.

Actions taken *ina abat* PN are the response to an oral command from above; there was also a phrase for oral requests from a colleague of equal rank within the administration, and that was *ana šipirti* "(acting) on a message from". While it cannot at present be proved, this seems likely to me to be distinct from the word *našpertu* (see above, § 2.7), which although from the same verbal root was probably always a "written message".[38] Thus in TR 3016 Mušabši-Šadana receives the tin/lead "on the message of Šadana-ašared"; in KAJ 118 it is two retainers of the household of Sikku who take delivery of the straw "on the message of PN, the steward of the household of Sikku"; and in VAT 9005 the 'debtor' takes (*ittiši*–no assumption of liability here!) corn and pig's fat "on the message of

[37] KAV 211.

[38] The translation of *ana šipirti* as "come garanzia?" (so C. Saporetti – K. Deller, Documenti medio-assiri redatti a titolo di ricevuta dietro parziale adempimento di un debito, in: Oriens Antiquus 9 [1970], 298 (TR 3016: 8) with commentary 304f.) does not carry conviction, nor the connection with *šapartu* "pledge" there advocated.

Gelzu".[39] Two Billa texts probably attest the same usage: No. 11 has the governor issuing corn to someone *ana šipirti* PN LÚ.ÌR LUGAL "on the message of PN, the royal servant", and this same phrase is surely to be restored in No. 26, where again we have items "in the charge of" ([*ša*] *qāt*) the governor, taken (*ittiši*) by Hubarzi "on the message of (*a-na ši-p*[*i*!-*ir-ti*]) PN, the herdsman".[40] All these texts look like relatively informal transactions in which one government department issues goods, etc., at the request of another; doubtless the formality of a proper written *našpertu* was not needed because of long-standing interaction between the two departments or officials concerned.[41]

§ 3.3 Written authorization

The complexity of some of the Middle Assyrian administrative documents results from the preference for written rather than oral authorization. Particularly where transactions took place at a distance from one another, a chain of administrative contracts was written, each specifying the action to be taken by one official before his part in the chain was fulfilled, and he might 'break his tablet'. For the duration of his role in the sequence, it seems that each official was liable for the entire amount of the obligation involved; although in fact his administrative duty was no more than the transmission of a documentary obligation to the eventual 'debtor'. In these circumstances, it was obviously essential that the nature and the origin of particular administrative obligations were carefully defined. Except in the rare cases of an oral command, the source of the obligation was another document, and we shall turn now to look at the terminology in use for this situation.

Rather unexpectedly, the word *pû* (still sometimes *pā'u*), literally "mouth" is used in our texts solely in the context of written documents. Often the most convenient translation in English is "wording" (cf. AHw 873b: Wortlaut). Where some clause is to be included in a document, the regular phrase is *ina pî ṭuppi* + *šakānu*: "he shall execute a tablet, and in the wording of the tablet he shall put as follows ..." (*ina pî ṭuppi akī'a išakkan* KAJ 83 : 15–18). In legal texts we have 40 GÁN A.ŠÀ *ina pî ṭuppi šiāti kī šaparti šaknūni* "... 40 *ikû* of field is put in the wording of that tablet as a pledge" (KAJ 165 : 10–12; cf. similar passages, KAJ 163 : 2–7, 8–10, 17f.).

The usage of *ana pî* is quite distinct: it refers to actions taken "in accordance with the wording of" a tablet. Thus "he shall clear [the field (?)] within 10 days in accordance with his tablets" (]*ana pî ṭuppāti-šu* [*ad*]*i 10 ūmāti* [. . .] *uzakka* KAJ 157 : 7–9), or "he received 100 homers of corn ... in accordance with a

[39] I am grateful to Dr. L. Jakob-Rost for permission to make use of the unpublished text VAT 9005, which belongs to the Ass. 14327 archive.

[40] For these Billa texts see J. J. Finkelstein, in: JCS 7 [1953], 126 and 129 with copies on 152 and 157.

[41] *šipirtu* is also a term in use in Babylonia at this date: cf. *kī šipirti* PN, which Gurney translates "on the instructions of PN" (O. R. Gurney, The Middle Babylonian Legal and Economic Texts from Ur, p. 71 on No. 19 : 1). He also quotes *kī šipirti šarri* in PBS VIII/2, No. 163 : 3. The circumstances of the first case seem to confirm that the original order was delivered orally, since otherwise one would expect to hear of a written document.

tablet of the king" (*ana pî ṭuppi ša šarri . . . imḫur* KAJ 234 : 6–11). That the phrase refers to the actions mentioned in the tablet, not (as with *ša pî* to which we shall come shortly) to the items, emerges clearly from KAJ 6, where "in accordance with the tablet of his father Ereš-ili... Nakidu is son, Keniya is his father, (and) he will respect him in town and country . . ." (*a-na pa-i ṭup-pí!-e ša-a a-bi-i-šu-ma* . . .). The structure of KAJ 143 is also instructive in this respect: here the text has "67 homers of corn . . . belonging to PN_1, PN_2 in accordan ce with a tablet (*a-na* KA-*i ṭup-pi*) of PN_3 has received". If the scribe had meant that the corn was specifically mentioned in the tablet (which it may have been), he would have phrased it instead as "67 homers of corn referred to in a tablet of PN_3" (*ša pî ṭuppi ša* PN_3). Finally we may quote VS 21 No. 6 : 88″–91″, where high officials are said to have reviewed the people "in accordance with the executed tablet of the tablet-house" (*ana pî ṭuppi ṣabitte ša bēt ṭuppāte ētašru,* see H. Freydank, in: AoF 7 [1980], 90); the persons were not listed in the 'executed tablet', rather, it must have imposed an obligation to take the action of reviewing the people, and hence the use of *ana pî*.[42]

Little remains to be said about *ša pî*. It too is perhaps best rendered in English as "according to" or "in accordance with", but this must be with the realization that it implies also "mentioned in" or "specified in". Thus in KAJ 122 we have corn and straw "in accordance with, i. e. specified in, an executed tablet of the sons of PN_1, which is written to the debit of PN_2" (*ša pi-i ṭuppi ṣabitte* . . .). The tablet both specifies the amounts in question, and attests the existence of the obligation. Sometimes *ša pî* has no expressed antecedent: *ša pí-i ṭuppi annīte arḫiš leqe'ā* "take what(ever) is mentioned in this tablet quickly" Manchester Cuneiform Studies 2 [1952], Pl.14, 1 : 17 f.), or "what(ever) is mentioned in this tablet PN has received" (*ša pí-i ṭuppi annīti* PN *maḫir* KAJ 165 : 21–22). Equally difficult to translate is the phrase *ṭuppāti šinātīna ū* A.ŠÀ *ša pí-ši-na* "those tablets and the fields mentioned in them" (KAJ 164 : 12–13). Of course, if the document in question was not a tablet, the same phraseology was used, so that corn etc. is referred to as "in accordance with 13 writing-boards" (KAJ 109 : 4; cf. 113 : 32; VS 21 No. 19 : rev. 11′). There is a slightly different nuance when men are referred to as "of the king's writing-board" (ÉRIN.MEŠ *ša lē'i ša šarri*, cf. above, § 2.6).

§ 3.4 Storage and transmission of tablets

One must presume that contract tablets remained in the possession of their 'creditors', and conveyances with the new owners of the property. There is no evidence for the deposit of copies of legal documents with any public authority, although one cannot rule out the possibility that official transcripts of legal judgements were retained by the courts. Occasionally our texts mention the place where a tablet is kept: the deed of manumission of the woman in KAJ 7 is "stored in the house of the same Amurru-naṣir" (*ina bēt Amurru-naṣir-ma šaknat*), and in

[42] Similar to *ana pī*, though not identical, is *kī pī*: *kī pī ṭuppi-ma ša ana šarri ū* DUMU-*šu tam'atāni tam'āta* "you are adjured in accordance with the very tablet by which you were adjured to the king and his son" (G. R. Driver – J. C. Miles, The Assyrian Laws, Oxford 1935, Tablet A, § 47 : 28–31).

one letter Babu-aha-iddina asks his agents to get out "the tablets of the house of PN which are stored in my bedroom" (*ṭuppāte ša bēt* PN *ša ina bēt majāliya šaknā-ni* KAV 102 : 11–16). Storage containers varied. There is a long list of "24 boxes of tablets" (24 *quppātu ša ṭuppāte*) stored in a lumber-room by Urad-Šerua (KAJ 310). The tablets are in separate containers classified by type of transaction or by the individual concerned. Most are in boxes (*quppu*—but this could also be a wicker container), other kinds of container listed are 4 "vats" (*marsattu* a *mišlu* ("half(-vessel)"), and a *tallu*. Some or all of these other containers may have been pottery vessels, and as at Kül Tepe in Old Assyrian times there is archaeological evidence that pots were used for the storage of tablets: a small private archive at Tell al-Rinah had been in a jar, and the archive of Mutta from the reign of Ninurta-tukulti-Aššur came from a single jar.[43] Some, at least, of the Aššur Temple offerings archive had been stored in ten pots, three of which had been labelled; the photograph of one (Ass. 18763) shows that the pot had been inscribed before firing, but unfortunately the text does not say explicitly that it was intended for tablets.[44] It is not stated whether either of the other inscribed jars were similar, or had been inscribed before firing, so that we cannot at present judge whether the four holes in Ass. 18763 were specially intended to aid the storage of tablets. Ass. 18782 (KAH II 64) was labelled "Container of the sealed tablets of the accounts of the brewers . . ." (*bēt kanīkāte ša nikkassē*, see above, § 2.4) Despite this, it is likely that *bēt ṭuppāte* in VS 21 No. 6 : 91" refers to a real "tablet-house", sc. administrative office, although a meaning "container for tablets" cannot be entirely ruled out.

Once in store, tablets did not remain undisturbed. On the contrary, they were continually consulted and passed from hand to hand. They were not infrequently sold, or passed on in connection with a sale. KAJ 172 records the transfer of a claim to a "palace share" (*zitti ēkalli*): "PN_1 has given that tablet with the royal seals, pertaining to that 'palace share' to PN_2, and PN_2 will locate and take (the share) referred to in the tablet". As evidence of the original royal assignation, such a tablet no doubt had especial force:[45] in other cases the tablet itself was not sold, but would have been transferred to the new owner of real estate as evidence of the previous holder's entitlement. Thus in KAJ 132 a sale document has been completed, but the previous title deed is apparently missing; the tablet then states "PN_1 has promised to give the 'strong' tablet to PN_2; if PN_1 does not give that tablet to PN_2, PN_1 will continue to bear the liability of clearing that land" (*pāḫat* A. ŠÀ *šuātu zakku'e* PN_1 *ittanašši*, 16–18). Perhaps possession of the earlier deed would have made the full 'clearing' process unnecessary (although it is stipulated in the law relating to sales[46]), but it clearly was possible to effect

[43] For the Ninurta-tukulti-Aššur archive see my article referred to in footnote 22 above (2. The archive of Mutta); for the group from Tell al-Rimah see D. Oates, in: Iraq 27 (1965], 75.

[44] See most recently my article referred to in note 22, under 1. The archive of Ezbu-lešir.

[45] For the most recent discussion of the *zitti ēkalli* tablets see C. Saporetti, in: Egitto e Vicino Oriente 2 (Pisa, 1979) 151–172 (with additional comment by the writer, in: M. A. Dandamayev et al. (eds.), Studies in honour of I. M. Diakonoff, Warminster 1982, 311).

[46] I. e. Tablet B § 6.

the sale without the earlier document, as we learn from KAJ 149 : 22–25 "The 'strong' tablet of that land, wherever it turns up, is cleared for Kidin-Adad".

Considering the formalities attending the creation of a 'strong' tablet, the loss of one must have been a comparatively rare event. For contract tablets this was apparently not so infrequent: at least, we often meet the statement "(that tablet) wherever it turns up is invalid, it is to be thrown away for breakage".[47] One particularly elaborate example from Tell al-Rimah may be quoted: "One tablet of 4 homers of barley, belonging to Kidin-Aššur, which is written to the debit of Šadana-ašared, and (in which) his houses in Šaidu are placed as pledge for 5 years, is invalid wherever it turns up, and is to be thrown away for breakage" (*ašar teliāni naḫrat ana ḫīpi nadât*, TR 3001).[48] The meaning of this clause is evident, and the function of documents containing it is neatly summed up by Deller and Saporetti's *per annullare un precedente contratto.* The "breaking" of the tablet was a well-known procedure; countless tablets end by saying that when the obligation is fulfilled the 'debtor' "may break his tablet" (*ṭuppu-šu iḫappi*); often the phrase is preceded by *ū*, implying a causal relationship, e. g. *imaddudu ū ṭuppu-šunu iḫappi'u* "they shall measure out (the corn debt) and then (*post hoc et propter hoc*) shall break their tablet" (OIP 79 Pl. 82 No. 5 : 15f, Tell Fakhariyah). This is a private document to do with a dowry; the Rimah text quoted above is also apparently private, and I can see no justification for the assumption of Koschaker that the *ṭuppu-šu iḫappi* clause is restricted to documents from the public sector (NKRA 140). It is more likely that its absence from many private transactions has to do with possible alternative procedures.

In the previous paragraph I wrote that the loss of contract tablets was apparently not so infrequent; the adverb is there because it seems to me unlikely that all the tablets which may "turn up" were really lost. It is true that Deller and Saporetti have restored two broken passages to refer to lost tablets, but neither restoration carries much conviction.[49] They are surely much closer the mark when they envisage the situation in which the debtor wishes to repay some or all of his debt, but the creditor is unable to produce the contract tablet in question because it has gone elsewhere: *perché ceduta ad un altro suo creditore o alla banca.*[50] The background to this is therefore the practice, well-attested in Old Assyrian times too, of trading in debt-notes. A whole group of texts includes the provision "to whoever is bearer of his tablet, he shall pay the lead/tin" *ana nāši ṭuppi-šu annaka ihiāt* (KAJ 22 : 16–17; cf. KAJ 40; 41; etc.). *našā'u* has no very specific connotation with tablets, as can be seen from the letter passage which reads "give (the textiles) to the men who are carrying my tablet" (*ana* LÚ.[MEŠ] *ša ṭup-pi na-ṣu-ú-ni,* KAJ 316 : 12–14). A rather more complex situation is recorded in KAJ 79: here Sin-naṣir, who had in his possession a debt-note for 5.2 homers of corn owed him by two brothers, sells the tablet to a third party,

[47] See Deller – Saporetti, Oriens Antiquus 9, 43–45.

[48] See Deller – Saporetti, Oriens Antiquus 9, 37.

[49] Deller – Saporetti, Oriens Antiquus 9, 31f. (Billa 19 : 7 – *qabā'u* generally means to "call (i. e. name)" or to "promise" in MA legal contexts); 289–290, on TR 102 : 3, but if the restoration *ḫ*[*ul*-]*qi* is correct, it would surely refer to lost *annuku*, not to a lost tablet (cf. also pp. 300f.).

[50] Oriens Antiquus 9 [1970], 49.

Kidin-Adad and his brother. Lines 14–21 then read: "Sin-naṣir has received [what was] mentioned in his tablet; Sin-naṣir bears the liability for calling-in that tablet. Whatever there is or is not (belongs) to Kidin-Adad and Bel-ahhe-šu" (*pāhat tīrubti ša ṭuppi šiāti Sin-naṣir naši; ibašši ū laššu ana Kidin-Adad ū Bel-ahhe-šu-ma*).

§ 3.5 Describing a tablet

When one document needs to make reference to another, there are various ways in which it may describe it:

a) first, of course, it may specify the type of document, that is whether it is a tablet, a board, an envelope etc., according to the terminology discussed already in § 2.

b) then it may mention the type of transaction recorded on it, e. g. *ṭuppi rabīte ša maḫār maḫār* (VS 19 No. 21 : 23; cf. above, p. 15), or *ṭuppu* ... *ša ipṭiri ša* FPN *ša zakā'i-ša* "the tablet ... of the manumission of FPN (and) of her being free from claims" (KAJ 7 : 30–32).

c) the persons involved may be specified. Most frequently a contract tablet is described as "which is written to the debit (lit. upon) of PN", e. g. KAJ 115 : 2–5 "1 tablet of 26 sheep and 1 lamb which is written to the debit of PN" (*ša i-na* UGU PN *šatrutūni*). More generally KAJ 310 can write simply "1 box of Šamaš-eriš' debits" (*1 quppu ša* UGU $^{1.d}$UTU.KAM, l. 11, cf. 13, 15–17 etc.). A more complex formulation which probably also names the creditor is found in KAJ 165 (see below). On other occasions a tablet is simply said to belong to someone (*ša* PN), on the understanding that the holder of the tablet is also the creditor (e. g. KAJ 115, see below).

d) perhaps a variation on c) is the mention of the sealing of the document. Compare, for example, "that tablet with the seals of the king" (*ṭuppa šiāti ša* NA_4.KIŠIB.MEŠ *ša* LUGAL, KAJ 172 : 5–6), or the envelope (*kiṣirtu*) with the seal of the provincial governor (VS 19 No. 49; see § 2.5 above). Other examples were mentioned under § 2.1. In contract-type tablets the person sealing is, of course, the 'debtor', and in conveyance-type tablets the seller (or, in the case of the king, the giver). Naming someone as the party who sealed the document therefore defines his part in the transaction (despite the fact that witnesses also sealed some documents); and one imagines that despite the occasional inscribed or otherwise unmistakable seal, the identity of the person would have been established from the main text, or from the Siegelvermerk.

e) finally, the object or commodity around which the transaction revolves may be specified. Many tablets begin "One tablet of x homers of corn" or "y sheep" or "z minas of tin/lead", and sometimes much more detail is included. No doubt the wording was often taken from the original tablet itself: thus, when in KAJ 115 the scribe writes "1 tablet of 26 pastured male sheep (and) 1 lamb ..., 1 tablet of 1 good 2-year-old cow ..., 1 tablet (of) 1 good 3-year-old cow ... in all 3 tablets of Urad-Šerua", and goes on to say that these tablets have been given to Ṣilliya the herding-contractor (*nāqidu*) for collection of the debts, we may be fairly certain that the scribe had the three tablets in front of him, and was copying the details directly from each one. This is an administrative text, but the same careful definitions are found in the case of contract and conveyance tablets alike: "1 tablet of 1 homer of corn and 3300 bricks" (KAJ 161), or "1 tablet of 35 minas of tin/lead (and) 20 harvesters and 20 *ikû* (of land) in its wording as a pledge" (KAJ 163), both contract-types, and "1 tablet of 4 *ikû* of land in the lot opposite the ruins, share of Urad-Šerua ..." (KAJ 164; a conveyance-text).

These were all severely practical documents, and such details are mentioned because they are needed to ensure the correct identification of the documents. Usually more than one of the possible means of identification are combined. Let us close with an elaborate example of tablet-description from KAJ 165: "1 tablet of 24 homers of corn ..., which is put to the name of A in the wording of that tablet and is written to the debit of B (and for which) 40 *ikû* of field is put as pledge on the wording of that tablet–C has sold that tablet to D for its full purchase price ... ".[51]

§ 4 *Accounts*

One scribal activity whose very essence is the manipulation of earlier records is the keeping of accounts. In English, at least, the word "account(s)" is used in two rather different contexts: the internal, administrative record of an establishment (whether a private household or government agency), and the documentation of bilateral transactions in a commercial context. With the Middle Assyrian predilection for the use of commercial forms in an administrative context, however, we should not be surprised to find that these two kinds of account overlap at times.

§ 4.1 Terminology (1): *nikkassū*

This word, originally Sumerian, is generally written and construed as a plural (NÍG.KA$_9$(=ŠID).MEŠ; once syllabically *ni-ka-se* VS 1 No. 105: 18). Two verbal phrases are regularly encountered with it: *nikkassē ṣabātu* and *ina nikkassē šakānu*. While their approximate meanings are evident–"to do the accounts" and "to put in the accounts"–to establish their more precise connotations it is necessary to look at some of the passages in detail. In VS 19 No. 23 Babu-šuma-ereš has been issued with a supply of cedar-resin; to fulfil his duty, we read that "he shall burn it all up, they shall do his accounts, (and) he may (then) break his tablet" (*išarrap ugammar*, NÍG. KA$_9$.MEŠ-*šu iṣabbutu ṭuppu-šu iḫappi*, 10–12). The point to stress here is that the anonymous "they" are to do the accounts, and so provide him with confirmation that he has discharged his obligation. The tablet to be broken is of course VS 19 No. 23 itself, with his seal impressed on it, and "they", presumably his administrative superiors, must have retained it in their possession until he supplied them with adequate accounts showing how the cedar-resin was used up. Such a commercial formulation of an admini-

51 ... *ša šūme* A *ina pī ṭuppi šiāti šaknūni ū ina muḫḫi* B *šaṭrutūni* 40 GÁN A.ŠÀ *ina pī ṭuppi šiāti kī šaparti šaknūni C ṭuppa šiāti ana šīmi ana šīm gamer ... iddin-ma ...* (ll. 4–19).

strative responsibility is entirely characteristic of the Middle Assyrian system, and other passages confirm that "doing the accounts" (*ṣabāt nikkassē*, KAJ 255 : 4) was a bilateral activity, not something that could be done by an individual on the basis of his own records. "I shall take [your tablet] and do your [accounts]" VS 21 No. 25 : 17, or "he shall do his accounts and they may (then) break their tablets" TR 2045 : 12′–14′ (context broken). There is no hint in our texts that any third party, or independent "auditor" was involved in the exercise.

§ 4.2 The formulation of account tablets

It is evident that, once the accounting procedure was complete, any remaining obligations in one direction or the other would need to be recorded, on a newly prepared tablet; this would in effect be a debt-novation or a record of prospective liability, and would no doubt have been formally authenticated with the 'debtor's' seal. While the creation of such a tablet appears to have been implicit in the procedure of "doing the accounts", it would, I believe, be a mistake to identify this usage too closely with *ṭuppa ṣabātu*, and suggest that *nikkassē ṣabātu* means to "execute an accounts(-tablet)", since other contexts make it clear that this phrase included the preliminary stages of the process as well.

Passages already quoted show that the documentary basis for an accounting might consist either of individual earlier bilateral documents (whether contracts between the two parties, or, for example, receipts which would serve as proof of proper disposal of assets entrusted to one of the parties), or perhaps of unilateral lists kept by one of the parties as evidence of disposal. It is obvious from VS 21 No. 19 (quoted below) that cumulative accounts of daily transactions were sometimes kept on writing-boards, and no doubt this is the kind of board referred to in KAJ 120: "after his accounts had been done, and everything had been deducted or included on the accounts in accordance with his writing-board" (*ištu nikkassē-šu ṣa[bt]ūni gabbu tušaharuṣūni lū [ša p]ī lē'i-šu ana [nikkassē] šaknūni*, 5–9). As an interim measure (even if not as a permanent record) the accumulated details must in some cases have been committed to clay, to enable the position to be agreed by both parties, but these details would not normally have been repeated in the final document. This interim stage would appear as some kind of Sammelurkunde, an example of which based on individual earlier contracts might be VS 19 No. 47, but I am aware of only one tablet which is explicitly designated as an account, VS 21 No. 19, an account of skins, where the summation reads: "Total . . . , of 2 years, according to the writing-boards (*ša pī lē'āni*) of offerings of the animal-fattener, which he received at various times (Gtn): settled accounts (NÍG.KA$_9$.MEŠ *ṣabtūtu*) of Amurru-šuma-uṣur, chief . . ." (rev. 10′–13′). This tablet was not sealed, and it makes no statement of any consequent obligation, so that one must imagine that a formal, sealed, tablet, lacking the detailed list, was subsequently drawn up. For a final document of that description we may take VS 19 No. 49, which is sealed. Here the first section (1–7) goes: "[From the month of] Sin, 18th day, eponymate of [Tiglath-]pileser king of Assyria, the accounts of Ezbu-lešir, offerings-supervisor, [in respect of (?)] 925.03 homers of corn of the contribution (*maddatte*) of the Assyrians, according to the envelope (*kiṣirte*) bearing the seal of Aššur-kitti-šeṣi, the governor of the land, have been settled (*ṣabtū*)." The next 3 sections list and total the disbursements he has made from this amount, and the last section (19–21) states: "745.805 homers of corn remains (*rēḫū*) (as an obligation) on Ezbu-lešir and Urad-Aššur". The basis for this conclusion will undoubtedly have been information contained in comprehensive lists of disbursements kept by the scribes of the offerings-supervisor's department. Examples of their activities have become available recently through the publication of VS 19 and 21, and we see a variety of records, from individual sealed receipts and contracts, through unsealed periodical listings, to texts of this kind.

§ 4.3 The timing and scope of the accounting procedure

The opening line of VS 19 No. 49 has been restored to begin [*iš-tu* ITI^{d}]*sîn* ("From the month of Sin . . .") on the basis of similar passages, where the scribe is concerned to make it clear that the newly defined obligation subsumes all debts and credits over a particular period. The formulation here, with the clause from [*ištu*] to *ṣabtu* in line 7 making an independent statement rather than being an introductory subordinate clause, is a compromise between two other applications of *ištu*, as exemplified in KAJ 80 : 1–5 "After (*ištu*) his accounts for (the period) from (*ištu*) the eponymate of A to the month of Qarrati, eponymate of B, had all been settled (*gabbu ṣabtūni*) . . ."; cf. KAJ 120, quoted above, and KAJ 107; 307. This is, of course, nothing more substantial than a question of drafting, but it does serve to underline the point that, to be serviceable, such formalizations of accounts need to be specific about their timing. Sometimes, as in KAJ 80, both beginning and end of the accounting period are specified; but we may suppose that generally any earlier accountings would be included with the other documentary evidence as a matter of course, making it unnecessary to specify the starting point, and that, although in VS 19 No. 49 the concluding date (which is the same as the date of the document) is explicitly stated, in most cases the document's date would be assumed tacitly to mark the end of the accounting period.

As for when the accounting took place, there is some evidence that, as one might expect, it was an annual event. Thus in KAJ 240 the scribe refers to skins "of the accounts of the eponymate of" three different *limmus*, and the same system is implied by VS 21 No. 19 (see above, § 4.1), or by VS 19 No. 56 : 68 (*maḫru ša limme* PN; from the Ezbu-lešir archive) and VS 21 No. 21 : 32. However, while I have not made a comprehensive search, a quick survey of Middle Assyrian documents does not suggest any concentration of accounting activity around the new year, whether in the last month, Hibur, or the first, Ṣippu; but since there is some slight evidence in Neo-Assyrian times that periodic accountings took place at the end of the 12th (and perhaps occasionally the 6th) month,[52] I am inclined to think that this is an accident of transmission, and that with the publication of more tablets the same pattern of activity will be revealed for the Middle Assyrian accountants.

52 Cf. Dalley – Postgate, The Tablets from Fort Shalmaneser p. 21.

For the position to be settled to their mutual satisfaction, it would be necessary for both sides to be quite clear which individual transactions were included in the calculations. Hence in KAJ 120 the text begins "Excluding (*uššer*) the sheep which have been given to him to hold in readiness . . ." (for continuation, see above, § 4.2; cf. also passages quoted under *ezib* c) in CAD E 430a). Compare also the note at the end of the biennial account of skins, VS 21 No. 19 : 19′: "The sheep of the shearing (? : *ka-aṣ-ṣi*) of the *naṣbutu*(-festival?) are not written, the tablet [. . .]". More often, though, it is the tablets recording the individual transactions which mention whether or not they are included in the general accounting. We read of sheep "which had been put to the debit of PN, the animal-fattener, at the settling of the accounts" (*ša ina ṣabāt nikkassē ina muḫḫi* PN *ša kuriltie iššaknūni*, KAJ 255 : 4–7), or "he shall collect their bread which had been put to his debit in the accounts from the 9th to the 11th day, (and then) do his accounts and break his tablet" (KAJ 107 : 7–15; cf. also KAJ 80 : 14–17 and KAJ 120 for this usage of *šakānu*).

§ 4.4 Terminology (2)

Like any accountants, the Middle Assyrian scribes had their own jargon, and since it differs slightly from others, it may be helpful to illustrate their procedures by mentioning some of their technical terms which have not already been discussed. Before drawing up some accounts, it was necessary to take stock, and check the items in question. For this the normal word was *ašāru*, and it is linked with the accounting process in KAJ 311: "These (are) the donkeys of the town . . . which Urad-Šerua checked and did the accounts of PN (in respect of them)" (*ša* URU.x *Urad Šerua ēšurūni* NÍG.KA$_9$.MEŠ *ša* PN *iṣbutūni*, 10–13). When something was to be included in the accounting, it was said to be "brought up", in a usage shared with the Nuzi diction (CAD E 132a, s. v. elû 10c): "the deficits owed by the sailors are not included with the corn" (*ina libbi še'im muṭṭā'ē ša muḫḫi* LÚ.MÁ.LAH$_6$.MEŠ *lā še-lu*, VS 21 No. 20 : 29; but cf. a different usage attested in MBab texts, CAD E 133b, s. v. elû 11a) 1′). The very same context also gives us for the first time in Middle Assyrian a clear instance of the word "to add", which turns out to have been *kamāru*, the term used by the Old Babylonian mathematical texts: *ana libbi še'im maḫri lā ka-mi-ir* "not added to the corn received" (VS 21 No. 20 : 28; cf. also VS 19 No. 21 : 30: *]la-a ka-mir* "not added"; broken context). The technical term for to "subtract" was probably also the same as that in use by the Old Babylonian mathematicians, *harāṣu*, but it is only attested at present in a Št form in KAJ 120 (see § 4.2 above): *tušaharuṣūni* "subtracted".[53] A word used for the concrete action of removing a quantity

[53] For **šutaḫruṣūni* with an additional *a* (cf. Deller – Saporetti, Oriens Antiquus 9, 45, for *naḫarat* and *reḫete*), and regular Middle Assyrian metathesis of the sibilant and dental. This metathesis is acknowledged by W. von Soden for Old Assyrian (GAG § 36a: *tišammeā*), further examples K. Hecker, Grammatik der Kültepe-Texte, Rome 1968 (An. Or. 44), § 41e; but it is also present in Middle Assyrian as the following examples show: *tušēbuli* VS 21 No. 17 : 99; *tusaḫḫuri* Assur 2/4 [1979], 98, and the PNs Adad-tišamme (unpub. text and perhaps VS 21 No. 25 : 19) and others composed with *tišmār* (from *šitmāru* AHw 1251b).

of corn from a larger amount is *našāru* (KAJ 119 : 5; 219 : 9; 220 : 4), but this is not strictly an accounting term.

Another term shared with Nuzi is the word for "deficit", by which is meant an amount owed to the administration because of underpayment of an obligation; the Middle Assyrian for "deficit" is *muṭṭā'ū*, written explicitly *mu-uṭ-ṭa-e* in VS 19 No. 56 rev. 54; "1.8 homers of sesame, which was written down to the deficit of the eponymate of A at the reading (?), ..." (*ša ina sassu'e ana muṭṭā'ē ša limme* A *šaṭrūni* ...). More often the word is written LÁ.MEŠ, suggesting that it is indeed, as suggested in AHw 691b, a plurale tantum: cf. "... corn, his deficit, received" (LÁ.MEŠ-*šu maḫir*, VS 19 No. 25 : 8), or "not included among the corn deficit ..." (*ina libbi še'i* LÁ.ME(Š) ... *lā šēlu*, VS 21 No. 20 : 28). This same text begins with two columns of figures, which distinguish corn "measured out (and) received into the palace" and that which is "deficit, in the hands of the boatmen" (LÁ.MEŠ *ina* ŠU LÚ.MÁ.LAḪ$_6$.MEŠ). Later on the second column is totalled: 20.4 homers of corn "he has 'deficited' (*um-ta-ṭí*) (and) has not brought" (Rev. 18).[54] There is a curious phrase in TR 2028, where Šamaš-šuma-uṣur is obliged to return and make payment of his *šulmānu* debt within a month, and "If he have not returned within 1 month, they shall give him to deficit" (*la-a it-tu-⟨ar⟩ a-na* LÁ.MEŠ *i-du-nu-uš*, 18–19). In many cases *muṭṭa'ū* seems to be a close equivalent of the Old Babylonian *ribbatum*, a word which does not occur in Assyrian, but survives, with its logogram LÁ.DÙ, into Middle Babylonian (AHw 980b). Apparently *ribbatum* is also absent at Nuzi, and it is probable, therefore, that despite the hesitation of CAD M/ii, 162a the word booked there as *muddû* and translated "outstanding balance, delivery due, deficit, leftover" (p. 161a) is identical with our Assyrian word.

Finally, the difficult word *talpittu*. The writer has suggested this form of the word in CTN II No. 64 : 4, but AHw retains the reading *ripītu*. It is admittedly worrying that we have no writing *ta-al-* in either Middle or Neo-Assyrian sources, but the long survival of 'Rimusu' instead of the correct Talmusu could serve as some alleviation of this anxiety. The only positive indication for *talpittu* instead of *ripītu* would be the form [*ta*]*l-pi-ta-a-te* (ARU 105 : 26, see J. N. Postgate, The Governor's Palace Archive, British School of Archaeology in Iraq 1973 (Cuneiform Texts from Nimrud [CTN] II), p. 99), but this single occurrence is not epigraphically certain. The form of the word suggests a verbal noun derived from the D stem of the verb, but unfortunately the only pertinent occurrences of *lapputu* in MAss texts are in KAV 195 : 8′ and 10′ (CAD L 91a), and these are now to be understood as forms of the adjective *laptu* in consequence of a new join, as Dr. H. Freydank kindly informs me. The usage of *talpittu* in the Middle Assyrian texts is certainly close to AHw's „etwa ‚Verbrauch' " (987); if we suppose that *lapputu* can mean "to book out" or "to write off", and so describe the action of a scribe or accountant when (unilaterally) recording an issue of some kind, a satisfactory solution is achieved. *talpittu* will refer to any item which has thus

[54] Against the dictionaries, I am also inclined to see *maṭā'u* (G) in two similar passages: "corn, completion-payment (*mullā'u*) of the granary of the palace which the men of Šibaniba were owing (*im*-DU-*ni*) ... is received" (Billa, No. 30: JCS 7 [1953], 130), and lost property which "the men of Matara ... were owing (*im*-DU-*ni*)" (TR 3011). However, an interpretation of this form as *emdūni* is obviously possible too.

been "written off", and this is supported by the contexts in which it is met, which tend to refer to expenditures for which no other written record is mentioned. In the 12th century Ninurta-tukulti-Aššur archive the sheep are often listed simply as *talpittu*–"disbursement"–but in other cases they are *talpittu ša* PN, where the PN is either Mutta or Buṣa, the two principal officials responsible for the animals; such passages should perhaps be understood precisely as "official unilateral disbursement by PN". The other passages listed by AHw can be readily accommodated to this meaning, and so too can recently published instances.[55] If there is a contemporary Babylonian equivalent it is perhaps *ṣītu* (ZI.GA); possible Neo-Assyrian equivalents are *akiltu* and *tidintu*, but there are so few elaborate accounts from the 1st millennium Assyrian scribes that this is very uncertain.

§ 4.5 The commercial sector

It should be stressed that the terminology discussed in the preceding section relates almost entirely to administrative transactions. If we translated *maṭā'u* as "to owe" it is only in the absence of a convenient alternative to render "to be behind in administrative payments"; in the commercial sphere it is probable that *ḫabālu* remained the word for "to owe".[56] However, we cannot be sure of this, because we have virtually no documents dealing with private accounts as kept between two parties. Undoubtedly a periodic adjustment of debts and credits will have been needed. The store-room inventory KAJ 310 reveals that several individuals had contracted enough debts to the Urad-Šerua family to occupy a tablet-basket to themselves: "1 basket (*quppu*) of Šamaš-eriš' debts" (*ša muḫḫi* Š.), similarly four other men (ll. 13, 15, 16 and 29), and a certain Riš-Adad, who is interesting because the store also contained some of his own tablets (cf. ll. 25, 27f.), so that he may have had some close association with the family in other ways. Evidently from time to time accounts were settled, whether or not the term for this was *nikkassē ṣabātu* as in the administration. This is the presumption lying behind those texts where we read "They shall deduct it from the tablet of his debt" (*ina ṭuppi ša muḫḫi-šu ukarrû*) or "from the wording of his executed tablet" (*ina pī ṭuppi-šu ṣabitte ukarrû*).[57] Here too the terminology differs from the administrative sphere, and underlines once again how biased our sources may be, in one way or another.

[55] See VS 19 Nos. 1. i. 60′, iv. 45; 18 : 2 (ÉRIN.MEŠ!); 51 rev. 9′; VS 21 No. 22 : 24, 27. Particularly telling is perhaps *ri*]-*mu-a-te ù tal-pi-te* [*ana lā mašā*]'*e šaṭir* " . . .] gifts and disbursement(s). Written down as a reminder" (AfO 10 [1935–1936], 33, l. 45), reflecting passages like *ana naptini ša Ninurta-tukulti-Aššur ū tal-pi-ti ša Ninurta-tukulti-Aššur-ma* "for the dinner of N. and for disbursement(s) of the same N." (V. Donbaz, Ninurta-tukulti-Aššur zamanına ait orta Asur idarî belgeleri, Ankara 1976 (TTKY VI/19), Text A. 113:19).

[56] The *muṭṭā'ū* restored in KAJ 159 by Deller – Saporetti, Oriens Antiquus 9, 286, is wrong, since we must read there rev. 7′ *i-na tu-*[*a*]*r ḫu-ra-di* (Studies in honour of I. M. Diakonoff 305). It remains therefore an administrative, not a legal, term.

[57] See the article of K. Deller – C. Saporetti (cf. footnote 38), in: Oriens Antiquus 9 [1970], 285–314.

BRIGITTE MENZEL, *Assyrische Tempel. I. Untersuchungen zu Kult, Administration und Perssonel. II. Anmerkungen, Textbuch, Tabellen und Indices* (Studia Pohl, Series Maior 10/I and II), Rome, Biblical Institute Press 1981. Pp. xv + 322; viii + 241* + 218 + 35 + 18.

A study of the temples of Assyria is, like most things Neo-Assyrian, long overdue, and we are fortunate that Dr Menzel has undertaken this with the painstaking philological standards that we have come to expect of Heidelberg students. As the subtitle to *Band I* makes clear, we should not expect a general survey, such as G. McEwan has more recently given us for Hellenistic Babylonia, and the author concentrates particularly on the evidence for the personnel and cultic events of the different temples in exhaustive detail; with over 4,000 footnotes, 218 pages of edited texts and excerpts, useful charts and indices in *Band II*, the reader is presented with all the components of a high quality do-it-yourself construction kit, and at times one feels that the author should have gone further in fitting some of the pieces together. Rather than list minor disagreements or corrections, therefore, the reviewer wishes to try and use Dr Menzel's work to resolve a question treated by her in *Exkurs I*: "Tempel-Schuldscheine" (*Band I*, 11-20), but without any fresh effort to find a solution ("Es bleibt abzuwarten, ob eine eindeutige Klärung ... im Zukunft einmal möglich sein wird", p. 21). Since these legal documents, which record loans or debts qualified in some way as temple offerings, are one of the few areas in which we see an interaction between the temples and the secular world, it seems a shame to leave the issue so much in suspense, and Dr Menzel's assemblage of the texts, new and old, gives a solid basis for further speculation.

Texts Nos. 73-130 in *Band II* are loans or debt-notes for silver, copper or corn apparently described as property of a deity (*ša* DN); usually it is also said to belong to a man or men as well (*ša* PN), and the essential problem concerns this apparent contradiction: how can it be described at one and the same time as the property of two different creditors? To this question we shall return below, but to illustrate the genre we will quote an unpublished text from the Musée d'Art et d'Histoire in Geneva. Thanks are due to Mlle C. Dunant, M. Georges Dossin and the Musée d'Art et d'Histoire for permission to publish this text.

MAH 16602 (Inner tablet, unsealed; 4.3 × 2.5 × 1.5 cm.)

Obv.	1	30 MA.NA 11 $^1/_2$ GÍN KÙ.BABBAR	30 minas 11 $^1/_2$ shekels of silver,
	2	SAG.MEŠ *ša* 15 *šá* ^{uru}*arba-ìl*	*rēšāti* of Ištar of Arbil,
	3	*ša* ^{1}*na-nu-u-ni*	belonging to Nanuni,
	4	*pa-an* ^{1}*na-nu-u-ni*	at the disposal of Nanuni,
	5	" ^{1}*qa-a-a*	ditto of Qaya,
	6	" ^{1}15-I	ditto of Ištar-na'id.
	7	ITI.BARAG UD.20.KÁM	20th day of Nisanu (I),
B.E.	8	[*l*]*im-mu* ^{1}EN-*šú-nu*	eponym-year of Bel-šunu.
Rev.	9	[*ana*] 4-*tú-šú* [*irab*]-*bi*	It shall bear interest at a quarter.
	10	IGI $^{1.d}$PA-⸢EN⸣-PAP.MEŠ-*šú*	Before Nabu-bel-ahhešu,
	11	IGI ^{1}EN (read *qáb*?)-*lu-aš-šur-aṣ-bat*	Before Qablu?-Aššur-aṣbat,
	12	IGI ^{1}*si-lim-aš-š*[*ur*]	Before Silim-Aššur,
	13	IGI ^{1}APIN-*eš*-DINGIR A.[X] GAB?	Before Ereš-ili ...

The vexatious SAG.MEŠ which here qualifies the silver in the same way as *ginû* in parallel texts, is discussed at length by Dr Menzel in note 155. Already in *Or.* NS XLII (1973), 444, the reviewer proposed identifying it with the word *rēšēti* in a Sennacherib inscription describing impositions on a recently annexed part of Babylonia: "1 ox, 10 sheep, 10 homers of wine, 20 homers of dates as its *rēšēti* (*re-še-ti/te-šú*) to the gods of Assyria I fixed" (Borger, *Babylonisch-assyrische Lesestücke*, II, 63). This reading of the logogram SAG.MEŠ had in fact been tentatively suggested already by Winckler (*Altorientalische Forschungen*, I, 248) for an Assurbanapli passage: *šallat-sunu kabittu* SAG.MEŠ *kaspu hurāṣu mimma aqru nakīrī šadlūti ana ilāni māt Aššur māt* [*Akkadi*] *aqīš ana qīšti*, "their heavy booty (as) SAG.MEŠ, silver, gold and all the valuable property of the numerous enemies I presented to the gods of Assyria and [Akkad]" (Streck, *Assurbanipal*, II, 168:34-5), and although he compares only the Sennacherib passage there is a syllabic writing in Assurbanapli's own inscriptions: UN.MEŠ *ū šallat Elamti ša ina qibīt Aššur ... ahbutu re-še-e-ti ana* DINGIR.MEŠ-*ia ašruk*, "The people and plunder of Elam which I had plundered at the command of ... the gods ... I presented to my gods (as) *rēšēti*" (Streck, *ibid.*, 58-60, vi.125-vii.1). Compare also *sattukkē ginê* SAG.MEŠ *Aššur ū Mulissu ū* DINGIR.MEŠ *māt Aššur ūkīn ṣēruš-šun*, "I fixed upon them regular offerings (and?) SAG.MEŠ of Aššur and Mulissu and the gods of Assyria" (Streck, *ibid.*, 40.106-7), and the earliest occurrence of the term, Assurnaṣirapli II's "I drew wine (and) libated (it as) SAG.MEŠ to Aššur ..." (see CAD Ṣ 60b), with the variant writing SAG.MEŠ-*te* in AKA 245:9. These historical contexts are ignored by Menzel, in accordance with a general reluctance to rely on texts not in Assyrian dialect (cf. her comment on the Assurnaṣirapli passage "in literarischem Kontext ein Ausdruck vorliegt, der die besondere Qualität des ... Weins beschreibt", *Band II*, 14*), but in this case her reluctance (which the reviewer admits at times to have experienced in excess himself) is misplaced. For the similarity with ADD 1013 rev. 12 (*issu libbi* SAG.MEŠ *ša muhhi māt Akkadi šarru* [*u*]*kinnūni*, "from the SAG.MEŠ which the king fixed upon the land of Akkad", see G. van Driel, *The cult of Aššur*, 207), serves to link the SAG.MEŠ = *rēšēti* of the historical inscriptions with SAG.MEŠ in administrative and legal texts, a connexion which also follows from the parallelism with *ginû* in the entirely different contexts of the two genres. As for the correct Neo-Assyrian normalisation of the word as *rēšāti*, this is probably given us by ND 10026:5 (J.V. Kinnier Wilson, *The Nimrud wine lists*, Pl.45) *ri-šá-a-ti*, since this is a term applied to a quantity of wine just like SAG.MEŠ in KAV 79 (not from *rēštû(m)* despite AHw 973b) and in ND 3486 (*Iraq* XV (1953), 148, coll.).

Having presented, I hope, evidence for the correct *reading* of SAG.MEŠ, it is time to consider its *meaning*. Apart from Dr Menzel herself, who expresses the tentative idea that SAG.MEŠ "möglicherweise die Grundversorgung der Tempel ist" (*Band II*, 15*), E. Lipiński has recently discussed the question in a study unavailable to Dr Menzel (*Orientalia Lovaniensia Analecta* VI (1979), 572 ff.). Following no doubt W. von Soden, AHw 972-3 s.v. rēštu(m) I, where most of the pertinent passages are cited, he favours reading *rēšēti/e* and writes that the term "s'entend généralement au sens de 'première qualité' ..." (p. 572). Since however we require a meaning comparable to *ginû* "regular offerings", this reviewer maintains with increased confidence his opinion that SAG.MEŠ/*rēšāti* are "(offerings of) first-fruits" to the temples. This rendering, first considered as an alternative to "first quality" by Streck (*Assurbanipal*, II, 40: "die Erstlinge"), is semantically plausible, and supported by the Biblical Hebrew *rēʾšît*, also contributions to a temple. Indeed, there is a much closer link with West Semitic in the shape of a word *rsh* quoted by Lipiński from Aramaic clay documents: *ksp rsh lhdd* "*rsh* silver of Hadad" and *ksp zy ḥrqy rsh zy ʾšr ʾrbʾlʾ* "silver belonging to Ḥrqy, *rsh* of Ištar of Arbil" (*op. cit.*, 573 and 581). This word is connected by Lipiński with the root *rsy* which expresses "l'idée de 'filtrer'... ou 'purifier'...", in order to supply a parallel for his interpretation of *rēšēti* as first quality (applied to pure silver), but it is surely a much easier solution to see here the exact transcription into Aramaic of *rēšāti*, cf. simply Aram. *srs* = Assyr. *ša rēšē* (S. A. Kaufman, *The Akkadian influences on Aramaic*, p. 100) and URU *ḫa-an-du-a-te* = *ḥdwh* (J. Kohler and A. Ungnad, *Assyrische Rechtsurkunden*, no. 313). Probably the same usage is to be recognised in West Semitic too (*rʾšt* from Cyprus, H. Donner and W. W. Röllig, *Kanaanäische und Aramäische Inschriften*, no. 31:1; *rst* from North Africa, *ibid.*, no. 120:2). It is true that as in Akkadian in all these cases it might be argued that the word refers to offerings which are "first (in quality)" rather than "first (in time)", so that *rēʾšît ha-bikkūrîm* would be "the choicest of the first-fruits", but even if this were correct, the basic point remains that the term refers to a particular kind of offering to a temple, and is not a general word with a vague meaning of "choicest".

Working then from the conclusion that SAG.MEŠ in the *Tempel-Schuldscheine* does not refer to the quality of the metal, but to a form of temple offering just as *ginû* does in Menzel's no. 78 (though probably not nos. 127-8, which have a *sūtu*-measure for *ginû*-offerings in the reviewer's opinion), let us revert to the underlying problem of these temple loans, which is how the metal ir corn owed could be both the property of the god and that of the creditor or "*ša*-Person". First let us exclude from consideration Menzel's second group (nos. 110-25) in which corn is described as the property in the god, and (except in no. 110) no other creditor is mentioned: it is clear that these are straightforward loans from the temple granary of Nabu at Kalḫu, and no. 110 may easily be explained by assuming Nabu-šumu-uṣur to be the responsible official. There is no problem of interpretation here. In all the other texts the "*ša*-Person" is named, and if anything is left out, it is the information that the object of the loan was connected with a temple at all: to this extent Lipiński is right to say that "le temple n'est aucunement partie dans les contrats en question" (*op. cit.*, 573). Compare BM 103392, a debt-note for silver which has the note SAG.MEŠ *šá aš-šur* added only as an afterthought on the side of the envelope (where it was missed by its copyist and also by Dr Menzel, see J. N. Postgate, *Fifty Neo-Assyrian legal documents*, no. 26), and ND 7088 (to be published as no. 39 in S. M. Dalley and J. N. Postgate, *Texts from Fort Shalmaneser*, forthcoming) has SAG.MEŠ *ša* ᵈNIN.LÍL on the tablet but no corresponding remark on the envelope. Hence we may conclude that the fact that the silver or copper in question was in some way classed as offerings to a deity was relevant, but not essential to the transactions, whereas the "*ša*-Person's" ownership of the capital *was* essential. Dr Menzel's discussion of this enigma quotes two possible explanations offered by R. Bogaert in *Les origines antiques de la banque de dépôt*: either that he was a "cessionaire" (who has borrowed directly from the temple in order to give credit to others), or that he was a simple intermediary (who acted on the temple's behalf but was not himself a functionary of the temple). However, neither of these carries entire convinction, as Dr Menzel admits, and this reviewer would like to propose a rather different reconstruction of the background to these transactions.

The central point is that in practice the "*ša*-Person" appears to be the real creditor, and the connection with the temple is a subsidiary consideration from a legal point of view. We suggest therefore that the wealthy used the temples as a kind of safe-deposit in which to store their capital in the form of silver (or, more rarely in the seventh century at least, in copper). In exchange for this service, the capital sum did not of course bear interest, and it was technically designated as one or another kind of temple "offering" (*ginê* or *rēšāti*), although in practice it, or an equivalent weight of the same metal, would remain at the disposal of the original depositor as though it were his own property. By this means the creditor would achieve religious and physical protection for his funds, the temples would secure a considerable holding in the currency of the time, and borrowers would know where to go for a loan with some protection against rapacious money-lenders. Without more specific evidence, we cannot reconstruct in detail the procedures for making such a loan, but two broad alternatives suggest themselves. Either the creditor negotiated himself directly with the borrower, and then authorised the temple staff to issue the amount of silver in question, or the transaction was concluded between the temple and the borrower, the creditor in this case accepting the temple virtually as his financial agents. There is no way for us to know at present whether each creditor's deposits were marked with his name, or the temple simply kept accounts of each man's deposits and withdrawals. In either case, it is likely that the interest from the loan partly or entirely accrued to the creditor and not the temple. Where the creditor and the temple belonged to the same town it is easy to imagine that the business was transacted within the precincts of the temple, whichever procedure was in use. However, one of the puzzling features of the *Tempel-Schuldscheine* is the occurrence of silver of Ištar of Arbil in loans from Balawat, Kalḫu, Nineveh and Ḫarran (*Band I*, 20; cf. also Lipiński, *op. cit.*, 573, for an Aramaic text of unknown origin). Our reconstruction would have to assume the presence of branches of the Arbil "head office" at other cities throughout the realm, which is compatible with the legendary wealth of this temple.

This reconstruction seems to us to make commercial sense, and to offer an explanation of the existence of temple offerings belonging to individuals. We should have hesitated all the same to make the proposal, were it not that there is a parallel already in the Old Assyrian documents, where the temples "mettaient à la disposition des marchands des biens appelés *ikribū*", and gold called *ikribū* might be stored in the temple under the individual merchant's private seal (see P. Garelli, *Les assyriens en Cappadoce*, 252-5). *ikribū* were certainly originally votive offerings, as can be seen in the contemporary dedications by the "sea-faring merchants of Ur" to the Ningal Temple, but Larsen has written recently that "It is clear that the temples in some way were engaged in the overland trade, for the texts quite often contain references to special shipments which are described as *ikribu*, a term which most probably designates temple investments" (*The Old Assyrian city-state and its colonies*, 149). There need not be an exact parallel with the administration of offerings by the Neo-Assyrian temples, but in each case it makes good sense to see the temples taking part in secular business affairs by using capital deposited with them.

In the space of a review it is not possible to follow up all the implications of our proposal. Probably the *Tempel-Schuldscheine* which make no specific mention of offerings, but describe the sum merely as "of DN" or as "capital (SAG.DU) of DN", can be accounted for in a similar way. On the other hand, some of the debt-notes from Balawat and elsewhere (e.g. nos. 103-6, 130) are supply contracts for temples, and it would have been illuminating if Dr Menzel had considered these in the general context of temple offerings, a subject which is frequently mentioned but does not receive any treatment in its own right. I would like to take this opportunity to thank Dr H. G. M. Williamson for guiding me to the West Semitic references.

TRINITY COLLEGE, CAMBRIDGE J. N. POSTGATE

Employer, Employee and Employment in the Neo-Assyrian Empire*

J. N. Postgate

Trinity College, Cambridge

1 *Introductory* Our sources cannot give us a balanced view of labour in Assyria. Since the majority of our texts come from palaces and temples, there must be a strong bias in favour of the public sector, and this only aggravates an inherent tendency of the documentary sources to stress the prevalence of large-scale organized labour, since it was there that most of the "paper-work" was generated. Although we do therefore know something about the organization of labour by the government, for the private sector we are, frankly, reduced to guesswork. Nevertheless, there is no harm in guessing, and since we shall be writing under the influence of our own more or less conscious assumptions about conditions in the private sector, we shall begin with a summary description of the employment scene in the Neo-Assyrian empire from the point of view of the employer, in the hope that this may at least expose some of these assumptions to scrutiny and lay them open to challenge.

First, though, a digression on a matter of terminology. In the original version of this paper I announced that I would enumerate "types of relationship between labourer and employer, and *not* a number of separate social classes." For this I was taken to task by I.M. Diakonoff, since in his words "according to the definition I am accustomed to, a social class is a group of persons differing from other groups by its relation to property in means of production and their share of the produce. That *is* a 'type of relationship between labourer and employer'. . . ." We cannot get immersed here in theories of social structure, but clearly I must explain what I *did* mean by the phrase. In many cases the relationship between the person doing the work and the person controlling it would indeed be a consequence or cause of their "belonging" to a group which can be defined by its relationship to property etc.; but not always. To use the words "social class" when referring to all such relationships rightly or wrongly suggests a degree of permanence, and excludes the possibility that the relationship is occasioned by other factors. To take one simple case, a man reaping a field on behalf of another may indeed be a "helot" acting for his owner, a free Assyrian, and these terms of themselves describe and explain the labour relationship between them. He could, however, have been another free Assyrian, fulfilling a contractual obligation to take part in the harvest, in which case the subordinate relationship, though

*Substantially rewritten version of my paper for the Edinburgh Congress, which was entitled "The organization of labour in Assyria." The present text does not consider the Middle Assyrian evidence. The paper takes into account the often constructive and always pertinent criticisms of I.M. Diakonoff on the original version. Where our views differ I have tried to quote the crucial words verbatim, but several criticisms have been tacitly incorporated into the recast text.

undeniable, is of short duration and scarcely differs from that of a labourer hired for the day. Surely this is a "type of relationship" which does not require the creation of a social class or even of a subdivision of one.

It is true, all the same, that in this example there is the kernel of a class distinction, created by the relation of the two parties to the means of production; in other words, it is the *impermanence* of the relationship that disqualifies it from being a "class." What concerns me more is to point out that the subordinate position of one worker could have a quite different origin. For one thing, the opposite to "permanent" is not only "temporary," but can be more specifically "seasonal" or "occasional"; there is a difference of kind as well as of degree here. Many services must have been rendered to city and country dwellers by specialist workers, whether resident or itinerant. This type of relationship cannot merely be described as that between one class and another. I am not sure how substantial the contact between two parties must be for a "labour relationship" to have been established, and since our sources are so scant, I have tended to include everything in this brief survey. Another factor which affects the type of relationship is whether the two parties live geographically apart, or share the same house or village. Finally, it is particularly important in Neo-Assyrian times to take account of *administrative* labour control: all classes and walks of life seem to have stood at one time or another in a "labour relationship" to the government, and it would not help our analysis to assume that the clear-cut administrative relationships coincided exactly with the boundaries of social classes in other contexts. Had we the sources, it might be feasible to tabulate all "labour" according to such different sets of variables (private : government—permanent : seasonal : occasional—direct control : indirect control—etc.), but the gaps in our present knowledge would make this a dubious procedure. Instead, we shall introduce the subject rather generally by concentrating on the employer, rather than the employed, so deferring the thorny problem of what to call the different classes, a side issue in this context. Then in sections 3 and 4 we sketch the picture from the point of view of the employee, while in section 5 the subject is approached from another angle by considering the kinds of employment in more detail. Inevitably this results in some repetition, but the different approaches seem to me to do justice to the complexity of the subject.

2 *Employer* Agricultural work in the private sector was presumably organized household by household, under the head of the family, whether the actual labour was done by free-born members of the family, by resident slaves, by hired workers, or by free men working off a debt. Persons distrained as a pledge are described literally as residing in the house of their creditors.[1] Except during harvest, it is likely that most of those working the land actually lived in the village within whose borders the fields lay. If the family owned land in distant places, a separate household would have to manage those fields—perhaps tenant-farmers, a (legally, or merely geographically) "divided" member of the family, or semi-free cultivators controlled by the family. The same must apply to families already permanently resident in the city, where it is

[1]"Is dwelling as a pledge" = *ana šaparti kammus(at)*; for this phrase and for *erābu*/*šērubu*, "to (cause to) enter" (the house of a creditor), and *palāḫu*, "to serve," see Postgate 1976:48.

unlikely that the actual cultivators lived in the city house (unless the family was wealthy enough to own land in the immediate vicinity). In both these cases the effective organizer of the labour must have been the man on the spot, and the relationship of the worker to the nominal head of the land-owning (or land-renting) family was a purely legal one.

Similar considerations must have applied to palace and temple estates, although for the palace at least procedures will have been more uniform. Work on the fields can only have been organized between the residents of the villages themselves, household by household as in the private sector, whatever their legal status. The alternative—that whole villages of "helots" were treated as a single labour gang jointly charged with cultivating the land under the supervision of government officials—contradicts what we know of Assyrian administrative traditions, could hardly have been efficient, and there is no evidence to suggest it. In each village there must of course have been someone representing its interests with the responsible government official, and vice versa; but although the terminology may have differed, the situation cannot have been unlike that of a free village, where the mayor (*ḫazannu*) served as the channel between the two parties when a tax-assessment or tax-collection was made. Overall conditions of work in the countryside must have been very uniform: no doubt some villages were part "private sector" and part "government owned," and belonging to the government may well have been less onerous than being the property of an absentee city landlord. Either way, fields had to be tilled, harvests gathered, threshed and stored, houses built, animals tended, and there was little that government or private landlords could do to affect the constraints of climate and geography.

In the cities the situation is naturally more complicated. Of course the domestic chores within each household can have varied little, and were performed by its resident members, whatever their social status. It is only as the size of the establishment increases that specialization is needed, and the duties of the individual become restricted to distinct tasks. Hence the various "professions" seem to be concentrated in the employ of palaces and temples, but this should not lead us to assume that some crafts, e.g., weaving, were not plied in the private sector—merely that they needed less documentation, and that what texts they did generate have yet to be discovered. The existence of private industrial establishments is hinted at by evidence discussed later (¶5.2), but they can never have remotely rivalled the palaces in size. Some idea of the range of palace employees in the early 8th century has been afforded us by the Nimrud Wine Lists, but they are of course confined to those actually resident in or near the palace. Later, perhaps under Tiglath-Pileser III, such workers were organized along military lines into cohorts (*kiṣru*), and there is no reason to doubt Esarhaddon's claim that he greatly enlarged this system: during the 7th century we do have firm evidence for cohorts of weavers, victuallers (*karkadinnu*), leather-workers, oil-pressers, iron-smiths, and shepherds.[2] The mention of shepherds

[2]For the extension of the *kiṣru* system to non-military employments see Postgate 1979a:210-212 with n.32 and especially p.219-220; we should now add *CT* 53 13, which is concerned with a cohort of state-employed iron-workers, and is translated in Fales 1980:148 n.8. For more on the *kiṣru* system, see also Postgate 1980b.

may cause some surprise, but in fact Esarhaddon mentions them too, along with farmers and gardeners, and it is clear that the palace adopted the military hierarchy as a means of organizing the vast numbers of civilian personnel within its employ. No doubt the process began with those crafts and trades which might supply ancillary military staff, such as cooks, leather-workers, or even scribes, but one suspects that later it became the means of assimilating to Assyria a large number of deportees who were not needed, or whose skills would have been wasted, on the land. It is very difficult to judge how significant the cadre of palace employees was, but it must have been an important component of the economy. The system was certainly introduced throughout the provinces, being attested near Carchemish,[3] and surely also in the Harran area census, where some farmers and gardeners are listed as being "from the cooks," "from the victuallers," or "from the weavers." Presumably these families are being redeployed within the palace system to a farmers' or gardeners' "cohort"—though these Doomsday Book passages are hardly sufficient grounds on which to reconstruct a chronic agricultural labour shortage![4]

The military hierarchy was very much in evidence in one sphere of labour which was virtually a monopoly of the palace, since only the palace required it. With no crucial irrigation system to maintain, "civil engineering" was confined to the major projects of the kings: canal systems, city walls, new palaces, etc. The use of large numbers of deportees and others under direct military command is well attested in various sources, including the letters of the kings and the provincial governors entrusted with the work (see below 5.3). Some of those employed may have been doing their *ilku* service, but there is no sign of the arrangement attested in Middle Assyrian times, when individual households could command and supply to the army large numbers of men (*ṣābu*). There is only a faint hint that such a system might have re-emerged at the very end of the empire when the king's power was slipping, if the passage from a text of Aššur-etelli-ilani is rightly translated: "Sin-šum-lešir, my chief eunuch, and the battle-troops of his own household which had stood with him. . . ."[5]

3 *The Employment of Free Persons* The "self-employed" of Assyria must have existed as an important part of the economy, whether they were farmers, craftsmen with small businesses, or merchants. However, in the complete absence of documentary evidence we have to pass over them with this bare mention.[6] Much better attested are various situations in which free persons are temporarily subordinated to other employers, and these are now discussed.

[3]See Postgate 1974a:360-362.

[4]See Fales 1973:123-124, quoting D. Arnaud's view that the redeployment was the consequence of a chronic shortage of agricultural labour. My assumption that the artisans belonged within the state cohort system provides the only precise explanation of the phrase *issu libbi* and accords excellently with my suggestion that the Doomsday Book is specifically concerned with royal lands [see Postgate 1974a:36-39].

[5]Postgate 1969 nos. 13:23-24 and 14:15-16, mutually restorable passages.

[6]For this summary dismissal of the self-employed I was taken to task by Diakonoff. It is true, as he commented, that we should like to know the answer to such questions about them as: did such a group exist at all? Did they supplement their own labour with that of slaves? Were they numerous or of marginal importance? To some extent I have given an opinion on these points, directly or indirectly, but my principal line of defence is that we just do not have the evidence to answer the questions.

3.1 *Free Persons Working for Hire* This group would include those attached to one particular employer on a more or less permanent, but voluntary basis (i.e., neither under economic nor under social coercion), and receiving a regular wage (not rations).[7] It must also include those, virtually self-employed, who undertook piece-work or contract work wherever they found it. This second group is known from work-contracts with builders, brickmakers, carpenters, etc.,[8] and the word for hire (*igru*), although rare, is found in the case of a goldsmith employed to do a specific piece of work probably connected with a wedding.[9] Recently an important new letter demonstrates the existence of a class of hired labourers not previously known, and it deserves to be quoted verbatim:[10]

1. *a-na* LUGAL EN-*a*	To the King, my Lord,
2. ÌR-*ka* $^{I.d}$*sa-am-nu-ḫa*-(U-PAP)	your servant Samnuḫa-bel-uṣur:
3. *šùl-mu a-na* LUGAL EN-*a*	Health to the King, my lord.
4. LUGAL *be-lí ú-da*	The King my lord knows,
5. *ki-i* ^{uru}*še*-[x]-KAN-*a-a*	that the people of . . . village
6. ^{lú}*mu-un-n*[*a-ag-r*]*u-te*	are hired workers.
7. *šu-nu-u-ni*	
8. *ina* KUR.KUR.MEŠ *ša* LUGAL	In the lands of the King
9. *in-na-gu-ru*	they work for hire.
10. [*l*]*a ḫal-qu-te šú-nu*	They are not fugitives,
11. [*i*]*l-ku il-lu-*[*k*]*u*	(but) perform *ilku* service;
12. [TA*? *lì*]*b-bi-šú-nu* LÚ.ERIN$_2$.MEŠ MAN	from among them they
13. [*id-d*]*u-nu*	supply "king's men."

Although this is indeed a first attestation in Neo-Assyrian texts of this usage of *agāru* N "to be hired, to work for hire," the letter as translated depicts an entirely plausible situation. Unfortunately we cannot identify the village in question, but the

[7]Diakonoff feels that this group "is purely imaginary. I cannot think of any real basis on which such a subgroup might have arisen." I could not myself be so emphatic: can we really be sure that it was not possible for a (legally) free Assyrian to work regularly for another free Assyrian without the coercion of debtor:creditor relationship, but more permanently than a seasonally hired worker or one carrying out a specific piece of contract work (see n.8 below)?

[8]For work-contracts, see Postgate 1976:33. Given the provenance of the majority of our texts, it is not surprising that one and perhaps both of the building contracts are with the palace. The contract for a boat or raft (*maškuru*) in *ARU* 640 was with a certain Kiṣir-Aššur, but he may of course have been acting as a state official; and in VAT 8683 K. Deller does not state whether the creditor in the transaction is mentioned. Nevertheless it seems to me perfectly likely that private individuals employed builders or other craftsmen on contract terms.

[9]See Postgate 1979b:101, ND 2310:22′.

[10]*CT* 53 87; remainder of obv. broken, rev. another matter. The text has also been treated in Fales 1980. Some notes here on details of the transliteration: *l*.5: Fales has ^{uru}*ša*[*d-di-*]*kan-a-a*, for which the copy does not seem to offer enough space; however, one should perhaps compare $^{[u]ru}$*še-di-*[*k*]*an*$^{?}$*-a-a* [*CT* 53 393:3′], with Fales. *l*.6: Fales has *mu-un-n*[*a-a*]*b-te*, which was also my initial reaction, but it does not fit the sense or the traces so well. *l*.10: [*k*]*i* (Fales) is to be excluded as one would expect *ki-i*. *l*.12: [*ina l*]*ìb-bi* also possible. *l*.13: [*i-d*]*u-nu* is another possibility, but a derivation from *tadānu* seems inescapable.

official explains to the king that its people go out and about through the lands of Assyria looking for employment. Nevertheless, they are loyal subjects, who do not duck their *ilku* obligations, and they supply soldiers for the royal army. It is a pity that the writer does not tell us what skills, if any, these villagers had to offer, but one imagines that they were most likely to find everyday agricultural labour. Since the writer goes to such lengths to describe their life-style to the king, it may be that it was not very common; but it could equally mean that he doubted the king's familiarity with such mundane topics.

3.2 *Free Persons Attached to Institutions or Households* It is likely that temples at least employed free persons who were nevertheless permanently attached to the temple and drew rations rather than wages. This is of course well attested in Babylonia, where the right to hold an office was sold formally by one holder to another for the profit it brought (German *Pfründe*), but we are not able to show its existence in Assyria, and if it did exist it was certainly less commercialized. A similar relationship may easily be imagined between a free person and a large household—e.g., poor relatives—but in neither case do our sources enable us to make the distinction between free persons and slaves. Moreover, in the case of temples there is a third category, formed by those dedicated to the service of the deity, who, however well born, can be classed as dependent ration-earning personnel.

3.3 *Free Persons Temporarily on State Service* Unless specifically exempted, free persons were liable to *ilku* service, either as a conscript in the army or by doing state corvée work (once at least called *dullu ša šarri*, "the king's work"). The length of time is not known, but could apparently run into years: "It is the third year since my cavalry was given leave; as the King knows, these men of the river-bank serve each for himself, and none of them is exempt."[11] ND 10,0013, an administrative document from the Arsenal at Kalḫu, suggests that some palace employees performed a variety of tasks as their *ilku* service, separately from their normal duties, and these tasks were defined as "from the 1st day of month A to the 30th day of month B."[12]

An entirely different obligation would result from the general call-up (*dikût māti*), but one suspects that during the later empire at least the free population was never conscripted en masse, either for a military campaign or for state corvée, so many labourers of the "helot" class being available.

3.4 *Free Persons Temporarily Enslaved* As already mentioned, free persons in debt might eventually be handed over to their creditor to reside in his house and work for him as a member of the household. There were various forms of debt pledge or enslavement: members of the debtor's family might be sent as pledges to the creditor, with the length of time prescribed in advance—usually a few years—but in other cases the person transferred approached more nearly to a slave, and to recover him

[11]Quoted from *ABL* 154:31-37 [see Postgate 1974a:259].

[12]Kinnier Wilson 1972 pl.49-50; an edition of this tablet will be included as no.89 in Dalley and Postgate 1984.

(or her) a conveyance tablet had to be drawn up, transferring the ownership back from the creditor to the original owner or household head. The distinction, both legal and practical, between debt-enslavement and ordinary pledge remains unclear to us, if indeed there was any distinction. In either case the transferred person was probably open to redemption, either by payment of a sum as agreed in the restricted conveyance under which the transfer took place, or as a result of an *(an)durāru* edict.[13]

The purpose behind the institution of personal pledge was to give the creditor access to the debtor's labour in return for interest on the sum borrowed (and, eventually, for the capital). In the countryside it seems possible that pledged persons (sometimes) and actual debt-slaves (usually) were left in their own houses and merely expected to work on the fields of their creditors, especially when the creditors were themselves city-dwellers. Their conditions would therefore have differed very little from those of the "helots."

Under this heading we should also mention apprenticeship, which is well known in contemporary Babylonia and presumably existed in Assyria too. However, no apprenticeship contracts have come down to us, and so we can only presume that the Assyrian apprentice (*talmīdu*) was usually the son of a free man, serving for a number of years in another household as though a dependant. We cannot exclude the possibility that slave children could also be apprenticed to a craftsman; this might be the situation in *ABL* 253, where apprentices are mentioned in connection with government-administered building works, and in the Harran census where we meet an apprentice iron-smith.[14]

4 *Employment of Unfree Persons* A recently published letter to the King Aššur-ban-apli draws a clear distinction between "slaves of the king" (*urdu ša šarri*), "slaves of an Assyrian," and, by implication, "Assyrians."[15] In other words, we seem to have three classes acknowledged: the free-born citizens of Assyria, the slaves legally, or in practice, owned by these citizens, and royal slaves, who may in theory have been servants of the state. All I wish to do here is to point out that in the Assyrian texts we have only the single term *urdu* to encompass all classes of unfree persons, so that if we wish to make distinctions within this group, we are obliged to coin our own terms. Without necessarily admitting more than a superficial resemblance, we have adopted the word "helot" advocated by I.M. Diakonoff, in preference to "serf," when describing the well known tied cultivators of the Neo-Assyrian empire.[16] There is no evidence known to me that their legal status differed in any way from that of a domestic slave legally the property of a free citizen: some may have been the *urdu* of the king, some of "an Assyrian," but all were *urdu*. Any apparent difference in

[13] On the difficult problem of personal pledge and the boundary between this and debt-enslavement, cf. Postgate 1976, Introduction ¶¶3.7.2, 3.7.4-5 and 3.7.7.

[14] PAP 22 SIMUG AN.BAR 1 *tal-mid* [*ADB* 7 = Fales 1973 no.22, Left Edge ii 3]; for *ABL* 253 see Deller and Parpola 1966:61 and also Fales 1980:141.

[15] See Postgate 1980a.

[16] Diakonoff 1974:64.

status—e.g., that some did and some did not draw rations—results from the fact that some lived apart from their owners, beyond immediate supervision.

Whether owned by the state or privately, the slaves were presumably either of immemorial servile stock or deportees from Assyrian campaigns. For a third possibility, the permanent enslavement of indebted families, we have at present no evidence; initially at least it seems unlikely that they would have been considered ordinary slaves and called *urdu*. To return to the deportees, we assume that they were normally settled in Assyria as "helots," and that the population of conquered lands was the principal source of the helot class in the 7th century at least. The transformation from a "deportee" to a "helot" probably did not involve any change in status, although for practical reasons the new arrivals in the central provinces must have received special treatment and have remained recognizably "captives" (*ḫubtu*) until they had been settled on their new land and assimilated into the local government structure.[17] Outside the central provinces, in recently conquered areas, we have no inkling of the technical status of the population. Prisoners of war taken during the fighting will normally have been deported and so—we presume—automatically have entered helot status; but what of the non-combatant inhabitants? Many of them must have been left to cultivate their hereditary lands, but were they also automatically degraded to the helot class, and if so, who were their owners? The king, the provincial governor, high officials, or a mixture of these? The sources do not tell us.[18]

5 *Types of Employment* We distinguish between agricultural and domestic labour, public works, and crafts and trades. Of these only the public works are restricted to one sector of the economy, and of course the actual work to be done was constant, whoever the employers and the employees. The preoccupations of royal correspondents in the Kouyunjik archives direct our attention especially towards the government's handling of the public works and crafts, but first we must sketch the more general agricultural and domestic labour scene.

5.1 *Agriculture* A farmer's life in northern Mesopotamia is characterized by long periods of relative inactivity punctuated by the need for frenzied work at harvest-time and, less acutely, at the autumn ploughing and sowing. There is none of the ceaseless vigilance required of the cultivator in south Mesopotamia, who must irrigate regularly and maintain the canals and their banks accordingly. There is good evidence, both documentary and archaeological, that the area under permanent

[17]For "deportees" (*ḫubtu*), see *ADB* 6 [= Fales 1973 no.5] vii 4 and other Gambulaeans, no doubt of the same origin, in *ADB* 5 [= Fales 1973 no.21] ii 26-28. For the treatment of deportees within Assyria, see now Oded 1979, Chapter III: The implementation of mass deportation. I should also refer here to the proposal of V.A. Jakobson that the term *šaknu* means "settled" and often applies to deportees settled in the countryside; unfortunately I cannot agree with this idea, and my own opinion is expressed in Postgate 1980b (high military officer!).

[18]For the questions of the identity and legal status of the population of the countryside in the Assyrian Empire, see van Driel 1970; Zabłocka 1971, 1972, 1974, 1978; Postgate 1974b.

cultivation was significantly increased during the later Assyrian empire, and since the growth in the army and government administration must have drawn, in the first instance, on the longer established sectors of the population, it is easy to see why a large proportion of the agricultural labour was supplied by the "helots". The replacement of "Assyrians" whose military or administrative duties prevented them from tilling their own lands, by the "helots" doubtless accounts for the large estates described in the royal land grants and similar texts, and can hardly have contributed to the stability of the empire. One might have expected the newly arrived deportees to be settled mainly in newly cultivated areas—such as that attested in the Ḫarran census for the settlement of the Gambulaean deportees. In fact, at least three of the late Assyrian kings (Sargon, Esarhaddon and Aššur-ban-apli) distributed large numbers of deported persons within the central provinces of Assyria ("Nineveh, Kalḫu, Kilizi, and Arbil"), a measure which was presumably intended to counteract a drift from the land and secure the continued full cultivation of these critical fertile areas.[19] One might be inclined to take the contracts with "harvester clauses" as evidence of a chronic shortage of agricultural labour, but these are a permanent component of the Mesopotamian scene, and really only reflect the inevitable surge of demand at harvest-time.[20]

Most private flocks and herds were doubtless tended by villagers by a variety of ad hoc arrangements, as happens today in the region. However, temples and government organizations maintained permanent shepherds, and even outside their direct employ the work was sufficiently full-time for individuals described as "shepherd" to be listed quite frequently in the Ḫarran census. At shearing time there must have been a need for extra workers, and this was used as the occasion for an annual accounting as well by the government, and doubtless between the shepherd and owners of the animals too. The very few contracts with shepherds, or otherwise concerned with sheep, do not give us enough on which to base a reconstruction of normal practice in the private sector.[21]

5.2 *Domestic Labour* For obvious reasons, there is little in our sources about conditions of domestic labour. We may reasonably assume that domestic slaves and debt-slaves were assigned the menial tasks common to any household—grinding the corn, perhaps spinning, weaving, etc. Women as well as men were obviously much used in domestic contexts, but it is known from a passage in Esarhaddon that male slaves, like Samson, might be used to grind corn: a figurine sent to the king as a symbol of submission was of a slave in chains, and had a grindstone "for performing the work of grinding."[22] Except in the large establishments of the highest officials there is no reason to think that single households employed large numbers of slaves,

[19]See Postgate 1979a:210 with notes 29 and 30.

[20]Harvester contracts: Postgate 1976:44-45; recent comment on the Middle Assyrian harvester clauses: Durand in Aynard and Durand 1980:31-33.

[21]Contracts involving animals: Postgate 1976 no.31 [= *ADD* 115+116], with comment on *BT* 138; also Dalley and Postgate 1984 nos. 9 and 17; Postgate 1973 no.68 (?).

[22]Borger 1956 ¶68.

and any surplus would perhaps have been directed into agriculture. There is however a possibility that some of the wealthier families followed the palace in maintaining their own industrial workshops. It would not be an innovation: in Old and Middle Assyrian Aššur a large household might employ a number of weavers—probably mostly female slaves—producing their own cloth for commercial purposes, and there is no obvious reason why this should not have continued into the first millennium as well.[23] My reason for thinking there may have been private workshops is the term *bēt qāti* (written É ŠU.^{II}), which I believe to mean "a workshop."[24] If this translation is correct—and it is not (yet) generally accepted—it is of interest because house conveyance texts several times mention a *bēt qāti* (and once, indeed, three of them) attached to the main house, implying the existence of private industrial establishments.[25] For further comment on crafts and trades, see below, section 5.4.

5.3 *Public Works* Both the royal inscriptions, the Kuyunjik and Nimrud letters, and the physical remains attest the large scale of building works undertaken by the late Assyrian kings in the central provinces. Some of these massive projects were probably conceived as much to find work for the numerous deportees as for any other reason—although we should not expect the kings to admit this. Certainly the construction of roads, fortifications, canals and palaces was generally initiated by the king, and the royal inscriptions make it clear that the deported populations were largely employed on these projects. However, the ordinary "Assyrian" could also be employed on the King's work as an alternative to service in the army in fulfilment of his *ilku* obligations.[26]

In the case of the construction of Sargon's new capital at Dur-Šarrukin the work force needed was so large, or the work was so dear to the king's heart, that it was administered directly by the king, like the standing army, rather than by the provincial governor. A number of letters from Kuyunjik mention affairs connected with the work at Dur-Šarrukin, and give us some insight into the procedures by which the labour force was collected and controlled. In *ABL* 1432 a provincial governor of Naṣibina relates that he ordered a captain (*rab kiṣri*) to "take your men (*ṣābu*) and come and do work (*dullu*) at Dur-Šarrukin."[27] From *ABL* 486, among other letters, it emerges that sections of the new city-wall were assigned to different

[23]See, e.g., Veenhof 1972:103-123; and the archives of Babu-aḫa-iddina, Shalmaneser I's chancellor, reveal a variety of crafts within his household [these archives to be re-edited by H. Freydank and C. Saporetti; provisionally cf. E. Ebeling, *MAOG* 7/I-II and especially E. Weidner, *AfO* 19 (1959-0) 33-39].

[24]Suggestion made in the edition of *KAV* 197 in Postgate 1974a:363-367; but cf. Postgate 1974c:66 "a room in which business was conducted or visitors received." I would now stress the first half of this definition.

[25]In house sales: *ADD* 326 (= *ARU* 173), 335 (= *ARU* 337), 341 (= *ARU* 353), 342 (= *ARU* 351); Postgate 1970:130 ("above the *bēt ubusāte*"). Also within the Arsenal (*ēkal māšarti*: *RMA* 240:9), and often when attached to temples (see Menzel 1981 I, 50, 77 and 79 for instances). Also attested in Middle Assyrian: *KAJ* 274:16.

[26]The *locus classicus* for the king's work is *ABL* 99 [Postgate 1974a:252-254]. A broken letter from Kuyunjik mentions a (or some) LÚ *e-piš dul-*[*li*]? [*CT* 53 no.614 rev.3].

[27]Translation in Postgate 1974a:301-302.

provinces, with each governor responsible for providing the labour force (and probably the materials too). Demarcation disputes naturally arose occasionally, and in this letter the Chief Steward Ṭab-šar-Aššur gives the king details such as "... three days ago when I was going over the wall they [the governors of Kalḫu and Arrapḫa] came to me and said 'Come and fix the (borders of) our sections between us,'..." or "... the section of the governor of Arrapḫa reaches from (brick?) 850 as far as the side of the city-gate 'The People's Tower'..." For obvious reasons we find that the far provinces are not represented, but labour forces were contributed by Arrapḫa and Naṣibina (each over 150 kilometres away), as we have seen.[28] Probably each force was composed of a mixture of Assyrians on state service and of helots; we do not know who took charge of the many deportees which Sargon tells us he brought into the area to take part in the work, although eventually some of them must have been settled in the area and have come under the governor of Dur-Šarrukin. In any case, whatever their legal or administrative status, the seasonal nature of agricultural labour gives us every reason to suppose that many of the state's labour gangs doubled up as farmers for the rest of the year.

As far as I know, there is no evidence for organized public works outside the government sector: conceivably individual communities, whether villages or cities, organized road-mending, well-digging, wall-building etc. on a communal basis, but this would hardly surface in the written documentation and does not in fact appear to be attested.

5.4 *Crafts and Trades* Outside the palace sector we know that temples might employ a variety of craftsmen,[29] and we assume that there was, in the cities at least, a class of "self-employed" craftsmen serving the needs of the general public. The possibility that the larger private houses may have employed craftsmen and run their own industrial ventures is mentioned above (5.2). We do not propose to list or even discuss the great variety of crafts and trades known to us in the Neo-Assyrian period, both from administrative and legal texts, and from the "practical" lexical lists.[29a] Unfortunately, it is normally not possible for us to be sure of the social status of an individual bearing a professional designation: for example, it *might* be the case that slaves could not properly be given a professional title, or that if they witnessed a document they would always be given the designation "slave," but we cannot prove this. Many of the craftsmen who appear as witnesses or otherwise in the legal documents may be free men, operating independently of the state sector, but since a great number of these texts come from the palaces themselves, it is perhaps more likely that they are within the government's administrative cadre. We simply do not know.

Cohorts of different kinds of craftsmen or specialist workmen are well attested in the 7th century, and have been mentioned already (section 2), when we also referred to the apparent transfer of government personnel from a craftsmen's cohort to

[28]For other occurrences of *pilku*, "a (work-)sector," see *AHw* 863 under *pilku(m)* I.5.

[29]See now simply Menzel 1981.

[29a]See, e.g., Henshaw 1980 *passim*.

agricultural life. The most illuminating document on the state organization of craftsmen is *KAV* 197, a long letter of complaint from a group (*kiṣru*) of oil-pressers to a high official, detailing the malpractices of their immediate superiors, probably of the rank of *rab kiṣri*, although this is not specified. This letter was taken by Ebeling as evidence of guilds in Assyria, not otherwise attested, but in fact it seems clear that the workers are state employees.[30] They are *ālik ilki ša šarri*, "*ilku*-performers of the king," and they are obliged to make *iškāru* payments, a system attested elsewhere in Neo-Assyrian texts, but still not fully understood. We presume that raw materials, called *iškāru*, were supplied to the craftsmen from government stocks, no doubt through a *rab kiṣri*, and in the original form of the system they then processed the materials, returning the finished product (still *iškāru*) through their officer to the government. In fact, though, the texts indicate that by the 7th century a change had taken place, and they were expected to sell off their products, returning to the government only a commuted *iškāru* payment in silver.[31] The original impetus for creating contingents of craftsmen was the government's (and especially the army's) real need for their products. Either, in later years, the system expanded beyond the needs of government, so that contingents continued to be created and the government merely profited from their labour as though a commercial concern, or else the interchange of commodities within the government departments was reorganized along commercial lines for greater efficiency, using silver as a currency, so that the craftsmen's products, though sold, were nonetheless destined for government use.

As the village of leatherworkers near Carchemish demonstrates,[32] not all government craftsmen lived in the towns, and no doubt the same might apply in the private sector. We know of villages called "Bakers' Village," "Goldsmiths' Village" and *kapru diqārāte*, "The Village of Pots," near Nineveh.[33] Some crafts are obviously better pursued outside the city, and pot-making is one, whether because of the proximity of good clay sources, or because of the nuisance which smoking kilns would inflict on an urban population; but goldsmiths and bakers would surely work in a city normally. So either these are lands held privately by a large family or group of specialist workers, or they are members of a government cohort, who have been settled in the countryside for one reason or another—various possibilities suggest themselves.

Other village industries must have flourished too, and it is probable that there were bands of tinkers or itinerant craftsmen—smiths, potters and the like—such as survived in Europe and the Near East until very recently. One such "tribe" in the Mesopotamian area was the Ṣlubba, who pursued an archaic existence in the desert between the Euphrates and Jordan, and whose services were esteemed by the *bedu*

[30]Ebeling 1950; revised translation: Postgate 1974a:363-367. Cf. also Postgate 1979a:212.

[31]For the details concerning *iškāru*, cf. Postgate 1974a:100-110; and for another discussion of the evidence, see Garelli 1979:13-15.

[32]For collated transliteration and translation of this text, see Postgate 1974a:360-362.

[33]Bakers: Postgate 1969 no. 32:23', 44', which also mentions a village of temple employees called *ērib bēti* (LÚ.TU.MEŠ É); goldsmiths: *ADD* 415 rev.9; pots: ^{uru}*ka-par-di-qa-rat* [ND 3469:9 in *Iraq* 15 (1953) 152] and URU.ŠE *di-qa-ra-te* [*ADD* 414 = *ARU* 210:41].

for their lore in metal-working, astrology and medicine.[34] It is the writer's suspicion that they are indeed an archaic survival, and that their ancestors are the *Šelappayu* of Neo-Assyrian (and indeed Middle Assyrian) texts, who have been recognized as smiths by J.V. Kinnier Wilson.[35] The name itself is close enough to be the same, and a life style of itinerant craftsmen would explain how the ethnic description in itself functions as a professional one. Admittedly, there is no clear evidence for an itinerant life style, but one would scarcely expect to meet such evidence in any case; and if the *Šelappayu*, like the Ṣlubba, were credited with supernatural or magical powers, it would explain a puzzling passage in a letter to King Esarhaddon about work on Esagila, which could not proceed because "the *Šelappayu* who was assigned to the work" refused to go and participate in laying the foundations, for the writer explains: "we are unable to lay the foundations without him" and concludes by asking the king to arrange for the delivery of "the spices, sweet oil, salve and stones" for the founding ceremony.[36]

[34]Exhaustive literature and discussion by Caskel 1967 (a reference I owe to Fabrizio Pennacchietti).
[35]Kinnier Wilson 1972:98-100.
[36]*ABL* 471. An association with ritual is perhaps suggested by *BT* 106 in which a *rab Š.* appears as witness before a priest (*šangû*); see *Iraq* 25 (1963) 91.

Bibliography

Aynard, M.J. and Durand, J.M. 1980: "Documents d'Epoque Medio-Assyrienne," *Assur* 3/I:1-3.

Borger, R. 1956: *Die Inschriften Asarhaddons, Königs von Assyrien* (*AfO* Beiheft 9).

Caskel, W. 1967: in M. von Oppenheim, *Die Beduinen*, IV/1:131-153.

Dalley, S.M. and Postgate, J.N. 1984: *The tablets from Fort Shalmaneser* (CTN 3).

Deller, K. and Parpola, S. 1966: "Die Schreibungen des Wortes *etinnu* 'Baumeister' im Neuassyrischen," *RA* 60:59-70.

Diakonoff, I.M. 1974: "Slaves, helots and serfs in early antiquity," *AAASH* 22:45-78.

Driel, G. van 1970: "Land and People in Assyria," *BiOr* 27:168-175.

Ebeling, E. 1950: *OrNS* 19:397-403.

Fales, F.M. 1973: *Censimenti è catasti di epoca neo-assira* (Studi economici e tecnologici 2).

Fales 1980: "New Assyrian letters from the Kuyunjik Collection," *AfO* 27:136-153.

Garelli, P. 1979: "Le système fiscal de l'empire assyrien," in H. van Effenterre (ed.), *Points de vue sur la fiscalité antique* (Publications de la Sorbonne, Série "Études," Tome 14), 7-18.

Henshaw, R.A. 1980: "Late Neo-Assyrian Officialdom" (review article on Kinnier Wilson 1972) *JAOS* 100:283-305.

Kinnier Wilson, J.V. 1972: *The Nimrud Wine Lists* (CTN 1).

Menzel, B. 1981: *Assyrische Tempel* (Studia Pohl, Series Maior 10/I-II).

Oded, B. 1979: *Mass deportations and deportees in the Neo-Assyrian Empire.*

Postgate J.N. 1969: *Neo-Assyrian Royal Grants and Decrees* (Studia Pohl, Series Maior 1).
Postgate 1970: "More 'Assyrian Deeds and Documents'," *Iraq* 32:129-164.
Postgate 1973: *The Governor's Palace Archive* (CTN 2).
Postgate 1974a: *Taxation and Conscription in the Assyrian Empire* (Studia Pohl, Series Maior 3).
Postgate 1974b: "Some remarks on conditions in the Assyrian Countryside," *JESHO* 17:225-243.
Postgate 1974c: "The Bit Akiti in Assyrian Nabu Temples," *Sumer* 30:51-74.
Postgate 1976: *Fifty Neo-Assyrian Legal Documents.*
Postgate 1979a: "The economic structure of the Assyrian Empire" in M.T. Larsen (ed.), *Power and Propaganda* (MesCop 7).
Postgate 1979b: "On some Assyrian ladies," *Iraq* 41:89-103.
Postgate 1980a: "'Princeps Iudex' in Assyria," *RA* 74:180-82.
Postgate 1980b: "The place of the *šaknu* in Assyrian government," *AnSt* 30:67-76.
Veenhof, K.R. 1972: *Aspects of Old Assyrian trade and its terminology.*
Zabłocka, J. 1971: *Stosunki agrarne w państwie sargonidów.*
Zabłocka 1972: "Landarbeiter im Reich der Sargoniden," CRRA 18:209-215.
Zabłocka 1974: "Palast und König," *AoF* 1:91-113.
Zabłocka 1978: "Zur Problem der neuassyrischen Dorfgemeinde," *Studia Historicae Oeconomicae* (Universitet im. Adama Mickiewicza) 13:61-72.

THE OWNERSHIP AND EXPLOITATION OF LAND IN ASSYRIA IN THE 1ST MILLENNIUM B.C.

J.N. Postgate

This article seeks to present a survey of our current knowledge of the conditions under which land was owned, leased, sold and otherwise exploited in Northern Mesopotamia during the first part of the 1st millennium B.C., especially from about 880 to 600 B.C., the period of the Neo-Assyrian empire. To avoid constant repetition and qualification, I would like to draw the readers' attention immediately to the heavy bias inherent in our sources, which come very largely from the last 100 years of this time, and almost exclusively from royal palaces or other administrative contexts. Although much of our information comes from legal instruments concerned with real estate of one kind of another, our attention will be concentrated on land used in agricultural and horticultural production, not for example on buildings and building land, and on the social and economic implications, rather than the legal principles, to be drawn from the texts.

§ 1 *Environmental conditions*

At its greatest extent the Assyrian Empire embraced lands as distant and diverse as Egypt, Palestine, Cappadocia and Elam, but the great bulk of our evidence for conditions of land tenure relates to the comparatively homogeneous stretch of territory which may broadly be called Northern Mesopotamia. This forms an arc bounded on the north and east by the foothills of the Anatolian and Iranian plateaux, and on the south and west by the desert, from the Euphrates at Carchemish to the Tigris at the latitude of Nineveh, and then across the two Zabs past Kerkuk (ancient Arrapha) almost to the Diyala.

Apart from the occasional outlier of the major mountain ranges (e.g. the Jebel Sinjar), the terrain is «undulating country with sandy gypsiferous soil and patches of loess and Quaternary alluvium»(1), intersected by occasional seasonal wadis. The agricultural regime here is today dependent on rainfall, and must also have been in the 1st millennium B.C. Although direct proof is hard to come by, one must assume that the great majority of the «fields» (A.ŠÀ(.GA) = *eqlu*) mentioned in our sources were devoted to rain-fed cereals, principally barley, and ploughed with oxen or by hand.

There are of course exceptions. At Assur and on the lower reaches of the Habur (south of that river's passage between the Jebel Sinjar and Jebel Abd-ul-Aziz) canals were constructed for miles along the edges of the river valleys, giving the benefits of gravity-flow irrigation to those who cultivated the rich alluvial soils of the valley beds(2). No doubt some such canals were also built (as already in the early 2nd millennium B.C.) along some stretches of the Euphrates between Terqa and Hit, although written evidence for this at our date is probably restricted to the activities of the early 8th century independent Governor of Suhu, Šamaš-rēš-uṣur(3). On such stretches, the exploitation of the river waters facilitated successful agriculture in a narrow strip (*Stromoasis*) well south of the limits of viable rainfall agriculture, and in these areas there can have been little permanent agricultural settlement outside the river valleys. Round the major population centers of the Assyrian Empire, like Arrapha, Arbil, Kalhu, Nineveh and the Upper Habur, irrigation was less necessary, though not unknown. Kings constructed cross-country canals, at least some of whose waters benefited the populace; but it is also likely that valley-bed canals were in use along the Tigris and the two Zabs, wherever the width of the bed offered enough ground to justify the effort(4). Even without gravity-flow irrigation, the fields in the valley-beds must always have attracted intensive exploitation, both because of

(1) Oates 1968, 3.

(2) For Assur, see Reade, *RA* 72 (1978) 170; the best textual evidence for the Habur is the inscription of Bēl-ēreš (Nassouhi, *MAOG* 3/1-2 (1927) 6-10), and archaeological details were presented at the 32nd Rencontre Assyriologique Internationale at Münster (Westf.) by H. Kühne.

(3) Weissbach 1903, 9-15; note that in fact the work is only the reconditioning of an existing canal. I have myself observed ancient rock-cut channels on the left bank of the river near Anah, but as far as I know their date has yet to be established. For early 2nd mill. practices, see Klengel, *AOF* 7 (1980) 77-87; also the Hana Dynasty (despite the doubts of Goetze, *JCS* 11 (1957) 63-4).

(4) For possible Assyrian canals along the Zabs, see Reade, *RA* 72 (1978) 172-4. From texts, cf. the *hirītu* (from the verb «to dig») in land-sales etc.: *ARU* 111; 135; 165; 397; also *ABL* 1180:9'. In *ARU* 101:36 there is a *gugallu* «canal inspector» as witness; here, to judge from the preceding line, we are in the region of Lahiru, and irrigation probably came from the right bank of the Diyala.

the quality of their soils, and because of the opportunities for using the river water afforded by the construction of temporary weirs or the use of buckets. Water-wheels were probably unknown in Assyrian times, but at least one text mentions plots of land irrigated in two different ways, *bēt šīqi* (canal-irrigated) and [*bēt*] *dalāni* (bucket-irrigated)(5).

In view of the extra potential of fields either in the river-valleys or canal-irrigated (or both), it is no surprise that these advantages are specified in many of the land sale documents: the distinction between fields «in the valley» (*ina ušalli*) or «on the heights» (*ina mûlê*) is standard, and not infrequently land is said to be *bēt šīqi* (canal-irrigated), in texts referring to the areas of Dur-Šarruken(6), Arrapha (= Kerkuk)(7), Šibaniba (= Tell Billa)(8), and the lower Habur(9), among others(10). No doubt there were many small irrigation systems which did not merit royal patronage and a mention in the royal inscriptions, sometimes in places we should not have predicted: at Tell Abta, about 35 km north of Hatra in the jazirah, some kind of canal system seems to have been in use(11), another canal (*hirītu*) is mentioned near Adian, probably in the Kerkuk area(12). Access to canal water in particular cannot have been an unmixed blessing: taxes were probably levied on their use(13), and a few legal documents specify the water-rights accompanying land which is being sold. One refers to continuous water(14), another specifies that «he may draw extra water for 2 days and 2 nights»(15). Although wells may change owners along with land, some must have been communal, and a sale of land at Dur-Šarruken states that «he may draw water from the well with (the rest of) his village»(16).

Apart from the availability of water, there is only one land-classification in use in the land-sale documents which seems to refer to its general agricultural quality. This is the phrase *ina maz(za)rûti* «in cultivation»; despite some ambiguity, it probably means that the fields are within the area of regular cultivation(17). The opposite to this may have been land «in the desert» (*ina madbāri/mudābiri*): despite the English translation, and the absence of this term from land-sale texts, some of these «desert» lands were certainly cultivated, and even supported villages(18). The term refers, in fact, to the ill-defined transitional strip between the unsettled semi-desert and the regularly farmed areas closer to the hills. In times of political stability this strip can be profitably farmed by those with alternative means of subsistence: in this century, by newly settled nomadic tribes on the one hand, and by wealthy urban land-lords (e.g. from Mosul) on the other(19). Although a harvest here may succeed only two years in five, the fertility of these jazirah lands makes this an attractive long-term investment, but not one compatible with subsistence farming.

Clearly we must expect very different land regimes in the two differing environments. Wirth observes that plots of land round Mosul are much smaller than the average holdings in the jazirah, which are mostly between 25 and 1000 ha(20). Then, as now, the amount of land assigned to the administrative area of particular villages must have decreased, as one came nearer to the desert proper, and we shall see below that this will have had consequences for the pattern of land holdings; furthermore, it is likely — although for this I can quote no modern confirmation — that the alternate-year fallow system was not applied, and perhaps indeed not needed, in areas where only two out of five harvests were likely to succeed. The fallowing system will be discussed below; the point is raised here only to underline the influence environmental conditions may have on patterns of land exploitation.

§ 2 *Types of real estate*

The great bulk of arable land which we have been considering was usually referred to simply as «field(s)» (A.ŠÀ(.MEŠ) = *eqlu*) and placed first in any enumeration of real estate. When the Assyrians give a general description of landed property, the fields are usually followed immediately by «orchards» (GIŠ.ŠAR = *kirû*): «he is giving them [the fugitives] fields, orchards and houses, is settling them on his land and they are dwelling there» (*ABL* 252:29-31), or «There are some servants of mine in the province of the Chief Butler, and some fields and orchards, but the servants of the Chief Butler wanted my orchards and took them» (*ABL* 353 rev. 8-13; cf. *LAS* No. 36). It is therefore no surprise to find orchards sold together with fields in the legal documents, or exchanged or leased. We know that a variety of fruit-trees was regularly cultivated in Assyria, and they must

(5) *CTN* 2 No. 64; cf. also two instances of the word *mašqītu* «a sluice(?)» (*CAD* M/1, 383a). Oates 1968, 48 writes that «the yield of irrigated barley has been estimated at a minimum of 300 kg. per donum, at least twice that of rain-fed crops».

(6) *CTN* 2 No. 64.

(7) *ARU* 444.

(8) *ARU* 187.

(9) *ARU* 211.

(10) *ARU* 105:3 (coll. Parpola, *Assur* 2/5 (1979) 176); *ARU* 171:6' (coll. Parpola, op.cit. 167); *ARU 408*:4.

(11) «(the city's) water he shall not divert into another channel» (see *CAD* B 357b, s.v. *butuqtu*). There is however a possibility that this is merely a repetition of a stereotyped clause.

(12) *ARU* 165.

(13) Cf. *TCAE* 131-2.

(14) *ARU* 107:3 (A.MEŠ *ka-a-a-ma-nu*).

(15) *FNALD* No. 4:36-7 (= *ARU* 373).

(16) *FNALD* No. 2:60; note that, against *FNALD* p.24, we should read EGIR *da-ra[!]-ri* in *ARU* 137/8 (after Parpola's collation *Assur* 2/5, 120), so that no water-rights are mentioned in this text.

(17) Cf. *Iraq* 32 (1970) 135.

(18) See my discussion, *JESHO* 17 (1974) 238.

(19) See Wirth 1968, 171 f.

(20) *Ibid.*, 171.

have been an important component in the agricultural economy of North Mesopotamia(21). Unfortunately the sale texts rarely if ever tell us what was grown in the «orchards» (with one exception), and even in the Harran census they are just described as «fruit orchards» (*kiri zamri*) without naming the species(22). The exception is the vineyard, also called *kirû*, but its size usually indicated by the number of vines (*tillutu*): they are counted in hundreds, and the Harran census mentions numbers ranging from 400 to 49,300. The land of Izalla, between Harran and Nisibis, was renowned for its wine(23), and viticulture was widespread elsewhere to judge from the sale documents; it is rarely possible to locate the area of an estate precisely, and we can only presume that the orchards and vineyards, as today, were concentrated in the foothills and wherever there was irrigation(24). Although the majority of the legal documents reflect holdings of the palace élite, our other sources, such as the letters, suggest that the ownership of land was often combined with orchards and vineyards.

Less often, though not seldom, we find small «vegetable gardens» (GIŠ.ŠAR Ú.SAR = *kiri urqi*). In both sales and cadastral texts these are usually counted, not measured (1, 5, or once even 1/2 vegetable gardens), and it is not always possible to decide if their area is included within the total area of land already listed. Presumably, though, they were relatively small plots, and one, sold in isolation at Kalhu in 779 B.C., measured only 46 x 30 cubits (about 15 x 22 m.). Obviously such areas could be kept watered by hand. In the Harran census we occasionally meet timber plantations, called *qablu*; these are usually of poplar (?: *ṣarbutu*), but other species are also mentioned(25). Plantations of timber are not frequently sold in the legal texts — I have noted only the stand of gall-oaks (*allānu*) in the Sinjar district, forming part of an estate bought by Remanni-Adad (*ARU* 445-6).

Especially when a complete estate is changing hands, often with its inhabitants, other features of the rural landscape are mentioned. Threshing-floors (*adru*, *adrāte*) are often included, and in one case sold in isolation, when it measures only 0.09 of a homer (ca. 10 x 10 m., a reasonable size(26)). Otherwise, like the vegetable gardens, their size is not specified. Wells (PÚ = *būr(t)u*) are not infrequently listed(27), and there is a type of real estate called *tabriu* (plural *tabriāte*) whose nature is unfortunately quite obscure; my guess would be that it has some connection with animal husbandry. In one case a stretch of the town fortifications is leased (*BT* 136), and in another an estate at Dur-Šarruken includes the village rubbish-tip(28). Sales often include a house and other buildings, or waste building plots, but I do not propose to deal with these special kinds of real estate in any detail, partly because there is no hint in the documents that they enjoyed any different legal status, and partly because they differ too much from one case to another to allow of any general inferences.

§ 3 *The documentation and administration of land ownership*

The owner of real estate was its «lord» (EN = *bēlu*), and his title to ownership will usually have derived from inheritance or purchase. For ancestral, inherited land it is unlikely that written entitlement was necessary, local tradition and existing land use probably being generally accepted. There is no evidence for a comprehensive cadastral register, even though the administration may have had lists of landowners for its own purposes(29). Certainly the 'Assyrian Doomsday Book' is nothing comparable to the Norman survey of England. For land sale/purchase, however, Middle Assyrian precedent strongly suggests that the change of ownership required to be documented in writing, and it is probable that the term *uppušu* in Neo-Assyrian land sales (and leases and pledges) implies the fulfilment of public notification and registration procedures, needed before a «valid tablet» of sale (*dannutu*) could be drawn up(30).

In the Middle Assyrian laws, which apply particularly to the city of Assur and its environs, the sale of land involves the participation of the mayor (*haziānu*) and elders (GAL.MEŠ = *rabûti*) of «the village of the house and field which he is buying». Although we have no comparable legal provisions from the 1st

(21) A brief survey of Assyrian fruit-trees is given by the writer in *Bulletin on Sumerian Agriculture* 3 (1987) 128-132.

(22) For (*a*)*zamru* «fruit» cf. *JESHO* 17 (1974) 226-7; *BiOr* 37 (1980) 68.

(23) *RlA* V/3-4, 225-6.

(24) See Wirth 1968, 173 for the characteristic configuration of a village and its orchards at the outflow of a water-course on to the plain.

(25) E.g. *šaššugu* (meaning uncertain) and *hilupu* (a kind of willow?), *CCENA* Nos. 1.ii.43 and 3.i.9 (sic; coll.).

(26) The homer (Assyrian *emāru*, originally «donkey(-load)») is a measure of area which cannot be accurately defined. The only evidence for its size comes from Nuzi in the mid-2nd millennium, and even that is uncertain, since the length of the GÌR is not known. It is more likely that the Assyrian homer was of similar size to that in use at Nuzi (and remained so during the 1st millennium) than that it was defined according to the entirely different system of 1st millennium Babylonia (which gave Meissner a value of 7340 m^2 for the homer). On the basis of the Nuzi evidence H. Lewy proposed 1 homer = 18000 m^2, but more recently Zaccagnini favours a figure of about 11000 m^2. In order to give an idea of the order of magnitude of the homer, I have occasionally used the equation 1 homer = 10000 m^2 or 1 hectare. See Zaccagnini, *Ugarit-Forschungen* 11 (1979) 853-6.

(27) For the problem of reading PÚ in Neo-Assyrian, see Deller, *OrNS* 35 (1966) 316f. (*būru* or *būrtu*?). Different from «well» is *iarhu* «a pool, cistern», which is also occasionally mentioned as a topographic feature in land sales.

(28) See *FNALD* No. 2:34; for the word *kiqillutu* see now the Aramaic *qlqlt'* in l. 22 of the Tell Fakhariyah statue (A. Abou-Assaf, P. Bordreuil & A.R. Millard, *La statue de Tell Fekherye et son inscription bilingue assyro-araméenne*, Paris 1982).

(29) Such as for instance some or all of the texts edited by Fales in *CCENA*.

(30) For detailed discussion of this point, see *FNALD* pp. 14-15; note that (in Neo-Assyrian times at least) not only sales but also leases of land used the *uppušu* formula.

millennium, there is ample evidence that the village remained the organization through which land law and customs were administered: as we have seen above, it was by the village (URU = *ālu*[?]) that the rights to use a well were arranged, and we shall see shortly below that *ilku* service and other forms of taxation were exacted through the villages (§ 6). Evidently it was known precisely which lands «belonged» to which village, and when a real-estate sale is for «a village in its entirety» (*ana gimirti-šu*) it includes the fields, orchards, etc. belonging to it. This is a situation resulting naturally from the interaction of two factors: the internal need for communal self-administration within each village, and the external need of the government to have a channel for the administration of taxes, military service, etc. in the countryside.

The social mechanisms for regulating land-tenure within a village must go back, in the abstract, to prehistoric times, and it is unlikely that Neo-Assyrian practice differed much from that of Middle Assyrian Assur. The needs were constant: a communal organization to represent the village in its dealings with other villages and with the governmental and judicial authorities, to administer the land within its own boundaries in accordance with the procedures determined by law and custom, and to organize whatever agricultural works required the collaboration of the community as a whole. In North Mesopotamia the control of irrigation and other water-rights is less critical than in the south, but there were other aspects which certainly did require communal administration. Principal among these was the regulation of the fallow system: an alternating biennial fallow regime is standard throughout the North Mesopotamian area today, and Neo-Assyrian land-lease texts in particular make it clear that it was regularly practised then, since a typical lease would specify «3 crop-years (*mērušu*), 3 fallow-years (*karaphu*), in all 6 years, he shall enjoy the land»(31). Common-sense suggests that the following description of a Turkish village in the 20th century A.D. would have applied verbatim to an Assyrian village of the 1st millennium B.C.: «One-half of the village land is sown one year, and the other left fallow and used for pasture. The village herds and flocks are transferred from one side to the other after the harvest, to glean the harvested fields and eat the stubble»(32). To ensure that everyone observes the same fallowing system requires co-operation, and the Middle Assyrian evidence from Assur shows that a two-tier system of land division was used, by which the lands in each 'half' of the village were divided into major tracts, in their turn subdivided into «lots» (*pūru*)(33). Our texts show that both in Middle and in Neo-Assyrian times the word «lot» should be understood literally: the land was indeed divided into carefully delimited «lots», which were numbered («third», or «ninth», for instance) ready for the annual(?) assignation to those participating in the draw(34). Details of the practice in the 1st millennium are very scarce, and virtually confined to *KAV* 186, a frustratingly damaged document concerned with the definition of «lots»: it specifies boundaries («above the royal road going to ...» or «opposite the gate-tower»), and begins with the phrase *ina qí-ri-te ša pu-ra-*[(*a-*)*ni*], which I suspect means «at the calling of the lots», with a «second calling» (*ina qí-ri-te* 2-*te*) later in the document. This would refer to the public ceremony at which the lots were drawn and the results announced. *KAV* 186 also uses the word *qutānu*, which is perhaps a further subdivision, and is otherwise known only from Neo-Babylonian texts.

In their relations with the outside world, the villages were normally represented by the *hazannu* (MAss. *haziānu*), an office also held in towns and cities and recognized by the government administration. His link to the provincial governor was probably the «village-inspector» (GAL URU.MEŠ = *rab ālāni*[?]) although we have no direct proof for this. Both men must often have had to deal with problems of land tenure, and hence they are sometimes named among those who might challenge the validity of a land-sale(35). The *hazannu* is also attested once as the first signatory of a ground-plot sale document, although not the owner, but this is the only unequivocal evidence known to me that the village and its officials exercised any *legal* control over the ownership of private land(36). Nevertheless, in practice they must have had some form of control: sale documents do envisage possible claims by both relatives and officials, and although a single person is usually named as seller, relatives and neighbours often appear as witnesses. Evidently, in areas of stable settlement, where land was allocated annually by lot, the co-operation of other members of a village would have been needed to accomplish a sale, and in such circumstances the account of a Turkish village in this century offered by Stirling may reasonably be applied once more: «under the present law, the cultivated land within the village territory belongs outright to its village owners, who can dispose of it as they choose. In practice, land is not often sold, and when it is, it is normally sold to close kin or to neighbours»(37). We must not, however, make the mistake of considering all villages to have been similar: many new villages were founded during the Neo-Assyrian period (see § 7 below), some of them the property of single owners,

(31) The formulary is described in *FNALD* pp. 29-30.

(32) Stirling 1965, 48.

(33) Recently summarized by me in Dandamayev et al. 1982, 309-10; for modern Syria, Wirth 1971, 227-8 (!).

(34) So *KAJ* 139: *pūra šanai'a/šalaši'a/rabai'a* and *KAV* 125-129: *pūru 4-ú/5-ši-ú/7-ú/9-ú*. A 7880, a Khorsabad tablet in Chicago to be edited by S. Parpola, is a description of *pūrāni* in the village of Babi.

(35) Cf. *FNALD* p. 19; for a *rab ālāni* [doubt exists as the Neo-Assyrian reading of URU], cf *CTN* 2 No. 17:14.

(36) *CTN* 2 No. 44.

(37) Stirling 1965, 49.

and it is obvious that there would not have been the same need for communal controls in such cases.

So far we have concentrated on the question of communal restraints on the private sale of land, but we must now turn to the problems of joint and communal land ownership. We must bear clearly in mind the difference between the ownership of land in common, and the existence of communal constraints on private ownership. Such constraints need not limit the right of the individual owner to sell: the land could not be removed from the village's territory by sale to an outsider, and the community's controls would be equally applicable to the new owner. Entirely different would have been the status of land owned in common by a village: this is hard to document, since by its very nature it could only rarely, if ever, have been sold, and on the few occasions where we have the sale of an entire village nothing is said of common land. Apart from special cases, like roads or threshing-floors, it is possible that villages did have a reserve of communally owned land in the Neo-Assyrian period, and in at least one instance land being sold is described as bordering on a plot belonging to a village(38).

Different again is the joint ownership of land by a number of individuals, which also existed. In some cases this was where sons had not yet formally divided their paternal inheritance (*bēt abi*); documents where several owners of a single plot are listed doubtless often result from this situation, but filiations are so rarely given in Neo-Assyrian texts that it is mostly impossible to know their relationships. How long property remained undivided after the father's death no doubt varied, according to local practices, family needs, and other factors we cannot hope to reconstruct. It was possible to sell or to pledge land even before a formal division had been made, either jointly or individually(39), and as far as we know there was an equal division between male heirs (i.e. no preferential share for the eldest). This at least seems to be the implication of a passage in a letter reading: «My father entrusted 6 homers of land to his brother, and my brother and I each took 3 homers (of this) ...»(40). It is important to realize that the technical division of an inheritance in law need not have entailed a corresponding separation of boundaries on the ground: each brother may merely have received an equal proportion of the land cultivated in common, and its exact location need only have been defined if it became necessary to sell to someone outside the family, in which case the co-operation of the other brothers would have been essential, but presumably not their formal consent as owners. No doubt such co-operative cultivation was common within the family, being an advantageous strategy to offset the damaging effects of partition into minute plots, and very likely extending to paternal cousins and even beyond; but there is no evidence that joint *ownership* could extend beyond brothers under normal conditions.

Of course other types of joint ownership did exist in special cases: in *ARU* 334 there are 5 joint owners of a threshing-floor, measuring only 0.09 homers and obviously not susceptible of subdivision, or in *CTN* 2, 35 we have a consortium of temple personnel as joint owners of land (4 singers and a lamentation-priest). We cannot, however, assume that in every sale of land by more than one owner there was joint ownership: thus in *ARU* 168 the owners are described as «in all, 10 men of the village of Danaya, owners of the village being sold in its entirety», and since they are all military personnel from the Nineveh élite it is unlikely that they were the ancestral joint owners of the lands(41). That the sellers are simply an aggregation of individual owners can be proved in such a case as *ARU* 413, where a royal eunuch buys 40 homers of land in a village, subdivided into 19 separate plots, with different (sometimes joint) owners specified for each plot. Such «aggregate sales» are no doubt for the convenience of the purchaser, and the apparent consortium of owners probably only came together because of the geographical fact that their properties were adjacent, and was disbanded once the purchase price had been appropriately allocated(42).

§ 4 *Temple lands*

The natural presumption that the Assyrian temples might own land is confirmed by the occasional text. We read of an «orchard of Nergal» at Nineveh(43); a land survey text from Nineveh mentions an entire «village of Nabû» in the land of Halahhu, and this may well have been the «village called Qurani in the land of Halahhu» where there was an estate of 400 (homers) of land taken by Sargon for the new temple of Nabû at Dur-Šarruken(44). It may be that the kings often gave land to the temples in this way, but we have more evidence for indirect support in the form of grants to the priests or other temple officials, or even to individuals otherwise apparently unconnected with the temple, on the understanding that the holders should supply offerings to the temple(45). The land so granted was usually exempted from state taxation, and it could apparently be sold, as in the sale of a vineyard in 682 B.C. where a note is added at the end of the text that «It is the vineyard of the

(38) *ARU* 413:11, cf. 21.

(39) Sale of «shares» (HA.LA = *zittu*) in *CTN* 2 No. 23; *ARU* 48; lease of a «share» in *TCL* 9 no. 66.

(40) *ABL* 1285 rev. 21-2; no doubt the uncle acted as guardian of the property of the two brothers.

(41) For other examples of multiple sellers to palace officials, cf. *FNALD* No. 2 and *ARU* 167.

(42) It is of course possible that in some cases the members of the consortium of sellers had previously formed a consortium of borrowers and are paying off their collective debt by means of the sale (cf. *FNALD* pp; 45-47 on multiple debtors).

(43) *ARU* 374.

(44) *CCENA* No. 24 rev. 14 and *ABL* 480; compare the «orchard of Ištar of Hu(zirina)» in *CCENA* No. 21.viii.16.

(45) Discussed in *NARGD* pp. 5-6.

regular offerings (*ginê*) of Aššur and Mulissu»(46). A more complex situation is reflected in another text relating to the construction of Dur-Šarruken, in which Sargon transplants the owners of some land, given some 100 years before to their ancestors by Adad-nirari III in return for an annual contribution (*sattukku*) of 10 homers of crushed corn to a temple, and instals them on an equivalent area in the environs of Nineveh(47).

Land could also be dedicated to the temples by private citizens, just like other property. The dedications are often said to be «for the life of» the king, and are to the deity (not to his priests)(48). As well as a few surviving dedication conveyances, like one for the life of Sin-šarru-iškun and his queen found in the Nabû Temple at Kalhu, we have the curious case of Ilu-iabi and the village of Elumu which he dedicated in its entirety to Sin «for the life of Assur-ban-apli»: unfortunately he had second thoughts and tried to repossess it, but then Assur-ban-apli himself stepped in and re-dedicated it to Sin «for my life»(49). The usual word for to dedicate is *šêlû*, and no doubt Ilu-iabi's original intentions were also those of «Adad-rimanni, the chief cook of Harran» who «dedicated the estate of Sin-ereš, the cook» in the Harran census(50). It is likely that land so dedicated by private individuals was, like royal grants to temples, thereby exempted from state taxation: this seems to follow from some of the clauses in dedication conveyances, and from the letter *ABL* 177, where an official complains to the king about a priest called Urad-Nabû (perhaps the priest of Nabû at Kalhu), who «has written the fields, house, people and children onto a sealed document (*unqi*) as dedications (*šêluāte*) and conveyed them to himself, so that I have no authority over them»(51).

§ 5 *State-owned land*

In the land grants of the 8th-7th centuries B.C. the Assyrian kings bear the sole title of *uklu* «overseer»(52). As has often been noted before, this term goes back to the early 2nd millennium, and is traditionally borne by the king when acting as head of the city-state of Assur, in which role he was, *inter alia*, the supreme authority in control of land. When he made a land grant, therefore, it was as custodian of the state lands, and we must presume that such land was strictly distinguished from any property he might hold as an individual in his own name, if only because normal inheritance procedures might otherwise lead to the fragmentation of the state lands among several brothers. For obvious reasons we have no sale documents relating to the personal property of the kings, and even government estates are hard to document. Probably the gifts of land to individuals, occasionally mentioned in the royal correspondence, are also from reserves of state land, and so too the substitute property found by Sargon for those he had compulsorily displaced to make space for his new capital at Dur-Šarruken(53).

While we cannot hope to establish the relative areas of state and private land, the administration of its land must have been one of the government's principal preoccupations(54). A great deal of land was probably entrusted to the direct administration of the provincial governors, but its exact legal status is often hard for us to establish, since the high officers of state could also hold prebendary lands in connection with their office, and private property of their own, within provinces assigned to other high officials. The clearest example of this is probably in the Harran census, where estates of 3 to 40 homers are attributed to high state officials like the Chief Butler (*rab šāqê*), the Palace Herald, the *sartennu*, three provincial gover-

(46) *ARU* 371.

(47) *NARGD* No. 32.

(48) For dedications see *FNALD* Nos. 15-16 with commentary.

(49) K 2564 (Th. Bauer, *Das Inschriftenwerk Assurbanipals* (Leipzig 1933), II, 90f.).

(50) *CCENA* No. 3.iii.9.

(51) A.ŠÀ É UN.MEŠ DUMU.MEŠ *šêluāte* ^IÌR-^dPA LÚ.SANGA *ina* ŠÀ *unqi issaṭar ana ramani-šu uttēri ū anāku ina muhhi lā šašluṭāku*. This Urad-Nabû seems likely to have been the priest of the Nabû Temple at Kalhu (see Menzel 1981, I, 107; also I, 26, although I do not agree with her interpretation of this passage).

(52) For these grants, see *NARGD*. For the term *uklu* see Diakonoff 1969, 219-220, where it is traced to an original function as «representative of the city-state community of Aššur which was the original actual owner of all land in the state». With the first part of this statement I would agree, but I can only envisage the city as the «administrator» (rather than «actual owner») of the land within its bounds.

(53) Instances of land granted to individual: *ABL* 421 («the father of the king gave me 10 homers of cultivated land in Halahhu»); *ABL* 414 (officials giving fields and orchards, in Syria); *ABL* 252 (foreign king giving fugitives from Assyria fields, orchards and houses). The state also gives people houses (when transplanting them forcibly, very often): *ABL* 190 (probably in Dur-Šarrukin); *ABL* 208 (eastern frontier; perhaps not a gift); *ABL* 314 (also official encouragement but perhaps not a gift); cf. also *NL* 102 (*Iraq* 36 (1974) 212-5), installing people in Huzirina (=? Sultan Tepe, near Harran). At times it is difficult to know whether «giving» villages is putting them into new legal ownership, or merely transferring them to another administrative sphere: cf. *ABL* 174, where it must refer to political control, and *ABL* 610 where the same may well be true: «I will give two or three villages from among them to Bel-duri, and I will give you (some) in their stead». Administrative control is probably not at issue in *ABL* 168 («why did you take (*tašši*) the villages and fields of Ilu-iada' which are in the province of Arrapha and in the village of Šamaš-naṣir?»). For the formal assignation of territory to a province, cf. the Hindana document in the form of a *kudurru* edited in *NARGD* pp. 115-7 with additional piece, Reade & Walker, *AfO* 28 (1981/82) 117-8.

(54) The correspondence of Tiglath-pileser III found at Kalhu is particularly full of messages about the farming of state lands. One example is worth quoting: 'The *turtānu* ordered me to plant 1000 (homers?) of seed corn, (but) the year has gone by and I cannot plant 1000 (homers) of seed corn... When the ploughs and oxen arrive I will plant as much seed corn as I can' (*NL* 79 (*Iraq* 27 (1965) 26-7), from a provincial official in Arpad, recently come under Assyrian rule). Similar reports on agricultural matters are to be found in *NL* 13:24-5; 20:25-8; 21:rev.2'-3'; 23:E:25-9 (all in *Iraq* 17); 24, whole letter (*Iraq* 18); 56:1'-13' (*Iraq* 21); and, in the reign of Sargon, *ABL* 128:rev.10:16 and 157:rev.8-12. This is not an exhaustive list.

nors (Nineveh, Halṣu and Tamnunu), and others(55). Another very clear statement is given in a letter written to Tiglath-pileser by a former governor of the province of Arzuhina (between Arbil and Arrapha): «The king my lord knows that the lands of the House of the *sukkallu* and of the House of the *sartennu* do not extend across the river Radanu: their border is the royal road which goes to Azari»(56).

The Assyrian usage is consistent: where lands are ascribed to an official by his title and not by his own name, the implication is that they are prebendary lands accompanying the office. This is made more explicit when they are said to belong to the official's «House». We meet the *sukkallu*'s and the *turtānu*'s Houses particularly often, perhaps because (like the *sartennu* but in contrast to the Chief Butler, Palace Herald, Chief Steward (*abarakku*) etc.), they did not also have provinces assigned to them. These estates might be extensive, encompassing entire villages, and they are not confined to any one part of the empire, since the *sukkallu* also held property in the Sinjar area, and on the northern frontier(57), the *sartennu* near Nineveh and Kurbail(58), and the *turtānu* on the northern frontier, round Kurbail and near Guzana(59). At times it seems as though the Houses are in fact miniature provinces, but they are not so (even though the term NAM = *pāhutu* is occasionally applied to them) because the phraseology «House of» is not used for a genuine province, but is used in the similar cases where a real provincial governor also administers estates within another province (e.g. the governor of Assur province in Guzana)(60) or for the estates of the Aššur Temple which were equally widely scattered(61). Nevertheless, the rights of the officers over their «Houses» were probably very similar to the rights of provincial governors over their provinces: they were not the rights of legal ownership, because real estate within their Houses could be conveyed from one private individual to another without the intervention of the head of the House(62). Quite possibly, therefore, they were expected to raise taxes and administer *ilku* obligations within their Houses, and it is likely that such estates were independent of the jurisdiction of the provincial governor in whose territory they lay, and thus effectively exempt from direct state taxation (see below, § 6)(63).

Even if the officials' control of such land fell short of direct administration for their own benefit, some of it must have been in effect prebendary land, and there is other evidence for the existence of state land assigned to employees for their subsistence(64). This has been identified with the word *ma'uttu*, which Parpola is probably right to equate with the Babylonian *mu'untu* occurring only in *ABL* 336: «(the village) Bit-Hussanni ... is 100 (homers?) of dates and 100 (homers?) of corn-land, *mu'untu* of the king»(65). «Prebend-land (*ma'uttu*) of the king» is also mentioned in 8th and 7th century texts from Assyria: a correspondent tells the king that he will «put harvesters on the prebend-land»(66) and another that «the prebend-lands of the king have been harvested»(67), while other documents show that regular taxes were levied on such land(68). That *ma'uttu* land was assigned to individuals follows from *ADD* 755, a list of lands which «Ahi-iaqamu enjoys (*ēkal*) in Halahhu», most of which he probably holds on lease or in pledge from the persons named, but in two cases *ma'uttu* land. Perhaps the most revealing passage is broken: in the royal grants of Assur-ban-apli he seems to be guaranteeing that «[(the recipient's sons)] are exempted (from taxation) like him; [(and ...)] perpetual prebend-land (*ma'uttu kabistu*) ...» — but the breaks forbid full understanding of the passage(69).

(55) *CCENA* No. 21; some of the estates in *NARGD* No. 27 (reign of Adad-nirari III) are probably prebendary lands going with various governorates.

(56) *NL* 41:16-20 (*Iraq* 20 (1958) 187-90).

(57) *sukkallu* (one or both): *NL* 41 (see n. 56); *ARU* 437 (Village of Goldsmiths of *bēt sukkalli*; occupied by Itu'aeans!). Without *bēt*: *ARU* 395:5; *ARU* 445 (orchard in Sinjar district). *ABL* 424:12 shows that some of the *sukkallu*'s estate was on the frontier with Urarṭu.

(58) *sartennu*: *NL* 41 (see n. 56); *CTN* 2 No. 15 (in Kurbail; PN *ša bēt sartenni*); *ARU* 657:20 (farmer of *s.*).

(59) *turtānu*: persons *ša bēt turtāni*: *CTN* 2 No. 15; 36 (Kurbail); *AfO Beiheft* 6, No. 25:8 (Guzana); *CTN* 2 Nos. 91:30, 35; 102:2; 110:6. Village of *t.*: *CTN* 2 No. 4:19 (but not *ARU* 387:3 after collation, Parpola, *Assur* 2/5 (1979) 164). Village of Hulī (or Allī?) in *bēt t.*: *ADD* 1176 and 1185. *Bēt t.* as administrative unit, parallel with the provinces: *NL* 51:12 (*Iraq* 21, 160); *ND* 2386+.i.4' (*Iraq* 23 (1961) 22); and in historical texts of TP III (see *AHw* 862b.4.b: NAM (= *pāhat*) *bēt turtāni*).

(60) *bēt šakin māti*: *AfO Beiheft* 6, No. 24; *bēt rab šāqê*: *TCL* 9 No. 67:11; *bēt abarakki rabî*: IM 76890, courtesy Dr. Bahijah K. Ismail. Note the land holdings in the Harran census, *CCENA* No. 21, including various governors.

(61) For the *pāhat bēt Aššur* see *NARGD* No. 27.

(62) As illustrated by *ADD* 1176 and 1185.

(63) It is understandable that such a situation would lead to disputes about ownership and administration. For examples of disputes, one need do little more than trace the occurrences of *puāgu* «to deprive of (wrongly)» in the letters: *NL* 95 (*Iraq* 28); *ABL* 174; 307; *CT* 53, 887. Cf. also *NL* 41; *ABL* 168; 353; 610; *CTN* 2 No. 196.

(64) I use the word 'prebendary' to refer to land held by the incumbent of an office (religious or secular) during and in consequence of that employment. This definition is intended to leave unsettled the question of whether he was expected to enjoy those lands for his own or for the employer's benefit.

(65) See Parpola, *ZA* 65 (1975) 295 ad p. 75; accepted in *CAD* M/ii, though in neither place is the plural *ma'uttāte* (rather than *ma'unāte*) explained. Prof. von Soden refers me to the 1st mill. plural forms of *piqittu* as a possible parallel.

(66) *NL* 24:24 (*Iraq* 18).

(67) *NL* 52:5 (*Iraq* 21).

(68) See *CTN* 3 Nos. 14-16. In earlier times in the south the word for this sort of land-holding was *šukūsu*, which is a Sumerian word, taking us back to the beginning of the ED III period, if not earlier.

(69) *NARGD* Nos. 9-10:38 [...] *kīma šāšu-ma zakû* 39: [...]*bu ma'uttu kabistu*. Neither *AHw* nor *CAD* gives the meaning «continue» for *kabāsu* (and hence «continuous» for *kabsu*, *kabistu*), but it is correct for Middle and Neo-Assyrian as some of the passages they quote can show: Ebeling, *SVAT* 14 No. IV rev. 9 (2 *šanāti ikabbas ana šalussi šatti ... iddan*) or *ABL* 537:rev.5-9:

Quite another form of land assignment from state reserves is probably represented by a single mention of a «bow-field». In *ABL* 201 the king (Sargon, probably) «has given instructions that (any) Itu'aean should be exempt (from taxes) on corn and straw ...»(70). The Itu'aeans are well known as the principal suppliers of mercenary or auxiliary foot-soldiers to the Assyrian army(71), and even without the clear parallelism with later Babylonian conditions as reflected in the Murašû archives, one would have deduced that a 'bow-field' was land assigned by the state as a reward for and/or condition of service in the army(72). Another trace of this system may survive in the phrase *bēl azanni-šu* «his quiver-master» (cf. Babylonian *bēl qašti-šu*) listed directly after the *bēl ilki-šu* in a late 7th century legal document(73), but it is pointless to speculate about the detailed arrangements without more evidence. Probably the state settled many of its auxiliaries as military colonists on long-standing state lands in need of cultivators, or on areas newly brought or brought back into cultivation, or even on newly conquered territory, and this leads us at length to consider the origins of state land and its status.

When the Assyrian kings decided to take territory under their direct rule, and thus «(re)turned it to Assyria» or «added to ... province», some part of the land was no doubt often added to state holdings in one form or another, but we must presume that the pre-existing rights of land-owners and the accepted customs of the area were generally respected. Even so close to home as Arzuhina, certainly under direct rule since the reign of Assur-naṣir-apli II (883-859 B.C.), conditions might vary from the norm: in a letter of about 730 B.C. from a former governor (already quoted above), we learn that «if land of the province Arzuhina is abandoned and without an owner, whoever wants it may divide it up and take it ...», showing both that local customs might vary, and that the king could be expected to honour them(74)

Some changes in land tenure must have been expected after a conquest. The private lands of a deposed ruler would presumably fall to the crown, at least if the conquest had not been peaceful, while state lands (if such a category already existed in the annexed territory) may be presumed to have remained such, and to have been added to Assyrian state land. Very likely other allocations were made — to members of the royal family, high officials or their «Houses», or to temples. Nothing is said explicitly about this process of land absorption, except in the early 9th century, when we find Adad-nerari II recording that he «counted the city of Saraku as my own property» or «counted his palaces as my own property» (*ēkallăti-šu ana ramaniya amnu*)(75). This is in territory that was probably incorporated into Assyria at the same time; a curious situation is revealed by his grand-son's account of a campaign into northern Syria: when he captured the fortified city of Aribua, belonging to Lubarna, king of Pattina, he says that «I took the city for myself ... and installed Assyrians in it»(76). He does not say that he incorporated it into Assyrian territory, and indeed it was not until the reign of Tiglath-pileser III, over a century later, that this part of the West was taken under direct Assyrian rule. It would appear that with Aribua Assur-naṣir-apli was adding a city in a foreign land to his personal estates: history does not record the fate of this royal possession, nor of its Assyrian occupants.

Conquest or peaceful annexation were not, of course, the only ways of enlarging the royal or state lands. From the reign of Tiglath-pileser I (1100-1077 B.C.) until Salmaneser III the kings vaunt their concern for revitalizing agriculture. Tukulti-Ninurta II writes: «I built palaces on the edge (*ina šiddi* — or «across the extent»?) of my land, and hitched ploughs on the edge of my land; I stored up in greater quantities than previously stores of grain for the needs of my land, and I added land to the land of Aššur, and people to its people»(77). The main thrust of this resettlement programme was surely southwards and westwards into the marginal lands of the jazirah, where the combination of political stability, and enterprises with a secure agricultural base in areas of more dependable rainfall, permitted renewed farming villages to survive. This is certainly the case in the early 8th century, when Palil-ereš in the Sinjar region and Bel-Harran-bel-uṣur at Tell Abta (north of Hatra) set up stelae to record resettlement programmes in the jazirah(78). By this time the majority of the farmers concerned will have been deportees from the Assyrian campaigns, and one specific instance is the body of Gambulaeans assigned with new plots of land to the high state officials in the Harran census, no doubt in the reign of Sargon(79). Some of the deportees also became the property of individuals, and these too may well have been installed as semi-free farmers on newly cultivated lands in the same part of the country(80); but it seems likely that the

«Let them return their families to them so that the workers will carry on with their work (*ikabbusu dullu eppušu*) and not have their minds constantly on their families (so that) they don't work». So also *ABL* 531:rev.16 («so that they may continue until the weather gets too cold»). Accordingly, the meaning of *kabistu* here is clearly «permanent, continuous».

(70) For the context, see the translation in *TCAE*, 263.

(71) See *RlA* V/3-4, 221-2.

(72) For the terminology in Babylonia, see *CAD* Q, 153-5 s.vv. *qaštu*, *bēl qašti* and *bīt qašti* A.

(73) *FNALD* No.15:18.

(74) *NL* 41:48-51 (*Iraq* 20 (1958) 187-90).

(75) Grayson, *ARI* 2, §§ 425-6.

(76) Grayson, *ARI* 2, § 585.

(77) Grayson, *ARI* 2, §478.

(78) Cf. *JESHO* 17 (1974) 237-8.

(79) For the text see *CCENA* No.21, esp. ii.25-8.

(80) «The remainder of them I distributed like sheep to my palaces, to my magnates, to the entourage of my palace, and to the population of Nineveh, Kalhu, Kilizu and Arbil» (Esarhaddon: see

king, as head of state, remained the principal landowner because of its initial role in the acquisition of the population and the absorption of the land.

§ 6 *Taxation and exemption*

Legal documents regularly specify the taxes payable on land being leased or taken as a pledge, but only occasionally on land being sold(81). Since in the sale texts the clause usually specifies tax-free status when it does occur, this was presumably the exception, and the implication is that taxes were normal, which is also implied by the exemptions given in the royal land grants (see below). Two of the taxes are in kind and generally occur together: *nusāhē* («extractions») are attested for corn-fields and orchards, and *šibšu* in Neo-Assyrian times is a tax on straw (called in the 9th century *miksē tibni*). Rates of 10 % for *nusāhē* (twice) and 25% on straw (once) are mentioned in the texts, but again the mere fact that they are specified leads one to suspect that these may not have been the regular rates. There is ample evidence that these taxes were exacted by the state through the civil administration headed by the provincial governors; they had their own officials, probably the «village-inspectors» (*rab ālāni*?), who dealt directly with the villages, represented by their *hazannu*(82). This is the natural consequence of the traditional role of the village's own authorities in the administration of the land within their territory, and they were doubtless communally responsible for collecting the taxes due from their members.

The other kind of tax associated with land tenure was *ilku* service. Its connection with land is illustrated by phrases such as «The taxes (*nusāhē*) of that orchard shall not be exacted, he shall not perform *ilku*-service with his village» (*ilku issi* URU-*šu la illak*) in a 7th century sale(83), or the mid-9th century texts from Šibaniba (Tell Billa) in which we have the very similar stipulation «they shall not pay straw-taxes (or) corn-taxes, they shall/shall not perform *ilku*-service with the village»(84). The problems of *ilku* have been discussed elsewhere, but it is at least clear that it was administered, like the other, agricultural, taxes, through the village. This was not, however, merely an administrative convenience, but results from the fact that in the 2nd millennium B.C. *ilku* obligations derived directly from the tenure, or perhaps more specifically ownership, of land. Opinions are divided as to whether these obligations were due to the state, in the form of military service, or to the village itself, in the form of communal labour; I believe that in Neo-Assyrian times at least it was primarily a state-imposed obligation to perform military or civil service, which could be commuted to some form of payment(85). As to the problems which resulted from the sale of *ilku*-liable land, the Neo-Assyrian sources are totally silent, and we can only say that *ilku* remained a heritable obligation(86); one must presume that some device was found whereby landless members of the Assyrian population could also be called up for service, but we have no idea how this operated.

In § 4 above we have already seen that lands dedicated by the king or one of his subjects to a temple may have been exempted from regular state taxes. Not infrequently in land sale and lease documents we meet private lands which have been exempted too (A.ŠÀ *zakûti*); in some cases the relief from tax may have been to the benefit of a temple instead, but in others they were exemptions by the king in favour of the individual. Presumably state lands farmed directly by the palaces or provincial governors did not pay taxes as such, but prebendary lands (*ma'uttu*) were not necessarily exempt(87). Disagreement between officials about whether agricultural taxes were to be paid on certain lands are often the subject of correspondence: «Let the king, my lord, question them, and if the king, my lord, did exempt the fields and give them to Tardit-Aššur, then in place of those fields let him release (some) of the fields of the [*ilku*]-performers»(88). When such exemption is claimed we cannot always be sure if it is on behalf of prebendary land or of private estates. Possibly the «Houses» of the high officials were automatically exempt, and the writer believes that the lands listed in the Harran census are probably all tax-exempt, for whatever reason. Otherwise, one letter is quite explicit: «The *sukkallus*(?) are not exempt; (only) whoever is in a sealed document of the king is exempt»(89). The word for such a charter is *unqu* (originally «(signet-)ring»), and we are fortunate that some of them survive, from the time of Tiglath-pileser and especially Assur-ban-apli and Assur-etelli-ilani(90). These do indeed grant tax-exemptions, and exhort future rulers to respect them: «do not neglect the charter» (*ištu pān unqi nadi ahi lā taraššī*)(91). What is not always clear is whether the king is actually granting land, or merely exemption(92): certainly they

Borger, *Die Inschriften Asarhaddons Königs von Assyrien*, p. 106:21-2).

(81) See *TCAE* 63-65 (*ilku*) and 175-181 (*šibšu-nusāhē*).

(82) See *TCAE* 194-7.

(83) *ARU* 114:rev.4-6.

(84) For the pertinent passages see *TCAE* 63 and 353-7.

(85) See Dandamayev et al. 1982, 306ff.

(86) On the basis of *ND* 5480, quoted in Dandamayev et al. 1982, 307.

(87) This follows from *CTN* 3 No. 14-16.

(88) *NL* 68 rev. (*Iraq* 25 (1963) Pl. XIII); for the appeal to the king on the Obv., cf my comments in P. Garelli (ed.) *Le palais et la royauté* (XIX° Rencontre Assyriologique Internationale), 422-3. Other disagreements on taxation status are to be found in *ABL* 442; *NL* 74; and *CTN* 2 No. 196, all quoted in *TCAE* 181-3.

(89) *NL* 74:9-11 (*Iraq* 27 (1965) 21-3); cf. *TCAE* 385; the translation uses a tentative reading LÚ.SUKKAL.ME(Š) in 1.93.

(90) Edited in *NARGD*; but note that *unqu* may refer to any documents sealed by the king such as a royal letter.

(91) *NARGD* Nos. 9-10:50.

(92) See the discussion in *NARGD* pp. 3-5.

occasionally gave land to faithful servants, but in spite of Assur-ban-apli's claim that he «exempted and gave» the land, he also specifies in the same document that it comprised «fields, orchards and people which he [the recipient] had acquired under my protection»([93])

§ 7 *Social aspects of land ownership and exploitation*

All that has been described so far is no more than the skeleton; and without better quantitative data, we cannot flesh it out enough to reconstruct a functioning organism. One of the difficulties is that almost all our sources refer to *changes* in the land regime — whether on the grand scale of conquest or only as the sale or lease of a small private plot. All the land holdings mentioned in our texts could only add up to a minute fraction of the total area in cultivation. I have not noticed any single holding of more than 1000 homers (say 1000 hectares = 1.0 km^2)([94]), and only lands of the crown prince and the Assur Temple reach this size([95]); the largest holdings mentioned in sale documents are only half this size, and this serves to remind us that such texts can only give us part of the complete picture([96]).

Sale documents cannot be taken as representative of private land holdings in general for various reasons. Not only do they come from the palaces, but the sale of land reflects a particular social situation and is therefore almost by definition unrepresentative: «a sale of land in Ancient Oriental times always indicates that the vendors are at the end of their economic resources» (I.M. Diakonoff)([97]). This principle may need slight qualification for the late Neo-Assyrian period, since we have the occasional transfer of land from one palace official to another, but the general rule holds good that land changes ownership from the poor to the rich. We can witness the process of accumulating estates by urban landlords at three stages in the Neo-Assyrian empire: at Kalhu in the 8th century by officials active in the provincial governorate([98]), in the early 7th century by Remanni-Adad, a royal charioteer, and in the late 7th century by another royal officer, Kakkullanu([99]). The estates of the Kalhu residents were widespread, though none further afield than Kurbail, north of Nineveh, and Bel-issiya's are often purchased from more than one owner, presumably with adjacent properties (cf. above § 3)([100]). This general pattern is repeated, with advantages, in the next century: Remanni-Adad's acquisitions stretch from an entire village with 580 homers in the district of Arrapha, through Nemed-Ištar and Sinjar, the middle Habur (Dur-Katlimmu), the Mardin area (Izalla) and Harran, as far as Arpad north of Aleppo, where again he buys an entire village from three men([101]). This dispersal is surely deliberate: as early as the reign of Adad-nirari III the steward of the Assur Temple had owned large estates in the provinces of Aššur, Kurbail and Guzana([102]), and this will have conferred an obvious economic advantage, since in drought years land at Kurbail or further north and west could produce a harvest when crops round Kalhu and beyond might fail altogether. It is noticeable that he does not appear to have bought much, if any, land close to the capital cities; perhaps it was too expensive, or simply not on the market. Kakkullanu, on the other hand, does seem to have been able to buy land in long-standing intensively settled areas, probably close to Nineveh: in *ARU* 210 his purchase of 21 homers is split into more than 20 lots, mostly of 1 homer or less. These were all the property of one man, Lulabbir-šarrussu; possibly he was himself an urban landlord, since many of his plots border on fields already owned by Kakkullanu or his colleagues in the military establishment, who also appear as witnesses. It is impossible for us to know whether this, and similar sales, were simply normal business transactions, or result from some economic distress of the previous owners, easily imaginable in the troubled conditions at the end of the empire. What is certain is that there must have been a strong tradition among the palace élites of maintaining rural estates.

Purchase was not the only strategy: it is clear from Kakkullanu's archive that his rural interests included lands leased as well as bought: *ARU* 120 shows him leasing 20 homers, probably the entire estate of Abu-eriba, for a six-year period, and in *ARU* 118 he takes 3 homers for the same length of time, in the same village as *ARU* 210, mentioned above as the location of one of his purchases. Such transactions represent distraint of land in respect of unpaid debts, as we can tell from the phrase *ana šaparti* «as a pledge», or from redemption clauses built into the formula([103]). Most such leases are for six or eight years, and they specify that the land will be left fallow in alternate years. Prices (per homer per annum) range from 1/2 to 1 2/3 shekels of silver([104]). For single years a

([93]) *ša ina ṣillīya iqnû* (l. 24; this is a phrase recurring in contemporary letters, see *CAD* Q, 91b).

([94]) For the conversion see note 26 above.

([95]) Crown prince: *NL* 74:rev.6' (*Iraq* 27 (1965) 21-3; cf *TCAE* 385-6). Aššur Temple (ex the *abarakku*): *NARGD* No. 27:5, 12. Cf. also *NL* 20 (*Iraq* 17 (1955) 139-41) where the governor of Arpad(?) reports that he will be harvesting an *extra* (*utru*) area of 1,000 homers. (The 1700 homers of *CCENA* No. 23:30 are in different areas).

([96]) 580 homers bought by Remanni-Adad in the Arrapha area (*ARU* 444); 500 homers leased from provincial authorities of Lahiru (*ARU* 116).

([97]) Diakonoff 1965, 25.

([98]) *CTN* 2 pp. 12-15.

([99]) For the texts relating to Kakkullanu see M. Falkner, *AfO* 17 (1954-56) 107-8, and the detailed study of F.M. Fales, *Dialoghi di archeologia* 3 (1981) 66-84.

([100]) *CTN* 2 pp. 12-13; Nos. 15-16, 33-35.

([101]) See G. van Driel, *BiOr* 27 (1970) 170 for Remanni-Adad's estates.

([102]) *NARGD* No. 27.

([103]) See *FNALD* pp. 29-32 for these pledge leases

([104]) Half a shekel: *ARU* 120. 1 2/3 shekels: *ARU* 119.

different legal form seems to have been in use, where the characteristic word is *gimru*([105]): these texts suggest that 1 year's rental cost between 1 and 2.86 shekels of silver per homer, which must of course be halved (i.e. 1/2 to 1 1/2 shekels per annum) for comparison with longer period rentals. The evidence is not yet sufficient to determine whether any of these transactions were at the initiative of the land-owner, rather than under the coercion of economic distress([106]). If we assume that 1 homer of land yielded about 600 kg. of barley these prices do not seem high, and suggest that in most cases there would have been some measure of economic coercion, or that the owners had more land than their available manpower could cultivate([107]).

It is instructive to compare the price of land when purchased, although the uncertainties are too great to permit any firm conclusions([108]). In the 7th century the currency is usually silver; prices range from a mere 1/3 (*ARU* 429) through 2 shekels (*ADD* 1156) to over 15 shekels per homer (*ARU* 54: 23 homers for 6 minas). Prices in copper, normal in the 8th century, go from 1 to 50 minas per homer([109])! Reasons for such differences are not far to seek: the value of the currency may change through time; prices will depend on the quality of land and availability of water([110]), and on whether the seller is under coercion and how demand relates to supply. Only occasionally, with contemporary texts from a single site, can we confidently suggest reasons for such variations: in *CTN* 2 Nos. 24 and 25 land in the valley (*ušallu*) costs 34 minas of copper per homer, whereas in No. 27 the land in the hills (*ina šadê*) is understandably only about half that price. The most expensive purchases in the 7th century Nineveh texts are *ARU* 54, 211 and 413, and in each case the land is obviously in an area of intense cultivation with dense, fragmented ownership: *ARU* 54 and 413 are divided into plots of no more than about 1 homer on average, while *ARU* 211 deals with irrigated land along the middle Habur. Other high prices can sometimes be accounted for because of the location of the land (e.g. *ina bāb āli, CTN* 2 No. 26: 60 minas of copper per homer; *qaqqerē puṣê* «clear (building) plot» in addition to orchard and land, *ARU* 165: 80 minas of copper, exact proportion uncertain).

That many of the land sales and leases are the consequence of deliberate estate-building is obvious from their size. If we accept the figures quoted by Oates([111]), a family of six (and there is no reason to think Assyrian families were any larger) would require a plot of 5 hectares(/homers), half in cultivation each year, for survival in irrigated conditions, and twice that for rain-fed land. Assuming area-yield was comparable in Assyrian times([112]), a minimal holding for a family would have been 10 homers or so in rain-fed areas([113]). Smaller plots would either represent only part of a family's property, or a final, residual holding of a family in dire straits. On the other hand, purchases of 20 homers or more can be fairly confidently seen as entrepreneurial acquisitions, and are not infrequent in both 8th and 7th century sale documents. It should be noted that plots of multiples of 10 homers are particularly frequent: the largest estates mentioned in our sources are of 1,000 homers([114]); Sargon gave 400 homers to the Nabû Temple([115]); in the Harran census plots issued to state officials are of 20, 10, or less homers each([116]), and in other census texts from Nineveh virtually every plot is a multiple of 10([117]). Undoubtedly these figures must represent some measure of approximation, the more so because they often come from non-legal texts, but equally much of the state land being assigned will have been in recently reclaimed areas out in the jazirah, where constraints were not imposed by existing land tenure, and estates could be parcelled out in convenient sizes. This was surely the case in the Harran text, and it is noticeable that when land grants (which must have the precision of legal documents) specify areas, these are also in multiples of 10 homers([118]).

As already remarked above, it would have been pointless to accumulate land without the labour to till it. Hence land grants and sales often include with the real estate the families living there. In long-established areas of cultivation, many of these people were doubtless previous owners of the land, who had been forced to pledge and then to sell it to urban creditors (rural land-owners must also have accumulated estates, but they are unlikely to surface in our sources). Some debt-enslaved families retained the legal option of re-purchasing their land (though it seems unlikely

(105) See *CTN* 3 No. 45, with discussion.

(106) The word for such a tenant-cultivator is probably *ārišu*, for such a tenancy *ārišūtu* (*ARU* 142 & 143; *ABL* 201).

(107) It is very difficult to establish normal prices of grain at this date:the evidence consists: (a) of abnormally high prices in drought years — K. Deller, *Or NS* 33 (1964) 257-61 on *Getreidekursangaben* and (b) the letter *NL* 52 (*Iraq* 21, quoted by Deller, *Ibid.*) which gives abnormally low prices, which vary up to 100%! On the question ofman-power, I have no figures for the area cultivable by a single family, but the limiting factor was presumably availability of labour at harvest-time (cf. *FNALD* pp. 44-5).

(108) Cf. van Driel's comments on the imperfect nature of the evidence supplied by land sales: *BiOr* 27 (1970) 170a.

(109) 1 mina: *CTN* 2 Nos. 33 and 34. 50 minas: *ARU* 165.

(110) Oates 1968, 45, suggests that irrigated land will yield twice the crop of rain-fed land, but specifically notes the difficulty of obtaining reliable data. For Syria, Wirth 1971, 234-6, suggests even greater variations.

(111) Oates 1968, 45-8.

(112) Perhaps an unjustified, and certainly an unjustifiable assumption (cf. for some Middle Assyrian data my review of *VS* 21 in *Or NS*, forthcoming).

(113) Hence, perhaps, the grant of 10 homers from the king, mentioned in *ABL* 421.

(114) See note 95.

(115) *ABL* 480.

(116) *CCENA* No. 21.

(117) I.e. *CCENA* Nos. 23-31.

(118) So *NARGD* Nos. 5 and 8 (Tiglath-pileser III), and No. 17 (7th century).

that they would often have been able to exercise it), and it is possible that such sales could also have been affected by *(an)durāru* edicts([119]); but even so the price of land purchase was not so much higher than land lease, and the transaction doubtless remained profitable to the creditor. By contrast, most of the families included in land grants from the kings are likely to have been deportees, installed directly on state farms on their arrival in Assyria. Most such land is likely to have been on the desert margins, and would have provided subsistence to its occupants only because the reserves of the state or other landowners accumulated from more favourable years and areas would have sufficed to see the 'helots' through the periodic droughts. The «desert villages»([120]) can hardly have been desirable environments, and it is noticeable that the purchases of Remanni-Adad and Kakkullanu seem to have been in much greener parts of the empire. When the Assyrian state collapsed, we must expect that many of the desert villages became uninhabitable almost at once, their population drifting into nomadism or a precarious existence further north. In the better lands, from Euphrates to Diyala, agricultural life no doubt survived much as before, and we can only speculate that occupation became nine-tenths of the law, and that ownership of most of the land became vested by tradition or *de facto* in those who cultivated it.

Bibliographical abbreviations follow W. von Soden, *AHw* III, with the following differences and additions:

ARI = A.K. Grayson, *Assyrian Royal Inscriptions I* and *II* (Wiesbaden, 1972 and 1976)

ARU = AR; *BT* = siglum for tablets from Balawat (Parker, *Iraq* 25 (1963) 86ff.); *FNALD* = FNAD; *NARGD* = NARG

NL = *Nimrud Letters*, edited by H.W.F. Saggs, *Iraq* 17 (1955) to 36 (1974)

Dandamayev M.A., et al. 1982 = *Societies and Languages of the Ancient Near East: Studies in Honour of I.M. Diakonoff* (Warminster: Aris and Phillips)

Diakonoff 1965 = I.M. Diakonoff, «Main features of the economy in the monarchies of ancient Western Asia», in *Troisième conférence internationale d'histoire économique*, Munich 1965 (Mouton), 13-32

Diakonoff 1969 = I.M. Diakonoff (ed.), *Ancient Mesopotamia: Socio-economic history* (Moscow: 'Nauka' Publishing House)

Menzel 1981 = B. Menzel, *Assyrische Tempel* (Studia Pohl, Series Maior 10/I-II; Rome: Biblical Institute Press)

Oates 1968 = D. Oates, *Studies in the ancient history of Northern Iraq* (London: British Academy)

Stirling 1965 = P. Stirling, *Turkish village* (cited after Science Editions: John Wiley & Sons, Inc., New York 1966)

Weissbach 1903 = F.H. Weissbach, *Babylonische Miscellen* (WVDOG 4)

Wirth 1962 = E. Wirth, *Agrargeographie des Irak* (Hamburger Geographische Studien, Band 13)

Wirth 1971 = E. Wirth, *Syrien: eine geographische Landeskunde* (Wissenschaftliche Länderkunden, Bd 4/5; Darmstadt, Wissenschaftliche Buchgesellschaft)

(119) See *FNALD* pp. 21-2.

(120) Cf. *NL* 88:13-14 «... let (the governors) write down their villages of the desert ...» (URU.MEŠ-*šú-nu ša mad-bar*), see *TCAE* 381. Some of the lands in *CCENA* No. 24 seem to have been in a *madbār* (cf. l. 33), but we do not know how these properties were acquired (grant or purchase).

THE ASSYRIAN PORSCHE?

J. Nicholas Postgate — Cambridge

One of the reasons why no really satisfying account of the Assyrian army has yet been written is the confusion caused by new scribal habits introduced in the 1st millennium, which are not explained in the regular Babylonian lexical repertoire. No doubt if we had a much more complete text of the Practical Vocabularies of Assur and Nineveh we should be less confused, but in many cases we can only penetrate the abbreviations and newly invented logograms of the Neo-Assyrian scribes by patient collection of examples and comparison of usages. The present note is an attempt to elucidate just such an obscurity which has hitherto left us very puzzled about the terminology of different types of chariot.

The proposal is simply to identify the epithet *pattute*, applied to the hunting chariot of the Assyrian kings from Tiglath-pileser I until Shalmaneser III, with the logogram DUH^{MEŠ} which is found after LÚ.^{GIŠ}GIGIR (and sometimes just after *ša* in later Neo-Assyrian administrative texts and letters. A selection of occurrences is given at the end of the article. It makes no claim to completeness, but the picture it gives is quite consistent. The instances for *pattute* are taken directly from *AHw.*, p. 849. The suggestion made there that this word is the feminine of *pattû*, i.e. the verbal adjective of *petû* D, is surely correct. Note in particular that it is applied to a single chariot before Assur-naṣir-apli II, and therefore that the ending in *-te* cannot be a plural, but must be feminine, so that the original form of the word must be *pattu'u* (otherwise there is no reason for the *u*). These chariots are therefore described as "open", or rather, "opened".

In the Nimrud Wine Lists three types of chariot troop are listed together, *ša* DUH^{MEŠ}, *ša* GÌR^{II}, and ^{GIŠ}TAH KAL (*NWL* 6, 34; same three in a different order in *NWL* 19, 9). Since I do not believe in "foot-chariots", I think these are classes of troops, not classes of chariots, and that the *ša šēpē* are (as long understood) a chariot contingent attached to the person of the king (hence my doubts expressed in *CTN* 3, p.34 n. 44). On the other hand, I agree with Dalley (*ibid.*) that Borger has hit upon the right explanation of ^{GIŠ}TAH KAL, i.e. to read *tah-líp* and compare the word *tah-li-pi* "(armour-)cladding" in the Tukulti-Ninurta Epic. There remains the *ša* DUH^{MEŠ} (often transcribed GAB^{MEŠ}). It cannot (despite, most recently, Kwasman in *NALK* p. 498a) be another writing for *tahlipi* because, as we have seen, it occurs side by side with ^{GIŠ}*tah-líp* in *NWL*. Instead, it must be a different type of chariot, and by far the most elegant solution is to read DUH^{MEŠ} as *pattu'u*, feminine *pattutu*: *non sunt multiplicandi aurigae praeter necessitatem*.

There are two points to be discussed about the logogram: the use of DUH or DU$_8$ for a form of *petû*, and the plural sign. The normal logogram for *petû* is BAD, and DUH stands more usually for *paṭāru*. It is possible that BAD was rejected because of the — significant — risk of confusion with SUMUN, "old". If the scribes were looking for an alternative Sumerian equivalent, DUH was not far to seek: the *AHw.* article for *petû* gives us for instance gag ì-du$_8$ = *pe-tu-ú sikkati* from lú = *ša*, and the equation $^{\text{tu-uh}}$ tuh = *pe-tu-ú šá pi-i*; also referring to *MSL* 4, 37: [111] (Emesal vocab.). For some bilingual passages see Deimel, *ŠL* 167, 26. As for the plural sign, it is important to note that it occurs in almost every case, both where a single chariot is mentioned and with the professional designation LÚ.^{GIŠ}GIGIR (in the two cases where just DUH is used, it refers to a man who is elsewhere given the full DUH^{MEŠ}). Particularly suggestive are the *NWL* passages where neither *ša* GÌR^{II} nor *ša* ^{GIŠ}*tahlip* are given a ^{MEŠ}, although in parallel usage. Note also that we never meet a writing like (LÚ.)^{GIŠ}GIGIR^{MEŠ} DUH^{MEŠ}: this may not be conclusive, but it would be surprising if only the plural adjective and never the plural noun were given the ^{MEŠ}. The explanation must surely rather be that as in other examples (ZI^{MEŠ} for *nasāhu* D, *AHw.* p. 751b; KUD^{MEŠ} for *parāsu* D, *AHw.* p. 831b), the ^{MEŠ} is here the marker of the D stem — hence a welcome convergence with the proposal to identify DUH^{MEŠ} with *pattû(tu)*.

The distinction between an "opened" chariot and an "armoured" one should be recognizable in the reliefs and other representations. The kind of chariot used by the king to hunt in Middle and early Neo-Assyrian representations can hardly be considered "closed" (cf. Ninurta-tukulti-Aššur, e.g. Frankfort, *Cylinder Seals* p. 192). In fact, though, the chariots used by the kings in battle, to judge from the reliefs, differed from their hunting chariots only by the addition of a heavily bossed shield at the back (see for instance B. Hrouda, *Kulturgeschichte des Assyrischen Flachbildes*, p. 94 with Taf. 23 Nos. 22-3; M.A. Littauer - J.H. Crouwel, *Wheeled Vehicles and Ridden Animals in the Ancient Near East* p. 103 — "Lion-head-bossed or toothed shields are often seen in profile as hung at the rear of these chariots"). Although it does not seem to me certain that these are shields, rather than a specially designed 'back-door' for the chariot cab, this single difference between the hunting and the battle version hardly appears sufficient to justify so clear and long-lived a polarity in the terminology, so that I cannot consider the issue resolved. Nevertheless, it is perhaps justifiable to wonder whether the "opened" sports-chariot was adopted by the army only later, after it had shown its worth in the hunt.

Appendix

A. Syllabic writings (after *AHw.*)

1. Tiglath-pileser I: *ina qitrub meṭlūti-šu ina* ^{GIŠ}GIGIR-*šu pa-at-tu-te*, "In his valiant onslaught in his open chariot ... ".
2. Aššur-dan: *i]na* ^{GIŠ}GIGIR-*ia pa-tu-te ina* GÌR$^{\text{II.MEŠ}}$-*ia lasamāte .... adūk*, "In my chariot (and) on my fleet feet I killed.".
3. Tukulti-Ninurta II: *ina* ^{GIŠ}GIGIR-*ia pa-at-tu-ti ina libbi-ia ekdi ina qitrub meṭlūti-ya ... adduak*, "In my open chariot with my raging heart in my valiant onslaught I killed.".
4. Adad-nirari II: *ina* ^{GIŠ}GIGIR-*ia pa-at$^{!}$-tu$^{!}$-te ina qitrub meṭlūti-ia ... adūk* (emended after *AHw.*), "In my open chariot in my valiant onslaught ... I killed.".
5. Assur-naṣir-apli II: *ina* ^{GIŠ}GIGIR^{MEŠ}-*ia pa-tu-te ina qitrub* EN-*ti-ia* ..., "In my open chariot(s) in my valiant onslaught ... ".
6. Shalmaneser II: *ina* ^{GIŠ}GIGIR^{MEŠ}-*ia pa-tu-te/i ... adūk*, "In my open chariot(s) .... I killed.".

Note: These all refer to hunting wild animals, in stereotyped phraseology persisting for over 2 centuries. Note that only in the texts of the last two kings is there a ^{MEŠ} written after GIGIR. It is not clear (as *AHw.*'s query implies) whether a plural is really intended, however, since we would need *pattu'āte* (^{GIŠ}GIGIR is certainly feminine in NA, see 1-*et* ^{GIŠ}GIGIR in *ABL* 241 and 242, even if it is to be read *mugerru*; unless it can still be read both *mugerru* and *narkabtu*, and the former is masculine, in which case one could postulate *patt(u')ūte* in the Assur-naṣir-apli and Shalmaneser passages).

B. Written DUH(^{MEŠ})(-*te*)

in administrative texts:
1. *ša* DUH^{MEŠ} *NWL* 6, 34 // *ša* GÌR^{II} and *ša* ^{GIŠ}*tah-líp*;
2. *ša* DUH^{ME} *NWL* 19, 19 // *ša* GÌR^{II} and *ša* ^{GIŠ}*tah-líp*;
3. PAP 28 DUH^{MEŠ} *CTN* 3, 111, 2' // GÌR^{II} (Sargon);
4. 2 *qur-but* GÌR^{II} DUH^{MEŠ} *ADD* 834(+), I, 4' (cf. 9');
5. 3 *qur-but* GÌR^{II} ^{GIŠ}x[(x)], 1 ... DUH^{MEŠ} *ADD* 971, II, 5;
6. [GIG]IR DUH^{MEŠ} *ADD* 835, 2';
7. PN LÚ.^{GIŠ}GIGIR DUH^{MEŠ} *ADD* 857, IV, 2 (cf. II, 24-27);
8. PN LÚ.^{GIŠ}GIGIR DUH^{MEŠ}-*te* *ADD* 912, I, 2;

(nos. 4-8 are post-Sargon).

in legal texts, witness lists:

9. PN ... LÚ.^{GIŠ}GIGIR DUH^{MEŠ} *NALK* 100 (=*ADD* 354), 11'; 236 (=*ADD* 60); 244 (=*ADD* 185), r. 18' but cf. 11'; 249 (=*ADD* 421), r. 21' (same man as 244 r. 11');
10. PN ... LÚ.^{GIŠ}GIGIR DUH *NALK* 244 (=*ADD* 185), r. 11'; 256 (=*ADD* 470), r. 35'.

Note: Although examples 1-3 show that "personal (chariotry of the king)" (*ša šēpē*) was sometimes distinguished from the "open-chariotry", it seems from example 4 that the two categories could be merged — "personal open-chariotry"? We are still inadequately informed to be sure of this, however.

There is a graphic problem with the sign group LÚ.^{GIŠ}GIGIR, since Parpola has shown fairly convincingly that it should be read *susānu* in NA texts (see SAAB II, p. 78 fn. 2, referring to his discussions and duplicate passages now in A. Livingstone, *SAA* III No. 38,15). It may be hard to conceive that LÚ.^{GIŠ}GIGIR DUH^{MEŠ} is to be read **susān pattute*, but note that examples 1-4 omit ^{GIŠ}GIGIR, rather implying that we should read *ša pattute*, "Open-chariot man". If so, there is nothing too implausible in reading DUH^{MEŠ} as *pattute* even where not preceded by *mugerru*/*narkabtu*, and this leaves the way open to take LÚ.^{GIŠ}GIGIR here as *susānu* after all, i.e. "open-chariot groom". Nevertheless, this is far from certain.

Corrigendum to p. 37 (3.vii.1992)

Chikako Watanabe pointed out to me that the passage assigned under citation 1. to Tiglath-pileser is in fact from Assur-bel-kala's Broken Obelisk (AKA 139:10), an error resulting from a homoioteleuton on my part. Interestingly, the Tiglath-pileser passage, which should have been cited as passage 1., reads: *i-na* GIŠ.GIGIR-*ia i-na pat-tu-te* "in my chariot, in the open (one)" (AKA 86 vi.80-81).

Sonderabdruck aus „Archiv für Orientforschung" Band XXIX u. Band XXX, 1983/84

In Zusammenarbeit mit Hermann Hunger herausgegeben von Hans Hirsch
Verlag Ferdinand Berger & Söhne Ges. m. b. H., A3580 Horn

The columns of Kapara

The amazing caryatid columns of the portico at Tell Halaf have suffered more than they deserve from the efforts of art-historians to date them, perhaps chiefly because they have no close parallels. By a small improvement in the reading of the cuneiform epigraphs, it is possible to suggest that they were indeed a freakish innovation of Kapara's, so that we would not expect any antecedents, and later imitations — had any been contemplated — may well have been forestalled by the advance of Assyrian arms and artistic conventions.

The cuneiform text on the goddess begins as follows: [1]É.GAL-*lim* I*ka-pa-ra* A I*ha-di-a-ni* [2]*šá* AD-*ia* AD.AD-*ia* TI ME [3]*la e-pu-šú-ni a-na-ku e-tap-ša* [Meissner, AfO Beiheft 1, 73]. The crux is posed by the last two signs of l. 2 (see Fig. 1): Meissner (ibid.) chose to read them as DINGIR-*lim*, taking this to mean that the ruler's forebears were deified, i. e. dead («Die Redensart 'Gott' bedeutet hier gewiß soviel wie 'gestorben' ....», ibid. p. 74). However, from the copy the Winkelhaken looks clearly to belong to the first sign, and although Meissner claims that his reading is «gesichert durch Nr. 57» (p. 72[2]), this is hardly the impression one receives from his copy.

Fig. 1

I therefore propose to read syllabically *ti-me* at the end of the line, and to translate «columns», *timmu* being the regular Assyrian word for an architectural column (AHw 1360a). Although the word order is admittedly somewhat strange, this gives excellent sense: «Columns, which my father and grandfather had not made, *I* have made». Unfortunately, inscriptions V (on the giant god) and III are broken at the critical point, but confirmation comes from inscription IV on the eastern sphinx: [1]É.GAL-*lim* I*ka-pa-ra* A I*ha-di-[a-ni]* [2]*šá* AD-*ia* AD.AD-*ia* NA_4 *t[im-me l]a e-pu-šú-ni* [3]*a-na-ku e-tap-šá* [Meissner, ibid, pp. 76—7; see Fig. 2]. While the restoration of *t[im-me* by itself might not be entirely convincing, the determinative NA_4 «stone» effectively banishes this element of doubt, given the fact that in all other respects the two epigraphs are duplicates.

Fig. 2

The implication of this text, which is significantly found only on the figures of the façade of the portico, is that Kapara proudly claims credit for their design. He does not mention the orthostats round the outside of the building, on which his name is carved, and it may well be correct to assign them to an earlier ruler, very likely his father or grandfather, who had lacked the initiative (or bad taste ?) to erect the caryatid columns of the portico!

Cambridge. J. N. Postgate.

The Land of Assur and the yoke of Assur

J. N. Postgate

The Assyrian state had its origins early in the second millennium, as the small self-governing merchant city of Assur, became a territorial power in the fourteenth to thirteenth centuries BC, and survived until 605 BC, by which time it had created an empire which set the pattern for its successors: Babylon, Persia and Macedon. Both as a phenomenon in its own right, and as the originator of the Near Eastern style of empire, Assyria demands to be included in any study of empires. For reasons of simplicity and space our attention will be concentrated on the western frontier, but much of what is described could be illustrated equally from the northern or eastern sectors.

The historical framework

For our purposes, Assyria's territorial history can be divided into four phases: the creation and original expansion in the period 1400–1200 BC, a long recession of varying intensity from 1200 to 900 BC, the progressive re-establishment of the earlier borders from about 900 to 745 BC, and then the final phase of expansion far beyond these borders into Egypt and Iran, 745 to 605 BC (see Table 1 and Figs 1–2). The form Assyrian control took varied: it did not emerge in a vacuum, and in each case it depended not only on the character of the central Assyrian government itself, but also on the political and social order in the lands absorbed. Both inside and outside Assyria the current realities were also tempered, and policies affected, by perceptions of precedents. It is therefore necessary to give an outline of these phases before examining the principles and practice of empire.

Phase 1 saw the transformation of the single city-state of Assur, under the domination, if not the direct rule, of the Mitannian kings, to a territorial state known as 'the Land of Assur', whose kings claimed equality with the Pharaoh and the Great King of the Hittites. From the land annexed by Assur in the fourteenth century, encompassing the cities of Nineveh, Kalhu, Kilizu and Arbil, the three thirteenth-century kings (Adad-nirari, Shalmaneser and Tukulti-Ninurta) swallowed up the remnants of the Mitannian kingdom in the Habur district, and so extended their direct administration to the Euphrates, which formed an acknowledged frontier with Hittite territory.

World Archaeology Volume 23 No. 3 Archaeology of Empires

Table 1 Chronological chart.

	King's name	*Regnal dates*
Phase 1	Aššur-rabi I	
	Aššur-nadin-ahhe I	
	Enlil-naṣir II	1432–1427
	Aššur-nirari II	1426–1420
	Aššur-bel-nišešu	1419–1411
	Aššur-rim-nišešu	1410–1403
	Aššur-nadin-ahhe II	1402–1393
	Eriba-Adad I	1392–1366
	Aššur-uballiṭ I	1365–1330
	Enlil-nirari	1329–1320
	Arik-den-ili	1319–1308
	Adad-nirari I	1307–1275
	Shalmaneser I	1274–1245
	Tukulti-Ninurta I	1244–1208
Phase 2	Aššur-nadin-apli	1207–1204
	Aššur-nirari III	1203–1198
	Enlil-kudurri-uṣur	1197–1193
	Ninurta-apil-Ekur	1192–1180
	Aššur-dan I	1179–1134
	Ninurta-tukulti-Aššur	
	Mutakkil-Nusku	
	Aššur-reš-iši I	1133–1116
	Tiglath-Pileser I	1115–1077
	Ašarid-apil-Ekur	1076–1075
	Aššur-bel-kala	1074–1057
	Eriba-Adad II	1056–1055
	Šamši-Adad IV	1054–1051
	Aššurnaṣirpal I	1050–1032
	Shalmaneser II	1031–1020
	Aššur-nirari IV	1019–1014
	Aššur-rabi II	1013–973
	Aššur-reš-iši II	972–968
	Tiglath-Pileser II	967–935
Phase 3	Aššur-dan II	934–912
	Adad-nirari II	911–891
	Tukulti-Ninurta II	890–884
	Aššurnaṣirpal II	883–859
	Shalmaneser III	858–824
	Šamši-Adad V	823–811
	Adad-nirari III	810–783
	Shalmaneser IV	782–773
	Aššur-dan III	772–755
	Aššur-nirari V	754–745
Phase 4	Tiglath-Pileser III	744–727
	Shalmaneser V	726–722
	Sargon II	721–705
	Sennacherib	704–681
	Esarhaddon	680–669
	Assurbanipal	668–627
	Aššur-etel-ilani	626–624?
	Sin-šumu-lišir	
	Sin-šar-iškun	–612
	Aššur-uballiṭ II	611–609

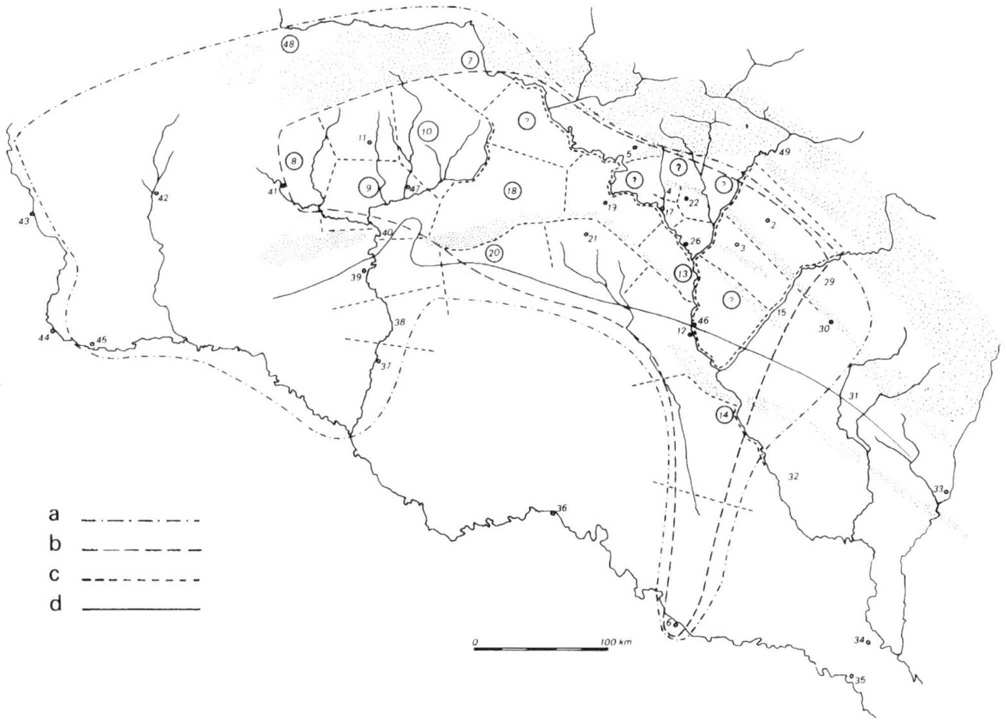

Figure 1 Map of Assyria, thirteenth to eleventh centuries BC, to show state and provincial boundaries: a. maximum extent of Assyrian territory (c. 1200 BC); b. extent of Assyrian territory c. 1100 BC; c. reconstructed provincial boundaries; d. 200mm reliable annual rainfall limit; stippling indicates relief (after Postgate 1985: 97, where the identification of individually numbered sites may be found).

Phase 2 could be subdivided, into a period of gentle recession, down to the reign of Tiglath-Pileser I (who was still in a position to march unopposed to the Mediterranean), and a much more intense loss of power which saw Assyrian control wither to the minimal core of Assur itself and the cities to its north on the Tigris (particularly Nineveh). The external political agents of this recession were not neighbouring states: Babylon was equally weak, the Hittite Empire had collapsed and fragmented, and the Mitannian state was only a memory. Rather, the damage was done by incursions of Aramaean tribes, who by 900 BC had established minor dynasties throughout most of North Mesopotamia and Syria. One contributory factor may well have been the climate, since poor rainfall both weakened Assyria's agricultural base and forced Aramaeans north in search of pasture.

Phase 3 Much of our knowledge of the dark years of Phase 2 comes from the accounts of later Assyrian kings who describe how Assyrian subjects had been forced to take refuge from famine in the mountains and how some of their towns and strong points had been taken over by the newcomers. In self-consciously reconstituting the former 'Land of Assur', they describe their programmes of agricultural reform in standard formulae which begin in the reign of Tiglath-Pileser I and persist almost 300 years into the time of Shalmaneser III. The re-establishment of the earlier frontier was a long process of picking

□	major towns
⊙	provincial capitals (site fairly certain)
○	provincial capitals (location uncertain)
•	other sites
▲	rock reliefs
△	stelae

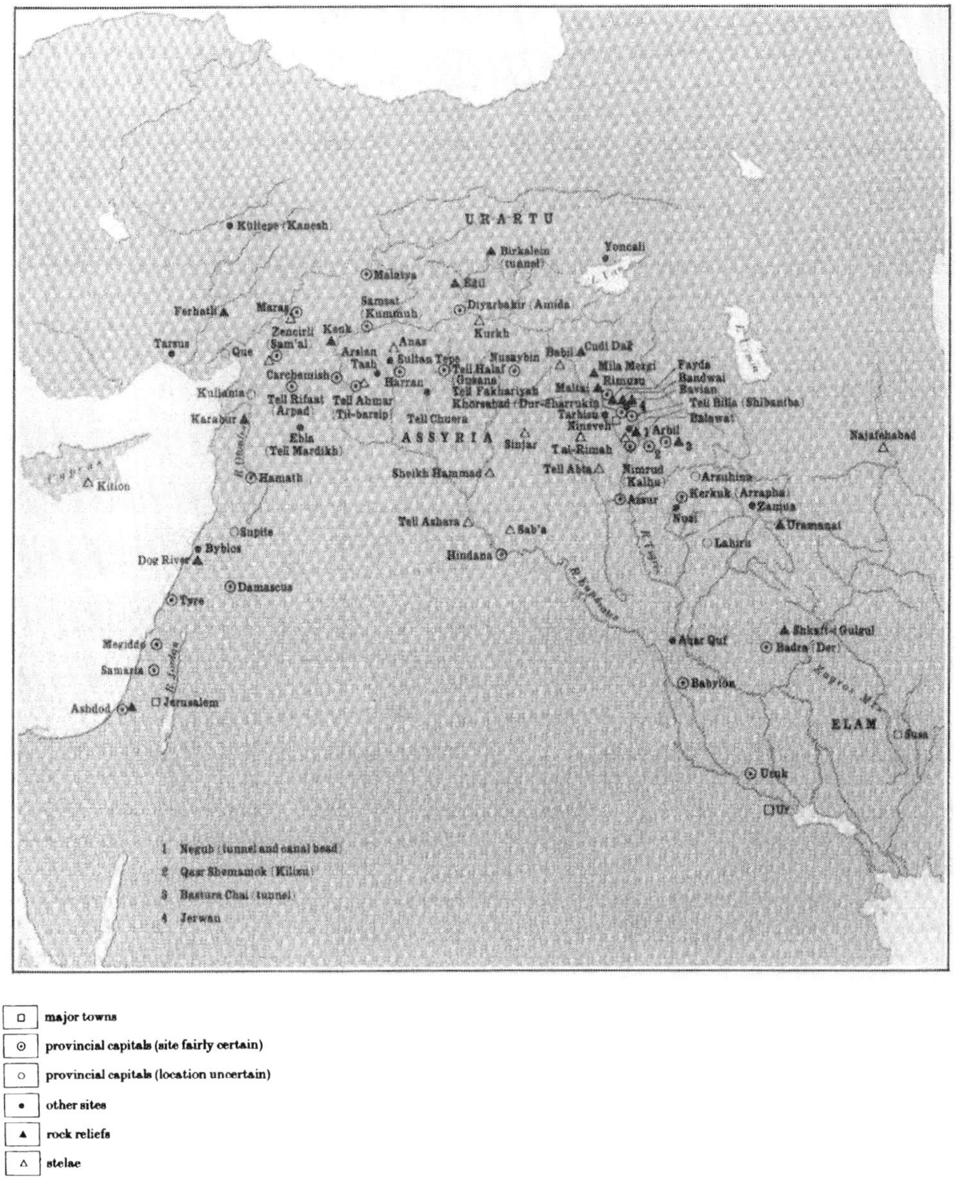

Figure 2   The Assyrian Empire in the first millennium BC, to show archaeological evidence for extent of empire (after *Cambridge Encyclopaedia of Archaeology*, p. 188).

off the mainly Aramaean states which now confronted the Assyrian kings, beginning very close to home with Assur-dan and Adad-nirari (934–912 and 911–891), and culminating with Shalmaneser's persistent series of campaigns into Syria and Anatolia, in territory still referred to as Hittite (the 'Land of Hatti').

Phase 4 The traditional Assyrian frontier in the west was the Euphrates. Although in the late ninth and early eighth century Assyrian influence was acknowledged by states beyond this line, there is no suggestion that the 'Land of Assur' crossed it too. The powerful Šamši-ilu calls himself 'administrator' (and not 'governor') 'of the land of Hatti', acknowledging thereby the separate identity of the western lands he controlled. Two recently published stelae show the Assyrian king arbitrating between local dynasts – with no visible inclination to annex their territory. This changed abruptly with the accession of Tiglath-Pileser III in 745, who conquered and annexed most of Syria and Lebanon, and initiated a policy of expanding the frontiers of 'The Land of Assur' which ended with Esarhaddon and Assurbanipal's annexation of Egypt and Elam, and abolished the intervening local states, thus setting the scene for the succeeding empires of Babylon, Persia and Macedon.

The forms of domination

The Assyrian imperial order differed from those of the Mitannians and Hittites, who incorporated a hierarchy of local dynasties into the same system as the high king's core domain. The formal pronouncements of the Assyrian kings distinguish clearly between territory directly administered and incorporated within the 'Land of Assur', and areas acknowledging Assyrian domination but retaining some form of autonomy. The examination of the documentary sources makes it quite clear that this distinction was not an empty formula, but corresponded with both practical arrangements and symbolic actions. Let us look first at 'Assyria proper', and then move to the satellites across the frontiers.

The Land of Assur: 'Assyria proper'

The Land of Assur is a phrase which is first used as the Middle Assyrian state came into being. It includes at first the 'Assyrian triangle' in the region of Nineveh, and is extended into the Habur region after the conquests of the thirteenth century. Thereafter, it remains the term for what we would call Assyria until the end. Territories freshly added to Assyria, or reclaimed, are said to be 'turned into' or 'returned to the land of Assur': 'to the land of Assur I added land, to its people I added people'. The name itself reflects the ideological centrality of the city of Assur, and the city-god, henceforth also the national god, who bears the same name. This one-to-one correspondence between the god and the city is underlined by the fact that, unlike most other major deities of the Mesopotamian scene, Assur has no other temples. His role, as the symbolic personification of the city and then state of Assur, is reflected in a system of offerings contributed, in a fixed rota, by the component parts of the Land of Assur, i.e. by the different provinces. These are not valuable items destined for the temple's treasury, but groceries for its daily menu. The system is best attested in the reign of Tiglath-Pileser I (1105–1077), but there is adequate evidence that it was still operating in the seventh century, both within some of the traditional central provinces and, newly imposed, in recently (and transitorily) annexed lands such as Egypt (Postgate 1980; 1985; Cogan 1974: 52).

For us, the significant point is that the contributors represent the constituent parts of Assyria proper: they do not include client kingdoms or other marginally autonomous areas. This is understandable: a central shrine embodies a territory's communal identity and, provided some measure of autonomy was maintained, any state would have its own symbolic centre in the shape of its traditional god, and could not serve two masters. Incorporation into Assyria meant participating in the cult of its god; it need not have meant abandoning the worship of the local deity, but it would have affected the significance of that cult as a political statement. The whole system stands in a tradition stretching back to the third millennium, whereby sharing responsibility for the provision of the daily sustenance of the Enlil Temple at Nippur was both the duty and the prerogative of those states (and, in Ur III times, provinces) which constituted part of 'Sumer and Akkad' proper (Steinkeller 1987).

The rota in Assyria too was shared between the provinces, and to this symbolic statement there corresponded practical aspects of government administration. Unlike the pyramidal structure of the Hittite and Mitannian empires, the Middle Assyrian kings governed through a single-tier system of provinces embracing all directly ruled Assyrian territory. While the provincial capitals were often the traditional local centres, the governors were usually (if not always) 're-deployed' members of the old families of Assur, rather than 're-employed' local dynasts. One family archive from thirteenth-century Assur shows how they harnessed the commercial traditions of the merchant houses, with their exact liability accounting, to establish a bureaucratic organization for the newly acquired territories, in town and country (Postgate 1988). Provincial governorships were sometimes, but not always, passed on within the family, but they were formally the king's appointments. In practice too, administration and economic exploitation were carried out by the governors on behalf of the king. This is made clear by the Assyrian coronation ritual in which their tenure of office was formally renewed each year, and by the detailed administrative correspondence of some of the governors.

This system survived until the end of the empire. There were, of course, changes: inevitably it shrank as the frontiers of Assyrian control contracted, and new provinces appear as the first millennium expansion followed; the rapid expansion of the state under Assur-nasir-apli and Shalmaneser in the ninth century led for a while to very large provinces (and perhaps correspondingly powerful governors), which were redivided under Tiglath-Pileser III after 745. But the theory and practice remain the same: the Land of Assur is a homogeneous territory divided into equal ranking provinces. If you are in Assyria, you are in a province; outside Assyria, not. Thus the list of provinces contributing to the Assur Temple in the reign of Tiglath-Pileser I tells us the extent of Assyrian territory in the eleventh century, and when new lands were added to Assyria by Tiglath-Pileser III in the eighth century, they were placed under a new governor, or, as he often says, 'I added that land to the province of x'.

The yoke of Assur: client kingdoms

The client kingdom (I use 'client' rather than 'vassal' on the firm insistence of Moses Finley to avoid feudal connotations), is an entirely different phenomenon and was so perceived by the Assyrians, as their terminology and actions make clear. First clearly attested under

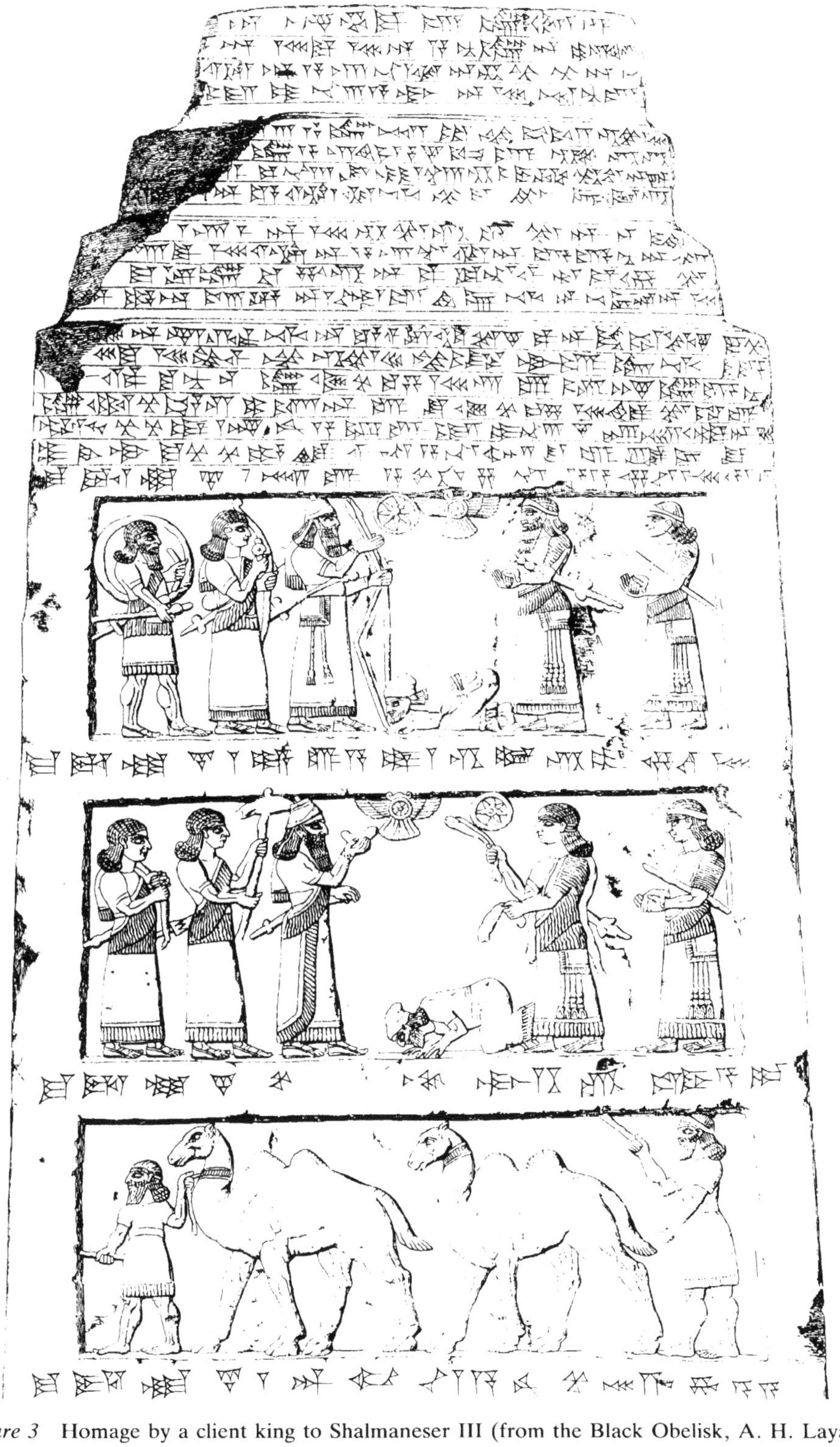

Figure 3 Homage by a client king to Shalmaneser III (from the Black Obelisk, A. H. Layard, *Monuments of Nineveh* I, Pl. 53).

Plate 1 Esarhaddon and client kings of the west (stele from Sam'al; F. von Luschan, *Ausgrabungen in Sendschirli* I, Taf. I).

Tiglath-Pileser I, by the first millennium BC it was a regular practice for the Assyrian king to exact annual tribute payments from those who 'bore the yoke of Assur', but these were quite different from the Assur Temple offerings. They were not basic foodstuffs but valuable gifts, whether in precious metal (in the eighth to seventh century often standard silver 'tribute bowls'), animals (especially horses), or other goods including local specialities. Although the inscriptions do sometimes refer to the 'tribute and forced labour of the god Assur', these contributions do not go to the temples but to the kings, and even to other members of the royal family and high state officials. This is readily understood. The relationship between the two states is a secular one between two rulers. Even before any form of overlordship was formally acknowledged, prudence will often have dictated a visit bearing gifts, or bribes, to deflect the marauding armies. Tribute from the client king is an institutionalized form of the same statement: the exact level of annual contribution would be fixed, and failure to make it would be construed as a political statement.

The local ruler (even if a puppet installed by the Assyrians) was king within his own country, which was not considered part of Assyria. All economic and administrative relations with the Assyrian state would have taken place at a high level, from apex to apex. The Assyrian administration would have had nothing to do with the internal affairs of the client state. Often, perhaps normally, the client king may indeed have been bound to the king of Assyria through some form of agreement. Without entering deeply into the debate about treaties, we may say that the Assyrians followed age-old practice in concluding formal agreements with such local rulers. Such agreements were reinforced by oaths and solemnized by religious sanctions, especially being witnessed by Assur and the local gods. To have broken such an agreement then constituted gross sin against Assur, and was seen as justification for punitive action on the part of the Assyrian ruler; but it was in fact a secular agreement between two humans, not a contract between the Assyrian god and a foreign ruler.

On the level of human gesture and social interaction the same ideology is apparent: defeated kings are subject to the king himself. In word and image they kiss his feet, are held by him on a leading-rope (Fig. 3, Pl. 1); Bar-rakab of Sam'al himself boasts that he ran at the wheel of Tiglath-Pileser's chariot. They do not join Assyria by becoming worshippers of Assur. Cogan has investigated carefully the idea that subjection to Assyria implied the worship of Assur, and found nothing to substantiate it. The 'symbol of Assur' (a dagger of iron, from the early second millennium when iron was precious) is attested as an object of reverence in the provinces under Tiglath-Pileser III, Sargon and Sennacherib, but not outside Assyria proper (Cogan 1974: 52). It is to the king in his palace that they bring their tribute around the New Year, not to him as High Priest of Assur.

The geographical pattern

I have stressed the distinction between these two forms of domination partly because it seems to me that Liverani's recent discussion of Assyrian expansion suppresses it unduly. He is of course well aware of the distinction: 'Already before the campaigns some places are "Assyrian" and do not pay tribute. These places alternate with places that pay tribute, there is no territorial continuity between Assyrian zones and tribute-paying or enemy zones, instead there is a structure of "islands" or outposts' (1988: 85). He goes on to conclude (p. 86) that 'the empire is not a spread of land but a network of communications over which material goods are carried'. The metaphors of a 'network whose mesh thickens' and a 'spreading oil-stain' for the expansion of Assyrian control in the first millennium BC do not seem to me to be mutually exclusive, and I am not sure that they are appropriate to his argument, which revolves round the piecemeal pattern of different forms of territorial control along the western frontier. Let me use them, though, to make some different points.

First, it is worth remarking that, as a description of the presence of the Assyrian army and civil administration, the image of a network rather than an oil-stain is indeed more apt: all territorial control must take such a configuration since people cannot be evenly distributed across a landscape and communications must be maintained between the groups. This applies at the level of villages, where it is unlikely that either civil or military personnel were billeted except in times or areas of insecurity; but similarly with towns and cities, certain places were suitable for political and strategic reasons for concentrating the Assyrian presence, and as long as this presence was successfully maintained there will inevitably have been interstices between the nodes. The image of a network should not be taken to imply a diminution of control in these areas, however: in an agricultural environment land is carefully monitored. Each farmer knows his fields, each village knows its boundaries, and the administration's rural network works through the village mayors.

At the same time, it seems to me that the 'oil-stain' metaphor is in fact appropriate for Assyrian territory proper, both because all such land was homogeneously administered through the provincial system and because within each province that administration was uniform. The empire, with all its tributary states, may not politically have been 'a spread of land', but Assyria proper certainly was, and was firmly perceived as such. Beyond the frontier, though, we could certainly envisage imperial control as a network, if that is taken to stress the single strand of communication between the centre and the local ruler's residence, and underline the absence of Assyrian intervention in the life of the town and countryside by contrast to its presence within the borders.

Transitional cases

In treating both classes as a single imperial system there is the risk not only of diverting attention from these very important differences, but also of glossing over a variety of marginal cases which fall between the two. Each will be different, as each constitutes an exception, but we may class them broadly as 'internal' and 'external' anomalies. Within Assyrian territory it need not surprise us if pockets of local autonomy persist until quite late, interrupting its continuity, as Liverani has stressed. There would have been no need to antagonize the local population and waste Assyrian resources in reducing polities which were clearly going to co-operate. Hence the survival of local dynasties in places like the Habur basin – firmly within Assyria by Assyrian reckoning – did create discontinuities in the oil-stain of direct Assyrian control: the best instance of this being Shadikanni, whose special status seems to reach back into the tenth century. On one level, this need not have been significant: to this day there are similar anomalies in Great Britain, with the Channel Islands and the Isle of Man retaining some legal and fiscal independence from the Westminster legislature, and no doubt other parallels could be found in medieval Europe or the Roman Empire. On the other hand, it would be wrong to blur the distinction between client status and direct administration, which must have been quite clear to those involved. With the passage of time these pockets were absorbed into the provincial system, and their survival can only have been the consequence of formal agreements to preserve an historical anomaly.

Beyond the frontiers there was a shifting ring of disparate satellites. In the early years of the Neo-Assyrian empire (the ninth, and perhaps the tenth, century), the political order was unstable even without Assyrian intervention, with recently established Aramaean dynasties not strongly territorial, and with boundaries often ill-defined. One curious case, mentioned by Liverani, is the fortified town of Aribua in Pattina. This must have lain far outside the limits of Assyria, but Assur-nasir-apli tells us that he adopted it as his own property and settled Assyrians in the city (Grayson 1976: 585). Another, in the Zagros, is referred to by Na'man (in Winter 1977: 377), who suggests that both colonies may have been intended as trading posts. I find it difficult to account for these in practical terms, and they suggest that we do not know enough about either Assyrian policy or the countries in question.

Easier to understand are examples of a half-way stage, in which a tributary state has not only tribute payments but also corvée imposed on it 'as on the people of Assyria'. The first Assyrian king to mention tribute payments, Tiglath-Pileser I, talks of forced labour in the same breath, and provided the labour is supplied centrally by the local ruler to the Assyrians, this could be seen as a different sort of 'tribute', not fundamentally affecting the formal relationship with the client state. However, Assur-nasir-apli II's inscriptions give more detail and tell us that construction supervisors (*urase*) were appointed to supervise the work. This certainly sounds like interference with the client state's internal affairs, and in fact it is probable that during his reign there was experimentation with a class of 'supervised client state'. This was not the same as the later practice of attaching an Assyrian agent to a local court, best attested in the Phoenician ports. Rather, it entailed replacing the local ruler by, or converting him into, a 'governor' answerable to the king, but probably not the incorporation of his territory or local administration into the Assyrian system proper, as they do not appear to have been provincial governors of the regular variety. One example of this is probably Adad-it'i of Sikani, whose colossal statue with a bilingual inscription calls him 'king' in the Aramaic version, but 'governor' in the Assyrian. Another may be the 'Governors of Suhi', although I suspect this is their own autonomous title (Cavigneaux and Ismail 1990). It suggests that Assur-nasir-apli was aiming to create a class of puppet rulers from the local élites of the satellite regions, without necessarily perpetuating the local dynasties.

This can only have been a transitory solution, and is hardly attested after the ninth century. There must have been strong pressure, both practical and ideological, to drop one side or the other of the divide. Practically, there was simply the convenience of conformity to a well-established pattern, creating comparability with other states in the same position. The case of Der, on Sargon's south-eastern frontier, where Ilu-iada', the local ruler who had controlled the city on a semi-independent basis, was simply transmogrified into an Assyrian provincial governor, shows the preference for avoiding transitional arrangements. Ideologically, the pressures were certainly strongest in north Mesopotamia, where it was a question of recreating the Land of Assyria as it had been in the second millennium. The kings lovingly record the resettlement of erstwhile Assyrians on erstwhile Assyrian land, and tell us in whose reign recaptured cities had fallen to the Aramaean intruders. The years when the Euphrates was the frontier to the west had not been forgotten. It was only under Tiglath-Pileser III that the 'Land of Assyria' and its associated provincial system broke with tradition and crossed the river.

Archaeological visibility

I do not propose to consider some of the more obvious but less informative archaeological debris of empire, such as frontier forts: they are described in the texts, but have hardly been broached by archaeologists. Nor shall I deal with their symbolic equivalents – those obvious relicts of imperial behaviour, the stelae and rock reliefs of the Assyrian kings, which have recently been reviewed with a consideration of their ideological significance by Morandi (1988). Instead I want to concentrate on the flow of élite goods and style. We are able to look at these through a combination of textual, iconographic and excavated data, giving a sharpness of focus which we should aspire to, but can rarely achieve from the archaeological record alone.

When dealing with artefacts, we need to guard against a tendency to equate cultural, or more specifically stylistic, influences with political relationships. A single political unit may have been or become culturally homogeneous, but it does not follow that a centre from which political power is exercised also diffused its cultural influence along the same lines. For Assyria, it is difficult to address the question of internal homogeneity, both because insufficient work has been done outside the major capitals, and because the best evidence comes from élite items less likely to be recovered in provincial contexts. Nevertheless, it would be no surprise if the political uniformity of the Land of Assur brought with it a strong trend towards cultural conformity, especially in the élite items. Governors represented the king, and no doubt adopted a toned-down version of the royal ceremonial. Both they and local notables will have emulated the royal palace and the society of the capital; a display of

Figure 4 The Assyrian king in state: from the provincial capital of Til-Barsip (F. Thureau-Dangin and M. Dunand, *Til-Barsib*, Pl. XLIX).

independent taste or influence from elsewhere is not to be expected and might not have been prudent. The best known provincial palace is at Til-Barsip on the Assyrian bank of the Euphrates, at times the residence of the most important governor in the west. It has many of the characteristics of a royal palace, including the throne room, but no reliefs: instead the walls were decorated with almost identical painted scenes (Fig. 4). It is 'provincial Assyrian', with hardly a breath of the Aramaean traditions of the immediate area or of the contemporary styles in use across the frontier.

The role of politics is hardly surprising in what is, after all, mostly visual propaganda. Equally, the evidence of the historical texts alone is enough to warn us that the movement of élite goods throughout western Asia must be tracked with a finger on the political map of the time. Even between equals, or before a subordinate relationship was established, élite goods would have passed from one ruler to another. Although products of Assyrian craftsmen found their way into other lands, whether by trade or as reciprocal complimentary gifts, there is little doubt that the bulk of the traffic was inwards to the Assyrian capitals. The royal annals record, and the royal palaces when excavated sometimes still contain, huge consignments of ivory or metalwork plundered or accepted as tribute. For the archaeologist, the issues surrounding the physical movement of artefacts are relatively simple. There is admittedly a problem with the known practice of importing, or deporting, foreign craftsmen bodily, and we are a long way from solving all the questions of schools of ivory carving; but in general, items of exotic manufacture will usually stand out and declare their provenance.

When we turn to the transmission of style, the issues are more complex. Like the objects themselves, cultural influences as shown in artistic style will not have been transmitted by some osmotic process of 'down-the-line' imitation, but by channels closely linked to the political order. They will have jumped by leaps and bounds from one political centre to another; and as the empire grew, the physical and cultural distances grew too. Some changes will have been triggered directly by the objects themselves, brought back as gifts or plunder in the hands of those who crossed their frontiers. Just as often, though, the stimulus will have come through the eyes of those who moved in either direction. Ambassadors of foreign states, whether tributary or not, came annually to Assyria to deliver their greetings and their 'gifts'; hostages often spent years at the capital. The process is easiest for us to document with the architecture, simply because buildings cannot have been transported physically. In their wall decoration, the palaces themselves conveyed a message, whether it was Assur-nasir-apli's depictions of his 'journeys of the mountain barriers of the land and sea and conquest of all lands', or the stately stone procession of exemplary tribute-bearers lining Sargon's throne-room; but the political message could not be divorced from artistic influence – the buildings, the wall decorations, and the furnishings would be seen and admired.

Assyrian influence is plainly visible across the frontiers: not as the homogeneous replication we would expect within Assyria, but as selective borrowings. The sheikh's hall at Tell Halaf is a wondrous amalgam of local and imported style, with its external dado and weird caryatid portico, but Assyrian-style glazed bricks and glazed wall-plaques in the throne room. On the other side of Assyria on the Iranian plateau, the characteristic local architecture of Hasanlu is also embellished with glazed wall-plaques, and we may well be right to assume that in each case the plaques were there to suspend tapestries with Assyrian

Plate 2 A client king at home: Bar-rakab of Sam'al and secretary (F. von Luschan, *Ausgrabungen in Sendschirli* IV, Taf. 60).

prototypes, if not actual imports. Similar eclectic borrowings can be seen in the eighth century: reliefs at Carchemish, which remained independent of Assyria as late as 716 BC, now display an accomplished Assyrian style of carving, while retaining their own architectural context and subject matter. The stela showing Bar-Rakab of Sam'al enthroned (Plate 2) is not an Assyrian phenomenon in itself, but his Assyrian leanings are mirrored in both the scene and the style of carving. These influences are indeed moving with the political flow, from centre to periphery, but as Winter (1977) has cogently shown in the case of Hasanlu, it is helpful to visualize the process from the standpoint of the recipient, as one of active emulation: we should not see the client rulers as cowering in their citadels waiting to be irradiated with Assyrian influence, but absorbing the scene in Nineveh, fingering the tapestries and envying the silverware.

The same process also worked in reverse: whatever the political order, there were things the Assyrians themselves were minded to emulate beyond their frontiers, whether they were being welcomed peacefully into their clients' palaces or sacking an opponent's residence. The stone reliefs which lined the interior walls of their palaces in the first millennium are rightly seen as the Assyrians' most characteristic achievement. Yet the evidence now strongly favours the view that they originate from the merging of two traditions: from the woven and painted wall decoration of Middle Assyrian palaces, and the use of rows of stone orthostats on exterior walls in the Aramaean and Neo-Hittite townships of northern Syria (Winter 1982). It does not seem far-fetched to suggest that Assur-nasir-apli, in whose reign this innovation was introduced, was inspired by such sculptured dadoes during his campaigns beyond the Euphrates.

This was not the only such emulation of the west. The statue from Tell Fakhariyah already mentioned is one of several such colossal statues of rulers from Assyria's north-western neighbours (e.g. Sam'al, Malatya). This was a tradition alien to Assyria, where most of the royal figures in the round which have survived are more like statuettes. However, fragments of one colossal statue (3 m high) are known from Assur, which is probably ninth century (Strommenger 1970: 11–13; the secondary inscription is of Shalmaneser III, but the statue may be earlier, i.e. Assur-nasir-apli?): this looks like a borrowing which did not catch on, and indeed the statue was quickly converted to a stela. In one case, we have the kings' own word for it that they borrowed from the west. The reception rooms of north Syrian palaces were columned porticoes along one side of a courtyard. More than one Assyrian king tells us that he built 'a portico, a replica of a palace of the land of Hatti, which they call a *bit hilani* in the language of the West' (Sennacherib; also Tiglath-Pileser III and Sargon). Although their architectural function was completely altered, these western imports are readily identified, with their carved stone column bases, in palaces at Nineveh, Nimrud and Khorsabad.

Such architectural borrowings are by no means exceptional. One need only think forward to the Egyptianizing buildings at Persepolis (built, of course, with the help of Egyptian masons), or look back to an early example of architectural plunder in the shape of the stone columns from Mitannian palaces brought back to Assur in the thirteenth century. Such borrowings by the political overlord can be seen in two ways. On the one hand, they are a tacit acknowledgement by Assyria of the worth of the cultural traditions of its western neighbours; on the other, the introduction of the exotic into their palaces is one facet of the imperial collector's urge which also led them to create zoological and botanical gardens (cf. Liverani 1979: 314). Like booty and tribute, they too are closely linked to the political order.

Conclusion

When examining the archaeological record of the Assyrian empire, one needs to be aware of the differences separating the Land of Assur from the client states. For most of her history (1300–745 BC), Assyria strove to form a homogeneous territorial entity in a north Mesopotamian homeland. Despite periods of weakness, she successfully digested Hurrian and Aramaean components, and re-expanded in the ninth century to match reality to her perceived ideal boundaries. Within these boundaries political unity promoted cultural conformity.

Beyond the frontier, the empire took the form of semi-autonomous states, whose ethnic and cultural diversity increased with the growth of Assyrian power. Here, close political bonds to Assyria did not suppress local traditions, and indeed there are clear instances of artistic and architectural influence operating 'in reverse', on Assyria from outside. Client dynasties maintained their own élite culture, not a mere scaled-down replica of the imperial court, but incorporating indigenous features and even influence from other quarters.

This describes the traditional order. Doubtless it needs modification after 745 BC, when the massive expansion of directly administered Assyrian territory must have placed strains on the concept of a 'Land of Assur': whereas the concept of a homogeneous Assyria had previously been compatible with historical fact and a degree of cultural uniformity, this could not be realistically extended to apply to Babylonia, Egypt and Elam, themselves major cultural and political entities. Nineveh in the seventh century was the centre of a cosmopolitan world of a quite new order, one which would require study in its own right.

23.viii.91

Faculty of Oriental Studies
The University of Cambridge
Sidgwick Avenue
Cambridge CB3 9DA

References

Cavigneaux, A. and Ismail, B. K. 1990. Die Statthalter von Suhi und Mari. *Baghdader Mitteilungen*, 21: 321–455.

Cogan, M. 1974. *Imperialism and Religion: Assyria, Judah and Israel in the Eighth and Seventh Centuries B.C.E.* Missoula, Montana: Scholars Press.

Grayson, A. K. 1976. *Assyrian Royal Inscriptions*, Vol. 2. Wiesbaden: O. Harrassowitz.

Liverani, M. 1979. The ideology of the Assyrian empire. In *Power and Propaganda. A Symposium on Ancient Empires* (ed. M. T. Larsen). Copenhagen: Akademisk Forlag, pp. 297–317.

Liverani, M. 1988. The growth of the Assyrian Empire in the Habur/Middle Euphrates area: a new paradigm. *State Archives of Assyria Bulletin* (Padua), 2: 81–98.

Morandi, D. 1988. Stele e statue reale assire: localizzazione, diffusione e implicazioni ideologiche. *Mesopotamia* (Firenze), 23: 105–55.

Postgate, J. N. 1980. Review of H. Freydank, *Mittelassyrische Rechtsurkunden und Verwaltungstexte. Bibliotheca Orientalis*, 37: 67–70.

Postgate, J. N. 1985. Review of K. Nashef, *Die Orts- und Gewässernamen der mittelbabylonischen und mittelassyrischen Zeit. Archiv für Orientforschung*, 32: 95–101.

Postgate, J. N. 1988. *The Archive of Urad-Šerua and His Family: A Middle Assyrian Household in Government Service*. Rome: Herder.

Steinkeller, P. 1987. The administrative and economic organization of the Ur III state: the core and the periphery. In *The Organization of Power: Aspects of Bureaucracy in the Ancient Near East* (eds McG. Gibson and R. D. Biggs). Chicago: Oriental Institute, pp. 19–41.

Strommenger, E. 1970. *Die neuassyrische Rundskulptur*. Berlin Abn. der Deutschen Orientgesellschaft 15.

Winter, I. J. 1982. Art as evidence for interaction: relations between the Assyrian Empire and North Syria. In *Mesopotamien und seine Nachbarn* (eds H. J. Nissen and J. Renger). Berlin, D. Reimer, pp. 355–81.

Winter, I. J. 1982. Art as evidence for interaction: relations between the Assyrian Empire and North Syria. In *Mesopotamien und seine Nachbarn* (eds H. J. Nissen and J. Renger). Berlin, pp. 355–81: D. Reimer.

Abstract

Postgate, J. N.

The Land of Assur and the yoke of Assur

Assyria's role in Near Eastern history was first to create a territorial kingdom in northern Mesopotamia, and then to absorb into this state and its administrative structure virtually the whole of the Near East. This short article looks at how, in the exercise of this imperial power and in its terminology, a sharp distinction was maintained between Assyria proper and the foreign states which acknowledged her overlordship. After describing these two forms of domination, we turn to consider the implications for the archaeological record, particularly in relation to the flow of élite goods and artistic and architectural style.

Rings, torcs and bracelets*

J.N. Postgate (Cambridge)

According to Xenophon, Cyrus honoured Syennesis the king of Cilicia with gifts considered honorific at court ἃ νομίζεται παρὰ βασιλεῖ τίμια : a horse with a gold-mounted bridle, a gold necklace and bracelets, a gold dagger and a Persian robe (Anabasis I.ii.27, after the Loeb translation of C.L. Brownson). In the Cyropaedia, he comments that „their purple tunics, and their mantles, the necklaces about their necks, and the bracelets on their wrists" are a Median (rather than Persian) feature. The honorific nature of the golden torc in the Achaemenid empire is referred to also by Josephus in the story of Mordechai: „If you wish to cover with glory the man whom you say you love let him ride on horseback wearing the same dress as yourself, with a necklace of gold, and let one of your close

*Bibliographical abbreviations (other than regular Assyriological):

Amandry 1958	P. Amandry, *Orfèvrerie achéménide*, Antike Kunst 1, 1958, 9-23.
Collon 1991	D. Collon, *Les trésors de Nimroud*, Le Monde de la Bible 71 July/Aug. 1991, 49-52.
Dalton 1964	O.M. Dalton, *The treasure of the Oxus with other examples of early Oriental metalwork*, London ³1964
Fiumi 1985	*La Terra tra i Due Fiumi* (Il Quadrante Edizioni: Torino) [the photo of the hoard published bottom left of p. 339 is now reproduced in Invernizzi 1992, Tav. 30].
Invernizzi 1992	A. Invernizzi, *Dal Tigri all' Eufrate, II: Babilonesi e Assiri*, Firenze 1992.
Hrouda 1965	B. Hrouda, *Die Kulturgeschichte des assyrischen Flachbildes*, SBA 2, Bonn 1965.
Jakob-Rost 1962	L. Jakob-Rost, *Zum Ohrschmuck der Assyrer*, Forschungen und Berichte 5, 1962, 34-9.
Kaufman 1974	S.A. Kaufman, *The Akkadian Influences on Aramaic*, AS 19, Chicago 1964.
Masson – Yoyotte 1988	O. Masson – J. Yoyotte, *Une inscription ionienne mentionnant Psammétique 1er*, Epigraphica Anatolica 11, 1988, 172-180.
Maxwell-Hyslop 1971	K.R. Maxwell-Hyslop, *Western Asiatic jewellery c. 3000-612 B.C.*, London 1971.
Roaf 1990	M.D. Roaf, *Cultural Atlas of Mesopotamia and the Ancient Near East*, New York-Oxford 1990.

For their help and advice during the preparation of this article I am very grateful to a number of colleagues: Leylâ Çehreli; Dominique Collon; Roger Dawe; Lamia al-Gailani-Werr; David Hawkins; Neil Hopkinson; Georgina Herrmann; John Ray; Julian Reade; Michael Roaf; Edward Ullendorf. I would also like to acknowledge gratefully the permission of the Trustees of the British Museum to collate the Sargon passage, to Simo Parpola for access to the files of the Helsinki State Archives of Assyria project, and to Elizabeth Postgate for drawing Figs. 1-4.

friends precede him" (AJ 11.6.10). That the torcs (in Greek usually στρεπτός περιαυχένιος) and bracelets (in Greek ψέλιον) had a significance directly related to the individual's status appears most clearly from Herodotus' comment about the selection of troops to remain in Greece by Xerxes' commander Mardonius, the first chosen being Persian „men wearing torcs" (στρεπτοφόρους) and „men wearing bracelets" (ψελιοφόρους), presumably of lesser status, and then Medians (Hdt. 8.113). Later on he describes how Persian corpses were stripped of their bracelets, torcs and golden daggers (ix.80). Indeed, the famous mosaic of the Battle of Issus shows the Persian king and his close aides wearing the twisted gold torc in the thick of the fray, and others with similar bracelets (e.g. Roaf 1990, 216-7).

The marks of esteem fall into four categories: a horse, golden rings round neck or arm, a golden dagger and purple robes. The comments of the Greek authors and the rarity of references to these items in a domestic Greek context make it clear that these were oriental specialities. The rings are most often mentioned. Already in the 7/6th century B.C. an Ionian who had served in Egypt was rewarded by the Pharaoh (Psammetichus I or II) with „a bracelet of gold and a city" (ψίλιόν τε χρύσεογ και πόλιν) „for his valour": both this phrase and such rewards are part of an old tradition in Egypt[1].

The same practice is not unknown in Mesopotamia before the Persian empire. When giving the background to land-grants rewarding those who had supported him in the internal dissensions surrounding his accession, Assur-etelli-ilani comments that „I clothed them with coloured robes, and bound their wrists with golden rings" (NARGD 13-14). Assurbanipal uses the same phrases to describe his rewarding of the local kings in Egypt (Streck, VAB 7, Annalen.ii.10-12, also a hoe of gold, the symbol of his royalty), and also of the rulers of Phoenician cities (ibid., ii.93-4). Sennacherib tells us that the Elamite nobles (LÚ.GAL.MEŠ) were equipped with a gold dagger (GÍR ***šibbi šitkunu***) and had their „wrists bound in rings of jasper, and red gold"[2]. The earliest reference to the practice that I have noted in the royal inscriptions is from Sargon, who tells us in his Prism B that he received heavy tribute from the ruler of Izirtu in the Iranian highlands, and then says „I clothed him with coloured linen garments, I bound his two wrists with inlaid rings, and he returned to his land rejoicing"[3].

These public claims by the kings are borne out by the ephemeral correspondence and administrative documents from the palace at Nineveh. The letter SAA

[1]Cf. Masson – Yoyotte 1988, 177; for Egyptian practices in the 2nd and 1st millennia see J. Vergote, *Joseph en Egypte*, Louvain 1959, 121-135; and D.B. Redford, *A study of the Biblical story of Joseph*, Vetus Testament, Suppl. 20, 1970, 208-226 (all references courtesy of J.D. Ray).

[2]See R. Borger, BAL II, 77.vi.13a, also III 114, ad loc. for the variant containing the rare word written KI.SAG.

[3]This translation corrects that of Luckenbill, ARAB II s. 211 which depends on the cuneiform of H. Winckler, *Sargon*, Plate 45 F. The passage (K 1671+1668) has been collated, and reads: ... *am-ḫur-ma it-ta-šíq* GÌR.2-*i*[*a*] / *lu-bul-ti bir-me* KAD *ú-lab-bi-s*[*u*] / ḪAR.MEŠ *tam-le-e tú-li-ma-nu-uš ar-kus-*[*ma*?] / *i-na ḫi-du-ut pa-ni i-tur* KUR-*uš-š*[*u*]. Note that despite Luckenbill's translation, the passage does not make any reference to the award of a golden dagger.

1, No. 29 was written to Sargon by Sennacherib who is looking after the country while his father is on campaign: he conveys reports on events in Urartu, and then mentions that „An envoy of the Mannaean (ruler) came to me, bringing me a horse as an audience-gift, and expressing the greetings of the Mannaean ruler. I clothed him and put a silver ring on him" (ḪAR KÙ.BABBAR *assakan-šu*). There is some evidence for the grant of special clothing as a mark of status. The term used is *labāšu* D, in both formal and informal contexts. Administrative texts talk of „robed" officials (*labbašūte*), using precisely the D stem of *labāšu*[4]. In the wine rations issued at Kalḫu in the 8th century some of the officials – chariot riders and singers – are classed as „robed". The term is usually met in a military context, and if ADD 696 is correctly understood, then „clothed" is almost the equivalent of „regular" or „uniformed", as opposed to hired by the day (*ša* UD.MEŠ). Compare also Mannu-ki-abi, the captain „who is not robed" *rab kiṣri ša la lab-bu-šú-u-ni* (ADD 1041: 5). These examples probably represent a somewhat different mark of status from the ambassadorial gifts of purple and linen robes.

But it is the rings which we meet most often. A very similar situation to Sennacherib's letter is reflected in the administrative account edited as SAA 7, No. 127, where envoys from Urartu each receive a pair of silver rings[5]. Equally instructive is SAA 7, No. 58, which also uses the less formal *šakānu* in place of *rakāsu* D „bind" of the royal inscriptions. It is a detailed list of gold and silver rings issued to the ambassadors from Assyrian vassals. The rings are noted by weight, with the lighter ones going to the attendants. Mostly they are described with the ordinary word for ring (ḪAR; see below for the Akkadian), but occasionally the scribes mention other kinds of ornament: the *kurinnutu* and the *qudāsu* (on which see below). The occasion of the gifts is not explained, but some of them seem to have been issued while the king, or at least his officials, were at Arbail, presumably on a military campaign[6]. This convergence of formal and informal documentary sources, and corresponding scenes shown on Assyrian reliefs, give us an opportunity to investigate the Assyrian vocabulary for personal ornament in the spirit of the *Kulturgeschichte des assyrischen Flachbildes*, to see if we cannot match some of the words with the archaeologically attested artefacts more precisely.

The reliefs give us an idea of the physical appearance ot these marks of status. The range of precious ornaments worn on the Assyrian reliefs is quite restricted. They have been described in Hrouda 1965, 51-54 (for deities), 55-59 (for men)

[4]Cf. CAD L, 23 s.v. *labbašu*, but at least the NA occurrences here should have been entered under *lubbušu* since *labbašūte* is only the plural form of the Assyrian D stem verbal adjective *labbušu* - with the *u* changing to *a* before the stressed *u*, as for example in *šaklalūte* (sing.: *šaklulu*) or *rakkasūte* (sing.: *rakkusu*).

[5]2-*šú* ḪAR KÙ.BABBAR; the difficult phrase *ša* UD.MEŠ which follows suggests that visitors of this rank were assigned a payment according to the length of time they remained guests of the Assyrian state.

[6]Zadok proposes to date this text to the reign of Sennacherib (WO 5, 1977, 35-37), but this would make it very unusual among the Kouyunjik archives, and Sargon still seems to me a better guess.

and 59 (for women)[7]. In general humans and gods, male and female, wear similar items. First and foremost, bracelets or rings worn on the arm, either above the elbow (hereafter: „arm-rings") or at the wrist (hereafter: „wrist-rings"); where it can be checked, both types are worn in pairs, one on each arm. Then there are of course ear-rings, hair bands or diadems, and necklaces. Existing translations have never been systematically compared with the data. To do this rigidly, by listing all the artefacts and then the vocabulary, would be laborious but also premature, given the wealth of new information to be expected from recent Iraqi discoveries. Instead I propose to take the more readily identified items first and gradually strike them off the list until we are left with the problematical cases.

1. *šewirum*, NA *šabirru*, *sabirru* (wr. ḪAR) = „ring", more specifically „arm-ring" or „wrist-ring".

This is the easiest term we have to deal with. It is a general term for ring, going back to at least the Old Babylonian period, and shared with Aramaic and Arabic (Kaufman 1974, 102). Our best detail is afforded by SAA 7, No. 73. This is a text listing gold rings given to (?) 9 Assyrian officials or dignitaries. Some are „wrist rings" (ḪAR *ritte*), some „arm rings" (ḪAR *durā'i*), and the first person also receives an additional item called *ku-ri-nat* (see 6. below). It would be reasonable to expect that the arm-rings were heavier, but this does not seem to be the case. In fact the wrist-rings vary from 15 1/2 to 56 shekels, the arm-rings from 15 1/3 to 19 2/3 shekels (some of the weights are broken or difficult to understand). There is a wide range here, but among the wrist-rings there are examples weighing 32 1/3, 30 1/2, 31 1/2, 31 1/2, 28 1/2 and 34 1/2 shekels, strongly suggesting that there was at least one class of wrist-ring intended to weigh half a mina (30 shekels), i.e. about 240 grammes. Similarly, the lightest rings may well have been intended to weigh 1/4 mina each.

This seems reasonable, since in the distribution of rings to ambassadors in No. 58 their weights are not specified with such precision, rather they are rounded off to the nearest quarter or third of a mina, or just called „light" (SIG = *qatnu*). Thus for gold rings we have, in descending weight.: 3/4, 2/3, 1/2, 1/3, 1/4 (?; or perhaps 3/4)[8] mina, and „light" (SIG). Silver rings are listed weighing: 1, 3/4, 1/3 mina, and „light" (of course there may well have been rings of other weights in the broken sections). This listing implies both that a rough classification was sufficient and that the rings did tend to fall into discrete groups by weight.

We need not be in much doubt about the identity of these rings. On the reliefs the most eloquent scene is that illustrated in SAA 1, p. 30 Fig. 11[9], where – as

[7] See also Maxwell-Hyslop 1971, 235ff.

[8] The uncertainty concerns the meaning of the four horizontal wedges used in this text: without a preceding 3 it seems rash to take these as short-hand for 3/4, but I do not know of a case where they are used alone for 1/4, which is usually written 4-*tú* (with the GAR sign) in Neo-Assyrian.

[9] This detail is not visible in the drawing of the relief A.H. Layard, *Monuments of Nineveh II*, London 1853, Pl. 35 but is clear on the SAA 1 photograph and on the stone itself.

recognized by J.E. Reade – an Assyrian spearman is having a ring fitted to his wrist by his senior officer, just as the royal inscriptions tell us the foreign dignitaries or loyal vassals were rewarded. This looks like a metal ring, of circular cross-section; it is not possible to tell whether they were solid or hollow, a detail which will only become clear with the detailed publication of concrete examples. On Sargon's and Sennacherib's reliefs the great majority of the courtiers and high officials wear both wrist-rings and arm-rings. The rings on the upper arms, above the elbow, are almost without exception spiral and open-ended; as with the wrist-ring being awarded to the soldier, they look solid, with a circular cross-section (Hrouda 1965, Taf. 9:8-11). Concrete Assyrian examples have been lacking until recently, but are now known in gold from Nimrud and in silver from the Assur hoard (Collon 1991, 52; Fiume n. 215), while many such rings are shown on the reliefs, often with animal-head terminals. They are the forerunners of the elegant Achaemenid bracelets referred to as ψέλια in the Greek authors, and discussed fully in Amandry 1958. The most splendid examples from the Oxus and from the Susa tomb are (or were) inlaid with semi-precious stones. Note that Sargon specifically mentions that he presented a pair of inlaid wrist-rings; he would not have mentioned this were it not a little special. „Gold rings inlaid with ivory" are mentioned in a list of precious ornaments given to Esarhaddon by his father Sennacherib from the booty of Bit-Amukani in Chaldaea (ARU 13.2: ḪAR.MEŠ KÙ.GI *tam-lit* ZÚ). The characteristic re-entrant curve opposite the finials, described by Amandry and best seen where rings are being brought as tribute, is not visibly present in the Assyrian period, but compare the flattened shape of the ring from Babylon (Fig. 1).

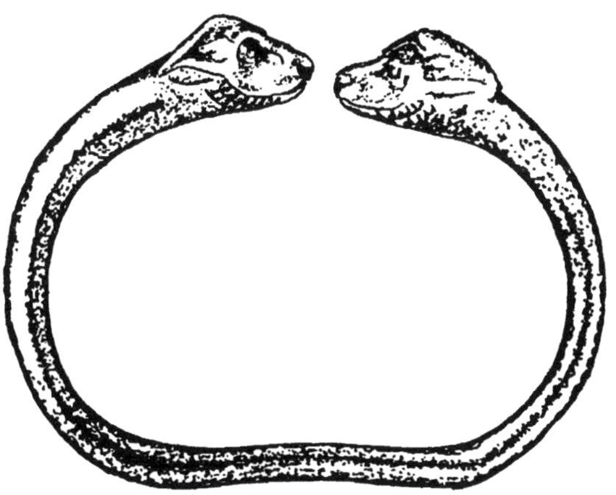

Fig. 1
IM 94362: Silver wrist-ring from the Temple of Ishtar, Babylon.
7th-6th century B.C. (7.5 x 6.15 x 1.0 cm.). Drawing: E.A. Postgate, after *Fiumi*, 339 and 418, n. 224.

It is of interest that many of the Achaemenid rings are surprisingly small, and that their weights tend to be in the region of 70 to 80 g., i.e. less than a quarter of a mina: are these the „light" rings of the Assyrian texts? Amand 1958 mentions weights of 82 g. (fn. 28), a pair of 76 and 72 g. (silver; fn. 84) and a pair of 65/68 g. (fn. 37). The small wrist-rings from the Oxus hoard range from 27 to 83 grammes[10]. The Oxus treasure also includes some heavier items. There seems to be a distinct group of medium-weight rings of between 200 to 235 grammes, about half a mina or 30 shekels (Nos. 117-118, 132, 138, 139); these are described by Dalton as „collar or spiral armlet", but as we have seen, their weight is consistent with wrist-rings. The largest piece is about 364 grammes in weight, or about 4/5 mina, 48 shekels; even this falls within the range of the ḪAR in the Assyrian texts.

2: *qūlu*[11] = „wrist-band"?

Round the wrist, however, there is a greater variety: as well as the open rings we have already discussed, there are flat bracelets of various shapes called by Hrouda „Rosettenarmringe" (Taf. 9:15-24). I shall refer to these as „wrist-bands". Most of those shown on the reliefs seem to be flat in cross-section and to have a circular decorative feature („rosette") on the back of the wrist, as a wrist-watch is usually worn. Examples of these are now to be found among the golden jewellery in the Nimrud queens' tombs, and the silver hoard from Assur also gives us examples of the real thing (Fig. 2: gold inlaid with agate, turquoise, etc.; Fiumi, pp. 339, 415 no. 214: silver with gold appliqué). A similar shape of wrist-band can be found among the Ziwiyeh treasure (cf. Amandry 1958, Pl. 13: 37-8). Sometimes a „rosette" or other decorative element extends well beyond the sides of the band, and it seems possible that these protrusions were deliberately designed to engage with the flesh of the wrist and so prevent the bracelet from slipping excessively. This would permit the diameter of the band to be large enough to allow it to pass over the hand onto the wrist without a separate opening device; unfortunately I cannot judge from the photographs whether the Assyrian examples could be opened and closed, but the Marlik example cited in Maxwell-Hyslop 1971, 250, suggests that some may have been hinged. In other cases, for example the pair worn in P. E. Botta, *Monument de Ninive I*, Pl. 43, the bracelets were evidently open at the back.

[10] Weights given in Dalton 1964 in oz. and grains have been converted to the metric system. Elsewhere unfortunately metal items are still sometimes published without their weight, which is the most important single piece of information when attempting to match artefacts with ancient terms.

[11] The Neo-Assyrian word should probably be normalized as *qūlu* (rather than *qullu*) cf. ND 2307 (FNALD No. 14) l. 11 *qu-ú-lu*. It seems unlikely to me that GUL-*lat* in SAA 7, No. 72 represents the plural of the same word.

Fig. 2

Inlaid gold wrist-band from tomb of Queen Yaba, Nimrud (8th century B.C.). Drawing: E.A. Postgate, after Nat. Geog. Magazine 179.5, May 1991, 111, and Roaf 1990, 165.

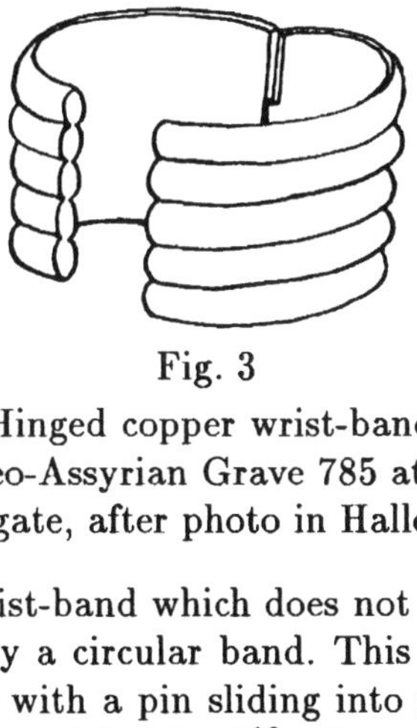

Fig. 3

Ass. 10744: Hinged copper wrist-band (or anklet) from Neo-Assyrian Grave 785 at Assur. Drawing: E.A. Postgate, after photo in Haller (see footnote 12).

There is a second type of wrist-band which does not have a circular disc or other central feature, but is simply a circular band. This is regularly hinged and has a closure opposite the hinge with a pin sliding into interlocking teeth. A copper example from Assur is illustrated in Fig. 3[12]; silver examples are attested in the

[12]Photo in A. Haller, *Die Gräber und Grüfte von Assur*, WVDOG 65, Berlin 1954, Taf. 17e with p. 68; it is described as a Beinring (i.e. anklet) and since from the scale in the publication it appears to be about 9 cm. in diameter, this may indeed be correct. However, the photograph in *Alef-Ba* 1077, Baghdad 1989, p. 5 shows golden rings of this type of two very different sizes (for wrist and ankle?), and some modern Iraqi examples are certainly worn on the wrist.

Assur hoard (on display in the Iraq Museum); gold at Nimrud (illustrated in *Alef-Ba* No. 1077, Baghdad 1989, cover and pp. 4-5; some of these appear to be much larger than others and may therefore be anklets); and the type is a standard item of feminine ornament in modern Iraq. It is of course possible that these should be classed with the ordinary „rings", but I prefer to think that their flat cross-section places them here with the „Rosettenarmringe".

Although they come in different shapes and types, wrist-bands seem to me to be clearly distinguished from wrist-rings in the reliefs, and they are not usually worn above the elbow like armrings. I assume, therefore, that we should look for a different name in the texts. My suggestion for this is *qūlu*, but it is no more than a guess. The word *qūlu*, like *sabirru*, is not confined to precious ornaments. It also occurs in Neo-Babylonian texts next to rings (CAD Q 298a), and is attested in association with lock mechanisms and in copper as ornaments on a chariot and on horse trappings. None of this is very specific. SAA 7, No. 126 r.3 lists a *qūlu* of „artificial stones" (NA4.MEŠ *kūri*), and a new usage is found in Nos. 130 and 131 which list gastronomic items including „birds of ^giš^*qu-li*"; I wonder if this refers to some form of restraint, like a collar or leg-ring. In SAA 7, No. 72 the summation of the text lists 15 *qu-li* between 34 BÀN.DA.MEŠ and 4 *ša tāmarti*. These terms are even less clear to us than *qūlu*, and hardly help. From the text we learn that the *qūlu* might be of silver or gold, and be inlaid with eye-stones (l. 24') or other stones (*muššāru*, r. 4'); may be qualified with *ṭūdi*, another obscure term; and, if my understanding of r. 11' is correct, be of wood bound in gold (1 *qu-lu* GIŠ *rakkusu neḫsu* KÙ.GI). None of this is decisive, or even particularly suggestive. Until we have better evidence I can only leave the proposal *qūlu* = „(wrist)-band" for further testing.

3. *qudāsu*[13] = „ear-ring"?

The word *qudāsu* certainly refers to a piece of feminine jewellery, although this would not of itself mean it was not worn by men. It is found also in Neo-Babylonian, and the same word is translated „ear-ring" when found in Aramaic and Syriac (Kaufman 1974, 86). It is however listed in the Neo-Babylonian text BIN 2 No. 126 next to *anṣabtu*, which is certain to be an ear-ring (cf. only the Descent of Ishtar). Although there are various types of ear-ring known from the reliefs and in the archaeological record (e.g. Maxwell-Hyslop 1971, 236-7; Jakob-Rost 1962), it is hard to identify two categories sufficiently distinct from each other that they could have been regularly referred to with two quite different words. This makes it doubtful that *qudāsu* could be translated as „ear-ring" in Neo-Babylonian, but since *anṣabtu* is not attested, and ear-rings are frequently encountered, in Neo-Assyrian contexts, the best solution is perhaps to adopt the CAD translation (Q 293-4) by translating „ring (worn by women)" but accept

[13] I am not sure how to normalize this word in Neo-Assyrian. Is it *qudassu* < *qudaštu*, as the plural *qudašāte* in LAS 121 would suggest? Or is it in fact an Aramaic loan-word so that the sibilant of the final radical need not have been *s*?

it as the normal Assyrian word for ear-ring. Other details from the texts do not contradict this: *qudāsu* could weigh only 5 shekels or less (CTN 2 No. 1:15[14]) and occur in relatively large numbers (20 in ND 2307 = FNALD 14), or in pairs.

4. sa'ūru = „hair-ring"?

The first difficulty with this word is how to read it. I have opted for *sa'ūru*, but the first *u* could be a long or a short vowel, and the glottal stop could technically be doubled (i.e. a *parrus* formation). The plural *sa'ūrāt(e/i)* is feminine. In three of the four mentions in the SAA 7 texts odd numbers are listed (5, 5 and 43), so they probably did not normally form pairs. Most illuminating is SAA 7, No. 67, where we have „5 *s.*, coils; 43 small *s.*" (i.4-5). Otherwise, except perhaps for *šá-'u-ur-tú* in a broken letter (CT 53 458: 8), the only occurrences of this word are in the 9th century inscriptions of Assur-nasir-apli, among valuable things taken from two of the Aramaeo-Hittite states:

AKA 365.62: „chairs inlaid with ivory, silver and gold, gold rings (ḪAR), *sa-'A-ru/ri* of gold with inlay (*tamlīte*), gold *gāgu*, a gold dagger" from the tribute of Aḫuni of Bit-Adini.

AKA 366.65: the tribute of Sangara king of Ḫattu (i.e. Carchemish): „20 talents of silver, *sa-'A-ri* of gold, ring(s) of gold, daggers of gold".

The only other similar word in the dictionary is that written once *šá-'u-ú-ra-a-te* and once *sa-'u-ú-ra-a-te* in the Neo-Assyrian ritual K 8669 (ii.18-19). It is an adjective describing cloths, and can hardly have the same meaning, since the context virtually imposes a translation „dirty", in contrast to those called „clean" (*zakuāte*). However, if, with AHw, we assign it to (Babylonian) *šu"uru(m)* meaning „hairy, covered with hair", the alternation of the sibilant in this word would give us a slight justification for connecting our ornaments with the same root as *šārtu* „hair" (*š'r*) and guessing that they are „hair ornaments". Spiral silver hair ornaments are in fact attested in the Assur silver hoard (Fig. 4), but the only ornaments worn in their hair by men on the reliefs are the head-bands or 'fillets' (cf. 9. below). This interpretation is no more than a guess, and it should be stressed that the etymological connection with *šārtu* is not certain.

Fig. 4

IM 91445/11: Silver hair ornament from hoard at Assur.
8th-7th century B.C. (1.7 x 2.6 x 0.38 cm.).
Drawing: E.A. Postgate, after *Fiumi*, 339 and 417, n. 220.

[14]I am uncertain whether *qu-da-si/e* here is singlar or plural.

6. *kurinnu* or *kurinnutu*, plur. *kurinnāt(e/i)*

This seems to be a minor item, mentioned after the rings in SAA 7, Nos. 58.iii.19 and 73.4; in the second text a weight of only 3 shekels is mentioned. Other occurrences of the word ***kurinnu*** confirm that it is a type of ornament, but the CAD translation „necklace" rests primarily on the ritual text TCL 6 49, where it is placed round the neck of the pregnant woman. A „(small) neck ornament" seems to be as close as we can come for now.

7. (KUŠ.)BÀN.DA (Akkadian reading unknown)

That this is a personal ornament does seem to follow from SAA 7, No. 72, where 34 of them are listed with 15 *qūlu*, and the similarity of the two items is underlined in r. 10'-11' where we have „[1] BÀN.DA of wood, bound with a gold band" followed immediately by „1 *qūlu* of wood, bound with a gold band". The Akkadian reading of the logogram is very problematic. In SAA 7 *šeršerrutu* meaning a „chain" is put forward, following a proposal of Parpola's (cf. p. xxvi). This would assume that BÀN.DA stands for *šerru*, and derive the first syllable *šer* from SU as a logogram for *šēru* „flesh" (not a regular equation). This reading is especially difficult in SAA 7, No. 72 which writes BÀN.DA without a KUŠ. It seems safer to accept KUŠ as an omissible determinative, suggesting that the essential item could be made of leather, but I have no satisfactory proposal for an Akkadian reading or meaning. Whatever it was, we do know that this item could be elaborate, made up of various components, including representations of birds, shells, etc. (see SAA 7, p. xxvi). It does not seem to come in pairs, and hence seems likely to be either a head, neck or breast ornament.

8. *gāgu* = „neck-ring"?

This word is rare in Assyrian. A golden *gāgu* is taken by Assur-nasir-apli II as booty from Aḫuni of Bit-Adini (see above, under 5.), another in the gift from Sennacherib to his son (ARU 13:3) came from Chaldaea; 2 silver ones are listed in the dowry text ND 2307 (=FNALD 14). It does not seem to be a common piece of Assyrian ornament, but ever since Streck compared it to an Ethiopic word it has been understood as a neck ornament[15]. If worn round the neck, either „torc" or „necklace" would be possible, with a marginal preference, in the light of the Ethiopic, for „necklace". Since it is listed in booty from Til-Barsip, perhaps we should look at ornaments illustrated in the west. Miss L. Çehreli refers me to two western rulers who wear neck rings unlike anything worn by Assyrian kings or

[15] Prof. E. Ullendorf, to whom I am very grateful for looking at the Ethiopic evidence, writes „In Ethiopic the word is virtually unknown outside translations of the Hebrew Old Testament where it occurs about a dozen times. Its meaning is very unclear, but it is certainly closer to „chain" than to „ring" ... in Deut. 28:48 it translates „yoke of iron", ... [Akkadian] *gāgi ḫurāṣi* is exactly reflected in Eth. gāgā zäwarq „gold collar" or „gold chain". Dillman also renders „catena" – 'quali monachi in Aethiopia affligendi corporis causa lumbos cingunt' " – which certainly sounds more like chains than rings.

courtiers. The Ain al-Arab statue of about the 9th century shows a North Syrian ruler boasting an elaborate ornament round his neck[16], and on the Ivriz relief the late 8th century Neo-Hittite king Warpalawas wears a solid, but delicately worked, neck ring. With this one exception, actual torcs, in the sense of solid metal rings worn round the neck, familiar from Celtic Europe, do not appear in the Near East before the Achaemenids.

9. *kililu* (wr. GIL) = „head-band"

This word is rarely mentioned (TCAE 283, Obv. 11 and Rev 5', in gold). For the reading cf. Borger, ABZ Add. Suppl. 1980. It is also attested in Neo-Babylonian (Camb. 193: 2) and among Sennacherib's gifts to his son from Chaldaea (ARU 13: 3 as corrected by ABL 1452). A stone(!) head-band seems to be listed in CTN 2, No. 1. Whether this word could refer to the tapering fillet with central rosette which is commonly shown on the reliefs (e.g. Hrouda 1965, Taf. 6 nos. 5, 7, 8; Maxwell-Hyslop 1974, 251-2) is not clear to me. We may prefer to think of the golden crown which is among the most splendid items recovered from the Nimrud tombs (National Geographic Magazine 179.5, May 1991, 111).

10. *unqu*

For the sake of completeness, we should list *unqu* (logogram ŠU.GUR), which certainly refers to finger rings, sometimes specifically a signet ring (incorporating a stamp seal).

In brief, there is good evidence for the use of arm-rings and especially wrist-rings in Assyria as honorific marks of status in the late 8th and 7th centuries B.C., although there is no reason to think this had been systematized to the extent of describing people as „torc-wearers" and „bracelet-wearers" like Herodotus, or that any of them were marks of a specific function (like a European mayor's chain of office). It is possible that the explicitly symbolic role of the bracelets was an idea imported via the Levant from Egypt, where it was already prevalent in the 2nd millennium, and it certainly was handed down to the Medes and Persians. In contrast, neck torcs did not yet serve this function, nor is there any clear evidence that another class of ornament, the *qūlu*, perhaps a wrist-band did so. Note, though, that among the bracelets handed out to visiting dignitaries by Sargon's officials there were probably ear and neck ornaments (*qudāsu* and *kurinnutu*). I have also listed some of the other terms for kinds of personal ornament, but even when they can be fairly securely identified with the objects themselves, there is no evidence that they had particular symbolic significance. In any case, the publication in detail of the great wealth of personal ornament from the royal tombs at Nimrud will revolutionize the entire subject, and this article cannot claim to do more than point out some of the outstanding issues which may be resolved.

[16]See W. Orthmann, *Untersuchungen zur späthethitischen Kunst*, SBA 8, Bonn 1971, 50, 476 and Taf. 4a; a similar neck ornament on the statue illustrated in W. Orthmann, Der Alte Orient, PKG 18, Fig. 411 ('Ain et-Tell, ca. 800 B.C.

Addenda (Dec. 1993)

(1) ad §1 note the Neo-Babylonian reference to a gold ring (ḪAR KÙ.GI) given to someone as a mark of office, cited by CAD Š/ii p.158 (CT 54 507 r.5).

(2) already under Assurnasirpal II we have a highly placed courtier bearing a dagger and a gold ring (ḪAR KÙ.GI) in the text published by Millard and Deller, Bagh. Mitt. 24 (1993) p.220 BM 36711 Vs. 16' with commentary p.227.

(3) ad §8 note that in ABL 653 (=SAA 10 189) a *gāgu* is mentioned among the symbols of royalty.

Middle Assyrian to Neo-Assyrian: the Nature of the Shift[1]

JOHN NICHOLAS POSTGATE
Cambridge

1 Introduction

It has often been recognized that Assyria had a special character of its own, which was retained through the centuries and marked it off from its neighbours. While boundaries are not always clear-cut, most of us would agree that it makes good sense to talk of "Assyrian dialect", "Assyria" and "Assyrian art", in both the 2nd and the 1st millennium. This does not of course mean that these Assyrian characteristics were unchanging: obviously while retaining a distinctive character, Assyria did change, and the generally accepted three-fold chronological division into Old, Middle and Neo-Assyrian comprises periods which are not just lengths of time, but display individual characteristics of their own. These divisions are valuable. There can be no disagreement about the significance of the break between Old and Middle Assyrian. Similarly – although in political affairs one could easily argue for a significant change with the accession of Tiglath-pileser III in 745 B.C. – on linguistic and art historical criteria there are important changes between 1050 and 900 B.C. which justify the traditional division.

Although for practical reasons political historians, philologists and art historians often confine their attention to one or other of these periods, the processes by which one phase of the culture is transformed into the next deserve to be studied in their own right. This is both difficult and essential for the same reason: the major transformations coincide with the periods of social unrest and political weakness (or 'Dark Ages'), and the body of evidence available from these times is notoriously scarce: kings cease to rebuild temples or write inscriptions about their conquests, economic activities are curtailed and are not documented, the output of craftsmen for wealthy patrons dries up. This is not coincidental, but it is frustrating: the changes cannot be observed directly, rather, we can only compare "before" and "after", analyse the changes and speculate about their causes. Such studies may be the only way to penetrate the gloom of the Dark Age and so give us a glimpse of how Assyria adapted and survived without losing its identity.

Change can come in different ways. One obvious question is whether a shift is due to external influence or completely internal. Answers can sometimes be given: for instance, there are Sumerograms in Middle Assyrian texts which are not current in Old Assyrian – a clear sign of borrowing from Babylonia, probably in the 14th century or so.[2] Less easy to identify is the difference between a single, deliberate act of reform (a political act presupposing a strong source of authority), and a gradual shift, which could be seen as an organic development of popular practice or taste. A further possibility is that a tradition may disappear totally, and then be replaced later by a new quite unrelated practice or documentary format. For each case of change observed, it is worth trying to classify it into one of these types, because each type of change will tend to be fostered by a different set of social or political conditions, opening the possibility of suggesting some deductions about the society and politics of the country at the time the change took place.

We cannot of course assume that changes in the different spheres we can observe – in administration, law, society, artistic style, language – all occur at the same moment. Major changes do seem to oc-

[1] The text has been considerably revised since it was delivered in Heidelberg, and documentation added. I would like to express my gratitude to the organizers of the Rencontre, and especially to Hartmut Waetzoldt, for the invitation to contribute to the meeting as an acknowledgement of my admiration and respect for Prof. Dr. Karlheinz Deller for his mastery of things Assyrian, and as an opportunity to wish him many further years of Assyriology proprement dit. I would also like to thank Prof. Ar. Theodorides, Prof. H. Limet and Prof. Ö. Tunca for their invitation to contribute to their inter-university session "Le vocabulaire juridique" held in Liège in November 1990, where I first had an opportunity to address some of these issues.

[2] These include Ì.LÁ.E(.MEŠ) for *šaqālu* (e.g. KAJ 12; TR 3021), Ì.ÁG.E for *madādu* (e.g. KAJ 67), ŠU.BA.AN.TI(.MEŠ) for *laqā'u* or *maḫāru* (e.g. TR 3022), and (MÍ.)KALAG.GA for *(ṭuppu) dannutu*.

cur often together (though not invariably), suggesting that stability and continuity in one sphere are accompanied by stability and continuity in another. Hence it is not sufficient to confine our attention to one sphere alone. Here I have taken the legal documents of the Middle and Neo-Assyrian period as a case study, but I am sure not only that a similar study of the transition from Old to Middle Assyrian legal documents and their formulae would be rewarding, but also that the shift from Middle Assyrian to Neo-Assyrian glyptic could be equally stimulating.

2 The tablets: document format

Let us begin with the external features of the tablets (Table 1[3]). That changes took place is obvious just from looking at them. There are three obvious variables to be observed: the shape of the document, whether it has an envelope or not, and sealing practices. While these may not be as explicit as the actual written text, they are practices, if not rules, which were systematically observed by the makers of the tablets, and they change with time. They are therefore quite appropriate for our purposes.

2.1 Conveyances

In both periods documents recording different kinds of transaction are treated very differently. I concentrate deliberately on the most frequent types of document, both because this improves the 'statistical validity' of the changes we see, and because changes in such a basic instrument of legal and social relations may reasonably be taken to reflect general changes in society better than differences between more specialized legal transactions of various kinds. The two commonest types are conveyances (principally sales) and contracts (loans, work contracts etc.).[4] With the conveyance texts the changes are quite minor. Whereas on our MA texts the seal occupies the head of the obverse, with a 'Siegelvermerk' distinguished from the main text (and often, I think, added later), by NA times a space is ruled off for the seal impression(s), and the Siegelvermerk is visually assimilated to the remainder of the text and obviously written at the same time as it. These are changes of presentation, not of substance, and we are handicapped by the fact that no certain MA final sale document is known, only interim texts which may or may not have received the same degree of formal presentation.[5] A more significant change may be in the persons sealing. In NA times, with rare exceptions, only the owner or owners of the property impress their seal, in the space ruled off on the obverse. It is possible that the MA sale document (*ṭuppu dannutu*), while undoubtedly sealed by the seller, was also sealed by some or all of the witnesses, like various other types of MA legal text; but again we lack a definite example.

2.2 Contracts

With contracts, that is to say a variety of transactions recording an obligation to be annulled in future, the situation is much more complex. In MA times the outward format of all such texts is fairly uniform. The regular MA format for loans and other types of contract, whether for silver, lead, etc., for commodities or even for labour, is a single, usually squarish, tablet, with no envelope, but with seals rolled all over (usually after the text was written). A space was left by the scribe at the top of the obverse for the debtor's seal, and his and the witnesses' seals (rolled on the reverse and the edges) were identified by a Siegelvermerk (KIŠIB PN). As set out elsewhere, there are reasons for thinking that the preparation

---

3 As a reminder that other (combinations of) formats are possible receipts have been included in the Table, although they are not discussed in the text.

4 For these two broad categories, which are as valid for Middle as for Neo-Assyrian, see FNALD pp. 11 (§ 2.0) and 32 (§ 3.1.0).

5 See BSOAS 34 (1971) 516, and AOF 13 (1986) 17–18.

of a legally valid contract of this kind was known as *ṭuppa ṣabātu*, and this phrase, and the practice, are attested in contemporary Babylonia.[6]

By the 7th century the situation is quite different. In no cases do witnesses seal the document, and there are two quite different kinds of document. For loans and debt-notes of silver small 'horizontal' (unlike the 'vertical' conveyances) tablets were encased in envelopes on which an approximate duplicate of the inner text was written and seals impressed (across the middle of the obverse, but without rulings). These are therefore double documents, one permanently open and available for consultation, the other protected from tampering and damage by its sealed outer version. By contrast, loans of grain and similar commodities are usually recorded on triangular clay lumps which were formed round string.[7] I believe it is now accepted as plausible that these too are all that remains of a double document: the clay bears the outer text and seals the string which secures the inner text, and the inner text must have been on a perishable scroll. The obvious reason for this extreme difference in documentary format is that the primary record of corn and commodity transactions at this time was in Aramaic, that for currency loans in Assyrian.[8]

When these formats were introduced, and why, is much less certain because we do not have enough documents from before the 7th century. I cannot for sure cite a single triangular docket earlier than the reign of Sennacherib,[9] but this is not significant since in fact there are hardly any commodity contracts from the reign of Sargon or earlier. One explanation could of course be that they were all (and only) written on perishable materials, but there are simply not enough texts from before Sargon's reign in general for this to be a necessary conclusion: they may have been on clay dockets or tablets which we happen not to have found. For silver loans the double format is apparently a late introduction.[10] Tablets without envelopes are still in use in the 730's, with a sealing or nail impression on the reverse (CTN 2 nos. 106, 107, both silver; cf. 109, bronze). These are distinguished from conveyances by being horizontal; earlier, in the 790's we have two 'vertical' tablets (CTN 2 no. 101, with nail impressions (bronze); cf. 102 (silver?)), but already one, unsealed, horizontal (CTN 2 no. 103 (people and bronze)). We therefore see a process of gradual change during the 8th century, followed by the universal adoption of a standardized double format in two very different forms. It is quite likely therefore that changes to the format of commodity loans happened about the same time as currency (silver and copper) loans were standardized, but we have no evidence for this.

3 The words: legal terminology

There are of course many changes in the vocabulary of legal documents between the Middle and the Neo-Assyrian periods. To some extent they may be attributed to an impoverishment of the range of legal transactions recorded, though in other cases it may not be more than a substitution of a new word

---

6 See AOF 13 (1986) 18–21.

7 See FNALD pp. 4–6; use of a triangular label was not however invariable for commodities (cf. ADD 127 = ARU 314 = SAA 6 46; ADD 147 and 148 = ARU 324 and 325); and the occurrence of triangular dockets with an Aramaic text for silver loans (among the Harran district documents cited in footnote 29) merely underlines the fact that the variation in document format is not rigidly dependent on the object of the transaction and must have some other explanation.

8 This interpretation of the dockets is, I think, implicitly accepted by H. Tadmor, in H.J. Nissen & J. Renger (eds.), Mesopotamien und seine Nachbarn (XXV. Rencontre Assyriologique Internationale; Berlin 1982), 453. However, he writes there "The triangular corn-loan dockets ..... are, in the order of their development, unilingual (= Akkadian), bilingual and unilingual (= Aramaic)"; while this may be presented as a **logical** development (assuming Akkadian priority), and is indeed the view espoused by myself in FNALD pp. 5–6, I do not believe that there are enough early dated dockets of the three kinds to demonstrate a **chronological** development, and so to contradict the view expressed here now, that the priority in the use of the dockets should go to Aramaic. F.M. Fales (Aramaic epigraphs on clay tablets, pp. 19–24) is therefore right to insist on the lack of any clear chronological sequence, although I cannot share his view that the loan dockets were either hung round a person's neck or attached to containers.

9 ADD 141 = ARU 304 = SAA 6 60: 704 B.C.

10 Cf. CTN 2, p. 19.

for an older.[11] Other symptoms of what we might term a decrease in sophistication are the abandonment of some elaborate Sumerograms used in the Middle Assyrian period (see note 2 above), and the loss of formality represented by the disappearance of patronymics. Here however I shall concentrate again on the commonest and simplest formulae for the same reasons (Table 2).

3.1 Conveyances

The principal changes may be described as follows:

a. MA *šīm gamer* is replaced by NA *kaspu gammur tadin*. This is not a deep change in the nature of the transaction, but simply moves the statement of "full price" from the operative clauses to the Schlußklauseln.

b. MA *ušabbi* "he has satisfied" is lost. The verb *šabā'u* is common in Old Assyrian commercial usage, but is not found in NA legal documents. This change probably reflects the disuse of the word as a legal term in vernacular,[12] oral contexts.

c. MA *uppu laqi* seems to become NA *zarip laqi*.[13] The similarity may however be deceptive, and cannot be taken as evidence that *uppu* and *zarip* are identical in meaning or function. If *uppu* is correctly derived from *wapû* D, it probably means "publicized" (by means of herald's announcement or other formalities needed to precede a legally valid sale). Whether the verb *zarāpu* bore the same meaning as *uppû* is hard to establish since we have neither etymological means nor sufficiently varied contexts to determine its underlying meaning. Nonetheless, this is clearly a modernization, since *uppû* is not attested in NA, and *zarāpu* not in MA, and it is not unreasonable to accept this as a case of legal formulae adapting to changes in the Assyrian vernacular.

d. NA *uppušu* is not used in MA legal documents. However, it does occur with *t/nadānu* in the Middle Assyrian Laws in the phrase, *eqla u bīta ana ukullā'i-ša ša 2 šanāti uppušu iddununeš-še* where local officials are empowered to sell an absentee's property to provide support for his wife ("they shall ... and sell for her for her sustenance for 2 years").[14] Again, for lack of varied contexts we can only guess at the precise meaning of *uppušu*. It is uncertain whether the two verbs should be taken together as referring to a single process or action (conventionally, though unsatisfyingly, referred to as a hendiadys[15]), or to two separate procedures. In other words, is the combination of *uppušu* with *t/nadānu* to be understood as simply "to sell", or rather as "to ... and sell"? My inclination is to take *uppušu* to mean "to carry out (certain procedures)", a meaning close to its well established usage with abstract nouns which can be rendered as "to exercise", e.g. *šarrūtu uppušu* "to exercise kingship". I would therefore opt for "to carry out (the legal preliminaries and) sell", hence "to sell legally". If so, it could contain within it some of the meaning of *uppu* in the MA formulary. In any case, this again looks like a case where a traditional legal formula has been replaced by a phrase borrowed from the vernacular.

e. In the early 8th century B.C. there was a change in the tenses used. Instead of *ilqe* (or in some conveyances *iddin*), we have the perfects *isseqe* and *ittidin*.[16] This seems to be another case of assimilation to the vernacular: as is well known, in the NA dialect the preterite is replaced in positive main clauses by

---

11 As examples of what is probably a simple substitution of one word for another we could cite *šēṣu'u* (NA) for *paṭāru* (MA) "to release (from pledge)", *kammusu* for *ušābu* "to reside, live", and *rubê* for *ṣibtu* "interest"; changes in phrasing, but probably not substance, are *ana šaparti šakin* for *ki šaparti ukâl* "is placed on pledge" for "he holds as pledge", and *ša marāqu ši* "it is to be crushed" for *ana ḫipi naṭat* "it is fit to be broken". On the other hand there are both words and legal clauses in MA texts which disappear from the repertoire without a replacement: *ḫiāṭu* "to pay out", *madādu* "to weigh out", *karrû* "to deduct", *naḫrat*, of a tablet "is invalid", and the *ina muḫḫi šalmi-šu u kēni-šu* phrases which go back to the Old Assyrian period. These are only a few randomly selected instances, a full study would doubtless reveal more but would also take up much space.

12 By vernacular, I mean the Neo-Assyrian dialect as spoken and known to us almost exclusively through letters.

13 See FNALD pp. 14–15 for these difficult terms.

14 Middle Assyrian Laws Tablet A § 45; cf. translation and discussion in BSOAS 34 (1971) 502ff.

15 Cf. F.R. Kraus, Sonderformen akkadischer Parataxe: Die Koppelungen (Mededelingen der Kon. Ned. Akad. van Wetenschappen, Afd. Letterkunde NR 50/i; 1987), for a different terminology.

16 Cf. FNALD p. 13 § 2.1.2 for conveyances, p. 37 § 3.2.4 for contracts.

the perfect.[17] Whether this assimilation dates back to the 9th century is unknown because we have no legal texts of that date; but in the 7th century the legal formulary reverted to the old preterite (with *-ma*, also archaizing), suggesting a deliberate attempt to enhance the document's formality.

To sum up, the changes between MA and NA include the adaptation of the traditional legal formulary to current vernacular usage, both by the substitution of lexemes, and by the updating of grammatical forms in accordance with Neo-Assyrian usage. There is no sign of influence, cultural or linguistic, from outside Assyria.[18]

3.2 Contracts

Here again the situation is quite different from conveyances. An entirely new formulation is adopted in the 1st millennium. Two levels of change have to be distinguished. Most significantly NA makes use of a single formulation to cover two situations which are regularly differentiated in MA. The ordinary loan in MA uses the active preterite verb *ilqe* "he took"; while a contract which records an obligation arising in some other way quite understandably avoids this positive statement and simply describes the liability with the phrase *ina muḫḫi*.[19] The difference in the two formulae reflects the fact that the loan texts record an action (of "taking"), while the debt-notes only describe a state or situation (which has not necessarily been created by an action in the same way). Turning to NA, we find that now the simple statement "item X, property of PN_1, is at the disposal of PN_2" serves for both types of contract. Where a loan is involved, a supplementary phrase (essentially *ina pūḫi ittiši*) is added making this clear. Before discussing the implications of this we may note some other detailed changes, which can be listed as follows:

a. The preterite of the MA formulae is replaced by the perfect, again in accordance with changes in the vernacular (see footnote 17).

b. In place of *ina muḫḫi* in the debt-notes, which describe the obligation as resting "on" the debtor, we see the introduction of *ina pān*, describing the item loaned or owed as being "at the disposal" of someone. This phrase is used in the vernacular (in the epistolary corpus) for people or things which are at the disposal of someone, and the same usage lies behind the legal phrase.

c. Unlike the conveyances, *laqāʾu* disappears. Where a verb is needed to describe the action of taking something, it is *našû*. This change is in accordance with vernacular usage. While both verbs are in use in both periods, in NA letters *našû* is frequent meaning "to take away", *laqāʾu* much less common. One reason for the divergence could be that *našû* is better suited (or *laqāʾu* not suited) to convey the positive action of **taking** the item owed, for it must be borne in mind that its use is broadly confined to the genuine loans with the *ina pūḫi* clause. Another (and not necessarily alternative) reason may be that *laqāʾu* remains in use in NA conveyance texts as the result of the greater formality of the conveyance as a legal deed, encouraging adherence to traditional vocabulary.

d. The KI ("from") used in the MA loan texts disappears entirely. This may in part be a purely linguistic phenomenon, because the distinction between the two prepositions *ištu* and *išti*, already uncertain in MA, virtually disappears in NA *issu/issi*, when TA is used as the sole logogram and the usage with verbs like *laqāʾu* (whether originally to be assigned to *ištu* "from" or *išti* "with") also disappears.[20] The

[17] The use of the perfect as the principal past tense in NA (with the preterite retained in subordinate clauses and negative sentences) was described, following Karlheinz Deller, in K. Riemschneider's Lehrbuch des Akkadischen (see also the English translation by T.A. Caldwell, J.N. Oswalt & J.F.X. Sheehan, An Akkadian grammar; Milwaukee 1974), Ch. 27.

[18] This in itself is perhaps a surprise: one might expect Aramaic influence, but perhaps not in legal environments, if one compares the basic phraseology of Aramaic legal documents (most recently F.M. Fales, Aramaic epigraphs on clay tablets of the Neo-Assyrian period; Rome 1986), even where the two languages share the same word or root no effort is made to assimilate one to the other, and lexical borrowings in legal terminology flow from Neo-Assyrian to Aramaic.

[19] The many texts in which someone's receipt of something is described (with the stative verb *maḫir*) are of course quite different, since they record not the creation of a future obligation, but the mere fact of the receipt (which may itself be the annulment of an existing obligation).

[20] See the dictionaries for the complex situation; and note in particular that the logogram KI in MA corresponds to the writing *iš-tu* although it is certainly equivalent to Babylonian *itti*, also used with verbs of taking.

loss of *ištu* meaning "from" before persons in the current vernacular may have encouraged the abandonment of the existing loan formula, and the adaptation of the *ša* PN debt-note phraseology to cover loans as well.

In general, despite the minor differences described as a. and b. above, it is probable that the standard NA loan formula (E) is derived from the MA debt-note format (D) with the addition of a supplementary clause. We may suggest this with greater confidence because signs of the change emerge already in the 2nd millennium. Two 13th century grain loan documents have operative sections with the *ša* PN_1 ... *ina muḫḫi* PN_2 ("belonging to PN_1, ... incumbent on PN_2") debt-note formula, and yet they are followed by a supplementary phrase "this grain he received on exchange" (ŠE-*um*.MEŠ *anniu ana pūḫi ilqe*).[21] They still retain MA features (*ana* – not *ina* – before *pūḫi*, *laqā'u* – not *našû*); and the supplementary phrase gives the impression of being colloquial and narrative, not a traditional legal formula.[22] A similar transitional stage is attested in the 11th century, but here too we still have *ša* PN_1 ... *ina muḫḫi* PN_2 "incumbent on", rather than *ina pān* "at the disposal of", and *ana* (not *ina*) *pūḫi* in a supplementary phrase.[23] The parallel with Neo-Assyrian usage, where it seems beyond doubt that *ina pūḫi* "on exchange" implies nothing more nor less than "as a loan", indicates that these texts too are recording loans, and the preterite (or later perfect) tense underlines the fact that the documents record an action, not just a situation (see above).

This then suggests that from at least the 13th century onwards the traditional formula for a loan was being replaced by the debt-note combined with a supplementary clause involving *ana pūḫi*. This phrase probably entered the legal formulary from the vernacular, but quite how it achieved this specific application to loans remains obscure. It is already present at Alalakh, where it is used with *leqû* in administrative (rather than strictly legal) documents for villagers taking loans of grain, in a situation remarkably similar to the MA texts already cited.[24]

4 Conclusions

In the absence of an up-to-date study of Middle Assyrian legal terminology, and given the very uneven chronological distribution of our texts, the foregoing discussion cannot be other than exploratory. Any conclusions will be liable to radical revision, and indeed my own views changed substantially both while preparing the spoken contribution to the Rencontre at Heidelberg and since then. Nevertheless, even as no more than the first step in a dialectic I hope it is worthwhile suggesting some ideas.

Conveyances display a measure of continuity, in both their outward format and their terminology. Contracts, on the other hand, change radically in their outward format, and in the formulation and terminology of the text. Perhaps the contrast is not too surprising: the importance and relative simplicity of a deed of sale can account for a degree of traditional formality and stability. Contracts are used for a much greater variety of transactions and are less formal and more transitory. This may indeed account in part for their greater changeability, but if examined more closely we find that contracts underwent at least three phases of change in different respects. First, within the Middle Assyrian period, there is a shift in basic format whereby traditional loan formulation with KI PN *ilqe* begins to be supplanted by debt-notes with the supplementary *ina pūḫi* clause. Next, at some period after the 11th century and before the 8th, there are lexical and grammatical changes reflecting the shift in vernacular dialect. Finally, probably at the very end of the 8th century, there are radical innovations in the outward form of the documents.

---

21 See Postgate, The archive of Urad-Šerua and his family (Rome 1988) Nos. 54 and 56.

22 Like others found after the operative section in relatively informal MA legal documents.

23 E.g. ŠE-*um*.MEŠ *annia ana pūḫi it-ta-x*, VAT 17918 (sic, instead of 17888 as given in Sumer, after information from H. Freydank): 13–14, Sumer 24 (1968) 18–19, 34. For the date of the archive from which these tablets come see Pedersén, Archives and Libraries in the City of Assur, Part I (Uppsala 1985), p. 44. The correct restoration of the verbal form still eludes me, but note that here, already in the 11th or late 12th century, the perfect tense now features in place of the preterite.

24 JCS 13 (1959) pp. 54–57; other references in G. Giacumakis, The Akkadian of Alalakh (The Hague 1970), p. 95.

That there are stages of change is hardly surprising. The great majority of MA texts belong to the 13th or 14th centuries, of NA texts to the 7th century, and we have virtually nothing from the 11th to 9th centuries inclusive. A "shift" spanning some six centuries is not a single process. Moreover, with so big a gap the perennial problem of the argumentum e silentio becomes especially acute. There is therefore plenty of scope for overturning some of the suggestions made here if documents from the intervening years turn up. Only then would we be able to see clearly whether certain changes coincide with periods of political disruption and economic distress, or with relatively stable and prosperous reigns such as those of Assur-naṣir-apli and Shalmaneser in the 9th century. In particular, there is no way of knowing whether the scarcity of private business documents from the centuries before 700 B.C. is because they were genuinely rare, or simply the consequence of accidents of archaeological preservation and discovery. It is well known that discoveries of documents, especially of the ephemeral contract type as opposed to conveyances, tend to cluster towards the end of historical periods when the sequence of continuous use of an archaeological context tends to be disrupted.[25] However, the variability of the 8th century contract texts mentioned above, when contrasted with the standardization and long-term stability of the 7th century type requires explanation. Is it that the genre was not in such regular use earlier, militating against the establishment of a standard format, that some degree of central (i.e. government) control and standardization was imposed later, or both, or neither?

And does any of this permit any deductions about social affairs? Historical and archaeological survey evidence indicate that in the 9th-11th centuries rural life was severely disrupted and it may be that the tradition of formal literate administration also evaporated. While it is clear that the basic NA contract formula was inherited, albeit with minor up-datings, from MA times, there may well have been a significant reduction in its use and uniformity. Many, perhaps most, commodity loans were made by urban creditors (wealthy families or institutions) to the rural population.[26] Not only were there probably less peasants actually in the countryside, but the instability will have reduced their contacts with the towns. Moreover the incentive to record loans in writing will always have come from the urban elite: peasants left to themselves are unlikely to have needed the legal sanction of a written document within a village environment, or to have increased the cost of borrowing by engaging the services of scribes. It therefore seems reasonable that the disruption of Assyria round the year 1000 reduced both the level of economic credit transactions, especially between the countryside and the cities (where all our tablets have of course been found), and undermined the social norms which required that they be documented in writing. Under these conditions, although the essential format of both conveyance and contract document remained constant, we need not be surprised to observe a process of modernization in the language of the texts, new terms and grammatical forms being introduced from the vernacular as centralized uniformity or the observance of formal legal phraseology slackened.

The same considerations may supply a background for the radical changes in outward format for contract texts, even though they occur late within our timespan. The triangular grain loan dockets are a specially striking innovation, requiring some explanation, but so is the adoption of the sealed envelope for currency loans. Much of the countryside abandoned around 1000 B.C. was subsequently resettled, some in the 10th century, some in the 9th or even early 8th.[27] With increasing stability and commercial links between town and country the documentation of credit transactions undoubtedly resumed. Most farmers require not silver loans but grain to tide them over the bad months; when the urban community began to reimpose written contracts on its rural clients, it would principally have been for commodity debts. There is no doubt that the new rural population was largely Aramaic speaking, whether descen-

[25] For the tendency for the numbers of cuneiform tablets recovered to increase towards the end of a period, cf. for instance M. Civil, in McG. Gibson & R.D. Biggs (eds.), The organization of power: aspects of bureaucracy in the ancient Near East (Chicago 1987), pp. 46–47.

[26] So for instance in the Alalakh texts cited in footnote 24, in the 13th century Assur texts such as Urad-Šerua Nos. 54–56 (cf. fn. 21), or in the early 7th century texts from the Nabu Temple at Nimrud edited by B. Parker in Iraq 19 (1957), pp. 125ff.

[27] For the record of settlement in the Assyrian plains cf. JESHO 17 (1974), pp. 225ff. and, for recent archaeological work pointing in the same direction, T.J. Wilkinson, Iraq 52 (1970) 57–60, 62.

dants of the 11th and 10th century invaders or deportees installed by the Assyrian kings themselves.[28] They would naturally prefer to have their debts recorded in a script they could read. We know little about the materials on which Aramaic was written before the 7th century, but it is not unreasonable to assume that a perishable roll of papyrus, leather or some other substance was normal. Unlike clay, this could not be directly sealed, so the string was secured by a clay sealing; and it is quite understandable that the text on the sealing was usually (though not always[29]) in cuneiform for the benefit of the urban Assyrian creditors.

So I overturn my earlier view, and now suggest that it was the double format of the commodity loans (on scroll and label) that gave the cuneiform scribes the idea of a double document for their silver and copper loans, which had not previously in Assyria been encased in envelopes. Currency transactions tended more to be within the urban and more traditionally Assyrian community and hence remained usually in cuneiform. Of course envelopes were still known and used for other purposes, but neither in Middle Assyrian times nor in the early and mid-8th century were they used on contracts, seals being rolled directly on the tablet. If this is a correct reconstruction of the sequence of events, it means that the external format of the Neo-Assyrian contract texts is not only a late development, but one triggered by the practices of the Aramaean component of society. Until we have a larger body of texts from the reigns of Sargon and his two predecessors, we cannot begin to judge whether the change was sudden, suggesting a measure of centrally controlled innovation, or more gradual. Perhaps, though, the reversion to the use of the preterite tense could be taken as a deliberate attempt to reinstate a level of formality in the formulation of legal texts, which would imply some measure of central intervention and may dispose us to guess that a self-conscious attempt at reform was made about this time.

In conclusion, for all the uncertainties, I hope that it has emerged that a study of the processes of change could be worthwhile, to illuminate both the continuities and discontinuities of the "Dark Ages" of Mesopotamia, and the operation of traditional pressures during better documented times. More specifically, I would urge that legal documents should be considered a specially sensitive indicator of such changes, both because of the social forces pressing for conservatism and because of the social context in which any legal document must be embedded. In studying such documents, we may take into account all their aspects: not only the terminology, but also their external characteristics which may or may not co-vary with the wording. Finally, we need to bear in mind that legal documents are only instruments of social relationships, and that one potent source of change will be social changes; and that the documents may change differently depending on their own social context. Hence grain loans have a different social role from silver loans, and conveyances of land or houses may last longer without change because of the relative stability of the property-owning urban classes.

---

28 See e.g. H. Tadmor, in H.J. Nissen & J. Renger (eds.), Mesopotamien und seine Nachbarn (XXV. Rencontre Assyriologique Internationale; Berlin 1982), 449–470; and B. Oded, Mass deportations and deportees in the Neo-Assyrian Empire (Wiesbaden 1979).

29 Examples in F.M. Fales, Aramaic epigraphs (see footnote 18), to be substantially enhanced when the archive from the Harran region being studies by E. Lipiński and P. Garelli is eventually published (cf. Fales, op. cit. pp. 270–273 for some preliminary citations; also P. Garelli in K.R. Veenhof (ed.), Cuneiform Archives and Libraries (XXX. Rencontre Assyriologique Internationale; Leiden 1986), 241–6, with D. Homès-Fredericq, ibid. pp. 247–59.

	Middle Assyrian		Neo-Assyrian			
CONVEYANCES						
Tablet shape	vertical	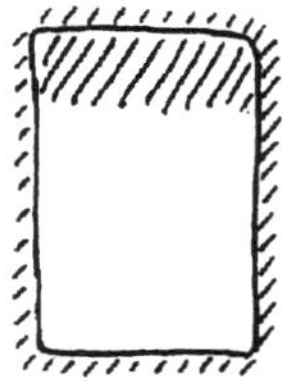	vertical	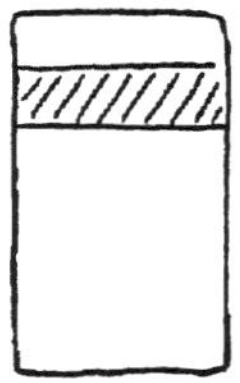		
Envelope	no		no			
Position of sealing(s)	top of Obv. (+ all over)?		top of Obv. (between rulings)			
Person(s) sealing	seller + witnesses		seller (not witnesses)			
CONTRACTS			silver		barley	
Tablet shape	square		horizontal	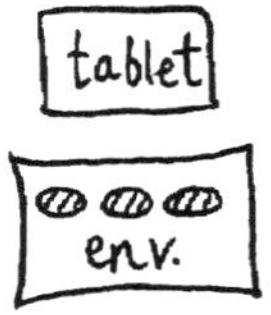	docket	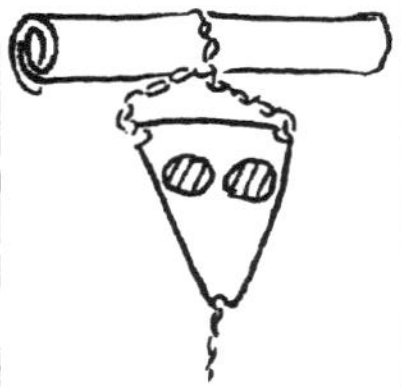
Envelope	no		yes		(docket + scroll)	
Position of sealing(s)	top of Obv. + all over		Obv. of envelope (no rulings)		Obv. of docket (no rulings)	
Person(s) sealing	debtor + witnesses		debtor(s)		debtor(s)	
RECEIPTS						
Tablet shape	horizontal		horizontal	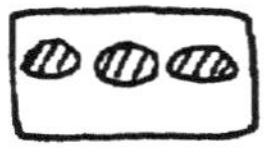		
Envelope	yes		no			
Position of sealing(s)	tablet: top of Obv. envelope: all over		Obv. (no rulings)			
Person(s) sealing	(uncertain)		recipient			

Table 1 Chart of document format (hatched lines indicate location of seal impressions)

CONVEYANCES

A (MA)		B (NA)
	seal identification	
Seal of PN_1 (= seller)		Seal of PN_1 (= seller)
	operative section	
Y (= object sold)		Y (= object sold)
ana šīm gamer		*uppiš-ma* PN_2 (= buyer)
ana Z (= purchase price)		
PN_1 (= seller)		*issu pān* PN_1 (= seller)
ana PN_2 (= buyer)		*ina libbi* Z (= purchase price)
iddin-ma ušabbi		*ilqe*
	Schlußklauseln	
kaspu gammur tadin		
uppu laqi		Y *zarip laqi*
tuāru u dabābu laššu		*tuāru dēnu dabābu laššu*
Z PN_1 *maḫir, apil zaku*		

CONTRACTS

C (MA loan)	D (MA debt-note)	E (NA loan on envelope)
seal identification		
Seal of PN_2 (= debtor)	Seal of PN_2 (= debtor)	Seal of PN_2 (= debtor)
operative section		
Y (= object owed)	Y (= object owed)	Y (= object owed)
ištu PN_1 (= creditor)	*ša* PN_1 (= creditor)	*ša* PN_1 (= creditor)
PN_2 (= debtor)	*ina muḫḫi* PN_2 (= debtor)	*ina pān* PN_2 (= debtor)
ilqe		
supplementary section		
	Y *anniu ana pūḫi ilqe*	*ina pūḫi ittiši*

Table 2 Comparison of MA and NA conveyance and contract formulae

Some Latter-Day Merchants of Aššur

J.N. Postgate / Cambridge, U.K.

The city of Aššur has long been famous for its mercantile role in the early 2nd millennium, but it has recently become apparent that it retained an affinity for commerce to the last centuries of the Assyrian state. There is a small number of Neo-Assyrian documents of a type known for many years in a single example published by Scheil, but first properly interpreted by Deller in the light of other unpublished Aššur tablets (Bagh. Mitt. 15 [1984] 240ff.). They record a transaction by which a group of merchants jointly borrow the capital for a trading venture. In some cases the creditor in fact appears as one of the debtors, whereby he is essentially spreading the risk of his investment by taking on business partners. The capital is stated in silver or in barley, but these bald little documents do not bother to tell us what commodity was being traded. However, some more Aššur texts newly published in transliteration by Fales and Rost in SAAB 5 (1991) lift the veil a little.

The trading contracts

In these texts the traders are called *bēl ḫarrāni* (EN.KASKAL; possibly rather *bēl ḫūli*). Since all the participants are so designated, the *bēl* in this phrase seems to me to mean no more than "person involved in" a trading venture, in other words effectively "trading partner, member of the consortium" (for the construction, cf. *bēl X tadāni* "person involved in the selling of X" in the Siegelvermerk of NA conveyances). The word *ḫarrānu* "journey" of course implies trade over a distance. It seems that both river traffic and overland caravans are involved. Some references to "journeys" are associated with *maškuru* "kelleks" (or similar) and no doubt refer to the Tigris trade. Thus SAAB 5 No. 27 refers both to 230 wine jars and to quite large quantities of silver "which is in the mountain" (*ša ina* KUR-*ú*) written down to a number of individuals in most cases; one entry of 2 minas is written to "the kellek of the Aššur-people" (*maškuru ša Libb-ālāyi*) and at the end the scribe has added "1 mina 8 shekels product of a barley(?) kellek" (*tēlīt ša maškiri ša* ŠE.BAR).

The text Scheil No. III (Bagh. Mitt. 15 241) points in a similar direction, adding at the end of the document "they shall give 6 pairs of shoes": we know from elsewhere in the ancient Near East that those engaged in much walking might receive appropriate footwear, whether humble shepherds under contract to the herd-owners, or ambassadors travelling from court to court. The Scheil text also mentions donkeys, and No. 12 in SAAB 5 refers to a servant lad and a donkey with its load (*adi ebissi-šu*), pointing unmistakably to a land route.

I strongly suspect that land transport also provides the background to two employment contracts also published by Fales and Rost (Nos. 46 and 48). The essential lines of No. 46 (Envelope) read: "He shall serve 10 months ... He shall bring the caravan in and send it out ([*a*]*laktuušērab ušēṣa*). If he misses a month he shall pay the silver two-fold". The *alaktu* clause is not present on the inner tablet, and it must therefore constitute an explanation of, or enlargement on, the verb *palāḫu* "to serve". The other text, No. 48, is more explicit, saying: "A has [taken] 32 1/2 shekels of silver, his wages for 10 months and will serve. For B, C and D he shall send the caravan out and bring it in (*alaktu ušēṣa ušērab*), (and then) shall take the remainder of his wages". There are some difficulties in interpretation here (the restoration of the verb at the end of l. 4, and whether to take *ana* B-D in ll. 6-8 with *palāḫu* or as part of what follows), but they do not materially affect the sense. In ll. 9-10 the first editors translate "He will cause the *traffic* to move out and in", and write in the commentary of "service", saying that *alaktu* "should be a task in the realm of production or of society" (p. 103). I believe that the concept of *alāku* "to serve", current of course in Neo-Assyrian in connection with *ilku*-service, is not relevant here, but that *alaktu* has rather the sense of "a (single) trip" especially with the concrete nuance of a merchant caravan. This usage is clearly present in contemporary Babylonian (CAD A/i, 299-300), and has recently turned up in the Ninurta-kudurru-uṣur texts from Anah, where it is used to refer to the camel-trains of the Arabian tribes (e.g. Cavigneaux & Ismail, Bagh. Mitt. 21 [1990] Text No. 2.iv.30'; Frame, RIMB 2 forthcoming). The contracts would therefore seem to be drawn up with a caravan leader or agent on behalf of a group of merchants supplying the capital for the venture. It is not clear whether we should assume that a single venture would last for a full 10 months, out and back, or several trips are envisaged. When further Aššur texts are published (note those referred to by Fales and Rost on p. 116 footnote 115, from the N9 archive described by Pedersén as "work contracts for several months"), it may become clear whether both our texts prescribe 10 months by coincidence or because it was a standard length of time.

In this context the question naturally arises of where these caravans were going. In the new texts no specific place names are mentioned, but the "mountain" already met in No. 27 is also found in No. 17:1 *qip-tú ša* KUR-*e* "An advance for the mountain, either wine or silver". The texts records that the relatives of one of two original partners have paid off their share, but otherwise all this can tell us is that, as in No. 27, the mountain trade involved wine and/or silver. Whether silver is involved purely as a currency, or the trade was actually concerned with tapping silver sources (which are mentioned, for instance, by Sargon in the Taurus), is hard to say. Wine is mentioned again in No. 64, where an advance of 6 minas of silver to a consortium of three merchants is accompanied by a closing proviso that "they shall pay a jar of wine in addition". Wine of course is known to have come from Izalla in the Anatolian foothills at this date and under the Neo-Babylonian kings, but it would go beyond the evidence to suggest that "the mountain" here refers exclusively to the Mardin area. The most it seems reasonable to say at present is that we have here evidence that some Aššur merchants traded in wine, which they imported from the foothills or mountains somewhere to the north of the city.

Almost certainly Aššur was also trading along other routes. The Middle Assyrian tablets from Khirbet ed-Diniyah on the Middle Euphrates attest to Aššur traders' ventures into the western desert to do business with the Sutû, and the new Ninurta-kudurru-uṣur inscriptions from that region show that the merchants of Tema and Saba in central and southern Arabia were already running caravans up to Hindanu near the modern Syria/Iraq border. This can hardly have been their final market, and one must presume that their route would then have led them to Aššur and thence to the rest of central Assyria. The goods coming in are as one might have predicted: coloured wool, precious stones and other desirable luxuries.

To conclude, I would like to put forward a more tentative proposal for a link between some of the new texts and trading ventures. In the late Assyrian empire the government had organized much of its labour force (frequently deportees from Assyrian military campaigns) into "cohorts" (*kiṣru*) modelled along military lines. There were *kiṣru* of shepherds, oil-pressers, gardeners etc. At Aššur one of these groups was composed of *ḫundurayyu*, to use the normalization of Fales and Rost in their discussion of the term, SAAB 5 21ff., and some of them were involved in the trading contracts just described. At first sight, of course, this designation seems to refer only to their geographical or ethnic origin, but the context in which we meet it shows that it functioned also as a professional designation, so that the Ḫundurayyu must have practised a specific type of employment. Agreeing with Fales and Rost that there is no reason to consider them bakers, and doubting that the evidence would support an identification with carpet-weavers (cf. SAAB 5 24), I would like to suggest that they were professional transporters. Given that the term alternates once with ^{lú}*ḫar-ḫar-a-a* it is clearly correct that we must see a connection with the Iranian town of Ḫundir mentioned on Sargon's Najafehabad stele in 716 B.C. However this provides no clue to their characteristic professional activity. The only such clue seems to be in the Neo-Assyrian letter KAV 112. Here one temple *laḫḫinu* writes to another as follows: "I have just sent you the" (or "some") "Ḫundurayyu. The day they arrive, give them immediately two sets of *masiku*-cloths, so that they can carry out their work with them in the king's service. Don't be negligent, put them immediately on the road, don't delay them, let them come to do their work" (*annurig ḫundurayyī assapra. ūmu ša iqarribūnini ana šinī-šu masikē arḫiš dinaš-šunu. dullu ina pānāt šarri ina libbi lēpušu. mēnuḫḫur lā tašīyaṭ arḫiš ḫarrānu/ḫūlu ina šēpē-šunu šukun lā tuparrak-šunu ina muḫḫi dulli-šunu lillikūni*). Although "put them on the road" can simply be used metaphorically, it is clear from this passage that these people have a specialized job to do for which they require a pair of the things called *ma-si-ki*. Unfortunately, the word's meaning is obscure. CAD (M/i 326) normalized *massaku* and hesitantly connects this Neo-Assyrian passage with a tow-rope attested in Old Babylonian texts, but neither the normalization nor the identification are decisive, and more passages are needed (a connection with Kassite *massiš* (AHw 619a) is tempting but scarcely probable). The TÚG determinative shows that it is some kind of textile (neither ZÍD nor ÉŠ seems plausible). The words *ana šinī-šu* show that they are normally in pairs or sets. Pace AHw 619a, it does not seem that it is a finished product like a carpet or rug, because the Ḫundurayyus' work is not to *make* the *ma-si-ki*, but has to be accomplished *with* (by means of) it, so that it should be some kind of tool or working equipment. Hence I would speculate that they are specialized items needed for transport. If in pairs, may be they were cloth saddle bags, nets or ropes for loading pack asses. On the other hand, the fact that these specialists originate in the Iranian highlands and the possibility that they were involved in transportation suggests another idea to anyone who has lived in Baghdad (where the specialist porters, who can balance amazing loads on their backs, come from Luristan), that perhaps the Ḫundurayyu were overland porters who needed specialist carrying equipment of some kind. Let us hope that at long last the gradual publication of the Neo-Assyrian texts from Aššur will continue, and that fresh clues to these enigmatic gentlemen will soon emerge!

Assyria: the Home Provinces

J.N. Postgate - Cambridge

By the "home provinces" I mean those which constituted the country known as *māt Aššur* before the reign of Tiglath-pileser III. This contribution is intended as a critical review of the relevant section of Forrer's *Provinzeinteilung* after seven decades and more. It is by no means exhaustive: a thorough revision of his work will be needed in due course, once the State Archives of Assyria project has covered the principal sources, and could easily occupy a substantial volume. My text does not list every known province in the 1st millennium, nor does it quote every attestation of the provinces it does discuss. In particular I have not prolonged my investigation beyond 695 B.C., when the traditional order of the eponym canon breaks down. The text takes for granted many of the results achieved by Salvini, Reade, and Kessler, as well as Nashef, RGTC 5 and recent articles in the *Reallexikon der Assyriologie*. For ease of comparison, I have adhered to Ungnad's dating (in RlA *Eponymen*), even though it may be a year out in the 9th century.

1. Terminology of the provincial system

1.1. *Ḫalṣu(m), ḫalzu(m)*

The correct translation of this word continues to give problems. It seems clear that in Old Babylonian texts a word normalized as *ḫalṣum* means both "fortress" (in omens) and "district" (especially at Mari). By Middle Babylonian and Middle Assyrian times this word seems to require normalizing with a *z*, since genitive forms are written with a *-zi* even in texts where the sign *ṣi* is normally used for the sound /ṣi/. The meaning in these texts is not "fortress", but "district", a meaning which according to Prof. Otten (orally) is valid for Hittite usage as well: so for instance URU.MEŠ *mādūte ša Karduniaš adi* URU.*ḫal-zi-šu-nu*[1] means "numerous cities of Babylonia together with their districts". In Middle Assyrian contexts *ḫalzu* or *ḫalṣu* tends to be associated with certain cities, including Ḫarran and Sudu[2] and Nineveh[3]. This same usage, of a district identified by its chief city, persists into Neo-Assyrian times. Assurnasirapli mentions URU (var. KUR)*ḫal-ZI-lu-ḫa*[4], which must undoubtedly[5] derive from *ḫalzi+eluḫat* "the district of Eluhat" and shows how indissolubly the word was attached to some place names. From the end of the 9th century note the revolt against Shalmaneser III (Fig. 4), which lists "27 towns (*māḫazē*) together with their districts (*ḫalZāni*)". NARGD No. 46, probably from the reign of Adad-nirari III, mentions the districts of Arbil and of Burallu, which is not attested as a province in the 1st millennium. The "district of Arbil" is still referred to in a late 8th or early 7th century text[6], and at this time there is both a province called simply Halṣ/zu, and another called Halzi-adbar (probably "Basalt District", see below, § 3.5). However, this should not be taken as evidence that the word is a technical term for "administrative province", and we cannot assume a priori that the "district of Arbil" would have coincided precisely with the "province of Arbil", for instance.

---

[1] Grayson, ABC, p. 168: 5.
[2] E.g. Adad-nirari I (RIMA 1, pp. 131: 13, 136: 40); Shalmaneser I (RIMA 1, p. 184: 83-84).
[3] ABC, p. 189: 12.
[4] RIMA 2, p. 200: 103.
[5] *Pace* the doubts of Liverani, ATA, p. 37.
[6] ADD 742: 7.

The picture is complicated by the fact that *ḫalṣu* reappears, written with the sign *ṣu* which unequivocally represents the sibilant /ṣ/, with the definite meaning of "fortress": it is clearly distinguished by this writing from the meaning "district" which uses *-zi*. (Writings ending with *-ṣi* or *-zu* seem not to be attested in Middle or Neo-Assyrian). The word is especially common in the routine reports at the beginning of letters to the king from his officials, and it has been suggested that the signs ḪAL.ṢU(M) are in fact a pseudo-logographic writing of the word *birtu*, meaning a fort. If this were always so, we lack Neo-Assyrian occurrences of *ḫalṣu* meaning a fort from which the writing must have derived, and it is difficult therefore to be certain where to draw the line.

The Mari, and perhaps generally North Mesopotamian, usage of *ḫalṣum* to mean a province seems to reappear in the later 2nd millennium with the term *ḫalzuḫlu* (and variants) well attested at Nuzi. This is composed with the Hurrian professional ending *-uḫlu*, and designates a high official. There is some disagreement about his precise function: I believe it is no more nor less than "provincial governor", but others prefer to connect this with the "fortress" meaning, and see him as a "garrison commandant". There is not enough evidence to determine whether *ḫasiḫlu* in Assyria is merely a vernacular term for provincial governor, identical with *bēl pāḫiti*, or a different position. My own inclination is to assume they are identical, but this cannot at present be proved.

1.2. *pāḫutu*

Already in Middle Assyrian times the provincial governor could be called *bēl pāḫiti*, as well as *šakin māt* X. This term is possibly a loan from Babylonia, where *bēl pīḫati* is also a provincial governor. While *pāḫutu/pīḫatu* derive from a stem meaning "substitute", and the term *bēl pīḫati* must begin life meaning "holder of a deputyship", its usage to mean "governor of a province" led to the identification of the rather abstract "responsibility" with a geographical concept, and already by the 11th century the vernacular was talking about *pāḫutu elītu* and *šaplītu* "the Upper" and "Lower Province" (cf. Fig. 2). By this time, therefore, *ḫalzu*, if it had had the technical meaning "province" in Assyrian, had probably lost it.

The term *bēl pāḫiti* survived into Neo-Assyrian times and is by far the most prevalent word for a provincial governor in the texts. A province is still called a *pāḫutu*, but usage of the term as borrowed into West Semitic, and in occasional Neo-Assyrian passages, suggests that in everyday speech the word *bēl* could be dropped, so that by the 7th century *pāḫutu* alone can also mean "governor" by itself[7].

2. The reform of the provincial system and its date

2.1. A theory put forward by Forrer[8], and which I for one have in the past accepted as a fact in print, involved a major reform of the provincial system by Tiglath-pileser III: "Entweder hat also Assur-nirari V. noch in seinen zwei letzten Jahren diese Neuerungen eingeführt, oder es war dies die erste Tat Tiglat-pilesers III. Letzteres ist mir das Wahrscheinlichere" (p. 10). The "innovations" to which Forrer refers were principally the introduction of the office of *bēl pāḫiti/pīḫati*, and the related use of the word *pāḫutu/pīḫatu* for a "province". He believed this terminology was introduced from Babylonia (p. 49: "In Babylonien bestand seit dem zweiten Jahrtausend eine Einteilung in Bezirke (*paḫâtê*). An der Spitze eines solchen standen der Statthalter und der Bezirksherr"), and replaced an earlier system under which the governors were called *šaknu* and their provinces were divided into Urasischaften. Even in 1920 some parts of this argument were suspect, but his basic tenet, that the *bēl pāḫiti* terminology was imported by, or just before, Tiglath-pileser, is contradicted by more recently published texts. In the first place, it is regularly in use in the Middle Assyrian period (e.g. in the Urad-

[7]Cf. AHw, p. 862b s. v. *pīḫātu(m)* I 5; S.A. Kaufman, *The Akkadian Influences on Aramaic*, Chicago 1974, p. 82.
[8]PAR, pp. 8 ff.

Šerua archive). Secondly, it is now firmly attested in the earlier Neo-Assyrian period. Just last year a fascinating text from the reign of Assur-naṣir-apli II was published, mentioning the "province" (NAM = *pāḫutu*) of Kalhu and "governors" (LÚ.EN.NAM.MEŠ)[9]. In the early 8th century, before the accession of Tiglath-pileser, Nergal- (or Palil-)ereš was the governor of the land of Raṣappa. In a *kudurru*-like stele discovered at Nineveh by Campbell Thompson the addition of the district of Hindana to his province was documented: he is referred to as the *šakin māt Raṣappa*, but we read that the new acquisition is "reckoned with the province of Raṣappa" (*itti pa-ḫa-at* KUR *Raṣappa mani*). This is a native Assyrian statement (not a Babylonianism) because *pāḫat* is the Assyrian form. In another text probably (but not certainly) from the early 8th century we have the EN.NAM of the province KUR Si'mē[10]. Finally, in a land grant of the time of Adad-nirari III, dated to 788 B.C.[11] a number of provinces within which fields were located are mentioned: they include the NAM (=*pāḫutu*) of Libbi-āli (=Assur), of Kurbail, and of Guzana, while one governor is referred to as the EN.NAM of Kurbail, though others are described as *šaknu* of Kalhu, Libbi-āli, Naṣibina and Kilizi.

There seems to be some disarray here (for a possible explanation see below, § 2.3) but that *šaknu* (or better: *šakin*-X) and *bēl pāḫiti* could refer to the same office is suggested by at least two of the governors of Kalhu, Bel-dan and Šarru-duri, who are referred to alternatively with either title[12]. As indicated there, the difference in these cases would seem to be a function of the context: *šakin*-X being used in formal, *bēl pāḫiti* in common usage. It is true that these two instances belong after the accession of Tiglath-pileser, but the evidence from the texts already cited show that there is certainly no basis for reconstructing a reform by which *šaknu* is replaced by *bēl pāḫiti* under Tiglath-pileser.

2.2. If Forrer's theory of the new introduction of the *bēl pāḫiti* system is thus invalid, are there any other aspects of his argument which favour an innovation by Tiglath-pileser? One of his points revolves round the disappearance of what we may call "sub-provinces": these he incorrectly refers to as Urasischaften, but in any case there is no evidence that they existed. For one thing, no term is found in the Assyrian texts for such a "sub-province". Forrer assumed from the inscriptions of Assur-naṣir-apli II that the officials called *urāsi* who are said to have been appointed in newly conquered territory were in effect sub-governors, and from this he deduced that there must have been sub-provinces for them to govern. These he recognized in the numerous administrative centres listed in texts of the time which do not themselves have provincial capital status, and are often mentioned as subordinate to a known capital. There is however no evidence for any formal category of subsidiary capital, and although we may freely concede that the major centres within a province served as administrative bases, there is no evidence that a formalized second tier of provincial administration was created, in the form either of specified centres or of specified officials. Forrer's assumption that the towns listed as having revolted against Shalmaneser were capitals of "Urasischaften" is doubtful even to him[13]. We may therefore exclude Forrer's sub-provinces from our discussion of the provincial system, and from any theory relating to a reform by Tiglath-pileser.

The next source of evidence comes from the nomenclature and territorial extent of the provinces themselves: with a major reform of the kind envisaged by Forrer, boundaries would have been changed, and the repertoire of province names would have to show changes too. A glance at the maps, and at the data of the eponym canon, makes it clear that if a reform took place it was almost certainly at the time of Adad-nirari III: in Table 1 the provinces are listed in the order of their first attestation, which is usually in the titulary of a *limmu*. We note that there is a sudden accretion of new provinces

[9] K. Deller and A.R. Millard: BaM 24 (1993), p. 242: 21 ff.
[10] NARGD 47.
[11] NARGD 27.
[12] CTN II, p. 8 n. 21.
[13] PAR, pp. 9-10; though no doubts e.g. about Dariga as an Urasischaft of Isana, p. 12.

Neo-Assyrian governors in the *limmu*-lists (down to 688)

	Anp II	Slm III A	Slm III B	Š-A IV	Adn III	Slm IV + Ad III	Asn IV	TP III	Sargon
HIGH OFFICIALS									
šarru	882	857	827	822	809	781/71	753	743	719
turtānu		856/3	[826]	814	808	780/70	752	742	
nāgir ēkalli		854/0	[823]	820	807	778	751	741	
rab šāqê		855	[825]	816	806	779	750	740	
abarakku		833	[824]	[821]	805	777	749	739	717
šakin māti (/libb(i)āli)	(/897)				804	776	748	738	/716
rab ša rēši					798				
PROVINCES									
Raqmat	[872]	836		812	795	773			?
Tušḫan (/Nairi)	(867)	(/849)			794	764		728	707
Kalḫu	(873)/864	851	829?		797	772	744	734	713
Naṣibina		852	831	815	800/782	774	746	736	715
Raṣappa		838			803	775	747	737	718
Nēmed-Ištar		(842)							
Aḫi/Ar-zuḫina		839/7			801	767		731	710
Ḫabruri		835		813	796	765		729	708
Ninua		834			789	761		725	704
Kilizi	(909)	832			788	760		724	703
Isāna			830?	817?	790	758			700
Arrapḫa			828?	811	802	769	745	735	714
Mā(t)zamua				810	783	768		733	712
Amedi					799	762		726?	705
Guzāna					793	763		727	706
Tillē					792	766		730	709
Šibḫ/ṭiniš					791	755			
Arbīl					787	759			702
Talmusi					786	754			696
Tamnu(n)na					785	756			697
Kurbail					784	757			699
Si'mē								732	711
Til-Barsip									701
Ḫalzi-adbar									698
Katmuḫi/Šaḫupa	(885)				(/*)				695
Dur-Šarrukēn									693
WESTERN PROVINCES									
Dimašqu									694
Arpaddu									692
Gargamiš									691
Samaria									690
Ḫatarikka									689
Ṣimirra									688

Thanks to A.R. Millard
(885) = information not from *limmu* lists
[821] = entry restored
(*) = attestation elsewhere

Table 1. - *Attestation of Neo-Assyrian provinces (principally from the eponym lists down to 688 B.C.). NB: The reign of Aššur-dan continues the Shalmaneser IV sequence with a break for the new king and the* turtānu *in 771-70.*

in the reign of Adad-nirari III: Amedi, Guzana, Tille, Šibhiniš, Arbil, Talmusi, Tamnu(n)na and Kurbail, all of which subsequently (except Šibhiniš) are regular members of the repertoire thereafter. Some of these, such as Arbil, are not remote from the centre, but occupy territory which must have been under Assyrian control since at latest the reign of Assur-naṣir-apli II. The sudden increment of provinces is therefore not the result of conquest, but must reflect a reorganization of the earlier system. This change is also evident if we compare Figs. 3 and 5: of the great baronial estates hinted at by Fig. 3, corresponding with the pluralism of the 9th century governors as recorded on their stelae, only two survive into the 8th century, Raṣappa under Palil-ereš and the lands west of the Habur under Šamši-ilu.

2.3. If we accept that some of the 9th century provinces were broken up into smaller units, it is worth briefly considering the earlier attribution of some of these new units. Amedi (799) will have been with Tušhan in the province also called Nairi. Guzana (793) was probably newly annexed to Assyria under Adad-nirari III, having been at least semi-independent in the 9th century. Tille (792) is more difficult, but was conceivably within the confines of Naṣibina. Šibhiniš (791) cannot be certainly located, but if the proposal made below (§ 3.5) were valid, perhaps it had belonged under the *abarakku*. Isana (791) is not certain for 830 and 817 B.C.; if it were a new province it would have been detached from Assur, i.e. the *šakin māti*. The appearance of Arbil (787) here for the first time is curious and poses questions which are at present unanswerable for me: who governed this region before, if it was not a province in its own right, or, if it was, why was such an important and ancient centre not higher up the cursus honorum? Talmusi (786; for location see below, § 3.5) could perhaps have fallen earlier under the *abarakku*, but this is by no means certain. Tamnu(n)na (785; for location see § 3.4) is perhaps more likely to have been under the *abarakku*. Kurbail (784) perhaps too, though less likely.

The governors of these new, smaller, provinces may have been accorded a lower status than the older ones. This at least would be one explanation for the differing terminology in NARGD 27: since Libb(i)-āli has a *šaknu* but is called a *pāḫutu*, one has to assume that *pāḫutu* is used equally for provinces with a *šaknu* and for those with a (mere) *bēl pāḫiti,* but the provinces with a *šaknu* (Kalhu, Libb(i)-āli, Naṣibina and Kilizi) are all old entities from before Adad-nirari's reign, whereas Kurbail with its *bēl pāḫiti* is one of the new creations. If this explanation were correct, the distinction was presumably lost by the reign of Tiglath-pileser III (cf. above, § 2.1, on the governors of Kalhu).

It is not difficult to suggest why such changes might have been introduced: the 9th century governors, who controlled these big provinces, were in some cases at least succeeded by their sons, suggesting the existence of local "dynasties". The major revolt at the end of the reign of Shalmaneser could not have taken place without the co-operation of some of the governors who controlled the individual provinces. The scale of this revolt is indicated on Fig. 4. It is noticeable that no places within the province of Raṣappa are mentioned in the revolt list: this suggests that its governor remained loyal to the winning faction, and was rewarded by no diminution of his territory. Further west, Tilabna and Huzirina should have fallen within the *turtānu*'s province; in this case, either the *turtānu*'s power was too strong, or the new appointee was not penalized for the disloyalty of these cities under his predecessor. I have suggested on previous occasions that it may have been at this time that the habit of using eunuchs as provincial governors was instituted. This too would be an effective means of curbing the hereditary power of governors.

3. The location of individual provinces

3.1. *The ex officio governorates*

By this I mean those provinces which were habitually attached to the major offices of state, specifically the *turtānu*, *abarakku*, *rab šāqê*, and *nāgir ēkalli*. Before we can move to suggest locations for the other provinces known by their own names, the spaces taken up by the ex officio provinces need to be determined. Their location was probably not constant, since in the 9th and early 8th century a few enumerations of the territories controlled by some provincial governors, on Assur stelae and other monuments, show that they controlled vast areas which were later broken up. Given that the location of some of the towns in these lists is known, it is possible to make suggestions as to the location of these provinces, but caution is required, because in two cases at least much of the territory seems to be entirely separate from the city after which the governor's office is named (Assur and Kalhu, see below § 3.3).

The association of certain provinces with specific high state officials persists into the reign of Tiglath-pileser III and beyond. At this time, both in Tiglath-pileser's inscriptions and in administrative documents these are explicitly designated as "the province of official x" (and therefore are difficult to identify with a specific land or city), but from Tiglath-pileser's inscriptions it becomes clear that three of these ex officio provinces were designed to form a bulwark on the difficult mountainous north-eastern frontier[14]. Their association persists into the 7th century, when the "lexical" list of Assyrian toponyms K 4384 (2 R 53, 1) lists:

"Province of the Steward (*abarakku*)
Province of the Palace Herald (*nāgir ēkalli*, in two writings)
Province of the Chief Butler"

3.1.1. *turtānu* "Field Marshal"

There are few problems about the location of the *turtānu*'s province. In the 9th century Bel-lu-balaṭ's territory was listed on his stele (No. 44) as: Tabiti, Harran, Huzirina, Duru, Qibani, Zallu, Balihu. Except for Tabiti, which is thought to be in the Habur basin (though not, to my mind, securely located), these names refer mainly to towns or districts in the Balih area. However, the inscriptions of the same governor at Tell Ahmar strongly suggest that this is where the *turtānu* was based, and that Til-barsip was his provincial capital. Proof of this is lacking, but we may note that there is equally no evidence at all for Forrer's theory that the *turtānu*'s capital was at Harran. In the 7th century Til-barsip (sometimes under its form Tarbusiba/i) was the capital of a province which bore its name; whether there remained a connection with the *turtānu* or not is unclear, and it must be admitted that the choice of Harran as the capital of refuge on the fall of Nineveh might constitute a hint that the ancient caravan city had acquired a political role, conceivably because in the 7th century the *turtānu*'s base had been moved there. The northern *turtānu* ("of the left"), first attested under Sargon, was based at Kummuh (presumably = Samsat).

3.1.2. *abarakku (rabû)* "the (Chief) Steward"

Under Shalmaneser III Yahalu was the Chief Steward (*abarakku rabû;* instead of *abarakku* it is possible the word is *mašennu*), and from his eponym lot[15] we learn that his governorate included the following places:

URU Kibšuni
KUR Qumeni
KUR Mehrani
KUR Uqi
KUR Erin[im?]

[14] Cf. generally Kessler, UTN, pp. 166 ff.
[15] YOS 9 73.

There is clear evidence that this territory is in the mountains north and east of the Al-Kosh plain, in the region of Atrush:

a) Qumani (sic) is a land attacked by Tiglath-pileser I in the 11th century[16]. He subdued their king and had the walls of "their royal city" Kibšuna razed. In the Šamši-Adad revolt text (Fig. 4) Kibšuna is listed after Tamnu(n)na and before Kurbail.

b) Within or near Qumani, or in neighbouring Muṣri, is the town of Hunusa[17]. This is the same as Hanusa (unstressed short *u* regularly changes to *a* in Neo-Assyrian before a long syllable). Hanusa[18] is reasonably identified with modern Hinis, next to which are the reliefs of Sennacherib at his canal head by Bavian.

c) Qumeni must not be confused with Kumme[19]. Kumme, surely the important Hurrian cult centre of Tešup in the 2nd millennium, is in the region of Zakho, and was still not firmly under Assyrian control in Sargon's reign[20]. Qumeni, on the other hand, is obviously Tiglath-pileser I's Qumani; and also Tukulti-Ninurta I's Uqumeni[21], which is mentioned in the same context as Mehru (cf. Yahalu's Mehrani) and (to judge from the geographical listings in his inscriptions)[22], lies east of Katmuhu and immediately east of Paphu.

d) It is probably significant that it was the *abarakku* Sin-taklak who in 739 B.C. led a campaign against Ulluba. Ulluba is known from the Mila Mergi inscription to be in the valley of the Lesser Habur, north of Dohuk[23]. Tiglath-pileser entrusted the newly conquered area (which had previously been under Urartian control) to one of his eunuchs, but does not specify which.

e) Kessler has shown that places listed by Tiglath-pileser III as within Ulluba turn up in his tablet ND 4301 in the province of the *abarakku* (p. 168).

f) The province probably has a border with the province of the *rab šāqê*. This seems to follow from Nimrud Letter 55 (ND 2978; Sargon?), where the author reports that all is well with "the province of the *abarakku* and the province of the *rab šāqê*"[24].

3.1.3. *rab šāqê* "the Chief Butler"

In Stele 47 (838 B.C.) the *rab šāqê* is governor of an enormous stretch of territory including KUR Nairi, URU Andi, URU Sinabu, URU Mallani and KUR Alzi. This belongs to a period when Assyria had recently annexed the area of the Tigris headwaters, and later, in 799, this area is still known as the province of Nairi but no longer governed by the Chief Butler (Stele 39). The location of the later province of the *rab šāqê* is discussed in detail by Kessler. I agree with him that there are no grounds for placing it west of the Tigris (as was done by earlier scholars), but I would locate it yet further east than he would, beyond but adjoining that of the *abarakku*.

---

[16]RIMA 2, pp. 24-25.
[17]RIMA 2, p. 24.
[18]OIP II, p. 20: 3.
[19]As has been done, e.g. by Kessler, UTN, p. 172, and others.
[20]Sumer 29 (1974), pp. 58-59.
[21]RIMA 1, pp. 234-235.
[22]E.g. RIMA 1, p. 240.
[23]Sumer 29 (1974), pp. 47-59.
[24]Cf. Kinnier Wilson, CTN I 14.

Pertinent points are:

a) The province should have a border with that of the *abarakku* (see above).

b) To the north-west of the *abarakku* lies Kumme in the Lesser Habur valley while Kurbail and other provinces seem likely to have bordered his province to the south-west. This leaves no room for the *rab šāqê*, and therefore it seems necessary to look further east.

c) Kessler cites the Sargon text ND 2640[25], which suggests that Dur-Enlil fell within the *rab šāqê*'s jurisdiction (the same association possibly also attested in Nimrud Letter 105)[26]. He does not however note that in the omen queries there is a Dur-Enlil which appears to be towards the border with the Mannaeans. If the same town, and there seems no call to doubt it, this strongly suggests a location east of the *abarakku*'s province.

d) Kessler's observations on Simerra, which belongs within this province but was also mentioned in the same context as Habruri, also suggest a location just to the west of Herir and the Palace Herald's province (p. 180).

On the basis of all these indications, it seems the best location for the *rab šāqê*'s province is approximately in the sector of Aqra. There do not seem to be any clear indications of the town which functioned as the capital of the province, unless it was Dur-Enlil (which presumably had a different, non-Akkadian name earlier in its existence). With Kessler[27] the earlier proposal that the town of Šabirē-šu was the capital of the *rab šāqê*'s province should be abandoned. However, I believe that this important road-station (whose location is discussed by Kessler exhaustively) is probably not to be sought on the east side of the Tigris. The Silopi plain on the east bank of the river opposite Cizre was still an area in which Sennacherib had to campaign at the end of the 8th century, and unlikely to have lain on a major internal Assyrian route (see also on Kumme above). Rather, I would suggest that Šabirē-šu "the place with the wells"[28] was a road station in the area north of the Jebel Sinjar, where the road from the Habur intersects with routes coming down from the Tur Abdin. One of several possible candidates could be Uweinat ("little wells", a loan translation).

3.1.4. *nāgir ēkalli* "Palace Herald"

Under Tiglath-pileser III, for at least part of his reign, the Palace Herald was Bel-Harran-bel-uṣur, who founded a town in the jazirah west of Assur (at Tell Abta); before him the office was held by Šamši-ilu, who was *turtānu* but also included *nāgir ēkalli* among his titles. A "Province of the Palace Herald" is not listed with other ex officio governorates in Tiglath-pileser's annals (ND 4301), but by the 7th century the title gives its name to a separate province, since it features as such in the geographical list K 4384 (see above). It is therefore possible that it was first created in the reign of Sargon, and we shall see that this might fit with historical circumstances.

The most specific evidence for its location is to do with the town of Hibtunu, as recognized by Deller, building on evidence cited by Zadok: Hibtunu was a town past which Sargon came when he debouched on to the Arbil plain from the mountains where he had been sacking Muṣaṣir: "I came out by the pass of Mt. Andarutta, a steep mountain above URU *ḫi-ib-tú-na*, and returned safely to my land". Hibtunu can be satisfactorily identified with Hefton, or Tall Haftun, in the Dasht-i Herir. The

[25]Iraq 23 (1961), p. 40.
[26]Iraq 36 (1974), pp. 218-220.
[27]UTN, pp. 122-149.
[28]Already attested in a Middle Assyrian text, cf. RGTC 5, p. 240.

Topzawa stele and its new duplicate confirm the connection between Muṣaṣir and Andarutta, and Deller gives other evidence for a close link between the *nāgir ēkalli* and the land of Urzana[29]. For the precise location of the province a distinct possibility is the plain of Rowanduz, lying east of Herir which is surely Hab(a)r(i)uri (as Kirruri is now to be read on the evidence of the Sultan Tepe *limmu* list, cf. RlA s.v. *Kirruri*), which had long been a province, and in this case the location for Muṣaṣir suggested by Boehmer, in a high valley north of the Rowanduz plain, is entirely plausible[30]. After Sargon's 8th campaign and the destruction of Muṣaṣir, he annexed the area and its population (TCL III 410) and created a province which he entrusted to the Palace Herald[31]. From the brief notice we have, one cannot say for certain whether a province of the Palace Herald already existed, and this was an extension thereof, or it was newly created.

3.2. *Named provinces: Middle Assyrian times* (Fig. 2)

Fig. 2 represents the Middle Assyrian provincial system in the light of information from the Assur Temple offerings archive which dates to the reign of Tiglath-pileser I in the 11th century. The details were discussed by the writer in AfO 32 (1985), pp. 95ff. and need not be repeated here. I do however want to draw attention to certain areas, marked with interrogation marks, whose name has not yet been established.

a) It is uncertain whether or not the land between Makhmur and the Tigris would have been a province separate from Assur.

b) The land north-west from Nineveh is in Neo-Assyrian times attributed to Kurbail, but that name is new and its 2nd millennium identity is unknown.

c) To the east of that, north of the Jebel Maqlub, no name is known (1st millennium: see Tamnu(n)na).

d) To the east again, between the Khazir and the Zab south of Aqra (1st millennium: see Šibhiniš).

e) To the north of Apku and west of the Tigris there is a large space without any major recognized centre, which also poses problems in the later 1st millennium. If Katmuhi is correctly located (as no. 7), there is a missing province here (1st millennium: see Barhalza, § 3.5, and on Šabirēšu under § 3.1 *rab šāqê*).

3.3. *Named provinces: 9th century* (Fig. 3)

Of the provinces listed before 799 B.C. in Table 1 the following deserve some comment for a variety of reasons:

Kalhu: Šamaš-belu-uṣur, governor of Kalhu in 864 and 851, controlled in addition to Kalhu itself places perhaps in the northern Habur basin: Hamedi, Sirgana, and Ialuna (Stele 42).

Aššur: Šarru-hatti-ipela, eponym in 831 and 815, according to Stele 41 governed Aššur, but also the eastern tract of the Habur basin including Naṣibina, Urakka, Kahat, and Masaka(ni). (This is no doubt one reason why Assur is mentioned after Urakka in the Shalmaneser revolt text). It is perhaps a little surprising to find him functioning in the same office (Governor of Assur) both before and after the revolt, but if the stele was erected on the occasion of his first eponymate, it may be that the province's lands were already curtailed in 815 when he served for the second time. This is more likely because later in Adad-nirari III's reign Assur province only encompassed Assur, Kar-Tukulti-Ninurta, Ekallati, Itu', and Ruqaha, the last two being tribal areas betwen Assur and Babylonia (Stele 38 from 804

[29] ZU, p. 121.

[30] *VIII. Türk Tarih Kongresi*, Ankara 1979, pp. 123-128.

[31] See Thureau-Dangin, TCL III, pp. 74-75.

B.C.). This is still a reasonably large tract, but occupies a continuous stretch of territory round the capital, with none of the Habur lands represented.

Raṣappa: The early 8th century governor of Raṣappa, Bel-Harran-belu-uṣur, controlled Nemed-Ištar, Apku, Mari, Raṣappi, Qatni, Dur-aduklim, Kar-Assur-naṣir-apli, Sirqu, Laqe, Hindanu, Anat, Suhi, Assur-aṣbat, in other words, the entire tract of territory forming Assyria's western front, from the Tigris bend near Eski Mosul to the Euphrates south of the Habur confluence[32]. As observed above, none of these places are listed as rebelling against Shalmaneser, and this may be one reason why this wide sweep of land survived our postulated reform intact, and indeed had Hindanu added to it during Adad-nirari's reign.

Raqmat: This place, whose name is usually written *raq-mat* has been read as Amat[33], and as Sallat[34]. The correct reading is suggested by the Sultan Tepe *limmu* list entry for 773 B.C. (STT I No. 46 r. 34'), as was recognized by H.F. Russell in his dissertation: URU *ra-qa?-ma?-tú*. This takes us straight back to the annals of Adad-narari II, who besieged the Temanaean ruler Muquru in his fortified town Gidara "which the Aramaeans call Raqamatu" (*ša* KUR *a-ru-mu*^{meš} URU.*ra-qa-ma-tu iqabbi-šuni*)[35]. This is in Hanigalbat, somewhere in the Habur triangle. Raqmat is listed in the Shalmaneser revolt list between Urakka (on the Habur) and Huzirina (Sultan Tepe), which suggests a westerly location within the area. This is plausible since it co-existed with the province of Naṣibina which extended as far south as Kahat, and thus occupied the eastern part of the triangle.

3.4. *The Shalmaneser revolt* (Fig. 4)

In his account of the disturbances which attended the end of Shalmaneser III's reign his successor Šamši-Adad V lists 27 cities which participated in a revolt. These are listed with Fig. 4: those which can be certainly located (either at a specific site or in an approximate area) are indicated with larger numbers, and it is obvious that they are in some degree arranged in a geographical order. Four places whose location is uncertain are indicated with smaller numbers enclosed in a circle. Here I wish to comment on these places, which are numbered 7-10 and all lie to the east of the Tigris.

No 7: *Šīmu:* This city is already attested as a province in the reign of Tiglath-pileser I, but not marked on Fig. 2 since the only criterion for locating it then is its listing after Šibaniba and before Kalhu, pointing inconclusively to a position east of the Tigris. This is supported by its position in the Shalmaneser revolt list, between Bit-šašširi and Šibhiniš. The principal difficulty with this name is whether or not it should be identified with Si'mē, attested in the post-745 period as a province and probably quite far east (see § 3.5). On balance, I think this is probably not the same toponym, but equally it is difficult to see where else the Middle Assyrian province of this name could be located.

Nos. 8, 9 and 10: *Šibhiniš, Tamnu(n)na and Kibšuna*: The sequence in the Shalmaneser revolt list seems to be moving from south-east to north-west, with Kurbail known to lie north or north-west of Nineveh on the east bank of the Tigris. Kibšuna, which had been the capital city of the Qumeni (see above, § 3.1.2), must have lain further east in the Al-Kosh plain, probably on its northern side, towards the mountains of Atrush; it presumably still lay within the province of the *abarakku* (and may indeed have been its capital city). Tamnu(n)na (previously sometimes read Parnunna; that CTN 2, 128: 9 ^{uru}*ta-ma-nu-n*[*i*] betrays the correct reading was recognized by Kessler) would have to be north

---

[32]See recently M. Liverani: SAAB 6 (1992), pp. 35-40.

[33]E.g. by Forrer, understanding the cuneiform as GEMÉ.

[34]E.g. Parpola, NAT, p. 300.

[35]RIMA 2, p. 150: 52; the writing *ra-dam-ma-te* ibid. 1.57, reflects Aramaic phonology as pointed out by A.R. Millard: JAOS 100 (1980), p. 369-b.

and east of the Jebel Maqlub and Jebel Baʾashiqa, and following the sequence backwards places Šibhiniš (which as far as I know occurs only here and as the name of an eponym's province) east of the Khazir; across the Upper Zab one imagines we would already be in the province of Arbil.

3.5. *Named provinces: 8th-7th centuries* (Fig. 5)

Fig. 5 shows the identifiable home provinces mentioned in the eponym canon in the period from 799 to 695 B.C. (after which Trans-Euphrates provinces are brought into the list, and the canonical ordering of provinces is abandoned). The solid thick lines are suggested provincial boundaries coinciding with obvious natural barriers, such as the river or a range of hills. Broken lines represent divisions proposed with less conviction.

Some of the earlier provinces survive, such as Raqmat (though it is likely that Guzana had encroached on its territory). Others are new creations although the towns after which they are named may be older. There remain certain spaces on the map which seem large enough to have been separate provinces but to which a name has yet to be assigned. These are labelled with letters, and I shall discuss their possible identity in alphabetical order. Some of these must be matched with names in the *limmu* list for this period whose location remains unknown: Šibhiniš, Talmusi, Tamnu(n)na, Si'mē, and Halzi-adbar. Several of these are clearly not linguistically Assyrian or Aramaic, and they are not mentioned by the royal annalists in any conquest accounts. This suggests that although linguistically (and ethnically) non-Assyrian they were in fact very early under Assyrian control, and that they make their appearance only later because in the 9th century they had been subsumed under one of the large provincial agglomerates. For this reason it seems likely that they should be sought in a kind of outer ring of home provinces in the foothills east of the Assyrian plain where the population was neither Assyrian nor Aramaic, and where there are unidentified spaces. Our discussion will concentrate first on the lettered spaces on Fig. 5.

A: To the north of Kurbail we assume the presence of the province of Talmusi, from which Sennacherib derived part of his irrigation scheme. A provincial boundary would naturally have lain along the ridge at Fayda, which reaches out towards the Tigris, and Reade's tentative identification with Gir-e-pan looks plausible[36]. What is less certain is whether a further province would have been created to the north and west of this, running up to the range of mountains which delimit the Lesser Habur valley and have to be crossed to reach modern Zakho. I have no suggestions for this space if it is not part of Talmusi.

B: This is the territory for which Tamnu(n)na was suggested on the basis of § 3.4 above, with the province of the *abarakku* stretching north from where the mountainous terrain begins.

C: Here again the Shalmaneser revolt text has suggested placing Šibhiniš. However, this gives a relatively large area, and we should consider the possibility that there are two provinces here. In that case, there is a possibility that the southern sector is the unidentified province of Si'mē. The reasoning is this: ADD 875 + 904 + Sm.1546 (presumably to be published in SAA 11) is a list of fugitives from the governor of Si'mē with their home towns or villages. These towns include one of some importance usually written ^{uru}DIŠ-*tú*. This may now with some probability be read Issutu (Lanfranchi, this volume), and features on the route towards Nineveh from the east[37], and can easily therefore have lain in the region between the Khazir and the Zab, south of the Jebel Zirga Bardaresh. A location not too far into the mountains is also suggested by the Semitic (Akkadian or Aramaic) appearance of some of the other place names in this text, e.g. Nahal-[...].

---

36 RA 72 (1978), pp. 159-161.

37 See ABL 891 discussed by K. Deller in ZU, pp. 120-121.

There is a second solution, which would be to assume that the province of Šibhiniš, which is attested in the late 9th and early 8th centuries, but not, to my knowledge, after the accession of Tiglath-pileser III, was renamed (with or without a change of borders) as the province of Si'mē, which first features as the province of the eponym for 732 B.C. The two province names complement one another chronologically very tidily (cf. Table 1), and on balance this seems to be a more probable solution.

D, E and F: East of Arbil the situation is very uncertain. At the north, bordering on the Upper Zab, there was Hab(a)r(i)uri (for identification with the Dasht-i Herir see above, § 3.1.4). Further south, separated from Arbil by a range crossed by the Salah-ed-din pass, Shaqlawa lies in a well-defined valley of its own; and south from here again is the Qoi Sanjak area running down to the Lower Zab, marked here as D. North-east of D is the Rania plain, in which Tell Shemshara is the best known site, and east of this again but still west of the Zagros chaîne magistrale lies the plain of Qala Dizeh, both geographical entities which might have deserved independent provincial status when Assyrian control reached them. However, it is quite possible that E and especially F may never have been annexed, and should be considered rather as outliers of Mannaea.

There is good evidence from earlier royal inscriptions that the land of Tumme was in this general region: it is the southern limit of Tiglath-pileser I's mountain campaigns, and one of the Nairi lands[38]. Perhaps therefore we should look here for the little known province of Tu'immu attested under Tiglath-pileser III and Sargon[39].

G: As in the Middle Assyrian period (§ 3.2), it is difficult to know whether this region west of the Jebel Makhmur belonged with the province of Assur or of Kilizi, or we need to look for a third province. No name immediately suggests itself in Neo-Assyrian times.

Other provinces: The province of *Barhalza* cannot be securely located. The texts describing the gates of Nineveh list the gate leading to the WSW (just south of the "Jezira Gate") as the "Gate of the sector of Barhalzi province" (KÁ.GAL *pilku* KUR *bar-ḫal-zi*). This might be taken to indicate that the province itself lay in this direction, but this is probably misleading. In the construction of Dur-Šarrukin the city-walls were divided into "sectors" for the construction of which different provincial governors were made responsible. Since Sennacherib built a brand new wall round Nineveh, it is likely enough that the work was organized along similar lines, and that this stretch of wall had been the responsibility of the Barhalzi governor. This does not therefore necessarily tell us anything about the direction in which to seek Barhalzi, and in fact it is possible that its mention in a tablet from Girnavaz should encourage us to seek a more northerly position[40]. Hence on Fig. 5 I have tentatively placed it between Apku and Naṣibina. The governor of *Halzi-adbar*, which appears to mean "Basalt district", appears in the eponym canon for 695 B.C. Given that *adbaru* stone seems to be volcanic, it is tempting then to seek this province in the area SW of Jebel Sinjar, which had a long-standing association with basalt, especially the alveolar pumice used for grindstones[41]. It could well have been created in the later 8th century from part of the province of Raṣappa which had remained so unusually big.

[38]RGTC 5, p. 264; Nashef writes "nach der Asn. II.-Stelle soll T. südl. von Kirriuri gelegen haben"; see Salvini, *Nairi e Ur(u)aṭri*, Roma 1967, pp. 21-22, with map p. 49; Liverani, ATA, pp. 19-20; and for the text now RIMA 2, pp. 196-197.

[39]To the reference in NAT add ND 2451: 17, r. 2; Iraq 23 (1961), pl. XIV; and CTN 3 No. 86: 14.

[40]Cf. V. Donbaz: SAAB 2 (1988), p. 6.

[41]M. Stol, *On Trees, Mountains, and Millstones in the Ancient Near East*, Leiden 1979, pp. 83 ff.

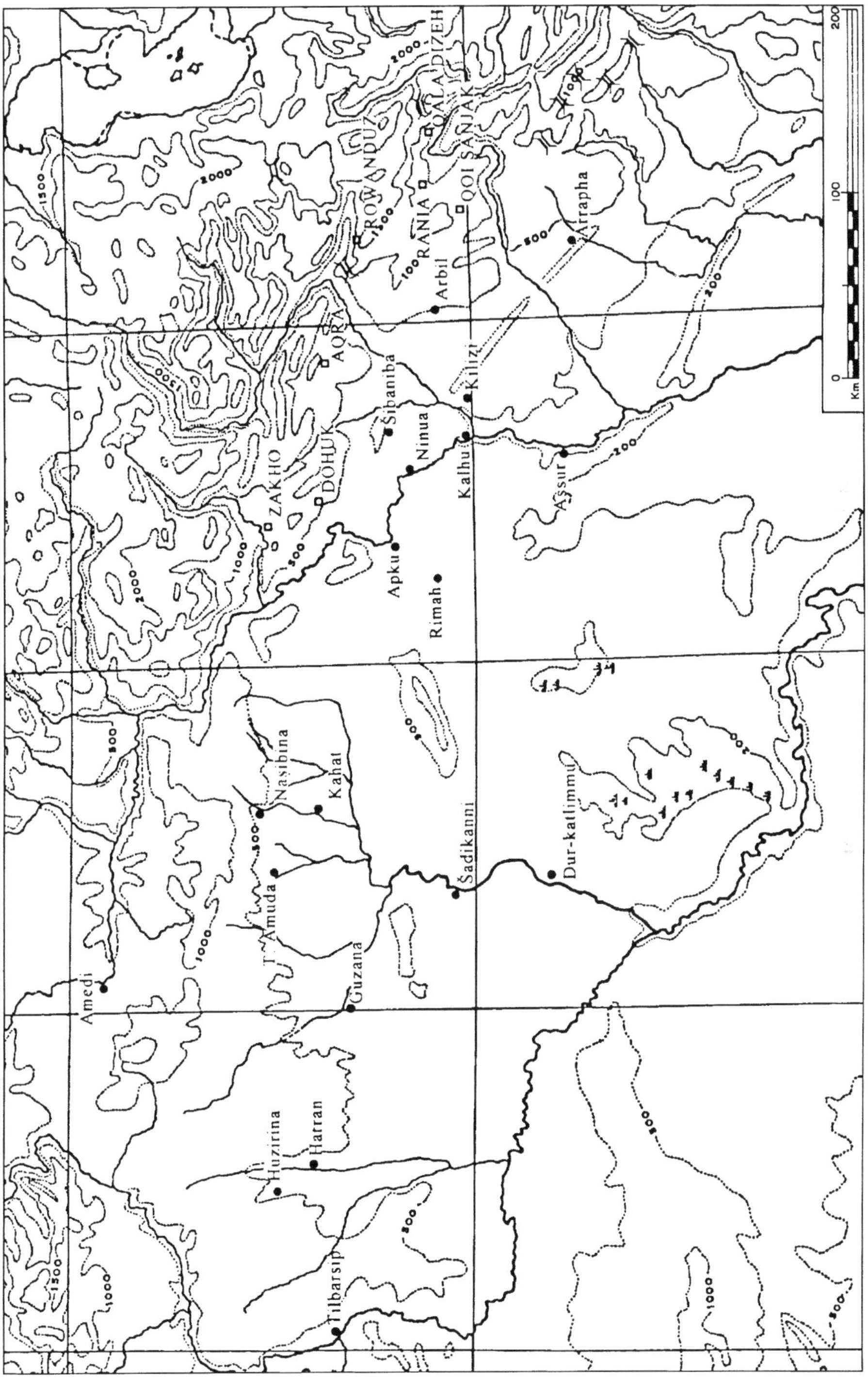

Fig. 1. - Principal identified locations and modern places. This map is intended to show the principal firmly identified Assyrian cities for the period under discussion, with a few additional sites, and the major modern towns in the north-eastern mountain area. To facilitate cross-reference, these dots and squares are repeated (without names) on Figs. 3-5.

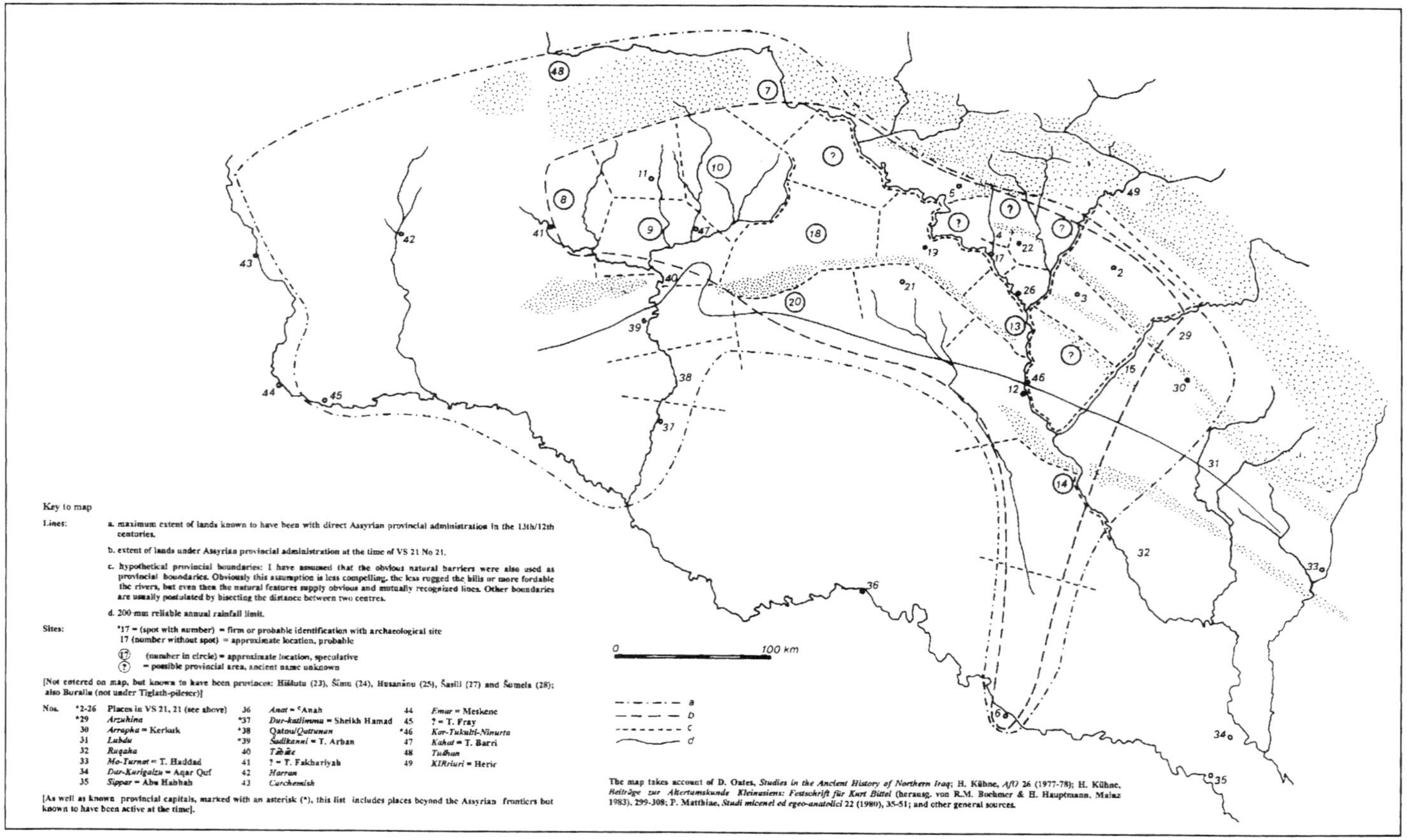
Key to map
Lines:
a. maximum extent of lands known to have been with direct Assyrian provincial administration in the 13th/12th centuries.
b. extent of lands under Assyrian provincial administration at the time of VS 21 No 21.
c. hypothetical provincial boundaries: I have assumed that the obvious natural barriers were also used as provincial boundaries. Obviously this assumption is less compelling, the less rugged the hills or more fordable the rivers, but even then the natural features supply obvious and mutually recognized lines. Other boundaries are usually postulated by bisecting the distance between two centres.
d. 200-mm reliable annual rainfall limit.
Sites:
*17 = (spot with number) = firm or probable identification with archaeological site
17 (number without spot) = approximate location, probable
(number in circle) = approximate location, speculative
= possible provincial area, ancient name unknown
[Not entered on map, but known to have been provinces: Hiššutu (23), Šimu (24), Husanānu (25), Šasili (27) and Šumela (28); also Buralla (not under Tiglath-pileser)]
Nos. *2-26 Places in VS 21, 21 (see above)
*29 Arzuhina
30 Arrapha = Kerkuk
31 Lubdu
32 Ruqaha
33 Me-Turnat = T. Haddad
34 Dur-Kurigalzu = Aqar Quf
35 Sippar = Abu Habbah
36 Anat = ᶜAnah
*37 Dur-katlimmu = Sheikh Hamad
*38 Qatnu/Qattunan
*39 Šadikanni = T. Arban
40 Tābāte
41 ? = T. Fakhariyah
42 Harran
43 Carchemish
44 Emar = Meskene
45 ? = T. Fray
*46 Kar-Tukulti-Ninurta
47 Kahat = T. Barri
48 Tušhan
49 KIRriuri = Herir
[As well as known provincial capitals, marked with an asterisk (*), this list includes places beyond the Assyrian frontiers but known to have been active at the time].
0 100 km
a
b
c
d
The map takes account of D. Oates, Studies in the Ancient History of Northern Iraq; H. Kühne, AfO 26 (1977-78); H. Kühne, Beiträge zur Altertumskunde Kleinasiens: Festschrift für Kurt Bittel (herausg. von R.M. Boehmer & H. Hauptmann, Mainz 1983), 299-308; P. Matthiae, Studi micenei ed egeo-anatolici 22 (1980), 35-51; and other general sources.

Fig. 2. - *The Middle Assyrian provinces. This map (reproduced previously but with excessive reduction in AfO 32 [1985], p. 97) shows the Middle Assyrian provincial system in the 11th century. Places No. 2-28, numbered after the lines of VS XXI 21, are as follows: (2) Arbail; (3) Kilizu; (4) Halahhu; (5) Talmuššu; (6) Idu; (7) Katmuhu; (8) Šudu; (9) Taidu; (10) Amasaki; (11) Kulišhinaš; (12) Aššur; (13) Lower Province; (14) Upper Province; (15) Turšan; (16) Libbi-ali; (17) Ninua; (18) Kurda; (19) Apku; (20) Addariq; (21) Karana; (22) Šibanibe; (23) Hiššutu; (24) Šimu; (25) Husananu; (26) Kalhu; (27) Šaṣili; (28) Šumela?.*

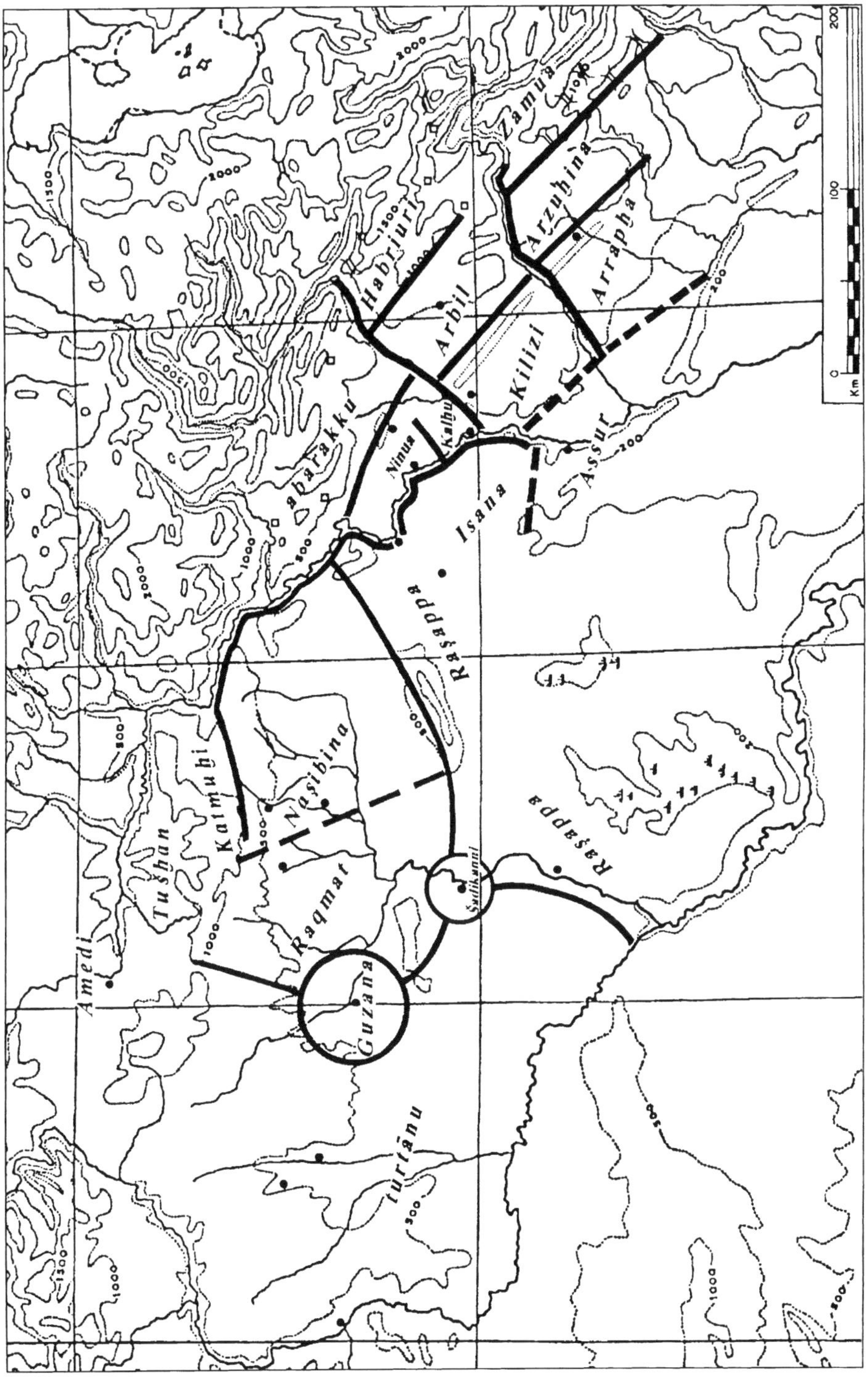

Fig. 3. - *The 9th century provinces. Provinces listed in the eponym list for the 9th century. Presumed natural borders, along rivers or ranges of hills, are suggested in solid black lines, broken lines indicate uncertainty about location or existence of border. Guzana and Šadikanni were independent for most of this time.*

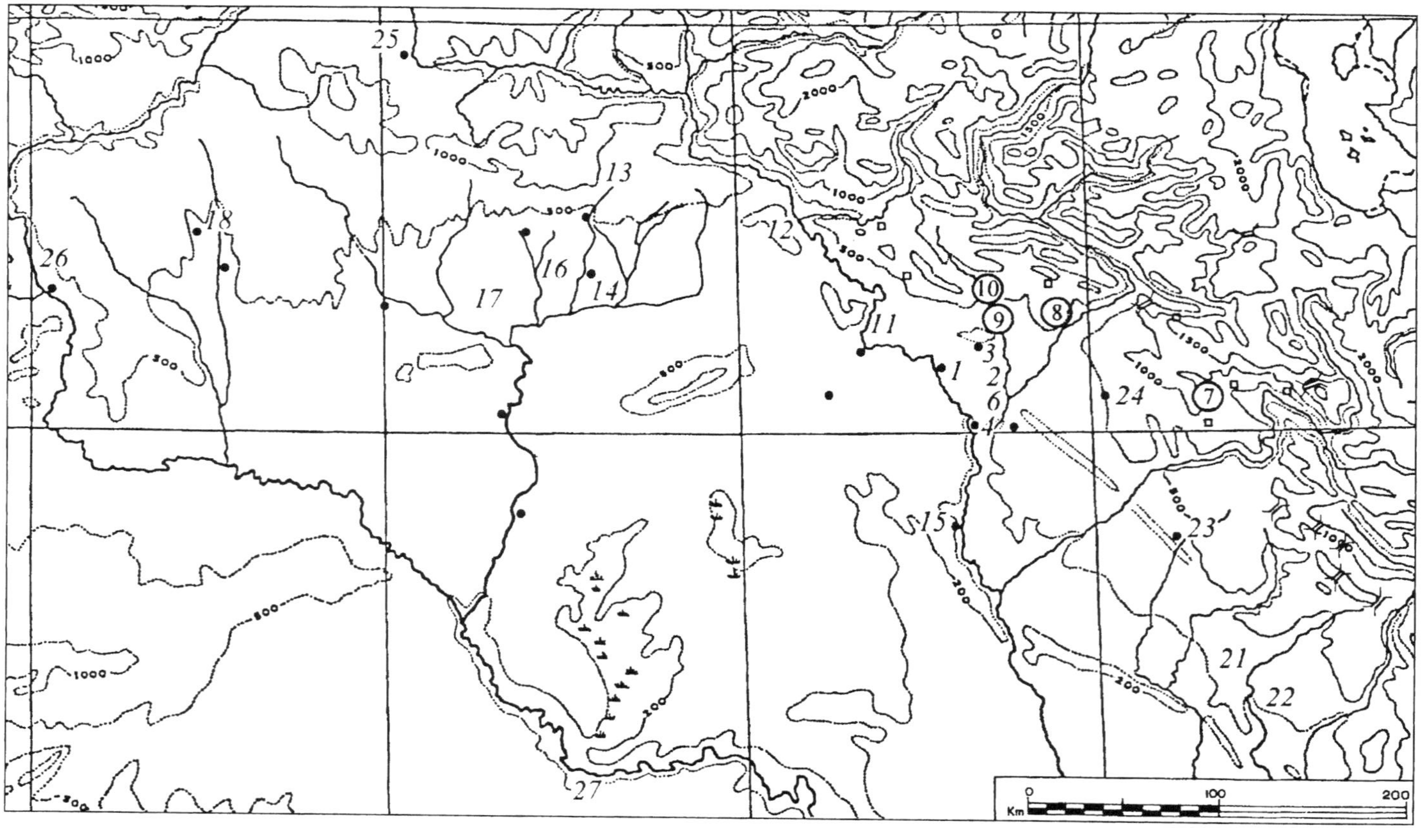

Fig. 4. - *The Shalmaneser revolt* (I R 29): *"(1) Nin(u)a; (2) Adia; (3) Šibaniba; (4) Imgur-ellil; (5) Išpalluri; (6) Bit-šašširi; (7) Šimu; (8) Šibhiniš; (9) Tamnunna; (10) Kibšuna; (11) Kurbail; (12) Tidu; (13) Nabulu; (14) Kahat; (15) Aššur; (16) Urakka; (17) Raqmat; (18) Huzirina; (19) Dur-balāṭi; (20) Dariga; (21) Zabban; (22) Lubdu; (23) Arrapha; (24) Arbail; (25) Amedi; (26) Tilabne; (27) Hindānu. Total: 27 cities with their districts, which revolted against Shalmaneser, king of the four rims". Numbers on the map correspond to the numbers in the list. Italic numbers on the map either are certainly located, or must be approximately correct. 7, 8, 9 and 10, enclosed in a circle, are tentative proposals.*

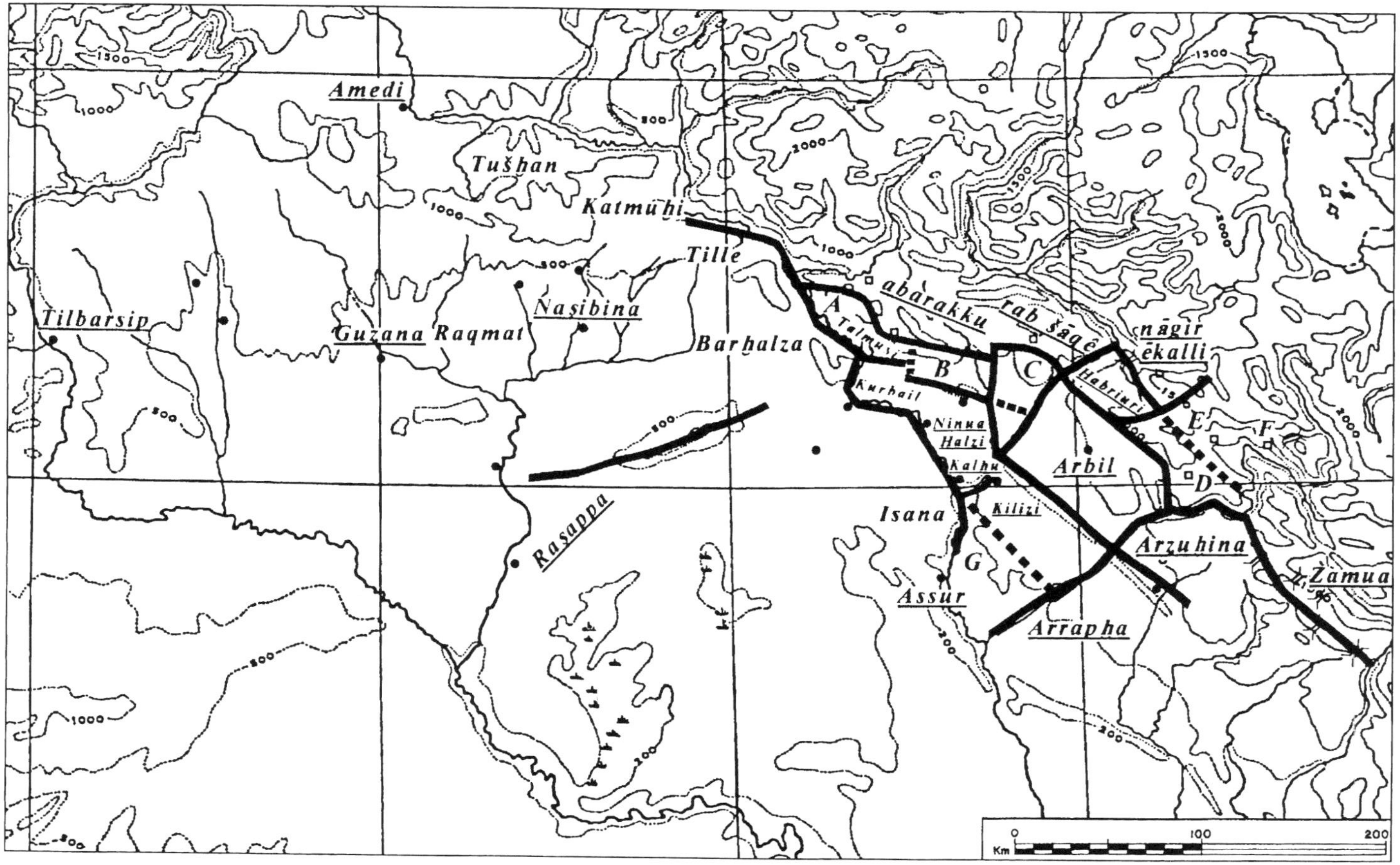

Fig. 5. - *Provinces 799-695 B.C. The provinces in the eponym canon for this time span which can be located with some confidence are underlined. Those less certain are not. Barhalza and Halzi are also included, though not in this part of the eponym list. Presumed natural borders, along rivers or ranges of hills, are suggested in solid black lines, broken lines indicate uncertainty about location or existence of border. Names of the areas lettered A to G are unknown (see § 3.5).*

THE ASSYRIAN ARMY IN ZAMUA

By J. N. POSTGATE

The article of Manitius published in 1910 has never really been superseded: that is because it was based on the Assyrian royal inscriptions, which were well understood at the time and to which there have been few major additions (and those principally from before the reign of Assur-naṣir-apli II). With new texts from Nimrud and new editions from Helsinki of the Kouyunjik archives, the time is overdue for a reassessment of the textual evidence for the composition of the Neo-Assyrian army. In any case Manitius only covered some aspects of military organization and he himself wrote that he hoped to publish a work which "would present the development of the whole military world of the Assyrians, exploiting the entire available material in literature and sculpture".[1] No doubt the Great War foiled these plans, and indeed there is still no comprehensive study of the Assyrian army which pulls together the evidence from both the texts and the reliefs. Two recent books on the Assyrian army have no illustrations (Malbran-Labat 1982; Mayer 1995). Yet the palace reliefs are an inexhaustibly rich mine of information which is always susceptible of further interpretation. The most important initiative in exploiting this resource and achieving Manitius's goal has been Reade's article of 1972, but the textual sources have improved significantly since then. This present article is thus a partial and belated response to his plea of a quarter of a century ago that "the epigraphists who are at present rewriting and re-interpreting" the administrative documents "will bear the evidence of the sculptures in mind" (p. 108).[2]

The article aims to do two things: to review in some detail the evidence of the administrative texts and letters with particular regard to terminology, and in the light of this review to begin to correlate the written sources more consistently with the evidence of the reliefs. As a starting point one cannot do better than use Nimrud Letter 89, excavated in the North-West Palace by Sir Max Mallowan in 1952 and first published in *Iraq* 28 by H. W. F. Saggs.[3] It gives a breakdown of the forces under the command of the governor of Mat-Zamua (the modern Shahrizur to the south-east of the Assyrian heartland) at one moment in the reign of Sargon. It is an indication of its value that it has been edited at least three times, most recently in 1990 by S. Parpola (SAA 5 215).[4] Even this version is not perfect, since it requires unjustifiable emendations, and more recently still I have found a way of making the scribe's arithmetic work without significant emendation of the text, which justifies presenting the revised text for a fourth time.

Transcription of Nimrud Letter 89

1 [*a-na* LUG]AL EN-*ia*
2 [ÌR-*ka*] $^{1.d}$IM–KI-*ia*
3 [*lu* D]I-*mu a-na* LUGAL EN-*ia*
4 [*š*]*a* LUGAL EN *ṭè-e-mu iš-ku-na-ni-ni*
5 *ma-a e-mu-qi ša* KUR-*za-mu-u-a*
6 *a-šur*$^!$ *šup-ra* 10 GIŠ.GIGIR.MEŠ
7 2 GIŠ *ut-tar-a-te* 10 *ša* ANŠE.KUR.RA.MEŠ
8 10 *ša* ANŠE *ku-di-ni* [P]AB 20 ANŠE *ú-ra-te*
9 97 ANŠE *pét-ḫal-lu* 11 LÚ *mu-kil*–KUŠ.PA.MEŠ
10 12 LÚ.3.U$_5$.MEŠ [( )]10 LÚ.A.SIG$_5$
11 53 LÚ.GIŠ.GIGIR.MEŠ [20 LÚ.GA]L *ú-ra-te*
12 PAB 1 ME 6 ERÍN.ME[Š] GIŠ.GIGIR.MEŠ
13 1 ME 61 LÚ *šá pet-ḫal-*[*a*$^?$*-t*]*e*$^?$ 1 ME 30 LÚ.GIŠ.GIGIR.MEŠ

[1] Manitius 1910, 117.

[2] Since Reade 1972 is an essential companion to this article, I have not duplicated any of its illustrations. Examples here and references in the text have been taken for convenience from the more accessible volumes rather than the fundamental but not widely accessible volumes of Botta, Layard and Place.

[3] Saggs 1966: copy Pl. LVI, edition pp. 185–7.

[4] The text will be included in Professor Saggs's forthcoming edition of the Nimrud letters.

14 52 LÚ *zu-un-zu-ra-ḫi* PAB 3 ME 43
15 LÚ.GIŠ.GIGIR.MEŠ 8 LÚ *šá* É 2-*e*
16 12 LÚ.KA.KÉŠ 20 LÚ.KAŠ.LUL
17 12 LÚ *kar-ka-di-ni* 7 LÚ.NINDA.MEŠ
18 10 LÚ.MU PAB 69 UN.MEŠ É
19 8 LÚ *um-ma-ni* 23 LÚ.UŠ.ANŠE.MEŠ
20 1 LÚ *mu-tir-ṭè-me* 80 LÚ *kal-la-pu*
21 PAB 6 ME 30 KUR *aš-šur-a-a*
22 3 ME 60 LÚ *qur-ru* 4 ME 40 KUR *i-tú*[( )]
23 PAB-*ma* 1 *lim* 4 ME 30 ERÍN.MEŠ MAN
24 *a-di pa-ni-ú-te ša a-na-ka-*[*ni*]
25 *a-di ša* LÚ *qur-bu-te na-ṣa-ni*
26 [*i-s*]*u-ri* [LU]GAL EN *i-qa-bi*
27 [*ma*]*-a re-*[*e*]*ḫ-te e-mu-q*[*i*] *a-le-e*
28 LÚ.GAL É-*i*[*a n*]*a-mar-ku re-eḫ-te*
29 *e-mu-qi ú-ba-lu*

Translation of Nimrud Letter 89

To the king my lord, your servant Adad-issiya, may it be well with the king my lord.

With regard to the king's instruction to me, that I should review the forces of Mat-Zamua and communicate (the result) to him:

Ten chariots, two wagons. Ten (teams) of horses, ten (teams) of mules, total twenty teams. Ninety-seven cavalry-horses.

Eleven chariot-drivers, twelve "third-riders", ten nobles, 53 grooms. [Twenty] team-commanders: total 106 chariot troops.

161 cavalry-men, 130 grooms, 52 *zunzurāḫu*, total 343 grooms.

Eight lackeys, twelve tailors, twenty butlers, twelve victuallers, seven bakers, ten cooks: total 69 domestic servants.

Eight scribes.

Twenty-three donkey-drivers.

One reporter.

Eighty *kallāpu.*

Total 630 Assyrians,

360 Qurraeans, 440 Ituaeans.

Grand total 1,430 "king's troops", including the previous ones who were here and those the aide-de-camp brought me.

In case the king my lord wonders where the rest of the forces are, my major-domo is delayed, and he is bringing the rest of the forces.

Philological notes on the text

Since SAA 5 215 is the most recent edition, readings adopted there and accepted here are not further discussed, but differences between the two are commented on. The transliteration in TCAE (Postgate 1974, 383–5) incorporates collations made by me in Baghdad in 1971 and again in March 1972; perhaps since these were not individually noted (although implicit in the Note to the Appendix on p. 246), they were not all taken up in SAA and some need to be reasserted here.

7. That the scribe could have written 20 by mistake for 2 is so improbable that any solution which avoids this assumption must be preferred.

8. The copy shows a slight space before the sign I have given as 20, offering support for taking the preceding sign as [PA]B, as already in TCAE after collation (Postgate 1974, 384). This resolves the uncertainties in ll. 7–8 by making this a total referring to the two types of team, horse and mule. The phrase *urâte ša sīsi/ē* or *ša kūdini/ē* "teams of horses" or "of mules" is more common in NA texts than the simpler construct-

plus-genitive construction, and evidently underlies the scribe's abbreviated formulation here.[5]

10. The profession (LÚ.)A.SIG$_5$ is problematic, although recently published Middle Assyrian texts from Sheikh Hamad have brought us a step forward. Writings using A or DUMU for the first component and SIG$_5$ or SIG for the second are most easily understood (with CAD M/i, 258) as *mār* (or the NA equivalent) *damqi*, though there are no syllabic writings for either component.[6] If correct, it would be tempting to see this term as the Assyrian equivalent of the contemporary Babylonian *mār banî* ("free person, citizen" or "nobleman" CAD M/i, 256–7, used with reference to Elam in an Assur-ban-apli inscription after a mention of bowmen). According to Deller and Millard 1993, 233, the logogram was first attested in a document from the reign of Assur-naṣir-apli II in the abstract formation LÚ*.A.SIG$_5$-*te*,[7] and they give its meaning firmly as "Kommandant des Streitwagens", "Streitwagenkämpfer", suggesting that it is successor to the second-millennium *mariyannu*.

Now, however, we have the following passage from a thirteenth-century letter from Dur-Katlimmu: "With respect to the troops DUMU.MEŠ SIG$_5$ and the weapons-troops who [...] were killed (or) captured, about which my lord sent me a message ..."[8] Earlier in the same letter the author mentions that 1,000 ERÍN.MEŠ A.SIG$_5$ are stationed under his aegis (*ina pittuya usbu*). The context of the letter is not as clear as we might like, but there is much to be gained from these passages. First it is clear that these "sons of the good" are soldiers, and that they are present in considerable numbers. Then we see that they are contrasted to "weapons-troops". Furthermore, as Cancik-Kirschbaum notes (p. 137) it is likely that the word *damqu* here, originally at least, denoted social standing by analogy with its use to describe court ladies (DUMU.MUNUS.MEŠ SIG$_5$) in her letter No. 10. In the light of this term, DUMU.MEŠ SIG$_5$ (not preceded by ERÍN.MEŠ) in Cancik-Kirschbaum 1996 No. 8: 46′ may indeed, as she suggests, refer to "nobles" in a non-military capacity. In other words, it now seems clear that the Neo-Assyrian charioteers with this title were indeed the successors to the higher ranks of Middle Assyrian society who, like the *mariyannu* further west, were chariot-fighters, with the bow as their principal weapon.[9]

11. If we retain the reading 10 in l. 10 of the editio princeps for the number of A.SIG$_5$, the total of 106 in l. 13 is short of twenty men. SAA's solution, to read 10 as [3]0, is not favoured by the copy. It is preferable to restore the twenty missing men in the second half of l. 11, and this points to [*rab*] *urâte*: restoring LÚ.GIŠ.GIGIR.MEŠ [ANŠ]E *ú-ra-te* "grooms of the teams" introduces a classification not otherwise attested and a fresh complication with this difficult term, whereas the *rab urâte* is a known military profession connected with horses and not listed elsewhere in the text. This also has the advantage of requiring only the 10 *mār damqi* in l. 10 and thus keeping the numbers of the three types of chariot-crew roughly equal. The implications of this line, if correctly restored, would be that the "team-commanders" were superior officers in charge of the *susānu*. If the proportion of men to animals in this chariot section of the list seems unduly high, we should note that the list of "other professions" later on includes no carpenters or other craftsmen whose skills might have been needed to effect running repairs to the chariots, suggesting that this task fell within the job-description of those in l. 11.

12. It seems unlikely that chariots should be totalled at this stage, since the author began by listing the horses and vehicles, and has now moved on to personnel. The 106 men totalled here are precisely "chariot troops", and this must be the author's meaning, as assumed by Saggs. The combination ERÍN.MEŠ GIŠ.GIGIR is found in a comparable context in ABL 1009 rev. 20′.

13. The double exclamation mark after 1-*me*-30 in SAA 5 is intended to justify an emendation to 1-*me*-50 which was, however, accidentally not made in the final version of the transliteration. The reason is that 161+150+52 gives a total of 363, twenty more than the clearly written total of 343 in l. 14, which is also required by the sub-total in l. 21. Although in the copy the sign 50 in l. 13 looks very clear, and it might seem easier to suppose that the damaged number at the beginning of this line was intended to be 40 (as already read by Saggs in his editio princeps), my own collation of the tablet as reflected in TCAE (Postgate 1974, 384) favoured reading 1-*me*-30 with SAA 5.

14. The word *zunzurāhu* is manifestly not of Assyrian origin but has not been recognized in any other languages, although AHw's suggestion of a Hurrian origin seems plausible (with the final -(*h*)*hu* being a frequent Hurrian ending). It is found abbreviated as LÚ *zu-un* in SAA 11 123 i 3′ alongside an equal number of *susānu* (read 4 here, rather than *šá*, as the total of 8 makes clear). These are the only two known occurrences; all one can say at present is that it seems to be an employment connected with cavalry, complementary to that of the *susānu*. One might, in view of the parallel listing of *susānu* followed by [*rab*]

[5] For the term *urû* "a stable" and "a team" see Deller 1958; Davies 1989. Both have the plural *urâte* (for "stable" see MacGinnis 1989, where there is no compelling reason to translate the word "trough") and it seems simplest to consider them as the same word, presumably because members of a team were stabled together. *Pace* AHw, there is no evidence for the existence of a word **urītu* (as suspected by Deller already and now confirmed by the collated version of ADD 753: 7 in SAA 11 77).

[6] Except in Neo-Babylonian, where texts from Darius have the writing *dam-qa* (see CAD M/i, 257 s.v. *mār damqa*, and A. L. Oppenheim in Pritchard 1969, 567 fn. 7).

[7] Also edited as SAA 12 83 (see rev. 24).

[8] Cancik-Kirschbaum 1996 No. 8: 38′–9′: *aššum* ERÍN.MEŠ DUMU.MEŠ SIG$_5$ *ù* ERÍN.MEŠ *ša* GIŠ.TUKUL.MEŠ *ša* [x-]x-*ni* / *dekūni ṣabbutūni*. Despite the uncertainty of the broken word at the end of l. 38′, the translation needs to be along these lines, since the two first words of l. 39′ are subjunctive statives not adjectives. The broken word is likely to have been either another subjunctive stative or an adverb.

[9] Note that a military rank or function in Hittite texts is written LÚ.SIG$_5$, sometimes with an Akkadian complement of -QU; see Haas and Thiel 1978, 159, citing *inter alios* S. Alp, *Belleten* 11 (1947) 411 ("etwa 'Unteroffizier'").

urâte in l. 11, go so far as to suggest that they fulfil a function similar to that of the *rab urâte* but in relation to cavalry.

15. The term used here for the total of cavalry-related troops is LÚ.GIŠ.GIGIR.MEŠ, which presents in its starkest form the apparent perversity of the scribal terminology. It seems almost incredible that a logogram which appears to mean "chariot men" could be used to refer to cavalry in contrast to "chariot troops" (ERÍN.MEŠ GIŠ.GIGIR.MEŠ) in l. 12, but such seems to be the case. In fact the term occurs three times in our letter: once describing a group of 53 men forming part of the chariotry arm, once as the 130 men working with the cavalry, and this third time where it seems to serve as the generic term for the cavalry arm. To unravel this we must concentrate on the underlying Akkadian words, rather than the logograms.

The solution seems to be in two stages: first, Parpola has made it probable that the logogram in fact stands for *susānu*;[10] second, this is a word which makes no reference to chariots and has an interesting pedigree. It must go back to *aššuššannu* with the loss of the initial syllable in the first millennium, paralleled in many other cases (e.g. *azamru*, *alaḫḫinu*, *ašarittu*, *Uqumānu*). The term is used in the Kikkuli horse training texts from Boğazköy.[11] Deriving from the Indo-Iranian *aswas*, better known to us as *equus* in Latin and *hippos* in Greek, the word meant originally something like "horse-person". Despite the misleading logogram, there is no difficulty in conceding that cavalry horses needed their trainers or grooms as much as the chariot horses did; as we shall see below, cavalry came later on the military scene and borrowed the grooms and their designation. There remains its use as a generic term for the cavalry arm. The explanation is perhaps that the scribe did not use *ša pētḫalli* in this context since it has already served to differentiate the horse-rider proper from his ancillary staff; however, precisely the same objection applies to *susānu*, and this remains a puzzle.

20. SAA's reading *kal-ba-te* goes back to the copy and the original edition, but the collation adopted in TCAE favoured reading *kal-la-pu* (Postgate 1974, 384), involving only a minimal adjustment to the copy. Writings of the plural of *kallāpu* attested elsewhere include *kal-la-pa-ni* (ABL 526 rev. 1), *kal-la-ba-a-ni* (TCL 3: 426), and *kal-la-ba-ni* (Tell Halaf 51: 3), not to mention the pseudo-logographic writing *kal-lab*.MEŠ. Examples of a feminine plural are lacking, and even without collation it would have been tempting to emend to *kal-la*!*-pu*!. How the word should be normalized is a problem. The persistent doubled writing of the *l* hints at a *parrās* form but no verb with radicals *klb* or *klp* is attested in Assyrian. The nature of the final consonant remains doubtful: a final *-bu* may equally well be read *-pu*, in singular forms *bi* alternates with *pi*, and *ba* with *pa* in the plural. The known alternation between /p/ and /b/ in Neo-Assyrian dialect makes it impossible to determine which is likely to be the older form. There is no basis for the connection with *kalappu* (a metal tool) assumed by the early Assyriologists, and the source of a proposed translation of "sapper, engineer". Since *kallāp/bu* looks like an acceptable Akkadian formation, one might even consider a word derived from *kalbu* "dog", but this is pure speculation. For the function of these troops see the discussion below.

22. The LÚ *qur-ru* undoubtedly represent the group previously called Gurraeans. Writings of the name in administrative documents and letters almost invariably use the sign GUR for the first syllable; the apparent evidence that the first consonant of the name is /g/ has evaporated with the collation of ABL 76 = SAA 10 59: 9, and a /q/ is suggested if the reading of ADD 680 = SAA 7 112 rev. 2 KUR? *qu-ra*?*-a-a* is correct, but also by ABL 685. Here a commander with responsibilities in the Lahiru region writes, "Fifty Ituaeans (and) thirty LÚ *qa*-ḪAR-*ra* [collated]: total eighty troops are inside (the fort)." As seen already in Parpola 1970, this writing can only refer to our Qurraeans: it ties in with the strange spelling in ABL 883 where in l. 19 we have the writing LÚ *qur*-ḪAR-*a-a* and in rev. 7 the phrase 10 [collated] LÚ *qur*-ḪAR-*a-a-e-a* "ten of my Qurraeans", parallel with 20 LÚ *i-tu-a-a-e-a* "twenty of my Ituaeans" in the next line. Obviously these writings pose a problem. To transcribe LÚ *qur*^{ur_5}*-ra-a-a*, improbable in itself, would not resolve the writing in ABL 685, and one must accept that in some cases the scribes were trying to indicate the presence of a consonant between the /q/ and the /r/. The easiest assumption would seem to be that an intervocalic /m/ was lost in pronunciation, as happens elsewhere in Neo-Assyrian dialect, so that we have a form /qamur-/ becoming /qa'ur-/ and thence contracting to /qûr-/; but even this is tricky, since in ABL 883 we would have to assume that the process of contraction has advanced enough to permit the writing with an initial GUR but not sufficiently to erase the memory of the syllable /mur/, which left the scribe in two minds. Unfortunately then the identity of this ethnonym remains a mystery. It is apparently unattested in the royal historical inscriptions, and since these auxiliaries were evidently distributed throughout the empire where regular troops were required, their presence in one place or another gives no clue to their origins.[12]

[10] Parpola 1976, 172; the equation is taken as established in the SAA series (and recently accepted also by Fuchs 1998, 109) but some caution is still warranted, since the "outright equation of the two terms provided by reciprocal variants in a 'literary' text" mentioned in SAA 11, xxvi, is not as decisive as it sounds. In the copy, at least, of LKA 71 the word is completely lost at its first occurrence, and it is not independently identifiable as LÚ.GIŠ.GIGIR at the second. The earliest attestation in NA may be Deller and Millard 1993, 221 BM 36711 rev. 14, written syllabically *su-sa-nu*.

[11] See e.g. Kinnier Wilson 1972, 54, and most recently Starke 1995, 116 ff. (on p. 118 n. 235 the form *šušānu* should have been identified as Neo-Babylonian, no doubt a mere *lapsus calami*).

[12] The only possible pointer is ADD 251 = SAA 5 53, where the contingent of a commander of fifty may be described as composed of "Mudurnaean Qurraeans". Unfortunately Mudurna as a place name is otherwise unknown, unless it be Me-Turnat, which is suggested by the SAA 5 edition and cannot be ruled out on philological grounds.

TABLE 1: Synopsis of Nimrud Letter 89

	Vehicles	*Animals*	*Men*					
Chariotry	chariots 10	horses 10	*mukīl appāte*	11	charioteers	106	Assyrians	630
		(TEAMS)	*tašlīšu*	12				
			mār damqi	10				
	carts 2	mules 10	*susānu*	53				
			rab urâte	[20]				
Cavalry		riding horses 97	*ša pētḫalli*	161	*susānu*	343		
			susānu	130				
			zunzurāḫu	52				
Logistical personnel			household staff			69		
			scribes			8		
			donkey-drivers			23		
			spy			1		
Infantry			*kallāpu*			80		
			Qurrāyu (Qurraeans)			360	auxiliaries	800
			Itu'āyu (Ituaeans)			440		
Total			"king's troops"					1430

Adad-issiya's enumeration is precise and logically arranged, and we can therefore tabulate the information as in Table 1. As the chart shows, the army as reviewed comprised 1,430 men, designated "king's troops". There are 630 Assyrians and 800 auxiliaries from two tribes, the Qurraeans and the Ituaeans. We shall come back to these Aramaeans later. The Assyrians are divided into four groups: the chariotry, the cavalry, the logistical personnel and foot-soldiers. This is an order followed in other contexts,[13] and we cannot do better than to follow the Assyrians' own arrangement and start with the traditional elite sector, the chariotry.

Chariotry — tradition

Composition of chariotry

The first section is the chariotry, and comprises the vehicles, the animals and the men. To go with ten chariots we have ten teams of horses and ten teams of mules. The term for team, *urû,* is used in detailed administrative lists like this where it must have conveyed a precise and therefore, one would imagine, invariable number.[14] This number is not explicitly stated for us anywhere in the written sources, but for chariotry in the ninth century, at least, it must have been three. There is evidence in the sculptures that ninth-century chariots had two horses under the yoke and a third unyoked but controlled by reins, to one side.[15] As pointed out by Deller 1958, the critical written evidence for three animals per team is a ninth-century administrative document from Tell Billa listing fifteen male horses and three mares, plus four male mules and five female mules, totalled as nine teams (9 *ú-ru-u*; Finkelstein 1955, 170 No. 72: 11–12). This must represent six teams of three horses and three teams of three mules. On the other hand, SAA 5 227 = ABL 408 does strongly suggest that a team of mules comprised just two animals. Possibly ABL 408 is concerned with animals being ridden, not towing chariots, and a *cavalry* team needed only two animals. There were "cavalry teams" identified already in the ninth century as *ú-ru-ú pet-ḫal* (Finkelstein 1955, 170 No. 72: 14) and the designation persists later, e.g. Tell Halaf 38 (late ninth/early eighth century), SAA 11 29 = ADD 1041 (late eighth/seventh century). We know from the reliefs that in the ninth century cavalry operated in pairs and single riders when not in battle

[13] E.g. at the end of Sargon's eighth campaign; Tukulti-Ninurta II (RIMA 2, 173: 37); Deller and Millard 1993, 220 BM 36711 obv. 22′; and in the omen queries (Starr, SAA 4). Also in ABL 1009, a letter from Nineveh similar to NL 89 which if complete would be an invaluable report on the forces under the command of the writer. It lists a motley collection of troops described by type of weapon, ethnic origin and other categories.

[14] For the word *urû* see above, note on l. 8.

[15] E.g. Kinnier Wilson 1972, 61 and Pl. 1; Littauer and Crouwel 1979, 113 with Fig. 53 showing three horses and six reins.

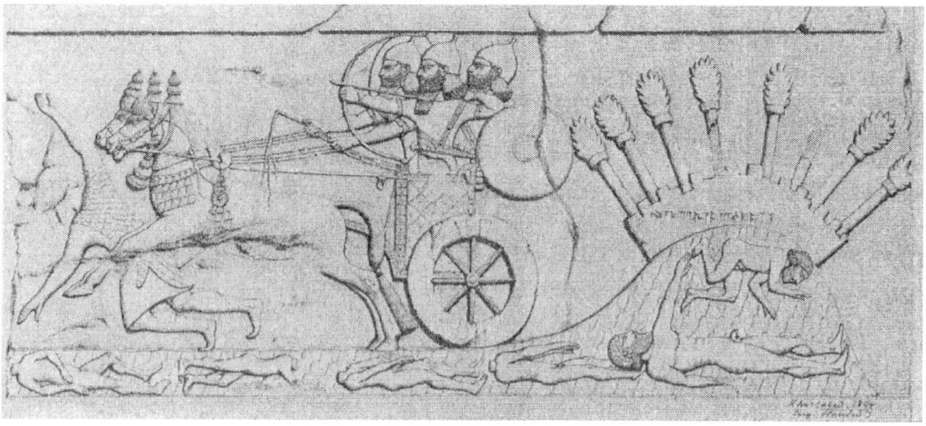

Fig. 1 Shield-bearing third man on chariot, reign of Sargon (after Albenda 1986, Pl. 123; reproduced by permission of the Bibliothèque et Archives de L'Institut de France).

often had two animals (Budge 1914, Pl. XVII); pairs of cavalry horses are shown under Tiglath-pileser III (Reade 1972, 103) and pairs of horses are brought as tribute in the Dur-Sharrukin reliefs (e.g. Albenda 1986, Pls. 25, 32–4). We could therefore reconstruct a situation where *urû* "team" without qualification meant three chariot horses (or mules) but *urû pēthalli* meant a pair of cavalry horses; but it seems a bit strained. It seems easier to assume that the normal team for chariotry was also reduced to two each from the time of Tiglath-pileser onwards, since only pairs of chariot-horses are shown in his reliefs.[16]

To return to Zamua, since there are far more mules than were needed to tow the two carts, they presumably stood in for the horses towing the chariots outside battle conditions, and this explains why they too were counted in teams. Since donkey-drivers are also listed later, some donkeys were presumably also present, but they seem not to have merited inclusion in the military calculations.

With the animals were 106 men. Listed first are the chariot crews: eleven drivers, twelve "third men" and ten "nobles". That the crew of each chariot involves three men seems likely in view of the approximately equal numbers of chariots and personnel of each type. On Assur-naṣir-apli's reliefs chariots in battle normally have a crew of two, a driver who uses both hands to control the reins and an archer. These are the *mukīl appāte* "rein-holder" and the "noble" (or *mār damqi*, see above on l. 10). A third member of the crew is rarely shown at this date; he can be seen standing precariously at the rear of the royal chariot (e.g. Budge 1914, Pl. XVI.3) or holding a shield before the driver (and presumably the king, ibid., Pl. XIV); in Barnett and Falkner 1962, Pl. CXVI, his two colleagues in front (who do not include the king) are in chain-mail but he is not. No doubt a three-man chariot crew of this kind is the GIŠ.GIGIR *šal-ši-it-te* or "triple chariot" mentioned in a ninth-century text.[17] On the reliefs the third man is still present in Tiglath-pileser's own chariot and holds the shield in battle at Khorsabad (Fig. 1).[18] He is evidently the *tašlīšu* who occurs here in NL 89 and frequently in other eighth and seventh-century texts. While the Akkadian reading of the logogram is still in need of final proof, the logogram itself (also LÚ.3-*šú*) clearly expresses the idea that this is the third member of a crew.

To return to the principal member of the crew, the *mār damqi*, Cancik-Kirschbaum suggested

[16] The evidence of the reliefs and other representations is not transparent. Four horses were sometimes harnessed together, occasionally already in the ninth century. Although normally only two horses are shown on Tiglath-pileser's and Sargon's reliefs, Littauer and Crouwel 1979, 114–15, assume that six or eight reins should be taken to imply three or four horses. The textual evidence does not really support this.

[17] Deller and Millard 1993, 220 BM 36711 obv. 11′; unless of course the term refers to the number of horses rather than the number of men employed. For the third man in the ninth century see Littauer and Crouwel 1979, 129.

[18] Albenda 1986, Pls. 121, 123; for a "shield third rider" see fn. 45 below.

that he is perhaps the equivalent of the Nuzi *rākib narkabti*, who also combines social standing with fighting in a chariot. The difficulty with this is that we can be fairly sure that at least some members of the nobility owning a chariot were known as EN GIŠ.GIGIR or "chariot-owner".[19] This is now known from eighth-to-seventh-century Nippur texts to have been read in Babylonian *bēl narkabti*, a term of sufficiently frequent oral use to have been worn down to *berkabtu*.[20] Whether this was also the Assyrian form or we should reconstruct a composite term with *mugirru* (as in the SAA indices) is impossible to say, but it can hardly have been identical with *mār damqi*. The clearest evidence for Assyrian "chariot-owners" in a military context is given by SAA 5 251 rev. 1–4, which is worth citing: 10 LÚ.EN.GIŠ.GIGIR.MEŠ 21 LÚ.ERÍN.MAN-*šú-nu* PAB 31 LÚ.EN.GIŠ. GIGIR.MEŠ *am-ru-te* "ten chariot-owners, their 21 king's troops, total 31 inspected chariot-owners". The ratio here of 1:2 strongly suggests that the "chariot-owners" were fulfilling the role of the *mār damqi*, with the other men providing the drivers and third riders. The different term may perhaps be explained as a difference of emphasis: just as the others are described as "king's troops", which refers to the system under which they were conscripted into the army (see below, p. 106), so we may assume the "chariot-owner" applies to a social status which has its own function within the army (as well as more generally to "charioteers", as this same passage illustrates), whereas perhaps by now the title *mār damqi* (which is attested much earlier) refers rather to the specifically military function of its holder within the chariot crew.

There follow 53 *susānu*, who must be the men who looked after the horses (and mules) and are therefore reasonably translated "grooms". They must have been responsible for the welfare of the animals outside the military context and presumably were not directly involved in combat. Their close relationship to the animals is stressed by a group of texts discovered in the Old Palace at Assur and discussed in CTN 3 (Dalley and Postgate 1984, 41–3),[21] texts which list *susānu* (written LÚ.GIŠ.GIGIR), each normally entrusted with two horses, as the totals make clear. No mention is made of chariots and each man comes from a different village, so that these texts certainly read as though the grooms cared for the animals at home, separately from the rest of the crew, over the winter months. Although they fall under the immediate command of either a *rab kiṣri* or a *rab ḫanšē*, one imagines their superior officers must also have included the *rab urâte*, as in l. 11 above.

Purpose of chariotry

Having looked at the internal composition of the chariotry, we need to examine its role within the army as a whole. The chariot was elite: the kings rode in chariots, both in battle and at other times, only occasionally transferring to sedan chairs or their own two feet when the going got too steep. The king in his chariot symbolized military might par excellence. In Middle Assyrian legal documents of the thirteenth century the phrase "wherever the chariot of the king traverses" is the equivalent of saying "wherever the king's rule is imposed",[22] and still in the eighth century Tiglath-pileser III uses the phrase "where the chariot(s) of the kings my fathers had not passed".[23] "Under

[19] Encountered by Tiglath-pileser III in the service of Rahianu of Damascus, see Tadmor 1994, 78–9: 5′; in the Nimrud Wine Lists, Kinnier Wilson 1972; from Que, incorporated into Sargon's army, SAA 5 68.

[20] See Cole 1996, 406.

[21] For the provenance see Pedersén 1985, I, 30 fn. 7.

[22] *Ašar mu-gi-ru ša šarri (bēli-šu) ibbalakkutūni* or *[ibb]alkitūni*, see Wilcke 1976, 214 note 30, for the two passages; as often with *mugirru* or *mugerru* there is doubt as to whether it meant "wheel" or "chariot". There is no doubt that the word *magarru* means "wheel" (note the lexical equivalence with giš.umbin), although as a *pars pro toto* it could sometimes stand for a chariot. The Assyrian *mugirru* is probably only a dialect variant of the same word (cf. perhaps NA *mud(a)buru* as a variant of *madbaru*). The doubt about the precise meaning persists into the NA period, especially in those cases where enemies fall "under the wheel", or the "tracks of the wheel" are mentioned; note that Assyrian vassals are said in the eighth century to "run at the wheel" (Aramaic *glgl*) of the king. The only absolutely clear passage seems to be ABL 1369 rev. 4. As Deller and Millard 1993, 230, point out, there is a Middle Assyrian profession "chariot carpenter" (LÚ.NAGAR GIŠ. GIGIR) who looks at first sight to be the same as the LÚ.NAGAR *mu-ger-ri* attested in the ninth-century text edited there. However, this does not amount to proof that GIŠ.GIGIR can be read *mugerru* (*pace* CAD M), since one may just as well be a "wheelwright" as a "cartwright".

[23] Tadmor 1994, 104: 20′–1′, KI MAN.MEŠ-*ni* AD.MEŠ-*a la e-ti-qa* ^{giš}*mu-gir-ra-šú-nu*.

the king's chariot" as a description of submission is still in use in the seventh-century royal correspondence.[24]

From Tukulti-Ninurta I down to Adad-nirari II in the ninth century the kings when speaking of their own and other armies say "my chariots and my heroes" or "troops" (*qurādēya* (Tiglath-pileser I) or *ummānāteya*), putting the chariots first.[25] This was of course a tradition which began in the Amarna age. One king writing to another will enquire after the well-being of his horses and chariots along with the royal family,[26] and the primary role of chariots is well attested in accounts of military activity from Babylonia to Egypt and the Hittite empire. Hence in Assyria, too, they were no doubt considered the elite arm of the fighting troops, but the prime question is whether their practical importance was equal to their symbolic value. There is no guarantee that they were numerically of great significance. Armies, perhaps especially those regularly victorious, may be slow to adapt to change.

If we are to believe the annals, in the ninth century both the Assyrians and their opponents in the west used chariots in hundreds,[27] and they are conspicuous in battle scenes on the first-millennium Assyrian reliefs. However this is a big "if": the annals are propaganda and the reliefs are propaganda in stone, and we have to enquire from other sources to establish the practical as opposed to symbolic worth of chariots in warfare. Hence the value of NL 89: in Mat-zamua at the end of the eighth century there are only ten chariots, as opposed to 97 cavalry mounts. Nevertheless, here they still are, and the Assyrians must have thought they served some purpose.

In the west, too, some chariots persisted into the eighth century. When Carchemish was finally absorbed into the empire in 716, Sargon's annals state that he took fifty chariots, 200 cavalry and 300 foot-soldiers (LÚ *zu-uk* GÌR.2) for incorporation into the royal corps.[28] These public statements are confirmed by the administrative lists from Fort Shalmaneser relating to preparations for Sargon's 710 campaign against Merodach-baladan: here we have groups of chariotry from Arbil, etc., but also Chaldaeans and Samarians. These late-eighth-century lists from Kalḫu come not from the royal residence on Kouyunjik but from a Review Palace which was undoubtedly concerned with the equipping of an army not a parade. The personal names of individual soldiers confirm that foreign men, as well as presumably their chariots and horses, were incorporated into the Assyrian army.[29]

The latest substantial written evidence for chariots outside the reliefs comes from the archives of the royal palace at Nineveh after the reign of Sennacherib. Two types of chariot are mentioned: one qualified as *taḫlīpi* (written *taḫ-líp*), the other as DUḪ.MEŠ. This latter qualification needs to be understood as *pattūtu* meaning "open"; it goes back to the Middle Assyrian period, when it refers to light two-wheeled chariots used by the kings for hunting.[30] Indeed, when hunting bulls Assur-naṣir-apli is shown on a chariot comprising a platform without any sides at all.[31] For hunting lions he prudently used one of the battle chariots shown on ninth-century Assyrian reliefs and described as "relatively small-wheeled, low-sided, basically two-man chariots",[32] which may also have a spiked shield hung on the back.[33] These are replaced on Tiglath-pileser's reliefs by

[24] SAA 10 33 (=ABL 385) rev. 14–15; ABL 620: 8; in SAA 10 (=ABL 80) rev. 8–12 the writer comments, "Why should I not embrace the tracks of the chariot (*ḫi-ir-ṣi mu-gi-ir-ri*) of the king my lord?" Notice that Assur-naṣir-apli's opponent in Zamua, Ameka, was deprived of "his possessions and his chariot" (RIMA 2, 206).

[25] So Tiglath-pileser I (RIMA 2, 14 i 71, ii 6; 15 ii 10; 19 iii 93, iv 69–70; and of the kings of Nairi, ibid., 19 iv 84–5); Assur-bel-kala (ibid., 91: 11′–12′); Assur-dan (ibid., 133: 25); Adad-narari II (ibid., 143: 10; 150: 51); Assur-naṣir-apli II (ibid., 196: 45 and often; of enemy army, ibid., 216: 58, 217: 63, etc.; note the variant GIŠ.GIGIR.MEŠ KAL-*tu* (var. *da-'a-tú*) *pit-ḫal-lu* SAG(.KAL)-*su* (var. *šá-ri-su*) "strong chariotry and outstanding cavalry", ibid., 205: 53; 210: 103; 246: 37; 260: 70). One exception: ERÍN.ḪI.A.MEŠ-*šu* GIŠ.GIGIR.MEŠ-*šú* LAL-*su* (=*rakissu*), ibid., 215: 45. These phrases are not used in the surviving inscriptions of Tiglath-pileser III.

[26] The Kassite king enquires about the "horses and chariots", Tušratta about the "chariots and horses"; whether the contrast has any significance is beyond me to judge.

[27] See e.g. Littauer and Crouwel 1979, 130; Mayer 1995, 451.

[28] Lie 1929: 75; see also Dalley 1985, 34–5.

[29] CTN 3 (Dalley and Postgate 1984); see Dalley 1985, 32–5.

[30] Postgate 1990; note in passing that in this article the first example on p. 37 is an accidental conflation of a passage from Tiglath-pileser I with one from Assur-bel-kala (for which see now RIMA 2, 103 iv 10).

[31] Budge 1914, Pl. XII.1.

[32] Littauer and Crouwel 1979, 128.

[33] For a shield on the back of a chariot see e.g. Littauer and Crouwel 1979, Fig. 53, pp. 103–4; they are in doubt whether chariots in the late eighth and seventh centuries still had separate shields, a doubt which is removed by the late-eighth-century administrative list of chariots CTN 3 No. 96, mentioning copper shields.

"bigger, heavier and higher-sided chariots".[34] Such chariots were undoubtedly sometimes also protected by metal reinforcements,[35] and this armour-plating must be what the term *taḫlīpu* refers to. The word itself is first used in the second millennium when the Tukulti-Ninurta epic says that the king entered battle *balum taḫlīpi* "without armour". Such armour is known archaeologically (e.g. Yadin 1965, 196–7), and a contemporary administrative document from Kar-Tukulti-Ninurta tells us that for his Kassite campaign a separate unit of donkeys was needed to transport the armour, designated with the foreign word *sariannu*.[36]

Like *taḫlīpu*, other words deriving from the D stem of *ḫalāpu* refer specifically to "armour". The term *taḫluptu*, which Sargon uses to refer to the armoured Urarṭian warriors,[37] is actually included in the garments section of ḪAR-*gud* (MSL 10, 140–1), and rightly translated "Panzerung" by AHw. The word for "armoured" is *ḫallupu*, though this has not always been recognized: in the eighth and seventh-century texts there is an item of clothing called the *šupalītu ḫalluptu,* which I translated as "reinforced ? lower-garment";[38] "armoured" would certainly have been better, and at this time both cavalry men and foot-soldiers are shown wearing a shirt or corslet of scale armour (Fig. 3). The feminine form *ḫalluptu* by itself can also mean "armour": in the definitive edition of Assur-naṣir-apli we read that the king took as booty from the ruler of Laqe on the Middle Euphrates "his chariots, his horses harnessed to the yoke, equipment for troops, equipment for horses", etc. (RIMA 2, 214: 22), and that from Bit-Zamani, the Diyarbakir region, he took as booty "fitted-out chariots, equipment for troops (and) horses, and 460 of his horses harnessed to the yoke" (ibid., 211: 120). The word translated "equipment" is *ḫallupti* (of ERÍN.MEŠ and ANŠE.KUR.RA.MEŠ) and we should in fact translate "armour for soldiers/horses". Indeed, Assyrian soldiers on foot and in chariots are shown wearing full-length coats of scale armour on the ninth-century reliefs and the Balawat Gates, and although Assyrian horses are not shown wearing body armour, this second-millennium practice obviously persisted elsewhere in the Near East, as we can see on a relief from Sakçagözü.[39] The Assyrian for "armourer(s)" is *ša ḫallupti-šu(nu)*: so already in the ninth century (see Deller and Millard 1993, 221 BM 367811 rev. 14, translating correctly "Hersteller von Panzern" with unduly diffident comment in the note on p. 231), and in the eighth/seventh century (SAA 7 115 rev. i 8). The only doubt is whether they are the manufacturers of the armour or ancillary personnel supplying and maintaining it.[40]

It therefore seems certain that the *taḫlīpi* chariots were those with armoured cars shown on the reliefs. Whether by the early seventh century either type was in general military use remains uncertain: the palace archives relate to the sector of the armed forces closest to the monarch (not, for instance, to the forces administered from the *ekal māšarti* at Nebi Yunus), and this can be expected to be the most traditional and ceremonial sector.

Indeed, on the basis of the reliefs it has been suggested by Duncan Noble that from the time of Sennacherib onwards chariots must have been purely ceremonial.[41] No relief of Sennacherib shows chariots in action and under Assur-ban-apli the sculptures only show them in use against the Arabs. There may be some truth in this, but in my view changes in the design of chariots[42] indicate that they cannot have been exclusively ceremonial white elephants — I do not suppose there have been any very significant design changes in the British monarch's coronation coach in recent years.

[34] Littauer and Crouwel 1979, 130.

[35] E.g. Barnett and Falkner 1962, Pl. LXXI (royal), Albenda 1986, Pls. 121, 123; such chequer-like patterns are also used to indicate reinforcements (probably metal) on the siege instruments (e.g. Yadin 1965, 422). On a Tiglath-pileser representation Madhloom 1969, 18 notes that "the design of concentric squares suggests actual plate armour as found in the excavations" (although the examples he cites from *Iraq* 20 (1958) Pl. XXXIV.3–4 are thought by Stronach to be from body armour). Outside Assyria see also Yadin 1965, 366, from Carchemish ("its sides are studded with metal disks").

[36] VS 19 1 rev. iv 43.

[37] TCL 3: 131, *qurādišu ša tahlupti.*

[38] SAA 7, xxix.

[39] Littauer and Crouwel 1979, Fig. 58.

[40] For the difficulty of establishing the precise meaning of this sort of Neo-Assyrian professional designation cf. Radner 1999, 125 (though I do not believe that "harness" is to be preferred to "armour").

[41] Noble 1990, 66–7; note Littauer and Crouwel 1979, 132: "Assyrian texts of the 8th and 7th centuries B.C. contribute little to this picture except to confirm the use of military chariots by Assyria and her enemies."

[42] See Littauer and Crouwel, 128; Madhloom 1970, 7–36.

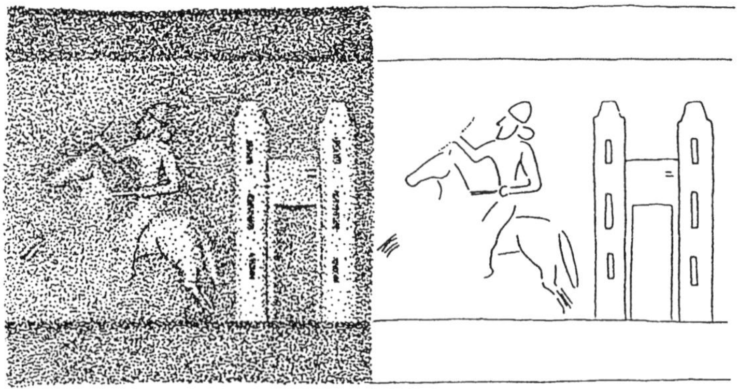

Fig. 2 Horseman, perhaps Ili-ipada. Impression on thirteenth-century tablet from Tell Sabi Abyad (Akkermans 1998, 253).

Alternative uses

There are perhaps indications that as they became less crucial as a fighting tool these traditional items were redeployed. A single chariot was less than effective in the front line, and using it as a mobile headquarters may well have made good sense. A late-ninth or early-eighth-century note from Tell Halaf[43] lists weapons which come in tens and imply a body of ten foot-soldiers,[44] but the list begins with a single chariot and this was doubtless intended for their commanding officer. It is noticeable that the "third riders" often function as agents or messengers,[45] and this may reflect the chariot's use as a communication centre. In some of the reliefs we see a single chariot at the back of the line-up, infantry and cavalry before them.[46] Thus it seems likely that at this time (in the late ninth/early eighth century) the commanding officer might, like the king, be distinguished by his chariot.[47]

Cavalry — innovation

The second millennium

As an arm of the military, cavalry does not figure in texts or images before the first millennium, but horse riders certainly had a role to play among the Hittites, Babylonians and Assyrians.[48] A cavalryman (*ša pe-et-ḫal-li*) turns up in the context of visiting dignitaries to the new Assyrian government in northern Syria in the thirteenth century;[49] and recently one of the contemporary Middle Assyrian administrative documents from Tell Sabi Abyad was found to have an impression of a remarkable seal (Fig. 2).[50] The rider here is holding a stick, a mace or some similar symbol of authority, and it has even been suggested that he may be the *sukkallu* himself. In any case, he is not in military mode.

Cavalry in first-millennium texts

By the first millennium the picture has changed. Tukulti-Ninurta II, in the early ninth century, is the first to mention cavalry in Assyria: "On the second day I ascended Mt Išrun after them on my own two feet, on the Mountain of Išrun one cannot cross either in my chariots or cavalry

[43] Tell Halaf 48.

[44] In my opinion this suggests that until the reign of Tiglath-pileser III the Assyrian army retained units of ten men like the Mitannian regime attested at Nuzi (an opinion shared by Mayer 1995, 425).

[45] So in, e.g., SAA 5 217 (=ABL 342) rev. 14 and s. 1; SAA 5 21 (=ABL 506) 7; SAA 5 33 (=ABL 705) 4′. The reference to a "shield *tašlišu*" in SAA 6 142 (=ADD 324) 4 cited by Cancik-Kirschbaum 1996, 136, may perhaps imply that only some of these "third riders" were still used as the defensive element in the chariot-crew (otherwise their connection with a shield would not have needed mention).

[46] E.g. Barnett 1976, Pl. XXXVI Slab 18, Pl. LXVII top left, Pl. LXIX.

[47] But later, perhaps, he abandoned the chariot in favour of a single horse: see below on the *rab kallāpi*.

[48] Mayer 1995, 456, cites BBSt 6 for cavalry in military use in Babylonia.

[49] Postgate 1988, No. 99.

[50] Akkermans 1998, 253 4 Fig. 10; my thanks go to Dr Akkermans for permission to reproduce the drawing. The seal is possibly of Ili-ipada himself, *sukkallu* of Hanigalbat.

(*pēthallu*)."[51] Assur-naṣir-apli, his son, mentions the cavalry alongside other sectors of the army: once he puts them into an ambush together with the kind of soldier called *kallāpu*,[52] and on other occasions he mentions that he took the cavalry and the *kallāpu* with him, e.g. on a march in the Shahrizur district of eastern Iraq.[53] One understands that chariotry might not be an ideal component of an ambush, and perhaps in the second case the terrain ruled out the use of chariots. In other cases the annals speak of the "strong chariotry and outstanding cavalry",[54] in each case in regions where there could have been flat terrain.[55] It is clear that the cavalry was by now a branch of the fighting troops, not confined to supplying messengers. The same applies to some of Assyria's enemies in the ninth century.[56]

Tiglath-pileser III's surviving inscriptions unfortunately give no detail. By the reign of Sargon it sounds as though the cavalry had taken over as the elite arm of the army. In the course of his eighth campaign Sargon sets off alone against the Urarṭian king, without waiting for his other troops, but "I fell upon him like a fierce javelin, with my solitary personal chariot, and the horses which go at my sides unceasingly in enemy or in friendly territory, the legion of Sin-aḫu-uṣur ..."[57] Since Sargon mentions that he was in the single chariot, and he would hardly have travelled surrounded by a group of unmounted horses, one must presume that these "horses" were cavalry, and indeed "one body of cavalry ... forms the core of the royal bodyguard from the reign of Sargon on."[58]

These statements by the annals, credible in any case since they represent a change from the earlier position rather than a rehearsal of conventional phrases, are confirmed by archival texts, including of course by NL 89 with its 97 horses and 343 cavalry men, as opposed to ten chariots and 106 chariot troops.

Cavalry on the reliefs

The hints of the texts are amply confirmed by the evidence of the reliefs. To judge from their dress and headgear, the cavalry were Assyrians like the chariotry, as we would expect in the light of NL 89. Careful observation of the reliefs has shown changes in the way the horses were used, which in part reflect the changing role of cavalry during the first millennium.[59] In the ninth century, under Assur-naṣir-apli, the horses are shown in pairs. The rider of one shoots his bow and has a shield slung on his back; the other rider holds the reins of both horses. The same arrangement is found under Shalmaneser (as shown on the Balawat Gates), except that the second man may have a spear or a shield in his spare hand.[60] Under Tiglath-pileser the reliefs show that the system had changed. The horses still come in pairs, but they are both ridden by identically equipped soldiers. These may wear quivers, indicating that they could use the bow, but usually charge, each holding a spear. As noted specifically by Noble, the riders' style has improved, with a secure seat well back on the animal and legs stretched out forwards.[61] On Sargon's reliefs cavalrymen still appear in pairs (e.g. Albenda 1986, Pl. 120), but also singly (ibid., Pl. 102). Finally by the seventh century the individual cavalryman has come of age. He is shown on the reliefs riding singly, but charging with a spear and, sometimes at least, still with a bow drawn (Fig. 3) or slung over the shoulder in its case.[62]

[51] RIMA 2, 173: 37–8.

[52] Ibid., 207: 70.

[53] Ibid., 246: 37; cf. 248: 88 and 207: 72 (both in Zamua).

[54] I note that in RIMA Grayson follows CAD A/ii 419 in translating *pēthallu šarissu* as "cavalry (and) crack troops". I prefer to see the two words as substantive plus adjective, in parallelism with the "strong (or big) chariots".

[55] RIMA 2, 246: 36–7 (same episode 205: 53, in the south-east, beyond the Diyala), 210: 103 (same episode 260: 70, in Tušḫan region, near Diyarbakir).

[56] Cf. Dalley 1985, 37–8, for the numbers of chariotry and cavalry mentioned in annals.

[57] TCL 3: 131. The word *pirru* goes back to the Middle Assyrian army, and refers to the enrolment of troops under different officers. I choose "legion" as a rendering since my English dictionary tells me that in Latin the word *legio* relates to *legere* "to levy".

[58] Reade 1972, 103, with reference to Botta and Flandin, *Monument de Ninive* 142 (see also Albenda 1986, Pl. 134; Gadd 1936, Pl. 13 opp. p. 60). Compare Herodotus's description of Xerxes' line of march, "... the king, who was immediately preceded by a thousand horsemen, the finest Persia could provide, behind whom marched a thousand picked spearmen ..." (vii 40; de Sélincourt 1954, 431). Cf. also Kinnier Wilson 1972, referring to Alexander's Immortals, and note that the Alexander mosaic reflects the same arrangement of the royal chariot surrounded by cavalry (e.g. Roaf 1990, 216–17).

[59] See Reade 1972, 103; Noble 1990; Littauer and Crouwel 1979, 134–7.

[60] Reade 1972, 103; Yadin 1965, 402–3.

[61] Noble 1992, 65.

[62] E.g. Yadin 1965, 458–9 (Assur-ban-apli).

Fig. 3 Cavalryman with armoured corslet, reign of Assur-ban-apli (Barnett *et al.* 1998, No. 328 b, Pl. 294; photograph courtesy of the Trustees of the British Museum, WA 124801 b).

I think it has rightly been said that the reliefs demonstrate that the traditional chariot crew, with its differentiated fighter and horse-controller, was transplanted from the chariot to horseback. If the cavalry evolved from the chariotry in this way, it is no surprise that the grooms who attended to the horses for the chariotry were also an essential component of the cavalry, and if indeed Parpola is right that these were the *susānu*, then the anomaly of the logographic writing with its apparent meaning of "chariot-man" is illusory and is merely an accident (see note on l. 15 above).[63]

The infantry — auxiliaries

The Ituaeans and other Aramaeans

Both the historical texts and the palace reliefs indicate that a variety of foot-soldiers served with the Assyrian forces. While some are described by their characteristic weapons or equipment,[64] many groups have ethnic designations. Of these the best attested textually are the Ituaeans, listed in NL 89 after the Qurraeans, on whom see the next section. The Ituaeans, in particular, were an essential component of the forces at the disposal of the Assyrian kings and their governors

[63] A *susānu* is no doubt shown in action in Budge 1914, Pl. XVI.1, rubbing the horse down.

[64] For troops designated by their weapon, cf. for instance SAA 11 127 (and 128): 350 shields (^{giš}*a-rit*), 240 bows (GIŠ.BAN); also ABL 1009 (see fn. 13).

throughout the empire.[65] They are not often, if ever, mentioned in the campaign accounts of which official royal annals are composed, but they are here in Mat-Zamua, and we know from other correspondence that Tiglath-pileser III used them in the late eighth century to sort out recalcitrant Phoenicians on the Lebanese hills (e.g. NL 12: Postgate 1974, 390–3). This and other mentions in letters and documents show that they were full-time professional soldiers. They are not found in association with horses, and NL 89 itself strongly suggests that they were foot-soldiers. Hence in NL 86: 13–14 ([*p*]*ét-ḫal-lum* LÚ *i-tú-u' i-si-šú-nu pi-qid*) we must understand "appoint cavalry (and) Ituaeans to be with them" (Saggs 1966, 181). There is no evidence that they were mercenaries serving in return for payment, but in one case it appears that an Ituaean was remunerated by the allocation of land, known as his "bow-field" in a formula familiar later in Babylonia.[66] This suggests that they were primarily archers. Whatever the terms of their service, it is clear that in the late eighth and seventh centuries they were an integral part of the imperial army, along with other ethnic groups.[67]

When did this first happen? The origins of (at least some of) the Ituaeans are known: they were a semi-sedentary tribe on the middle Tigris, around Samarra, in the early ninth century when Assur-naṣir-apli's father, Tukulti-Ninurta II, marched to Dur-Kurigalzu. At that time they obviously retained a degree of independence. Sheikhs of the Ituaeans are mentioned as late as Sargon, and of course it has often been observed that tribal members not engaged in sedentary farming practices would have been better able to enrol as year-round fighters than the peasants further north. It has been tempting to guess that the exploitation of the Ituaeans and other such groups may have been an innovation of Tiglath-pileser III, who was responsible for the definitive imposition of Assyrian military supremacy in the mid-eighth century. Just recently, though, we have acquired a little scrap of evidence that Ituaeans were already serving with the Assyrian army before Tiglath-pileser: two small cuneiform tablets were excavated at the site of Tell Baqqaq on the east bank of the Tigris north of Nineveh by an Iraqi expedition.[68] One, listing helmets, swords, bows, arrows and quivers, is dated to the reign of Shalmaneser III (eponym Iahalu: 833 or 824 or 821 BC). The other, which is likely to belong with it, records an issue to the Utu'aya, using the older form of the name. These two notes would indicate that the Ituaeans already formed part of an Assyrian garrison or expedition on the northern fringes of Assyria in the ninth century.

This is perhaps supported by evidence that another Aramaean group entered the service of the Assyrian army as early as the reign of Assur-naṣir-apli. The initial clue comes from another tablet from the North-West Palace, ND 2646.[69] It is unfortunately badly damaged but would in its intact state have been an extremely valuable document. On one side it lists numbers of troops, beginning with [(x+)]123 Ruqahaeans, 136 Hallataeans, [(x+)]359 Habinu and 33 Hamataeans. The territory of the Ruqahaeans is listed along with that of the Ituaeans among the lands under the governor of Assur province in the late ninth and eighth centuries, and was thus no doubt on the Tigris between Assur and Babylonia. The Hallataeans are another group from the lower reaches of the Tigris; both are known from ABL 94=SAA 1 91 to have served as "king's troops".[70] Here, though, it is the 359 men designated "Habinu" who interest us. This seems to be a group named after an individual called Habinu (his name is duly provided with the "Personenkeil"), but quite as large as other ethnically designated groups. Another tablet from the same context, ND 2619, mentions numbers of Aramaean troops, including "117 people of Habinu in Naṣibina", again with the "Personenkeil" preceding the name.[71] It cannot be a coincidence that one of the military administration tablets from Tell Halaf listing iron and copper helmets, ten daggers, 700 arrows, five bows and a quiver, concludes tersely with the single name Habinu.[72] The contexts suggest

[65] See in general Postgate 1977.

[66] See Postgate 1974, 263 ABL 201: 6, "Let the Ituaean be exempt. His bow-field is exempt from (taxes on) straw and barley." For the "bow-fiefs" in Achaemenid Babylonia see Stolper 1985, 25: "Types of fiefs were more specifically named for the type of soldiery they were intended to support. The chief terms were 'bow land' (*bit qašti*), 'horse land' ... and 'chariot land'."

[67] See Cooper 1988; I am grateful to Dr Cooper for allowing me to consult her thesis, which offers a much more substantial study of the role of Aramaean auxiliaries in Assyria than can be undertaken here.

[68] Ismail 1989.

[69] Parker 1961, 40–1, Pl. XXI.

[70] Obv. 13–rev. 2: *ina muḫḫi ša kutal ṣāb šarri ša* KUR *ru-qa-ḫa-a-a ša* KUR *ḫal-lat-a-a*.

[71] Parker 1961, 38 and Pl. XIX, ND 2619 rev. 21–2: 1 ME 17 ZI *ša ḫa-*[*bi-*]*ni* / *ina* uru *na-ṣib-na*.

[72] Tell Halaf 49, reign of Adad-nirari III.

Fig. 4 Aramaean auxiliary archer (after Albenda 1986, Pl. 98; drawing E. A. Postgate)

that this must have been a tribal group, similar to the other Aramaean auxiliaries but referred to by a personal name, and I think we can probably identify its origin. In the ninth century Assur-naṣir-apli tells us that he took the chariots, cavalrymen and foot-soldiers (*kallāpu,* see below) of Ahuni with him (presumably incorporating them into his forces),[73] but he also says, "At that time I received the tribute of Ahuni of the land of Adini, and of Habinu of the city of Til-Abna."[74] It seems a fair guess that at the same time he incorporated a group of auxiliaries from Til-Abna as well, a group which survived bearing the name of their original leader in the service of the Assyrian kings for over 150 years into the reign of Sargon, if not longer. It is easy to see that a close-knit tribal group like this, with an *esprit de corps* and professional pride, could soon become extremely important to the military establishment. Whether they would consider themselves Assyrian subjects, or an independent body voluntarily serving with the imperial army, is not clear. While Assur-naṣir-apli says more than once that he "took along with him" troops from conquered states, we have never been able to see how fully they were integrated into the army.

Aramaean auxiliaries on the reliefs

If we look on the reliefs for groups of infantry differentiated from the Assyrians proper, they are not hard to find. The situation is described succinctly by Reade: while Assyrian foot-soldiers also exist (see below), some of them archers, they are identifiable by their pointed helmets. By contrast a good many of the archers share identifying features of shorter hair, held in place by a headband, and a skirt cut well above the knee. Some are already seen in Assur-naṣir-apli's reliefs, but they feature regularly from Tiglath-pileser on (Fig. 4). They are not all the same: there are variations in their kit and some, especially later, look more assimilated to Assyrian fashions.[75] That some of them are Aramaeans is suggested by the similar, even identical, appearance of enemies in some of the Assyrian campaigns.[76] It is particularly striking that the patterns on their dress reappear in the reigns of Tiglath-pileser III and Sargon and in the seventh century, confirming

[73] This immediately poses the question of whether the various bodies of troops of Bit-Adini listed in ND 2619 also owe their origins to Assur-naṣir-apli's Syrian campaigns. However, there is a problem in that Bit-Adini in southern Babylonia was also the victim of the attentions of the Assyrians under Shalmaneser V and Sennacherib (see Brinkman 1968, 244 with fn. 1567).

[74] RIMA 2, 216 iii 55 ff.; also ibid., p. 217 iii 63–4, "At that time the tribute of Habini of Til-Abna — four minas silver, 400 sheep — I received from him, and ten minas silver I imposed on him as yearly tribute."

[75] Reade 1972, 104–5.

[76] The evidence cited for this by Reade ("especially along the Euphrates and in Babylonia") is Budge 1914, Pl. XIII (archers with beards, long hair and hairbands widening over the forehead; still the fashion in the seventh century, cf. Barnett 1976, Pl. XXXIV.c and (rather less convincingly) King 1915, Pl. LXV (Band XI.6).

Fig. 5 Auxiliary spearman (after Albenda 1986, Pl. 96; drawing E. A. Postgate).

that these are not random rabbles recruited *ad hoc*, but a stable and well-recognized component of the fighting force.[77]

The Qurraeans

In NL 89 the 440 Ituaeans are listed after 360 Qurraeans (see above on l. 22 for the name). These two ethnic groups are encountered elsewhere listed side by side, often in approximately equal numbers,[78] and it is plain that they must have each fulfilled a differing but complementary function. If the Ituaeans are the auxiliary archers par excellence, then the other group can hardly have been other than the auxiliary spearmen, as already hinted by Reade.[79] These are seen on the reliefs alongside the auxiliary archers, identifiable by their round shields, crested helmets and crossed chest-straps (Fig. 5).[80] They first appear under Tiglath-pileser III and remain instantly recognizable through the reign of Sargon down to Assur-ban-apli in the seventh century. The Qurraeans are also attested in the texts until at least the reign of Esarhaddon. As we have seen (above on l. 22), their name does not help us to fix their geographical origins, but the reliefs offer some help. The Anatolian affinities of their helmet crests are documented by Barnett and Falkner 1962, xix–xx, who also compare the discs with crossed straps with a disc shown on an Urarṭian bronze figurine from Toprakkale, which might also suggest a northern origin for this type of equipment.[81] From their dress they are plainly not Assyrian units nor Aramaeans, but they are not likely to have originated from a single place. Reade has pointed out that in the eighth century there is variety in the helmet crests shown, and that certain foreign features, such as boots with up-turned toes, disappear later (no doubt assimilating to normal Assyrian fashion). Perhaps more than one ethnic group contributed to the auxiliary spearmen, and Reade suggests that some may have been enrolled from Carchemish after its defeat in 716 BC, wearing what Barnett and Falkner 1962, xx, refer to as "the N. Syrian-Hittite type of helmet as illustrated at Carchemish, with angular ridge and crest". It seems entirely plausible that such soldiers were recruited from more than one source along the northern and western frontiers, but I am unable to identify any other obvious candidates for non-Aramaean auxiliaries in the textual evidence. Perhaps this does not matter: if the Qurraeans and the Ituaeans were the largest contingents of auxiliary spearmen and

[77] I discuss Assyrian military dress in an article in a forthcoming volume edited by W. van Soldt.

[78] E.g. ABL 685 rev. 22 (50 Ituaeans and 30 Qurraeans); ABL 388 (50 Qurraeans and 50 Ituaeans); ABL 883 (10 Qurraeans and 20 Ituaeans; rev. 7 [collated] has a clear figure 10 at the beginning of the line).

[79] Reade 1972, 106.

[80] Reade 1972, 105–6.

[81] Barnett 1954, Pl. II.2: to judge from the inadequate photograph the figure has a crested helmet as well as a disc, but straps are not shown. A northern origin is already advocated in Billerbeck and Delitzsch 1908, 99 fn. 2; cf., for example, the crested helmets of the Urarṭian captives on the Shalmaneser Balawat gates, Billerbeck and Delitzsch 1908, Pl. I B.u.6.

archers respectively, maybe each term could be used to include their less numerous colleagues in general parlance, and should be understood as "Qurraeans *et al.*" or "Ituaeans and the other Aramaean auxiliaries".

The infantry — Assyrians

What does seem clear is that these spearmen with crossed straps are not *Assyrian* foot-soldiers. On the reliefs the Assyrians are marked out by their pointed helmets and properly curled and trimmed beards. Archers are shown in groups, or singly with each archer accompanied by a shield-bearer. Other Assyrians carry a short sword (or dagger), shield and usually also a spear. This component of the fighting force is identifiable on the reliefs from at least Shalmaneser to Assur-ban-apli.

However Assyrian foot-soldiers are not so readily identified in the texts. Rather surprisingly, we are still unsure of the everyday Neo-Assyrian word for infantry. The literal phrase "foot-soldier" (LÚ.ERÍN.MEŠ GÌR.2.MEŠ) is found once, in SAA 5 88 (=ABL 380): 4, where three thousand of them are mentioned, but it is probably not coincidental that the writer is referring here to an Urarṭian army. There is also the word *zūku*, which is rendered in AHw as "Infanterie". It has no transparent etymology and is not attested before the first millennium BC. We first meet it in Assur-naṣir-apli passages in the sequence chariots–cavalry–*zūku*, and it is also used in the Synchronistic History after chariots (the absence of cavalry may reflect the fact that the battle described is in the second millennium). In eighth and seventh-century royal annals (Tiglath-pileser, Sargon, Sennacherib) the phrase used is *zūk šēpē*, but this combination has not appeared in the archival texts, and we are left uncertain whether the phrase is merely pleonastic — "foot infantry" — or *zūku* has a wider meaning. There are two occurrences of *zūku* by itself; each is suggestive but neither is decisive. In SAA 1 11 = ABL 304, a letter from Sargon to Mannu-ki-Adad, we read:

> 1,119 LÚ.ERÍN.MEŠ KALAG.MEŠ ... *ana* LÚ *zu-ku ša* É.GAL *tadnū kī piqitti ina pānī-ka paqdū atta atâ tanašši annûti ana* [lú]*raksūti annûti ana* LÚ.A.SIG.MEŠ *annûti ana* [anše]*ša pētḫallāti ana kiṣri ša ramini-ka tutâr-šunu*
>
> 1,119 grown troops ... were given for *zūku* of the palace and entrusted to your care as a responsibility. (So) why are you taking and redeploying them to your own contingent, some as recruits, some as chariot-men, some as cavalry?

Unfortunately, although some of these troops were actually being assigned to serve with chariotry and cavalry, this does not necessarily mean they were not infantry, since using them for a purpose other than "*zūku* of the palace" may itself have been part of Mannu-ki-Adad's misdemeanour.

The other occurrence of *zūku* in the Neo-Assyrian correspondence is equally difficult to interpret. This is CT 53 150 (cited below), where LÚ *zu-ku* are mentioned after four different groups of *kallāpu*. It is not clear from the context whether the *zūku* include the *kallāpu* or form a separate group, but it does direct our attention towards this class of soldier. For in NL 89 we have not yet identified any foot-soldiers within the Assyrian section, and the only substantial body of troops not yet accounted for there are the eighty *kallāpu*. This alone is enough to suggest that we might have here the missing word for the Neo-Assyrian infantry. In Assyriological literature the *kallāpu* have had a chequered career (see above *ad* l. 20). More recently AHw followed Weidner and rendered "courier", the SAA series offers "outrider"[82] and "mounted scout",[83] and Dalley "dispatch riders".[84] On the other hand, CAD K 77 offers "member of the light troops", and Malbran-Labat "une sorte d'infanterie légère" (1982, 82–3). An identification as infantry is therefore controversial and requires a review of the evidence.

The word is so far unknown before the first millennium. In the ninth century Assur-naṣir-apli mentions them twice in the same context as the cavalry — that is to say, in an ambush and over rough terrain.[85] Sargon's letter to Assur concludes with a formulaic statement of casualties,

[82] SAA 1 5.

[83] SAA 4.

[84] See Dalley and Postgate 1984, 229; also p. 34 with mention of my own opinion in a footnote.

[85] RIMA 2, 207 ii 70, 72; in each case without chariots. Elsewhere in his annals where the regular sequence (chariotry–cavalry–infantry) is used, the third component of the army is called *zūku* (ibid., 216: 58, 60, 63 etc.).

perhaps the earliest known censored military press-briefing: "One charioteer, two cavalrymen and three *kallāpu* were killed."[86] Note that this follows the same order as the Zamua review in NL 89 (chariots–cavalry–*kallāpu*), and that they do not bother to mention non-Assyrians. At the beginning of Sargon's campaign we read: "I took the head of my host, I had the chariotry and the cavalry, the battle troops who go at my side, fly over the mountain like heroic eagles, and I made the plebeian troops, the *kallāpu*, take up their rear."[87] The phrase for plebeian troops is *ṣāb ḫupši*, which is applied again to the *kallāpu* by Sargon in l. 258. It does not belong in the current vernacular but goes back to the world of the Bronze Age, when we know that a person's social status determined the arm of the army in which he fought. There is nothing here which proves that *kallāpu* were mounted or foot-soldiers: that they are mentioned directly after the cavalry could be *either* because they are also cavalry, of a different sort, *or* because they are not.

To my mind, the decisive evidence is provided by ND 2646, another North-West-Palace text from the reign of Sargon, which we have already mentioned when discussing the Aramaean auxiliaries. On the reverse we read, "in total they took 2,079 *kallāpu*." It seems improbable that there would be over two thousand messengers or sappers, and hence probable that without qualification the word must refer to a body of "infantry" included within the Assyrian sector of the army. That there were different groups of *kallāpu* is clear from CT 53 150: 5′–11′, where four are listed: *kallāp qurbu*, *kallāp ma-'*A*-x*, *kallāp* ^{uru}*ár-*[*x*], *kallāp ša* É.[GAL]. At least three of these categories bear comparison with the divisions of the other Assyrian sectors: chariotry and cavalry may be *qurbu* "close (to the king)", "of the palace", and indeed in some cases "of Arbil" or "Arrapha".[88] No doubt the *kallāpu qurbu* did fight near the king, and they are perhaps the forerunners of the Ten Thousand Immortals who accompanied the Persian monarch.[89]

Why, then, is the opinion that the *kallāpu* were mounted couriers so widespread? It derives from the occurrence of the term in two combinations, *kallāp šipirti* and *rab kallāpi*.[90] Since *šipirtu* means a "written message", the former of these was undoubtedly a "messenger", in the sense of a person who carried the message (as opposed to a *mār šipri* who was much more of an "envoy" with powers to represent and negotiate). In this role it is obviously possible, but not certain, that the individual *kallāpu* could have been mounted. As for the "commander", there is indeed one tablet from Fort Shalmaneser in which 32 horse teams are assigned to *rab kallāpi* officers.[91] This may appear to be proof that they were cavalry or perhaps even chariotry, but appearances can be deceptive. We have already seen a single chariot with a group of foot-soldiers at Tell Halaf, and there is nothing implausible in having a mounted cavalry officer assigned to an infantry corps. Indeed, Yadin has already called attention to one scene in which a contingent of Assyrian foot-soldiers seems to be under the command of a mounted Assyrian officer (Fig. 6).[92]

To sum up, the *kallāpu* are a regular component of the Assyrian sector of the army and they occur in too great numbers to be specialists like engineeers or messengers. Against the idea that they were "mounted as light, mobile and versatile troops" (Dalley and Postgate 1984, 34), is the absence of any such distinct body of troops identifiable on the reliefs. If the foot-soldiers who appear on the reliefs as a regular component of the Assyrian sector are not *kallāpu* we have no other term for them. It seems better to identify *kallāpu* with the class of troops who did exist than with a class which is not visible.

[86] TCL 3: 426; that this was a formalized topos is plain from the incomplete draft for Esarhaddon's letter to Assur, which has the identical report on casualties (Borger 1956, 107: 25). Note also that the sequence chariotry–cavalry–*kallāpu* here is paralleled in Sargon's annals where the same three classes of fighter from Carchemish are described as chariotry–cavalry–*zūk šēpē*.

[87] TCL 3: 25–6.

[88] See Dalley and Postgate 1984, 36–7. For the third group the CT 53 copy suggests *ma-'a-da* "much" but although this is initially the most obvious restoration it makes little sense. Collation does not favour a form of *ma'assu*, but does suggest that the final sign could rather be read *ba*, which would oblige us to assume we have here a body of infantry recruited from Moab, historically not impossible.

[89] See also LÚ *kal-la-pu qur-b*[*u* in ADD 855: 9 (=SAA 11 126, cf. Dalley and Postgate 1984, 43–4; in the light of CT 53 150 there is no call to restore *-te* after *qur-bu* here).

[90] For *rab kallāpi* see Deller and Fadhil 1993, 253 No. 9 rev. 5′ (790 BC) and 263 No. 19 rev. 8 (788 BC) wr. GAL *kal-la-bi*, and the approximately contemporary tablet ibid., 264 No. 20 rev. 3 and 5, wr. GAL *kal-la-pi*. The plural of this title is evidently *rab kallāpāni*.

[91] CTN 3 No. 112 rev. 10–11: PAB 32 *ú-ru-ú* [LÚ.]GAL *kal-la-pa-n*[*i*]. This follows fifteen personal names, suggesting they had a team of two animals each.

[92] Yadin 1965, 458; Barnett 1976, Pl. XXXIV, cf. also Pl. LXVIII, lowest register on left.

Fig. 6 Infantry being directed by a mounted officer, perhaps a *rab kallāpi* (Assur-ban-apli; AO 19912, photograph by kind permission of Mme A. Caubet, Musée du Louvre; copyright Photo RMN).

The king's troops

NL 89, 23 shows that the term *ṣāb šarri* "king's troops" embraced both Assyrians and auxiliaries. It is known from other contemporary letters that some of the king's troops were performing their *ilku* service, and these were presumably Assyrians.[93] Nothing is known of how the obligation to perform *ilku* service was assessed, who precisely was liable and the length of time served. Only some of the people recruited under the *ilku* system ended up in the army: others were assigned to public works. The *ilku* system undoubtedly has its roots in the second millennium, and the term *ṣāb šarri* has now turned up in two thirteenth-century administrative documents.[94] This is not the place to discuss the Middle Assyrian system in detail, but it appears likely that the men so conscripted were assigned at the enrolment process (*pirru*) to the command of one of a number of high officials, including the king himself, and their names listed on the writing-board (*lē'u*) of that official. As an echo of that practice, Neo-Assyrian sealings, almost certainly from writing boards, and found in the Review Palace at Kalḫu, state "reviewed king's troops" (ÉRIN.MEŠ MAN *ašrūte*) and specify their commanding officer (CTN 3 Nos. 21–2; one is a *šaknu*). It seems clear that not all of the "king's troops" were recruited through the same procedures. SAA 5 251, quoted above, shows that the ordinary "king's troops" could be differentiated from "chariot-owners", who were perhaps, in view of their chariot-owning status, more permanently part of the military establishment. Similarly, it is probable that the auxiliaries, Aramaeans and others, served more continuously with the army. In any case, it is plain from NL 89 that the essential standing forces at the disposal of the provincial governors were collectively known as the "king's troops".

Other categorizations

Having considered in some detail the terminology of Adad-issiya's letter we should conclude by noting some of the categories he does not mention. Although he distinguishes chariotry, cavalry and infantry, he does not identify his soldiers by their characteristic weapons. Such categories, like "archers", "shield-bearers", "slingers" and "lancers", are used both in the royal annals and

[93] See Postgate 1974, 218–24 for a discussion of the term.

[94] Both from Kar-Tukulti-Ninurta: VS 21 1 vii 26, where a list of more than fifty men is summarized baldly as ERÍN.MEŠ LUGAL; and Postgate 1979, MAH 16086, which lists military garments including *kusi'ātu ša ṣāb šarri* (TÚG.BAR.DUL.MEŠ *ša* ERÍN.MEŠ LUGAL).

in other letters,[95] but apparently this information was not needed on this occasion. Nor does he make any mention of the hierarchical structure of the army. We would expect from other sources that the different sectors would have been divided into "cohorts" (*kiṣru*) under the command of a *rab kiṣri*, and that above them there were also "captains" (*šaknu*). However, we still do not know how many men (and horses) made up a cohort, and the relationship between the *rab kiṣri* and the "chief of fifty" (*rab ḫanšē*) has not to my knowledge been convincingly explained.

If we choose to view the "king's troops" as the standing army of the Assyrian empire, which appears reasonable, we have to differentiate them from the "royal cohort". This is referred to in the annals as the *kiṣir šarrūti*. Manitius, who gives an excellent account of it on the basis of the annalistic texts, considered it to be effectively a contingent which stood permanently under the king's direct command, a "stehende Königsschar".[96] This still seems to be a valid conclusion but there are questions still to be resolved. Was, for instance, the "legion of Sin-aḫu-uṣur" (see above and fn. 57) a part of the "royal cohort" or separate from it? In this context, we may note that in the thirteenth century the king was only one of a number of high officials on whose "boards" conscripted men were enrolled (see p. 106 above). Further, there is the "new cohort" of Sennacherib, whose relationship to the royal cohort needs to be determined.[97] Finally, we should note that the Zamua roll-call does not identify any separate "foreign" or "provincial" units, like the Samarian or Arzuhina units mentioned in the Sargon lists from Fort Shalmaneser. Such units were certainly included in the royal cohort, as the annals and the archival texts make clear,[98] and could also have been present in the provinces. In Adad-issiya's letter they would not be subsumed under the auxiliaries, but it is conceivable that some at least may have been present as "Assyrians".[99]

Bibliography

Akkermans, P. M. M. G. 1998. "Seals and seal impressions from Middle Assyrian Tell Sabi Abyad, Syria", *Subartu* IV/1, 243–58.

Albenda, P. 1986. *The Palace of Sargon, King of Assyria* (Paris).

Barnett, R. D. 1976. *Sculptures from the North Palace of Ashurbanipal at Nineveh (668–672 BC)* (London).

Barnett, R. D. and M. Falkner 1962. *The Sculptures of Aššur-naṣir-apli II (883–859 BC) Tiglath-Pileser III (745–727 BC) Esarhaddon (681–669 BC) from the Central and South-West Palaces at Nimrud* (London).

Barnett, R. D. *et al.* 1998. R. D. Barnett, E. Bleibtreu and G. Turner, *Sculptures from the Southwest Palace of Sennacherib at Nineveh* (London: British Museum Press).

Billerbeck, A. and F. Delitzsch 1908. *Die Palasttore Salmanassars II von Balawat* (Beiträge zur Assyriologie 6/i).

Borger, R. 1956. *Die Inschriften Asarhaddons Königs von Assyrien* (Graz: AfO Beiheft 9).

Brinkman, J. A. 1968. *A Political History of Post-Kassite Babylonia 1158–722 BC* (Rome: Analecta Orientalia 43).

Budge, E. A. W. 1914. *Assyrian Sculptures in the British Museum. Reign of Ashur-nasir-pal, 885–860 BC* (London).

Cancik-Kirschbaum, E. C. 1996. *Die mittelassyrischen Briefe aus Tall Šēḫ Ḥamad* (Berichte der Ausgrabung Tall Šēḫ Ḥamad/Dūr-Katlimmu 4).

Cole, S. W. 1996. *The Early Neo-Babylonian Governor's Archive from Nippur* (Chicago: OIP 114).

Cooper, E. N. 1988. "The Organization of the Neo-Assyrian Army: The Presence of Aramaean Soldiers in the Assyrian Forces" (University of Cambridge, M.Phil. dissertation).

Dalley, S. 1985. "Foreign chariotry and cavalry in the armies of Tiglath-Pileser III and Sargon II", *Iraq* 47, 31–48.

Dalley, S. and J. N. Postgate 1984. *The Tablets from Fort Shalmaneser* (London: CTN 3).

Davies, G. I. 1989. "*'urwōt* in I Kings 5:6 (EVV. 4:26) and the Assyrian horse lists", JSS 34, 25–38.

Deller, K. 1958. Review of A. Salonen, *Hippologica Akkadica* in Or NS 27, 311–14.

Deller, K. and A. R. Millard 1993. "Die Bestallungsurkunde des Nergal-āpil-kūmūja von Kalḫu", *Baghdader Mitteilungen* 24, 217–42.

Finkelstein, J. J. 1953. "Cuneiform texts from Tell Billa", JCS 7, 111–76.

Fuchs, A. 1998. *Die Annalen des Jahres 711 v. Chr.* (Helsinki: State Archives of Assyria Studies 8).

95 See Manitius 1910, 125 ff.; above, fn. 64.

96 Manitius 1910, 114 ff. Doubt as to its identity with *kiṣir šarri* in legal documents is expressed in my contribution to the proceedings of a conference in Copenhagen in May 1999 (edited by M. T. Larsen).

97 Cf. Dalley and Postgate 1984, 41.

98 See Dalley 1985.

99 The author wishes to thank both the editors for important corrections.

Gadd, C. J. 1936. *The Stones of Assyria* (London).
Haas, V. and H. J. Thiel 1978. *Die Beschwörungsrituale der Allaituraḫ(ḫ)i und verwandte Texte* (AOAT 31).
Ismail, B. K. 1989. "Two Neo-Assyrian tablets", SAAB 3/ii, 61–4.
Kinnier Wilson, J. V. 1972. *The Nimrud Wine Lists* (London: CTN 1).
Lie, A. G. 1929. *The Inscriptions of Sargon II King of Assyria* (Paris).
Littauer, M. A. and J. H. Crouwel 1979. *Wheeled Vehicles and Ridden Animals in the Ancient Near East* (Leiden: E. J. Brill).
MacGinnis, J. D. A. 1989. "Some inscribed horse troughs of Sennacherib", *Iraq* 51, 187–92.
Madhloom, T. A. 1969. *The Chronology of Neo-Assyrian Art* (London: Athlone Press).
Malbran-Labat, F. 1982. *L'armée et l'organisation militaire de l'Assyrie* (Geneva/Paris).
Manitius, W. 1910. "Das stehende Heer der Assyrerkönige und seine Organisation", ZA 24, 97–149, 185–224.
Mayer, W. 1995. *Politik und Kriegskunst der Assyrer* (Münster: Abhandlungen zur Literatur Alt-Syrien-Palästinas und Mesopotamiens 9).
Noble, D. 1990. "Assyrian chariotry and cavalry", SAAB 4/i, 61–8.
Parker, B. 1961. "Administrative tablets from the North-West Palace, Nimrud", *Iraq* 23, 15–67.
Parpola, S. 1970. *Neo-Assyrian Toponyms* (AOAT 6).
Parpola, S. 1976. Review of J. V. Kinnier Wilson, *The Nimrud Wine Lists*, in JSS 21, 165–74.
Pedersén, O. 1985. *Archives and Libraries in the City of Assur*, 2 vols. (Uppsala).
Postgate, J. N. 1974. *Taxation and Conscription in the Assyrian Empire* (Rome: Studia Pohl sm 3).
Postgate, J. N. 1977. "Itu' ", *Reallexikon der Assyriologie* 5, 221–2.
Postgate, J. N. 1979. "Assyrian documents in the Musée d'Art et d'Histoire, Geneva", *Assur* 2/iv (Malibu: UNDENA Publications).
Postgate, J. N. 1988. "Middle Assyrian texts (Nos. 99–101)", in I. Spar (ed.), *Cuneiform Texts in the Metropolitan Museum of Art* I (New York), 144–8.
Postgate, J. N. 1990. "The Assyrian Porsche?", SAAB 4/i, 35–8.
Pritchard, J. B. 1969. *Ancient Near Eastern Texts Relating to the Old Testament*, 3rd edn (Princeton).
Radner, K. 1999. "Traders in the Neo-Assyrian period", in J. G. Dercksen (ed.), *Trade and Finance in Ancient Mesopotamia* (Leiden: Nederlands Historisch-Archaeologisch Instituut te Istanbul), 101–26.
Reade, J. E. 1972. "The Neo-Assyrian court and army: evidence from the sculptures", *Iraq* 34, 87–112.
Roaf, M. D. 1990. *Cultural Atlas of Mesopotamia and the Ancient Near East* (Oxford).
Saggs, H. W. F. 1963. "Assyrian warfare in the Sargonid period", *Iraq* 25, 145–54.
Saggs, H. W. F. 1966. "The Nimrud letters, 1952—Part VIII", *Iraq* 28, 177–91.
de Sélincourt, A. 1954. *Herodotus: The Histories* (Harmondsworth: Penguin Books).
Starke, F. 1995. *Ausbildung und Training von Streitwagenpferden. Eine hippologisch orientierte Interpretation des Kikkuli-Textes* (Wiesbaden: Studien zu den Boğazköy-Texten 41).
Stolper, M. W. 1985. *Entrepreneurs and Empire. The Murašû Archive, the Murašû Firm, and Persian Rule in Babylonia* (Leiden).
Tadmor, H. 1994. *The Inscriptions of Tiglathpileser III King of Assyria* (Jerusalem).
Wilcke, C. 1976. "Assyrische Testamente", ZA 66, 196–233.
Yadin, Y. 1965. *The Art of Warfare in the Ancient Near East* (London).

ASSYRIAN FELT

J.N. POSTGATE

In Helmut Freydank and Claudio Saporetti's edition of the Bābu-aha-iddina archive, the tablet VAT 8863 is given in transliteration, in advance of the hand-copy published as WVDOG 92 no. 64. The tablet is a letter from the great man himself to his administrators at Assur, and like many of his letters it gives instructions on a variety of matters. The first matter dealt with in this letter is the manufacture of boots (*šuhuppātu*), and ll. 5-19 may be translated as follows:

> «Instruct Ilu-ki-abiya the leather-worker as follows: "Hurry and make one pair of boots in the Assyrian mode, and one pair of boots in the Katmuhaean mode". Read the tablet out before him and appoint witnesses to his words. If he says to you "There is no *taḫapšu* for the boots in the Assyrian mode», take *taḫapšu* from the department of the Chief *sāpiu* (GAL *sa-pi-e*). Take madder (for?) skins, ..., ... give (it) to him, so that he can make (them) quickly.»

The association of the *rab sāpê* with *taḫapšu* is attested also in WVDOG 92 No. 59. Here a certain Amurru-šuma-uṣur, with this title, issues:

2 PA.MEŠ *ša ta-ḫap-še* 18 MA.NA *ana* KI.LÁ
   «2 poles(?) of *taḫapšu* weighing 18 minas,
ša ina libbi SÍG.MEŠ *ša pitti* GAL.MEŠ ASGAB.MEŠ *sa-ri-a-ni*
   which (come) out of the wool of the department of the Chief Armour-Leather-workers .....
ana ^{giš}*ša šadādi ša šarri*
   for the royal sedan chair».

Here again *taḫapšu* is associated with leather-workers, but there is a strong suggestion that it is a woollen product. Dr. Freydank has already observed the association of the *rab sāpê* with a variety of materials. He refers to Deller's rendering «Abdecker», which reflects the association with animal skins (AfO 34 (1987) 62f.), and comments himself that the *sāpi'u* «dürfte eine weit über diese Tätigkeit hinausgehende produktive handwerkliche Arbeit verrichtet haben, die neben Leder auch aus Haar und Wolle hergestellte Materialien wie etwa Filz zum Gegenstand gehabt haben mag» (WVDOG 92, p. 15). We will return, briefly, to the terminology of the craftsman below, but for the present must concentrate attention on the product.

First one other Middle Assyrian text, WVDOG 92, No. 53, in which the same *rab sāpê* is responsible for items of *taḫapšu,* needs to be cited in extenso:

> 310 TÚG.SAGŠU.MEŠ *ša ta-ḫap-še* 46.5 MA.NA *ana* KI.LÁ
> «310 hats of *taḫapšu*, 46.5 minas in weight
> *ša Amurru-šuma-uṣur* GAL *sa-pe-e*
> belonging to Amurru-šuma-uṣur, the Chief Felt-worker,
> *Uṣur-namkur-šarri u Ubru ana ēkalli maḫru*
> Uṣur-namkur-šarri and Ubru have received for the palace,
> *ša* [lú]*sa-pi-ú* KUR *ḫa-at-ta-iu-ú ša ḫu-up*[?]*-šu-te ēpušūni*
> which the Hittite felt-worker manufactured for[?] the troops[?]».

There are two difficult points here. One is the identity of the logogram in l. 1. The same logogram is found in WVDOG 92 No. 12, edited by Freydank in AOF 21 (1994) 31-33, where a gift of garments is made to a Hittite interpreter. The sign looks like UGU (U+KA), not the U(or ŠÚ)+SAG expected. This is not an error of the copyist, who explicitly considered the possibility of a reading SAGŠU (see WVDOG 92, p. 12 ad loc.), but notwithstanding this the weight of the contexts, in my opinion, favours interpreting this sign as the Middle Assyrian writing for *kubšu* «a hat». The other tricky point is the word *ḫupšūte.* I owe to Dr. Stefan Jakob the suggestion that this is a plural adjectival form from *ḫupšu*, at this date «footsoldiers» or similar.

The word *taḫapšu* was known before, but until now most translators have not felt able to say more than «(a textile)». However, in the course of writing this contribution I secured a copy of T. Kendall's dissertation on *Warfare and military matters in the Nuzi tablets* (Ph. D., Brandeis University 1975): there in his discussion of *taḫabšu*, which in the Nuzi passages is mostly used for horse-armour, he writes «perhaps *taḫapšu* was similar or identical to the «*namad*», which is still made in Luristan today, and which was described to this writer by Richard Frye, Professor of Iranian, Harvard University. This is a non-woven, felt-like, material, often as much as an inch thick ...» (p. 314). Another description of felt-making in Persia is given in H.E. Wulff, *The traditional crafts of Persia* (Massachussetts Institute of Technology 1966), pp. 222-4. Kendall must have been on the right lines, since the new passage from Assur shows beyond doubt that this material was needed for the manufacture of Assyrian-style boots, and a review of the other instances allows us to propose with some confidence a translation «felt».

No doubt the suspicion that *taḫapšu* might mean «felt» had already crossed Dr. Freydank's mind too, and it may cut a long story short if at this stage we cite some words from an article of P. Steinkeller's in which, again foreshadowed but not forestalled by no less a scholar than Leo Oppenheim, he nailed the Sumerian for felt as **túg.du$_8$.a**, and the craftsman producing it as the **túg.du$_8$**: «we can conclude that the basic task of the **túg-du$_8$** was to manufacture felt and to turn it into finished goods, such as mattresses, cushions, caps, etc. It appears that the **túg-du$_8$** also used felt to line various containers, pieces of furniture, wagons, etc., and to pad shoes and sandals. ... Finally, the **túg-du$_8$** also seems to have produced ropes and belts from goat hair and low quality wool ... there is no evidence (*other than his common association with leatherworkers* [my italics]) that he worked with leather» («Mattresses and felt in early Mesopotamia», *Oriens Antiquus* 19 (1980) 93). The earlier Akkadian words for «felt» and «felt-worker» are not clearly identified yet, since *kiššu* and *kašāšu* (mentioned by Steinkeller, p. 89) attested in lexical texts, have not yet been observed in economic contexts.

Our reasons for suggesting that, from 1500 BC on, felt was called *taḫapšu* will now be evident. First, it seems not so much to be a type of textile, as a substance used to make a variety of products. Then it seems to be derived from a «wool department», but used in association with leatherwork. Apart from armour, the items so far encountered are hats (*kubšu*), boots (*šuḫuppātu*), and the upholstery of a royal vehicle, all items which can well involve felt and feature in Steinkeller's list cited above. Like **túg.du$_8$.a** in Ur III times, *taḫapšu* is worked by a craftsman who is associated with the leatherworkers (*aškāpu*). Let us now take the equation as proven, and, after a digression on the form of the word, review other occurrences of the term.

Kendall opted to connect the word with the root *ḫbš*, with the meaning «chop up into pieces». This is attractive at first sight, but the principal drawback is that a **tapars-* form (rather than *tapras-*) would be hard to explain. It is true that occasionally in Middle Assyrian an extra *a* is sometimes written after a syllable closed by a *ḫ* (two clear examples cited by W. Mayer, AOATS 2, p. 19, are *tušaḫaruṣūni* and *naḫarat*), but to my knowledge this is not attested in Babylonian dialects, whereas the form of our word is consistent in the Kassite texts, at Nuzi and in the west. It is safer, therefore, and probably better, to eschew an Akkadian etymology, and (with AHw) to suspect a Hurrian word, and Prof. G. Wilhelm confirms to me orally that an ending in *-(a)pšu* could well be of Hurrian origin.

Also possibly in favour of a Hurrian source is the early attestation in the west. From Alalakh we have the Hurrian professional designation for felt-maker *taḫapšuḫuli* (JCS 13 55:301, 8.10), with an Akkadian version *ēpiš taḫapši* at Boğazköy and also at Alalakh. Von Soden (AHw 1301) also cites the Ugaritic *tġpṯm* (PRU 5 113.6).

In Mesopotamia the earliest attestations are probably at Nuzi. Kendall's discussion of the term shows that *taḫapšu* was used with leather for the manufacture of horse-armour, but also for padding under a yoke (p. 314). The three Middle Babylonian occurrences cited by J. Aro, *Mittelbabylonische Kleidertexte der Hilprecht-Sammlung Jena*, p. 33, agree with our Middle Assyrian evidence: caps (*patinnu*) are made of *taḫapšu*, and in HS 187 the fabric is mentioned together with leather. Another Kassite tablet (CT 51 Pl. 7 No. 16:5-6) lists wool for various purposes, including «2 minas for the *ta-ḫap-ši* of a travelling chair (GIŠ.GU.ZA KASKAL - reading thanks to C.B.F. Walker, who copied the text) and its wash-bowl (GIŠ.NÍG.ŠU.LUḪ.ḪA-*šu*)». It was used on horses, perhaps as a saddle, in the Middle Assyrian horse-training texts (E. Ebeling, *Bruchstücke einer mittelassyrischen Vorschriftensammlung*, p. 46), and in the Marduk Ordeal text A. Livingstone translates the word as «saddle» (SAA 3 p. 88 No. 35:23). A connection with horses or chariots is probably responsible for the word's position in the Practical Vocabulary of Assur, where it comes right at the end of the textile section, after *nakbusu,* which is known to be used in chariots in Middle Assyrian times (see WVDOG 92, 5:34') and for etymological reasons may well be a «mat», and *kirbinu* of uncertain meaning (ll. 292-4, AfO 18 (1957-58) 331).

Other lexical passages are unhelpful, except that they tend to suggest a rather general meaning like «cover, rug». The equation túg.líl.lá = *ta-ḫap-šú* features in the Nineveh exemplar of HAR-ra-hubullû XIX, 276 (MSL 10, p. 135) followed by *taktīmu* («covering»), but is absent from the Ras Shamra Forerunner. *taḫapšu* also appears in the right-hand column of HAR-gud, without an entry in the middle (original Akkadian) column, which supports a post-Old Babylonian adoption of the word. It is preceded in Recension C by *šuḫattum*, which also features in the Practical Vocabulary of Assur as the next entry after *taḫapšu* (AfO 18 331:295 TÚG *šu-ḫa-ta-ti*) (MSL 10 p. 140 r.7) and is followed in Recension D by *taḫluptu*, which is, at least for us, an equally non-specific word for a covering (p. 141, l. 432). On the other hand, the entries in synonym lists *[ṣu]bat t*., *tēdeq t.* (CT 18 11.28f.) indicate again that *taḫapšu* was considered a material, rather than a specific finished product in itself.

Thus we may say that the evidence now strongly favours translating *taḫapšu* as «felt», describing an unwoven woollen fabric used for some kinds of rugs, including horse blankets or saddles, and for padding yokes, armour, boots and hats, often in conjunction with leather. Later it seems that the word by itself could refer to a felt blanket or saddle used on horses.

217

In conclusion a few words about the felt-worker. In Middle Assyrian contexts the craftsman associated with the manufacture, or at least the transformation of felt into finished items, was called a *sāpiu*, Babylonian *sēpû*; the Assyrian logogram for this profession is given clearly by the lexical texts as MUG (CAD S 227), which unfortunately invites a serious risk of confusion, at least among modern scholars, with the cuneiform signs for the «bow-maker» (ZADIM = *sassinnu*) and the «leather-worker» (ASGAB = *aškāpu*) - cf. CAD S 192 and A/ii, 443-4. Etymology does not help much with reconstructing the literal meaning of the word, because the precise meaning of the verb *sepû* is uncertain (CAD S 226-7), but that it was an activity in the production of fabrics seems to follow not only from the lexical entries under that verb mentioning wool and hair, but also from the «Practical List» from Sultantepe which puts the profession *sēpû* firmly into a section of textile-workers (MSL XII 233-4, ll. 7-16). I think we may safely understand «felt-worker», and pace Deller, AfO 34 pp. 62-3, see the felt-working as his primary activity in preference to the connection with leather.

ASSYRIAN UNIFORMS

J.N. Postgate, Cambridge

"The Pisidians carried little ox-hide shields and a pair of hunting-spears of Lycian workmanship, and wore bronze helmets, crested, and decorated with the ears and horns of an ox, also in bronze. Their legs were bound with strips of crimson cloth ... The Milyans carried short spears and had their clothes fastened with brooches; some of them were also armed with Lycian bows and wore leather casques."[1] These are just two of the many and varied units which Herodotus tells us composed Xerxes' army. Less than two centuries earlier the Neo-Assyrian army, as in most other empires of antiquity, not least the Persian and the Roman, included a similar variety of ethnic groups, each of which had its own weapons, dress, and fighting specialities.

While there are at least three substantial studies which address the representation of military and civilian personnel on the Neo-Assyrian palace reliefs,[2] there has been no comparable attempt by philologists to respond with a study of the textual data. With the advancing publication of the Helsinki State Archives of Assyria volumes the excuse that the state of the texts made them almost unusable is being rapidly eroded, and this short tribute to the guru of Assyrian textiles of an earlier age is only a first step on this road, since the wealth of information in the reliefs will merit further and deeper study. The Assyrian palace sculptures show a range of kit used by different military units. When trying to identify them it is tempting to concentrate on their weapons, which are readily differentiated and for which the Akkadian terms are mostly known. However, the dress and hairstyle of the different kinds of soldier are also significant, though much trickier to differentiate with confidence, and to match with the Assyrian terminology. We must try, though: the sculptors would have been aware of the implications of slight variations in formal and informal dress which may not be apparent to us today, and they are entitled to our respect. We must assume that recurring differences and similarities in the uniforms shown on the reliefs were deliberate, and we are obliged to find an account of the military which will be consonant with them.

I use the word "uniform" deliberately: with all the implications of standardization, formality, and identity that it carries, it is surely the right word. The choice of garment may of course be governed by practical considerations, reflecting the activities of the different units (e.g. whether or not they need to sit astride a horse), but particular styles spoke of group identity, and sometimes rested on a long tradition, since we see some uniforms persisting from the mid-9th century reliefs of Assur-naṣir-apli down into the 7th century. Of course, as in almost every army, dress could also mark out hierarchical differences[3]. Those who have commented on the representations of the

---

[1] de Sélincourt 1954, 441-2 Book vii.76.

[2] In particular Hrouda 1965; Madhloom 1970; Reade 1972.

[3] Note that eunuchs and royal aides (*qurrubūtu*) had their distinctive garments in Neo-Babylonian times, to judge from Wiseman 1967, 496-7 ll. 16'-17'.

Fig. 1. Arslan Tash: soldier and officer (after Thureau-Dangin, *Arslan-Tash* Pl. X).

military in the reliefs have had no difficulty in distinguishing "officers" by observing the combination of their clothing and role in each scene. At its simplest note the distinction between officer and private on the reliefs from Arslan Tash (Fig. 1). Unfortunately the texts we have do not mention any garments specific to any particular rank, although one might expect to find such. One usage which does confirm the symbolic importance of uniform in general is reflected in passages which talk of soldiers being "clothed" (*labbušu*; regular NA pl. *labbašūte*, cf. GAG §15f).[4] *SAA* 11 29 r.3-5 mentions a cohort-commander "who has not been clothed" (*ša la labbušūni*), but *SAA* 11 122, a note of soldiers and horses, is the most explicit text.

6 *labbašūte* 208 *ša* UD.MEŠ	PAB 214 *ša* PN_1 *naṣanni*
8 *labbašūte* 96 *ša* UD.MEŠ	PAB 104 *ša* PN_2 *naṣanni*
PAB 14 *labbašūte* 304 *ša* UD.MEŠ	PAB 318 LÚ.ERÍN.MEŠ 177 KUR.MEŠ

Although laconic, the text's mention of horses confirms the military context, and the small numbers and prior listing of the "clothed" soldiers suggest that they were in authority, if not technically officers. In the royal annals kings talk of the "clothing" of visiting dignitaries as a form of honour, along with the presentation of rings and torcs; the slightly different usage in these administrative documents must imply that becoming "clothed" (*labbušu*) was a formal procedure signifying, and thereafter attesting to, the acquisition of status. The term *ša* UD.MEŠ for the remaining troops is difficult, but since the contrast is presumably between officially uniformed and less

[4] For "uniformed rein-holders" (*mukīl appāte lab-ba-šú-te*) cf. Kinnier Wilson 1972, 144 (No. 16:14), though I fail to understand the significance of the opposition to *ša mu-gir-a-te* (if that is indeed the correct interpretation).

definitively enrolled troops, I suspect that these are "day" troops serving out their time as conscripts.[5]

Because of the need for standardization, and perhaps because of the economic circumstances of the ordinary soldier, the manufacture or at least the supply of uniforms would normally be a concern of the military administration. Some of the clearest evidence for this comes in fact from as far back as the 13th century, and since other features of the Neo-Assyrian army can be traced back into the 2nd millennium, it can do no harm to examine the evidence of the Middle Assyrian texts first. Two tablets, both perhaps originating from Kar-Tukulti-Ninurta, are especially pertinent: VAT 18045 (Freydank 1994, No. 5; Ass. 14466, not listed in Pedersén), and MAH 16086 which must also derive from the German excavations though it somehow found its way to Geneva.

As noted by Freydank (1994, p. 9), both texts list a similar range of clothing and other items, but before considering the terminology in detail, let us try to reconstruct the administrative context into which these documents must be fitted. VAT 18045 is divided into sections listing small numbers of garments and a quantity of wool, next to the name or title of a woman, including in one case the "chief of the female weavers" (GAL MÍ.UŠ.BAR.MEŠ). The final section states GIŠ.GÀR.MEŠ (= *iškārāte*) *ša ab-ba-še ša lime* PN "work quotas of the ... for the eponymate of Ber-[...]" (l. 40'). This could be a list of delivered items, but since the tablet itself is probably dated to the same *limmu* (the name in l. 42' also begins Ber-[ ), it seems more likely that they are the projected quotas required of each woman. The word *abbāšu* is not yet well understood, but is possibly some kind of textile-worker.[6]

MAH 16806 is different. Here each section of the text concludes with the name of a person or "house"; because of damage to the tablet their role is usually unclear, but if we can be guided by the verb *iddunu* "they shall give" at the end of A.i.11 they are mentioned as contributors of the garments listed, which are thus being transferred from the private sector into the hands of the state administration. Working out the relationship between these contributions and the work quotas of the female weavers is beyond the scope of this article. One possibility might be that the weavers are producing the clothes within the central administration, while the contributors in MAH 16806 are required to organize their own production and supply finished products. Alternatively, since Freydank has restored the name Marduk-tabni-šuklil in both VAT 18045, 41' and MAH 16806 A.ii.4, it is possible that the Berlin tablet gave a detailed breakdown of this person's production

[5] Compare, in the context of *ilku* service, *ūma ina libbi* UD.MEŠ-*ia* ...... *imaḫḫarranni* "Now during my period of service he receives from me ..." (ND 3467, see Postgate 1974, 399).

[6] It turns up otherwise in the Geneva text (MAH 16086), but in the unhelpful phrase Á.MEŠ *šá ab-ba-še* (A.i.2), where the broken text and the ambiguity of the logogram Á obscure the meaning, and in the Assyrian coronation ritual which is even less enlightening. One possibility is that we have here the nomen professionis from a verb describing textile manufacture whose existence has always been rather shadowy because it gets absorbed in the common verb *epēšu*. Discussions of it can be found in Landsberger, *AfO Beiheft* 17, 24 (with fn. 70-71) and in Durand, *ARM* 26/i, no. 57 note (b). It is perhaps to be recognized in the other Geneva text concerned with textiles, MAH 15854, whose sections end typically n MA.NA SÍG.MEŠ TA.A.AN UB-BU-*ša* "each (of these textiles) ...ed with n minas apiece". This phrase reminds us of the MB stative *up-pu-us* (or *ub-bu-us*) listed in Aro 1970, 34, where the context suggests some meaning like "interwoven with" or "decorated with", but even if these are all the same word referring to textile manufacture, I prefer to leave unresolved whether it is a specialist usage of the common verb *epēšu*, or a separate lemma (as the *b* in *abbāšu* and the MB sibilant might suggest).

quota, which was summarized along with others' in one section of the Geneva text (though the two did not necessarily apply to the same time period).

Here however we must concentrate on the products themselves, some of which from their descriptions were intended for military use (as indeed all may have been). The items most regularly listed by MAH 16086 are:

lippu (+ É.ḪI.A) *ša birme*	"*lippu* ," (sometimes with "houses"[7]), "with coloured trim"
naḫlaptu (ša birme) šanāʾītu	"coat," (sometimes "with coloured trim,") "2nd class"
naḫlaptu ša dīkāti ṣaʾuptu qatattu	"coat, for battles, embroidered, fine"
(ṣubātu) ša tusaḫḫuri ša dīkāti mašru	"(cloth) for winding, for battles, teaselled"
(ṣubātu) ša tusaḫḫuri adi sūni-šu ša UD.MEŠ	"(cloth) for winding, with its fringe?, everyday?"
kusītu ša ṣāb šarri	"robe of king's troops"

These items, like others mentioned in the text, pose numerous problems of interpretation and translation, only a few of which can be addressed below.

lippu

The identity of this item is not known. My transcription follows the most recent discussion of the term by Donbaz (1991, 79)[8] and implies a connection with *lapāpu* "to wrap". The *CAD* (L 200) conflates a NA word *li-ip-pu* with the word *lappu* found in medical texts and translated by them as a wad or tampon. However, that meaning is inappropriate here, and if correctly reconstructed the *pirsum* formation *lippum* may need to be kept separate from the *parsum* formation *lappum*. On the other hand we should note that the scribes do not write the *p* double, and a connection with *lawûm* "to surround" cannot be ruled out.[9] Etymology is not specially helpful therefore in identifying this item, and the only indications we have are that they are usually (including *VS* 19 24 and Donbaz 1991, though not in Freydank 1994 No. 5) designated as *ša birme* "with coloured trim", and that they can be manufactured as part of an annual *iškāru* arrangement.

More enigmatic is the phrase *ša kī lēʾi ša PN* "as on the writing-board of PN".[10] The equivalent phrase in VAT 18045 has "in accordance with the writing-board of the palace" (*ša pī lēʾi ša ekalli*). At first sight, this might seem to refer to the writing-boards named after either the king or one of four to five high officials which are mentioned in contemporary 13th century texts in contexts which make it clear they were lists of Assyrians recruited to serve in the army. However, in these textile lists the phrase is tightly associated with the particular garment called *lippu/lību*, not with the soldiers. The "translation" should run e.g. "4 *lippu* garments (and) 6 'houses', with

[7] The items written É.ḪI.A remain completely obscure to me, unless it is a writing for the textile item *ša bētāte*; they appear to be closely associated with the *lippu*.

[8] The passage in question reads 5 TÚG *li*-BU *ša bir-me ištu lubultu(!) ša tupnini ša Kilizi šeluʾatanni ana* FPN *tadnu* GIŠ.GÀR *ša* [uru]*Ikkib-Marduk ša limme* PN "5 *lippu/lību* textiles with coloured trim were given to FPN when the clothing of the chest of Kilizi was brought up. *Iškāru*-quota of the town of Ikkib-Marduk, for the eponymate of PN"

[9] As suggested in Postgate 1979, 98.

[10] The correct reading of *lēʾu* here was recognized by Freydank 1994, p. 9.

coloured trim, which are in accordance with the writing-board of Uṣur-namkur-šarri, cohort(?; *gildu*) which is with Aššur-tukulti-kēni" (A.ii.6). It seems to show that the precise specification for these items was recorded on a writing-board, and since the number is already specified, it would seem that different clients (whether a highly placed individual or the palace itself) had different specifications. It is tempting to suggest, therefore, that the designs, or perhaps specifically the decorations, of these coloured items distinguished one sector of the army from another. Whatever they were, the designation *lippu/līpu* does not reappear in the 1st millennium.

naḫlaptu

CAD N/i 138a "wrap, outer garment"; *AHw* 715a "Gewand, Mantel". Two versions of this piece of clothing are listed in MAH 16806:

naḫlaptu (ša birme) šanāʾītu	"coat" (sometimes "with coloured trim"), "2nd class"
naḫlaptu ša dīkāti ṣaʾuptu qatattu	"coat, for battles, embroidered, fine".

In the British army "battle dress" is tougher and more smartly cut than everyday wear, and it seems as though much the same was true for the Middle Assyrian soldier. One MA context (*KAJ* 77, 9) offers the writing *na-ḫa-ÁB-tu*; I have dithered as to how this should be read (e.g. Postgate 1988, 127) but in the light of MAH 16806 the following adjective *šanāʾīta* favours the *CAD*'s suggestion that *naḫlaptu* is meant here too.[11] However, rather than restore a missing <*la*> we should assume that the word was actually pronounced without it, since in *SAA* 7, 112 r.1 and 115.ii.18 Parpola has recognized a Neo-Assyrian form *naḫaptu* used with reference to Qurraean uniform.

Elsewhere in Neo-Assyrian texts the word is rather uncommon, and it may well not be coincidental that in *ABL* 473 the writer is explicitly describing non-Assyrian troops[12], but in the Neo-Babylonian textile documents discussed by Matsushima 1995 it appears frequently in the dress of statues of goddesses along with *kusītu* (see Salonen 1980, 143 for examples). The same association seems to be present already in our Middle Assyrian Aššur lists, but as with other instances of garments listed together, it is hard to know whether they were worn regularly together, or were alternatives to each other. Matsushima notes that the *naḫlaptu* is of wool, but lighter and used in greater numbers than the *kusītu* (on which see below). She suggests that it "must be a light and auxiliary garment", perhaps "a shawl or the like, just to cover the shoulder" (1995, 246-8). In the 2nd millennium it could be either of linen (at Nuzi and Aššur) or of coloured wool (Nuzi, Babylonia and Aššur). MAH 16806 tells us further that they were worn in battle, and decorated. Against seeing it as a simple shawl is the detail in VAT 18045 that, in addition to 9 minas for the main garment, 2/3 mina of purple wool was allocated for the sleeves (*aḫātu*, wr. Á.MEŠ) and "fronts" (GAB.MEŠ). Hence I have opted to translate "coat", rather than use the word "cloak", which is normally thought of as sleeveless in English.

---

[11] Note the corresponding Nuzi term for "second-class" *šinaḫilu* applied to a *naḫlaptu* in *HSS* 14, 523 cited *CAD* N/i, 139b.

[12] In the Babylonian tribute(?) list edited in Wiseman 1967, 5000 *naḫlaptu bir-mu* are listed immediately before leather shields, and may therefore have been intended for military use.

kusītu

CAD K 585 "(an elaborate garment)"; *AHw* 514 "Gewand"; *SAA* "robe". This garment is well attested in both Assyrian and Babylonian contexts, although when the *CAD* entry was compiled there were no Middle Assyrian attestations. In MAH 16086 the phrase *ša* ERÍN.MEŠ LUGAL does not apply to all the garments in a section, but must be a specific qualification of the *kusītu*. Hence the preferable interpretation of the phrases concluding sections in MAH 16086 is "5 king's-troops-*kusītu*-garments PN [shall give?]". In other words, some, though not all, *kusītus* were specified as uniform for the king's troops. VAT 18045 gives confirmation that this item was made of wool, to judge from the context, and produced as part of their *iškāru* work by women; there are virtually no other mentions of *kusītu* in Middle Assyrian.

We have no usable representations of Middle Assyrian uniforms, though a clue to the possibilities might be taken from Egyptian representations of Asiatic soldiers: long mail-clad robes are shown in the grave of Rameses III, and with blue trimmings among gifts to the pharaoh in the tomb of Ken-Amun at Thebes.[13] A charioteer wearing a similar long robe features in Thutmosis IV's battle against the Syrians, but others wear a long elaborately decorated cloth robe, and archers have a short coat of mail over this.[14] To try to achieve a more precise identification we must turn to the 1st millennium evidence, both written and carved. One source is the group of textile labels and related lists found on Kouyunjik (*SAA* 7 95-109), perhaps of the early 7th century.[15] These labels were sealed, and some list large numbers of items (833 woollen textiles in *SAA* 7 108); they gave a whole range of information about the number, colour, fabric, shape, and weight of the items they list. Unfortunately the scribe's space-saving fondness for the ditto sign means that they are not always transparent, a typical translation of one of the entries being: "ditto ditto ditto ditto, textile, ..., knotted, 1 1/2". However, they plainly are the product of an office involved in the provision of clothing for government servants, and given their provenance (from the royal palaces, not from the Review Palace on Nebi Yunus), these are likely to have been personnel in the service of the king himself. Some of the types of garment listed are known to have been worn by soldiers, while others are probably not military wear, although this would not preclude their wearers' being members of the military establishment, which was expanded in the 7th century to embrace civilian professions.

In the Neo-Babylonian texts the *kusītu* are of wool and always seem to be worn by goddesses (Salonen 1980; Matsushima 1995, 234). They are mentioned in Neo-Assyrian religious texts as the dress of a deity (Dumuzi and Šakkan), but also turn up in other contexts which makes it clear that they could be worn by soldiers and officials. They are listed occasionally in the textile labels, where they may be qualified as "with coloured trim" (GÙN *SAA* 7.99) or "red ..." (SA_5 KUR *SAA* 7 105.6'-7').[16] As an honorific form of dress they are also encountered among the funerary gifts for a royal burial (MacGinnis 1987), and in *ABL* 473 where eunuchs are said to be "clothed with

---

13 Wolf 1926, 96-7, Abb. 67, 69; N. de G. Davies, *The Tomb of Ken-Amūn at Thebes, I* (N.Y. 1930) Pl. XVI and in colour on Pl. XXIX. My thanks to Barry Kemp for steering me to these Egyptian representations; also illustrated Yadin 1963, 196-7.

14 W. Wreszinski, *Atlas zur altägyptischen Kulturgeschichte II*, Taf. 1.

15 For these labels see *SAA* 7, pp. xxvi-xxix. The two dated (but not typical) sealings Nos. 93 and 94 come from 681 and 658 B.C.

16 Perhaps this should be "red (and) blue", if, by analogy with SA_5, KUR in these textile labels can be taken as an abbreviation for SÍG.ZA.GÌN.KUR.RA = *takiltu*.

kusītu robes and adorned with rings", plainly in imitation of court ceremony. As in Babylonia, the robes were made of wool in Assyria since in *ABL* 413, when the king enquires whence some *kusītu* robes are to be provided, the reply comes that the people in question will be given purple wool (SÍG SA_5, perhaps for SÍG.ZA.GÌN.SA_5 = *argamannu*) and they will have them made themselves, with the assistance of weavers from Arbil.

To identify this garment does not seem very difficult. Goddesses were represented in 1st millennium seals wearing long flounced robes (e.g. Teisssier 1984, No. 217). If we look in the Neo-Assyrian sculptures too, we can identify individuals who wear long robes falling straight to the ground. The king himself wears an elaborately decorated one when in battle, and it is normal wear for high ranking civil and military personages (e.g. Fig. 2). The Arslan Tash reliefs (Fig. 1) give the simplest opposition between the officer in a long robe and his soldiers, but the same distinction is present in many scenes of battle and ceremony. This robe, or gown (Hrouda: langes Hemd) must be the *kusītu*.

Often the robe is worn on its own, but it can be worn with a garment over it. The eunuch archer probably wears a robe with a tasselled hem underneath a mail shirt (e.g. Fig. 3).[17] A fringed shawl is sometimes worn over it. In formal dress this may reach from the shoulders to the feet (see Hrouda 1965 Taf. 2; Assur-naṣir-apli II), or be wrapped round the waist so that the lower

Fig. 2. Assyrian wearing a *kusītu* under a shawl (Sennacherib: after Barnett et al. 1998, 659a).

Fig. 3. Eunuch archer in mail-shirt over robe at the capture of Ekron (Sargon: after Albenda 1986, Pl. 136).

17 Frequent in Sargon battle scenes; similarly Tiglath-pileser III, with broad belt at waist, Barnett & Falkner 1962, Pl. LXXIII.

part of the robe is left free and the fringe encircles the legs horizontally and is then slung diagonally across the upper body (e.g. Fig. 4).[18] In these cases as it crosses the chest the extra garment seems to be more fringe than shawl, either because it has become more of a sash than a shawl, or because the cloth has been rolled up for its upper part.

If we seek for an Akkadian term perhaps we may find it in *SAA* 7, 112, 6' where someone "has given upper garments and robes" (TÚG.AN.TA.MEŠ TÚG.BAR.DIB.MEŠ); the item translated "upper garment", *el(ēn)ītu*,[19] could presumably be such a shawl. It is attested several times in the textile labels, once specified as "purple" (SA_5), and two black ones are included in a list of items supplied to Urartian emissaries (*SAA* 7, 127). There is a problem with the literal interpretation of the term, in that it is unclear whether "upper" means "for the upper part of the body" or "outer". I am inclined to take it as "outer", hence an "overgarment", in opposition to the "undergarment" (*šupālītu*, see below). This would also permit identification with the shawl, but this must remain no more than a guess for the time being.[20]

* * * *

Fig. 4. Fringed shawl draped over upper body (Sargon: after Albenda 1986, Pl. 86).

Fig. 5. Auxiliary archer in short kilt showing fringed edge (Sargon: after Albenda 1986, Pl. 98).

[18] So also Hrouda 1965 Taf. 49.2 (Arslan Tash); Houston 1954, 149 Fig. 147; Parrot 1961, Fig. 112 (Til-Barsip).

[19] No definite equivalent is known, but in the light of the NB syllabic writing TÚG *e-le-ni-tum* (*CAD* E 83 s.v. elēnītu B) the longer form is probably correct.

[20] For a different suggestion for the identification of the shawl, see above under *naḫlaptu*.

While officers and officials retained the traditional robe (*kusītu*), with or without a shawl, it is obvious from the reliefs that the ordinary soldier's uniform was quite different. Unfortunately, determining the precise nature of even these commonest items of dress is less easy than it might seem at first sight. Since our texts are principally late 8th and early 7th century, for our comparisons we need to concentrate on the relief corpus from the reigns of Sargon and Sennacherib.

Kilts (*Hrouda: Schurzrock*)

The easiest garment to define is the kilt, which can be worn alone, and is essentially a rectangular piece of cloth wrapped around the waist. Short kilts, evidently formed like this and with a decorated fringe falling below the hem-line, are already shown at Boğazköy and in Egyptian paintings of Aegean emissaries of the 2nd millennium (see Barber 1990, 337 Fig. 15.20 and 15.18-19) and on the 9th century Tell Halaf reliefs (Madhloom 1970, 89 with Pl. XLVIII.2). In Assyria too there are short kilts, often worn without any clothing on the upper body, from the 9th century at latest. Both the short versions of the Aramaean and other auxiliaries (Fig. 5), and the slightly longer kilts worn by Assyrians have the fringed outer edge positioned at the wearer's right side, and with the Assyrian kilts the long tassels forming a fringe hang down below the hem. This is clearly shown in the Arslan Tash procession (Figs. 1 and 6; and countless other instances), where those soldiers moving to our right, and thus exposing their right side to the viewer, show the

Fig. 6. Arslan Tash: soldier moving to left (after Thureau-Dangin, *Arslan-Tash* Pl. IX).

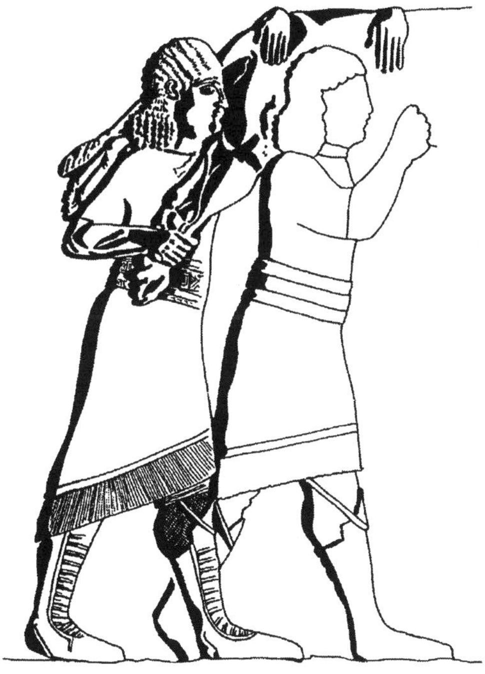

Fig. 7. Work tunic worn by servants (Assurbanipal, after Barnett 1976, Pl. XLIII).

tasselled fringe falling vertically down from the waist-band, while with those moving in the opposite direction and showing their left side to the viewer we can only see the extremity of the fringe as it appears below the hem on the far side.

Tunics (Hrouda: kurzes Hemd) and shirts (Bluse)

The word "tunic" means different things to different writers. I am using it to mean a close-fitting tailored garment on the upper body, reaching to the wearer's knees or somewhat higher. It differs from a shirt in that it drops below the waist, and from the robe in being shorter. Such a garment is frequently shown on the reliefs (see Fig. 7). Its characteristics are that it is close fitting, with short tight sleeves ending above the elbow, and a plain or sometimes fringed horizontal hem, usually above the knee. Some version of the tunic is worn by a wide variety of people, with or without a belt. Menial tasks, whether military or civilian, are often performed by men wearing this garment alone: by the foreign (Aramaean?) labourers, with a belt of some kind at the waist (Barnett et al. 1998 Fig. 536a); by grooms (ibid. Fig. 584) and by hunt attendants (e.g. Fig. 7; cf. Madhloom 1970, 71). Horse-riders often have a longish version which is cut on a slant rising towards the front to expose the knees (e.g. Barnett 1976, Pl. L; note that the slant is equally present when the rider is dismounted). Even the king himself wears an elaborate version of the same garment. Over it both cavalry and infantry often wear a mail-shirt, usually sleeveless (see Fig. 8; military scribes in Barnett et al. 1998 Pl. 252), or, in the case of helmeted auxiliaries, under the crossed straps attached to a wide belt shown in Fig. 9.

Fig. 8. Mail-shirt over tunic (Sennacherib: after Barnett et al. 1998, Pl. 55).

Fig. 9. Auxiliary spearman, crossed straps over tunic (Sargon: after Albenda 1986, Pl. 96).

In many cases it is impossible to be certain whether we are looking a single knee-length garment, or a separate shirt and kilt. As Hrouda comments "Über die Verbindung von Rock und Bluse geben die Darstellungen keine Auskünfte, weil die "Nahtstellen" immer durch den Gürtel verdeckt werden" (1965, 25). In other cases the waist area is concealed by the base of a mailshirt. Because kilts usually have a pendent fringe, and always show their fore-edge when the wearer is moving to the right, we are probably entitled to assume a tunic is intended if there is a straight hem-line without a pendent fringe, and certainly when the right side of the body is shown without the fore-edge of a kilt (e.g. Barnett et al. 1998 Fig. 645a, bottom right; Madhloom 1970, Pl. XLVI.3).

But may we assume conversely that if there is a pendent fringe the garment can only be a kilt starting from the waist, and any clothing on the upper body a separate shirt? Perhaps not. On the one hand, one must, I think, agree with Hrouda 1965, 25, that it is hard to imagine a single garment which combined a close-fitting sleeved upper part like a shirt with a wrapped and fringed lower part like a kilt. So where we see a kilted figure with pendent fringe and a sleeved upper garment, as in Figs. 1 and 7 (Arslan Tash) we must assume he is wearing a waist-length shirt (Bluse). On the other hand, we cannot always be sure the fringe belongs to a kilt. Assyrian soldiers in the late 8th and 7th century often show a pendent fringe which is not formed from the vertical fore-edge of a kilt, as in the Arslan Tash examples, but seems to fall straight from the waistband after having been pulled diagonally up across the right hip (e.g. Fig. 10; or the slingers shown in Barnett et al. 1998, Fig. 516).

Fig. 10. Fringe falling from waist-band
(Sennacherib: after Barnett et al. 1998, 584).
Albenda 1986, Pl. 96).

In some Sennacherib scenes this feature may distinguish a superior rank (ibid. Fig. 370a, the leading spearman in the middle register). In others it differentiates two classes of spearmen: in Fig. 348b those with pointed helmets have a pendent fringe, but not those with crests, although their skirts look virtually identical. With Houston 1954, 138-9, I suspect that the fringe belongs to a "small wrap-around shawl" worn over a knee-length tunic. Thus from the reign of Sargon the rabbit-hunter in Albenda 1986 Pl. 85 is wearing a typical Assyrian kilt, and presumably above this a shirt, but the officer on the bottom right of Pl. 87 will be wearing a tunic with a fringed shawl draped round it. It is admittedly difficult always to be sure of this distinction, and Hrouda sees this style rather as a development of the "Zipfelschurzrock" (1965, 32, with Taf. 44, 3).

* * * *

To sum up, the evidence of the reliefs suggests that in addition to the robe (*kusītu*) items of military clothing we should expect to encounter regularly in administrative texts are (1) the kilt; (2) the knee-length tunic (3) the shirt; and (4) the mail-shirt or corslet. If we can securely identify some or all of these, some progress will have been made. TH No. 48 is an administrative list of the late 9th or early 8th century from the provincial capital of Guzana. After "1 chariot, 4 horses and 2 donkeys" it enumerates weapons: "10 bows, 10 daggers, 10 spears, 10 helmets, 10 quivers, 10 shields". This is followed by "10 *gulēnu,* 10 KUŠ.*me*-[*x-x*], 10 *sāgu*". Ignoring the leather item for the time being, it is obvious that at least the *gulēnu* and the *sāgu* were components of infantry uniform. They are associated also in later contexts of the late 8th and early 7th century. In a list of allocations to palace personnel the palace supervisor (*ša pān ekalli*) and his scribe each receive 6 *gulēnu*, 4 *sāgu*, a pair of saddle-bags(?), a sheep and a bowl of wine (*SAA* 11, 36.ii.13). Since the palace supervisor himself also receives a pair of donkeys, it seems likely that these items of clothing were intended for their more humble and unlisted employees involved in the physical task of transporting the palace supplies. What is not of course stated is whether they were worn together, or are alternatives. Let us examine the evidence for each term more closely.

sāgu

CAD S, 27-8 "(a piece of clothing)"; *AHw* 1003a "ein Arbeitsschurz ?"; *SAA* "sash"; *SAA* 7 p. xxix "loin-cloth". We can certainly come a bit closer than *CAD*, because both lexically and elsewhere there is a clear connection between *sāgu* and the waist or hips (*qablu*). This is tacitly acknowledged in the following article (*sāgu* in *ša sāgāte-šu*, p. 28) where *CAD* translates "belt(?) peddler". In Middle Assyrian texts, apart from the harem edict passage, cited by both dictionaries, which reveals that the *sāgu* would have been "tied" (*rakāsu*), it is found in two lists of miscellaneous items along with containers (e.g. *kukubu* pots and *naruqqu* sacks, VS 19 7:18 and VS 19 29:21). This suggests that it may be an Assyrian variant of the Babylonian *saqqu(m)* (*CAD* S 168-9, which also means both a sack and a type of cloth.[21]

In Neo-Assyrian texts where the word is given a determinative it is TÚG, so that it was of textile not leather. The Neo-Assyrian passages cited in the *CAD* article make it plain that this was a very basic item of equipment, often issued along with water-skins.[22] There was a profession

21 The one possible Ugarit passage is very doubtful, according to van Soldt, *Orientalia* NS 60 (1991), p. 117.

22 *Sāgu* are mentioned along with *ḫimtu* "water-skins" at Tell Halaf (no. 52:11) and in NL 25 (*Iraq* 18, 1956, 41). In later texts *sāgu* are similarly listed together with *ma(z)zā'u* (see simply *CAD* S 27b; the

devoted to its manufacture or supply (*CAD* S p. 28, cf. above). Discounting the possibility that it was merely a loin-cloth worn out of sight, two options may be considered (1) with *SAA*, a textile belt or "sash" worn round the waist or (2) a garment worn round the hips (so *AHw*). There is indeed a broad cummerbund or girdle worn round the waist with a variety of garments (Hrouda 1965, 47-8 with Taf. 7.13-24; in red and blue in Parrot 1961 p. XVII and Fig. 347). This is clearly some form of textile, although it may have incorporated a narrower leather belt, and it is so common that it must be mentioned somwhere in our sources. However, a better candidate than *sāgu* for this is *ṣipirtu* (see *CAD* Ṣ 201 "(a sash woven or treated in a special technique)"; *AHw* 1103b "Band oder Schärpe aus Textilgeflecht ?"). On the grounds, therefore, that it refers to a commonly worn garment worn round the hips, I would propose *sāgu* as the best candidate for the "kilt", always leaving open the possibility that special types of kilt had names of their own.

gulēnu

SAA "cloak"; *CAD* G, 127 "(a coat)"; *CAD* S 27 "cloak"; *AHw* "ein Obergewand". *Gulēnu* is a 1st millennium word. The possibly cognate Aramaic word *glīmā* is a garment worn across the shoulders, as can be seen from a (much later!) Genizah marriage document which refers to all someone's property "even from the shirt off his back".[23] From the Practical Vocabulary of Assur 247 we learn that the *gulēnu* might have red ZAG.MEŠ; unfortunately the correct reading and meaning of ZAG in this context are still unknown (see *SAA* 7 p. xxviii for the reading *pūtu* "front-piece", but this is only a guess). *SAA* 7 96:4' mentions 45 *gulēnu* ; in the following line we have 2, perhaps with a red "front-piece" (ZAG SA_5; so also in Nos. 98:8' and 107.r.8'), followed by 30 "old" ones. Note too that ladies might also have a *gulēnu* (Parker 1954, 37:35). Further confirmation of *gulēnu* as one of the basic pieces of uniform comes from *SAA* 1 193 (=*ABL* 642) a letter attributed on the basis of scribal ductus to an official at Carchemish called Nabu-pašir. He replies to the king's request for an issue of uniforms to foreign troops apparently stationed or detained: he has sent 200 *gulēnu* to men of At[...] in one city [name lost], and 200 to the troops of PN who are in Til-Barsip, and 700, apparently, to some other destination. We cannot say that these were exclusively for military use, but in such numbers they must have been a standard item of apparel.

Much the most explicit attempt to identify the *gulēnu* is Weidner's: "Es dürfte sich um das bis zu den Knien reichende, kurzärmelige Gewand handeln, das an den Hüften von einem doppelten Gürtel zusammengehalten wird und über den der Bogenschütze mitunter das Brustkoller trägt." (*AfO Beiheft* 6, 34).This garment is the "tunic", as defined above,[24] and certainly remains a strong candidate for the *gulēnu*. However, there does not seem to me to be any decisive reason why it should be a tunic rather than a shirt. Indeed, if we suppose that the soldiers in the *TH* 48 and the officials in *SAA* 11 36 are unlikely to have been issued with two different outfits, then a better solution would be to translate *gulēnu* as "shirt", to go with *sāgu* "kilt". Otherwise we would have to suppose they received both a tunic and a kilt to be worn as alternatives, but no shirt. This is

---

correct restoration of *TH* 48:11 KUŠ *me*-[remains doubtful) and I guess this is also a (new?) word for "water skin". It is perhaps literally a "squeezer".

23 *mglymʾ dʾl ktpyh* (Friedman 1980, II, p. 124-7 l. 20; my thanks to Geoffrey Khan for steering me to this passage).

24 As a modern English translation, neither "cloak" nor "coat" is really suitable, since both are outer garments worn off the shoulders, either short or full length. The difference is that a coat has sleeves, whereas a cloak at the most has armholes and is worn much more loosely.

also possible, of course, since soldiers clad in just a kilt are not uncommonly shown on the reliefs.

* * * *

A rather more varied military wardrobe is recorded by a Nineveh text, *SAA* 11 28, which lists contributions for a soldier performing *ilku* service. The clothing section of the list reads:

11 TÚG.KI.TA *ḫal-lu-up-tú* TÚG.*gul*-IGI(=*inu*)
12 TÚG.SAGŠU TÚG.*ṣi-pir-tú*
13 [TÚG].*ur-nu-tú* 6 MA.NA SÍG.MEŠ
14 [x x TÚ]G.*sa-a-gu* 2 KUŠ.MEŠ *ma-za-ʾi*
15 [*a-na* (x)]x-*šú* KUŠ.E.SI[R.M]EŠ GIBIL.MEŠ

"(One) armoured under-garment; a *gulēnu*; a headband; a girdle; an *urnutu*; 6 minas of wool; [a] *sāgu*; 2 leather water-skins(?); [2?] new pairs of shoes/sandals; ...".

Here in addition to the *sāgu* and *gulēnu* we have two garments which recur frequently in both the textile labels and other Neo-Assyrian contexts, the *urnutu* and the *šupālītu ḫalluptu*. Let us take first the "armoured under-garment" which is common enough for the scribes to abbreviate it occasionally down to KI *ḫal*. For *šupālītu* *AHw* 1278b "Untergewand" and *CAD* Š/iii 314 "undergarment" are better than "lower garment" (my rendering in *SAA* 7), since it must have been an "undergarment" (worn closer to the body than another) rather than a "nether garment" (worn on the lower body). Though usually qualified by *ḫallupu* (see below), it could also be "black" (*SAA* 7 127, 9') or "white" (*SAA* 7 94:1), and in Neo-Babylonian texts of linen. As for its usual epithet *ḫallupu*, since coining the awkward *SAA* translation I have become more confident that its precise meaning is "armoured".[25] It was probably manufactured, or at least distributed, by a special profession *ša ḫallupti-šunu* who received a talent of fibre (wool or linen) in *SAA* 7 115.i.8. An identification as a mail-shirt is satisfactory, because we require a word for the scale armoured corslets, with or without short sleeves, which are frequently worn by regular soldiers on the reliefs (e.g. Fig. 3). Presumably it was named in contrast to the *elēnītu* which is also worn over as formal a garment as the *kusītu*. In *SAA* 11 28 (and also *SAA* 7 94) it is listed next to the *gulēnu*: perhaps it was worn over another shirt or a tunic, but it seems more likely, since one would not choose to wear a mail corslet 24 hours a day or to multiply layers of close-fitting clothes in the Mesopotamian climate, that it was an alternative.

Finally, in l. 13, the *urnutu*, plural *urnāt(e)*. *AHw* 1431b ein Gewand (aus Filz, Leinen); *SAA* (a garment, perhaps "tunic"). Frequent in the textile labels, probably usually woollen but also of linen (*SAA* 7 96 r.3) or of *biršu* (probably a rough fabric, with *CAD* B 261a, rather than felt which is *taḫapšu*). Coloured woollen and linen ones feature in a dowry (Parker 1954, 37:15-18). They can be black and red (*SAA* 7 109.ii.2'ff.) and also from Byblos (*gu-ub-li*, 108. r.ii.4'). *SAA* 7 115.ii.10 lists 20 talents of madder(?) for 600 *maqāṭu*-garments and 600 *urnutu*, confirming at least that they might be provided centrally. Depending on the correct identification of *gulēnu*, this is probably either a shirt or a tunic, but more than that it is premature to say.

---

25 See Postgate 2000 for *ḫallupu*; in connection with the *šupālītu* this meaning of *ḫallupu* is also supported by the Neo-Babylonian term TÚG *širʾam šupālītu* (see *CAD* Š/iii.314a), since *širʾam*, though of textile in NB texts, begins life as a coat of mail.

There are plenty of other terms, of which *maqāṭu* itself is just one, which still require investigation, but there we must stop for now. The net result of this process is to suggest the following equivalences:

kusītu	"robe"
naḫlaptu	(some kind of coat)
elēnītu	"fringed shawl"
sāgu	"kilt"
ṣipirtu	"woven girdle"
gulēnu	"tunic"
šupālītu	"shirt"
šupālītu ḫalluptu	"mail shirt"
urnutu	(a shirt or tunic)

There are plenty more terms to be discussed, but if these prove satisfactory we shall have made a start.

Bibliography

Albenda, P. 1986, *The Palace of Sargon, King of Assyria*, Paris.
Aro, J. 1970, *Mittelbabylonische Kleidertexte der Hilprecht-Sammlung Jena*, Sitzungsberichte der Sächsischen Akad. d. Wiss. zu Leipzig, Pl.-Hist. Kl. 115.2; Berlin.
Barber, E.J.W. 1990, *Prehistoric textiles: the development of cloth in the Neolithic and Bronze Ages with special reference to the Aegean*, Princeton U.P.
Barnett, R.D. 1976, *Sculptures from the North Palace of Ashurbanipal at Nineveh (668-627 B.C.)*, London: British Museum Press.
Barnett, R.D. & M. Falkner 1962, *The sculptures of Aššur-naṣir-apli II (883-859 B.C.) Tiglath-Pileser III (745-727 B.C.) Esarhaddon (681-669 B.C.) from the Central and South-West Palaces at Nimrud*, London: British Museum.
Barnett, R.D. et al. 1998, *Sculptures from the Southwest Palace of Sennacherib at Nineveh*, by R.D. Barnett, E. Bleibtreu and G. Turner, London.
de Sélincourt, A. 1954, *Herodotus: The Histories*, Penguin Books.
Donbaz, V. 1991, "The date of the eponym Nabû-bēla-uṣur", in D. Charpin & F. Joannès (eds.), *Marchands, diplomates et empéreurs: Études sur la civilisation mésopotamienne offertes a Paul Garelli*, 73-80, Paris.
Freydank, H. 1994, *Mittelassyrische Rechtsurkunden und Verwaltungstexte III*, *WVDOG* 92, Berlin.
Friedman, M.A. 1980, *Jewish marriage in Palestine*, Tel Aviv/New York.
Houston, M.G. 1954, *Ancient Egyptian Mesopotamian and Persian costume and decoration* (2nd ed.), London.
Hrouda, B. 1965, *Die Kulturgeschichte des assyrischen Flachbildes*, Bonn.
Kinnier Wilson, J.V. 1972, *The Nimrud Wine Lists*, *Cuneiform Texts from Nimrud*, 1.
MacGinnis, J.D.A. 1987, "A Neo-Assyrian text mentioning a royal funeral", *SAAB* 1, 1-12.
Madhloom, T.A. 1970, *The chronology of Neo-Assyrian art*, London; The Athlone Press.
Matsushima, E. 1995, "Some remarks on the divine garments: *kusītu* and *naḫlaptu*" *Acta Sumerologica* 17, 233-249.

Parker, B. 1954, "The Nimrud tablets, 1952 - business documents", *Iraq* 16, 29-58.
Parrot, A. 1961, *Nineveh and Babylon*, London: Thames and Hudson.
Postgate, J.N. 1974, *Taxation and conscription in the Assyrian Empire.*
Postgate, J.N. 1979, "Assyrian documents in the Musée d'Art et d'Histoire, Geneva", *Assur* 2, 93-107.
Postgate, J.N. 1988, *The archive of Urad-Šerūa and his family. A Middle Assyrian household in government service*, Rome: Herder.
Postgate, J.N. 2000, "The Assyrian army in Zamua", *Iraq* 62, forthcoming.
Reade, J.E. 1972, "The Neo-Assyrian court and army: evidence from the sculptures", *Iraq* 34, 87-112.
Salonen, E. 1980, *Neubabylonische Urkunden verschiedenen Inhalts* III, Helsinki.
Teissier, B. 1984, *Ancient Near Eastern cylinder seals from the Marcopoli Collection.*
Wiseman, D.J. 1967, "A Late Babylonian tribute list?", *Bulletin of the School of Oriental and African Studies* 30, 495-504.
Wolf, W. 1926, *Die Bewaffnung des altägyptischen Heeres*, Leipzig.
Yadin, Y. 1963, *The art of warfare in Biblical lands*, London.

All Figures were drawn by Elizabeth Postgate.

XII

SYSTEM AND STYLE
IN THREE NEAR EASTERN BUREAUCRACIES

Those seeking to reconstruct the palatial administration of the Mycenaean and Minoan world understandably cast their eyes east from time to time to see what might have been going on across the sea (though not so often to Egypt, where palace archives are noticeably unforthcoming). This is partly a general comparison of one palace-centred system with another, and partly much more specifically to see how written documents might operate within that culture. Such comparisons may not always have been as illuminating as hoped. One reason is that cuneiformists, floundering in the sheer volume of documentation, have not always thought as long or as clearly about the operation of their bureaucracies as Linear B pundits. Another is that there are of course as many different bureaucratic systems as there are palace archives, and each is subtly or even not so subtly different. Here I have chosen to pick out three of these systems, and try to use the benefit of distance to apply some clarity of perspective. This should help to reveal some aspects of the system which are not made explicit by the documentation and hence are rarely discussed, and thus to underline the variability.

The three systems have been selected not because there is any suggestion of a 'genetic' relationship between them and Minoan and Mycenaean practices, but precisely in order to underline their diversity in general, and in particular to illustrate the varying role of the written document within the different systems. They are the Ur III kingdom (2100–2000 B.C.), the First Dynasty of Babylon (1800–1550 B.C.) and the Middle Assyrian kingdom in the 13th century B.C. For archaeologists these are at first sight very unsatisfactory choices, because in no case are we dealing with an archive neatly housed within the confines of an excavated palace building; but apart from Mari, we hardly have examples to compare with Pylos or Knossos, and in any case, as will become apparent, a system and its documentation are not necessarily contained within such confines.

Although other matters do of course crop up, it is broadly fair to say that the principal subjects of the written archives are the movement of commodities and the control of persons. Important as it is, there are huge gaps in what we know, or even think we know, about the exploitation of labour in all these cases, and for this reason among others, when examining bureaucratic procedures it will be easier to concentrate on the commodities. Given that writers about early states often single out *redistribution* as one of their attributes, it should be salutary to look critically at how such redistribution might have worked in reality.

Before descending into detail, we need to define some of the ways in which the systems differ. If we look at each document as a cog in the system, it is evident that its significance can only be appreciated if we know how the rest of the machine is operating. Sometimes the other cogs, or to use the terminology I have suggested below, the *transactions*, are also represented by documents, but sometimes not. Hence the need to separate out in our minds the transaction itself and the written record of it: in some systems it seems there is a written record at every stage, in others the scribes do not seem to have been put to work much. I have described the extent to which written instruments are used as *documentary coverage*. In fact the three examples I have chosen are all fairly enthusiastic about documentary coverage of the system: for obvious reasons, we know less about those parts of the system which did not merit documentary coverage, and less about those systems which are less enthusiastic in their use of documents. The Neo-Assyrian empire got by with a great deal less in the way of 'paper' work, and differences of this kind must reflect a differing ethos. Whether the ethos is the product of the bureaucratic system, or vice versa, is a further question which would take us too far in this context.

In any case, since we recover our view of the administrative system very largely through written texts, it is obviously essential to establish the role of the texts within the system before we can use them to reconstruct it. This requires us to employ our terminology with care, and to start with I would like to identify some general concepts which can be applied to our different case-studies and so aid the process of comparison.

transaction

The documentation generated by an administrative system is very largely concerned with the transmission of commodities from one person or organization to another: a written text will regularly be created at the time (and often place) when/where such a transmission takes place. In what follows I shall use 'transaction' to refer to this occurrence; it does not imply any financial or commercial component.

transmission of instruction

Within a system the individuals at each point of transaction are acting under some kind of instruction. Such instructions can be conveyed in different ways, not all mutually exclusive:

— direct oral instruction

— indirect oral instruction (i.e. via an intermediary)

— written personal instruction (i.e. a letter, a 'letter-order')

— written formalized liability (i.e. a 'legal-type' document or contract)

Further, all these may relate to a single occasion or (as must often have been the case) initiate a series of recurrent transactions without need for further authorization.

We could think in terms of 'standing orders', and we can envisage situations in which a system operates smoothly on the basis of standing orders (whether written or orally defined), and resorts to fresh written instructions which might have been preserved for us only when something abnormal crops up.

duties and liabilities

A system's mode of instruction will be intimately bound into the ethos of service. To generalize wildly: a system that operates exclusively orally will depend on personal loyalty and tasks will be carried out from a sense of duty. One that uses written instruments extensively can have a more commercial ethos and tasks can be formulated as legal obligations or liabilities.

In some systems the duties of a junior official may be no more precise than to carry out his superior's wishes and instructions, leaving wide scope for interpretation and presupposing mutual understanding. This may have been the case in the Neo-Assyrian empire (and this is one reason why it does not feature among my examples). At the other end of the spectrum, if the ethos requires it, he may be neither empowered nor required to take any action without explicit authorization from above, and in different ways the Ur III and the Middle Assyrian kingdom offer instances of this.

Administrative tasks are not the same as commercial debts in the shape of material commodities, but they can be described in words and formulated as liabilities. When a task to be performed is formulated in writing, there are at least three components which it might comprise:

— liability for materials involved in the task
— liability for correct execution of the task
— liability for correct documentation of the task

This is of course a banal observation, since any shop assistant making a sale today is simultaneously incurring liabilities under all three headings, but one way in which administrative systems may differ from one another is the extent to which they choose to take account of more or fewer of these different types of liability.

administrative reach

By this I mean the extent to which the central administration controlled the economic transactions in which it was involved. 'Reach' is not an ideal word for what I mean, but must suffice until a better one is found. The image of an administrative net or network is also helpful in general, but in any one context this may be less appropriate because we tend to be looking more at a linear system than a chessboard. By reach I mean how far the administrative control of *transactions* stretches (see Fig. 1). Some regimes extended their administrative reach to all corners of society, others were content to draw in their horns and allow production and commercial activities to take place in what today we might call the private sector. This involves questions that are integral to the nature of the redistribution which is often seen as characteristic of early

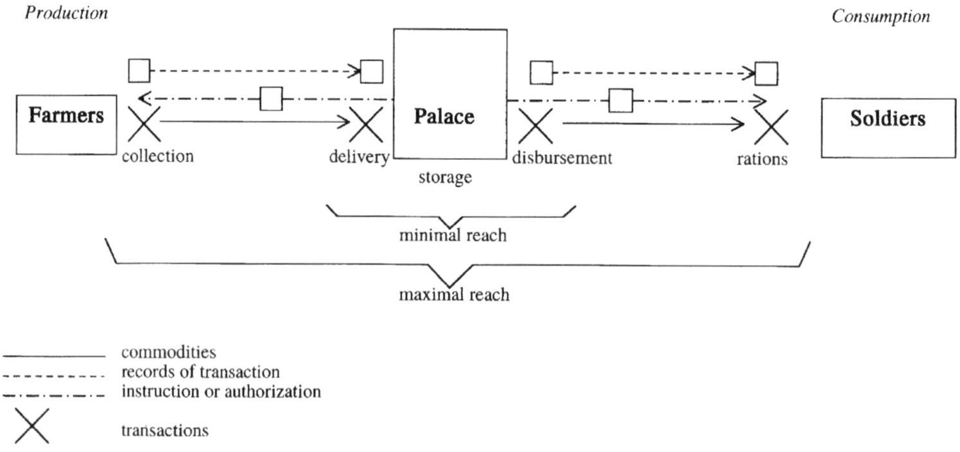

Fig. 1. Documentary coverage and administrative reach – a hypothetical example

states. In order to secure its bread, did the state, palace, or temple organize the labour force which dug the canals and planted the seed, and marshal the harvesters, threshers and grinders of the grain? And when it had its granaries full, did it issue every last bushel to some of those same workers? Or did it let the farmers get on with the job and only send out tax-collectors once the grain was on the threshing floors? Or was it even more relaxed, relying on agents to collect the taxes and to retail the surpluses?

What delimited the administrative reach in each case may have varied: in some cases it may be that the regime would have liked to extend its reach but did not have the power to; in other cases it may have deliberately chosen to shrink its administration, and voluntarily abandon parts of the society and economy to the private sector, something not unknown in the 20th century A.D. In such cases we can suppose that there may have been a perception that the reach *could* always be extended out again.

documentary coverage

Administrative reach does not refer to the coverage of written documentation, which is a different (though of course related) issue. *Documentary coverage* refers to the extent to which the network of administrative *transactions* is matched by the creation of written records. The word 'documentary' is not ideal; I wish one could use *schriftlich*, as 'written' is a bit too informal. To use the net image, the system has nodes at each transaction within its administrative reach and the degree of documentary coverage determines what percentage of these nodes generate a corresponding written instrument. This varying degree has much to do with the differences in bureaucratic style we shall be observing below.

bilateral and unilateral

If we view the economic system as a whole, it is obvious that the extent of the palace's administrative reach may affect both the documentary coverage, *and* the nature of the documents. Where a tightly controlled unitary system is operating, with superiors and subordinates in close contact, many transactions can take place without constant monitoring, and this will tend to reduce the need for dense documentary coverage. Moreover, the documents that are generated will tend to be for the benefit of the archives, written by the bureaucracy for its own data base. I find it helpful to refer to such texts as 'unilateral'. A *unilateral* document is generated within an institution for its own reference. It may record a transaction, and it may state the existence of liabilities, but since it is not authenticated by the party liable, it cannot be said to create the liability or even to prove it (i.e. it is neither a constitutive nor an evidentiary legal or quasi-legal document). In contrast, a *bilateral* document records and provides legal evidence for a transaction, and most of those we meet in administrative contexts document an individual's liability. To be valid, it normally requires the party placed under the liability to acknowledge the liability by the application of his seal or some comparable act. As we shall see, such liabilities could be within the system's administrative reach or beyond it, but they resemble one another and it is often difficult to be certain which side of the frontier they belong.

1. The Ur III system: an archival mode

The administration of the Third Dynasty of Ur deserves it reputation as the bureaucracy par excellence. No corner of Ur III production or labour seems to be free of state control, and the means of control seems to have been the written document. There are more than 25,000 published documents from the administration of the Ur III state, and heaven knows how many more still unpublished in museums and even private collections. The great majority of these come from illicit excavations at just three sites: Tello (= ancient Girsu), Tell Jokha (= ancient Umma) and Drehem (= ancient Puzriš-Dagan). Other archives were excavated by archaeologists, at Ur, Nippur and in the Diyala region east of Baghdad, and one has to suppose that there are at least one million Ur III tablets still lying underground in south Iraq. There are of course problems of interpretation with the language and technical vocabulary of individual documents, but the principal obstacle to understanding the system derives from the need to place each text within its archival context.[1] The association of the texts, which at the three main sites were probably stored on shelves or in baskets in purpose-built archive rooms, has been lost by the tablets' dispersal on the antiquities market, and we can only use internal criteria. Happily the subject matter and to some extent the physical appearance of the tablets do differ from site to site, and Ur III specialists are usually able to assign a tablet to its

[1] Recent writings on the Ur III system include Jones 1976; Civil 1987; Englund 1990.

city of provenance. In this they are also helped by the insistence of the system that even the least considerable transaction be dated, and the anomaly that different cities retained differing calendars. I say anomaly, because it is plain that the bureaucratic ethos which generated this huge volume of paperwork was the product of the reign of the second king of the dynasty, Šulgi, and that it was part of a more extensive reform of government aimed at forging his state into a single organism.[2] One might therefore have expected the local calendars to have been centralized; that they were not probably reflects respect for local sentiment, no doubt largely because calendars were closely integrated with local cults.

We need to reconstruct archives not only to understand the substance of what was going on – which commodities were being transferred, in what quantity, how frequently, and from whom to whom – but also how and why it was happening. Once one archive has been partially reconstructed, we can hope to look for others which may link to it, either via the commodities themselves or via the personnel. A study of such archive-linking is given by Steinkeller,[3] and although it is concerned with labour management rather than commodity movement, it may serve as an example. The documentary coverage of timber exploitation in the province of Umma is summarized in Fig. 2, with the instances of tablets marked by hollow squares. It is fair to say that the coverage is dense.

	responsible official	location of commodity	nature of transaction	document created	sealed?
1.	overseer (ugula tir)	forest (tir)	felling timber	[41] 3.1.3 review of workers	no
2.		[warehouse]	delivery to store	[42] 5.2.2.1 delivery note	no
3a.	governor or head office		authorization for withdrawal	[ ] 5.2.2.3 letter order	yes
3b.	[various officials]	[various uses]	withdrawal from store	[ ] 5.2.2.4 receipt (šu ba-ti) tablet & envelope sealed by withdrawing official	yes
4.	[scribes]		accounting process [18] 5.2.2.6 individual account	[19] 5.2.2.5 annual ledger [60] 5.2.2.7 7-year ledger	no no?

Fig. 2. The Ur III forest paper-trail.

[2] Opinions differ as to how much Šulgi was responsible for the centralization and standardization; see Steinkeller 1987a but more cautiously Waetzoldt 1991.

[3] 1987b.

Let us turn now to look at the documents themselves. The most striking Ur III documents come from each end of the size spectrum. We have little square tablets which record items as banal as the death of a single sheep, duly provided with the name of at least one responsible person and a date to day, month, and year, and then we have tablets with multiple columns each side, summarizing commodity movements for periods of a year or more. And there is everything in between. My impression is that the majority of the Ur III documentation is internal and unilateral, within the same system as the monthly or annual account texts. In other words, individual components of the government's data base, supplying information to the system about the occurrence of a transaction rather than providing evidence for an individual that he has fulfilled a liability.

The matter of sealing comes into play here since it is later closely identified with bilateral documentation. There is a short 'letter-order' from this time which includes the phrase 'let him not refuse on the ground that the tablet has not been sealed'.[4] This could mean one of two things: either, for the present moment, the tablet would need to be sealed in order to prove the authority of the sealing official before the recipient accepts the instruction, or it might need to be sealed to provide the recipient with proof of liability for future use. If the latter, it would hint at a move towards a bilateral mode, which is not impossible. Bureaucracies do not always stagnate, and it has recently been established that the sealing of Ur III administrative tablets at Drehem was not the norm during the long reign of Šulgi, but comes in first during the reign of Shu-Sin.[5] This marks a shift from unilateral to bilateral, which probably reflects the demand for the system's chains of authority and liability to operate where no previous personal relationship existed. In any case, whatever adaptations may have been introduced, the Ur III system constitutes our prime example of comprehensive administrative reach matched by dense documentary coverage.

2. *Old Babylonian procedures: a legal mode*

There is a fair amount of varied documentation about sheep-farming from different times within the Old Babylonian period. For instance, we have:

— full-blown institutional accounting for state flocks from Larsa before the unification under Hammurapi;[6]

— private contracts between shepherds and owners;[7]

— documentation relating to contracts between merchants as collection and retail agents for the palace.[8]

[4] Sollberger 1966, no. 305.

[5] Sigrist 1992, 102.

[6] Kraus 1966.

[7] Postgate and Payne 1975.

[8] Stol 1982; Charpin 1982.

I want to begin with the private contracts, because they illustrate a pattern which, as we shall see, was imported into the palace administration. In a largely agricultural society livestock is a principal form of investment and large flocks may be owned by well-heeled urban families. These obviously are not kept in the city; in south Mesopotamia sheep and goats may be able to survive grazing off fallow fields, young crops and field or canal margins, or they can be fattened in pens, but even within our lifetimes larger flocks are often walked considerable distances following the vegetation.[9] The shepherd was therefore in charge of the flocks for months at a time without any possibility of supervision; moreover, he may have looked after animals belonging to more than one owner, and only the shepherd could know which lambs came from which ewes. If an animal died or was killed, whose was it, and how could the shepherd prove that he had not simply sold the live animal and pocketed the proceeds? The Code of Hammurapi mentions procedures adopted to regulate such issues: parts of the dead animal to be produced as evidence of the death, oaths to be sworn in the temple where proof was not forthcoming. These obviously reflect conventions which operated in illiterate contexts, but during the Old Babylonian period even something as old as the relationship between a flock owner and his shepherd was committed to writing. A systematic approach to the relationship took the form of an annual accounting procedure in which the animals and other products were counted and matched to figures prescribed by a contractual formula (see Fig. 3). Growth of the herd was anticipated and the shepherd was expected to produce at least the prescribed increase in numbers of animals, while in some cases wool and cheese were included in the accounts. Direct payments to the shepherd were minimal, more 'expenses in employment', and his real recompense would lie in the margin by which the actual

	responsible party	location	transaction	document	sealed?
1.	"owner"	shearing	annual accounting	annual ledger	no
2.	shepherd	pasture	entrustment of flocks	herding contract	yes
3.	a. "owner" et al.		order for delivery of sheep	(letter-order)	(yes)
	b. [various recipients]	[various uses]	delivery of sheep as per 3a.	receipt for sheep	yes
	c.	abattoir	delivery of skins of cadavers	receipt for skins	yes
4.(=1)	"owner"	shearing	annual accounting	annual ledger	no

Fig. 3. The Old Babylonian sheep count.

[9] Kraus 1976.

growth and produce exceeded what he was contractually obliged to render up. Obviously in a bad year, or for a bad shepherd, this might be a negative recompense.

There is no need to get immersed in the technical details, because our purpose here is to describe the pattern of employment. The shepherd can be viewed as a self-employed person, having freedom of movement, and able to work for more than one employer at the same time. He has the possibility of accumulating personal wealth, and presumably at an annual accounting it would be open to him to return to the owner a flock in accordance with his liability, and walk away without further restraint. This is the simple situation between a private citizen and his shepherd. It must have been a social strategy which was basic to much of Mesopotamian society before and after the Old Babylonian period, and it is only thanks to the exceptionally literate ethos of that time that it was actually committed to writing. The written record is less surprising in the case of the institutional Larsa archives, and here in any case the situation is more complex, because there is a state-employed herding-contractor (*nāqidum*) who was not himself a shepherd but functioned as an agent. Nevertheless, the same underlying principle applied: that the shepherds were obliged to meet a certain quota of flock-growth and product delivery, and could retain the excess over that. I am not sure where the 'administrative net' stopped and started – whether the 'herding-contractor' was 100% a government employee, or it was only a free contractual relationship – but the underlying ethos was the same: that as long as the state recouped an agreed level of income from its capital, it was satisfied. In this way it was accepting the reality that it could not supervise the shepherds, and was relieving itself of any supervisory burden beyond the edge of the net; and where the edge was reached, by analogy with the private herding contracts, we would expect a bilateral document to have been made out.

In this way, contractual relationships which include profit-making opportunities for the palace's direct or indirect employees were introduced into the 'public sector'. After the unification of south Mesopotamia under Hammurapi this 'privatization' of state enterprises moved further still (see Fig. 4). We find the palace delegating much of the organization of its agricultural investments to agents designated 'merchants' (*tamkārum*). They seem to have negotiated with the palace concessions to a variety of its products, which they were then entitled to take delivery of directly from the producers (such as tenant farmers or shepherds). They then disposed of the goods on the open market, no doubt at a satisfactory profit, and made (or owed) to the palace a pre-agreed payment. For reasons not yet clear to us, these contracts were usually for a bundle of fairly staple products, including dates, (dried) fish, wool. However this arrangement started, by the end of the First Dynasty it had become a well-established practice, to the extent that special provisions have to be made in the *seisachtheia* edicts to protect the agents from unfair losses when a tenant's arrears in delivery of produce, to which the agents had bought entitlement, were cancelled by edict.[10] Later in the dynasty, the palace seems to have moved towards a deliberate farming enterprise which concentrated on breeding calves (for plough teams) and growing sesame for the general

[10] See Postgate 1992, 197–200.

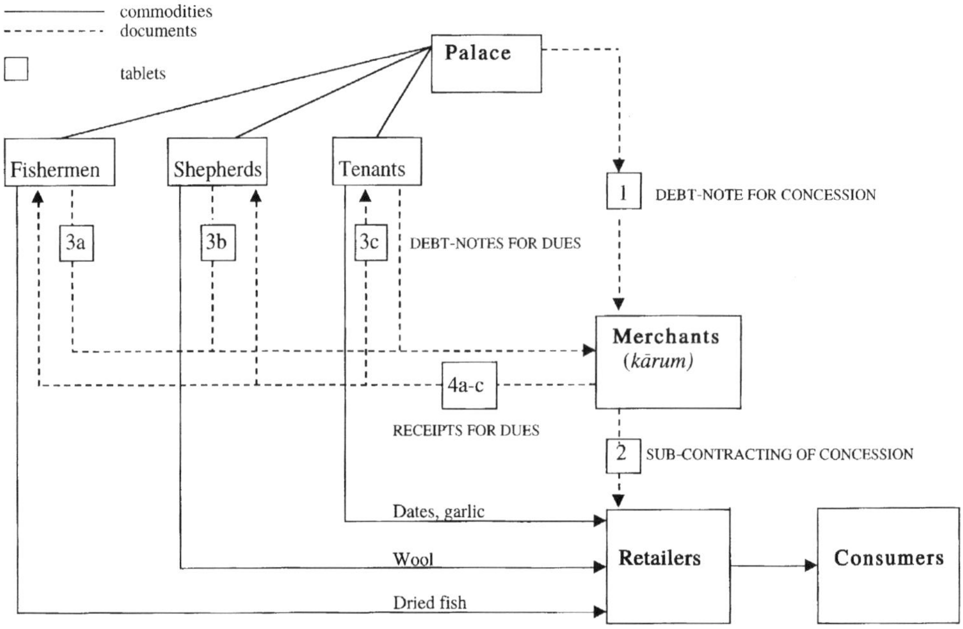

Fig. 4. Old Babylonian surplus produce concessions.

market, administered by the merchants under the same contractual arrangements.[11] It meant that the paperwork was greatly reduced: the palace could leave it to the merchants to recoup its profits from its tenants and other employees, and received its payment from the merchant in silver or another currency. Only one set of accounts to maintain.

I have described these Old Babylonian practices as the 'legal' mode because sectors of the redistributive enterprise have been hived off, privatized, handed over to private contractors under arrangements governed by public legal forms. Thus the documentation between the agents and the palace relates to transactions which take place outside its administrative reach, and the documents are accordingly bilateral. It must be stressed that these are just two instances, and there was certainly a great variety of practice in the four centuries or more between the end of the Ur III Dynasty and the collapse of the First Dynasty of Babylon. Nevertheless, I think it is fair to say that by comparison with Ur III we see here a reduction in the reach, and probably the intensity, of public administration, in favour of contractual relationships with outside parties. It would be very difficult to prove that the administrative cadre of the Ur III period was denser than in the Old Babylonian kingdoms; but the written documents we see suggest that the later system would have permitted economies in man-power, and common sense suggests that this would have been the motive for going down the contractual route.

[11] Charpin 1982.

3. The Middle Assyrian system: a commercial mode

With the Middle Assyrian kingdom we come closer in time to Pylos and Knossos, but perhaps not in ethos. In contrast to my two earlier examples we also know something about the archaeological provenances of the archives.

Because I have written at length on Middle Assyrian bureaucratic practice elsewhere this section has been kept short.[12] From the archaeological provenance of the archives it is plain that much of the central administration's work was carried out not on the palace premises, but in the household establishments of the responsible officials. Some of these were high court officials, including the Chancellor or 'Chief Victualler' *(abarakku)*, others were provincial governors who still maintained a home base in the capital city of Assur. In the 13th century B.C. the Middle Assyrian government operated through these governors, who were, at least in some cases, members of the traditional élite families of the capital city of Assur. We have a group of documents in which the governors of a north-western province are tasked by the central government with the distribution of rations to deported populations within their district.[13]

These illustrate two main features of the system:

(i) the administrative net reaches to the limits of the redistributive process;

(ii) there is dense documentary coverage of the system.

Thus, on the one hand, administrative *duties* are defined in writing and converted to a *liability* which is fulfilled by carrying out the task and, usually, receipt of another written document providing evidence of this; both the transmission of commodities and liability to execute are regularly documented at each transaction node. On the other hand, administrative liability may be explicitly differentiated from a commercial obligation. Tablets recording an administrative liability are not always witnessed, sometimes not sealed, and they often contain the phrase 'he will do x, and then may break his tablet', which occurs only very rarely in legally formulated documents from the commercial sphere.

This may be illustrated by the three fairly typical Middle Assyrian administrative texts summarized in Fig. 5.[14] They belong to the archives of a family which held governorships in the north-western provinces. In No. 22 Aššur-aha-iddina is the 'creditor', but Ištar-kidinni's liability is not so much for the 2000 litres, although this is presumably incidentally part of it, as for the task imposed on him, which is to deliver the grain to Lullayu and ensure that the document with which Lullayu acknowledges receipt includes a particular repayment provision. No doubt his fulfilment of the task would be demonstrated by producing the sealed document. No. 28, in which the creditor is Aššur-aha-iddina's son Melisah, is not dissimilar. The task of the 'debtor' here is to distribute grain from a granary under Melisah's control, and replace it wholly or in part

[12] Postgate 1986.

[13] See Postgate 1988.

[14] Taken from Postgate 1988 (=CMA 1).

CMA 1 No. 22

Contract to deliver grain and draw up the pertinent document of liability

Seal of Ištar-kidinni

❑ 2000 litres of grain of Assur-aha-iddina (is) owed by Ištar-kidinni

❑ "He (=Ištar-kidinni) shall give the grain to Lullayu
and draw up a tablet "of" Lullayu,
in which there will be the provision that:
the capital of the grain will be paid back at harvest or bear interest.

Witnessed and sealed

No. 28

Contract to distribute grain

❑ 1190 litres of grain (withdrawn from the granary within the walls)

of Melisah (is) owed by Mannu-gir-Assur

He shall have this grain distributed
and shall deposit in the granary the new grain
that was given to him for distribution

and break (t)his tablet.

Witnessed and sealed

No. 36

Contract to collect an administrative debt

Seal of Marduk-[bel-išmanni]

❑	4530 litres of grain + 3668 litres of malt	owed by Assur-ereš
❑	2.25 talents of tin	owed by Samedu
❑	1000 litres of grain	owed by Iddin-Nergal
❑	500 litres of grain	owed by Ašaredu

❑ Total 4 tablets of Urad-Šerua

given to Marduk-bel-išmanni for collection.

when he has collected the debts, he may break (t)his tablet.

Witnessed and sealed.

Fig. 5. Three Middle Assyrian documents.

with a new supply. It is not specified, but we would probably be right to assume that he would secure sealed documents from the recipients as evidence that he had carried out the distributions; while, since the amount of the 'new grain' is not specified, it is likely that this transaction was governed by a separate document. In any case, the concern of No. 28 is that the task of distribution be carried out, and it is only by fulfilling this task that the liability is acquitted, and the tablet may be retrieved from Melisah (who doubtless retained it) and broken. That it survived with other tablets in the archive to be discovered by the German excavators suggests that this was one liability that

Mannu-gir-Aššur failed to fulfil. Finally, No. 36 has Melisah's son as the creditor. Here the 'debtor' is being charged with the collection of four miscellaneous unpaid debts. As with the others, his liability is for the execution of the task: this may have involved having the repaid commodities within his possession for a while, but it could also have been discharged by securing delivery of them directly to Urad-Šerua or his household. Thus each of these three documents illustrates the Middle Assyrian practice of formulating an administrative task as though it were a commercial liability, even though in some or all cases it also included temporary responsibility for the commodity involved in the transaction.

There is a now-famous passage from the correspondence of an Assyrian chancellor with members of his household staff, giving minute instructions on the unsealing and re-sealing of a storeroom. I cite it in order to emphasize the awareness of such procedures in contemporary consciousness, rather than for its detailed content.

> Together open the storeroom and get out the chest with (dyed textiles) in it; get out two pairs of (dyed textiles) ... (Then) seal the chest with my seals and return it to the storeroom. Seal the storeroom with this seal (i.e. the one accompanying the letter), and seal my sealing with your seals. Then let PN take the textiles and the seal and bring them to me.[15]

A similar preoccupation with water-tight documentation is betrayed by Middle Assyrian administrative texts that often include phrases prescribing how given transactions should be documented. Recently excavated documents from the north-western provinces (Dur-katlimmu, Tell Sabi Abyad and Tell Chuera) reveal a complex procedure for enclosing letter orders passing from one provincial centre to another in sealed envelopes, using formulae which incorporate explicit instructions to the receiving official for the next stage in the documentation process.[16] Unfortunately one significant part of the record is missing, and that is what was written on wooden writing boards. We know, from references in the clay tablets, that these were used within the administration, probably only as unilateral documents, listing both people and commodities. It always raises the question in my mind, to what extent the clay tablets of the Mediterranean constitute the complete written record.

To conclude, the Middle Assyrian system resembles the Ur III, to the extent that administrative control reaches to the limits of the redistributive system (in some cases, at least), and that there is dense documentary coverage of the system. Nevertheless, the written formulation of administrative tasks as liabilities is strange to the earlier systems, and I have called this Middle Assyrian system 'commercial' because it is my conviction that what we see is the redeployment in public administration of a mercantile ethos in which both commodities and tasks to be executed were regulated by legal instruments.

15 Freydank and Saporetti 1989, KAV 105.
16 Discussed in Postgate forthcoming.

Summary

One essential aspect of a bureaucratic system is the placement of institutional boundaries. Thus, for instance, with a redistributive system the state organization could encompass all stages in the process of redistribution – that is to say the production, collection, storage, transport and ultimate delivery to end-user. The state could monitor all stages, or it could delegate, devolving responsibility to others. Written documentation will reflect these differences, but there are also differences in the way the written record is used, even where the processes were identical. Where all processes took place within the confines of the state organization, one can see that with a tight hierarchy no bilateral documents were needed: unilateral documents could be kept as a source of information for future reference, but would not need to be kept where the administrative network was dense. An increase in bilateral documents perhaps could reflect a slackening of the bureaucratic mesh: as personal oversight became less automatic, a written testimony could substitute for it. As we have seen, at Drehem in the Ur III period, tablet sealing came in only under Shu-Sin, and this may have been a delayed response to the increasing distance between officials.

Of course the limit of the net is not a mere formality: those directly under the net are not their own masters, whereas an independent contractor would at least in theory have the freedom to choose what services to render and when, leaving him free to undertake other activities outside the institutional framework. Whether the relationship between a supplier and the institution was contractual or hierarchical will have depended on the choices of the institution backed by state power, but also on the nature of the source of supply: a shepherd by the nature of his work was not permanently under the observation of the bureaucrat, and the same applies to the merchants who brought materials in from abroad.

Perhaps the Ur III kings would have latched on to the Middle Assyrian system with glee. That they did not is probably because documentary coverage and the legally recognized format of documents had not developed to such a degree in the 3rd millennium private sector. It may not be too bold to suggest that the initiative in the application of written instruments to transactions shifted from the state sector to the private sector after the collapse of the Ur III system. In response to this, in Old Babylonian times the state began to borrow private administrative practice and to farm out much of its system to the private sector, reducing its administrative reach. The Middle Assyrian kings retained their reach, and merely borrowed and adapted the documentary ethos of the private sector.

Trinity College, Cambridge J. NICHOLAS POSTGATE

Charpin, D. 1977. "Marchands du palais et marchands du temple", *Journal Asiatique* 270, 25-65.
Civil, M. 1987. "Ur III bureaucracy: quantitative aspects", in Gibson, McG. & Biggs, R.D. (eds.), *The organization of power. Aspects of bureaucracy in the ancient Near East* (Studies in Ancient Oriental Civilization 46), 43-53.
Englund, R.K. 1990. *Organisation und Verwaltung der Ur-III Fischerei* (Berliner Beiträge zum Vorderen Orient 10).
Freydank, H. and Saporetti, C. 1989. *Bābu-aha-iddina. Die Texte.*
Jones, T.B. 1976. "Sumerian administrative documents: an essay", in Lieberman, S.J. (ed.), *Sumerological Studies in honor of Thorkild Jacobsen on his seventieth birthday, June 7, 1974* (Assyriological Studies 20) 41-61.
Kraus, F.R. 1966. *Staatliche Viehhaltung im altbabylonischen Lande Larsa.*
– 1976. "Akkadische Wörter und Ausdrücke: nawûm", *Revue d'Assyriologie* 70, 172-79.
Postgate, J.N. 1986. "Middle Assyrian tablets: the instruments of bureaucracy", *Altorientalische Forschungen* 13, 10-39.
– 1988. *The archive of Urad-Šerua and his family: a Middle Assyrian household in government service* (Corpus Medio-Assiro 1).
– 1994. *Early Mesopotamia: society and economy at the dawn of history.*
– forthcoming. "Documents in government under the Middle Assyrian kingdom", in Brosius, M. (ed.), *Archives and archival traditions. Concepts of record-keeping in the ancient world.* [reprinted here as No. 27].
Postgate, J.N. and Payne, S. 1975. "Some Old Babylonian shepherds and their flocks", *Journal of Semitic Studies* 20, 1-21.
Sigrist, M. 1992. *Drehem.*
Steinkeller, P. 1987a. "The administrative and economic organization of the Ur III state: the core and the periphery", in Gibson, McG. and Biggs, R.D. (eds.), *The organization of power. Aspects of bureaucracy in the ancient Near East* (Studies in Ancient Oriental Civilization 46), 19-41.
– 1987b. "The foresters of Umma: toward a definition of Ur III labor", in Powell, M.A. (ed.), *Labor in the ancient Near East* (American Oriental Series 68), 73-115.
Stol, M. 1982. "State and private business in the land of Larsa", *Journal of Cuneiform Studies* 34, 127-30.
Waetzoldt, H. 1991. Review of Gibson McG. and Biggs, R.D. (eds.), *The organization of power. Aspects of bureaucracy in the ancient Near East* (Studies in Ancient Oriental Civilization 46), *Journal of the American Oriental Society* 111 (3), 637-41.

Business and Government at Middle Assyrian Rimah

J.N. Postgate

Introduction

Although the Middle Assyrian texts from Tell al Rimah have been understandably eclipsed by the Old Babylonian archives they do make a significant contribution to the history of the site itself and of changing patterns of settlement in the Jezirah. Tablets were found in 1964, 1965 and 1966.[1] Most of them were found together in the scrappy Middle Assyrian layers on the south side of the temple courtyard, and they have been used to date the end of Level Ib to around 1200 BC (Postgate, Oates and Oates 1997, 26). Like many Middle Assyrian archives they had probably been stored in large jars, sherds of which were found with them. A smaller group, also associated with a jar, was found just below the surface on the floor of a Level 1 room built over the Old Babylonian brickwork of the temple antechamber. Plainly the condition of the Level 1 architecture here does not offer meaningful detailed contexts, but the temple was rebuilt in Level 1 (Postgate, Oates and Oates 1997, 25–26), and both locations were presumably still within the precincts of the main temple. As David Oates himself commented, we do not 'know why commercial archives should have been kept in such close proximity to the temple; it is possible that one or more of the principals in the transactions held office in the temple or town' (Oates 1967, 91). I hope to show in the following pages that this possibility is indeed a near certainty, and that the Rimah Middle Assyrian texts shed an interesting light on life in a rural centre.

Family archives

To identify the 'owner' or keeper of an archive most private legal documents can be placed in one of two classes: those recording the conclusion of a bilateral act, primarily sale documents, which serve as evidence of ownership for retention by the new owner (usually a purchaser); and those providing evidence of the creation or existence of a liability (which may derive from a loan but could have other origins), normally kept by the person to whom the liability is due (such as a commercial creditor). At Rimah there are only a few texts concerned with purchases, and those there are are poorly preserved and give no real pattern. Moreover, sale documents are a dangerous indicator of archive ownership, as they could be handed over to a third party along with the property in a future sale. A more promising approach is therefore to look at the debt-notes of various kinds, which would in principle have been retained by the 'creditor'. Texts concerned with the division or bequest of an estate can also be taken as characteristic of a family archive, and although they are much less frequent, as it happens they are represented in both of the Rimah tablet groups (105; 117; 2037; 2016; 2099).

Let us deal first with the 1964 archive, which was found separately. Although the tablets were found close to the mound surface and their texts are fragmentary thanks to their eroded state, four generations of a family can be reconstructed (Deller and Saporetti 1970a, 58), and members of the two later generations (i.e. Ilu-naṣir and his children) feature as the creditors in most of the documents.[2] This group has every appearance of being from the archive of a commercial family, making small loans of grain, tin, and in one case of garlic. Two texts (105 and 117) dealing with divisions of estate underline the private nature of the archive. There are few overlaps with the prosopography of the texts from 1965 and 1966, but that the two groups are at least in part contemporary is clear from 115 (edited in Deller and Saporetti 1970a, 35–36), referring to a loan taken out by Ilu-naṣir from 'Kidin-ilāni and his brothers, sons of [Takla-šemati] daughter of Erīb-ilu', since these are members of the best-attested family in the second, larger, group of texts, now to be considered.[3]

These include 2037, a testamentary deed of Erīb-ilu, son of Athi-nada, in favour of his daughter,[4] which establishes a presumption that we may be dealing with his family's archive, and confirmation comes from the debt-notes. There are at least 11 'creditors' in the group, of whom Mušēzib-Adad, son of Šadânu-ašarēd, son of Haburraru, son of Erīb-ilu, is the most frequently attested. He lends grain, with the supply of harvesters built into the repayment, in 3015, 3022, and 3014; 2903 is also a grain loan, though without the harvester obligation, and it is made to the same borrower as in 3014, Abeli from the village of Hamaraza. In 3022 too the home town of the debtor is stated: Qaṭara. Whether or not this is Rimah,[5] the debtor in 3015 is probably a Rimah resident, as he is the son of Haburraru, who (provided it is the same person) belongs to the third generation of the family of Athi-nada, and is indeed the uncle of the creditor. Note that 3015 and 3022 come from the same year, though different months, but that 3014 and 2903 are dated to two other years, so that this was a recurrent activity. There is perhaps enough here to allow us to say that Mušēzib-Adad is a member of a family long resident in the town, with access to grain supplies which he lends to urban and rural clients.[6] In 3013, in yet another year, his son Nahiš-šalme is probably continuing the family business when he loans grain to Izbu from the city of Arbail.

It is no surprise that an archive should include documents relating to more than one generation of a family, but in fact six generations of this family descended from Athi-nada can be identified in the texts.[7] At least two of the tablets go back to Erīb-ilu in the second generation.[8] Mušēzib-Adad is one of his great-grandchildren in the fifth generation and Nahiš-šalme belongs to the sixth and last attested generation. One of Mušēzib-Adad's brothers is called Abu-ṭāb: his house is mentioned in 2022, and he features as the creditor in 2910, loaning three homers of grain to Abi-ili, son of Amurru-aha-iddina of the town/village of Rakmi. Other documents which relate to the private affairs of Athi-nada's descendants include 3007 (Haburraru) and 2096 (name lost) from the third generation, and 3016 (Haburraru's son Šadânu-ašarēd) from the fourth. Others may belong, but unfortunately the name Abu-ṭāb, which is borne by one of Mušēzib-Adad's brothers, is too common at Rimah: hence we cannot tell if Šamaš-kitta-e-tamši whose father was called Abu-ṭāb (2055, 2060, 2065, 2906; possibly 2084A) is a member of the same family or not.

This tempting assumption would be all the more dangerous because in fact the next best attested 'creditor' is Abu-ṭāb son of Šadânu-bēl-nišēšu, not demonstrably from the same family. He lends tin in 2913 to a borrower from a village whose name is damaged. In 2911 a man whose name begins Ahu-[owes him a sheep;[9] and he is also creditor in 2087, which seems to be concerned with army provisions and is discussed below. He also features in 2015 and 2057, as the person making a repayment recorded on a receipt-tablet. This class of legal text is unusually frequent at Rimah by comparison with Middle Assyrian archives from other sites. Receipts served a variety of purposes, but for some reason alone among Middle Assyrian legal texts, they usually had envelopes (cf. Postgate 1986, 15–16). Normally when a debt was repaid the only action needed was the destruction of the tablet recording the debt, so that there was no need for a fresh tablet embodying evidence of receipt. Hence we find that receipt texts are used when the debt could not be annulled by the destruction of a previous debt-note for one of three reasons: the debt-note had existed but was not available, the sum being repaid did not coincide precisely with the amount of the debt on the original debt-note, or no previous debt-note tablet existed because the liability had not arisen in the form of a recorded debt. The first two types of receipt were studied in detail by Deller and Saporetti, largely on the basis of the new material from Rimah, and so can be described here summarily.

Debt-note lost or not available (Deller and Saporetti 1970a)

These are documents drawn up to affirm that another tablet is null and void (*nahrat*, derivation uncertain but approximate meaning obvious) and should be destroyed 'where it turns up' (*ašar tēlianni*). Sometimes the reason for this statement is given, e.g. that the debt recorded on the absent tablet has 'been received' (*mahir*): thus in Billa 18, 19, and TR 115, 2061, which are therefore a form of receipt tablet. On other occasions, all as it happens associated with real-estate, either pledged or inherited, it is not stated that the amount of the debt has been received (KAJ 142, TR 3001, 3002, 3012). The reason in KAJ 142 is clear: the debt was not repaid within a time-limit, and in consequence the title to the property (here a field) has passed to the creditor, and the original debt is thereby annulled. The same explanation is probably valid in TR 3001 and 3002, where houses in a town called Šaidû had been pledged to cover debts of 4 homers of grain (3001) and 3 talents of tin (3002). The texts do not usually explain why the original tablet is unavailable, but the formula prescribing its destruction is fairly consistent, and it does not sound like an exceptional occurrence. Sometimes there is a time gap, so perhaps the original has just vanished with the passage of time. On other occasions it may be a matter of geographical distance, but examples of this are easier to spot in the next class of receipt document.

Debt reduction receipts (Deller and Saporetti 1970b)

Although one similar text was identified from Aššur (KAJ 159), the remaining 12 examples of this type of document studied by Deller and Saporetti come from Rimah. Their common feature is that they record that a payment of grain or metal has been received (*mahir*). The reason for drawing up a receipt in these cases was that the repayment did not coincide precisely with the amount owing. The texts state that the repayment is to be deducted from the amounts owed and recorded on another tablet or tablets. There are several variants of this phrase (see Deller and Saporetti 1970b, 306). The simplest is in 2015: 'they shall deduct (the amount) from the (debt on the) tablet incumbent on him' (*i-ṭuppi ša muhhi-šu ukarrû;* similarly 2058; 2062; 2065; 3011; 3016). Other examples are: 'they shall deduct (the amount) from the (debts on the) formally executed tablets incumbent on his father' (100), where the debt-notes sealed by his father may either have been absent or for different amounts; 'from a(ny) tablet which turns up' (102), where a corresponding debt-note is obviously not present and cannot be cancelled; and 'from the formally executed tablet for 30 minas of tin which is incumbent on him' (2057A+B).

Noting the relative frequency of this sort of transaction at Rimah, Deller and Saporetti comment that Rimah 'appears in a different light from other known cities, perhaps in consequence of a different economic structure' (Deller and Saporetti 1970b, 314). That seems rather a bold conclusion, but some explanation is certainly required. What these texts must surely indicate is that there is a well-established commercial community of families operating in the Rimah context. Each text requires there to have been a persisting relationship between creditor and debtor: there is the original loan, which is followed by a full or partial repayment; but because the loan document itself cannot be cancelled, an adjustment will have to follow on a third occasion. Moreover, where the amount of the repayment is to be deducted from a (presumably) larger amount or sum of amounts, we must assume that the debt relationship will continue even after the content of the receipt tablet we have has been accounted for. Hence it is plain that in some, if not all, of these cases the creditor–debtor relationship is an abiding one, and the transaction a normal episode within a larger context.

When we consider how these receipt texts fit into the reconstruction of the archives, it is obvious that the tablets should have been retained by the person making the repayment, as proof that it had been made, and that the recipient of the repayment was an earlier creditor of theirs or of the person whose debt is being repaid. Hence, with 100 and 102 it is entirely expected that the (now absolved) repayers are sons of Ilu-naṣir, since the tablets come from his family archive, and the same applies to 3016 where the repayment is made by Šadânu-ašarēd, from the fourth generation of Athi-nada's family.

No previous debt-note

Finally, there are receipts which relate not to the repayment of an earlier loan, but to the acquittal of some other kind of liability. These are actually commoner than the others among the texts so far published from Aššur, where they tend to acknowledge payment of tax or offerings to an official.[10] At Rimah too they tend to record administrative rather than commercial transactions. We have receipts of customs dues (3019), and some receipts of military supplies or equipment (3006; 3023). Two tablets seem to be concerned with the issue of materials in response to an order from central government (2014 and 3018). All these rather special cases are discussed below. More generally, there are a good number of receipt texts which make no mention of a previous debt-note, and are probably part of day-to-day administration. They can differ from commercial receipts in some or all of the following respects: the use of the phrase *ša qāt* 'in the charge of' (frequent; see below), no witnesses (e.g. 2039), no date (e.g. 2086, 3009), though even where there are no witnesses or date there is sometimes, perhaps always, a seal impression (e.g. 2039, 2086, 3009). They can be concerned with items which do not usually feature in commercial contexts, such as straw, horse fodder, garlic, and pieces of equipment (including the enigmatic É *na-zi-qi* in 2086 and 3009?). Or they may look very like ordinary commercial transactions, distinguishable only by the phrase *ša* (or once *ina*) *qāt*. This phrase conveying administrative responsibility is not confined to this group of receipts, since it turns up for instance among the debt reduction receipts, e.g. 2057, 2065, 2906. The tablet and envelope of 2057 record a payment made by Abu-ṭāb, son of Šadânu-bēl-nišēšu, to Nābudu of the town of Unina. The text had the usual provision that the amount paid out should be deducted from the debt of 30 minas of tin recorded on a 'formally executed tablet' (*ṭuppi ṣabitte*), but this does not mean that this was not a public transaction, and indeed it is by no means certain that Nābudu was a creditor, in the sense that he had loaned the money, as it may rather be that the payment was transmitted to him for some unstated administrative purpose.[11]

Official administration

That there should have been a mixture of public and private documents in a single collection of tablets is no surprise, since family archives at Aššur itself included documents which derived from the members' private and public activities; and we may now turn to consider the nature of public administration at Rimah. Wiseman identified three potentially official documents from 1966 as 'written in a skilled hand on a fine reddish clay' (*Iraq* 30, 175). These are 3017, 3020 and 3024. The first of these gives a detailed description of some real estate, which probably includes 3 storerooms (*huršu*), a stable (*bīt sīsē*) and an 'old stable'. Locations are given, and also in one case dimensions, and since the tablet was sealed on the left edge (by a certain Šadânu-[...]), it is likely that this was a property sale, which would explain why the tablet was well prepared and carefully inscribed. 3020 is a short note of 3 lots (*pūru*) of arable land which could have served either a public or a private purpose, and 3024 seems to be an unusual text which is difficult to characterise.

The palace

It is easier to use the content of the texts rather than their appearance to identify the public documents. A few texts mention 'the palace'. One of the few letters from the archive is 2031, concerning a 'palace farmer' last seen in Qaṭara, implying that some peasants were owned or at least administered by 'the palace'. In 2048, a badly broken though potentially very interesting text which is hard to assign to any legal category, we find that miscellaneous equipment *ša ēkalli* was left in the city of Hu[...], in the charge of (*ša* ŠU) Adad-šar-nišē. Another broken text, 2045, mentioned a quantity of grain 'belonging to the palace, [in the charge] of(?) Puhunu, the [eun]uch? of the king' ([*ša* Š]U? ^I^*pu-hi-ni* [LÚ.S]AG? LUGAL). Most of the text is lost, but it concludes 'He shall do his accounts and they shall break their tablets', making it clear that this was an administrative transaction probably involving distribution of supplies to different officials. Finally 3031 is the cancellation (probably) of a tablet which had recorded a debt of 1 mina of tin owed by Šadânu-[...], son of Haburraru, to the palace, in the charge of Saniqi? son of Adad-šumu-ereš. In these last three cases (2048, 2045, 3031) goods said to be 'belonging to the palace' are also said to be 'in the charge of' (*ša qāt*) a person, underlining that they are acting here in their capacity as public officials. Unfortunately, none of these texts tells us where 'the palace' was. Indeed, we cannot be certain that the phrase refers to any individual institution or building, since the phrase *ša ēkalli* in Middle Assyrian contracts often seems to be the equivalent of 'government property'. Therefore, while I think we can be certain that there was a branch of the official administration at Rimah, we cannot be equally certain that it was based in a 'palace', although it seems likely.

The officials

There are remarkably few professional designations in our texts, people being identified by their father's name rather than their profession.[12] Undoubtedly some of the persons in whose 'charge' (*ša qāt*) commodities are said to be must have held official posts but these are not identified for us. This, the opposite of Neo-Assyrian practice, is also true of similar archives from Aššur, and it does not mean that the persons visibly engaged in public affairs had no formal office, merely that the practice was to formulate public liabilities along the lines of commercial debts. Government employees from outside Rimah itself do sometimes have their profession indicated. The government at Aššur used 'royal delegate(s)' (*qēpu/ūtu (ša) šarri*) to liaise between the capital and the provinces. One such is probably mentioned in 2038:10 (*qí-pu*), some kind of record of administrative or commercial proceedings to do with tin, sadly too fragmentary to yield much sense. More revealing are the two receipts 2014 and 3018. These two unwitnessed texts bear the impression of the same seal, presumably that of 'Rēš-Adad, son of Qibi-Aššur, royal delegate' (2014, 13–14; 3018, 12–13; see Parker 1977, 259 with fig. 6 on Pl. XXVII). The item received seems in each case to have been a quantity of straw; and the purpose was for the production of baked bricks for a temple, probably that of

Ištar.[13] A metropolitan connection is also suggested by the phrase 'on? the (writing-)board of Lulāyu' (3018, 5–6),[14] and it was probably connected with some special event, because 3018, 7ff. says 'on the day the king dedicated .... to ...'.[15]

Military service

A group of six texts are probably all to do with the provision of military service or supplies in one form or another. They are not a coherent group, each dated to different *limmu* years, and not conforming to any formula. 3023 is a receipt attesting that Sikku has received grain for the fodder of horses and some straw and fat 'from the *ilku* of Abu-ṭāb'. It does not explicitly state from whom he received them, but we may perhaps assume it was Abu-ṭāb himself. The text is unwitnessed, patronymics are not given, and this was therefore probably an internal administrative note. Another reason for the informality may have been that the people were well known to each other, since they are also involved as principals in 3010: this tablet, which is witnessed, states that (with effect) from the eleventh day of Hibur in the eponymate of Adad-bēl-gabbe Abu-ṭāb and Sikku have settled their accounts. Their *ilku* has been performed through the agency of *(ina qāt)* Sikku'. Again the fathers' names are not specified, which is frustrating, since one would like to know whether or not they were brothers: a Sikku is son of Šadânu-ašarēd (3014; 3015) and brother of Mušēzib-Adad (see above), and so is one Abu-ṭāb. However as we have seen, there are several Abu-ṭābs at Rimah and the evidence of 2087 may suggest that this one is not Sikku's brother, since the creditor here is Abu-ṭāb, son of Šadânu-bēl-nišēšu, and it is a similar debt-note in which a certain Aššur-damiq who comes from a village (the *dunnu* of Šulmānu-naṣir) is made liable for 6 [or more] homers of grain, 53 minas of tin and 3 *qû* of fat. The second half of the document specifies that he shall pay on demand 'the grain (as) fodder for the horses, the fat, the tin (as) hire of a chariot-man and [horse?], the straw? for 4 m[onths?]'.[16] 3005 is a strange document because neither 'creditor' nor 'debtor' is specified. This means that it must have been written for retention in a context where the principal players were taken for granted, although the seal impression on the reverse makes it more than a mere internal memo. The text states simply: '1 homer 20? *qû* grain, 3 *qû* marsh-pig fat, 3 minas of wool, of the army of Nihria who performed *ilku*-service with his brothers'. This passage, with its explicit mention of pig's fat, suggests that the same substance (and not 'oil') is meant by *šamnu* (IÀ) in 2087 and 3023. A liability for pig's fat is also mentioned in an administrative (*ša qāt* PN) text from Tell Fakhariyah.[17] An answer to why it occurs in military contexts is provided by a passage from a Sabi Abyad text which refers to more than a homer of marsh-pig fat 'for ointment for the horses' (*ana piššete ša sīsē*).[18] 3006 is a receipt text which belongs less certainly in a military context; reasons for considering it here are the mention of horses, in l. 2, and the 'profession' *pahnu* of the recipient.[19] It too was a relatively informal document, since the only witness is the scribe, and the filiation of Abu-ṭāb is not given. Unfortunately the central section of the text remains undeciphered. Finally we have 2021(+2051) which is formulated like a normal private debt-note. The unusual feature is that the item borrowed is a spear or javelin, which is to be given back 'on the return of the army' *(ina tuār hurādi)*. In l. 4 the palace is mentioned; the rest of the line is undeciphered, but plainly it may be that the weapon was in some way palace property, although it is firmly said to be 'of Aššur-damiq' in the phrase normally used of the creditor in a contract; interestingly, it is the same Aššur-damiq, son of Munnabitu, who is required to make the contributions in 2087 (see above).

It is difficult to decide whether the occurrence over a number of years of transactions concerned with military service reflects the public administrative responsibilities of one or more of the archive-owners, or their interaction with the authorities in connection with their personal obligations to military service. On the one hand the informality of some of the texts, especially 3005, suggests they are internal to the administration; on the other hand 3023 and 3010, which certainly relate to military service, seem to be private transactions between Abu-ṭāb and Sikku.

Taxation

Links between the town's residents and the central administration are also indicated by a few documents concerned with the payment of customs dues (*miksu*). The most informative is 3019, which records that a tax-collector (*mākisu*) has received 50 minas of tin 'of the customs-dues of a 2-year old mare which came out from the Nairi land, which Uballissu-Marduk the merchant brought out from the Nairi land, belonging to Abu-ṭāb, son of Šadânu-ašarēd'(see Postgate 1983–84, 233b for the collated Akkadian). The phraseology, with the Š stem of *waṣûm* describing the merchant's activity of 'bringing out' from a specified foreign country, recurs in at least two other Middle Assyrian documents referring to regular trading activities, as shown by Saporetti (1977, 97). Dues were exacted on a horse in 3025 too: here the sons of Šadânu-ašarēd accept liability for three separate items, including a debt ascribed to Abu-ṭāb, a lawsuit to do with a house, and 'the merchant who taxed the horse which he gave to Šadânu-ašarēd'. The main text of 3027 seems to have ended *[e-ta-]mar [im-ti]-ki-si* 'he has seen and taxed', but all other details are really lost. That this restoration is broadly correct follows from 2059, cited with the generous permission of H.W.F. Saggs. This states that a tax-collector (*mākisu*) called Sin-šumu-lēšer saw and taxed (*ētamar imtikis*) a 3-year-old donkey in Qaṭara, which a lady called Ṣalimtu had acquired from a Sutian tribesman (*su-ti-e iu-ú-ra-ie-e*). The text is remarkably similar to one in the Louvre from the antiquities market published in Aynard and Durand 1980, 44–46. This records that a tax-collector called Ṣilli-Idiglat 'has seen and taxed' a sheep 'belonging to Ubru, which he had acquired in Kulišhinaš from a Sutian' of the same tribe (*su-ti-e i-iu-ú-ra-ie*). A similar customs receipt for a cow imported from the Sutians (*ša iš-tu su-ti-e še-ṣi-a-ni-ma ...*) was also issued in Kulišhinaš (Aynard and Durand 1980, 36).

šulmānu *text*

Other documents which reflect the interaction between the private citizen and the administration are 129 and 2028, representatives at Rimah of a class of text known from Aššur and Tell Billa. Several such texts are found in the archive of Urad-Šerua's family (see Postgate 1988, pp. xiii–xvi). It was noted there that in the majority of cases the litigant comes from outside Aššur, often probably from a village, and here too the sheep to be paid are owed by someone from other places, Urbadalbe in 2028, and Ša[...]be in 129, each otherwise unknown but presumably in the Rimah district. In 2028, to judge from ll. 11–13, which seem to read *ištu b[ēt?] uššuri-š[u] iqbiūni* 'from the time he ordered his release', the litigant may in fact have been buying his way out of custody.[20]

Rural connections

The impression that the inhabitants of Rimah had wide ranging interests in the countryside is borne out by a miscellaneous assemblage of details in various texts. Well known cities are occasionally mentioned, Arbail (3013), Kalhu (119) and Aššur (Libb-āli: 119 and 2906). Less well known places are more frequent. Texts which actually involve transactions in other places include 2048 (Hu[...]), 3001 and 3002 (houses in Šaidû), 3012 (house in Ešarrazki), 3020 (field in the Village of PN), and 2910 where the creditor receiving a repayment is also the scribe who wrote the tablet, and belongs to ^{uru}*ra-aK-mi*. 2907, which mentions at least three places, is too broken to be enlightening. 3025 concerns in part a lawsuit to do with a house in a town whose name begins Pa[...]. In 2069A one of the witnesses is rather unusually given his home town (Sinanu). A number of debtors or recipients of repayments are identified not only by their name and father's name, but by their place of origin: 100 (Tarbaṣu), 2028 (Urbadalbe), 2903 and 3014 (Hamaraza), 2913 (A...abi), 2087 (*dunnu* of Šulmānu-naṣir). In 3007 a late repayment of the grain loan is specified to be made in Tarmali(?); this may be an unusual arrangement, and the quantity of 145 homers is considerable. In 2066 a resident of Da?sakate? has sold a slave-woman to Mušēzib-Adad 'of Qaṭara'. Most of these look like private transactions; 2049 seems to be a case where an official of a town [...]manite (same place probably in 2905) has issued a commodity, while in 2057 it is Nābudu, the recipient of an administrative issue made by Abu-ṭāb (son of Šadânu-bēl-nišēšu), who comes from Unina; the same Nābudu is also the recipient in 2039 and 2065, although here his place of origin is not specified.

Conclusion

To sum up, the Rimah texts illustrate the activities of a rural centre with a seat of official administration and links with the countryside, both sedentary farmers and the nomads (who are regularly referred to as Sutian).[21] Some of the administrators had private commercial interests of their own, stretching back a number of generations, presumably into the early part of the 13th or later 14th century BC.[22] The Assyrian presence at Rimah would therefore precede the annexation of the western part of Hanigalbat, which has so strikingly been illuminated by the recent discoveries of archives at Sheikh Hamad, Sabi Abyad and Chuera.[23] If the governing class at Rimah in the late 13th century were largely Assyrian, to judge from their names (though there are Hurrian names too), for how long had this been the case? Was there an Assyrian presence in the town before Assyrian independence? If we look back before the Mitanni dynasty to the Mari period, the Rimah texts reveal the mixed population of North Mesopotamia, principally comprising people with Amorite and Hurrian names. Aššur merchants must certainly have passed through there in Old Babylonian times (with donkey caravans, Dalley 1984, 174), but there are very few Assyrian names in the contemporary archive from the site (most conspicuously Aššur-kīma-abiya, Dalley *et al.* 1976, no. 203:8). The Old Assyrian routes from Aššur to Cappadocia remain far from precisely known.[24] One useful crumb of evidence is the Old Assyrian 'treaty' from Tell Leilan,[25] which confirms that the Aššur merchants passed through the upper Habur triangle, and gives a glimpse of how their relations with the polities they passed through were organised. Moreover although at that time the *lingua franca* of the region was North Mesopotamian Babylonian, it is noticeable that the Aššur dating system by *limmu* was generally adopted even in places well outside the political control of the city (and after the reigns of Samsi-Addu and his sons, who were of course in no sense Assyrian themselves), suggesting the pervasiveness of the Aššur commercial tradition.

From those days there must have been some continuity of occupation, since the list of Middle Assyrian provinces includes not only Karana but also Kurda and Andariq, all three of which are minor states familiar in the Mari correspondence and located in the northern Jezirah between the Habur and the Tigris; Qaṭara too was closely associated with Karana in the Old Babylonian period. Another continuously inhabited site was no doubt Dur-Yaggitlim, which has become Dur-katlimmu by Middle Assyrian times and has yielded a large administrative archive which is in the process of publication. The evidence of these Sheikh Hamad texts suggests that this town, well south of the Jebel Sinjar – Jebel Abd-al-Aziz line, served as a secondary capital for the territory west of the Habur, and that a cross-desert route from Aššur to the lower Habur was in regular use. Rimah was on a different route to the west, one which would have taken off from the Tigris in the vicinity of Qayyara and then struck west–north-west roughly parallel with the Jebel Ibrahim ridges and then below Sinjar to the Habur. There is not a modern road on this line but when the area was well settled (and to judge from the ancient tells littering the landscape it was) it must have been an easy option, and Rimah could easily have been a staging post under both Mitannian and Assyrian domination. Whether Assyrians were there under Sauštatar must remain an open question: none of the personal names in the three 'Nuzi type' tablets (124, 125; and Dalley *et al.* 1976, no. 341) looks Assyrian, most being uncompromisingly Hurrian. All the same, one cannot rule out the possibility that Aššur merchants had footholds in long-established cities under the aegis of the Mitannian dynasty. Equally, though, they may only have arrived at the same time as Assyrian political and military control of the region, perhaps in the reign of Aššur-uballiṭ.[26]

Notes

1. The Rimah Middle Assyrian tablets were published in *Iraq* 30 (Saggs 1968, Wiseman 1968). To save space, the tablets are referred to here by their excavation catalogue numbers, which should cause no problems, as they are in that order in the publication. In detail, from 1964 TR 100–15, 117–19, 121, 129, 132, 134–35 and 137 are published in copy on Pl. LXVII-LXXIV, and catalogued on pp. 196–97. From the 1965 season TR 2001, 2006, 2008, 2014–18, 2020–22, 2024-26, 2028, 2031, 2033–34, 2037–39, 2044–45, 2048–49, 2052–53, 2055–58, 2060–66, 2069, 2078, 2080–81, 2083–84, 2086–87, 2090, 2095–96, 2903–07, 2909–10, 2913 are published in copy on Pl. XLIII–LVI, TR 2029 in photograph on Pl. XLII, catalogued on pp. 198–202. The texts of these and other pieces are transliterated or mentioned on pp. 157–74. The remaining pieces from 1965 were small or illegible fragments, with the exception of TR 2019, 2032+2054, 2046, 2050 and 2059, publication of which was deferred pending collation. TR 2037 has also been edited by Wilcke (1976) and after collation by the writer (Postgate 1979, 89–91). TR 2083 was joined to TR 2084 A+D and a composite edition presented in *Iraq* 41 (Postgate 1979, 92–93). From the 1996 season TR 3001–31, 3036–39 are published in copy on pls. LVII–LXVI, catalogued on pp. 204–05, and edited on pp. 177–85. The seal impressions on the entire collection were published by Barbara Parker (1977, 257–68). Photographs of 39 of the tablets are included there on pls. XV–XXVI. The drawings for this article were made by Carolyn Postgate; some results of my collations of the tablets made in connection with this work were incorporated in Freydank and Saporetti (1979), insofar as they concerned the personal names, and others are used here.
2. Except for three tablets (111, 112 and 119) which ought to have been in the possession of Aššur-šuma-uṣur (son of Adad-dayyān, who is said to be from Kalhu in 119), and perhaps 106 where he is the debtor.
3. Note also that a Nābudu is mentioned as the father of a witness in 100 and 113, and as a recipient in 2039, 2057 (from Unina) and 2065. A detailed study of the prosopography, which might provide interesting insights into the community, would take too much space here, and in any case would really need to wait until conditions permit a full-scale collation of all three groups of tablets in the Iraq Museum.
4. Edited by Wilcke 1976 on pp. 224–29, and (after collation) by the writer in Postgate 1979, 89–91.
5. This remains unresolved (see D. Oates, in Postgate, Oates and Oates 1999, 18–20); in 2066 a Mušēzib-Adad 'of Qaṭara' buys a woman for 7 talents 20 minas [of tin]; unfortunately his patro-

nymic is lost, but if this is *our* Mušēzib-Adad it tilts the scales towards Qaṭara as the Middle Assyrian name of Rimah. Note that in 3022 his father's name is probably written ^{d}*ša-da-na*-SAG, supplying further evidence for reading the enigmatic and so far exclusively Rimah deity ^{d}KUR.NA as Šadâna (see Deller and Saporetti 1970a, 55–56; also footnote 15 below).

6. Mušēzib-Adad (son of Šadânu-ašarēd) also features in 3006, dealing with military service, discussed below.
7. See Wilcke 1976, 229ff.
8. 2037 (see above) and 3030, a tin loan.
9. No copy of this tablet is published and I have only a rough note of the first 4–5 lines.
10. See Postgate 1986, 13–15.
11. Probably a similar administrative transaction (though not technically a receipt) is 3003, recording that an Abu-ṭāb had secured the payment of a cow owing to the administration and then entrusted it to a state cowherd.
12. Professional designations (other than tax-collector and (royal) delegate, both mentioned below), are 'mayor' (*ḫaziānu*: 2020, 2083A+), (horse) 'trader' (3019; 3025), 'commander of 50 troops' (2030), 'cowherd' (3003), 'palace cultivator' (2031), and of course scribe. The goldsmith in 2906 comes from Aššur.
13. If the reading of ^{d}*iš*$_8$*-tár* in 3018:10 is confirmed by collation, this would provide Middle Assyrian support for attributing the main Rimah temple to Ishtar (cf. Postgate, Oates and Oates 1997, 26).
14. Since Lulāyu is one of a small 13th-century group of high officials with a 'board' (listing 'king's troops') named after them (see e.g. Freydank 1991, 163).
15. A full collation of these two badly damaged tablets is needed, but preliminary sight of them permits mutual restorations and indicated the following readings in the most significant lines. TR 2014: 1: 1 *a-za-i-*[*lu* ( )] IN.NU. 2: *ša*$^?$ ^{I}*a-bu*-D[ÙG.GA. 8: *ša*$^?$ SIG$_4$.MEŠ *gur-ri-te*. 9: *ša x x x* É ^{d}[x] 10: *a-na la-ba-a-ni* 11: *ub-lu-ni-ni*. TR 3018: 1: ... *a-*]*za-il-lu* IN.NU. 5:]*i+na le-'i*. 6: *ša* ^{I}*lu*$^?$*-la-ie-e*. 9: *a-na* KUR$^?$.NA$^?$ *ú-še*$^?$*-lu*$^?$*-ú-ni*. 10: x SIG$_4$.MEŠ *ša* É ^{d}*iš*$_8$*-tár*$^?$. 11: *ša gur-ri-te la-ba-ni*. 12: *ub*$^?$*-lu*$^?$*-ni-ni*. The form *gur-ri-te* must be the Assyrian form of *agurratum* 'baked-bricks'. If the reading of KUR.NA in 3018:9 were confirmed, it might contribute to the enigma surrounding the ^{d}KUR.NA, who seems to be a Rimah speciality (here read Šadânu following Saggs, but cf. Deller and Saporetti 1970a, 53–57 and note 5 above; Freydank and 1979, 115-6), suggesting that he may have had a shrine here (though the lack of a divine determinative is a worry).
16. The text of these lines was restored with the benefit of collation in Postgate 1982, 304. Since then the correct restoration of l. 12 has occurred to me, so it is worth repeating the lines: 10. ŠE-*um* PAD-*at* 11. [AN]ŠE.KUR.RA.MEŠ 12. [AN.N]A *ig*$^!$*-ru* 13. ša LÚ.GIGIR *ù* ANŠE.[(KUR.RA)] 14. IN.NU *ša* 4 I[TI(.MEŠ)] . (There are remnants of a date on the left side, Nabû-bēla-[uṣur], Saporetti 1979, 119.)
17. Güterbock 1958, no. 7, pl. 84.
18. T93–10, quoted by courtesy of F.A.M. Wiggermann, who tells me that the quantity of 1.2 homers was spread over a period at less than half a *qû* per day.
19. Which is also attested in KAJ 307, a settling of accounts similar to 3010, which includes the statement that 'they did not give a spear (*ulma*) or an axe (*haṣinna*) to their *pahnu*' (cf. Postgate 1982, 305–06).
20. 2903 is also identified as a *šulmānu* document (Saggs 1968, 171) and may indeed have been one, although the critical word *šulmānu* is very difficult to recognise in the visible traces of l. 9.
21. Sutians are found involved in the animal trade at Rimah and Kulišhinaš (see above on 2059) and in the purchase of a slave woman (2083A; see Postgate 1979, 92–93). They also appear in the archives from Sabi Abyad, Chuera, and Sheikh Hamad (e.g. Arnaud 1991, No. 105; C. Kühne 1995, 207 (cf. p. 220, 92.G.214:18, 26); Cancik-Kirschbaum 1996, 231). They are sometimes qualified by a narrower tribal designation (e.g. Yurayu at Rimah and Kulišhinaš, Tahabayu at Rimah, and Qairanayu at Dur-Katlimmu and Sabi Abyad).
22. For the chronology of the Rimah texts cf. Wilcke 1976, 229–33.
23. Cf. in general Harrak 1987.

24. Cf. in general Nashef 1987. One Middle Assyrian route to the Carchemish stretch of the Euphrates through Chuera is discussed e.g. in C. Kühne 1996, 5.
25. Eidem 1991.
26. Three tablets from the smaller 1964 archive seem to mention a father and son from one of the elite families at Aššur from which provincial governors were chosen (as recognised by Saporetti 1970, 149). These are the *šulmānu* text 129 where the 'creditor' may be Urad-Šerua, son of Melisah; 119:8, where Melisah's role unfortunately remains obscure, and possibly 114:18 (as the father of a witness [Urad-^{d}Š]e-ru-ia). If this is the same man as the Governor of Nahur under Shalmaneser, whose son was Urad-Šerua, as proposed by Saporetti, then the family's interests outside Aššur will have included Rimah as well as Kurda and Karana (if Karana is not itself Rimah); cf. Postgate 1988, pp. xx, xxv and texts 50; 56. The identification is made more plausible by the mention of Aššur (URU ŠÀ.URU) in 119:11, and the presence of a *šulmānu* text suggests that they may have exercised some administrative power over the Rimah area.

Bibliography

Arnaud, D. 1991. *Textes syriens de l'Age du Bronze Récent.*

Aynard, M.-J. and Durand, J.-M. 1980. 'Documents d'époque médio-assyrienne', *Assur* 3/i, 1–63.

Cancik-Kirschbaum, E.C. 1996. *Die mittelassyrischen Briefe aus Tall Šēḫ Ḫamad.*

Dalley, S. 1984. *Mari and Karana: Two Old Babylonian cities.*

Dalley, S., Walker, C.B.F. and Hawkins, J.D. 1976. *The Old Babylonian tablets from Tell Al Rimah.*

Deller, K. and Saporetti, C. 1970a. 'Documenti medio-assiri redatti per annullare un precedente contratto', *Oriens Antiquus* 9, 29–59.

Deller, K. and Saporetti, C. 1970b. 'Documenti medio-assiri redatti a titolo di ricevuta dietro parziale adempimento di un debito', *Oriens Antiquus* 9, 285–314.

Eidem, J. 1991. 'An Old Assyrian treaty from Tell Leilan', in Charpin, D. and Joannès, F. (eds), *Marchands, diplomates et empereurs: Etudes sur la civilisation mésopotamienne offertes à Paul Garelli*, 185–208.

Freydank, H. 1991. *Beiträge zur mittelassyrischen Chronologie und Geschichte.* Berlin: Schriften zur Geschichte und Kultur des Alten Orients, 21.

Freydank, H. and Saporetti, C. 1979. *Nuovi attestazioni dell'onomastica medio-assira* (Incunabula Graeca 74).

Güterbock, H.G. 1958. 'The cuneiform tablets', in McEwan, C.W., Braidwood, L.S., Frankfort, H., Güterbock, H.G., Haines, R.C., Kantor. H. and Kraeling, C.H. *Soundings at Tell Fakhariyah* (Oriental Institute Publication 79).

Harrak, A. 1987. *Assyria and Hanigalbat: A historical reconstruction of bilateral relations from the middle of the Fourteenth to the end of the Twelfth Centuries BC* (Texte und Studien zur Orientalistik 4).

Kühne, C. 1995. 'Ein mittelassyrisches Verwaltungsarchiv und andere Keilschrifttexte', in Orthmann, W., Hempelmann, R., Klein, H., Kühne, C., Novak, M., Pruß, A., Vila, E., Weichen, H.-M. and Wener, A. *Ausgrabungen in Tell Chūera in Nordost-Syrien, I,* (Saarbrücken: Saarbrückerei und Verlag), 203–25.

Kühne, C. 1996. 'Aspects of the Middle Assyrian Ḫarbu archive', *State Archives of Assyria Bulletin* 10/ii, 3–7.

Nashef, K. 1987. *Rekonstruktion der Reiserouten zur Zeit der altassyrischen Handelsniederlassungen.*

Oates, D. 1967. 'The excavations at Tell al Rimah, 1966', *Iraq* 29, 70–96.

Postgate, J.N. 1974. 'Review of C. Saporetti, *Onomastica medio-assira*', in *Oriens Antiquus* 13, 65–72.

Postgate, J.N. 1979. 'On some Assyrian ladies', *Iraq* 41, 89–103.

Postgate, J.N. 1981. 'Nomads and sedentaries in the Middle Assyrian sources', in Castillo, J.S. (ed.), *Nomads and sedentary peoples* (XXX International Congress of Human Sciences in Asia and North Africa, Mexico 1976), 47–56.
Postgate, J.N. 1986. 'Middle Assyrian tablets: the instruments of bureaucracy', *Altorientalische Forschungen* 13, 10–39.
Postgate, J.N. 1982. '*Ilku* and land tenure in the Middle Assyrian kingdom – a second attempt', in Dandamayev, M.A. *et al.* (eds), *Societies and languages of the ancient Near East,* 304–13.
Postgate, J.N. 1983–84. 'Review of P. Machinist, *Provincial government in Middle Assyria and some new texts from Yale*', in *Mesopotamia* 18/19, 229–34.
Saggs, H.W.F. 1968. 'The Tell al Rimah tablets, 1965', *Iraq* 30, 154–74.
Saporetti, C. 1970. 'Rapporti Assiria-Anatolia negli studi più recenti (I)', *Studi Micenei ed Egeo-Anatolici* 11, 146–51.
Saporetti, C. 1973–74. 'Gli eponimi medioassiri di Tell Billa e di Tell al Rimāḥ', *Mesopotamia* 8/9, 167–79.
Saporetti, C. 1977. 'La figura del *tamkāru* nell'Assiria del XII secolo', *Studi Micenei e Egeo-Anatolici* 18, 93–101.
Wilcke, C. 1976. 'Assyrische Testamente', *Zeitschrift für Assyriologie* 66, 196–233.
Wiseman, D.J. 1968. 'The Tell al Rimah tablets, 1966', *Iraq* 30, 175–205.

The invisible hierarchy: Assyrian military and civilian administration in the 8th and 7th centuries BC. *

Introduction

How the Assyrian empire functioned remains obscure because the royal inscriptions, of which we have many, are not concerned to convey such information, and the administrative texts and archives we have are neither as voluminous nor as transparent as in some other periods of Mesopotamian history. At first sight it seems as though the written word and an elaborate bureaucratic hierarchy were relatively unimportant under the Neo-Assyrian kings, and in what follows an attempt is made to test this impression by examining some aspects of Neo-Assyrian administrative procedure.

By hierarchy, I mean both the personnel through whom the activities of government were administered, and the chain of authority and command which placed one official below or above another, thus obliging one person to carry out the instructions of another by virtue of their respective positions in the system. This is I hope not a controversial definition, but it is worth noting that it already uses some words, like "instruction" or "authority", which presuppose some aspects of the system worthy of further investigation.

Before we can understand *how* the hierarchy functioned, we have to remind ourselves *what* it was supposed to be doing. As the representative of the god Assur, the king was in charge of the administration of the land of Assur. The king was responsible for the prosperity of the land, and in the coronation ritual is explicitly required to enlarge it: "extend your land with your just sceptre" (*ina ešarti haṭṭi-ka māt-ka rappiš*).[1] Accordingly aspects of the government of the country of direct concern to the king will have included: defence of the realm,

---

* The origin of this text is my contribution to a conference on Palace, King and Empire held at the Carsten Niebuhr Institute in May 1999. This was revised and enlarged for the publication of the proceedings in 2000 and minor changes made in 2003. The current version, updated bibliographically but not significantly otherwise, is published here in advance of the conference volume by kind permission of Prof. Mogens Trolle Larsen. Normal Assyriological abbreviations are used (as in W. von Soden, *Akkadisches Handwörterbuch*); note that although letters are where possible cited after their edition in the *State Archives of Assyria* (SAA) series, the ABL reference has often been left in to facilitate comparison with earlier literature which uses the ABL numbers.

[1] Müller 1937.

construction of public buildings and irrigation works, agricultural reform, judicial administration, and observance of ritual conformity.

If we ask how the king carried out these responsibilities, or from a different standpoint, how the establishment used the monarchy as an instrument of rule, we have to look both at the reality, and at the ideological vocabulary: how was the king's will converted into action by his subjects on the ground, and how was the chain of command described, i.e. what terminology was in use to describe the formal hierarchical structure, and what everyday vocabulary was applied to its functioning? One of the frustrating but familiar aspects of Assyria is that in the inscriptions which are the closest our Assyrian informants come to writing history we have few statements about anything other than the actions of the king himself, and we are obliged to glean hints from the letters and administrative documents which were themselves components of the machinery of government.

Royal or state sector

Before examining the administration in detail, we need to define which sector of society we are talking about. One important distinction is made for us in a letter to the king concerned with how he should deal with people who had appealed to him for justice - *ša a-bat šar-ra-a-te* [*izkarūni*].[2] The writer defines two categories of person who might have made an appeal: a slave of the king, or a slave of an Assyrian (*šumma* ÌR *ša* LUGAL ... *šumma ur-du ša aš-šur-a-a*). While all subjects of the king must in one sense have been his "slaves", this passage makes it clear that one sector of the populace was considered to be employees of the king.[3] Exactly what this implies is not immediately self-evident. To us it seems reasonable to make a distinction between those in "state" employment, charged with carrying out the civil administration of the country as a whole, and those employed as members of the royal household. In this letter the writer is surely thinking of state, rather than royal, servants. This seems to follow from his expectation that the "slave of the king" would have made his appeal either to his "captain" or to his provincial governor (*ina* [UGU] LÚ.*šak-ni-šu ina* UGU LÚ.NAM-*šú iq-ṭi-bi*). These are two ranks in the upper echelon of state administration, not falling within the royal household.

Nevertheless a royal sector of some nature and size must have existed. Kings, or at least their families, had personal identities independent of their state function, which would involve the possession or at least the occupation of buildings, i.e. palaces, the private ownership of land, the ownership of slaves, not to mention a harem, and the employment of "free" staff (i.e. not slaves) for a variety of purposes which were not part of state administration. It is likely they also engaged in productive activities. When we come across "weavers of the king",[4] there is a temptation to assume that they served the king himself, rather than the

---

2 CT 53, 78+426. A first attempt at an edition in Postgate 1980b.

3 The precise definition of an "Assyrian" remains to be established (see Postgate 1980b); one might be tempted to say that we see here three categories of Assyrian subject: free Assyrians, their slaves, and state or royal slaves. But provisionally, it is not certain that the free Assyrians were not themselves "slaves of the king".

4 MÍ.UŠ.BAR.MEŠ *ša* LUGAL (SAA 1, 33:24).

state as a whole, and it would not be surprising if there were many other employees, whether service personnel or craftsmen, who fall into this category. It seems to me likely that there was a "private" royal sector which was distinct in practice and distinguished in theory, but this is hard to prove, and for our present purposes, it is not specially important. Obviously we cannot always expect to be able to determine whether a single professional title, or a particular administrative action, fell within a separate royal sector or formed part of state administration, but the procedures and ethos are likely to have been similar. We shall be dealing in principle with the state sector, but if some instances derive from "royal" contexts it will not greatly matter.

Military and civilian

The state sector must have comprised an extensive cadre of officials to whom the king's duties of state were delegated.[5] Quite apart from military field officers, tax collectors and recruitment officers were needed, and the provincial governorates required civil administrators for town and countryside. The supply of clothing and other equipment for the army and public works, whether through the *iškāru* system or from some other source, will have required managers, and the activities of all these officials required monitoring and remunerating by someone (not all can have been allocated land holdings). One issue which needs to be addressed immediately is summed up by the words "military and civilian" in my title, which mask an ambiguity: are we looking at one hierarchy or two? Did the Assyrian government have a single system or two separate branches for the administration of military and civilian affairs? In the case of the Ur III kings P. Steinkeller has reconstructed a dual system comprising a "Civil Service", based on the traditional governing mechanisms in the different city-states, and a military command, presided over by the *šagina/šakkanakkum*, which was centrally run and co-existed with the civilian regime in each province.[6] Hence the possibility that in the Neo-Assyrian empire the military and civilian branches of the administration were separate is one that must be seriously considered. This is obviously a fundamental question which needs to be resolved before we can look in more detail at what the administrative system really consisted of, and at how it relates to the buildings in which we usually assume it operated.

Generally, we need to bear in mind that the bulk of the correspondence relating to government administration tends to be about military matters, or at least the spin-off from military matters. This is no doubt partly because of the importance and unpredictability of military events, requiring urgent and irregular actions and accordingly generating correspondence. Thus letters not infrequently deal with the disposition of deported populations. This is something which also features in archives of the Middle Assyrian period, and reasons are presumably that these were exceptional events which required ad hoc arrangements, and also events which crossed the boundary between one governor and another or between one governor and the central administration.

---

[5] How "extensive" we are unable to say, as we have no comprehensive statements in our sources. Apart from military lists, cf. the round numbers in SAA 7, 21 and 22, with comment on p. XIX; there are 28 procurement-officers (*mušarkisu*) listed in CTN 3, 99 section J.

[6] Steinkeller 1987.

This said, the evidence does seem to point in one direction:

• Provincial governors, who certainly had responsibility for the conduct of civilian affairs in their provinces, also had military duties. To cite just a few cases, the royal inscriptions of Sargon tell us that they could be expected to prepare stores of flour and wine for military purposes,[7] and that they were expected to mount campaigns (e.g. under Sargon on the Iranian front).[8] At Guzana under Adad-nirari III the governor receives an instruction, to be forwarded to his colleague, to send troops to a campaign.[9]

• We know that some of the Assyrian subjects recruited into government service under the *ilku* system became "king's troops" (*ṣāb šarri*), but that others were used "to do the king's work".[10]

• Under Esarhaddon the *kiṣru* (or cohort) system was greatly expanded from its military role into an organization of groups of craftsmen, shepherds etc. under government control (see further, below).

• As we have seen above, CT 53 78+426 distinguishes plainly between persons in state service, who are called "slaves of the king", and those in the private sector who are called slaves of an Assyrian. Those in state service are identified as coming under a governor and a *šaknu*, which is often a military rank, and there is no attempt to identify whether they are in military or civilian posts.

For all these reasons, in discussing the administrative hierarchy of the state sector, we have to assume that province by province the individual governors were head of both civilian affairs and the military hierarchy. Beneath them, moving down the hierarchy, tasks must obviously have become more specialized, and no doubt most posts were carried out in either a civilian or a military environment. This does not necessarily mean that the titles of offices can always be confidently assigned to one or the other, and indeed, as just mentioned, the military hierarchical structure seems to have been replicated in civilian contexts.

The administrative ethos

The terminology of appointments.
For the system to work, spheres of responsibility need to be well-defined, and appointments to be formal. Certain important appointments were reinforced by ritual. At the highest level each provincial governor mirrored the range of royal functions in his own sub-set of the land, probably exercising the same judicial and military (though perhaps not religious) roles. The ministers of state were chosen as

[7] TCL 3, l. 53.

[8] E.g. Fuchs 1993, p. 156, l. 319.

[9] Weidner 1940, p. 9 Text 1.

[10] See Postgate 1974a, 218-224.

eponyms by the same procedure as the king, and in the coronation ritual were formally reinvested with their sceptre of office by the king.[11] From the omen queries we know that some appointments were submitted to divine approval. In SAA 4 we have queries relating to the suitability of a priest (*šangû*), a temple-auditor (*šatammu*), the chief eunuch, and the governor of Ur (*qēpu*). The phraseology of these queries gives us words used to describe official responsibility (*piqittu, bēl piqittūti*), and the act of appointment *(paqādu, šazzuzu)*:

• "should he appoint him to an official post?" (*ana bēl piqittūti lipqid-su* SAA 4, 166)

• "for as long as he carries out that office" (*adi ūmē mal piqittūta šātu ippušu* SAA 4, 156)

• "should he let (him) serve with him?" (*ina panišu lušazziz[-su]* SAA 4, 152*)*.

In the contemporary correspondence also the normal term for nominating a person to an office is *paqādu*, with its derivative *piqittu* "an appointment". The phrase *bēl piqitti* is current in the letters too, and does not refer to a specific office, but to any "official" or to the "official responsible". Thus the king may ask a governor "Is there an official of yours over them?" and be told that "The mayor of the village and the chief scout have been appointed as my officials in charge of them" (*bēl pi-qit-te-ka-a ibašši ina pānišunu hazannu ša* URU *rab dayyāli bēl pi-qit-ta-te-ia [in]a muhhi-šunu paqqudu* SAA 1, 239). Other examples are "I have sent an official with them" (SAA 1, 248) and "Let me appoint my major-domo with the (other) officials" (SAA 1, 264).

To "stand before" is used not only of courtiers, but of civilian service in general:

• "(a scribe) came two years ago and served with Ilaya-bel" (*ina pa-an* PN *it-ti-ti-zi*, SAA 1, 204)

• "I despatch him to right and to left, (and) he serves with me" ([*ina*] IGI-*ia i-za-az* SAA 5, 63).

We have seen the causative "appoint to serve" above, in SAA 4, 152; in the letters *šēšubu* "to instal" is more common. The everyday word for "to dwell" in Neo-Assyrian is *kammusu*, while *ušābu* often, though not exclusively, refers to the occupation of a post.[12] See SAA 1, 12, cited below, or "he installed his eunuch into the mayoralty" (LÚ.SAG-*šú a-na* LÚ *ha-za-nu-ti ú-se-še-eb*, ABL 473:6-7), in SAA 1, 171:6 (=NL 18) of the king installing a baker in Hatarikka, if rightly

[11] *attamanu bēl pāḫete ša ukallūni .... [paḫ]assu luka'il* (Müller 1937, p. 14).

[12] My thanks to Dr. R. Whiting for providing me with a list of occurrences of *ušābu* from the Helsinki data base. We also find *ušābu* used of government allocation of people to new residences. With the Š stem we need to bear in mind that there may not have been an appropriate causative stem to go with *kammusu*. The same uncertainty about the meaning ("occupy (dwelling or post?)") affects *mūšubu*, e.g. in SAA 7, pp. 9-11 (cf. my hesitation there on p. xvii).

restored, and of military service "he installed his elder brother" (SAA 1, 205 (=ABL 154):17).

This last passage is concerned with service in the army, either as a *mār damqi* (charioteer) or as a *raksu* (meaning unknown). Here the verb in use for "serve" is *lasāmu* "to run", and these soldiers could be variously serving in the palace contingent, or with the author in Raṣappa, or with the king himself. In the other similar context for *lasāmu* the service is also under a *rab kiṣri* within the military system: "I appointed him to be under PN, another cohort-commander, but he did not consent, saying "I shall serve in my own *group*" ..." (*ina kal-zi-a-ma a-la-su-u[m]*, SAA 1, 236).[13]

If there was a formal or informal process of appointment, such that it was clear to all concerned whether someone held an appointment or did not, there must obviously have been a process of dismissal too. The term for this in Neo-Assyrian is *pattu'u* (*petû* D):

• "I sacked him from the post of major-domo and removed him, but you installed him in his house in the centre of Arrapha ..." (TA* *pan rab-bētūte up-ta-at-ti-šú attiši ina qabsi Arrapha ina bētišu tussēšibšu*, SAA 1, 12).

• "Just as the king my lord commanded we divided them up, and I appointed a "palace slave" to be in charge of them, but PN dismissed him" (*up-ta-ti-šú*, NL 68, *CTN 5, p. 205*).

• "The king my lord wrote to me to say "You dismissed him from the post of cohort-commander"... (but) I did not dismiss him at all, he is (still) a cohort-commander" (TA* *muhhi rab-kiṣirūte tu-up-ta-ti-šú ... laššu la ú-pat-ti-šú rab-kiṣri šū*, SAA 1, 235).

Compare SAA 10, 364 (cited below), where the dismissal is carried out by an aide and his deputy at the royal behest. The same word can also be used of foreign governors and local dignitaries outside the Assyrian hierarchical system (ABL 638, of Ilu-yada' of Der; ABL 645, of a city-ruler in the Zagros).

Thus, to sum up, although the officials involved in administrative activities are usually referred to by their name, not by their office, the well developed terminology of appointment and dismissal is consistent with the ethos of a formally regulated administration.

Delegation of authority

Although, as shown below, the king was recognized as the ultimate source of authority, in practice as well as in theory, most of the time his authority was of course delegated so that officials could take action and make decisions without constantly referring back up the chain of command. The concept of authority, and

---

[13] The precise meaning (as indeed the reading) of *KALzu* (which is attested mainly in Neo-Assyrian contexts, but can now be recognized in a Middle Assyrian palace edict of Assur-uballiṭ, AfO 17 (1954/6) 268, 1:4) remains in doubt.

of authorization, is current, and expressed with the verb *šalāṭu* "to have authority":

• "I have no authority over anyone in my own department" (*ina muḫḫi memēni ina bēt bēlēya lā šalṭāk* ABL 84).

• "The priest wrote down the dedications in a sealed document and diverted (them) to himself, and I am not given authority in the matter *(anāku ina muḫḫi lā šašluṭāku* SAA 13, 126 =ABL 177).

When we come to look at how authority was delegated and instructions transmitted we have a problem in that our source for such procedures is itself the instrument, causing the risk of circularity in our argument. Put another way, this is a question of administrative style, and the style needs to be understood not only for its own sake, but also because it determines the nature of the written documentation available to us. The royal inscriptions are irritatingly silent about any of the machinery of government or of military command. Much the most informative body of material on this subject is provided by the royal correspondence from Kalhu and Nineveh. There are also what we class broadly as "administrative" documents from both sites, or more precisely, from three main palaces, the South-West Palace at Nineveh, and at Kalhu the North-West Palace and Shalmaneser's Review Palace. The problem is, these are not systematic archives mapping the regular activities of the administration, such as we do have for some sectors of government at other places and times. They give the impression of being, and I am sure they mostly are, pieces of writing produced by officials as part of their official activities *only as and when an occasion demanded.* They are not usually quasi-legal documents constituting proof of a liability, in the way that much of Middle Assyrian administration seems to have been carried out, but notes or accounts written for one official or his department for its own internal reference. There are of course exceptions, but looking at what we have one cannot resist the conclusion that in general administrative commands and decisions were transmitted orally without parallel documentation, and that the system worked via word of mouth within the framework of a recognized hierarchy.

If this is correct, and of course it is partly an *argumentum e silentio* and hence susceptible to disproof or at least disbelief, it has obvious implications for any effort to reconstruct the reality of the administrative structure. Where each administrative liability is not expressed in writing as a legal obligation, the guarantee that the system will work must depend on an ethos of service. Whether the duty of each official is perceived as owed to the system, or to an official or officer immediately above him in the system, the reason for fulfilling that duty is a mixture of loyal conscientiousness -- perhaps even pride -- in fulfilling the assigned role, expectation of reward and improved security in employment, and fear of the consequences of failure. The system will also require common acceptance of the validity of oral commands, and will depend heavily on the mutual acquaintance of at least some of the parties involved. The non-use of regular written instruments in the bureaucracy must have limited the ability of the system to function as single undifferentiated whole in which *any* higher official could give commands and expect performance from *any* lower official. To achieve this in a given situation, it may have been necessary for officials to climb up the administrative tree until they reached a point where the official they were seeking to control also fell under the same higher command; and sometimes this may have been the king himself.

Those documents from the administration which we have will tend to reflect the exceptional, and not the normal, and need to be treated with caution as a basis for reconstructing the system as a whole. And of course it must always be borne in mind that we cannot recover a representative sample of the complete range of the documents that *were* written, because not all were clay tablets. The problem of perishing Aramaic scrolls may not be too significant here, since we have no evidence that papyrus (or leather) was used for everyday administration. More of a problem is the loss of the wooden writing boards inscribed in cuneiform, which we know were used for making lists of people, for instance.

So to sum up, reconstructing the bureaucratic hierarchy on the basis of the surviving cuneiform documents is doubly difficult, because most routine administration was *not* committed to writing, and what we do have is biased precisely because it records the exceptional. Nevertheless, it is plain from the terminology of appointment and dismissal that a well-defined administrative hierarchy was in place.

The king's role

There is plenty of evidence in the royal correspondence from the late 8th and 7th centuries that the kings played an integral role in the exercise of government, and that they played this role in person. It is noticeable that we not infrequently find letters from persons who have failed to see the king in person, although they plainly would have preferred this. Either they are simply too far away by virtue of the task they are carrying out, or they cannot secure an audience. Writing a letter is a second-best; an audience with the king is much better. SAA 1, 160 (=ABL 843) is a letter Tariba-Issar found himself forced to write because, as he explains, he "stood by the Royal Road in front of the orchards, but the king did not pay attention to me (because) he was talking to Raṣappaya. I went to Adian and spoke before the *rab mūgi* but no-one came out and greeted me and I was scared". Seeking (and getting) an audience with the king is of course *šarru maḫāru*. Another word is *qarābu* "to approach (with a request)". ABL 333 is a plea for justice to "the king of righteousness" (*šar kēnāte*) from a subject who had been told by the king to "approach" (*qirib*) him, but "was weeping and did not approach" (*abakka lā aqrib*). Although his full meaning is lost in breaks, the end of this letter is concerned with the circumstances under which the king's servants should or should not approach him. We have already seen CT 53, 78+, a letter advising the king how to deal with appeals to him by "slaves of the king" or by slaves of Assyrian citizens. It seems a subject was entitled to question the authority of a superior officer or a local official by appealing for justice directly to the king, in a procedure known as "to speak the king's word" (*abat šarri zakāru*). In several cases a royal correspondent mentions that he has received such an appeal, and that he has sent the appellant to the king in person. Where it is possible to tell, these appeals are not made through the process of the law-courts, but through government officials against administrative injustices.[14]

Such cases were no doubt the exceptions. In the correspondence officials make it clear that they are prepared to take action without consulting the king. As in any efficient administration, they would know the limits of their responsibilities and powers, and would not have required separate authorization on each occasion, either by word of mouth or in writing. Nevertheless, to judge from the correspondence it often seems to have been a very "hands-on" system. The king interferes in a great variety of matters, and in various ways, and we frequently come across cases where, for one reason or another, the king's permission, influence or authority is sought. Sometimes a correspondent feels it necessary to alert the king to the action he is intending to take (SAA 1, 177) or to advise him, *ex post facto*, of actions already taken. There are of course cases where others, officials or not, protest about the action and have recourse to royal intervention. Thus SAA 1, 205 (=ABL 154) is only one instance where an official (Zeru-ibni) assures the king that he has not done the deeds for which the king has upbraided him (and of which another official, or Marduk-eriba himself, has presumably accused him). These are mostly no more than demarcation disputes between officials, or grievances being taken higher up the chain of authority to outrank an official. In other cases the direct hierarchical chain might be by-passed for purely administrative reasons. The king or central authority may have wished to impose an exceptional request on the official, and/or the job to be undertaken involved two or more officials in different chains, whose co-operation needed to be secured by delegation from higher up the tree. It is worth looking at these instances of "by-pass", or "administrative short-cuts" in more detail.

Direct royal intervention

First, there are the occasions where the king intervenes in person. The initiative usually comes from the top, but it may also be in response to complaints by those lower in the hierarchy, on either public or private matters. The king is ready to intervene directly in matters which are certainly within the responsibilities of an official, either at the urging of some other equal ranking or lower official, or because he is himself dissatisfied. And his interventions are crisp and business-like:

• king writes a brusque note to confirm to a correspondent that he is to have the use of a group of Nabataeans (*ina pāni-ka šunu* SAA 1, 5)

• king writes directly to masons (*urāsē* SAA 1, 25)

• king writes about large quantities of straw and reeds (SAA 1, 26)

---

14 Postgate 1974b, 423ff. In this context it may be worth raising the possibility that the *sartennu* was responsible for dispensing justice in the public domain, and the *sukkallu* within the administration. Compare the joint activities of these two officials in Assyrian and Babylonia, e.g. Mattila 2000, 90.

• king writes to Mannu-ki-Adad about his folly in distributing his 1000 men to different military tasks (SAA 1, 11)

• appeal to the king from local kinglets obliged to carry out public works under one of the governors (SAA 1, 146; cf. 147)

Such examples could be multiplied. Obviously the degree of royal intervention, and the areas in which it was prevalent, will have depended partly on the character of the king himself. These cases are from Sargon's reign, and he may have been more inclined to intervene in every day matters than some of his successors, but we cannot judge this.

The royal seal

There are many mentions of the royal seal in Neo-Assyrian letters and in those from Babylonia. Its use can be well illustrated by two such passages:

• "On the 27th day in Anisu the cohort-commander of the Chief Eunuch brought for me a sealed letter of the king" (*rab kiṣri ša rab ša rēši un-qi šarri ina libbi* uru*anisu ina muhhi-ia naṣa* SAA 1, 145 (=ABL 173)).

• "PN the captain (*šaknu*) who is appointed in Nippur for forwarding the sealed-orders and/or messengers of the king" (PN *šaknu ša ana šūtuqūti ša un-qa-a-ti u* LÚ.A.KIN *ša šarri ina* NIBRU.KI *paqdu* ABL 238).[15]

• "without a royal sealed-order and/or without a royal aide I will not hand him over to to you" (ABL 336).

These last two citations are from Neo-Babylonian letters, and similar instances from the south are found e.g. in ABL 259 and 281.

Unqu is of course in origin a signet-ring, which then (like *kunukku*) came to stand for the document sealed by it. The royal seal itself, with its design of the king in single combat with a lion, is attested in many impressions on royal grants and on labels.[16] It plainly had a variety of uses and probably existed in numerous examples. I tend to assume that these "sealed-orders" were cuneiform tablets with a stamp-seal impression, but this is perhaps not a foregone conclusion. One cannot *a priori* rule out the possibility that a signet-ring itself was carried by a royal representative as token of his authority, or that a scroll (papyrus or leather) was held by a clay sealing. However, another passage does at least make it clear that the *unqu* was itself an inscribed text:

---

[15] Cf. also SAA 10, 359, and SAA 5, 98 (=CT 53, 42) PN, the aide who brought the sealed-order to me ..." (*ša un-qu ina muh[hi-ia] naṣani*). In this passage it is not specified that the sealed-order came from the king, though there is no clear instance of such an order from anyone else.

[16] See Sachs 1953; Millard 1965; Millard 1978; and comprehensively Herbordt 1992, 123-34.

• "The king my lord will say 'The ...-men are not exempt. (Only) those who are in the sealed-document of the king are exempt'" (*ša ina libbi un-qi šarri zakû* NL 74: 9-11, CTN 5 p. 132, see Postgate 1974a, p. 385).

This was surely not so much a letter as a sealed grant, as it must be in SAA 13, 126 (=ABL 177) "PN the priest has inscribed the field, the house and the sons of votaries on a sealed document *(ina libbi un-qi issaṭar)* and diverted them to himself, but I am not empowered in the matter." We know, from the Assurbanapli grants, that they were sealed by the king's signet-ring (e.g. "I sealed with my signet of royalty" *[ina u]n-qí šarrūti-ya aknu[k]* SAA 12, 25:27), and examples of such sealings go back at least as early as Adad-nirari III (SAA 12, 6).

I am not aware of any letter attested with the royal stamp seal, but despite this in most cases the royal *unqu* was probably a sealed letter of instruction, rather than a land grant.

Royal representatives

Where the king wanted his wishes to be carried out and a simple message, oral or written, was insufficient, for various reasons, he used specially designated representatives. Sometimes, it is true, we find the king delegating his authority to eunuchs,[17] emissaries, or to "third-riders",[18] but the royal representative par excellence was the *ša qurbūti.*[19] This term, which is conventionally translated "bodyguard, Leibgardist", is not to my knowledge found in the 2nd millennium. It is generally accepted that his title means "the one of proximity", and refers to his role in the immediate entourage of the king (or other member of the royal family), probably referring both to his physical proximity, and to his role as a trusted confidant privy to the royal will. The term "bodyguard" does of course express the physical proximity, but if we seek an English term which also expresses the more metaphorical closeness, I would prefer "aide-de-camp", or simply "aide".

He is first attested as a type of official in the Nergal-apil-kumua edict (SAA 12, 82-84) from the reign of Assur-naṣir-apli II. In one context (83 r. 24) he is mentioned after charioteers (LÚ.A.SIG$_5$-*te*), which suggests a military context. In the reign of Adad-nerari III it is listed as a profession, e.g. in designation of witnesses, cf. CTN 2 p. 278, or in SAA 12, 76:14' as a class mentioned in the same breath as *urad-ēkalli*, neither context explicitly military.

The role of the *ša qurbūti* in the 8th and 7th centuries was very well described by Klauber 1910, p. 105-111 (under the incorrect transcription *mutīr pūti*), and can accordingly be briefly summarized here.[20] They turn up in the lists of members of the administrative hierarchy found in the omen enquiries, in what seems to be a

---

[17] E.g. SAA 1, 11; 124.

[18] Third man as messenger e.g. SAA 5, 217 (ABL 342) r.14 and s.1; 21 (=ABL 506):7; 33 (=ABL 705):4'; in SAA 13, 83 (=ABL 683) "third men" as a group.

[19] in the 7th century perhaps also simply *qurbūtu*, with the loss of the *ša* comparable to the late Neo-Assyrian loss of *bēl* before *pāḫiti* in the word for provincial governor.

[20] For a representative collection of instances see CAD Q, 315-7.

generally military part of the list, between "cavalry-captains" (LÚ.GAR.MEŠ *pét-hal*) and *ša šēpē* (SAA 4, 142:6), between "team-commanders" (*rab urâte*) and *ša šēpē* (SAA 4, 139:7), and after "cohort-commanders" (LÚ.GAL KA.KÉŠ.MEŠ; SAA 4, 144:6 - the following profession is broken away). They are also mentioned in an explicitly military context in Sennacherib's royal inscriptions "with my select personal aides" (*itti* LÚ *qur-bu-ti šēpēya nasqūti* OIP 2 36.iii.81) and "my perfect personal aides, my heroic battle-troops" (LÚ *qur-bu-tú*.MEŠ *šēpēya gitmalūti ṣābē tāhāziya qardūti* OIP 2 74:66).[21]

In the 7th century palace archives from Kouyunjik we find mention of a *ša qurbūti* of the Crown Prince (SAA 7, 5.ii.17; 7 r.ii.3; 9 r.ii.8, 20; ABL 600:10; ADD 207:6), and also the Queen Mother (SAA 7, 5 r.i.42; 9 r.i.22). A *ša qurbūti* of the Crown Prince (referring presumably to Sennacherib) turns up in a large administrative tablet to do with deported foreigners from the North-West Palace at Kalhu (ND 2803.ii.26, r.i.8; *Iraq* 23 (1961) 56); probably this was during the time when Sargon himself was on his Babylonian campaign and Sennacherib was left in charge of Assyria.

Criteria for reconstructing the function of the *ša qurbūti* are really only available from the correspondence of Sargon and his successors, but from these texts a clear pattern of use does emerge. Specific points are:

- He acts as agent representing the king (or the Crown Prince)
  SAA 1, 29 (=ABL 198); 10, 349 (=ABL 476); 364 (=ABL 1214)

- He is appointed (*paqādu*), to supervise others
  ABL 127; 415; 552; SAA 10, 349 (ABL 476)

- He is sent (*šapāru*), with a message or task
  SAA 1, 29 (=ABL 198+); 10, 338 (=ABL 667); 369 (=ABL 339); 13, 124 (=ABL 558); NL 103 (*CTN 5, p. 199*)

- He escorts troops, horses
  ABL 226; 760; SAA 1, 99 (=ABL 99); 5, 215 (=NL 89); 10, 348 (=ABL 340); *Iraq* 27 (1965) 16, no. 6; delivers ice (sic!) to king NL 31 (*CTN 5, p. 204*)

- He appears as the highest agent in an administrative situation
  SAA 5 78 (=ABL 246); 82 (=ABL 1012); 104 (=ABL 206); 105 (=ABL 544)

- Two together in a judicial context *Iraq* 32 (1970) 133, new edition Jas 1996, 52-3.

- A reliable (*taklu*) one
  ABL339 r.11; SAA 10, 253(=ABL 956)

---

21 "Personal aides" (*ša q. ša šēpē*) are also attested as witnesses in ADD 177 and other Kouyunjik legal documents; for *ša šēpē* see below.

Taking this range of activity together, we can say that the *ša qurbūti* works usually on his own or in collaboration with a local official, in which case he is generally the higher ranking officer. He is frequently appointed by the king (or some other official on behalf of the king) to take control of a situation. He is a mobile official: he is sent to a new place, either to deliver and execute fresh instructions, or to exercise his own authority in the situation, or to collect and escort a person, animals, or a commodity from one place to another. The *ša qurbūti* are expected to cope with affairs related to the military, but also cover what we would consider civilian matters. They do not occupy a fixed position within the chain of command, and they were thus in effect the oil between the different cogs of the administrative machinery. It is time now to turn to the silent majority of the system, which needed no such oiling.

It is important, before moving on, to stress again that although there seems to have been no hesitation about direct royal involvement, and it is frequently mentioned in the Neo-Assyrian letter corpus, it was probably nevertheless relatively exceptional. Our letters come from the royal palaces, and are therefore representative of the business which reached the king or his close staff, and completely unrepresentative of the great majority of administrative business beyond the palace limits. There we must expect that the system of delegated authority would normally have operated without the necessity of constant written authorization or consultation with the king.

The military hierachy

Although we have seen above that military and civilian affairs were dealt with by the same overarching provincial authorities, we also noted that further down the system the distinction between the two sectors must have been clear, and in search of a well-defined hierarchy we cannot do better than to start with the military. Any attempt to reconstruct the Neo-Assyrian military hierarchy has to choose between, or perhaps better bring together, two approaches. On the one hand there is inescapably a model in our own minds of how it might have worked, informed perhaps by comparisons with later or earlier systems, on the other there is the range of technical terms we encounter which may give clues to their relationship to one another and thus to the wider structure. This is not the place to undertake a survey of the entire army personnel, but in our attempt to reconstruct the ancient ethos it seems appropriate to start from their own terminology.

There are many terms used to refer to fighting men in the Neo-Assyrian documentary and inscriptional texts, but they are not all on the same level. At the least one may distinguish terms referring to rank, activity or function, ethnic or geographical origin, and status or sector.

(1) Activity
Of itself, defining a soldier by his characteristic weapon (e.g. "bow-man, shield-man") or similar function (e.g. *ša pēthalli* "horse-rider") tells us nothing about his

position in the hierarchy (although once the system is constructed, and hence to his contemporaries, it may have implied it).[22]

(2) Origin
Some ethnic designations may have had equally specific implications for the position of their holders in the system. The best known are the Ituaeans and the Qurraeans, who are known to be included within the "king's troops". They were so well established that they actually feature in a lexical text,[23] but other ethnic units, probably mostly Aramaean, are attested and for most if not all of these we may assume that the unit had a recognized position within the system and characteristic equipment and functions.

(3) Rank
Terms implying command over other troops are the most explicit, but the fact is that we have only the slenderest evidence on which to reconstruct a military hierarchy.

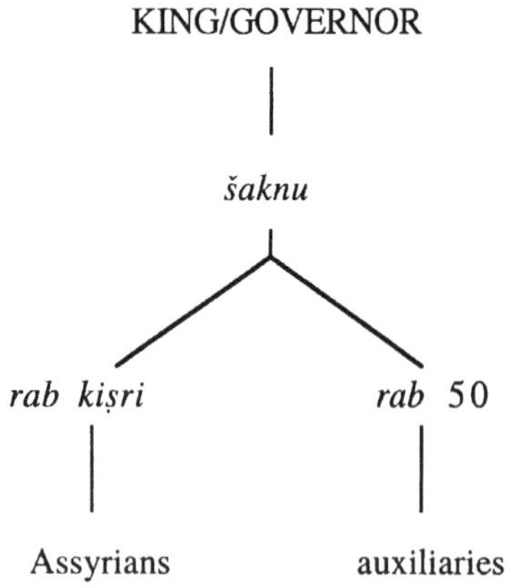

Diagram 1: the basic module

The ranks we can identify are principally *rab kiṣri* "cohort-commander", *rab 50* "commander of 50", and *rab ešarti* "decurion". In all these cases the term *rab* is taken by us to imply command, but obviously other terms may refer to hierarchical command positions without stating so explicitly. I would claim *šaknu* as one of these on the basis of a study of context.[24] There seems to have been a very

---

22 So e.g. Manitius 1910, 118-133, Malbran-Labat 1982, 59-88.

23 MSL 12, 238 i.13-14.

24 I think the position of the military *šaknu* as an officer above the *rab kiṣri* has been sufficiently established (Postgate 1980a), and his position immediately below the governor seems to follow from CT 53 78+, 6-7 (see Postgate 1980b). The principal difficulty still revolves round the relationship between the *rab kiṣri* and the *rab haššē*, on which cf. Postgate 1974a, 221. They seem to be of approximately equal rank, so perhaps the "commander of 50" exercised a function similar to that of the "cohort-commander" in a sector of the administration which was not divided into cohorts (*kiṣru*). Note that correspondents in letters do not usually

simple four tier "module", with the governor at the top, beneath him the military *šaknu*, then the cohort-commander (or the commander of 50), and the ordinary soldier or private. I believe this was a regular chain of command from the reign of Tiglath-pileser III onwards, whereas there is some evidence that the "decurion" (*rab ešarti*) was the lowest officer in the reign of Adad-nirari III and back into the 2nd millennium. This rank disappears from military contexts later on, but the title survives among the court diviners.

While this module was no doubt developed in the army, in the 7th century the *kiṣru* system also embraced non-military occupations, and we can expect to encounter the module in civilian contexts as well. Hence to progress further with the broad sectors of the administrative hierarchy we need to sort out the terms describing status.

(4) Status

This deliberately vague term applies to designations which seem to refer to a person's position or role within the military establishment (as opposed to role on the battlefield). These are the most difficult to pin down. They may include *ṣāb šarri, raksu, ša šēpē, qurrubu* and *ša qurbūti.*

It will be obvious that a single person could be classed under three or even all four of these headings. Thus one could be a commander (3) of archers (1) drawn from the Ituaeans (2) who belonged within the "king's troops" (4). Some titles are a combination of two classes, e.g. *rab urâte* "team-commander", and which of the varied terms in (4) are incompatible with terms in (1)-(3), either by definition or because of the structure of the army (e.g. only Assyrians were horsemen), has to be worked out laboriously case by case. Even when this has been done (and it cannot be attempted here), there remain further issues to be addressed before we can hope to achieve a clear view of the military hierarchy: who served, and for how long? what was the basis on which they were conscripted? was the conscription process organized by local communities or by the central administration? which officials commanded them once conscripted? There are not likely to be single answers to all these questions. We may expect, by comparison with similar systems, that within the army some personnel served on a different basis from others, but this does not necessarily mean that they came under a separate command structure. There are however two major divisions of the army, the king's troops and the royal cohort, and since they served different functions, it will be as well to consider them separately.

The "king's troops"

The evidence of NL 89,[25] supported by plentiful other indications, tells us that the core of the forces at the disposal of provincial governor was formed by "king's

talk of bodies of troops in terms of one or more *kiṣru*, but rather specify numbers, often in multiples of 50 or 100 [e.g.ABL 273; 521; 561; 622; SAA 5, 33 (=ABL 705)]. Perhaps this means that (like many modern armies) the number of men in contingents with the same designation could vary significantly, and that specifying a number of *kiṣru* did not give sufficiently accurate information.

25 A new edition of this letter is offered in Postgate 2000.

troops", who included among their number both Assyrians and auxiliaries. The Neo-Assyrian evidence for this class of soldier is clear on some points:

• the "king's troops" (*ṣāb šarri*) served in a **military** body (e.g. NL 89)

• some at least were conscripted under the *ilku* system, and they were a selected group, since other such conscripts acted as reserves (*ša kutalli*) and yet others as corvée labourers, doing the *dullu ša šarri* (see simply SAA 1, 99 (=ABL 99)).

• they were "reviewed" (*ašāru*) and lists of their names were kept on boards (CTN 3, 21-22).

• some, if not all, auxiliary units, such as the Ituaeans and the Qurraeans, were included within the "king's troops" (NL 89); it is unclear whether or not these would have fallen under the *ilku* system of conscription (in favour of this note that at least one Ituaean had a "bow-field" (SAA 5, 16 (=ABL 201)).

• they came under the command of provincial governors: NL 89; SAA 1, 149 (=CT 53, 108); SAA 1, 236 (=ABL 639); and probably SAA 1, 91 (=ABL 94). Taklak-ana-Bel is another case of a governor in charge of both military and civilian personnel (e.g. SAA 1, 235 (= ABL 1432), though these soldiers are not explicitly stated to be *ṣāb šarri*).

It is clear that these are the king's troops in the sense that they are recruited into the service of the state. Nevertheless, they do not serve directly under the king but are at the disposal of the governor in his role as the head of the provincial administration. Some may have been professional Assyrian soldiers for whom the army was a career, not a temporary obligation, while others may be auxiliaries under different conditions of service. It seems possible, though, that the majority of the "king's troops", especially those technically considered "Assyrians" (cf. NL 89), were recruited to serve in the army under the terms of the state-wide *ilku* system.

A text from Tell Billa[26] demonstrates that *ilku* obligations were administered at provincial centres in the 9th century, and there is every reason to think that at least the theory behind *ilku* service went back into the 2nd millennium. Middle Assyrian military records from Kar-Tukulti-Ninurta indicate that there were at least 4 "boards" (*lē'u*) named after the king or one of a few high officials, and listing the soldiers falling under each person's command. These were described as *ṣāb šarri.*[27] The procedure for conscripting these men was probably known as the

---

[26] JCS 7 (1953) 141 texts 86-90; note that, as hypothesized by Finkelstein, these pieces probably all belong to a single tablet, and some of them can now be physically joined, as I was able to establish when collating these pieces in 1989. My thanks to Prof. Å. Sjöberg and the late Father Hermann Behrens for their assistance on that occasion.

[27] Middle Assyrian instances of *ṣāb šarri* are both from Kar-Tukulti-Ninurta: VS 21 1.vii.26 and Postgate 1979a, MAH 16086, which lists military garments *ša ṣāb šarri* (see Postgate 2000, 106 fn. 94).

pirru,[28] and this is relevant, because in Sargon's 8th campaign one of the crack regiments is described as the *pirru* of Sin-ahu-uṣur (Sennacherib's brother): although there is a gap of 500 years, I think it is reasonable to assume that the core army which served under the king was still composed of regiments or legions, each under the command of a highly-placed member of the elite. However, it seems likely that such troops formed part of the royal cohort. Whether they were also *ṣāb šarri* still is impossible to say at present.

The "royal cohort"

As already stated, in Neo-Assyrian times the royal core of the army was known as the *kiṣir šarrūti*.[29] This term is attested in Old Babylonian texts, but not at present in Middle Assyrian contexts.[30] In seeking a precise definition of this body the word *kiṣru* itself is unhelpful because it has several usages. In administrative and legal texts it is of course the word for the cohort of an unknown number of men commanded by a *rab kiṣri*. In his 8th Campaign letter Sargon uses it in the plural: *lā upaḫḫira kiṣrē-ia* ("I did not gather my cohorts" l. 230), and elsewhere tells us that his provincial governors had their cohorts (LÚ.*šu-ut*-SAG.MEŠ-*ia* LÚ.EN.NAM.MEŠ *a-di ki-iṣ-ri-šu-nu*, TCL 3, l. 333) and that Merodachbaladan "gathered his cohorts" (*upaḫḫira kiṣrē-šu*, Fuchs 1993, p. 138 l. 266). When Sargon states that he added troops to his "royal cohort" the numbers involved make it clear that he is not talking about a cohort of the size usually commanded by a *rab kiṣri*, and indeed it must presumably have contained within it many such cohorts.[31] On the other hand a smaller body is obviously in question when a correspondent writes to the king about "the Palestinians whom the king formed into a cohort (*ki-iṣ-ru ik-ṣur-u-ni*) and gave to me" SAA 1, 155 (=ABL 218). In the Nimrud Wine Lists there is also a "cohort of Šamaš", of unknown size. Hence in any given context we can only guess how large a *kiṣru* is meant from the context itself.[32]

---

28 This term, and the related adjective *perrūte* (if it exists and is not *utrūte*), remain difficult. "Enrolment or taxation (procedure, centre)" seems to be the approximate meaning.

29 This phrase is found in the royal inscriptions. The phrase *kiṣir šarri* is attested as the "profession" of four witnesses to a slave sale dating to 682 B.C. in the reign of Sennacherib (=SAA 6 192 (=ADD 276) r.5'-8'), and of at least one witness in SAA 6 246 (=ADD 251) r. 2' (probably reign of Esarhaddon to judge from the other texts of the same purchaser). The obvious assumption would be that this was the vernacular equivalent of *kiṣir šarrūti* (as proposed e.g. by Mattila 2000, 149, but on reflection this seems less likely because at this time the "royal cohort" was so extensive that membership of it would hardly act as an identifying profession. Conceivably this phrase is here used for a much smaller body or troops closely attached to the king (in which case its relationship to the groups known as *qurrubu* and *ša šēpē* would need elucidation). See also foonote 31 below.

30 Even if the term *kiṣir šarrūti* was ever used in the Middle Assyrian period we do not know enough about the composition of the army to be able to guess what it might have referred to (e.g. the contingent listed on the "king's board", all the contingents listed on boards, or an entirely separate (and smaller) body of permanent professional soldiers accompanying the king). Given the high-ranking title *rab kiṣri* at this date (see below, footnote 32), it seems likely that *kiṣir šarrūti* was not in current use.

31 Manitius 1910, 114 remains an adequate source for this.

32 I know of no evidence that this *kiṣru* commanded by a *rab kiṣri* existed before the 8th century. The identical title, *rab kiṣri*, is used on three late 2nd millennium stelae: Nos. 57, No.

The classic statement on the *kiṣir šarrūti* is in Manitius 1910, 114-117, and there is still little that can be added to it. This is because the term *kiṣir šarrūti* itself is known exclusively from passages in the royal inscriptions of the last four major kings. In one recurring topos they report the addition of personnel from defeated enemies to their *kiṣir šarrūti*. Under Sargon and Sennacherib these are a variety of fighting men, under Esarhaddon and Assurbanapli they also include craftsmen.[33] In the inscriptions of Sargon and Sennacherib the kings also mention occasions when they sent their "royal cohort" to assist their governors with local campaigns in Elam and in Anatolia.[34] A further complication in the 7th century is the existence of a "new cohort", which is mentioned in administrative documents. It occurs twice in the title of Nabû-šarru-uṣur "Governor of Nineveh, New Cohort of Sennacherib" (SAA 7, 3.i.5-6; 4.i.7-8). In the first case his entry follows Ahu-ilaya, who is simply styled "Governor of Nineveh". In three other passages the "Review Palace, New Cohort" follows on from "Review Palace, Central Nineveh" (SAA 7, 23), or from both "Central Nineveh" and "Review Palace, Nineveh" (SAA 7, 115.i.2-4; 148.ii.13-15). Plainly this was an organization which required a governor and a separate Review Palace, and we can only assume that enough troops had indeed been added to Sennacherib's "royal cohort" to warrant the creation of a new establishment parallel to that which already existed under Sargon for the administration of his *kiṣir šarrūti*. The use of Sennacherib's name in these phrases would probably only have begun after his death, and certainly SAA 7, 3-4 come from late in the reign of Esarhaddon or early in his successor's reign (cf. SAA 7 p. xix).[35]

Location and composition of the "royal cohort"

Along with Manitius and his successors I imagine that the *kiṣir šarrūti* was a body of troops not commanded via the provincial governors but under the separate

67 (of Marduk-uballissu and Ninurta-apla-iddina, see Saporetti 1979, 21 with fn.6) and No. 58 (of Ipparšidu, whose sole title is GAL *ki-iṣ-ri*, Saporetti 1979, 154-5). The stele must imply a high rank, so this can hardly be the equivalent of the later Neo-Assyrian title, but more than that it is hard to say.

33 For the non-military *kiṣru* see Postgate 1979b, 210-1 with footnotes; CT 53 13 probably exemplifies a cohort of ironsmiths. For Esarhaddon's account see Borger 1956, 106, iii.14-20. For Assurbanipal see Borger 1996, 58-9 "I added to my royal cohort bowmen, shieldmen, specialists, craftsmen whom I had plundered from inside Elam, and the remaining ones I distributed like sheep to my governors, magnates, cult-centres, and the whole of my camp" (in text F; a standardized phrase going back to Sargon).

34 Sargon: Fuchs 1993, p. 178, l. 404 (Kummuḫ); Sennacherib: Luckenbill 1924, 61 ll. 69-71 (Cilicia); 62 ll. 6-8 (Tilgarimmu); 87 ll. 29-30 (Elam).

35 Although Esarhaddon writes at some length in his inscriptions about his expansion of the system, he does not state that he created a new *kiṣru*, merely added to his own *kiṣir šarrūti* (l. 15), and to "the *ki-ṣir* of the earlier kings his (fore)fathers" (l. 19; this was perhaps the Sennacherib *kiṣru*). In one legal document from his reign Nabû-belu-uṣur the eponym for 672 BC is uniquely given the designation "cohort of (*ki-ṣir*) Esarhaddon, King of Assyria". Since he was Governor of Dur-Šarrukku both before and after the date in question (Millard 1994, 104), he can hardly have been commander of a cohort, and I suspect this refers to membership of a much smaller group, and is equivalent to the titles *kiṣir šarri* used in other texts from Esarhaddon's reign (see above, footnote 29).

command of the king. If so, it, or much of it, would have been based at the seat of government, hence at Kalhu up until the move to Dur-Šarruken, and at Nineveh from Sennacherib's reign onward. Within each city it seems fair to assume that the main military component of the *kiṣir šarrūti* would have been based at the Review Palace (*ēkal māšarti*), which the royal inscriptions tell us were designed as military headquarters. I also suspect that it was under the command of the chief eunuch (*rab ša rēši*). The military role of the chief eunuch was already remarked on by Manitius and Klauber, and he is the only high officer of state ("magnate") without responsibilities away from the capital.[36] This remains only a best guess: we do not have any compelling evidence associating him either directly with the command of the *kiṣir šarrūti,* or with the Review Palace.

In administrative contexts we occasionally come across troops "of the palace". These include:

- chariotry (GIŠ.GIGIR.MEŠ *ša* É.GAL SAA 1, 10 (= ABL 306)r.14)
- a charioteer (LÚ.A.SIG *ša* É.GAL SAA 1, 205 (=ABL 154):12)
- cohort-commanders (LÚ.GAL *ki-ṣir.*MEŠ *ša* É.GAL SAA 11, 36 (=ADD 1036).iii.19-20); and
- Ituaean auxiliaries (LÚ.*i-tú-'a-a ša* É.GAL SAA 5, 3 (= ABL 424) r.10).

That it is a precise designation is clearest from SAA 1, 205, a letter which is explicitly concerned with the details of army service. The most revealing instance is however in the horse lists from Fort Shalmaneser. Here, in CTN 3, 103 r.ii.4-6 we have "Total 373 horses: the procurement-officers of the palace chariotry" (LÚ.*mu-šar-kis*.MEŠ *ša* GIŠ.GIGIR É.GAḶ), and they are contrasted with an earlier section of the list, of which the only surviving part is the end of the last line: "[Total n horses]: the procurement-officers of the *qurrubtu* chariotry" (LÚ.*mu-šar-kis*.MEŠ *ša* GIŠ.GIGIR *qur-ub-te*). Since this refers to a muster at Borsippa in Babylonia, it is plain that these two groups remained identifiably separate even away from their base. The question is: which palace? To judge from the provenance of the tablet, these troops came under the administration of the Kalhu Review Palace, and there is no reason to think, here or in any other passage, that they came from one of the governors' palaces. Indeed, since the writers do not specify which palace is meant, it must be self-evident, and from the time of Shalmaneser III we know that it was the *ēkal māšarti* which served as the headquarters for the Assyrian army par excellence, and is regularly described as designed for the administration and equipment of the army.[37] The only alternative would seem to be that they were troops serving directly under the monarch, and hence based at the principal residential palace - in Kalhu the North-West Palace. This cannot be completely discounted, but in CTN 3 no. 103 the "palace" troops are expressly differentiated from a sector of the army designated *qurrubtu*, and this seems much more likely to refer to the king's sector and to have been based at the residential palace.

---

[36] See Mattila 2000, 163-4.

[37] See already CTN 3, p. 29 n. 15. If the much-quoted statements to this effect by Sennacherib and Esarhaddon are not thought sufficient, the variety of military administrative documents found in the Kalhu Review Palace should be enough to satisfy us.

qurrubtu

Philologically this word poses problems which cannot be resolved in this context. No-one doubts that it is related to *qurbu* "close, near", but is it just the feminine *qurubtu*, or are the writings with *qur-ru-* to be taken as conveying a genuine geminated consonant, in which case it could presumably be a D-stem adjective (for **qarrubtu*)? Whichever it is, the meaning is not much affected, as it is generally agreed to refer to bodies of troops or individuals serving in close proximity to the king. Esarhaddon lists *qurrubtu* chariotry and *qurrubtu* cavalry (Borger 1956, 106 16), units which are also attested in the administrative records.[38] It remains unclear whether all *ša qurbūti* were members of a *qurrubtu* unit, and/or all members of a *qurrubtu* unit could be called *ša qurbūti*. I suspect not,[39] as it is plain that not every *ša qurbūti* formed a member of the king's *qurrubtu* unit, since some served the Crown Prince and the Queen Mother (cf. again CAD Q, 317). On the other hand, the not infrequent appearance of *ša qurbūti* in the Kouyunjik legal documents is consistent with their attendance in the entourage of the king, and there may well have been a considerable overlap (cf. also footnote 38 for Kalhu). For practical reasons, I would assume that the *qurrubtu* contingents were much smaller in total than the rest of the *kiṣir šarrūti*, and within the contingents a yet smaller group was known as *ša šēpē*, generally recognized as those in the immediate entourage of the king himself.[40] The qualification "right" and "left" applied to *ša qurbūti* in CTN 3, 108.i.7-8 may refer to these aides' positions by the side of the royal person, to judge from their place near the beginning of the list.

The "standing army"?

We have therefore two main sectors of the Assyrian empire's military establishment: the "king's troops" under the command of provincial governors and therefore distributed throughout the empire, and the "royal cohort" based at one of the capital cities under the king in theory, and in practice perhaps under the Chief Eunuch. Although we have some evidence about the composition of these two

---

38 Chariotry: ABL 1009 7 *ša* GIŠ.GIGIR *qur-x*[traces (coll.) insufficient to identify the broken sign; cavalry: ND 2386+ (*Iraq* 23 22 cf. Postgate 1974a, p. 372) ii.15'-17' *ša pét-ḫal qur-u[b(-x)]*). Two contexts in the Nimrud ration lists are atypical: bread rations for LÚ.EN GIŠ.GIGIR.MEŠ *qur-ub-tú* ND 2489 (*Iraq* 23 32, CTN 1 No. 35) i.7-8; and to *ša qur-ru-ub-tú* and EN GIGIR.MEŠ *qur-ru-ub-tú* ND 2371 (*Iraq* 23 21, CTN 1 p. 154-5 No. 34) 7-8. Note that unlike the wine lists, these come from the North-West Palace, where the king resided.

39 Pace CTN 3 p. 32ff. Although they look similar at first sight, the graphic habits of the scribes keep the terms distinct, as indeed they are grammatically. The word *qurrubtu* comes of course from the same root as *ša qurbūti*, but in Assyrian texts a distinction is clearly maintained between the individual professional title, where the *qur* sign is followed directly by the *b*, and the designation of a body of troops, where the *qur* sign is followed by *ru* or *ub*. In Babylonian texts the individual profession is also given as *qurrubtu*, but whatever the pronunciation of the words in Assyria, scribal practice maintains a distinction, and we should observe this. For this reason I would take the phrases LÚ.GAL *kiṣir qur-but* SAA 6, 323 (=ADD 115) and LÚ.GAL *ki-ṣir šá qur-but* ADD 211; 235; SAA 6, 329 (=ADD 444) as meaning either "cohort-commander **and** aide" or "commander of a cohort **of** aides". Note that pace CTN 3 p. 33 with note 37, Sargon's inscriptions do not explicitly identify the 1000 cavalry which accompanied the king as *qurubtu*.

40 CAD Q 317a-b; with reference to CTN 3 p. 39 with note 73, note that it is only in l. 150 of the annals (Fuchs 1993, 114) that the cavalry is designated "personal" (GÌR.2-*ia*), because in the other passages where the phrase occurs it applies to his "single chariot".

sectors, we have seen little to tell us how permanent these two sectors were. Manitius identified the *kiṣir šarrūti* as a "stehende Königsschar", a standing body of troops attached to the king himself, rather than to individual governors. In this sense he remains correct, and it is unfortunate that he also uses the phrase "**the** standing army" (**des** stehenden Heeres), because there were also regular bodies of troops under the command of the governors. Since we guess that both the royal and the provincial sectors were in existence throughout each year the phrase "standing army" should apply to both, in contrast to a force raised seasonally from among the civilian population (the *dikût māti*).

Even if correctly used, the phrase "standing army" conceals a large area of ignorance, since it need only imply that the army as a whole remained ready under arms throughout the year, without specifying the terms of service of the individual soldier. We need to know how permanently they served: in each sector were some or all of them a "conscript army" composed of young recruits serving out a short period of state service, or full-time, professional soldiers? Did they live in barracks 12 months a year, and did they spend more than a few years as soldiers? No administration will take kindly to feeding and housing a large body of idle troops. It is plainly conceivable that the Assyrian governors had lists of current king's men who were technically in service but not physically armed and assembled, but since we have a term for "reserve", *ša kutalli*, it seems reasonable to assume that those designated as *ṣāb šarri* were currently in service under military command. As for how many years one served, that remains an area of complete ignorance. There is evidence for time-accounting of *ilku* service in the Middle Assyrian period, but nothing really comparable in the 1st millennium (with the possible exception of ND 3467 mentioned below). Nevertheless, the link with *ilku* does suggest that service with the king's troops was something one did for a limited period, and not a lifetime's employment (compare SAA 1, 205 (=ABL 154)). That said, we need to bear in mind that some of the king's troops were professionals: the Ituaeans and others, and also presumably some of the officers.

Military rank was of course formally recognized, as shown by ABL 85 (quoted below), where the king is elevating people to the ranks of *rab kiṣri* (cohort-commander), *tašlīšu* ("third-rider") and *ša qurbūti*, and note in particular that the third-rider's post is specified as "permanent" (*kayyamāniu*). Some other instances of this word, written logographically SAG.UŠ have recently been identified (SAA 7, 150.ii.3'; 154.r.ii.19', both *tašlīšu*; 152.r.i.9 without further specification). Some "permanent" soldiers were no doubt "Assyrians" (whatever that precisely implied[41]), but it seems likely that most of the foreign contingents which we know to have been incorporated into the *kiṣir šarrūti* were also long-term professional soldiers who did not disperse annually to their places of origin in the off-season.

As we should expect and as the evidence of the sculptures makes clear, the rank and affiliation of soldiers were reflected in their uniform. In the texts there are a few allusions to this, which have been discussed by the author elsewhere (Postgate 2001). In SAA 11, 30.r.3-5 Mannu-ki-abi is identified as a cohort-commander

---

41 On the term "Assyrian" in an administrative context cf. Postgate 1980b.

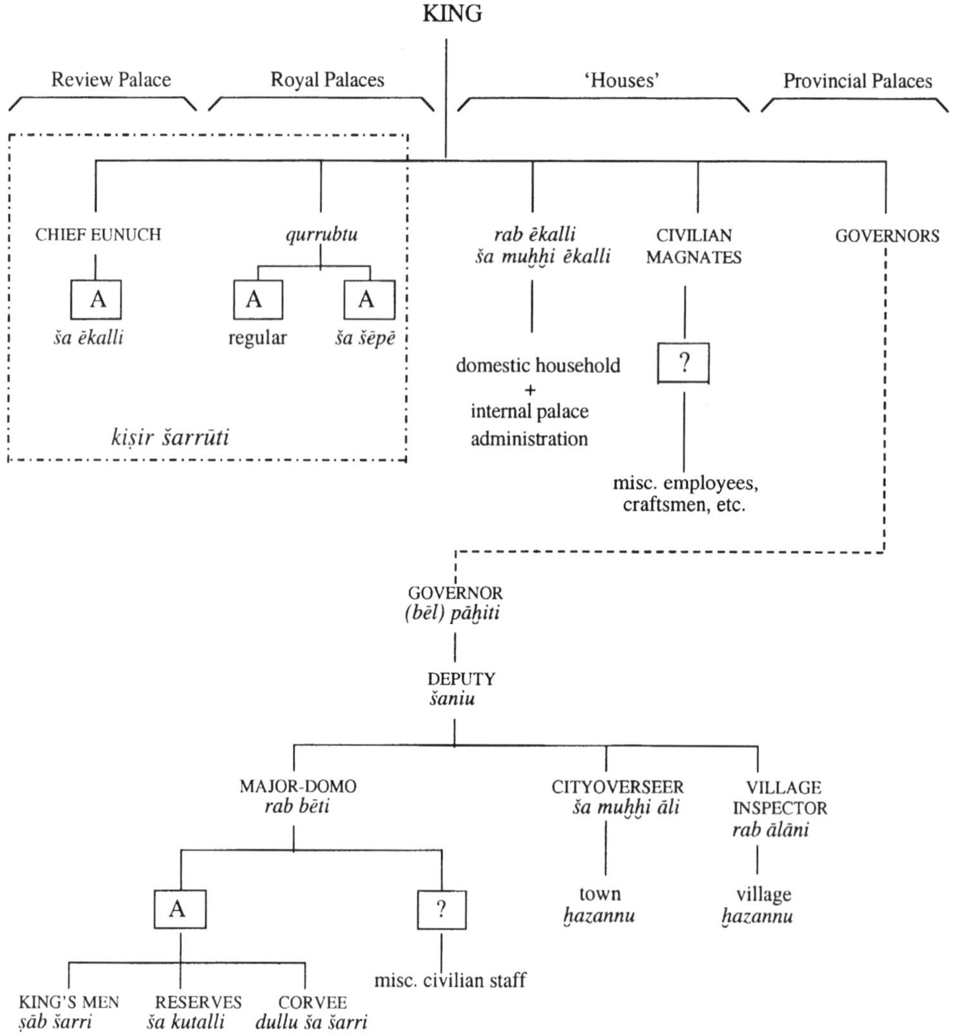

Diagram 2: hypothetical reconstruction of the principal sectors of the administration. The boxes marked A represent the basic module as shown in Diagram 1.

"who has not been uniformed" (*ša la labbušūni).* One of the pertinent texts is SAA 11, 122, where the numerical contrast of 6 or 8 "uniformed" (*labbušu*) to 208 or 96 "daily" (*ša ūmē*) troops is intriguing. It seems plain that the contrast is between officially uniformed and less definitively enrolled troops.[42] Although the meaning of *ša ūmē* is not transparent, the best explanation may be that these are conscripts serving out their "days" of *ilku*-service owed to the state. Such "days (of

[42] For *labbušu* "uniformed" see also CTN 1, p. 144 No. 16.

service)" are probably referred to in ND 3467 which is a list of *ilku* contributions in kind received "during my days" (*ina libbi* UD.MEŠ-*ia*; see Postgate 1974a, p. 399). In that case, we may not be looking at the *kiṣir šarrūti*, but at a governor-commanded force of "king's troops". At least the newly incorporated personnel of the *kiṣir šarrūti* in the 7th century were plainly "slaves of the king",[43] who were by definition permanently in royal service, and there is no evidence that any of the "king's troops" served in the *kiṣir šarrūti*. Nevertheless, if the provincial levies were to be competently commanded, there must have been some exchange of personnel between one sector and the other.

Palaces and houses

Even if the administration is invisible in the texts, it can hardly have been invisible on the ground, but where, in practice, did it operate? As we all know, the kings had a variety of palaces, some in different cities, sometimes more than one in the same city. In the 10th and 9th century the kings resettling the countryside built "palaces", and while theoretically no doubt these were outposts of the main royal palace, they must also have served as the places of work, and probably residences, of the local governors. Palaces were also storehouses, and when Sargon tells us that Ullusunu had stocked up flour and wine for his army just like his own provincial governors, we are entitled to assume that it was in their palaces that they kept these supplies.[44] This in any case is the clear implication of SAA 1, 160 where the author is involved in storing grain for the king in three different palaces, Arbil, Kilizi, and Adian (which was probably not a provincial capital).

While the provincial palaces, like Til-Barsip or Dur-katlimmu, may have contained all the functions - residence, ceremony, administration and storage - in one, in the capital cities some of these functions were separated out. The Review Palace (*ēkal māšarti*) not only acted as a place where the army was reviewed, but also stored military equipment, incorporated a harem area, housed the administration including the scribes, and no doubt acted as a residence for some of the personnel who worked in the palace. At Kalhu and Nineveh the Review Palace was at some hundreds of metres from the principal royal palace and cannot just have been an enlargement of its administrative functions. As far as I am aware, apart from the palatial residences of members of the royal family, no other buildings were known as "palaces". If there were other buildings which housed government administration, they were probably "houses" of one kind or another. This brings us to look at one recurrent phrase in the Neo-Assyrian texts which does seem to have a specific reference to the administrative system.

---

43 For the ÌR *ša šarri* contrasted with *urdu ša aššurāyi* ("slave of an Assyrian") cf. CT 53, 78+426, above, p. 2 with footnote 3.

44 TCL 3, l. 53.

"Their Master's House"

ABL 85 is a letter from Bel-iqiša to the king Assurbanipal (Baker, PNA 1/ii, 316 no. 10) complaining about some of his colleagues within the administration:

5	ÌR.MEŠ *ša* É.EN.MEŠ-*ia*
6	*ša* LUGAL *be-lí* UD-*mu*
7	*an-ni-ú ú-par-ri-su-u-ni*
8	^{1}*tab*-URU-*a-a* DUMU ^{1}EN.KASKAL--PAB--PAB
9	*ša a-na* LÚ*.GAL *ki-ṣir-u-te*$^{!}$
10	LUGAL *be-lí ú-še-lu-u-ni*
11	$^{1.d}$PA--*sa-kip ša* TA* LÚ*.3.U$_5$.MEŠ
12	*ka-a-ma-nu-te*$^{!}$
13	LUGAL *be-lí ú-še-lu-u-ni*
r.1	^{1}IGI.LÁ--^{d}ŠÚ
2	*ša* TA* LÚ* *qur-but.* MEŠ
3	LUGAL *be-*<*lí*> *ú-še-lu-u-ni*
4	3 *an-nu-tú* ÉRIN.MEŠ
5	*šá-ak-ra-nu-tú šú-nu*
6	*ki-ma i-šak-ki-ru*
7	LÚ GÍR AN.BAR
8	TA* *pa-an me-hi-ri-šu*
9	*la ú-sa-ah-ra*

"The servants of my government department whom the King allocated(?) today - Tabalayu, son of Bel-Harran-ahu-uṣur whom the King promoted to a cohort-commandership; Nabû-sakip, whom the King promoted to(?)/from(?) the permanent 'third-riders'; Atamar-Marduk whom the King raised to(?)/from(?) the *ša qurbūti* - these three men are drunkards. When they get drunk one man does not turn (his) iron dagger away from his colleague."[45]

This same Bel-iqiša is also the plaintive author of ABL 84, in which he maintains that "Since the time the King appointed me to my government department, I have had no authority over anything (or: anyone ?)." (TA* É LUGAL EN *ina* É EN.MEŠ-*ia ip-qid-da-ni-ni ina* UGU *me-me-ni ina* É EN.MEŠ-*ia la šal-ṭa-ak,* r.4ff.), and goes on to explain how his secretary is in control.

These two letters may serve as a starting point for consideration of the phrase *bēt bēlēya*, literally "house of my masters", which I have translated "my government

45 There are uncertainties about the correct translation. In the first place it is not clear to me whether the *ana* in l. 9 has the same meaning as TA* in l. 11 and r. 2, hence my hesitation between "to" or "from" in these two cases. Secondly, I am unsure whether LÚ*.3.U$_5$.MEŠ *ka-a-ma-nu-te* and LÚ* *qur-but.*MEŠ are to be understood as plurals, or abstracts ("from/to the permanent 'third-riders'" or "from/to a permanent 'third-ridership'"). Whether plural or abstract, I have no idea if the form in r. 2 should be taken as simply (*ša) qurbūti* or (*ša) qurbūtūti*!

department". It is plainly important for us.[46] In CTN 2 p. 186 I wrote that: "*bēt bēlē* "masters' house" is a phrase used (with suitable changes of suffix), to refer to the administrative department under which a person works" (with references to CAD B 195a and K. Deller, Or NS 35 (1966) 312). This still appears to be a reasonable approximation,but some examples will help to sustain it.[47]

The phrase "Masters' House" is attested already in a Middle Assyrian administrative context (AfO 19 Taf.VI see Freydank & Saporetti 1989, p. 52 Rs. 17-19), where members of Babu-aha-iddina's household are not to take garments out of "their Masters' House", but to check them within it. In this archive it is almost certain that the textile store belonged to Babu-aha-iddina, which suggests that already in the 13th century the phrase referred not to some other unspecified superiors but to the establishment by which an official was employed. In Neo-Assyrian contexts the concept certainly seems to have this meaning: in ABL 561 the king himself writing to some correspondents shows that it should be loved: "you are people who love your Masters' House" (*rā'imūte ša bēt bēlē-kunu attunu*). In ABL 778 the king again writes "I shall hold you to account for the work of your Masters' House" (*dullu ša bēt bēlē-ka ina qātī-ka uba'a*), and his subject replies "I am doing ... the work of my Masters' House, I am keeping guard for my Masters' House" (... *dulli ša bēt bēlē-ya eppaš, maṣṣartu ša bēt bēlē-ya anaṣṣar*). Revealing also is ABL 415, written to the king by a *rab bēti* and his scribe.[48] They complain that "our Masters' House" is being despoiled by the Governors, and more specifically the Governor of Arrapha.[49]

Of course the two components of the phrase, "house" and "master", can each be used independently of the other with specific reference to the administrative system. A Babylonian letter associates the phrase *bīt bēlī-šu* with the term "master" (*bēlu*): "a man who loves his Masters' House, and who sees and hears (anything) will open the ears of his masters" (ABL 288). This satisfactorily confirms that the "Masters" in the phrase are indeed the writer's administrative superiors. As for the "House", although the word obviously has a wide variety of usages, it can also have a precise meaning in an administrative context. In ABL 84, cited above, Bēl-iqīša's rival says "I will cut you off from this House" (*anāku*

46 After the text had been submitted I received the substantial study of Fales 2000 devoted to this phrase. This is not the place to comment on his discussion in detail, but our understanding of most of the contexts is broadly similar, and where he detects a different nuance it does not seem to me that this affects the situation as I have described it.

47 In addition to passages cited in the text, I have noted the following instances (the list is unlikely to be complete, cf. now Fales 2000): Neo-Assyrian: ABL 523; 620; 845; 1101; SAA 1, 223 (=CT 53, 87); 5, 31 (=ABL 139); 154 (=ABL 787); CTN 2, 186; ADD 62 (see Postgate 1974a, pp. 303-5; SAA 6, 95, not an improvement); SAA 11, 202(=ADB 2).ii.14'-15'; Neo-Babylonian: ABL 897; 1119.

48 For the role of the scribe here, compare the pertinent comments of Kinnier Wilson 1972, 95-97.

49 Read at the end of l. 9 *ub!-ta-di-du!* (coll.). Typically the writers mention neither the identity of their "House" nor the office of their "Master" (who was recipient of a gift from the king, but has failed to engage in litigation). In the context, he does not seem likely to have been a provincial governor, reminding us that each department, not only provincial governorates, probably had a *rab bēti*.

TA* É *annî aparras-ka*), with the consequence that later "he has gathered my entire Masters' House, and put it under his control" (*bēt bēlē-ya gabbi iktirik šapluš issakkan*). In ABL 415 the king is exhorted by the major-domo and his scribe to "appoint an aide over his servant's House, to carry out the House's legal cases" (*ša qurbūtu ina muḫḫi bēt urdi-šu lipqid dēnāni ša bēti lēpuš*); here the house described by the two officials as "our Masters' House" is described, from the king's viewpoint as "his servant's house".[50] From such passages it is clear that such a "House" was a specific entity within the administrative system. Compare also SAA 1, 12 (=ABL 1042) where the king, probably, describes how a man he had dismissed from his post of *rab bēti* had then been installed by the recipient of the letter "in his House inside Arrapha". Later in the same letter the king says "He is not a good man in the field, and in the House he is not one who organizes(?) his Masters' House" (*la ina* É-*im-ma ka-ṣi-ru ša* É EN.MEŠ-*šú šu-ú*).

The variety of usages of *bētu* has already been mentioned. The question arises of any "House" whether it is to be understood as an administrative department, a private (if extensive) domestic establishment, a complete agricultural "estate", or a combination of one or more of these. The Crown Prince and the Queen Mother had their own "House". For the meaning "estate" SAA 11, 221 (=ADD 675) is valuable, since it proves that the term *bētu* can include a house, people, fields, orchards and sheep. Four of these estates belonged to magnates (the *sartennu*, *sukkallu*, Chief Eunuch, and Deputy Treasurer), but since they are mentioned by their personal names, like the other estate-owners listed in the text, we should probably see these "houses" as their personal property, but the magnates also had administrative "Houses" attached to the office.[51] These are likely to refer to entire organizations rather than single buildings as such, if only because in the provincial capitals, at least, the governors had "palaces" *(ēkallu)* at their disposal. We also have Houses under less exalted officials, such as the House of the Chief Cook (É LÚ.GAL MU.MEŠ, SAA 11, 90 (=ADD 754)). In SAA 7, 115 (=ADD 953), a list of raw materials for textile production, we meet the House of the Carpet-worker (É LÚ *ka-ṣir*) three times, but also the House of the Cupbearer (r.ii.8; presumably not the Chief Cupbearer), and the House of the Deputy (É LÚ.2-*e*, r.ii.9, also, without the LÚ, i.12).[52] Where it is used to describe a sector of the administration, we can hesitate as to how exactly it achieved this meaning. Was the shift in meaning from *house* to *office-building* to *government agency* housed within it? Or from *house* to *members of household* to *administrative staff* to *government agency*? However it arose, in the phrase "Masters' House" *bētu* plainly refers to an administrative department, although that does not necessarily mean there was not also an identifiable building with the same designation.

---

50 The "legal cases" would presumably have been aimed at recouping the depredations of the provincial governors, which sheds rare light on the level of formality prevalent in relations between departments.

51 Mattila 2000, 143; Postgate 1989, 147 dicusses the prebendary land-holdings or estates attached to the offices of some magnates. These are called É, and are particularly difficult to distinguish from administrative households.

52 The use of the determinative LÚ obliges us, I think, to translate "House of the Deputy" (pace the SAA edition), and to adopt the same translation for i.12 in the same text, where no LÚ is written, which admittedly makes it difficult to differentiate from the "Second House".

Sometimes the subject matter does betray the nature of the department. Some are clearly operating in a military context. Our plaintive Bel-iqiša in ABL 84 is involved in horses, and horses belong in the army. Other passages confirm that the concept of the "Masters' House" operates within the military administration.

• ABL 617: "twice or three times we have sent messages to our Masters' House for horses".

• CTN 2, 186 "I sent a message to PN saying 'The forces of their Masters' House are assembled in Halzi'".

• SAA 1, 223 (=CT 53, 87) "Let the king give orders that each man should go to his Masters' House. The troops should not be weakened, not one man should [be missing] from the campaign".

Almost the only official who we know for certain served on the staff of a provincial governor was the *rab bēti*, the "major domo", both for civilian and military affairs. In SAA 1, 264 the author (if the editor is right, perhaps the Governor of Isana) writes "Let me appoint my *rab bēti* along with the responsible officials" to deal with grain supplies. In NL 89 the remainder of the provincial army is delayed, but "the major domo will bring (them)"; similarly in ABL 242 (cf. Postgate 1974a, p. 269).[53] He plainly acted as deputy to provincial governors, and we may guess that some of the "Masters' Houses" we encounter in the correspondence were simply provincial governorates. We have already seen that these had both civilian and military functions. Under the governors came an unknown (and no doubt variable) number of *šaknūte*. I see no evidence at present that they had "Houses" of their own, but equally, it can not be ruled out. On the other hand, there must have been government departments which did not fall under the provincial governors, either inside or outside the "royal cohort", and it seems probable that these too were designated "Houses". One example is probably to be found in ABL 415 (see above). Questions that remain to be addressed include the place of work of the members of the administration - were there specially designated government buildings dedicated to certain administrative activities outside the palaces, or were some functions exercised from home?

While the "Masters' House" thus refers to the government department in which someone works, unfortunately the use of this phrase conceals from us the identity and functions of the department in general and of its officials in particular. The problem is that the texts never, or hardly ever, tell us WHO these masters are. It is almost as though the different government departments had responsibilities so nebulous and ill-defined that they did not have designations of their own. Officials writing letters do not specify their own rank or office, and when referring to their superiors they just talk about their "Masters' House". If only they had mentioned their own or their masters' title(s), we should be much better informed as to the

53 For examples of the *rab bēti*'s military role cf. CTN 2, p. 15, footnote 27. However, the fusion of military and civilian administration means that there is no need to maintain my opinion expressed there, that "his original association with the household seems to have become secondary".

structure of the Neo-Assyrian administrative machinery. Nevertheless, one thing does seem clear, that, as we might deduce from the phrase, there was an identifiable *bētu* or department, even if its masters are not specified. Any diagram representing the system would have to take account of these "houses".

Conclusions

My conclusions are

• that the Neo-Assyrian administration was not bureaucratic, and depended on a sense of institutional loyalty and personal interaction up and down the system.

• that the administrative ethos was nevertheless well-developed, with well formulated concepts of responsibility and authority, and of appointment to and dismissal from, offices.

• that the hierarchy of posts within the system is largely invisible to us because of the combination of the non-bureaucratic ethos, and the tantalizing usage of the phrase "Masters' House".

Bibliography

Borger, R. 1956 *Die Inschriften Asarhaddons Königs von Assyrien* (AfO Beiheft 9).
- 1996 *Beiträge zum Inschriftenwerk Assurbanipals* (Wiesbaden).
Fales, M.F. 2000 "bīt bēli: an Assyrian institutional concept", in E. Rova (ed.), *Patavina Orientalia Selecta* (History of the Ancient Near East. Monongraphs IV; Padua), 231-49.
Freydank, H. & Saporetti, C. 1989 *Bābu-aḫa-iddina. Die Texte* (Rome: Corpus Medio-Assira 2)
Fuchs, A. 1993 *Die Inschriften Sargons II. aus Khorsabad* (Göttingen 1994).
Herbordt, S. 1992 *Neuassyrische Glyptik des 8.-7. Jh. v. Chr.* (Helsinki: SAAS 1).
Jas, R. 1996 *Neo-Assyrian judicial procedures* (Helsinki: SAAS 5).
Kinnier Wilson, J.V. 1972 *The Nimrud Wine Lists* (CTN 1).
Klauber, E. 1910 *Assyrisches Beamtentum nach Briefen aus der Sargonidenzeit* (Leipziger Semitistische Studien V/3).
Luckenbill, D.D. 1924 *The Annals of Sennacherib* (OIP 2).
Malbran-Labat, F. 1982 *L'Armée et l'organisation militaire de l'Assyrie* (Librairie Droz, Genève-Paris)
Manitius, W. 1910 "Das stehende Heer der Assyrerkönige und seine Organisation" *Zeitschrift für Assyriologie* 24, 97-224.
Mattila, R. 2000 *The King's Magnates: A study of the highest officials of the Neo-Assyrian Empire* (SAAS 11).
Millard, A.R. 1965 "The Assyrian royal seal type again", *Iraq* 27, 12-16.
- 1978 "The Assyrian royal seal: an addendum", *Iraq* 40, 70.
- 1994 *The eponyms of the Assyrian Empire* (SAAS 2).
Müller, K.F. 1937 *Das assyrische Ritual. Teil I: Texte zum assyrischen Königsritual* (MVAeG 41/iii).
Postgate, J.N. 1974a *Taxation and Conscription in the Assyrian Empire* (Studia Pohl, Series Maior 3; Rome, Pontifical Biblical Institute).
- 1974b "Royal Exercise of Justice under the Assyrian Empire", in P. Garelli (ed.), *Le palais et la royauté* (Compte Rendu de la XIXe Rencontre Assyriologique Internationale, Paris 1971), 417-26.
- 1979a "Assyrian documents in the Musée d'Art et d'Histoire, Geneva", *Assur* (UNDENA Publications, Malibu) 2/iv.
- 1979b "The economic structure of the Assyrian Empire", in M.T. Larsen (ed.), *Power and propaganda. A symposium on ancient empires* (Copenhagen: Mesoptamia Vol. 7), 193-221.
- 1980a "The place of the *šaknu* in Assyrian government", *Anatolian Studies* 30, 67-76.
- 1980b ""Princeps Iudex" in Assyria", *Revue d'Assyriologie* 74, 180-2.
- 1989 "The ownership and exploitation of land in Assyria in the 1st Millennium B.C.", in M. Lebeau & P. Talon (eds.) *Reflets des deux fleuves. Volume de mélanges offerts à André Finet,* 141-52
- 2000 "The Assyrian army in Zamua", *Iraq* 62, 89-108.
- 2001 "Assyrian uniforms", in W.H. van Soldt (ed.), *Veenhof Anniversary Volume* (Leiden: Nederlands Instituut voor het Nabije Oosten), 373-88.
Sachs, A.J. 1953 "The Late Assyrian Royal-Seal type", *Iraq* 15, 167-170
Saporetti, C. 1979 *Gli eponimi medio-assiri* (Bibliotheca Mesopotamica 9; UNDENA Publications, Malibu).
Steinkeller, P. 1987 "The administrative and economic organization of the Ur III state: The core and the periphery", in McG. Gibson & R.D. Biggs, *The organization of power.*

Aspects of bureaucracy in the ancient Near East (Chicago: Studies in Ancient Oriental Civilization 46), 19-41.

Weidner, E.F. 1940 "Die Keilschrifttexte vom Tell Halaf. 1. Das Archiv des Mannu-ki-Aššur", in J. Friedrich, G.R. Meyer, A. Ungnad & E.F. Weidner, *Die Inschriften vom Tell Halaf* (AfO Beiheft 6), 8-46.

6

Documents in Government under the Middle Assyrian Kingdom

J. N. POSTGATE

1. Introduction

In about 1450 BC the whole of north Mesopotamia, by which I mean the lowland parts of northern Iraq and of north-east Syria and Turkey as far west as the Euphrates, was under the political domination of the Mitanni kingdom with its centre in the Habur basin. We have virtually no archives which date to this time, but there are two major bodies of cuneiform texts which come from this region somewhat later in the second millennium (fourteenth–thirteenth century BC). These are the Nuzi texts, from a small provincial princedom near Kerkuk on the south-east wing of the Mitannian empire, and the texts from Assur, the capital of the newly formed state of Assyria which by 1200 BC had completely supplanted Mitanni and absorbed the entire north Mesopotamian area.

The Middle Assyrian texts from Assur are very varied in character, provenance, and date. The Nuzi archives are much less varied, being principally family legal dossiers, although with some texts from public administration, and cover a much shorter time-span. My own familiarity is with the Assur material, to which can be added miscellaneous archives from provincial centres, including Tell Billa, Tell al-Rimah, Sheikh Hamad, and several others.[1]

Note. For bibliography see p. 137.

[1] On the basis of this material I devoted quite a long article to Middle Assyrian documentary format and associated issues, which covers most of the issues under consideration here in relation to the texts published at that time (Postgate 1986*b*). A brief account of the different archives at Assur itself was given in Postgate (1986*a*), and the details in this were comprehensively overhauled by Pedersén (1985), with

2. The Written Documents: Physical Characteristics

Most documents were written in cuneiform script on clay tablets, which varied in size in response to the amount of information to be recorded. Some tablets were impressed, while still damp, by rolling cylinder seals over the surface. In legal transactions these were the seal of the party ceding a right or acknowledging liability, placed at the head of the obverse above the text proper, plus the seals of some or all of the witnesses, rolled wherever else space could be found, often but not always on uninscribed parts of the edges. The individual impressions are usually identified by an accompanying written note ('seal of PN'). By contrast, sealed administrative texts usually bear only the seal of the person accepting liability, and they are not usually witnessed.

Some tablets are enclosed in clay envelopes (Postgate 1986*b*: 13–16). Sometimes these are letters,[2] but rather surprisingly—by comparison with other Mesopotamian documentary traditions—the remainder seem to be administrative receipts (texts attesting the receipt of some commodity).[3]

In Assyria certain administrative records were kept on wooden writing-boards, probably in most cases a hinged diptych, on the waxed inner surfaces of which cuneiform could be written. Their function is described below in greater detail (see pp. 133–6). As far as I am aware, their use is not attested in the Nuzi texts, but they

data taken from the unpublished excavation archives and photographs. Thus the basic outlines of the Oxford workshop theme had already been laid down for the Middle Assyrian system. The following general discussion of the role of documents in government administration at this time can be correspondingly brief, but takes account of new texts published in the last ten years, encouraging the treatment of certain points in greater detail. For these texts see Freydank (1994); Kühne (1995); Cancik-Kirschbaum (1996) has only letters, but some details of unpublished texts from Sheikh Hamad, Tell Chuera, and Tell Sabi Abyad are known to me from the '2. Internationaler Workshop zur Mittelassyrischen Zeit', organized by Prof. Dr Hartmut Kühne, Dr Helmut Freydank, and Dr Eva Cancik-Kirschbaum in Berlin in Apr. 1997. The text of the present article is virtually unchanged from the workshop contribution; for two other contributions relevant to this theme, each written and published since the Oxford workshop, see Postgate (2001), esp. 191–3, and Postgate (2002).

[2] See below, sect. 3, under *našpertu*.

[3] The detailed terminology and function of such envelopes is discussed below, pp. 131–3.

are known at this time at Emar (on the Euphrates near Aleppo) and in Anatolia (cf. Symington 1991: 118).

3. The Written Documents: Assyrian Terminology

Since the correlation of certain types of transaction or record with certain formats of document is plainly deliberate, one would not be surprised to find that the Assyrian scribes had their own terminology for different document types. Terms used for describing documents in the Middle Assyrian texts are:

ṭuppu 'tablet': general term for clay tablet of any kind.

ṭuppu dannutu 'strong tablet': technical term for a legal conveyance document (e.g. land or slave sale).

ṭuppu ṣabittu 'executed tablet': probably refers to a tablet which has been formally sealed and witnessed and which provides evidence for an administrative (or legal) transaction.[4]

kanīku 'sealed (tablet)': the only two Middle Assyrian examples seem to refer to tablets which are lists which have been sealed to give them authoritativeness and a guarantee on the part of the person(s) sealing. However, this is too small a sample to establish so precise a meaning, and the word is used in other dialects and probably had a wider range of meanings.

kiṣirtu (original meaning uncertain): this problematic term was discussed by me (Postgate 1986*b*: 21–2), and was taken to refer to an envelope, both in the Middle Assyrian texts and in Neo-Assyrian times. It has recently been discussed again by Radner (1997: 63–5), who suggests a Neo-Assyrian meaning of *Hüllentafel* (i.e. a tablet and its envelope), with which I would not quarrel. The precise meaning 'tablet-in-envelope' rather than just 'envelope' could also

[4] This interpretation of *ṣabātu* is still controversial. The issue, discussed at length in Postgate (1986*b*), 18–21, is admittedly complex, and the precise meaning of the phrase remains elusive, but that this interpretation is broadly correct for Middle Assyrian seems fairly certain to me. Whether the same applies to Middle Babylonian usage (cf. Postgate 1986*b*: 20–1) is less easy to determine. For the Neo-Assyrian period a comprehensive presentation of the evidence is given in Radner (1997), 89–106; she reaches a different conclusion. Further discussion of the Neo-Assyrian position is therefore needed, and should take account of *dannutu ṣabātu* in Fales and Jakob-Rost (1991), no. 38, where the editors translate 'seize' but I believe a radically different interpretation of the text is required.

be correct in Middle Assyrian contexts, but the implications of this need renewed discussion in the light of fresh evidence from Tell Chuera (see below, pp. 131–3).

lē'u 'board': for the writing-boards see below, pp. 134–6.

našpertu 'missive': this term, sometimes preceded by *ṭuppi* ('missive tablet'), certainly refers to an administrative order conveyed by letter, in accordance with which an official is expected to act. In Postgate (1986*b*), 26, I surmised that 'some of these message-tablets were sealed', and suggested that VS 19: no. 39 might be one such tablet. Although it has no surviving envelope, it is sealed on both faces and dated, and is addressed to the governor of Amasaki by the chancellor, Babu-aha-iddina. New texts from Tell Chuera fit the same pattern exactly, being sealed and dated letter-orders addressed to a governor, but they actually retain their envelopes. This term to my mind can now be identified with such administrative letter-orders with some confidence. That it sometimes has an envelope, but is not a *kiṣirtu*, may have implications for the correct interpretation of *kiṣirtu* (see below, pp. 131–3).

4. Storage of Archives

The evidence for archive storage comprises both archaeological finds and references in the texts.[5] To start with the archaeology, the best evidence comes from the temple of the god Assur at the site of Assur, where some 600 tablets were found deriving from the office of the 'regular offerings overseer' (*rab ginā'ē*). The archive room lay on the south-west side of the outer courtyard of the temple, and the tablets had been stored in eight or ten large pottery jars. Three of these pots bore cuneiform inscriptions identifying the contents (Postgate 1986*a*: 170; Pedersén 1985: archive M 4). One of them identified itself as the 'sealed-tablet container [*bīt kanīkāte*] of the accounts of the brewers of the temple of Aššur'. Another says 'of the victualler and oil-presser of the temple of Aššur', and the third merely 'of Šamaš-aḫa-eriš son of Riš-Marduk'.[6]

Several other Middle Assyrian archives from Assur were found

[5] An excellent survey for readers of Danish remains Weitemeyer (1955); see now Pedersén (1998) for a comprehensive survey of the later material.

[6] Described and full texts translated in Grayson (1976), 42–1: nos. 26* and 27*; for a photograph see Haller and Andrae (1955), pl. 49.

in, or in association with, a pottery jar. The archive of Mutta comprised 112 tablets stored in a jar, to do with a year's transactions concerning sheep (Postgate 1986*a*: 171–2; Pedersén 1985: archive M 6). The archive of Ubru included 57 or 58 tablets inside a pottery vessel near the western city wall (Postgate 1986*a*: 172–4; Pedersén 1985: archive M 8). Ad-mati-ili's family archive, composed of 54 (or 60) tablets, was found in a pottery jar in a house in the south-west quarter of the city. This pot was stored along with many others in a small storeroom attached to the entry vestibule of the house (Postgate 1986*a*: 180–1; Pedersén 1985: archive M 12).

Tablet jars are also normal further afield. At Tell al-Rimah (some 60 km. west of Nineveh) the main body of Middle Assyrian tablets came from within the old temple, but one group of about 20 private legal documents was found in 1964 in a pottery jar close to the surface of the mound (see Wiseman 1968: 186 ff.; Oates 1965: 75; Postgate 2002). At Tell Chuera at the western corner of the Habur basin, although the majority of cuneiform documents was found in and around a niche in the wall of room 3, where they had plainly been stored, an inscribed vessel was found near the surface in the same context as the fragments of a tablet.[7] At Tell Sheikh Hamad the tablets in building P were found in association with large jar sherds (Cancik-Kirschbaum 1996: 8). It is clear that clay jars were regularly used for both public and private archives. This was of course an ancient practice, since archives in the Old Assyrian colony at Kültepe were regularly kept in (sometimes sealed) jars.[8]

As for the textual references, undoubtedly the most illuminating is a tablet from a thirteenth-century family archive at Assur which lists the contents of one of their storerooms. This begins with parts of a chariot and concludes with miscellaneous things like furniture and other metal and wooden objects. The middle of the list is summarized as '24 chests of tablets'. The term for chest is *quppu*, which may be of wood or reed; included within the list are two or three other container types, which include a 'vat' (*marsattu*). The text gives considerable detail about the types of tablet stored in this archive. They were classified by their subject matter, and in this context it seems worthwhile citing the text to illustrate the variety

[7] Kühne (1995), 203. Built-in niches for tablet storage are well attested in the 1st millennium BC, e.g. in Sargon's Nabu temple at Khorsabad or the temple library at Sippar.

[8] For the use of jars in Mesopotamia throughout the ages see Weitemeyer (1955), 65–6. See also Veenhof, this volume.

of both the documentation this family had seen fit to conserve and the containers in which they stored it.[9]

1 chest [*quppu*] of (obligations) on Šamaš-eriš.
1 chest of clearance(s) of people and fields, of the town of Šarika.
1 chest of (obligations) on Aššur-tahatti.
1 *ditto* of expropriated tablets of (obligations) on citizens of Aššur.
1 *ditto* of (obligations) on Aššur-mušabši . . .
1 *ditto* of (obligations) on Ištar-eriš; 1 chest [of . . .] of the town of Karana.
1 *ditto* of (obligations) on craftsmen; 1 chest of cattle and donkeys owed by citizens of Aššur.
1 *ditto* of (obligations) on Riš-Adad; 1 chest of herald's proclamations for houses in the inner city.
1 *ditto* of sheep owed by citizens of Aššur.
1 *ditto* of grain owed by citizens of Aššur.
1 *ditto* of mixed silver owed by citizens of Aššur.
1 *ditto* of . . . and donkeys owed by shepherds.
1 vat [*marsattu*] of tablets of Riš-Adad.
1 chest of tablets of the palace owed by the horse-trainer.
1 chest of envelopes [*kiṣrāte*] of Riš-Adad.
1 half-vessel [*mišlu*] of . . . of the provinces (?).
1 vat of (obligations) on Uqa-den-ili (?).
1 pot [*tallu*] of Arzuhina workmanship (of) Mannu-gir- . . . and his brothers and Sin-šeya.
1 vat of tablets of [PN], the butler.
1 chest of . . . of clearances (?).
1 chest of . . . of . . . of Ištar-ummi and Šamaš-lu-dayyan.
1 vat (and?) 1 vessel of letters (?).
TOTAL: 24 chests of tablets [*ṭuppāte*].

5. Types of Administrative Document

Middle Assyrian legal documents known to us conform to a banal norm and will not be considered here further. Administrative texts, on the other hand, vary in response to the variety of situations they reflect, and deserve more extensive discussion. Rather than attempt a detailed categorization of the precise function of every administrative document, for which neither time nor space is sufficient, there follow some brief general observations, followed by

[9] Full edition in Postgate (1988), no. 50, with commentary on pp. 116–19.

two sections dealing with particular types of document which pose problems.

A first fundamental point to be established about any administrative record is whether it is 'unilateral' or 'bilateral'. By this I mean, whether it is a record produced and kept by one person (or institution) for their own purposes, or one which records a transaction or other relationship between two parties and is acknowledged as valid by each side, and retained by one side (or sometimes both) as evidence for the resulting liability. Normally the bilateral nature of a document is implicit in the wording of the text, but by the late second millennium BC the acknowledgement of liability was usually also expressed physically on the document, with a seal impression. In this respect it resembles a private legal transaction.

One characteristic bilateral Middle Assyrian government document is the job contract. This resembles a private commercial debt-note, but without the witnesses required for a legally valid document. The obligation recorded may be simply to supply a commodity, to receive a commodity (as *iškāru*) and having worked with it to return a finished product, or to collect a commodity from a third party and deliver it. A time limit is usually prescribed, and the text states that once the commodity is delivered 'he may break his tablet'. This basic formula is infinitely adaptable, and so is applied to virtually any administrative transaction which involves one official (or privately contracted person) carrying out a prescribed task for another.

Unilateral documents are primarily identifiable by negative criteria, i.e. the absence of any sealing (or envelope), the lack of mention of one or both parties, the absence of any statement of liability (e.g. *ina muḫḫi*), and the absence of any 'verb of transmission' (e.g. *laqā'u*, *tadānu*, *maḫāru*). There is ample evidence from Assur for unilateral administrative lists of expenditures and receipts, usually of foodstuffs and materials for craft production. The Assur archives have less to say about the administration of agriculture, but I believe that we can expect much in this sphere from the provincial centre of Dur-katlimmu (Sheikh Hamad on the lower Habur). All such lists known to me record past events—I am not aware of any 'planning' documents which record estimates or prescribe future payments.

On small memorandums the scribes often wrote 'written down so as not to forget' (*ana lā mašā'e šaṭir*; see Freydank 1994: no. 18). As far as I know, plain memorandums and unilateral account texts were not sealed.[10] Since they were accounts of past events, there would have been no need to update them, and the thirteenth-century Assur texts are crammed in ruled-off sections on to large clay tablets without much concession to the user by way of layout within each section (see Freydank 1994: nos. 1, 3). However, it is worth noting that the wording of such an account tablet could resemble, and perhaps also form the basis of, a bilateral receipt text (cf. Postgate 1986*b*: 14–15). The process of 'doing the accounts' (*nikkassē ṣabātu*) was sometimes certainly a bilateral one, even though both parties were within the administration. I am not aware of any document which says that 'the accounts between A and B have been completed and A (or B) now owes nothing'; this would have been superfluous, and it is probable that a sealed document would only be produced if any outstanding liabilities remained (one example is KAJ 80 = Postgate 1988: 40). The Old Assyrian merchants talked of 'uncovering the jars', which evidently meant taking out all the previous period's records and compiling them into a statement of the current mutual obligations.[11] In an efficient administration such procedures take place at regular intervals, and there is some evidence that government offices kept annual accounts.[12] Some texts also suggest that months were used as convenient divisions of time for accounting purposes, such as Freydank (1994), no. 1, which is a bread receipt and expenditure account starting on 1 Kuzallu and dated 30 Kuzallu).[13]

6. *Kiṣirtu*, *kaṣāru*, and Related Problems

In Middle Assyrian texts at least, the meaning of *kiṣirtu* cannot be established without taking into account the associated usage of *kaṣāru*. In an earlier discussion it was concluded that 'whether or

[10] Readers should be aware that in earlier publications philologists did not always record information about seal impressions, so that statements of this sort are always liable to be invalidated.

[11] The phrase is *qablītam errûm* (from *erûm*, 'naked', misunderstood by both *CAD* and *AHw* in different ways).

[12] Cf. Postgate (1986*b*), 36–7. A new example for recording by *limmu* is given by Freydank (1994), no. 30.

[13] Freydank (1994), no. 3, is perhaps similar, recording grain issues and with its final words 'of the month of Ša-sarrāte'.

not *kaṣāru* is to be understood literally as 'to apply the envelope', it . . . implies some form of authentication or "endorsement" by a superior official' (Postgate 1986*b*: 22). This is confirmed by a new phrase which has turned up in the Middle Assyrian documents from Tell Chuera: *ṭuppi tūbala ana kunukki ša kiṣrāte tutâr. šumma adi uraḫ ūmāte lā tattabal lā tuttaer lā ikaṣṣurūnikku* (cf. Kühne 1995: 216 ff.). This I would understand as 'you will bring my tablet and convert it into "seals of case-tablets/envelopes". If after one month you have not brought it and converted it, they will not *kaṣāru* for you.' The background to this is that the recipient of the letter is being told how to extract from the administration formal acknowledgement of the expenditure he will have to incur as a result of the instructions issued to him in the letter. This recognition evidently has to take the form of one or more sealed *kiṣirtu*, and the process of creating such a document is called *kaṣāru*. There are still uncertainties about the technical phraseology, especially the words *kunukki ša kiṣrāte*, but taken together these new instances do strengthen the conclusion that the procedure is 'some form of authentication or "endorsement" by a superior official'.

It remains hard to decide whether *kaṣāru* refers to the physical act of applying an envelope and associated sealing (and *kiṣirtu* accordingly to the envelope or tablet-in-envelope), or to 'binding' in a metaphorical sense (and *kiṣirtu* accordingly to a 'bond'); and whether the actual letter-tablet we have would be 'converted' into a *kiṣirtu* by the application of an envelope, or an entirely new document is to be created in its stead. Since this difficult issue relates to the use of envelopes, it does perhaps merit further exploration. The answer is that it seems more likely that an entirely new document was created, given that the Tell Chuera phrase (envisaging a *future* procedure called *kaṣāru* and resulting in a *kiṣirtu*) comes from at least four letters (perhaps we should call them 'letter-orders' to use a term introduced for Ur III Sumer), each of which *already* consists of a sealed tablet enclosed in a sealed envelope bearing the same text as the tablet (see also below, p. 136, on sealed *boards* in a Hittite context). This suggests that *kiṣirtu* refers not specifically to an envelope, or to a tablet-in-envelope, but only to a certain type of document which (sometimes, usually, always?) takes the form of a tablet-in-envelope.

The physical evidence for tablets-in-envelopes suggests that these are documents I have termed generally receipts (Postgate

1986*b*: 13–14), in other words, texts which state that certain commodities have been 'received' (*maḫir*). However, that is not the only verb used, and we also find *madid* 'measured out', *tadin* 'given out', *ētaklu* and *ultākilu* 'consumed/caused to be consumed'. Thus these documents state that the commodity has reached its intended destination, and give that statement official confirmation by sealing the tablet and enclosing it in a sealed envelope. This agrees satisfactorily with the scenario reflected in the Tell Chuera letters, and suggests that we could paraphrase *kaṣāru* as 'to certify properly expended' and *kiṣirtu* as a 'certificate of proper expenditure'.

This is different from a normal receipt document, which usually confirms receipt of a commodity by an individual, for whatever purpose, and would be retained by the previous 'owner': here the confirmation is that the administration has received a satisfactory account of the ultimate disposition of the commodity, but the two types of document belong together in that they are both *concluding* documents, recording the completion of a bilateral relationship, rather than *initiating* documents, recording the creation of a liability. In some systems it might have been felt sufficient for the administration to prepare a unilateral statement and thereby satisfy itself that its delegate had fulfilled his obligations. That a need was felt for this elaborate sealing and enveloping mechanism was typical of the Middle Assyrian ethos, on which more below.

7. Writing-Boards

Plenty of evidence exists for wooden writing-boards in Mesopotamian administration after 1500 BC, and this is summarized for Middle Assyrian in Postgate (1986*b*), 22–6. The evidence for such boards in Anatolia, and at Emar and Ugarit, is collected by Symington (1991). They were probably always a hinged diptych (polyptychs are attested in the first millennium for scholastic texts) with wax inlaid on the inner surfaces to take the script. There is specific mention of wax in connection with these boards in texts from Hattusas, Ugarit, and Assur (and quite likely elsewhere).

What were the reasons for using a wooden board rather than the more traditional cuneiform tablet? We presume that the advantages of boards over cuneiform tablets were that they offered a larger surface and so could accommodate longer texts, and that the malleability of the wax allowed the addition and removal of entries. We know from the cuneiform texts that boards could be used for long lists of personnel and/or commodities, for transmission from one geographical centre to another, and that they could be sealed.[14] The only contemporary example of a wooden writing-board comes from the Ulu Burun shipwreck. By comparison with wooden and ivory writing-boards of the first millennium it was very small (9.5 × 6.2 cm.), and could not have accommodated some of the lists known to have been kept on boards at Assur in the thirteenth century (see below). It seems possible that it belongs in an east Mediterranean environment, where boards were used for the whole range of purposes fulfilled by clay tablets in cuneiform contexts. Boards must have been more expensive (cf. Payton 1991: 106), and hence one would perhaps not expect to find such small wooden writing-boards in Assyria, where clay was the norm. In the west there is a complication in that boards were probably the normal vehicle for hieroglyphic (as opposed to cuneiform) script, so that the usage of the vehicle for the script reflects a much deeper difference than merely the type of administrative operation involved.

That in Assyria boards had a role in government administration is plain from passages like KAJ 260 (Postgate 1986*b*: 23), 'they looked in the earlier and later boards of grain received', or KAJ 109, where a large quantity of grain is described as being 'in accordance with thirteen boards which the deportees . . . received' (Postgate 1988: no. 34). This latter instance implies that on these boards the central administration had inscribed lists, evidently specifying the numbers of deportees and their domestic animals, and *perhaps* also the exact amounts of grain due to each, which had then been entrusted to the (officials in charge of) the deportees themselves for subsequent conversion into grain at their destination.

Another instance of the central administration establishing lists of personnel on waxed boards is provided by a particular group of boards referred to in texts from the reign of Tukulti-Ninurta I (*c.*1244–1208 BC) as 'the board of PN', and also a 'board of the king'. It is clear that these boards listed men in connection with military service, with over 2,000 men on a single board. I concluded earlier that 'these lists of soldiers . . . served more than one purpose: as

[14] For possible ways of sealing a board see Payton (1991), 103–5. Note that a few Neo-Assyrian clay sealings excavated in the Review Palace at Kalhu (Nimrud) are perhaps from boards listing reviewed soldiers (Dalley and Postgate 1984: nos. 21–3).

well as the essential record of persons under each command, they were used to supply the same information for the benefit of those responsible for the issue of rations to them' (Postgate 1986*b*: 24–5). Since this was written, fresh evidence has come from the provinces that this system was well established, and that it operated between different administrative centres.

The 'board-owners' listed in VS 19: no. 1 are: the king; Lulayu; Sin-ašared; Šamaš-apla-uṣur;[15] and Adad-šamši. Boards of the king and of Šamaš-apla-uṣur and Adad-šamši are also listed in VS 21: no. 17; and of Lulayu, Sin-ašared, Šamaš-apla-uṣur, and Adad-šamši in VS 19: no. 9. Collation of an Assur tablet by Dr Helmut Freydank allows an improved understanding of KAJ 245 (Postgate 1988: no. 45).[16] Here the name Adad-šamši is now to be restored in l. 13 in place of my queried Sasi. This means that the tablet now has a 'board of the king' a 'board of Aššur-si . . .', a 'board of Šamaš-aha-iddina', and a 'board of Aššur-šamši'. Further, a new text from Tell Sheikh Hamad also mentions persons 'of the board of PN', where the PNs are Lulayu, Sin-ašared, Šamaš-aha-iddina, and Adad-šamši.[17] The new occurrences serve to reinforce the conclusion that these boards were used to record the assignation[18] of conscripted troops to one of about five high officials. It is relevant here to note, as Wolfgang Pempe pointed out to me, that the texts mentioning these board-owners cover a span of more than twenty years, and it is thus reasonable to conclude that the boards were in effect standing registers of men integral to the organization of the Middle Assyrian army. They were kept for reference by the administration not only in respect of the identity of the individuals concerned, but also when organizing and recording the distribution of commodities to the army.

Looking beyond Assyria, there are a few mentions of boards in contemporary texts from Babylonia which show that here too they could be used for a standing list or register for consultation (see *CAD*: L 157a). Whether boards were also in use in the admin-

[15] This is how the name, written [Id]UTU-A-PAP, was read in Postgate (1986*b*), but there is now complex evidence suggesting that it could be read as Šamaš-aha-iddina (Freydank 1990: 308, citing other examples given in Pedersén 1985: 107–8 n. 5).

[16] This reading was proposed in Freydank (1990), 308, and kindly confirmed for me by collation by Dr Freydank (letter of 25 May 1997).

[17] DeZ 3374; information courtesy of Wolfgang Pempe (letter of 26 May 1997).

[18] The technical term for such assignation may have been *tabāku* (see Postgate 1988: no. 54. 18).

istrative system of the Mitannian kingdom and its component or successor kingdoms is less certain. They are apparently not referred to in the Nuzi archives (unless in the most recently published material, which I have not searched), but they did have a role within the (post-Mitannian) administrative system at Emar in the thirteenth century (Symington 1991: 118) and at Ugarit (Symington 1991: 121 ff.). Within the Hittite empire there is evidence that officials travelling on state business might be given sealed boards authorizing them to withdraw state commodities from various places: this is different from the attested Assyrian usage, and sounds like the equivalent of the sealed tablets in a sealed envelope (see above) now known from both Tell Chuera and Sabi Abyad (cf. Symington 1991: 120 and n. 6).

8. Public vs. Private

I have more than once suggested that Middle Assyrian administrative practice was borrowed from procedures used by the private commercial sector. This makes it difficult at times to determine whether the liabilities expressed are private and commercial, or public and administrative, or indeed, whether that distinction is universally valid. Various criteria can be used to identify the public and administrative transactions (Postgate 1988: xxiv with n. 24). The consequence of the application of private commercial practices, with the ethos of an audit culture, must have been stultifying to government. Where not only the nature and quantity of commodities as they passed through the administrative machine, but also the administrators' abstract responsibilities in respect of them, are recorded in writing at every stage, rather than relying on the reciprocal expectations of an orally administered hierarchy, flexibility in response to change is lost and bureaucratic paralysis will tend to set in. This is not to deny that other aspects of the commercial tradition, such as company loyalty, may have had compensating advantages, but anyone looking in detail at the documentation required of a Middle Assyrian provincial governor can hardly doubt that he must have experienced some impatience with the 'paperwork'.

A reasonable explanation of the dominance in Assyria of the private transaction as a model for public administration would be that the commercial enterprises of the city of Assur were already highly sophisticated centuries before the inhabitants of the city found themselves called on to administer the newly acquired territories to the north and west. On the other hand, when we look at neighbouring Nuzi, the situation is very different. Here we do not see the network of administrative liabilities expressed in the same terms as commercial debts, nor are the administrative texts drawn up with the same regularity and formality as in Assyria. Although Nuzi had participated in the network of Old Assyrian trade-routes, it was not a major trading centre itself, and although it borrowed from Babylonian and Assyrian scribal practice, it is entirely possible that its administrative ethos was fundamentally different.

BIBLIOGRAPHY

Cancik-Kirschbaum, E. (1996), *Die Mittelassyrischen Briefe aus Tall Šēh Hamad* (Berichte der Ausgrabung Tall Šēh Hamad/Dur-katlimmu, 4, Texte, 1; Berlin).

Dalley, S. M., and Postgate, J. N. (1984), *The Tablets from Fort Shalmaneser* (Cuneiform Texts from Nimrud, 3; London).

Fales, F. M., and Jakob-Rost, L. (1991), 'Neo-Assyrian Texts from Assur: Private Archives in the Vorderasiatisches Museum of Berlin, Part 1', *SAAB* 5/1–2: 1–157.

Freydank, H. (1990), review of Postgate (1988), in *ZA* 80: 306–8.

—— (1994), *Mittelassyrische Rechtsurkunden und Verwaltungstexte*, vol. iii (WVDOG 92; Berlin).

Grayson, A. K. (1976), *Assyrian Royal Inscriptions*, vol. ii (Wiesbaden).

Haller, A., and Andrae, W. (1955), *Die Heiligtümer des Gottes Assur und der Sin-Šamaš-Tempel in Assur* (WVDOG 67; Berlin).

Kühne, C. (1995), 'Ein mittelassyrisches Verwaltungsarchiv und andere Keilschrifttexte', in Orthmann *et al.* (1995), 203–25.

Oates, D. (1965), 'The Excavations at Tell al Rimah, 1964', *Iraq*, 27: 62–80.

Orthmann W., et al. (eds.) (1995), *Ausgrabungen in Tell Chuera in Nordost-Syrien*, vol. i (Saarbrücken).

Payton, R. (1991), 'The Ulu Burun Writing-Board Set', *AnSt* 41: 99–106.

Pedersén, O. (1985), *Archives and Libraries in the City of Assur: A Survey of the Material from the German Excavations*, pt. 1 (Studia Semitica Upsaliensia, 16; Uppsala).

—— (1998), *Archives and Libraries in the Ancient Near East: 1500–300 BC* (Bethesda, Md.).

Postgate, J. N. (1986*a*), 'Administrative Archives from Assur in the Middle Assyrian Period', in Veenhof (1986), 168–83.
—— (1986*b*), 'Middle Assyrian Tablets: The Instruments of Bureaucracy', *AoF* 13: 10–39.
—— (1988), *The Archive of Urad-Šerua and his Family: A Middle Assyrian Household in Government Service* (Rome).
—— (2001), 'System and Style in Three Near Eastern Bureaucracies', in Voutsaki and Killen (2001), 181–94.
—— (2002), 'Business and Government at Middle Assyrian Rimah', in Werr *et al.* (2002), 297–308.
Radner, K. (1997), *Die neuassyrischen Privatrechtsurkunden als Quelle für Mensch und Umwelt* (State Archives of Assyria Studies, 6; Helsinki).
Symington, D. (1991), 'Late Bronze Age Writing-Boards and their Uses: Textual Evidence from Anatolia and Syria', *AnSt* 41: 111–23.
Veenhof, K. R. (ed.) (1986), *Cuneiform Archives and Libraries: Papers Read at the 30e Rencontre Assyriologique Internationale, Leiden, 4–8 July 1983* (Leiden).
Voutsaki, S., and Killen, J. (eds.) (2001), *Economy and Politics in the Mycenaean Palace States: Proceedings of a Conference Held on 1–3 July 1999 in the Faculty of Classics, Cambridge* (Cambridge Philological Society, suppl. 27; Cambridge).
Weitemeyer, M. (1955), *Babylonske og assyriske archiver og biblioteker* (Copenhagen).
Werr, L. Al-Gailani, *et al.* (eds.) (2002), *Of Pots and Plans: Papers on the Archaeology and History of Mesopotamia and Syria Presented to David Oates in Honour of his 75th Birthday* (London).
Wiseman, D. J. (1968), 'The Tell al Rimah Tablets, 1966', *Iraq*, 30: 175–205.